Worlds in Our Words

CONTEMPORARY AMERICAN WOMEN WRITERS

EDITED BY

MARILYN KALLET

University of Tennessee, Knoxville

PATRICIA CLARK

Grand Valley State University

A BLAIR PRESS BOOK

Prentice Hall, Upper Saddle River, NJ 07458

Library of Congress Cataloging-in-Publication Data

Worlds in our words : contemporary American women writers / [edited by Marilyn Kallet and Patricia Clark].
p. cm.
Includes index.
ISBN 0-13-182130-X (pbk.)
1. American literature — Women authors. 2. Women authors, American — 20th century — Interviews. 3. Women — United States — Literary collections. 4. American literature — 20th century.
I. Kallet, Marilyn. II. Clark, Patricia.
PS508.W7W67 1996
810.8′09287 — dc20 96-25044
CIP

Editorial/production supervision: Julie Sullivan
Interior design: Melodie Wertelet
Cover design: Karen Salzbach
Cover image: Synthia Saint James
Buyer: Bob Anderson

A BLAIR PRESS BOOK

A Pearson Education Company
Upper Saddle River, NJ 07458

Printed in the United States of America
10 9 8 7 6 5 4 3 2

ISBN 0-13-182130-X

Acknowledgments appear on pages 760–766, which constitute an extension of the copyright page.

Prentice-Hall International (UK) Limited, London
Prentice-Hall of Australia Pty. Limited, Sydney
Prentice-Hall Canada Inc., Toronto
Prentice-Hall Hispanoamericana, S.A., Mexico
Prentice-Hall of India Private Limited, New Delhi
Prentice-Hall of Japan, Inc., Tokyo
Pearson Education Asia Pte. Ltd., Singapore
Editora Prentice-Hall do Brasil, Ltda., Rio de Janeiro

Worlds in Our Words

Preface

As teachers of literature and creative writing, we became frustrated in trying to find for our classes an anthology that would include writers of diverse cultural and ethnic backgrounds — including white authors. As women writers, we wanted to learn more about how women authors in our century have represented themselves and their cultures within America. Even in the 1990s, many mainstream anthologies of literature still underrepresent women, particularly women of color. Furthermore, we wanted to choose a book that would include a variety of genres. And we sought enough of a historical range to enable us to trace developments in American women's writings, not merely to highlight the most recent works. Could we also find a text that featured outstanding new writers as well as American classics? We needed many worlds in one text. We realized with a growing sense of adventure that we would have to create this book ourselves.

Each of the selections in *Worlds in Our Words: Contemporary American Women Writers* has its own integrity — chosen for its formal beauty and formal risks; for its depth and range of emotions; for the liveliness and freshness of language. Each adds to the ensemble, where both variety and connectedness are hallmarks, where women's voices and women's strengths are highlighted. Juxtaposed with voices we have come to rely on for substance and for beauty — such as those of Alice Walker, Leslie Marmon Silko, Maya Angelou, and Cynthia Ozick — it is refreshing to find the vitality of newer writers such as Janice Eidus, Amy Ling, and Luci Tapahonso. Many of our authors speak of concerns that are larger than the personal — their works give voice to the aspirations of their communities as well as to their own feelings. Adrienne Rich, Tillie Olsen, Alice Childress, and Irena Klepfisz come to mind as examples of writers whose concerns are no less than the destiny of humankind. In each section of our book, women's voices are eloquent in fiction, nonfiction, drama, and poetry. As poets ourselves we took particular delight in choosing poems that we admire and in selecting prose as finely crafted as the poetry.

Our thematic organization offers a clear starting point for discussion and increases enjoyment of the narrative elements throughout the book. These themes emerge clearly in writings by women: Finding Words, Family Album, Histories, Transformations, Working Life, Many Loves, Spirit and Song, and Happiness. Of course, these themes sometimes overlap, and the works themselves in their artfulness resonate beyond single categories. We trust that teachers and students will question the connections we are making. What are the vital differences between the works we have juxtaposed? Our instructor's manual can assist with suggestions for class discussion and assignments.

The thematic sections mark a journey — from struggle to joy, from silence to story and song. The positive and affirming quality of women's writings has long been underestimated. No matter how difficult the struggle, most of our selections contain joy in the art of using language. The sections on "Spirit and Song" and "Happiness" emphasize many forms of joyful spirit.

Another unique feature of our book consists of the interviews we conducted with eight authors. These interviews, which appear one per section, enhance the thematic organization and add to our understanding of the creative process. Judith Ortiz Cofer, Linda Hogan, Colleen McElroy, Sylvia Watanabe, May Sarton, Nancy Willard, Joy Harjo, and Joyce Carol Thomas — these noted authors speak to us in personal voices, offering insight into their lives and work.

Worlds in Our Words aims to be both new and familiar, adding emerging writers to the readers' lists of favorites. Our introductions for each section and for each selection and our biographical notes for each author should help teachers and students to understand and enjoy the richness that is multicultural women's writing in contemporary America. The face of American literature is changing to include more women writers and more women of color, and with this anthology we are proud to be an active part of that change.

ACKNOWLEDGMENTS

In assembling this anthology we were fortunate to have the assistance of expert reviewers in literature, women's studies, and writing: Muriel Brown of North Dakota State University; Janet Ellerby of the University of North Carolina, Wilmington; Elaine Ginsberg of West Virginia University; Andrea C. Holland of Virginia Polytechnic Institute and State University; Libby Falk Jones of Berea College; Sue V. Lape of Columbus State Community College; and Amy K. Levin of Central Missouri State University. Professors Deborah Castillo-Chavez and Nellie Furman of Cornell University's Women's Studies and Literature programs provided useful suggestions at the start, as did drama specialist Professor Deborah R. Geis of the City University of New York. Professor Lisa Johnston, head of Public Services and bibliographer for Gay and Lesbian Studies at Sweet Briar College Library, helped us with our research. Professor Michael Keene of the University of Tennessee encouraged us and offered practical advice as to textbook creation. Steve Pensinger also gave invaluable editorial advice.

We are most grateful to the authors whom we interviewed: Judith Ortiz Cofer, Linda Hogan, Colleen McElroy, Sylvia Watanabe, Joy Harjo, May Sarton, Nancy Willard, and Joyce Carol Thomas. These writers were particularly generous with their time and ideas.

MARILYN KALLET: Julia Demmin has encouraged me in this project from the start — in her friendship I have been very fortunate. Several research assistants, sponsored by University of Tennessee Graduate Studies in English, have offered valuable input into this book: Katharine B. Emanuel, Sara Melton, Eileen Joy, Toby Emert, and Elaine Oswald deserve our gratitude. Professor Mary Papke, Associate Head of Graduate Studies, provided suggestions and support. Professor La Vinia Jennings shared her expertise in African-American literature, particularly on Alice Childress. Professor Kenneth Mostern, specialist in Ethnic Studies, provided insight. Professors Judy Lee Oliva and Bonnie Gould of the University of Tennessee Theatre Department assisted us in the selection of plays. Fine writers and scholars also helped with research: Emma Williams, Florence McNabb, Carol Devenski, Claire Taft, Kecia Driver, Lance Dean, Lee Papa, Keith Norris, David Taylor, Chad Sexton, and Rose Raney. Under the supervision of Marie Garrett, the research librarians at John C. Hodges Library facilitated our work; Felicia H.F. Hoehne was particularly helpful. Library-Express under Sugg Carter and then William De Leonardis also enabled our research. Betty Morgan at Central Duplicating worked tirelessly on our manuscript. We thank the John C. Hodges Better English Fund, which helps to fund scholarship and creative writing, and Professor Allen Carroll, Head of the English Department, for his support of faculty projects.

PATRICIA CLARK: I would like to thank John Gracki, head of Research and Development, Forrest Armstrong, dean of Arts and Humanities, and Mack Smith, chair of the English Department, all at Grand Valley State University, for their encouragement and financial support of this project. I also wish to thank colleagues Kathleen Blumreich, Linda Chown, Milt Ford, Roberta Simone, and Lois Tyson. Thanks also to freelance writer and friend Sue Stauffacher.

For bibliographic support and other kinds of encouragement, thanks to Stanley F. Krohmer at the Milton S. Eisenhower Library of Johns Hopkins University.

Project manager Julie Sullivan provided outstanding skills — and patience. We were fortunate to have Nancy Perry of Blair Press/Prentice Hall as our editor — one with vision, courage, and a fine sense of humor. Women editors are the hope of women writers in our country, and Nancy Perry stands out as the best of the best.

Marilyn Kallet
Patricia Clark

Contents

Finding Words

Finding Words

◎ ◎ ◎

For writers, language is our vital necessity. In our narratives, poems, and plays, language enables us to express ourselves, to discover and integrate feelings and ideas. Our writings help us to bring communities together; through words we inscribe our memories and link generations. In the following selections we find vivid images of women talking and listening to one another, as Paule Marshall describes her mother and her mother's friends talking in the kitchen, exulting in their control of language; with Judith Ortiz Cofer we sit in the shade of the mango tree and listen to Mamá, a consummate storyteller. In these and other selections, language strengthens bonds between women. Though they are not bread or mangoes, stories and poems have the potential to nourish us, to teach us about our lives and the lives of others.

Some of the stories included here warn about treachery in language. Leslie Marmon Silko's "Lullaby" bears witness to crimes committed against Native people through the manipulation of words. Historically, American writers whose native language is not English have been robbed and oppressed; today they encounter discrimination. Many of the writers in this book live in more than one world linguistically. Bilingualism and multilingualism involve tensions that these authors have transformed into artistic riches.

Unlike our own media-blitzed society, in societies based on oral tradition a word has power in itself; a name calls up being. The importance of poems and stories for traditional cultures can still be felt in the writings included here.

In Alice Walker's "Everyday Use," the author's concern with language and naming is present throughout the narrative concerning a family reunion of three women. The narrator, the mother, speaks plainly and says what she means. Her daughters, Maggie and Dee, are very different from each other — scarred and shy, Maggie has remained at home with her mother; Dee has gone off to school in Augusta and puts on airs. Dee uses language to browbeat her family: "She used to read to us without pity; forcing words, lies, other folks' habits, whole lives upon us two, sitting trapped and ignorant underneath her voice." When Dee tries to take the family quilts her mother has been saving for Maggie, the mother firmly refuses. Dee would have used them as decoration. Maggie will "put them to everyday use." Writers also make a choice when they rely on the words of "everyday use" to render their poems and stories.

The theme of how people use language is central to Janice Eidus's "Robin's Nest." Rachel and Ambrose, sixth graders, are creating their own private language. Rachel's mother, Robin, stopped speaking in the sixties. Her husband, the plastic surgeon, discovered Robin in a hospital where she had been sent after taking LSD. He wanted to "take her home" in order to reshape her thoughts, to "be a plastic surgeon of the mind." Touched by the children's idealism, Robin finally speaks to Rachel and Ambrose. The mother's healing takes place through the children's compassion and creativity.

Leslie Marmon Silko's "Lullaby" tells a difficult story with no waste of words. Ayah, a Navajo mother, has been pressured into signing a document that permits doctors to take away her young children. Ayah cannot read; she knows only how to sign her name. For Native people, the holocaust wrought by massacres, wars, and resettlement, treaties not honored, and children shipped off to boarding schools where they learn to forget their tribal language and tradition, continues. A guardian of culture, Silko ends her story in a traditional manner with a Navajo lullaby.

In Judith Ortiz Cofer's "Tales Told Under the Mango Tree," Mamá, the author's grandmother, creates worlds through her storytelling under the mango tree in Puerto Rico. This excerpt begins with the tale of María Sabida, the smartest woman on the island. The women and girls of Cofer's family sit in the shade of the mango tree absorbing lessons about survival that are implicit in Mamá's entertaining stories. In this memoir, where stories and nonfiction and poems mingle, Cofer says, "It was under the mango tree that I first began to feel the power of words."

Audre Lorde's essay "Poetry Is Not a Luxury" makes the eloquent argument that poetry helps us to live, to shape our future. An integrated self is necessary for survival, and poetry offers that place "where survival and change [are] first made into language, then into idea, then into more tangible action." Poetry makes it possible to "give name to the nameless so it can be thought."

Paule Marshall's memoir "From the Poets in the Kitchen" celebrates the many purposes of the language women use in her aunt's Brooklyn kitchen. Hard-working women gather there to talk "endlessly, passionately, poetically, and with impressive range." More than therapy, their "highly functional" talk integrates art and life "in keeping with the African tradition. . . ." Talk is a "refuge" for them in the complex new culture; it rescues them from "their invisibility, their powerlessness." They "[fight] back, using the only weapon at their command: the spoken word."

In "A Starfish in Mott," Kathleen Norris celebrates one of her young students, "Hidasta, or Sioux," whom the other children treat "as if she were invisible." The girl has so many poems at her desk that Norris remarks: "You must love to write." The girl's reply is a poem in itself.

Cassandra Medley's one-act play *Waking Women* conveys a serious message while celebrating the music and vigor of everyday speech. The setting is a "working-class black neighborhood," and the only speaker is Ms. Edie, who is ostensibly paying her neighbor Lucille a condolence call. But Ms. Edie cannot control her dismay about the pregnancy of her fifteen-year-old niece, Pinkie. Most of her talk is a diatribe against her sister-in-law, who did not discuss birth control with Pinkie. The language of the monologue is lively, conveying humor even as Edie tries to convince us of the need for our children to be informed about sexuality.

More than any other genre, poetry brings home to us the power of words. Leslie Marmon Silko's poem, which begins with "Ts'its'tsi'nako, Thought-Woman," is an invocation of the sacred. Silko places this poem at the beginning of her novel *Ceremony.* In this way the poem calls upon the novel's connection with Creation, with language as a generative act, and with the power of the female imagination. Silko, who is of the Laguna Pueblo, is one of Thought Woman's powerful descendants: "I'm telling you the story / she is thinking."

The speaker in Lorna Dee Cervantes's "Refugee Ship" grieves for the Spanish language, which is her Chicana heritage. But, she tells us, "Mama raised me without language. / I'm orphaned from my Spanish name." The poet reclaims her language by using Spanish for the last line, creating a haunting bilingual refrain.

Those who shop at the Latin Deli of Judith Ortiz Cofer's poem will pay more for their food than at the A&P, but they can find "the comfort / of spoken Spanish." The ample shop owner is "Patroness of Exiles" — exiles from Cuba, Puerto Rico, Mexico. In Paterson, New Jersey, customers read the package labels out loud as if they were "the names of lost lovers: *Suspiros, / Merengues,* the stale candy of everyone's childhood."

In Marilyn Chin's "First Lessons," language and behavior come together in a brutal way. The word *goodness,* taught "before I learned my name," puts the young girl at the mercy of rougher girls. Marilyn Chin "learned the strokes" of the word *goodness* in Chinese, but rebellious, she never learned its message.

In "For Alva Benson, and for Those Who Have Learned to Speak," Joy Harjo draws connections between the earth, women's power to give birth, and women's eloquence: "And the ground spoke when she was born." Even when Navajo women in urban society must resort to impersonal hospital delivery rooms, the "body [goes] on talking." The child in this poem is born with "both voices," speaking Navajo and English. She herself becomes a poet connecting traditional and contemporary worlds.

As a black lesbian-feminist, Audre Lorde dedicated "A Litany for Survival" to "those of us" who are marginal to society. The poem articulates the fears of those "who live at the shoreline," and it urges us to speak despite fear, though "We were never meant to survive."

"Turning to you, my name," Lisa Suhair Majaj feels that she can finally "claim" the name *Lisa* and the half of her heritage that is Iowan. Her Palestinian name, *Suhair,* is more distant, a "little star in the night." Since childhood the author has felt a "rending split" in herself between cultures. Yet the poem ends with an integration of selves. A hint of music like the sound of the Arabic flute, *nai,* suggests "some possible language / all our tongues can sing."

According to Naomi Shihab Nye, *adios* "is a good word," one that we all need to know, "no matter what language you were born with," for loss is a universal experience. The poet knows how to celebrate this constant, how to "wear it on every finger / till your hands dance, / . . . letting everything, easily, go."

Margaret Walker's poetry and novels have provided strong models for many African-American writers over the last fifty years. "I Want to Write" is an incantation celebrating and embodying a language that will provide "the songs of my people." The ambition is larger than the personal, and it is sacred; "I want to frame their dreams into words; their souls into notes."

In an interview, Judith Ortiz Cofer tells us that she wants to invite the reader into her work. Spanish is included in the English text not for decoration, but because it is essential, used where English could not convey the meaning or emotional impact. *Casa,* for example, speaks worlds about the atmosphere that the women of Cofer's family created in their homes both in Puerto Rico and in New Jersey. Having learned well the art of story-telling from her grandmother, Cofer has shaped her own voice in a language of "plenitude," a language that offers a feast for our imagination in several different genres. "The art of not forgetting" her past and her cultural heritage is a "spiritual matter" to the author and a gift to the readers.

◎ *ALICE WALKER*

Alice Walker was born in 1944 in Eatonton, Georgia. She attended Spelman College and received a B.A. from Sarah Lawrence College. She is the author of five novels, two books of short stories, two essay collections, and five volumes of poetry, the most recent of which is Her Blue Body Everything We Know *(1991). In 1983 her novel* The Color Purple *won the National Book Award and a Pulitzer Prize, and was shortly thereafter made into a feature film by Stephen Spielberg. Walker's most recent book is* The Same River Twice: Honoring the Difficult *(1994), composed of essays and articles about the film* The Color Purple, *an original screenplay for the film, entries from Walker's journals, and correspondence. Walker has rescued important writers from neglect, most notably Zora Neale Hurston, whose works she edited. She lives in the San Francisco area, where she has established a small press, Wild Trees, which publishes deserving lesser-known writers.*

"Everyday Use" was originally published in Alice Walker's first collection of stories, In Love and Trouble: Stories of Black Women *(1973). "Everyday Use" gives us a portrait of attitudes towards identity in the early 1970s, reflected in the names chosen by Dee and her mother. Walker creates a touching and sometimes humorous story/ensemble about a family of women, reminding us that language, like quilting, embodies our cultural histories.*

Everyday Use

for your grandmama

I will wait for her in the yard that Maggie and I made so clean and wavy yesterday afternoon. A yard like this is more comfortable than most people know. It is not just a yard. It is like an extended living room. When the hard clay is swept clean as a floor and the fine sand around the edges lined with tiny, irregular grooves, anyone can come and sit and look up into the elm tree and wait for the breezes that never come inside the house.

Maggie will be nervous until after her sister goes: she will stand hopelessly in corners, homely and ashamed of the burn scars down her arms and legs, eying her sister with a mixture of envy and awe. She thinks her sister has held life always in the palm of one hand, that "no" is a word the world never learned to say to her.

You've no doubt seen those TV shows where the child who has "made it" is confronted, as a surprise, by her own mother and father, tottering in weakly from backstage. (A pleasant surprise, of course. What would they do if parent and child came on the show only to curse out and insult each other?) On TV mother and child embrace and smile into each other's faces. Sometimes the mother and father weep, the child wraps them in her arms and leans across the table to tell how she would not have made it without their help. I have seen these programs.

Sometimes I dream a dream in which Dee and I are suddenly brought together on a TV program of this sort. Out of a dark and soft-seated limousine I am ushered into a bright room filled with many people. There I meet a smiling, gray, sporty man like Johnny Carson who shakes my hand and tells me what a fine girl I have. Then we are on the stage and Dee is embracing me with tears in her eyes. She pins on my dress a large orchid, even though she has told me once that she thinks orchids are tacky flowers.

In real life I am a large, big-boned woman with rough, man-working hands. In the winter I wear flannel nightgowns to bed and overalls during the day. I can kill and clean a hog as mercilessly as a man. My fat keeps me hot in zero weather. I can work outside all day, breaking ice to get water for washing: I can eat pork liver cooked over the open fire minutes after it comes steaming from the hog. One winter I knocked a bull calf straight in the brain between the eyes with a sledge hammer and had the meat hung up to chill before nightfall. But of course all this does not show on television. I am the way my daughter would want me to be: a hundred pounds lighter, my skin like an uncooked barley pancake. My hair glistens in the hot bright lights. Johnny Carson has much to do to keep up with my quick and witty tongue.

But that is a mistake. I know even before I wake up. Who ever knew a Johnson with a quick tongue? Who can even imagine me looking a strange white man in the eye? It seems to me I have talked to them always with one foot raised in flight, with my head turned in whichever way is farthest from them. Dee, though. She would always look anyone in the eye. Hesitation was no part of her nature.

"How do I look, Mama?" Maggie says, showing just enough of her thin body enveloped in pink skirt and red blouse for me to know she's there, almost hidden by the door.

"Come out into the yard," I say.

Have you ever seen a lame animal, perhaps a dog run over by some careless person rich enough to own a car, sidle up to someone who is ignorant enough to be kind to him? That is the way my Maggie walks. She has been like this, chin on chest, eyes on ground, feet in shuffle, ever since the fire that burned the other house to the ground.

Dee is lighter than Maggie, with nicer hair and a fuller figure. She's a woman now, though sometimes I forget. How long ago was it that the other house burned? Ten, twelve years? Sometimes I can still hear the flames and feel Maggie's arms sticking to me, her hair smoking and her dress falling off her in little black papery flakes. Her eyes seemed stretched open, blazed open by the flames reflected in them. And Dee. I see her standing off under the sweet gum tree she used to dig gum out of; a look of concentration on her face as she watched the last dingy gray board of the house fall in toward the red-hot brick chimney. Why don't you do a dance around the ashes? I'd wanted to ask her. She had hated the house that much.

I used to think she hated Maggie, too. But that was before we raised the money, the church and me, to send her to Augusta to school. She used to read to us without pity; forcing words, lies, other folks' habits, whole lives upon us two, sitting trapped and ignorant underneath her voice. She washed us in a river of make-believe, burned us with a lot of knowledge we didn't necessarily need to know. Pressed us to her with the serious way she read, to shove us away at just the moment, like dimwits, we seemed about to understand.

Dee wanted nice things. A yellow organdy dress to wear to her graduation from high school; black pumps to match a green suit she'd made from an old suit somebody gave me. She was determined to stare down any disaster in her efforts. Her eyelids would not flicker for minutes at a time. Often I fought off the temptation to shake her. At sixteen she had a style of her own: and knew what style was.

I never had an education myself. After second grade the school was closed down. Don't ask me why: in 1927 colored asked fewer questions than they do now. Sometimes Maggie reads to me. She stumbles along good-naturedly but can't see well. She knows she is not bright. Like good looks and money, quickness passed her by. She will marry John Thomas (who has mossy teeth in an earnest face) and then I'll be free to sit here and I guess just sing church songs to myself. Although I never was a good singer. Never could carry a tune. I was always better at a man's job. I used to love to milk till I was hooked in the side in '49. Cows are soothing and slow and don't bother you, unless you try to milk them the wrong way.

I have deliberately turned my back on the house. It is three rooms, just like the one that burned, except the roof is tin; they don't make shingle roofs any more. There are no real windows, just some holes cut in the sides, like the portholes in a ship, but not round and not square, with rawhide holding the shutters up on the outside. This house is in a pasture, too, like the other one. No doubt when Dee sees it she will want to tear it down. She wrote me once that no matter where we "choose" to live, she will manage to come see us. But she will never bring her friends. Maggie and I thought about this and Maggie asked me, "Mama, when did Dee ever *have* any friends?"

She had a few. Furtive boys in pink shirts hanging about on wash-day after school. Nervous girls who never laughed. Impressed with her they worshiped the well-turned phrase, the cute shape, the scalding humor that erupted like bubbles in lye. She read to them.

When she was courting Jimmy T she didn't have much time to pay to us, but turned all her faultfinding power on him. He *flew* to marry a cheap city girl from a family of ignorant flashy people. She hardly had time to recompose herself.

When she comes I will meet — but there they are!

Maggie attempts to make a dash for the house, in her shuffling way, but I stay her with my hand. "Come back here," I say. And she stops and tries to dig a well in the sand with her toe.

It is hard to see them clearly through the strong sun. But even the first glimpse of leg out of the car tells me it is Dee. Her feet were always neat-looking, as if God himself had shaped them with a certain style. From the other side of the car comes a short, stocky man. Hair is all over his head a foot long and hanging from his chin like a kinky mule tail. I hear Maggie suck in her breath. "Uhnnnh," is what it sounds like. Like when you see the wriggling end of a snake just in front of your foot on the road. "Uhnnnh."

Dee next. A dress down to the ground, in this hot weather. A dress so loud it hurts my eyes. There are yellows and oranges enough to throw back the light of the sun. I feel my whole face warming from the heat waves it throws out. Earrings gold, too, and hanging down to her shoulders. Bracelets dangling and making noises when she moves her arm up to shake the folds of the dress out of her armpits. The dress is loose and flows, and as she walks closer, I like it. I hear Maggie go "Uhnnnh" again. It is her sister's hair. It stands straight up like the wool on a sheep. It is black as night and around the edges are two long pigtails that rope about like small lizards disappearing behind her ears.

"Wa-su-zo-Tean-o!" she says, coming on in that gliding way the dress makes her move. The short stocky fellow with the hair to his navel is all grinning and he follows up with "Asalamalakim, my mother and sister!" He moves to hug Maggie but she falls back, right up against the back of my chair. I feel her trembling there and when I look up I see the perspiration falling off her chin.

"Don't get up," says Dee. Since I am stout it takes something of a push. You can see me trying to move a second or two before I make it. She turns, showing white heels through her sandals, and goes back to the car. Out she peeks next with a Polaroid. She stoops down quickly and lines up picture after picture of me sitting there in front of the house with Maggie cowering behind me. She never takes a shot without making sure the house is included. When a cow comes nibbling around the edge of the yard she snaps it and me and Maggie *and* the house. Then she puts the Polaroid in the back seat of the car, and comes up and kisses me on the forehead.

Meanwhile Asalamalakim is going through motions with Maggie's hand. Maggie's hand is as limp as a fish, and probably as cold, despite the sweat, and she keeps trying to pull it back. It looks like Asalamalakim wants to shake hands but wants to do it fancy. Or maybe he don't know how people shake hands. Anyhow, he soon gives up on Maggie.

"Well," I say. "Dee."

"No, Mama," she says. "Not 'Dee.' Wangero Leewanika Kemanjo!"

"What happened to 'Dee'?" I wanted to know.

"She's dead," Wangero said. "I couldn't bear it any longer, being named after the people who oppress me."

"You know as well as me you was named after your aunt Dicie," I said. Dicie is my sister. She named Dee. We called her "Big Dee" after Dee was born.

"But who was *she* named after?" asked Wangero.

"I guess after Grandma Dee," I said.

"And who was she named after?" asked Wangero.

"Her mother," I said, and saw Wangero was getting tired. "That's about as far back as I can trace it," I said. Though, in fact, I probably could have carried it back beyond the Civil War through the branches.

"Well," said Asalamalakim, "there you are."

"Uhnnnh," I heard Maggie say.

"There I was not," I said, "before 'Dicie' cropped up in our family, so why should I try to trace it that far back?"

He just stood there grinning, looking down on me like somebody inspecting a Model A car. Every once in a while he and Wangero sent eye signals over my head.

"How do you pronounce this name?" I asked.

"You don't have to call me by it if you don't want to," said Wangero.

"Why shouldn't I?" I asked. "If that's what you want us to call you, we'll call you."

"I know it might sound awkward at first," said Wangero.

"I'll get used to it," I said. "Ream it out again."

Well, soon we got the name out of the way. Asalamalakim had a name twice as long and three times as hard. After I tripped over it two or three times he told me to just call him Hakim-a-barber. I wanted to ask him was he a barber, but I didn't really think he was, so I didn't ask.

"You must belong to those beef-cattle peoples down the road," I said. They said "Asalamalakim" when they met you, too, but they didn't shake hands. Always too busy: feeding the cattle, fixing the fences, putting up salt-lick shelters, throwing down hay. When the white folks poisoned some of the herd the men stayed up all night with rifles in their hands. I walked a mile and a half just to see the sight.

Hakim-a-barber said, "I accept some of their doctrines, but farming and raising cattle is not my style." (They didn't tell me, and I didn't ask, whether Wangero [Dee] had really gone and married him.)

We sat down to eat and right away he said he didn't eat collards and pork was unclean. Wangero, though, went on through the chitlins and corn bread, the greens and everything else. She talked a blue streak over the sweet potatoes. Everything delighted her. Even the fact that we still used the benches her daddy made for the table when we couldn't afford to buy chairs.

"Oh, Mama!" she cried. Then turned to Hakim-a-barber. "I never knew how lovely these benches are. You can feel the rump prints," she said, running her hands underneath her and along the bench. Then she gave a sigh and her hand closed over Grandma Dee's butter dish. "That's it!" she said. "I knew there was something I wanted to ask you if I could have." She jumped up from the table and went over in the corner where the churn stood, the milk in it clabber by now. She looked at the churn and looked at it.

"This churn top is what I need," she said. "Didn't Uncle Buddy whittle it out of a tree you all used to have?"

"Yes," I said.

"Uh huh," she said happily. "And I want the dasher, too."

"Uncle Buddy whittle that, too?" asked the barber.

Dee (Wangero) looked up at me.

"Aunt Dee's first husband whittled the dash," said Maggie so low you almost couldn't hear her. "His name was Henry, but they called him Stash."

"Maggie's brain is like an elephant's," Wangero said, laughing. "I can use the churn top as a centerpiece for the alcove table," she said, sliding a plate over the churn, "and I'll think of something artistic to do with the dasher."

When she finished wrapping the dasher the handle stuck out. I took it for a moment in my hands. You didn't even have to look close to see where hands pushing the dasher up and down to make butter had left a kind of sink in the wood. In fact, there were a lot of small sinks: you could see where thumbs and fingers had sunk into the wood. It was beautiful light yellow wood, from a tree that grew in the yard where Big Dee and Stash had lived.

After dinner Dee (Wangero) went to the trunk at the foot of my bed and started rifling through it. Maggie hung back in the kitchen over the dishpan. Out came Wangero with two quilts. They had been pieced by Grandma Dee and then Big Dee and me had hung them on the quilt frames on the front porch and quilted them. One was in the Lone Star pattern. The other was Walk Around the Mountain. In both of them were scraps of dresses Grandma Dee had worn fifty and more years ago. Bits and pieces of Grandpa Jarrell's Paisley shirts. And one teeny faded blue piece, about the size of a penny matchbox, that was from Great Grandpa Ezra's uniform that he wore in the Civil War.

"Mama," Wangero said sweet as a bird. "Can I have these old quilts?"

I heard something fall in the kitchen, and a minute later the kitchen door slammed.

"Why don't you take one or two of the others?" I asked. "These old things was just done by me and Big Dee from some tops your grandma pieced before she died."

"No," said Wangero. "I don't want those. They are stitched around the borders by machine."

"That'll make them last better," I said.

"That's not the point," said Wangero. "These are all pieces of dresses Grandma used to wear. She did all this stitching by hand. Imagine!" She held the quilts securely in her arms, stroking them.

"Some of the pieces, like those lavender ones, come from old clothes her mother handed down to her," I said, moving up to touch the quilts. Dee (Wangero) moved back just enough so that I couldn't reach the quilts. They already belonged to her.

"Imagine!" she breathed again, clutching them closely to her bosom.

"The truth is," I said, "I promised to give them quilts to Maggie, for when she marries John Thomas."

She gasped like a bee had stung her.

"Maggie can't appreciate these quilts!" she said. "She'd probably be backward enough to put them to everyday use."

"I reckon she would," I said. "God knows I been saving 'em for long enough with nobody using 'em. I hope she will!" I didn't want to bring up how I had offered Dee (Wangero) a quilt when she went away to college. Then she had told me they were old-fashioned, out of style.

"But they're *priceless!*" she was saying now, furiously; for she had a temper. "Maggie would put them on the bed and in five years they'd be in rags. Less than that!"

"She can always make some more," I said. "Maggie knows how to quilt."

Dee (Wangero) looked at me with hatred. "You will not understand. The point is these quilts, *these* quilts!"

"Well," I said, stumped. "What would *you* do with them?"

"Hang them," she said. As if that was the only thing you *could* do with quilts.

Maggie by now was standing in the door. I could almost hear the sound her feet made as they scraped over each other.

"She can have them, Mama," she said, like somebody used to never winning anything, or having anything reserved for her. "I can 'member Grandma Dee without the quilts."

I looked at her hard. She had filled her bottom lip with checkerberry snuff and it gave her face a kind of dopey, hangdog look. It was Grandma Dee and Big Dee who taught her how to quilt herself. She stood there with her scarred hands hidden in the folds of her skirt. She looked at her sister with something like fear but she wasn't mad at her. This was Maggie's portion. This was the way she knew God to work.

When I looked at her like that something hit me in the top of my head and ran down to the soles of my feet. Just like when I'm in church and the spirit of God touches me and I get happy and shout. I did something I never had done before: hugged Maggie to me, then dragged her on into the room, snatched the quilts out of Miss Wangero's hands and dumped them into Maggie's lap. Maggie just sat there on my bed with her mouth open.

"Take one or two of the others," I said to Dee.

But she turned without a word and went out to Hakim-a-barber.

"You just don't understand," she said, as Maggie and I came out to the car.

"What don't I understand?" I wanted to know.

"Your heritage," she said. And then she turned to Maggie, kissed her, and said, "You ought to try to make something of yourself, too, Maggie. It's really a new day for us. But from the way you and Mama still live you'd never know it."

She put on some sunglasses that hid everything above the tip of her nose and her chin.

Maggie smiled; maybe at the sunglasses. But a real smile, not scared.

After we watched the car dust settle I asked Maggie to bring me a dip of snuff. And then the two of us sat there just enjoying, until it was time to go in the house and go to bed.

◎ JANICE EIDUS

Janice Eidus was born in New York, and grew up in the Bronx. She has an M.A. in Writing from Johns Hopkins. Eidus is the author of the novels Urban Bliss *(1994) and* Faithful Rebecca *(1986) and the short story collection* Vito Loves Geraldine *(1990). She has won two O. Henry Prizes for her short fiction, as well as a* Redbook *Magazine Prize. Her books and stories have been published throughout Europe and in South America, Japan, and Greece. Her work also appears in many anthologies, including* Mondo Elvis *and* Growing up Female: Stories by Women Writers from the American Mosaic. *Her novel* The Celibacy Club *will be published in 1996.*

"Robin's Nest," appears in Vito Loves Geraldine. *Eidus has commented: "I believe in the triumph of the imagination. It's a theme that recurs repeatedly in my novels and stories. I believe that the first step toward change of any kind — and toward being able to overcome obstacles, both external and internal, is to imagine — to envision — that change. 'Robin's Nest' explores this theme: Through the invented-imagined language of Ooola, Rachel and Ambrose (and finally even the disillusioned, mute Robin) are able to feel hope; and with hope, there is always the possibility of a better world for all of us becoming a reality" (Letter from Eidus to Kallet, February 26, 1996).*

Robin's Nest

Mr. Rosen, my social studies teacher, is standing in front of the blackboard and talking about the Vietnam War, which took place in the nineteen sixties. Mr. Rosen is my favorite teacher this year. For one thing, he has a red mustache, and I've loved red hair ever since I was a little girl. Robin, my mother, has red hair. But Mr. Rosen talks a lot, really fast, and Robin doesn't talk at all. Ever.

Mr. Rosen's hair isn't as beautiful as Robin's, though. Nobody has hair that beautiful. And I bet that if Robin could speak, her voice would be beautiful, too.

Ambrose, my boyfriend, also has red hair. Ambrose is in the sixth grade, like I am, but he goes to the Emerson School, which my dad says is too unstructured. I go to the Smythe-Durham School, which is very structured. I also like Mr. Rosen because he used to teach at the Emerson School, but I've never told my dad that. Right now, Mr. Rosen is saying that innocent people, even women and children, were killed during the war. I try to take notes while he speaks. But it's hard because I keep picturing the women and children, and they all start to look like me and Robin, and then I can't concentrate on his words. But I have to concentrate so that I can pass. I've been failing English since last year, and if I start to fail social studies too I don't know what my dad will do. It makes me nervous just thinking about it. So I start writing really fast, trying to copy down everything Mr. Rosen is saying. "President Johnson," I write down. "Amnesty for draft resisters," I write that down, too, but I'm not sure I know what amnesty means. Mr. Rosen must have said, but I guess I wasn't concentrating. Amnesty is a pretty word, though. I like the way it sounds. Maybe Ambrose and I can use it in Ooola, which is the private language he and I are inventing. Nobody in the whole world will know how to speak Ooola except me and Ambrose. But I can't think about Ooola now. I have to pay attention. Mr. Rosen is saying something about the draft resisters having to move to Canada. I know that my dad didn't like the draft resisters. My dad was an officer in the Marines in Vietnam, and he says that he lost close friends there, and that he and his friends were patriots, and that it was a good war. In Ooola, patriot means cappuccino. My dad says that the people who protested against the war were so self-indulgent and immature that they thought sex and rock 'n' roll were more important than freedom and honor. Or else they were crazy. He says that history will prove him right. Robin was a war protestor. Mr. Rosen is saying that he was a war protestor, too. "War protestor," I write down. I wonder if Robin and Mr. Rosen used to know each other during the nineteen sixties. Maybe Mr. Rosen even lived on Robin's commune with her.

Another thing I like about Mr. Rosen is that he talks about things I care about. For instance, last week he talked about the people in America who are so poor they have to live out on the streets, and how they get malnourished and freeze to death and other terrible stuff. He calls them "the homeless." I see them, these homeless people, every day, when I walk through the park on my way to and from Smythe-Durham. Sometimes I even see homeless mothers with homeless children. I shiver when I see them. My dad forbids me to give them dimes or quarters or anything. He says it could be dangerous because they're crazy. But I don't think most of them are crazy. And even the ones who are deserve some dimes and quarters. But Ambrose's father, who's a plastic surgeon like my dad, says that it's good to give them dimes and quarters, so Ambrose gives for both of us. Robin never carries money, but one day last winter, she and I were walking in the park and we passed a homeless woman who was only half dressed. Robin was wearing a big baggy black coat. She took it off and gave it to the woman. I bet my dad wouldn't have liked that if he'd been with us.

The bell rings. I close my notebook. Mr. Rosen says that the only homework we have tonight is to think about whether it's okay to disagree with your government. Or with your parents. He smiles. He has a nice smile.

Next I have my session with Ms. Ullman, the psychologist at Smythe-Durham. Last year when I started failing English, the headmaster, Dr. Prescott, who has almost no hair at all, called me into his office, which was filled with ships in bottles. He said, "Your reading scores are extremely high, young lady. You shouldn't be failing English." I didn't say anything. So he said that he was going to send me to see Ms. Ullman. He said my dad had called him and was very unhappy that I wasn't passing English. And he said he didn't want my dad to be unhappy.

I knock on Ms. Ullman's door and she says, "Come in, Rachel." Ms. Ullman's office is nice, much nicer than Dr. Prescott's office, and I like sitting in the big brown leather chair across from her. Above her desk there's a painting of a big red bird sitting on the branch of a tree. I once asked Ms. Ullman if the bird was a robin, and she said she didn't think so. She said it was more like a bird painted from the artist's imagination. I like to look up at the red bird when we talk because that bird's eyes are big and sad, like Robin's.

Ms. Ullman and I talk a lot about birds, because when I was little I used to think that Robin wasn't really my mother, but that she was some strange bird that had flown into our apartment. I figured that she had a broken wing and couldn't fly home. Sometimes I thought that she was a lost bird from another planet.

The thing is, Robin really does look more like a bird than a mother. At least, she doesn't look like the mothers of the other kids I know. And she doesn't act like them, either. Ambrose's mother, for example, is tall and she wears high heeled shoes which make her look taller and blouses with padded shoulders and she talks all the time. But Robin is very small, and she wears simple dresses that just slip over her head, and flat sandals. And she's always looking over her shoulder, like birds do. And she has those big sad bird eyes. Even sadder than the eyes of the red bird on Ms. Ullman's wall. And she has long hair that goes way past her waist, so that sometimes it looks like bright red feathers are growing down her back. Ms. Ullman thinks it's good that I've accepted that Robin really is my mother, and not a bird.

Ms. Ullman and I also talk a lot about my dad. My dad does nose jobs and face lifts and tummy tucks and breast enlargements. Sometimes he calls himself a "sculptor." He also calls himself "Pygmalion," which Ambrose says is the title of a play about a rich man who wants to make a poor woman act rich. Most of my dad's patients are women. They come from all over the world, he says, "because I speak their language, Rachel. They all want to be beautiful, and I speak the language of beauty." Sometimes he tells me and Robin stories about his patients, like the woman who had a nose like Jimmy Durante's, but wanted a nose like Marilyn Monroe's, or the woman who was flat-chested and had never had a boyfriend but after my dad gave her bigger breasts she had two boyfriends. "I gave her perfect breasts," he said, looking right at Robin who has really tiny breasts, almost no breasts at all, and what she has she hides completely underneath baggy dresses. Robin looks over her shoulder when he says things like that. But I say, "Really, Daddy?" and "Wow, Daddy," because I'm too scared not to act excited about his work. I'm scared that when I grow up he's going to want to do those jobs on me, too. Ambrose says I shouldn't be scared, that he won't let him. But I don't know. I'm afraid that if I don't grow up to be beautiful enough, he'll start sculpting me.

Since Ms. Ullman encourages me to talk to her about my fears, I've told her that lately I've noticed that my nose is starting to grow. "It's not a tiny pug nose any more like it was when I was little, and I'm afraid my dad will notice it soon," I say.

"You have a lovely nose, Rachel," Ms. Ullman says. "Honestly."

I don't ever want my dad to meet Ms. Ullman. I'm afraid he'll want to do something to her nose, too. Ms. Ullman has short frizzy brown hair, but sometimes, when the sun shines through her office window, her hair looks almost red. And she has big thick eyebrows and a long hooked nose with a bump on it. Ambrose met her one Saturday morning when he and I were sitting on a bench in the park, practicing Ooola and counting out change to give to homeless people. Ms. Ullman walked by. She looked different in blue jeans and a sweatshirt. She came over and said, "How nice, that you both care so much about the less fortunate." "She's intense looking," Ambrose said after she left. But I don't think my dad would find intense beautiful.

The very first thing Ms. Ullman ever said to me during our very first session was, "So I hear you're having some trouble in your English class." But I just shrugged. I didn't want to talk about English class. I looked up at the painting of the red bird. "Is it okay if we forget the English class stuff today?" I asked. "Can I tell you something else instead?"

She didn't answer right away. And then she gave me a big smile and said, "Shoot!" So I took a deep breath, and I told her the story of how my dad met Robin and why Robin doesn't ever speak. I told it exactly the way my dad tells it to me. "Robin was in a hospital because she'd taken all this LSD during the nineteen sixties and it had made her stop speaking," I said. Ms. Ullman began taking notes. "My dad says that LSD is a drug that makes you see the world as though you're crazy. It ruins your mind like a . . ." But I had to stop there because my dad always says, "like a bump and a hook ruin a nose," and I didn't want to repeat that in front of Ms. Ullman. So I just said, "Anyway, Robin had taken a lot of it. My dad was working in the hospital. He says that from the first moment he saw her, sitting on top of her bed in her hospital gown, staring over her shoulder, he knew what he wanted. 'I wanted to take her home, Rachel,' he says. 'To heal her, to make her whole again. I saw that there was something special about her. Her suffering had enriched her. It was my duty. I would be a plastic surgeon of the mind. Instead of a nose job, I would give your mother a mind job.' "

Ms. Ullman looked up from her notes. "A mind job?" she asked. "Those are your father's words?"

I nodded.

"Did he . . . smile when he said it?" she asked.

I shrugged. "I can't remember."

"Well . . . just what is a . . . mind job?"

"I'm not sure," I said. "I think he . . . talked to her a lot. About the things he wanted her to believe in. Things that would make her less crazy. Things for her . . . own good."

Ms. Ullman took a wrinkled handkerchief from her desk and blew her nose.

"Anyway, he took her home and married her. And he gave her the mind job. And then they had me." I didn't say anything else because I wasn't sure what else to say. That's where my dad always stops when he tells the story.

"A mind job," Ms. Ullman said again. She was writing really fast now.

"I'm afraid," I said.

"Afraid, Rachel?" Ms. Ullman put down her pen and leaned forward and looked into my eyes. "What are you afraid of?"

"I'm afraid that a mind job hurts."

"Oh," she said. "Well, has Robin . . . gotten better?"

"My dad says yes," I said. "He says that even though she doesn't speak she's not crazy or unhappy anymore and that she believes in all the right things and that she would never do the kinds of things she used to do like protest against the Vietnam War and take drugs and live in a commune and dance naked at hippie festivals and not buy from the military-industrial complex and not give money to taxes because the money is spent on weapons and things like that . . . ."

"And what do you think?"

"I don't know." And then I told her that when I used to think Robin was a bird from another planet I also believed that she was really speaking all the time, but that people on earth just couldn't hear her because her language was on a higher frequency than earth ears could hear. "Even though she doesn't say so, I know Robin loves me," I explained to Ms. Ullman. I told her that Robin takes me on long walks through the park and that when I have a fever she sits by my bedside for hours and holds my hand and puts wet towels on my forehead, and that she sometimes sits with me and Ambrose and we all eat tuna fish sandwiches together. Ms. Ullman said that Robin sounded like a very caring person, and I felt happy when she said that.

Sometimes Ms. Ullman doesn't say anything at the beginning of the session. She just lets me start talking about anything I want to. But other times she starts by asking me a question, and today the first thing she asks me to do is describe our apartment. "I'd like to have a sense of your home," she says. "Tell me about it, Rachel."

"It's very big," I tell her. "My dad has a bedroom and a study, and Robin and I each have a bedroom, and there's a living room and a kitchen and a dining room. And last year my dad put this white furniture all over the place. It's kind of like a hospital now, and he doesn't like it if there's the slightest bit of dirt on anything."

Ms. Ullman waits for me to say something else. But I don't have anything else to say about the white furniture.

"Any other thoughts about your home?" Ms. Ullman runs her hand through her frizzy hair.

So I tell her about how one day I told my dad that I felt guilty about how big our apartment was, because there are so many homeless people. I said maybe we had more than our fair share of space. He said that I shouldn't feel guilty, that most of the homeless people wouldn't know how to survive in an apartment building like ours anyway, that they wouldn't want the responsibilities of mortgages and coop board meetings and things like that, and that chopping a bedroom or two off of our apartment wouldn't solve the homeless problem. Ms. Ullman asks, "Did he smile when he said those things?" But I shrug. "I can't remember."

Then Ms. Ullman says, "You're a very caring girl, Rachel."

I'm glad that Ms. Ullman thinks I'm a caring girl. I also hope she thinks I'm pretty just the way I am. Sometimes my dad takes my face in his hands and looks at it from different angles and I get very scared.

"So," Ms. Ullman says, leaning back, "how's Ooola going?" Ms. Ullman asks me about Ooola a lot during our sessions. After I'd had a few sessions with her, I told her about it because I knew I could trust her. I told her that sometimes Ambrose and I invent brand new words to mean things, words which sound like nonsense to anyone else. And that other times we take words that already mean something in English but we make them mean something else, which is just as good as inventing a new word, and that we're going to have a whole Ooola dictionary some day which only we'll know how to read. And a grammar handbook, too.

"Ambrose found the word ablutions in the dictionary yesterday," I tell her. "It means a ceremonial washing of oneself." Ms. Ullman may know this already, but I can't be sure. "But in Ooola, it's going to mean sad." Sometimes I tell Ms. Ullman a few words in Ooola. Ambrose says it's okay, because even if I tell her a few words, she still won't know enough to speak it. "Today after school Ambrose and I are going to invent words for colors," I tell her. "Last week we invented words for the seasons. Cratoup means winter."

"Cratoup," she repeats, blowing her nose.

She puts away her handkerchief and looks serious for a minute. "Maybe, Rachel," she says softly, "the reason you're inventing Ooola has something to do with the reason you're not passing English. What do you think of that idea?"

I don't say anything. Ms. Ullman comes up with weird ideas like this all the time.

"Well, I'm afraid that our time is up for today," Ms. Ullman says, looking at her watch.

"Arugula," I say to her, which is Ooola for goodbye.

"Arugula," she says.

My next class is English. I dread it. This year I was put in a slow class, even though Dr. Prescott said my reading scores are so high. It's a punishment for failing, I guess. Ms. Buschel is my English teacher. She's got blonde hair and a tiny nose. She's the type, I think, that my dad has in mind when he fixes noses. I always sit in the back of the room, hoping that she won't remember I'm there. Today she tells us to write, stories about anything we want. I wish I could write my story in Ooola. But if I did that I'd be afraid Ms. Buschel would show it to Dr. Prescott and then they'd send me to a hospital like Robin was in. And then my dad would definitely want to do a mind job on me. I force myself to pick up my pen and write.

Ms. Buschel says, "Okay, that's enough writing time. Now we'll call on a few of you to share your stories. How about Carl first?" Carl walks to the front of the room. He licks his lips. His story is about a little boy who wants a donkey for Christmas more than anything else in the world, and then on Christmas morning Santa Claus gives him one. Everyone applauds. Ms. Buschel says, "Okay, everyone, let's give Carl some feedback." Annie raises her hand and says, "It made me feel good that he got the donkey." "Very perceptive, Annie. And thank you, Carl, for sharing your story," Ms. Buschel smiles.

I pray that Ms. Buschel doesn't call on me next. "Nancy," she says. Nancy walks to the front of the room. She holds the paper right in front of her face while she reads. Her story is about a little girl who wins a pie baking contest and starts a pie business and becomes a millionaire. Everyone applauds. Ms. Buschel asks for feedback. "It's good because she succeeds," Nicky says. "Very insightful, Nicky. And thank you, Nancy, for sharing that," Ms. Buschel says.

I pray again that Ms. Buschel doesn't call on me. But this time I'm not so lucky. "Rachel," she says. I walk to the front of the room. I clear my throat and read. "There was a little girl whose mother was a beautiful silent bird from another planet. The little girl's father said the little girl's mother was crazy. So he gave her mother something he called a mind job. But a mind job hurts. It pushes words down into your brain. So the little girl started to speak a special, secret language that nobody else would understand. That way nobody could ever give her a mind job." Nobody applauds. Nobody gives feedback. Ms. Buschel doesn't thank me for sharing my story. So I sit down and some other students get up and read their stories, but I don't pay any attention. Instead, I think about what amnesty could mean in Ooola and about Ambrose and Robin and the red bird on Ms. Ullman's wall.

English is the last class of the day, and when the bell rings, I race out. Ambrose is waiting for me on the corner. "Mubbles," I say to him, which means hello in Ooola. "Mubbles, Rachel," he says.

I met Ambrose last year when my dad was giving a speech about a new technique in nose jobs. It was a whole afternoon of plastic surgeons speaking about cutting and pulling and bending. I went because it seemed like a way for me to act really interested in my dad's work. I was sitting by myself in the front row. I was the only kid in the whole auditorium. But then Ambrose came in.

He sat down right next to me. He pointed towards the doctors sitting on stage waiting for their turns to speak. "That one's mine," he pointed to a roly-poly, red-headed man on the left side of the stage. "Which one's yours?"

Ambrose's father is really different than my dad. His father mostly works on people who've been burned in fires or injured in accidents. He tries to make them look the way they looked before they got hurt.

I fell in love with Ambrose the instant he sat down next to me. He says that he fell in love with me right then too. He says that unconsciously we'd already begun communicating with each other in Ooola. I was nervous about what Ambrose would say the first time I brought him home and introduced him to Robin, but he didn't blink an eye. He's very sensitive. He writes love poems to me in both English and Ooola. He's even asthmatic, which makes me love him more. Because I know he needs taking care of.

Ambrose takes my hand as we walk across the park. The Smythe-Durham School is on the east side of the park, and I live on the west side. I'm glad because that way we get to walk through the park every day and Ambrose can give quarters and dimes to the homeless people who live in the grass and trees. Sometimes he drops the money into their cups, sometimes right into the palms of their hands. Some of them say "God bless you." Some of them say, "Hey, Carrot Top." And some of them don't say anything. I wonder if the ones who don't say anything are really speaking to us in a language on another frequency.

When we get to my building, the doorman, Billy, who likes Ambrose, gives him a special handshake. "It's from the nineteen sixties," Billy says. "It's called a power-to-the-people shake." Ambrose and I give power-to-the-people shakes to each other in the elevator on the way upstairs. I wonder if Robin used to shake hands like that before she took too much LSD. In the elevator, Ambrose also gives me a little kiss right on the tip of my nose, which I'm sure he does because I told him that it's growing. "Swampy," I say to him, which means thank you in Ooola.

We walk inside the apartment. The first thing I always do is look around for Robin. When I was little I used to look around because I was worried that she'd flown away while I was gone, but now I do it just because I like to. But I don't see her, so I figure she's in her bedroom. Ambrose and I go into the kitchen and make tuna fish sandwiches. I like mine with more onions than he does and he likes his with more mayonnaise. What we both like is to make them thick, with lots of lettuce and tomatoes crammed in. And we both like them on hard rolls with seeds. My dad disapproves of the way I eat. He tells me I'm not too young too start counting calories. But since he won't be home until much later, I stuff my sandwich to the limit.

Then Ambrose and I pour ourselves some cherry seltzer, which is my favorite flavor, and we go into the living room and get ready to work on inventing words for colors. We sit on the rug, and we surround ourselves with all of my dad's dictionaries and thesauruses. We even take his medical dictionaries out and use words from them. For instance, in Ooola, Cortisone means dinnertime, and Tetracycline means helicopter. We have to be very careful not to get tuna fish on the white rug.

Robin wanders in. I'm happy to see her. I smile at her. She's wearing a baggy light blue dress. She takes tiny bird steps. She smiles back at us and wanders past us into the kitchen.

Ambrose says, "How about sponge for blue?"

I try it out. "Robin is dressed in sponge today."

"Now I'm not sure," Ambrose says. "Did that sound right to you?"

"Well, let's think about the meaning of blue." That's how we work. We think about what words mean to us. I once explained our method to Ms. Ullman and she told me that what we do is called free associating.

I begin. "The sky."

"The sea," Ambrose says.

I say, "My dad says that women with blue eyes get the most upset if their noses are big because they feel gypped, like since they got the blue eyes they should have also gotten the tiny noses."

"Bluefish," Ambrose says.

"My dad says that the blue in the black and blue marks that women get on their skin after face lifts is a unique shade of blue, not found anywhere else."

"Singin' the blues," Ambrose says.

Robin comes in from the kitchen and sits down with us. She tucks her legs under her dress. She's made herself a tuna fish sandwich too. She hardly uses any mayonnaise or onions at all, and her sandwich is much thinner than ours. Ambrose and I take big bites of our sandwiches. Robin takes tiny bird-sized bites. I want to say something to her but I don't know what to say. When I was little I used to say things like, "Pretty bird, fly." But now I'm usually just quiet around her. What I want to say most of all is that I hope it didn't hurt too much when my dad gave her the mind job. I believe that my dad wouldn't hurt her deliberately. I believe that he loves her too. But he has this saying that he uses a lot, "The end justifies the means." Ms. Ullman says if I want to ask Robin about the mind job, maybe I should just come out and ask.

"Listen," I say to Ambrose instead, "I think I like sponge for blue."

Ambrose smiles. He has these wonderful crooked teeth that braces just don't seem to help. "I get the sponges most every night," he says.

Robin takes a sip from my glass of cherry seltzer. And then she clears her throat. It's a tiny sound. Ambrose and I both stare at her. I've never heard any noise come from her throat before. Robin turns away from us and looks over her shoulder. Then she turns back and takes another sip of seltzer. She clears her throat again. Ambrose takes my hand. I hold onto his hand for dear life. We keep staring at her.

"Children," Robin says.

I hear it clearly. It's the first word Robin has ever spoken to me. Her voice is soft and sad. It's the voice that birds really would speak in if they could, I'm sure.

"Children," Robin says again.

I can't say a word. I look at Ambrose. He's having trouble breathing. I'm afraid he's going to have an asthma attack and I won't be able to take care of him because I'm in a state of shock. But luckily Ambrose calms down. He takes deep breaths and counts to ten. He begins breathing normally again and color returns to his face. And he actually answers her, like he's just having a regular conversation with anyone. "Uh huh?" he asks.

Robin looks over her shoulder and then back at us. I'm sure she won't answer. Maybe someone put LSD into our tuna fish sandwiches and Robin never spoke at all. Maybe we just imagined her voice. But I'm wrong. She answers. She speaks very slowly. She stops between words. She looks as though she's concentrating and working very hard on speaking. "Children. I know that . . . you are inventing . . . new words. . . . A new . . . language."

"Mother," I say, finally, putting down my sandwich, "Why haven't you spoken all these years?" My hand in Ambrose's is all sweaty. I feel like a very very little girl, much younger than eleven. I also feel like an old woman, maybe a hundred years old. I can't believe that I'm asking her this and that she's going to answer me.

Robin waits a minute before speaking. This time her words come more quickly. She's not stumbling so much. "I chose not to speak. It was my own choice. I'd grown very sad. But now . . . I speak because I'm so very pleased . . . that you care so much, Rachel . . . the way I did."

I don't say anything for a minute, I feel so surprised. All these years Robin could have talked, but she didn't want to because she was sad. I remember a word my dad used once. "Disillusioned," he said. "Your mother, Rachel, had grown disillusioned." I keep staring at Robin and I start to feel very sad, myself. I don't like the sound of the word disillusioned. I don't want to include it in Ooola.

Ambrose squeezes my hand and says, "It's spaghetti." Spaghetti means okay in Ooola. I squeeze his hand back. And then I take Robin's hand and I squeeze it, too. She squeezes back. She holds my hand tight.

And I think that maybe Ambrose and I don't need to keep Ooola a secret from everyone. Maybe it would be wonderful if one day everyone in the whole world spoke only Ooola. And there wouldn't be any words in Ooola for homelessness or crime or prisons or wars or mind jobs and nobody would want a different skin color or a smaller nose or larger breasts. Everyone would feel fine just the way they were. And Robin would talk all the time, because she wouldn't be disillusioned, and my dad would only do plastic surgery on people who'd been injured. Even though Robin didn't know about Ooola during the nineteen sixties, I guess that was the way she wanted it too. But she failed. At least, she thought she failed. But maybe what she's saying now is that, because of me, she hasn't really failed.

I feel shy and I look at Ambrose. Ambrose says, "It's spaghetti."

◎ *LESLIE MARMON SILKO*

Leslie Marmon Silko, born in 1948 in Albuquerque, New Mexico, is of mixed Laguna, Mexican, and white ancestry. She grew up on the Laguna Pueblo reservation and considers Laguna culture to be her way of knowing the world. Silko graduated from the University of New Mexico and has been on the faculties of the University of New Mexico and the University of Arizona. She spent two years in Ketchikan, Alaska, when she was provided with an artist's residence by the Rosewater Foundation-on-Ketchikan Creek. There she wrote her novel Ceremony *(1977). She has received an award for poetry from the* Chicago Review, *and a MacArthur Foundation Fellowship, among many honors. Silko's latest novel,* Almanac of the Dead, *came out in 1991.*

"Lullaby" first appeared in the Chicago Review *in 1974. In the text,* Yeibechei *refers to the Navajo Night Chant, a ceremony of healing; a* hogan *is a traditional, six-sided Navajo dwelling.* BIA *is the U.S. Bureau of Indian Affairs. In the Navajo lullaby that concludes this story, Silko evokes the continuity of the oral tradition and of maternal love. The lullaby offers the last word in this story, restoring balance where healing might have seemed impossible.*

Lullaby

The sun had gone down but the snow in the wind gave off its own light. It came in thick tufts like new wool — washed before the weaver spins it. Ayah reached out for it like her own babies had, and she smiled when she remembered how she had laughed at them. She was an old woman now, and her life had become memories. She sat down with her back against the wide cottonwood tree, feeling the rough bark on her back bones; she faced east and listened to the wind and snow sing a high-pitched Yeibechei song. Out of the wind she felt warmer, and she could watch the wide fluffy snow fill in her tracks, steadily, until the direction she had come from was gone. By the light of the snow she could see the dark outline of the big arroyo a few feet away. She was sitting on the edge of Cebolleta Creek, where in the springtime the thin cows would graze on a grass already chewed flat to the ground. In the wide deep creek bed where only a trickle of water flowed in the summer, the skinny cows would wander, looking for new grass along winding paths splashed with manure.

Ayah pulled the old Army blanket over her head like a shawl. Jimmie's blanket — the one he had sent to her. That was long time ago and the green wool was faded, and it was unraveling on the edges. She did not want to think about Jimmie. So she thought about the weaving and the way her mother had done it. On the tall wooden loom set into the sand under a tamarack tree for shade. She could see it clearly. She had been only a little girl when her grandma gave her the wooden combs to pull the twigs and burrs from the raw, freshly washed wool. And while she combed the wool, her grandma sat beside her, spinning a silvery strand of yarn around the smooth cedar spindle. Her mother worked at the loom with yarns dyed bright yellow and red and gold. She watched them dye the yarn in boiling black pots full of beeweed petals, juniper berries, and sage. The blankets her mother made were soft and woven so tight that rain rolled off them like birds' feathers. Ayah remembered sleeping warm on cold windy nights, wrapped in her mother's blankets on the hogan's sandy floor.

The snow drifted now, with the northwest wind hurling it in gusts. It drifted up around her black overshoes — old ones with little metal buckles. She smiled at the snow which was trying to cover her little by little. She could remember when they had no black rubber overshoes; only the high buckskin leggings that they wrapped over their elkhide moccasins. If the snow was dry or frozen, a person could walk all day and not get wet; and in the evenings the beams of the ceiling would hang with lengths of pale buckskin leggings, drying out slowly.

She felt peaceful remembering. She didn't feel cold any more. Jimmie's blanket seemed warmer than it had ever been. And she could remember the morning he was born. She could remember whispering to her mother, who was sleeping on the other side of the hogan, to tell her it was time now. She did not want to wake the others. The second time she called to her, her mother stood up and pulled on her shoes; she knew. They walked to the old stone hogan together, Ayah walking a step behind her mother. She waited alone, learning the rhythms of the pains while her mother went to call the old woman to help them. The morning was already warm even before dawn and Ayah smelled the bee flowers blooming and the young willow growing at the springs. She could remember that so clearly, but his birth merged into the births of the other children and to her it became all the same birth. They named him for the summer morning and in English they called him Jimmie.

It wasn't like Jimmie died. He just never came back, and one day a dark blue sedan with white writing on its doors pulled up in front of the boxcar shack where the rancher let the Indians live. A man in a khaki uniform trimmed in gold gave them a yellow piece of paper and told them that Jimmie was dead. He said the Army would try to get the body back and then it would be shipped to them; but it wasn't likely because the helicopter had burned after it crashed. All of this was told to Chato because he could understand English. She stood inside the doorway holding the baby while Chato listened. Chato spoke English like a white man and he spoke Spanish too. He was taller than the white man and he stood straighter too. Chato didn't explain why; he just told the military man they could keep the body if they found it. The white man looked bewildered; he nodded his head and he left. Then Chato looked at her and shook his head, and then he told her, "Jimmie isn't coming home anymore," and when he spoke, he used the words to speak of the dead. She didn't cry then, but she hurt inside with anger. And she mourned him as the years passed, when a horse fell with Chato and broke his leg, and the white rancher told them he wouldn't pay Chato until he could work again. She mourned Jimmie because he would have worked for his father then; he would have saddled the big bay horse and ridden the fence lines each day, with wire cutters and heavy gloves, fixing the breaks in the barbed wire and putting the stray cattle back inside again.

She mourned him after the white doctors came to take Danny and Ella away. She was at the shack alone that day they came. It was back in the days before they hired Navajo women to go with them as interpreters. She recognized one of the doctors. She had seen him at the children's clinic at Cañoncito about a month ago. They were wearing khaki uniforms and they waved papers at her and a black ball-point pen, trying to make her understand their English words. She was frightened by the way they looked at the children, like the lizard watches the fly. Danny was swinging on the tire swing on the elm tree behind the rancher's house, and Ella was toddling around the front door, dragging the broomstick horse Chato made for her. Ayah could see they wanted her to sign the papers, and Chato had taught her to sign her name. It was something she was proud of. She only wanted them to go, and to take their eyes away from her children.

She took the pen from the man without looking at his face and she signed the papers in three different places he pointed to. She stared at the ground by their feet and waited for them to leave. But they stood there and began to point and gesture at the children. Danny stopped swinging. Ayah could see his fear. She moved suddenly and grabbed Ella into her arms; the child squirmed, trying to get back to her toys. Ayah ran with the baby toward Danny; she screamed for him to run and then she grabbed him around his chest and carried him too. She ran south into the foothills of juniper trees and black lava rock. Behind her she heard the doctors running, but they had been taken by surprise, and as the hills became stepper and the cholla cactus were thicker, they stopped. When she reached the top of the hill, she stopped to listen in case they were circling around her. But in a few minutes she heard a car engine start and they drove away. The children had been too surprised to cry while she ran with them. Danny was shaking and Ella's little fingers were gripping Ayah's blouse.

She stayed up in the hills for the rest of the day, sitting on a black lava boulder in the sunshine where she could see for miles all around her. The sky was light blue and cloudless, and it was warm for late April. The sun warmth relaxed her and took the fear and anger away. She lay back on the rock and watched the sky. It seemed to her that she could walk into the sky, stepping through clouds endlessly. Danny played with little pebbles and stones, pretending they were birds eggs and then little rabbits. Ella sat at her feet and dropped fistfuls of dirt into the breeze, watching the dust and particles of sand intently. Ayah watched a hawk soar high above them, dark wings gliding; hunting or only watching, she did not know. The hawk was patient and he circled all afternoon before he disappeared around the high volcanic peak the Mexicans called Guadalupe.

Late in the afternoon, Ayah looked down at the gray boxcar shack with the paint all peeled from the wood; the stove pipe on the roof was rusted and crooked. The fire she had built that morning in the oil drum stove had burned out. Ella was asleep in her lap now and Danny sat close to her, complaining that he was hungry; he asked when they would go to the house. "We will stay up here until your father comes," she told him, "because those white men were chasing us." The boy remembered then and he nodded at her silently.

If Jimmie had been there he could have read those papers and explained to her what they said. Ayah would have known then, never to sign them. The doctors came back the next day and they brought a BIA policeman with them. They told Chato they had her signature and that was all they needed. Except for the kids. She listened to Chato sullenly; she hated him when he told her it was the old woman who died in the winter, spitting blood; it was her old grandma who had given the children this disease. "They don't spit blood," she said coldly. "The whites lie." She held Ella and Danny close to her, ready to run to the hills again. "I want a medicine man first," she said to Chato, not looking at him. He shook his head. "It's too late now. The policeman is with them. You signed the paper." His voice was gentle.

It was worse than if they had died: to lose the children and to know that somewhere, in a place called Colorado, in a place full of sick and dying strangers, her children were without her. There had been babies that died soon after they were born, and one that died before he could walk. She had carried them herself, up to the boulders and great pieces of the cliff that long ago crashed down from Long Mesa; she laid them in the crevices of sandstone and buried them in fine brown sand with round quartz pebbles that washed down the hills in the rain. She had endured it because they had been with her. But she could not bear this pain. She did not sleep for a long time after they took her children. She stayed on the hill where they had fled the first time, and she slept rolled up in the blanket Jimmie had sent her. She carried the pain in her belly and it was fed by everything she saw: the blue sky of their last day together and the dust and pebbles they played with; the swing in the elm tree and broomstick horse choked life from her. The pain filled her stomach and there was no room for food or for her lungs to fill with air. The air and the food would have been theirs.

She hated Chato, not because he let the policeman and doctors put the screaming children in the government car, but because he had taught her to sign her name. Because it was like the old ones always told her about learning their language or any of their ways: it endangered you. She slept alone on the hill until the middle of November when the first snows came. Then she made a bed for herself where the children had slept. She did not lie down beside Chato again until many years later, when he was sick and shivering and only her body could keep him warm. The illness came after the white rancher told Chato he was too old to work for him anymore, and Chato and his old woman should be out of the shack by the next afternoon because the rancher had hired new people to work there. That had satisfied her. To see how the white man repaid Chato's years of loyalty and work. All of Chato's fine-sounding English talk didn't change things.

It snowed steadily and the luminous light from the snow gradually diminished into the darkness. Somewhere in Cebolleta a dog barked and other village dogs joined with it. Ayah looked in the direction she had come, from the bar where Chato was buying the wine. Sometimes he told her to go on ahead and wait; and then he never came. And when she finally went back looking for him, she would find him passed out at the bottom of the wooden steps at Azzie's Bar. All the wine would be gone and most of the money too, from the pale blue check that came to them once a month in a government envelope. It was then that she would look at his face and his hands, scarred by ropes and the barbed wire of all those years, and she would think, this man is a stranger; for forty years she had smiled at him and cooked his food, but he remained a stranger. She stood up again, with the snow almost to her knees, and she walked back to find Chato.

It was hard to walk in the deep snow and she felt the air burn in her lungs. She stopped a short distance from the bar to rest and readjust the blanket. But this time he wasn't waiting for her on the bottom step with his old Stetson hat pulled down and his shoulders hunched up in his long wool overcoat.

She was careful not to slip on the wooden steps. When she pushed the door open, warm air and cigarette smoke hit her face. She looked around slowly and deliberately, in every corner, in every dark place that the old man might find to sleep. The bar owner didn't like Indians in there, especially Navajos, but he let Chato come in because he could talk Spanish like he was one of them. The men at the bar stared at her, and the bartender saw that she left the door open wide. Snowflakes were flying inside like moths and melting into a puddle on the oiled wood floor. He motioned to her to close the door, but she did not see him. She held herself straight and walked across the room slowly, searching the room with every step. The snow in her hair melted and she could feel it on her forehead. At the far corner of the room, she saw red flames at the mica window of the old stove door; she looked behind the stove just to make sure. The bar got quiet except for the Spanish polka music playing on the jukebox. She stood by the stove and shook the snow from her blanket and held it near the stove to dry. The wet wool smell reminded her of new-born goats in early March, brought inside to warm near the fire. She felt calm.

In past years they would have told her to get out. But her hair was white now and her faced was wrinkled. They looked at her like she was a spider crawling slowly across the room. They were afraid; she could feel the fear. She looked at their faces steadily. They reminded her of the first time the white people brought her children back to her that winter. Danny had been shy and hid behind the thin white woman who brought them. And the baby had not known her until Ayah took her into her arms, and then Ella had nuzzled close to her as she had when she was nursing. The blonde woman was nervous and kept looking at a dainty gold watch on her wrist. She sat on the bench near the small window and watched the dark snow clouds gather around the mountains; she was worrying about the unpaved road. She was frightened by what she saw inside too: the strips of venison drying on a rope across the ceiling and the children jabbering excitedly in a language she did not know. So they stayed for only a few hours. Ayah watched the government car disappear down the road and she knew they were already being weaned from these lava hills and from this sky. The last time they came was in early June, and Ella stared at her the way the men in the bar were now staring. Ayah did not try to pick her up; she smiled at her instead and spoke cheerfully to Danny. When he tried to answer her, he could not seem to remember and he spoke English words with the Navajo. But he gave her a scrap of paper that he had found somewhere and carried in his pocket; it was folded in half, and he shyly looked up at her and said it was a bird. She asked Chato if they were home for good this time. He spoke to the white woman and she shook her head. "How much longer?" he asked, and she said she didn't know; but Chato saw how she stared at the boxcar shack. Ayah turned away then. She did not say good-bye.

She felt satisfied that the men in the bar feared her. Maybe it was her face and the way she held her mouth with teeth clenched tight, like there was nothing anyone could do to her now. She walked north down the road, searching for the old man. She did this because she had the blanket, and there would be no place for him except with her and the blanket in the old abode barn near the arroyo. They always slept there when they came to Cebolleta. If the money and the wine were gone, she would be relieved because then they could go home again; back to the old hogan with a dirt roof and rock walls where she herself had been born. And the next day the old man could go back to the few sheep they still had, to follow along behind them, guiding them, into dry sandy arroyos where sparse grass grew. She knew he did not like walking behind old ewes when for so many years he rode big quarter horses and worked with cattle. But she wasn't sorry for him; he should have known all along what would happen.

There had not been enough rain for their garden in five years; and that was when Chato finally hitched a ride into the town and brought back brown boxes of rice and sugar and big tin cans of welfare peaches. After that, at the first of the month they went to Cebolleta to ask the postmaster for the check; and then Chato would go to the bar and cash it. They did this as they planted the garden every May, not because anything would survive the summer dust, but because it was time to do this. The journey passed the days that smelled silent and dry like the caves above the canyon with yellow painted buffaloes on their walls.

He was walking along the pavement when she found him. He did not stop or turn around when he heard her behind him. She walked beside him and she noticed how slowly he moved now. He smelled strong of woodsmoke and urine. Lately he had been forgetting. Sometimes he called her by his sister's name and she had been gone for a long time. Once she had found him wandering on the road to the white man's ranch, and she asked him why he was going that way; he laughed at her and said, "You know they can't run that ranch without me," and he walked on determined, limping on the leg that had been crushed many years before. Now he looked at her curiously, as if for the first time, but he kept shuffling along, moving slowly along the side of the highway. His gray hair had grown long and spread out on the shoulders of the long overcoat. He wore the old felt hat pulled down over his ears. His boots were worn out at the toes and he had stuffed pieces of an old red shirt in the holes. The rags made his feet look like little animals up to their ears in snow. She laughed at his feet; the snow muffled the sound of her laugh. He stopped and looked at her again. The wind had quit blowing and the snow was falling straight down; the southeast sky was beginning to clear and Ayah could see a star.

"Let's rest awhile," she said to him. They walked away from the road and up the slope to the giant boulders that had tumbled down from the red sandrock mesa throughout the centuries of rainstorms and earth tremors. In a place where the boulders shut out the wind, they sat down with their backs against the rock. She offered half of the blanket to him and they sat wrapped together.

The storm passed swiftly. The clouds moved east. They were massive and full, crowding together across the sky. She watched them with the feeling of horses — steely blue-gray horses startled across the sky. The powerful haunches pushed into the distances and the tail hairs streamed white mist behind them. The sky cleared. Ayah saw that there was nothing between her and the stars. The light was crystalline. There was no shimmer, no distortion through earth haze. She breathed the clarity of the night sky; she smelled the purity of the half moon and the stars. He was lying on his side with his knees pulled up near his belly for warmth. His eyes were closed now, and in the light from the stars and the moon, he looked young again.

She could see it descend out of the night sky: an icy stillness from the edge of the thin moon. She recognized the freezing. It came gradually, sinking snowflake by snowflake until the crust was heavy and deep. It had the strength of the stars in Orion, and its journey was endless. Ayah knew that with the wine he would sleep. He would not feel it. She tucked the blanket around him, remembering how it was when Ella had been with her; and she felt the rush so big inside her heart for the babies. And she sang the only song she knew to sing for babies. She could not remember if she had ever sung it to her children, but she knew that her grandmother had sung it and her mother had sung it:

The earth is your mother,
    she holds you.
The sky is your father,
    he protects you.
Sleep,
sleep.
Rainbow is your sister,
    she loves you.
The winds are your brothers,
    they sing to you.
Sleep,
sleep.
We are together always
We are together always
There never was a time
when this
was not so.

◎ JUDITH ORTIZ COFER

Judith Ortiz Cofer was born in the Puerto Rican town of Hormigueros in 1952 and spent one part of her childhood on the island with her mother's family and the other part in Paterson, New Jersey. She is the author of a novel, The Line of the Sun *(1989), and of personal essays,* Silent Dancing *(1990). The title essay was picked by Joyce Carol Oates for* The Best American Essays, *(1991). Cofer has also published two books of poetry,* Reaching for the Mainland *(1987) and* The Latin Deli: Prose and

Poetry *(1993), which won the Anisfield Wolf Book Award; her work has been selected for* O. Henry Prize Stories *and a Pushcart Prize as well. Her most recent collection is* An Island Like You: Stories of the Barrio *(1995). An associate professor of English and creative writing at the University of Georgia, Cofer divides her time between Athens and the family farm in Louisville, Georgia.*

"Tales Told Under the Mango Tree" is included in Silent Dancing: A Partial Remembrance of a Puerto Rican Childhood, *Cofer's memoir about moving between cultures. Mamá, Judith's maternal grandmother from Puerto Rico, is the center of the book, for she is a source of stories. The excerpt opens with Mamá's tale of María Sabida, the smartest woman on the island, a story that influenced Cofer in her thinking about womanhood.*

Tales Told Under the Mango Tree

María Sabida

Once upon a time there lived a girl who was so smart that she was known throughout Puerto Rico as María Sabida. María Sabida came into the world with her eyes open. They say that at the moment of her birth she spoke to the attending midwife and told her what herbs to use to make a special *guarapo,* a tea that would put her mother back on her feet immediately. They say that the two women would have thought the infant was possessed if María Sabida had not convinced them with her descriptions of life in heaven that she was touched by God and not spawned by the Devil.

María Sabida grew up in the days when the King of Spain owned Puerto Rico, but had forgotten to send law and justice to this little island lost on the map of the world. And so thieves and murderers roamed the land terrorizing the poor people. By the time María Sabida was of marriageable age, one such *ladrón* had taken over the district where she lived.

For years people had been subjected to abuse from this evil man and his henchmen. He robbed them of their cattle and then made them buy their own cows back from him. He would take their best chickens and produce when he came into town on Saturday afternoons riding with his men through the stalls set up by farmers. Overturning their tables, he would yell, "Put it on my account." But of course he never paid for anything he took. One year several little children disappeared while walking to the river, and although the townspeople searched and searched, no trace of them was ever found. That is when María Sabida entered the picture. She was fifteen then, and a beautiful girl with the courage of a man, they say.

She watched the chief *ladrón* the next time he rampaged through the pueblo. She saw that he was a young man: red-skinned, and tough as leather.

Cuero y sangre, nada más, she said to herself, a man of flesh and blood. And so she prepared herself to either conquer or to kill this man.

María Sabida followed the horses' trail deep into the woods. Though she left the town far behind she never felt afraid or lost. María Sabida could read the sun, the moon, and the stars for direction. When she got hungry, she knew which fruits were good to eat, which roots and leaves were poisonous, and how to follow the footprints of animals to a waterhole. At nightfall, María Sabida came to the edge of a clearing where a large house, almost like a fortress, stood in the forest.

"No woman has ever set foot in that house," she thought, "no *casa* is this, but a man-place." It was a house built for violence, with no windows on the ground level, but there were turrets on the roof where men could stand guard with guns. She waited until it was nearly dark and approached the house through the kitchen side. She found it by smell.

In the kitchen which she knew would have to have a door or window for ventilation, she saw an old man stirring a huge pot. Out of the pot stuck little arms and legs. Angered by the sight, María Sabida entered the kitchen, pushed the old man aside, and picking up the pot threw its horrible contents out of the window.

"Witch, witch, what have you done with my master's stew!" yelled the old man. "He will kill us both when he gets home and finds his dinner spoiled."

"Get, you filthy *viejo*." María Sabida grabbed the old man's beard and pulled him to his feet. "Your master will have the best dinner of his life if you follow my instructions."

María Sabida then proceeded to make the most delicious *asopao* the old man had ever tasted, but she would answer no questions about herself, except to say that she was his master's fiancée.

When the meal was done, María Sabida stretched and yawned and said that she would go upstairs and rest until her *prometido* came home. Then she went upstairs and waited.

The men came home and ate ravenously of the food María Sabida had cooked. When the chief *ladrón* had praised the old man for a fine meal, the cook admitted that it had been *la prometida* who had made the tasty chicken stew.

"My what?" the leader roared, "I have no *prometida*." And he and his men ran upstairs. But there were many floors, and by the time they were halfway to the room where María Sabida waited, many of the men had dropped down unconscious and the others had slowed down to a crawl until they too were overcome with irresistible sleepiness. Only the chief *ladrón* made it to where María Sabida awaited him holding a paddle that she had found among his weapons. Fighting to keep his eyes open, he asked her, "Who are you, and why have you poisoned me?"

"I am your future wife, María Sabida, and you are not poisoned, I added a special sleeping powder that tastes like oregano to your *asopao.* You will not die."

"Witch!" yelled the chief *ladrón,* "I will kill you. Don't you know who I am?" And reaching for her, he fell on his knees, whereupon María Sabida beat him with the paddle until he lay curled like a child on the floor. Each time he tried to attack her, she beat him some more. When she was satisfied that he was vanquished, María Sabida left the house and went back to town.

A week later, the chief *ladrón* rode into town with his men again. By then everyone knew what María Sabida had done and they were afraid of what these evil men would do in retribution. "Why did you not just kill him when you had a chance, *muchacha?*" many of the townswomen had asked María Sabida. But she had just answered mysteriously, "It is better to conquer than to kill." The townspeople then barricaded themselves behind closed doors when they heard the pounding of the thieves' horses approaching. But the gang did not stop until they arrived at María Sabida's house. There the men, instead of guns, brought out musical instruments: a *cuatro,* a *güiro, maracas,* and a harmonica. Then they played a lovely melody.

"María Sabida, María Sabida, my strong and wise María," called out the leader, sitting tall on his horse under María Sabida's window, "come out and listen to a song I've written for you — I call it *The Ballad of María Sabida.*"

María Sabida then appeared on her balcony wearing a wedding dress. The chief *ladrón* sang his song to her: a lively tune about a woman who had the courage of a man and the wisdom of a judge, who had conquered the heart of the best bandido on the island of Puerto Rico. He had a strong voice and all the people cowering in their locked houses heard his tribute to María Sabida and crossed themselves at the miracle she had wrought.

One by one they all came out and soon María Sabida's front yard was full of people singing and dancing. The *ladrones* had come prepared with casks of wine, bottles of rum, and a wedding cake made by the old cook from the tender meat of coconuts. The leader of the thieves and María Sabida were married on that day. But all had not yet been settled between them. That evening, as she rode behind him on his horse, she felt the dagger concealed beneath his clothes. She knew then that she had not fully won the battle for this man's heart.

On her wedding night María Sabida suspected that her husband wanted to kill her. After their dinner, which the man had insisted on cooking himself, they went upstairs. María Sabida asked for a little time alone to prepare herself. He said he would take a walk but would return very soon. When she heard him leave the house, María Sabida went down to the kitchen and took several gallons of honey from the pantry. She went back to the bedroom and there she fashioned a life-sized doll out of her clothes and poured the honey into it. She then blew out the candle, covered the figure with a sheet and hid herself under the bed.

After a short time, she heard her husband climbing the stairs. He tip-toed into the dark room thinking her asleep in their marriage bed. Peeking out from under the bed, María Sabida saw the glint of the knife her husband pulled out from inside his shirt. Like a fierce panther he leapt onto the bed and stabbed the doll's body over and over with his dagger. Honey splattered his face and fell on his lips. Shocked, the man jumped off the bed and licked his lips.

"How sweet is my wife's blood. How sweet is María Sabida in death — how sour in life and how sweet in death. If I had known she was so sweet, I would not have murdered her." And so declaring, he kneeled down on the floor beside the bed and prayed to María Sabida's soul for forgiveness.

At that moment María Sabida came out of her hiding place. "Husband, I have tricked you once more, I am not dead." In his joy, the man threw down his knife and embraced María Sabida, swearing that he would never kill or steal again. And he kept his word, becoming in later years an honest farmer. Many years later he was elected mayor of the same town he had once terrorized with his gang of *ladrones.*

María Sabida made a real *casa* out of his thieves' den, and they had many children together, all of whom could speak at birth. But, they say, María Sabida always slept with one eye open, and that is why she lived to be one hundred years old and wiser than any other woman on the Island of Puerto Rico, and her name was known even in Spain.

"Colorín, colorado este cuento se ha acabado." Mamá would slap her knees with open palms and say this little rhyme to indicate to the children sitting around her under the giant mango tree that the story was finished. It was time for us to go play and leave the women alone to embroider in the shade of the tree and to talk about serious things.

I remember that tree as a natural wonder. It was large, with a trunk that took four or five children holding hands to reach across. Its leaves were so thick that the shade it cast made a cool room where we took refuge from the hot sun. When an unexpected shower caught us there, the women had time to gather their embroidery materials before drops came through the leaves. But the most amazing thing about that tree was the throne it had made for Mamá. On the trunk there was a smooth seat-like projection. It was perfect for a story-teller. She would take her place on the throne and lean back. The other women — my mother and her sisters — would bring towels to sit on; the children sat anywhere. Sometimes we would climb to a thick branch we called "the ship," to the right of the throne, and listen there. "The ship" was a thick limb that hung all the way down to the ground. Up to three small children could straddle this branch while the others bounced on the end that sat near the ground making it sway like a ship. When Mamá told her stories, we sat quietly on our crow's nest because if anyone interrupted her narrative she should stop talking and no amount of begging would persuade her to finish the story that day.

The first time my mother took my brother and me back to Puerto Rico, we were stunned by the heat and confused by a houseful of relatives. Mamá's *casa* was filled to capacity with grandchildren, because two of the married daughters had come to stay there until their husbands sent for them: my mother and the two of us and her oldest sister with her five children. Mamá still had three of her own children at home, ranging in age from teenage daughter to my favorite uncle who was six months older than me.

Our solitary life in New Jersey, where we spent our days inside a small dark apartment watching television and waiting for our father to come home on leave from the navy, had not prepared us for life in Mamá's house or for the multitude of cousins, aunts and uncles pulling us into their loud conversations and rough games. For the first few days my little brother kept his head firmly buried in my mother's neck, while I stayed relatively close to her; but being nearly six, and able to speak as loudly as anyone, I soon joined Mamá's tribe.

In the last few weeks before the beginning of school, when it was too hot for cooking until it was almost dark and when mothers would not even let their boys go to the playgrounds and parks for fear of sunstroke, Mamá would lead us to the mango tree, there to spin the web of our *cuentos* over us, making us forget the heat, the mosquitos, our past in a foreign country, and even the threat of the first day of school looming just ahead.

It was under that mango tree that I first began to feel the power of words. I cannot claim to have always understood the point of the stories I heard there. Some of these tales were based on ancient folklore brought to the colonies by Spaniards from their own versions of even older myths of Greek and Roman origins — which, as I later discovered through my insatiable reading, had been modified in clever ways to fit changing times. María Sabida became the model Mamá used for the "prevailing woman" — the woman who "slept with one eye open" — whose wisdom was gleaned through the senses: from the natural world and from ordinary experiences. Her main virtue was that she was always alert and never a victim. She was by implication contrasted to María La Loca, that poor girl who gave it all up for love, becoming a victim of her own foolish heart.

The mango tree was located at the top of a hill, on land that belonged to "The American," or at least to the sugar refinery that he managed. *La Central*, as it was called, employed the majority of the pueblo's men. Its tall chimney stacks loomed over the town like sentinels, spewing plumes of grey smoke that filled the air during cane season with the syrupy thick aroma of burnt sugar.

In my childhood the sugarcane fields bordered both sides of the main road, which was like a part on a head of spiky, green hair. As we approached the pueblo on our way coming home, I remember how my mother sat up in the back seat of the *carro público*, the taxi, we had taken from the airport in San Juan. Although she was pointing out the bell tower of the famous church of La Monserrate, I was distracted by the hypnotizing motion of men swinging machetes in the fields. They were shirtless, and sweat poured in streams down their backs. Bathed in light reflected by their blades, these laborers moved as on a ballet stage. I wondered whether they practiced like dancers to perfect their synchronicity. It did not occur to me that theirs was "survival choreography" — merely a safety measure — for wild swinging could lead to lost fingers and limbs. Or, as I heard one of the women say once, "there are enough body parts in the cane fields to put one whole man together."

And although trucks were already being used in most *centrales*, in our town, much of the cane harvest was still transported from the fields to the mill in oxen-drawn carts which were piled so high with the stalks, that, when you followed one of them you could see neither the cart driver nor the beasts in front: It was a moving haystack.

To car drivers they were a headache and a menace on the road. A good wind could blow the cane off the top of the cart and smash a windshield. But what most drivers hated was getting stuck behind one that would take up the whole road traveling at five miles per hour and ignore the horn, the mad hand waving and the red-faced man shouting invectives. In later years this vehicle would be almost totally replaced by the open-bed trucks that were also loaded to the limit, traveling the roads of the Island at sixty or seventy miles per hour, granting no other vehicle (except police cars) right-of-way. The driver would keep his hand on the horn and that was all the warning a passenger car received. Pulling over as if for an emergency vehicle, was usually the best plan to follow.

We sucked on little pieces of sugar cane Mamá had cut for us under the mango tree. Below us a pasture rolled down to the road and the cane fields could be seen at a distance; the men in their perpetual motion were tiny black ants to our eyes. You looked up to see the red roof of the American's house. It was a big white house with a large porch completely enclosed by mosquito screens (on the Island at that time this was such a rarity that all houses designed in that way were known as "American"). At Mamá's house we slept cozily under mosquito nets, but during the day we fought the stinging, buzzing insects with bare hands and, when we lost a battle, we soothed our scratched raw skin with calamine lotion.

During the first few weeks of our visits both my brother and I, because we were fresh, tender meat, had skin like a pink target, dotted with red spots where the insects had scored bulls-eyes. Amazingly, either we built up a natural resistance, or the mosquitoes gave up, but it happened every time: a period of embarrassment as pink "turistas," followed by brown skin and immunity. Living behind screens, the American couple would never develop the tough skin needed for Island survival.

When Mamá told stories about kings and queens and castles, she would point to the big house on the hill. We were not supposed to go near the place. In fact, we were trespassing when we went to the mango tree. Mamá's backyard ended at the barbed-wire fence that led to the American's pasture. The tree stood just on the other side. She had at some point before my time, placed a strong stick under the barbed wire to make an entrance; but it could only be pulled up so much, so that even the children had to crawl through. Mamá seemed to relish the difficulty of getting to our special place. For us children it was fun to watch our mothers get their hair and clothes caught on the wire and to listen to them curse.

The pasture was a magical realm of treasures and secret places to discover. It even had a forbidden castle we could look at from a distance.

While the women embroidered, my girl-cousins and I would gather leaves and thorns off a lemon tree and do some imaginative stitch work of our own. The boys would be in the "jungle" gathering banana leaves they built tepees with. Imitating the grownups who were never without a cigarette hanging from their mouths, we would pick the tightly wrapped buds of the hibiscus flowers, which, with their red tips, looked to us like lighted cigarettes. We glued wild flower petals to our fingernails and, although they did not stay on for long, for a little while our hands, busy puncturing the leaves into patterns with lemon tree thorns, looked like our mother's with their red nail polish, pushing needle and thread through white linen, creating improbable landscapes of trailing vines and flowers, decorating the sheets and pillowcases we would sleep on.

We picked ripe guavas in their season and dumped them on Mamá's capacious lap for her to inspect for worms before we ate them. The sweetness of a ripe guava cannot be compared to anything else: its pink, gooey inside can be held on the tongue and savored like a caramel.

During mango season we threw rocks at the branches of our tree, hanging low with fruit. Later in the season, a boy would climb to the highest branches for the best fruit — something I always yearned to do, but was not allowed to: too dangerous.

On days when Mamá felt truly festive she would send us to the store with three dollars for ten bottles of Old Colony pop and the change in assorted candies: Mary Janes, Bazooka gum, lollypops, tiny two-piece boxes of Chicklets, coconut candy wrapped in wax paper, and more — all kept in big glass jars and sold two for one penny. We would have our reckless feast under the mango tree and then listen to a story. Afterwards, we would take turns on the swing that touched the sky.

My grandfather had made a strong swing from a plank of heavy wood and a thick length of rope. Under Mamá's supervision he had hung it from a sturdy lower branch of the mango tree that reached over the swell of the hill. In other words, you boarded the swing on level ground, but since the tree rose out of the summit, one push and you took off for the sky. It was almost like flying. From the highest point I ever reached, I could see the big house, as a bird would see it, to my left; the church tower from above the trees to my right; and far in the distance, below me, my family in a circle under the tree, receding, growing smaller; then, as I came back down to earth, looming larger, my mother's eyes glued on me, reflecting the fear for my safety that she would not voice in her mother's presence and thus risk overriding the other's authority. My mother's greatest fear was that my brother or I would hurt ourselves while at Mamá's, and that she would be held accountable by my excessively protective father when he returned from his tour of duty in Europe. And one day, because fear invites accident, I did fall from a ride up to the clouds.

I had been catapulting myself higher and higher, when out of the corner of my eye I saw my big cousin, Javier, running at top speed after his little brother, swinging a stick in front as if to strike the younger boy. This happened fast. The little boy, Roberto, ran towards Mamá, who at that moment, was leaning towards my mother in conversation. Trying to get to his brother before he reached safe haven, Javier struck, accidentally hitting my mother square on the face. I saw it happening. I saw it as if in slow motion. I saw my mother's broken glasses fly off her face, and the blood begin to flow. Dazed, I let go of the swing ropes and flew down from the clouds and the treetops and onto the soft cushion of pasture grass and just rolled and rolled. Then I lay there stunned, tasting grass and dirt until Mamá's strong arms lifted me up. She carried me through the fence and down to her house where my mother was calling hysterically for me. Her glasses had protected her from serious injury. The bump on her forehead was minor. The nosebleed had already been contained by the age-old method of placing a copper penny on the bridge, between the eyes. Her tears upset me, but not as much as the way she made me stand before her, in front of everyone, while she examined my entire body for bruises, scratches, and broken bones. "What will your father say," she kept repeating, until Mamá pulled me away. "Nothing," she said to my mother, "if you don't tell him." And, leaving her grown daughters to comfort each other, she called the children out to the yard where she had me organize a game of hide-and-seek that she supervised, catching cheaters right and left.

When it rained, the children were made to take naps or play quietly in the bedroom. I asked for Mamá's monumental poster bed, and, when my turn came, I got it. There I lay four or five feet above ground inhaling her particular smells of coconut oil, (which she used to condition her thick black hair) and Palmolive soap. I would luxuriate in her soft pillows and her mattress which was covered with gorgeously embroidered bed linens. I would get sleepy listening to the drone of the women's conversation out of the parlor.

Beyond the double doors of her peacock blue bedroom, I could hear

Mamá and her older daughters talking about things that, at my age, would not have interested me: They read letters received from my father traveling with the navy in Europe, or letters from any of the many relatives making their way in the barrios of New York and New Jersey, working in factories and dreaming of returning "in style" to Puerto Rico.

The women would discuss the new school year, and plan a shopping trip to the nearest city, Mayagüez, for materials to make school uniforms for the children, who by September had to be outfitted in brown and white and marched off to the public school looking like Mussolini's troops in our dull uniforms. Their talk would take on more meaning for me as I got older, but that first year back on the Island I was under María Sabida's spell. To entertain myself, I would make up stories about the smartest girl in all of Puerto Rico.

When María Sabida was only six years old, I began, she saved her little brother's life. He was dying of a broken heart, you see, for he desperately wanted some sweet guavas that grew at the top of a steep, rocky hill near the lair of a fierce dragon. No one had ever dared to climb that hill, though everyone could see the huge guava tree and the fruit, as big as pears, hanging from its branches. María Sabida's little brother had stared at the tree until he had made himself sick from yearning for the forbidden fruit.

Everyone knew that the only way to save the boy was to give him one of the guavas. María Sabida's parents were frantic with worry. The little boy was fading fast. The father tried climbing the treacherous hill to the guava tree, but the rocks were loose and for every step forward he took, he slipped back three. He returned home. The mother spent her days cooking delicious meals with which to tempt her little son to eat, but he just turned his sad eyes to the window in his room from where he could see the guava tree loaded with the only food he wanted. The doctor came to examine the boy and pronounced him as good as gone. The priest came and told the women they should start making their black dresses. All hope seemed lost when María Sabida, whose existence everyone seemed to have forgotten, came up with an idea to save her brother one day while she was washing her hair in the special way her grandmother had taught her.

Her mamá had shown her how to collect rainwater — water from the sky — into a barrel, and then, when it was time to wash her hair, how to take a fresh coconut and draw the oil from its white insides. You then took a bowl of clear rainwater and added the coconut oil, using the mixture to rinse your hair. Her mamá had shown her how the rainwater, coming as it did from the sky, had little bits of starshine in it. This starstuff was what made your hair glossy, the oil was to make it stick.

It was while María Sabida was mixing the starshine that she had the brilliant idea which saved her brother. She ran to her father who was in the stable feeding the mule and asked if she could borrow the animal that night. The man, startled by his daughter's wild look (her hair was streaming wet and she still held the coconut scraps in her hands) at first just ordered his daughter into the house, thinking that she had gone crazy with grief over her brother's imminent death. But María Sabida could be stubborn, and she refused to move until her parents heard what she had to say. The man called his wife to the stable, and when María Sabida had finished telling them her plan, he still thought she had lost her mind. He agreed with his desperate wife that at this point anything was worth trying. They let María Sabida have the mule to use that night.

María Sabida then waited until it was pitch black. She knew there would be no moon that night. Then she drew water from her rainbarrel and mixed it with plenty of coconut oil and plastered her mule's hoofs with it. She led the animal to the bottom of the rocky hill where the thick, sweet smell of ripe guavas was irresistible. María Sabida felt herself caught in the spell. Her mouth watered and she felt drawn to the guava tree. The mule must have felt the same thing because it started walking ahead of the girl with quick, sure steps. Though rocks came tumbling down, the animal found footing, and in so doing, left a shiny path with the bits of starshine that María Sabida had glued to its hoofs. María Sabida kept her eyes on the bright trail because it was a dark, dark night.

As she approached the guava tree, the sweet aroma was like a liquid that she drank through her nose. She could see the fruit within arms-reach when the old mule stretched her neck to eat one and a horrible scaly arm reached out and yanked the animal off the path. María Sabida quickly grabbed three guavas and ran down the golden trail all the way back to her house.

When she came into her little brother's room, the women had already gathered around the bed with their flowers and their rosaries, and because María Sabida was a little girl herself and could not see past the crowd, she thought for one terrible minute that she was too late. Luckily, her brother smelled the guavas from just this side of death and he sat up in bed. María Sabida pushed her way through the crowd and gave him one to eat. Within minutes the color returned to his cheeks. Everyone rejoiced remembering other wonderful things that she had done, and why her middle name was "Sabida."

And, yes, María Sabida ate one of the enchanted guavas herself and was never sick a day in her long life. The third guava was made into jelly that could cure every childhood illness imaginable, from a toothache to the chicken pox.

"*Colorín, colorado . . .*" I must have said to myself, "*Colorín colorado . . .*" as I embroidered my own fable, listening all the while to that inner voice which, when I was very young, sounded just like Mamá's when she told her stories in the parlor or under the mango tree. And later, as I gained more confidence in my own ability, the voice telling the story became my own.

◎ AUDRE LORDE

Audre Lorde was born in 1934 to Grenadian parents who lived in Harlem. She was educated at the University of Mexico, Columbia University, and Hunter College. Her many published works include From a Land Where Other People Live *(1973),* The Cancer Journals *(1980), which charts her own struggles against cancer, as well as* Zami: A New Spelling of My Name, *a fictionalized account of growing up lesbian and black (1982).* The Black Unicorn *(poems, 1978), incorporates the myths of Dahomeyan Amazons as useful to the contemporary urban poet. In 1993* The Marvelous Arithmetics of Distance: Poems, 1987–1992 *was issued posthumously. Lorde received a grant from the National Endowment for the Arts (NEA) in 1990, and she held an honorary doctorate from Oberlin College. Lorde taught English, creative writing, and literature at John Jay College, City College of New York, and Hunter College, among others. At her death in 1992, she was living in St. Croix.*

"Poetry Is Not a Luxury" was first published in Chrysalis: A Magazine of Female Culture *in 1977. It is included in Lorde's* Sister Outsider: Essays and Speeches *(1984). Though Audre Lorde defined herself as a poet rather than as a theorist, there is a consistency in her thinking about the necessity for women to speak out, to break silences.*

Poetry Is Not a Luxury

The quality of light by which we scrutinize our lives has direct bearing upon the product which we live, and upon the changes which we hope to bring about through those lives. It is within this light that we form those ideas by which we pursue our magic and make it realized. This is poetry as illumination, for it is through poetry that we give name to those ideas which are — until the poem — nameless and formless, about to be birthed, but already felt. That distillation of experience from which true poetry springs births thought as dream births concept, as feeling births idea, as knowledge births (precedes) understanding.

As we learn to bear the intimacy of scrutiny and to flourish within it, as we learn to use the products of that scrutiny for power within our living, those fears which rule our lives and form our silences begin to lose their control over us.

For each of us as women, there is a dark place within, where hidden and growing our true spirit rises, "beautiful / and tough as chestnut / stanchions against (y)our nightmare of weakness / and of impotence.

These places of possibility within ourselves are dark because they are ancient and hidden; they have survived and grown strong through that darkness. Within these deep places, each one of us holds an incredible reserve of creativity and power, of unexamined and unrecorded emotion and feeling. The woman's place of power within each of us is neither white nor surface; it is dark, it is ancient, and it is deep.

When we view living in the european mode only as a problem to be solved, we rely solely upon our ideas to make us free, for these were what the white fathers told us were precious.

But as we come more into touch with our own ancient, noneuropean consciousness of living as a situation to be experienced and interacted with, we learn more and more to cherish our feelings, and to respect those hidden sources of our power from where true knowledge and, therefore, lasting action comes.

At this point in time, I believe that women carry within ourselves the possibility for fusion of these two approaches, so necessary for survival, and we come closest to this combination in our poetry. I speak here of poetry as a revelatory distillation of experience, not the sterile word play that, too often, the white fathers distorted the word *poetry* to mean — in order to cover a desperate wish for imagination without insight.

For women, then, poetry is not a luxury. It is a vital necessity of our existence. It forms the quality of the light within which we predicate our hopes and dreams toward survival and change, first made into language, then into idea, then into more tangible action. Poetry is the way we help give name to the nameless so it can be thought. The farthest horizons of our hopes and fears are cobbled by our poems, carved from the rock experiences of our daily lives.

As they become known to and accepted by us, our feelings and the honest exploration of them become sanctuaries and spawning grounds for the most radical and daring of ideas. They become a safe-house for that difference so necessary to change and the conceptualization of any meaningful action. Right now, I could name at least ten ideas I would have found intolerable or incomprehensible and frightening, except as they came after dreams and poems. This is not idle fantasy, but a disciplined attention to the true meaning of "it feels right to me." We can train ourselves to respect our feelings and to transpose them into a language so they can be shared. And where that language does not yet exist, it is our poetry which helps to fashion it. Poetry is not only dream and vision; it is the skeleton architecture of our lives. It lays the foundations for a future of change, a bridge across our fears of what has never been before.

Possibility is neither forever nor instant. It is not easy to sustain belief in its efficacy. We can sometimes work long and hard to establish one beachhead of real resistance to the deaths we are expected to live, only to have that beachhead assaulted or threatened by those canards we have been socialized to fear, or by the withdrawal of those approvals that we have been warned to seek for safety. Women see ourselves diminished or softened by the falsely benign accusations of childishness, of nonuniversality, of changeability, of sensuality. And who asks the question: Am I altering your aura, your ideas, your dreams, or am I merely moving you to temporary and reactive action? And even though the latter is no mean task, it is one that must be seen within the context of a need for true alteration of the very foundations of our lives.

The white fathers told us: I think, therefore I am. The Black mother within each of us — the poet — whispers in our dreams: I feel, therefore I can be free. Poetry coins the language to express and charter this revolutionary demand, the implementation of that freedom.

However, experience has taught us that action in the now is also necessary, always. Our children cannot dream unless they live, they cannot live unless they are nourished, and who else will feed them the real food without which their dreams will be no different from ours? "If you want us to change the world someday, we at least have to live long enough to grow up!" shouts the child.

Sometimes we drug ourselves with dreams of new ideas. The head will save us. The brain alone will set us free. But there are no new ideas still waiting in the wings to save us as women, as human. There are only old and forgotten ones, new combinations, extrapolations and recognitions from within ourselves — along with the renewed courage to try them out. And we must constantly encourage ourselves and each other to attempt the heretical actions that our dreams imply, and so many of our old ideas disparage. In the forefront of our move toward change, there is only poetry to hint at possibility made real. Our poems formulate the implications of ourselves, what we feel within and dare make real (or bring action into accordance with), our fears, our hopes, our most cherished terrors.

For within living structures defined by profit, by linear power, by institutional dehumanization, our feelings were not meant to survive. Kept around as unavoidable adjuncts or pleasant pastimes, feelings were expected to kneel to thought as women were expected to kneel to men. But women have survived. As poets. And there are no new pains. We have felt them all already. We have hidden that fact in the same place where we have hidden our power. They surface in our dreams, and it is our dreams that point the way to freedom. Those dreams are made realizable through our poems that give us the strength and courage to see, to feel, to speak, and to dare.

If what we need to dream, to move our spirits most deeply and directly toward and through promise, is discounted as a luxury, then we give up the core — the fountain — of our power, our womanness; we give up the future of our worlds.

For there are no new ideas. There are only new ways of making them felt — of examining what those ideas feel like being lived on Sunday morning at 7 A.M., after brunch, during wild love, making war, giving birth, mourning our dead — while we suffer the old longings, battle the old warnings and fears of being silent and impotent and alone, while we taste new possibilities and strengths.

◎ KATHLEEN NORRIS

Kathleen Norris was born in 1947 in Washington, D.C., and was educated at Bennington College. In 1972 Norris received the Provincetown Fine Arts Center fellowship, and the following year she was awarded a Creative Artists Public Service grant by the state of New York. She has also received awards from the Guggenheim and the Bush foundations. Norris has published two books of poetry, Falling Off *(1971) and* The Middle of the World *(1981).* Dakota: A Spiritual Geography *won the 1993 New Visions Award from the Quality Paperback Book Club and the Society of Midland Authors Annual Award. Norris lives in Lemmon, South Dakota.*

Kathleen Norris' memoir "A Starfish in Mott" is a part of Dakota: A Spiritual Geography, *which evokes the Great Plains and their influence on the human spirit. Norris left Manhattan, where she worked at the Academy of American Poets, in 1974 to move to South Dakota. She has lived there ever since.* Dakota *is described by a* New York Times *reviewer as being "a deeply spiritual, deeply moving book."*

A Starfish in Mott

> An abba said, "The prophets wrote books, then came our fathers who put them into practice. Those who came after them learnt them by heart. Then came the present generation, who have written them out and put them into their window seats without using them."
>
> — *The World of the Desert Fathers*

The girl has scarcely looked at me. She's been drawing and writing furiously all during class. When the bell rings she hurries up to me with more than twenty sheets of paper. She's Indian — Hidatsa, maybe, or Sioux — and the other children let her pass as if she were invisible.

The morning star dances in a red circle, singing a song about his girlfriend Sheila; the angel Gabriel stands before Mary, his blue wings ablaze with stars. His mouth is open wide and notes are coming out, each one a different color. A woman with green hair holds her hands up to the sky and says:

> These are secret words,
> Say them after me.
> May all the plants and flowers rise
> And all people rise from death.

I look up from the paper: a dusty shelf, a starfish in a jar caked with dust beside dusty petri dishes. I see shades of blue: the globe cerulean, the sky bleached out. And out the window, above the children's heads, topsoil, the residue of ancient oceans, swirling like a thumbprint in the playground, wind pushing the empty swings.

"So many poems," I say, smiling at the girl. "You must love to write." She shifts from foot to foot and weaves her hands in air. "I don't have paper at home," she says, "so I keep them in my head. That's where they live until I write them down."

◎ *PAULE MARSHALL*

Paule Marshall was born in 1929 in Brooklyn and grew up there. Her parents had emigrated to New York from Barbados during World War I, so she writes from the perspective of two different cultures. Marshall was educated at Hunter College and Brooklyn College. Her first novel, Brown Girl, Brownstones *(1959), was adapted for a CBS Television Workshop. In the same year Marshall was awarded a Ford Foundation grant. Since then she has published three other novels, a book of novellas, two books of short fiction, and several essays. Marshall has taught creative writing at Yale University, Columbia University, the University of Massachusetts at Boston, and the Iowa Writers' Workshop. She is Professor Emeritus of English at Virginia Commonwealth University.*

"From the Poets in the Kitchen" is an autobiographical essay that introduces her collection, Reena and Other Stories *(1983). The essay was first published in* The New York Times Book Review *series "The Making of a Writer."*

From the Poets in the Kitchen

Some years ago, when I was teaching a graduate seminar in fiction at Columbia University, a well known male novelist visited my class to speak on his development as a writer. In discussing his formative years, he didn't realize it but he seriously endangered his life by remarking that women writers are luckier than those of his sex because they usually spend so much time as children around their mothers and their mothers' friends in the kitchen.

What did he say that for? The women students immediately forgot about being in awe of him and began readying their attack for the question and answer period later on. Even I bristled. There again was that awful image of women locked away from the world in the kitchen with only each other to talk to, and their daughters locked in with them.

But my guest wasn't really being sexist or trying to be provocative or even spoiling for a fight. What he meant — when he got around to explaining himself more fully — was that, given the way children are (or were) raised in our society, with little girls kept closer to home and their mothers, the woman writer stands a better chance of being exposed, while growing up, to the kind of talk that goes on among women, more often than not in the kitchen; and that this experience gives her an edge over her male counterpart by instilling in her an appreciation for ordinary speech.

It was clear that my guest lecturer attached great importance to this, which is understandable. Common speech and the plain, workaday words that make it up are, after all, the stock in trade of some of the best fiction writers. They are the principal means by which characters in a novel or story reveal themselves and give voice sometimes to profound feelings and complex ideas about themselves and the world. Perhaps the proper measure of a writer's talent is skill in rendering everyday speech — when it is appropriate to the story — as well as the ability to tap, to exploit, the beauty, poetry and wisdom it often contains.

"If you say what's on your mind in the language that comes to you from your parents and your street and friends you'll probably say something beautiful." Grace Paley tells this, she says, to her students at the beginning of every writing course.

It's all a matter of exposure and a training of the ear for the would-be writer in those early years of apprenticeship. And according to my guest lecturer, this training, the best of it, often takes place in as unglamorous a setting as the kitchen.

He didn't know it, but he was essentially describing my experience as a little girl. I grew up among poets. Now they didn't look like poets — whatever that breed is supposed to look like. Nothing about them suggested that poetry was their calling. They were just a group of ordinary housewives and mothers, my mother included, who dressed in a way (shapeless housedresses, dowdy felt hats and long, dark, solemn coats) that made it impossible for me to imagine they had ever been young.

Nor did they do what poets were supposed to do — spend their days in an attic room writing verses. They never put pen to paper except to write occasionally to their relatives in Barbados. "I take my pen in hand hoping these few lines will find you in health as they leave me fair for the time being," was the way their letters invariably began. Rather, their day was spent "scrubbing floor," as they described the work they did.

Several mornings a week these unknown bards would put an apron and a pair of old house shoes in a shopping bag and take the train or streetcar from our section of Brooklyn out to Flatbush. There, those who didn't have steady jobs would wait on certain designated corners for the white housewives in the neighborhood to come along and bargain with them over pay for a day's work cleaning their houses. This was the ritual even in the winter.

Later, armed with the few dollars they had earned, which in their vocabulary became "a few raw-mouth pennies," they made their way back to our neighborhood, where they would sometimes stop off to have a cup of tea or cocoa together before going home to cook dinner for their husbands and children.

The basement kitchen of the brownstone house where my family lived was the usual gathering place. Once inside the warm safety of its walls the women threw off the drab coats and hats, seated themselves at the large center table, drank their cups of tea or cocoa, and talked. While my sister and I sat at a smaller table over in a corner doing our homework, they talked — endlessly, passionately, poetically, and with impressive range. No subject was beyond them. True, they would indulge in the usual gossip: whose husband was running with whom, whose daughter looked slightly "in the way" (pregnant) under her bridal gown as she walked down the aisle. That sort of thing. But they also tackled the great issues of the time. They were always, for example, discussing the state of the economy. It was the mid and late 30's then, and the aftershock of the Depression, with its soup lines and suicides on Wall Street, was still being felt.

Some people, they declared, didn't know how to deal with adversity. They didn't know that you had to "tie up your belly" (hold in the pain, that is) when things got rough and go on with life. They took their image from the bellyband that is tied around the stomach of a newborn baby to keep the navel pressed in.

They talked politics. Roosevelt was their hero. He had come along and rescued the country with relief and jobs, and in gratitude they christened their sons Franklin and Delano and hoped they would live up to the names.

If F.D.R. was their hero, Marcus Garvey was their God. The name of the fiery, Jamaican-born black nationalist of the 20's was constantly invoked around the table. For he had been their leader when they first came to the United States from the West Indies shortly after World War I. They had contributed to his organization, the United Negro Improvement Association (UNIA), out of their meager salaries, bought shares in his ill-fated Black Star Shipping Line, and at the height of the movement they had marched as members of his "nurses' brigade" in their white uniforms up Seventh Avenue in Harlem during the great Garvey Day parades. Garvey: He lived on through the power of their memories.

And their talk was of war and rumors of wars. They raged against World War II when it broke out in Europe, blaming it on the politicians. "It's these politicians. They're the ones always starting up all this lot of war. But what they care? It's the poor people got to suffer and mothers with their sons." If it was *their* sons, they swore they would keep them out of the Army by giving them soap to eat each day to make their hearts sound defective. Hitler? He was for them "the devil incarnate."

Then there was home. They reminisced often and at length about home.

The old country. Barbados — or Bimshire, as they affectionately called it. The little Caribbean island in the sun they loved but had to leave. "Poor — poor but sweet" was the way they remembered it.

And naturally they discussed their adopted home. America came in for both good and bad marks. They lashed out at it for the racism they encountered. They took to task some of the people they worked for, especially those who gave them only a hard-boiled egg and a few spoonfuls of cottage cheese for lunch. "As if anybody can scrub floor on an egg and some cheese that don't have no taste to it!"

Yet although they caught H in "this man country," as they called America, it was nonetheless a place where "you could at least see your way to make a dollar." That much they acknowledged. They might even one day accumulate enough dollars, with both them and their husbands working, to buy the brownstone houses which, like my family, they were only leasing at that period. This was their consuming ambition: to "buy house" and to see the children through.

There was no way for me to understand it at the time, but the talk that filled the kitchen those afternoons was highly functional. It served as therapy, the cheapest kind available to my mother and her friends. Not only did it help them recover from the long wait on the corner that morning and the bargaining over their labor, it restored them to a sense of themselves and reaffirmed their self-worth. Through language they were able to overcome the humiliations of the work-day.

But more than therapy, that freewheeling, wide-ranging, exuberant talk functioned as an outlet for the tremendous creative energy they possessed. They were women in whom the need for self-expression was strong, and since language was the only vehicle readily available to them they made of it an art form that — in keeping with the African tradition in which art and life are one — was an integral part of their lives.

And their talk was a refuge. They never really ceased being baffled and overwhelmed by America — its vastness, complexity and power. Its strange customs and laws. At a level beyond words they remained fearful and in awe. Their uneasiness and fear were even reflected in their attitude toward the children they had given birth to in this country. They referred to those like myself, the little Brooklyn-born Bajans (Barbadians), as "these New York children" and complained that they couldn't discipline us properly because of the laws here. "You can't beat these children as you would like, you know, because the authorities in this place will dash you in jail for them. After all, these is New York children." Not only were we different, American, we had, as they saw it, escaped their ultimate authority.

Confronted therefore by a world they could not encompass, which even limited their rights as parents, and at the same time finding themselves permanently separated from the world they had known, they took refuge in language. "Language is the only homeland," Czeslaw Milosz, the emigré Polish writer and Nobel Laureate, has said. This is what it became for the women at the kitchen table.

It served another purpose also, I suspect. My mother and her friends were after all the female counterpart of Ralph Ellison's invisible man. Indeed, you might say they suffered a triple invisibility, being black, female and foreigners. They really didn't count in American society except as a source of cheap labor. But given the kind of women they were, they couldn't tolerate the fact of their invisibility, their powerlessness. And they fought back, using the only weapon at their command: the spoken word.

Those late afternoon conversations on a wide range of topics were a way for them to feel they exercised some measure of control over their lives and the events that shaped them. "Soully-gal, talk yuh talk!" they were always exhorting each other. "In this man world you got to take yuh mouth and make a gun!" They were in control, if only verbally and if only for the two hours or so that they remained in our house.

For me, sitting over in the corner, being seen but not heard, which was the rule for children in those days, it wasn't only what the women talked about — the content — but the way they put things — their style. The insight, irony, wit and humor they brought to their stories and discussions and their poet's inventiveness and daring with language — which of course I could only sense but not define back then.

They had taken the standard English taught them in the primary schools of Barbados and transformed it into an idiom, an instrument that more adequately described them — changing around the syntax and imposing their own rhythm and accent so that the sentences were more pleasing to their ears. They added the few African sounds and words that had survived, such as the derisive suck-teeth sound and the word "yam," meaning to eat. And to make it more vivid, more in keeping with their expressive quality, they brought to bear a raft of metaphors, parables, Biblical quotations, sayings and the like:

"The sea ain' got no back door," they would say, meaning that it wasn't like a house where if there was a fire you could run out the back. Meaning that it was not to be trifled with. And meaning perhaps in a larger sense that man should treat all of nature with caution and respect.

"I has read hell by heart and called every generation blessed!" They sometimes went in for hyperbole.

A woman expecting a baby was never said to be pregnant. They never used that word. Rather, she was "in the way" or, better yet, "tumbling big." "Guess who I butt up on in the market the other day tumbling big again!"

And a woman with a reputation of being too free with her sexual favors was known in their book as a "thoroughfare" — the sense of men like a steady stream of cars moving up and down the road of her life. Or she might be dubbed "a free-bee," which was my favorite of the two. I liked the image it conjured up of a woman scandalous perhaps but independent, who flitted from one flower to another in a garden of male beauties, sampling their nectar, taking her pleasure at will, the roles reversed.

And nothing, no matter how beautiful, was ever described as simply beautiful. It was always "beautiful-ugly": the beautiful-ugly dress, the beautiful-ugly house, the beautiful-ugly car. Why the word "ugly," I used to wonder, when the thing they were referring to was beautiful, and they knew it. Why the antonym, the contradiction, the linking of opposites? It used to puzzle me greatly as a child.

There is the theory in linguistics which states that the idiom of a people, the way they use language, reflects not only the most fundamental views they hold of themselves and the world but their very conception of reality. Perhaps in using the term "beautiful-ugly" to describe nearly everything, my mother and her friends were expressing what they believed to be a fundamental dualism in life: the idea that a thing is at the same time its opposite, and that these opposites, these contradictions make up the whole. But theirs was not a Manichaean brand of dualism that sees matter, flesh, the body, as inherently evil, because they constantly addressed each other as "soully-gal" — soul: spirit; gal: the body, flesh, the visible self. And it was clear from their tone that they gave one as much weight and importance as the other. They had never heard of the mind/body split.

As for God, they summed up His essential attitude in a phrase. "God," they would say, "don' love ugly and He ain' stuck on pretty."

Using everyday speech, the simple commonplace words — but always with imagination and skill — they gave voice to the most complex ideas. Flannery O'Connor would have approved of how they made ordinary language work, as she put it, "double-time," stretching, shading, deepening its meaning. Like Joseph Conrad they were always trying to infuse new life in the "old old words worn thin . . . by . . . careless usage." And the goals of their oral art were the same as his: "to make you hear, to make you feel . . . to make you *see*." This was their guiding esthetic.

By the time I was 8 or 9, I graduated from the corner of the kitchen to the neighborhood library, and thus from the spoken to the written word. The Macon Street Branch of the Brooklyn Public Library was an imposing half block long edifice of heavy gray masonry, with glass-paneled doors at the front and two tall metal torches symbolizing the light that comes of learning flanking the wide steps outside.

The inside was just as impressive. More steps — of pale marble with gleaming brass railings at the center and sides — led up to the circulation desk, and a great pendulum clock gazed down from the balcony stacks that faced the entrance. Usually stationed at the top of the steps like the guards outside Buckingham Palace was the custodian, a stern-faced West Indian type who for years, until I was old enough to obtain an adult card, would immediately shoo me with one hand into the Children's Room and with the other threaten me into silence, a finger to his lips. You would have thought he was the chief librarian and not just someone whose job it was to keep the brass polished and the clock wound. I put him in a story called "Barbados" years later and had terrible things happen to him at the end.

I sheltered from the storm of adolescence in the Macon Street library, reading voraciously, indiscriminately, everything from Jane Austen to Zane Grey, but with a special passion for the long, full-blown, richly detailed 18th- and 19th-century picaresque tales: "Tom Jones," "Great Expectations," "Vanity Fair."

But although I loved nearly everything I read and would enter fully into the lives of the characters — indeed, would cease being myself and become them — I sensed a lack after a time. Something I couldn't quite define was missing. And then one day browsing in the poetry section, I came across a book by someone called Paul Laurence Dunbar, and opening it I found the photograph of a wistful, sad-eyed poet who to my surprise was black. I turned to a poem at random. "Little brown-baby wif spa'klin' / eyes / Come to yo' pappy an' set on his knee." Although I had a little difficulty at first with the words in dialect, the poem spoke to me as nothing I had read before of the closeness, the special relationship I had had with my father, who by then had become an ardent believer in Father Divine and gone to live in Father's "kingdom" in Harlem. Reading it helped to ease somewhat the tight knot of sorrow and longing I carried around in my chest that refused to go away. I read another poem. " 'Lias! 'Lias! Bless de Lawd! \ Don' you know de day's / erbroad? / Ef you don' get up, you scamp / Dey'll be trouble in dis camp." I laughed. It reminded me of the way my mother sometimes yelled at my sister and me to get out of bed in the mornings.

And another: "Seen my lady home las' night / Jump back, honey, jump back. / Hel' huh han' an' sque'z it tight . . ." About love between a black man and a black woman. I had never seen that written about before and it roused in me all kinds of delicious feelings and hopes.

And I began to search then for books and stories and poems about "The Race" (as it was put back then), about my people. While not abandoning Thackeray, Fielding, Dickens and the others, I started asking the reference librarian, who was white, for books by Negro writers, although I must admit I did so at first with a feeling of shame — the shame I and many others used to experience in those days whenever the word "Negro" or "colored" came up.

No grade school literature teacher of mine had ever mentioned Dunbar or James Weldon Johnson or Langston Hughes. I didn't know that Zora Neale Hurston existed and was busy writing and being published during those years. Nor was I made aware of people like Frederick Douglass and Harriet Tubman

— their spirit and example — or the great 19th-century abolitionist and feminist Sojourner Truth. There wasn't even Negro History Week when I attended P.S. 35 on Decatur Street!

What I needed, what all the kids — West Indian and native black American alike — with whom I grew up needed, was an equivalent of the Jewish shul, someplace where we could go after school — the schools that were shortchanging us — and read works by those like ourselves and learn about our history.

It was around that time also that I began harboring the dangerous thought of someday trying to write myself. Perhaps a poem about an apple tree, although I had never seen one. Or the story of a girl who could magically transplant herself to wherever she wanted to be in the world — such as Father Divine's kingdom in Harlem. Dunbar — his dark, eloquent face, his large volume of poems — permitted me to dream that I might someday write, and with something of the power with words my mother and her friends possessed.

When people at readings and writers' conferences ask me who my major influences were, they are sometimes a little disappointed when I don't immediately name the usual literary giants. True, I am indebted to those writers, white and black, whom I read during my formative years and still read for instruction and pleasure. But they were preceded in my life by another set of giants whom I always acknowledge before all others: the group of women around the table long ago. They taught me my first lessons in the narrative art. They trained my ear. They set a standard of excellence. This is why the best of my work must be attributed to them; it stands as testimony to the rich legacy of language and culture they so freely passed on to me in the workshop of the kitchen.

CASSANDRA MEDLEY

Cassandra Medley was born in Detroit. Her plays include Dearborn Heights, By the Still Waters, Waking Women, Terrain, *and* Ma Rose, *for which she received the Walt Disney Screenwriting Fellowship in 1990. Medley has also received the 1986 New York Foundation for the Arts Grant, a 1990 NEA Grant in Playwriting, the 1995 New Professional Theatre Award, and the 1995 Marilyn Simpson Award. Medley has taught playwriting at Sarah Lawrence College and Columbia University and has also been a guest artist at the University of Iowa Playwrights Workshop. Currently she lives in New York City and is writing for television.*

"Waking Women" was published in 1991 in Antaeus: Plays in One Act, *selected by Daniel Halpern "to celebrate the play as an act of 'recorded literature.'" Medley wrote the play in 1985, inspired by her father's wake.*

Waking Women

The setting is a closed-in porch of a neat A-frame house in a working-class black neighborhood in a midwestern city. At rise the porch is empty. Sunshine streams through the screen windows, glistening on the potted and hanging plants that are placed on the banister in great profusion. Birds can be heard as well as the barking of unseen nearby dogs and the occasional passing of a car.

The sound of banging is heard as if someone is knocking on the screen door, Ms. Edie enters as if coming from the direction of the street. She is a black woman in her mid to late fifties, dressed in a plain housedress and slippers. She is carrying a rattan hand fan in one hand to beat off the heat and a potted plant tied with a white ribbon in the other. Her hair is done up in curlers with a hair net tied securely on her head. She has a sorrowful expression on her face as she addresses the unseen woman before her. Throughout the monologue she speaks to the audience as if speaking directly to her close friend and confidante, Lucille.

MS. EDIE: Lucille! . . . I was *so* sorry to hear about it! Girl, you *know* I was gonna make it over soon as I could, you *know* I was gonna be over to see 'bout you just as soon as I was able . . . honey, I was so surprised! Gina Hawthorne just called me just now and *told* me! I said to her, I said, "*Passed?*" Whose husband done passed? . . . "Well, when did it happen?!"

My goodness. 'Cause seem to me that I saw Coleman out working in the yard just last week, seem to me, and he looked to be so *healthy*, and now you tell me he done passed! have mercy! and when's the funeral? [*Pauses.*] Oh, I see . . . [*Pauses, listening.*] Well, where your in-laws spring from? ah, so his people from Ohio! Ah-so . . . you don't say . . . and you gonna have the wake at night . . . [*Nods her approval.*] Well, that's good, that's good. Well, sir, I was *so* sorry to hear . . . [*Points to herself.*] Me? [*She leans back and fans herself vigorously.*] Aw, girl, I'm all right, I guess I'll do. [*She is frowning and scowling.*] Chile, it's just that I'm so outdone so, till I don't know *what* to do! [*Pauses.*] Hon-nee, I just can't tell you! [*Pauses.*] Well, what time is it . . . ? Okay, well, hon-nee, get ready for this . . . Pinkie's in labor! [*Fanning herself with indignation.*] that's *right!* Yeah, girl, Pinkie done been in labor since . . . well, she went in at four this morning and here it is what . . . ? Twelve-thirty? Okay, so she's still, yeah, chile . . . well, you know they say that first baby is always the hardest. So she's in there now and uh . . . took her down at four o'clock, her water broke at three-thirty . . . um-hum . . . Oh, yeah, that's what they say . . . the first one . . . yep . . . count on that to be the hardest. Well, now, course with me, they just "dropped" . . . I was real lucky . . . 'cause I weren't in there *no* time and 'fore I knew nothing, I was just opening up m'legs and look like my boys just "dropped" out the barrel, but hon-nee, poor Pinkie, she's up in there now and she's having a time of it. . . . [*Pauses, then with disapproval as if answering a question.*] . . . "De-troit General." . . . Yeah, that's where . . . um-hum . . . yeah [*Fans vigorously.*]

[*She pauses abruptly and with scowling reacts to the unseen woman's question.*]

Girl don't ask! and ain't no sense in me troubling you with *my* trouble in *your* time of trouble! I don't even want to bother you. Naw-naw, you just rest. Never mind 'bout Pinkie, you just take it easy yourself . . . Naw-naw, never mind . . . [*Suddenly.*] Well, chile, it's just a shame! Just a sin and a shame, and that's *all* I'm gonna say!

[*She seems to have closed the subject for a few beats; then she suddenly launches into a tirade.*]

Shooo! That silly sister-in-law of mine! that's Gladys! best good common sense my brother ever had was to *leave* that woman . . . girl, the way she brought up that poor Pinkie! [*Pause*] Say what? Now, girl, you mean to tell me you been living in this neighborhood all this time and you *don't* know? Ha! "Paulette." yeah! "Paulette," but we been calling her Pinkie ever since she first drew breath, 'cause she was such a pretty lil "pink" thing when she come. [*Pause.*] Oh, chile, I just don't even wanna get into it 'cause you got *enough* on your mind as it is, but hon-nee, do you know, that Pinkie, that child ain't *never* been to a picture show in her *life!* Now you know that's a shame! That's the gospel truth! Fifteen years old and ain't never *ever* been to the movies in her life! I ain't telling no tale. Cause my damn sister-in-law, 'scuse my French, cause my sister-in-law Gladys just keeps Pinkie all locked up in the house *all* the time! Oh, I don't know *what* be going through Gladys's mind! She think she be sheltering Pinkie or "protecting" her or I don't know what. Keeps Pinkie in the house *all* the time! Don't let her go *nowhere.* Don't let her go out shopping with her little friends . . . *parties?* You better forget it! *Sleepovers?* Forget it! *Dances?* Forget it! Join a club? Forget it! After-school home games and whatnot? [*She waits for Lucille to silently answer back "forget it," and she nods "correct."*] You got it! and like I told Gladys, I said, "Gladys," we was sitting out on the porch and I said, "Gladys" . . . 'cause you know me, I speak my mind, if that's one thing about me, I'm gonna pull your coat from the jump. I said, "Gladys you just can't keep your daughter locked up under lock and key in the house like that," I said, "Gladys, that ain't right! 'cause *you* know and I know we was all young once, and Gladys, you just can't keep Pinkie under your nose all the damn time."

Now I know for myself, see I'm gonna tell ya, when I was young, see, I was "fast." I'm gonna tell you like it is; I was "fast." And here I was dark skinned and considered "ugly" and the boys was after me? And here Pinkie is, light skinned and with straight hair! Well, now, you *know* the boys gonna be after her! And here she can't even go to the picture show and ain't never been in her life! And I told Gladys, I said, "Gladys," "Gladys," I said, "You know that now we have got to face reality. It ain't like when we was coming up, no, it ain't. It ain't like back when they didn't talk about nothing and you weren't supposed to know nothing and when your first time of the month first come on you, you thought you was bleeding to death and all that, 'cause you didn't know no better and all, like y'know, when we come up. After all, this is 1991 and my goodness, and things have changed and you gotta face up to it!" And I told my ole silly sister-in-law, "Gladys, you just can't rule that girl like that!" I've told Gladys time and time again, "We have got to face reality here, and we have got to tell these kids 'bout birth control and whatnot," and hon-nee, ooohhh! What did I want to say that for? Chile, do you know she looked at me like I was the devil's own *slut?* Oh, yes, she did!

[*Pause. She studies Lucille, nodding as to answer a retort.*]

Well, now, I know, I *know* that, hon-nee, I know what you mean 'bout "sin," and I'm as religious as the next one, I'm as upstanding as any one of the rest of your friends, Lucille, but keeping these kids *ignorant* ain't keeping them from "sin." How's *that* s'pposed to "keep 'em from sin" . . . ? [*Pauses.*] See what I'm saying? [*Pauses.*] I mean, I mean, yeah, I see what *you* saying, but do you see what *I'm* saying? . . . So anyway, okay . . . so I said to myself right there and then, I said, *all right! so be it! lemme just shut up and back off, lemme just shut my mouth!* so I shut my mouth.

Yessir, here I am trying to plead with that ole sanctified heifer — 'scuse my talk, Lucille, in your time of sorrow, but it just makes me so "outdone" and dang-blasted put-out so, till I don't know what! naw, naw, Gladys just gonna make Pinkie stay up in that house all the damn time; make her come home from school and lock her up in that house and not let her go *nowhere.*

Well, course, now, my brother? I blame him as much as anybody. He just *had* to go 'head and marry and father a child by that ole light-skinned dumb bunny — I mean y'know, hey . . . let's just admit it and call the card like it is — just 'cause he thought she was educated and pretty and proper and holy! Well! He left her and left poor Pinkie *with* her, and you see what happened, don't you? Gladys call herself keeping Pinkie pure, and Pinkie *still* ended up here with the big belly! In *my* family! a relative of *mine,* a relation to *me* with *my* family name and ending up out of wedlock and "big"!

See, 'cause these kids these days, they gonna get out here, they are curious. And a young girl like that? Huh! Pretty as she is? You *know* she gonna be wanting to find out and to experiment and whatnot . . . with what it's like to have a boy kissing her and — and holding her and hon-nee, . . . humph! [*Fans herself vigorously.*] That's just nature, wanting somebody to be rubbing up 'gainst ya and thing. . . . Course, now that ole fool I married, well, *my* time is now dried up. . . .

[*Suddenly she stops, throws her hand to her mouth, gasps in embarrassment and running on in such a way.*]

Oh, my goodness, chile, listen to me carrying on at "this" time! Why didn't you stop me; oughta be 'shamed of myself . . . ! [*Pauses.*] Darlin', Lord hamercy, forgive me, pardon me, this ain't the time for none of this kinda talk. . . . Naw-naw, I ain't going no further. Let me stop, let me just stop. [*Pauses.*] Yeah, you may *think* you "okay" and that it "don't bother you," but I'm gonna just *stop.*

[*Silence for several beats; she folds her hands in her lap.*]

[*Unable to contain her frustration.*] But you *see* what I'm saying, though! I mean this chile is young, fine, "new minted" and shuuuu!! [*Nodding in agreement with Lucille.*] Who you telling? That age you be *wanting* to be held and have your toes curl up and . . . whew! yes ma'am! And see, when you raising these here kids nowadays, you got to face it! face that fact! things are *not* like when we was coming up. See and Gladys wanna get sour faced with me when I tell her like it is. See 'cause, I ain't gonna hold back, you know me girl, if it's gotta be *looked at* then I'm gonna make you lay it out flat in the sun and take a good look at it, yessir, whatever it is! I'm gonna get you told about it!

Well, now, I'll tell how it went down, see . . . Here all these weeks and weeks and carrying on, see, and I'm steady coming over visiting Gladys, and here I'm noticing that Pinkie up here always got on the *same* top, day after day, week after week, the same kinda blouselike thing, like a navy blue, you know like them navy blue nylon button-down things, like a jacket, and she's wearing this thing day in and day out, from "can't see to can't see," and I'm steady coming over. Well, one day, Gladys is out of earshot, and I say to Pinkie, "Say, Pinkie? honey, you gotta change that top, girl, I think you gonna have to wash that blouse, 'cause you know how 'navy' is now, that 'navy' get's that funk in it, and you can't wash it out. . . ." I said, "Well, Pinkie, uh, you gotta change your blouse *sometime* uh . . ." and I'm thinking to myself, well what is going on? And Gladys ain't saying nothing, and I'm waiting for her to notice or say something or *something.* I guess she ain't seen it, 'cause she ain't said nothing. Gladys got her head so stuck in them prayer books — 'scuse me for saying so, Lucille, on such a sad occasion — but she can't half see no way. I mean — I mean, the Lord said for us to "pray," well, okay, but not to go deaf, dumb, and blind in doing it! And then if I try and say, "Gladys, ain't Pinkie got another jacket or something to put on?" Then Gladys think I'm trying to talk bad about her, and she wanna rile up and jump up in *my* face and jump bad with me. And look like to me every time I turn round here come Pinkie in that same navy blouse, jacket-type blouse thing, so I'm thinking, *What is* with *this child?* and I said to Gladys finally, I said, "Gladys, Pinkie's wearing that thing out"! And Gladys come talking 'bout [*Imitating a high-pitched voice.*] "Well, if that's what she wants to wear, then that's what she wants, what you trying to make something of it? what you trying to start?" so I said to myself, "Well, hell, I'm gonna just let well enough alone then!" And what happened? The next thing I know Bernadette from 'cross the street come calling me, calling *my* house, talking 'bout how her daughter Carol, who's Pinkie's best friend, told *her* that Pinkie up at the school told *Carol* that she thought she *may* be pregnant and that Pinkie told Carol "not to tell nobody," but that Carol just now *told* her! Well, I said, "*Whaaaaa?*" Say *what?!* Well, hon-nee, I said to myself, *Let me go down here to Gladys's* and see what is what, see just *what* is going on here!" Well, so, hon-nee . . . I couldn't get out m'house fast enough! My phone come ringing off the hook, and who's on it but Gladys, weeping and wailing and having conniptions and pleading with me as the "Auntie" to come over and "have a word with Pinkie." Uh-hum *See!?* And far be it for me to say, "I told you so," far be it from me to say, "I told you the pony was gonna jump the stable!"

See, and she wanna jump up in my face when I was trying to *tell* her something way back, but now, now when it come down to the get-go, you *see* who she called on, now don't you! [*Pauses in fury.*] I'm telling you, girl! see, now that the monkey's out the bag, now that she finds out the cards done *already* been shuffled, *then* she come calling on me "to deal!"

Hon-nee, I was so outdone! So I come over there to the house, I come over saying to myself, "Oh, Lord ha-mercy! Oh, Lord!" 'Cause you know honey, I been *seeing* that navy blue top day in and day out. . . .

Well, honey! Get down to the house and what do I find? Gladys sitting up there with Pinkie looking all long face and looking like she been nailed to the cross and Pinkie's all wide-eyed and mystified! And Gladys acting like she ain't never left Sunday school, just hedging and swallowing and ducking and dodging! Don't know what's *with* that woman; act like she ain't never see the "wee-wee" on a dog! Don't know *how* my brother ever got a child with that woman, my goodness — that's the ole sanctified church mess. They ain't like *our* kind of Christian; them people crazy — way she act you'd think she ain't never seen herself "down there," I swear! You shoulda seen her, [*Imitating a high-pitched, awkward voice.*] "uh . . . uh, P-P-P-P-P-P-Pinkie? P-P-P-P-P-P-Pinkie?" She wanna beat round the bush and hesitate and germinate and I don't know what else. "P-P-P-P-P-P-Pinkie . . . have you — have you *done* . . . have you been doing anything?" And Pinkie she just stares at Gladys wide-eyed and shakes her head back and forth [*She shakes her head in no response.*] "Uh-uh" . . . Shit, girl!! — 'Scuse me, 'scuse me, Lucille, this is not the place and this is not the time, but I was so outdone, I said, Well, hell! I mean hell! later for all this! Let's get it all out here in front and the hell with beating round the bush and carrying on and acting all prettified and citified. I said, Well, hell, let's just get it out in the open. I said, "Pinkie have you *fucked?!*" I mean, you know, *Let's just get it out here!*

Well, her Mama wanted to have a seizure, but I ain't studyin' that woman. I said to Pinkie, I said, "Pinkie, well, when was your last time you had your period?" I mean, you know, let's call a "trump card" a "trump," let's say it like *is,* let's bring it all out here! Later for all this shucking and jiving and ducking and dodging and conniving and hiding and carrying on!

Well, hon-nee, I am here to tell you, Pinkie went up to that calendar and hon-nee, them pages of that calendar went to . . .

[*She illustrates with her hands flipping the air.*]

. . . flipping and ah flipping and ah flipping and ah flipping and ah flipping . . . [*Her voice trails off.*] And I said, uh-oh-oh, Lord! oh, Lord ha-mercy! well, well sir, I walked up to her and hon-nee, I lifted up that ole navy blue blouse, jacket, whatever the hell it was, and that belly was ah sitting up there just as pre-tee!

And see Gladys all this time wanna keep hiding Pinkie way from the world and keeping her at home and keeping her under lock and key and keeping her all closed up and keeping her way from the boys and what happened? You *see* what happened! And I said to her, "Pinkie, when did this happen?" Well, it turns out she was sneaking some little boy round here, right in the very house of her so sanctified mama! Honey, it's the gospel truth! [*She throws her hands in the air.*] If I'm lying, Lord choke me! Right there in the basement, right under our noses. I was probably sitting up there, too, with Gladys upstairs, probably watching tee-vee with her and here Pinkie supposed to be following Gladys's ole-timey rules and regulations, supposed to be "in the bed." Ha, she was "in the bed," all right, "in the bed" down in the basement with that boy!"

And Gladys wanna act all horrified and carrying on. She wanna come talking 'bout, "If your father was still living here, if your father was still right with the Lord, then this never would have happened." I said, "Gladys, Gladys, the Lord ain't got nothing to do with it! You can't keep locking the girl up under lock and key and anyway, 'The fox has got the hen' *now,* so what we carrying on about?" And I dunno what Gladys getting all upset for, anyway, 'cause see [*She whispers very low.*] girl, I had to bite my tongue, see, 'cause Gladys don't know that I know, but I know, 'cause see my brother *let me* know, that 'fore she married my brother, the "stork had already given notice as to Pinkie," if you know what I mean. . . .

So anyway . . . yeah . . . Pinkie's laying up there now, she's laying up there in labor, and I'll tell you one thing, my dear. . . . Now she's fifteen and having this baby. . . . Oh, Gladys is gonna help take care of it, and Gladys and me we gonna hog whip that chile if she don't *stay* in school. . . . But honey . . .

[*Her face is suddenly a portrait of sadness, foreboding, and old hidden recollections.*]

Her childhood is *over* . . . her childhood is up! Them days of being a little carefree little girl? She can just lock 'em up. . . !

[*She struggles to fight back tears.*]

. . . 'Cause raising up a baby and raising up a child and being a child your own self and with no man? Trying to raise yourself plus raise something all by yourself? [*Pause.*] Talk about being "grounded in the house"? Now she *really* gonna be "grounded"! [*Pause*] She's on the killing ground now . . . yes, Ma'am!! Pinkie's gonna be a mama! She's on the killing ground now. . . ! [*Pauses and recovers herself.*]

So anyways, Lucille, I was so, so sorry to hear that Coleman passed . . . and now what day is the viewing of the body? Oh, that's good. Let him be laid out for a couple days. That way everybody that wants to can pay they respects; that's good. . . .

[*Her voice trails off, she nods to Lucille's remarks as the lights fade.*]

That's good . . . right . . . right. . . . Amen. . . .

Fade out.

◎ LESLIE MARMON SILKO

*Leslie Marmon Silko (**see also page 24**) prefaces her novel* Ceremony *(1977) with a three-part poem connecting the words of the contemporary narrator with the sacred tradition of Thought-Woman, or Grandmother Spider, the source of names and stories, creator of all things in the Laguna Pueblo tradition. The passage included here is the first part of an incantation and dialogue between female and male, health and illness, balance and imbalance. This opening passage of Silko's novel integrates poetry and fiction, tradition and contemporary voices in a healing ceremony of words.*

from the prologue to Ceremony

Ts'its'tsi'nako, Thought-Woman,
is sitting in her room
and whatever she thinks about
appears.

She thought of her sisters,
Nau'ts'ity'i and I'tcts'ity'i,
and together they created the Universe

this world
and the four worlds below.

Thought-Woman, the spider,
named things and
as she named them
they appeared.

She is sitting in her room
thinking of a story now

I'm telling you the story
she is thinking.

◎ LORNA DEE CERVANTES

Lorna Dee Cervantes was born in San Francisco in 1954 and she was raised in San Jose. She graduated from San Jose State University and studied at the University of California, Santa Cruz. She was a member of the Chicana Theatre Group and organizer for the Centro Cultural de la Gente. She also founded a small press, MANGO, *which published a literary magazine and books of poetry by Chicano and Chicana poets and other multicultural works. Cervantes was awarded a fellowship in poetry at the Fine Arts Work Center in Provincetown, Massachusetts. She has published two volumes of poems,* Emplumada *(1981) and* From the Cables of Genocide: Poems on Love and Hunger *(1991). Cervantes now lives in Boulder, Colorado, and coedits* Red Dirt, *a cross-cultural poetry journal.*

Cervantes' poem "Refugee Ship" was first published in 1975 and is included in her first book, Emplumada. *The poet coined the word* emplumada *— a cross between* emplumado, *"feathered, in plumage, after molting," and* plumada, *a feminine noun for "flourish of the pen." Cervantes' title combines creative display and flight, transformation, and serious delight in writing. The poems in* Emplumada *trace her emerging identity as woman, Chicana, and poet.*

Refugee Ship

Like wet cornstarch, I slide
past my grandmother's eyes. Bible
at her side, she removes her glasses.
The pudding thickens.

Mama raised me without language.
I'm orphaned from my Spanish name.
The words are foreign, stumbling
on my tongue. I see in the mirror
my reflection: bronzed skin, black hair.

I feel I am a captive
aboard the refugee ship.
The ship that will never dock.
El barco que nunca atraca.

MARILYN CHIN

Marilyn Chin was born in 1955 in Hong Kong. Her education includes a B.A. from the University of Massachusetts at Amherst and an M.F.A. from the University of Iowa. She has received many awards for her work, including the Mary Roberts Rinehart Award, a Stegner Fellowship at Stanford University, and a grant from the National Endowment for the Arts. Since 1988 she has been a professor of creative writing at San Diego State University. Her publications include two volumes of translations and a book of poetry, Dwarf Bamboo *(1987). She also edited* Writing from the World *(1985).*

"First Lessons" is from Marilyn Chin's first book of poetry, Dwarf Bamboo. *Memory is a powerful tool for poets; here the speaker of the poem remembers schoolyard lessons as well as language lessons. A child struggles to understand a word's meaning, especially when actions witnessed by the child seem to offer contradictions.*

First Lessons

(dedicated to the character 好 *or "goodness")*

1

I got up; a red shiner bloomed
like a rose in my eye. She said,
"A present fit for a queen . . . served
by the hand which fed you, soothed you
and presently, slaps you to your senses.

"Your goddess of Mercy has spoken."

She ran, blonde hair ablaze,
dust settling on asphalt.

I did it again.
I got up from the blood and the mud
crying like a bullcalf,
not for the wound but for the dress.

2

This is how I remember *goodness.*

A woman whose lipstick smells of lilac leans over a child.
She says, "Have you been good?"
The child, kneels like a supplicant,
looks up, whispers, "always."

3

Dust we are made, dust we leave behind —
The dress shall be clean no matter the circumstance.
My friend, my foe, wearing worn Levis and a T-shirt,
hides in the schoolyard, now, with her black labrador.

4

I learned *goodness* before I learned my name.
I learned the strokes, their order, but never the message:

that the good shall never rise from their knees is my
river-to-cross.

◎ JUDITH ORTIZ COFER

"The Latin Deli: An Ars Poetica" is the title poem of Judith Ortiz Cofer's volume of poetry and prose The Latin Deli *(1993) (see also page 31). The poem is an ars poetica because it evokes the two cultures Cofer draws upon in her writing and suggests how Spanish evokes a homeland for Hispanic "exiles" in New Jersey. As Cofer has explained: "My Puerto Rican heritage is the life-giving fountain for much of my work, poetry and prose. . . . My work is an attempt to make sense of the complexities of a life*

lived between two quite different cultures: and of the words I heard spoken in two languages — hoping that the synthesis of these collected glimpses of experience will lead me to the heart of this, my reality" (Cofer to M. Kallet, 1994).

The Latin Deli

Presiding over a formica counter,
plastic Mother and Child magnetized
to the top of an ancient register,
the heady mix of smells from the open bins
of dried codfish, the green plantains
hanging in stalks like votive offerings,
she is the Patroness of Exiles,
a woman of no-age who was never pretty,
who spends her days selling canned memories
while listening to the Puerto Ricans complain
that it would be cheaper to fly to San Juan
than to buy a pound of Bustelo coffee here,
and to Cubans perfecting their speech
of a "glorious return" to Havana — where no one
has been allowed to die and nothing to change until then;
to Mexicans who pass through, talking lyrically
of *dolares* to be made in El Norte —

all wanting the comfort
of spoken Spanish, to gaze upon the family portrait
of her plain wide face, her ample bosom
resting on her plump arms, her look of maternal interest
as they speak to her and each other
of their dreams and their disillusions —
how she smiles understanding,
when they walk down the narrow aisles of her store
reading the labels of packages aloud, as if
they were the names of lost lovers: *Suspiros,*
Merengues, the stale candy of everyone's childhood.

She spends her days
slicing *jamon y queso* and wrapping it in wax paper
tied with string: plain ham and cheese
that would cost less at the A&P, but it would not satisfy
the hunger of the fragile old man lost in the folds
of his winter coat, who brings her lists of items

that he reads to her like poetry, or the others,
whose needs she must divine, conjuring up products
from places that now exist only in their hearts —
closed ports she must trade with.

JOY HARJO

Joy Harjo was born in 1951 in Tulsa, Oklahoma, an enrolled member of the Muskogee tribe. She graduated from the Institute of American Indian Arts and from the University of New Mexico, and attended the Anthropology Film Center in Santa Fe. She received her M.F.A. in Creative Writing from the University of Iowa. Harjo published her first chapbook at Ishmael Reed's press when she was an undergraduate. Since then she has published five books of poems, including *She Had Some Horses* (1983) and *In Mad Love and War* (1990), which won the William Carlos Williams Award from the Poetry Society of America for best poetry book of 1991. Her most recent book of poetry is *The Woman Who Fell from the Sky* (1994). With photographer/astronomer Stephen Strom, Harjo published *Secrets from the Center of the World* (1989). Her anthology of Native American women's writing, *Reinventing the Enemy's Language*, is forthcoming. Harjo plays tenor saxophone with her band, Poetic Justice.

"For Alva Benson, and for Those Who Have Learned to Speak" is from *She Had Some Horses*. Herself a mother of three and a grandmother, Harjo compares traditional and modern experiences of giving birth. In the early 1970s Harjo worked as a nurse's assistant in the maternity ward of an Oklahoma hospital. Her article "Three Generations of Native American Women's Birth Experiences" appeared in *Ms.* in 1991. Her poem draws connections between the creativity of women's bodies and women's experiences of language and culture.

For Alva Benson, and for Those Who Have Learned to Speak

And the ground spoke when she was born.
Her mother heard it. In Navajo she answered
as she squatted down against the earth
to give birth. It was now when it happened,
now giving birth to itself again and again
between the legs of women.

Or maybe it was the Indian Hospital
in Gallup. The ground still spoke beneath
mortar and concrete. She strained against the
metal stirrups, and they tied her hands down
because she still spoke with them when they
muffled her screams. But her body went on
talking and the child was born into their
hands, and the child learned to speak
both voices.

She grew up talking in Navajo, in English
and watched the earth around her shift and change
with the people in the towns and in the cities
learning not to hear the ground as it spun around
beneath them. She learned to speak for the ground,
the voice coming through her like roots that
have long hungered for water. Her own daughter
was born, like she had been, in either place
or all places, so she could leave, leap
into the sound she had always heard,
a voice like water, like the gods weaving
against sundown in a scarlet light.

The child now hears names in her sleep.
They change into other names, and into others.
It is the ground murmuring, and Mt. St. Helens
erupts as the harmonic motion of a child turning
inside her mother's belly waiting to be born
to begin another time.

And we go on, keep giving birth and watch
ourselves die, over and over.
And the ground spinning beneath us
goes on talking.

◎ *AUDRE LORDE*

Audre Lorde's "A Litany for Survival" is included in The Black Unicorn *(1987). The poem repeats its invocation to "those of us" who are marginalized by society, "For those of us / who were imprinted with fear," and, "For all of us / this instant and this triumph" is the poem's triumph in speaking out even though we are afraid.* *(For more on Lorde, see page 42.)*

A Litany for Survival

For those of us who live at the shoreline
standing upon the constant edges of decision
crucial and alone
for those of us who cannot indulge
the passing dreams of choice
who love in doorways coming and going
in the hours between dawns
looking inward and outward
at once before and after
seeking a now that can breed
futures
like bread in our children's mouths
so their dreams will not reflect
the death of ours;

For those of us
who were imprinted with fear
like a faint line in the center of our foreheads
learning to be afraid with our mother's milk
for by this weapon
this illusion of some safety to be found
the heavy-footed hoped to silence us
For all of us
this instant and this triumph
We were never meant to survive.

And when the sun rises we are afraid
it might not remain
when the sun sets we are afraid
it might not rise in the morning
when our stomachs are full we are afraid
of indigestion
when our stomachs are empty we are afraid
we may never eat again
when we are loved we are afraid
love will vanish
when we are alone we are afraid
love will never return
and when we speak we are afraid
our words will not be heard
nor welcomed

but when we are silent
we are still afraid.

So it is better to speak
remembering
we were never meant to survive.

LISA SUHAIR MAJAJ

Lisa Suhair Majaj is a Palestinian American born in Iowa, raised in Jordan, and educated in Beirut. She is completing her dissertation on Arab American literature in the department of American Culture at the University of Michigan. Her work has appeared in Red Dirt, Worcester Review, Women of Power, *and* Mr. Cogito, *among other literary journals, and is in a forthcoming anthology of Arab American women's writing. Majaj lives in Cambridge, Massachusetts.*

"Recognized Futures" appeared in the cross-cultural anthology of poetry Unsettling America *(1994). Majaj yearns not merely for a personal integration of her split heritage — Palestinian and American — but on behalf of all of us she hopes for "some possible language" enabling expression, communication, and connections. In the poem, the word* nai *refers to an Arabic flute.*

Recognized Futures

Turning to you, my name —
this necklace of gold, these letters
in script I cannot read,
this part of myself I long
to recognize —falls forward
into my mouth.

You call my daily name, *Lisa,*
the name I've finally declared
my own, claiming a heritage
half mine: corn fields golden
in ripening haze, green music

of crickets, summer light sloping
to dusk on the Iowa farm.

This other name fills my mouth,
a taste faintly metallic, blunt
edges around which my tongue
moves tentatively: *Suhair,*
an old-fashioned name, *little star*
in the night. The second girl,
small light on a distanced horizon.

Throughout childhood this rending split:
continents moving slowly apart,
rift widening beneath taut limbs.
A contested name, a constant
longing, evening star rising mute
through the Palestine night.
Tongue cleft by impossible languages,
fragments of narrative fractured
to loss, homelands splintered
beyond bridgeless rivers,
oceans of salt.

* * *

From these fragments I feel
a stirring, almost imperceptible.
In the morning light these torn
lives merge: a name on your lips,
on mine, softly murmured,
mutely scripted, both real
and familiar, till I cannot
distinguish between your voice
and my silence, my words
and this wordless knowledge,
morning star rising
through lightening sky,
some music I can't quite
hear, a distant melody,
flute-like, *nai* through
the olives, a cardinal calling,
some possible language
all our tongues can sing.

◎ NAOMI SHIHAB NYE

Naomi Shihab Nye was born in 1952 in St. Louis, Missouri, to a Palestinian father and an American mother of German descent. She was educated at Trinity University and has worked since then as a freelance visiting writer. Most recently she was a visiting writer at the University of Texas at Austin. Her awards include the Voertman Poetry Prize from the Texas Institute of Letters in both 1980 and 1982 for her books Different Ways to Pray *and* Hugging the Jukebox. *She has also received three Pushcart Prizes and the I. B. Lavan Award from the Academy of American Poets. She has published six volumes of poetry in addition to* Words Under the Words: Selected Poems *(1995).*

"Adios" is found in Words Under the Words. *Nye's tone in this poem is jubilant as she celebrates words and the silence that follows them.*

Adios

It is a good word, rolling off the tongue
no matter what language you were born with.
Use it. Learn where it begins,
the small alphabet of departure,
how long it takes to think of it,
then say it, then be heard.

Marry it. More than any golden ring,
it shines, it shines.
Wear it on every finger
till your hands dance,
touching everything easily,
letting everything, easily, go.

Strap it to your back like wings.
Or a kite-tail. The stream of air behind a jet.
If you are known for anything,
let it be the way you rise out of sight
when your work is finished.

Think of things that linger: leaves,
cartons and napkins, the damp smell of mold.

Think of things that disappear.

Think of what you love best,
what brings tears into your eyes.

Something that said adios to you
before you knew what it meant
or how long it was for.

Explain little, the word explains itself.
Later perhaps. Lessons following lessons,
like silence following sound.

◎ *MARGARET WALKER*

Margaret Walker was born in 1915 in Birmingham, Alabama. Eighty-one years old at this writing, she still gives lectures and poetry readings. She received an M.A. from Northwestern University and a Ph.D. from the University of Iowa. She has been a social worker, a newspaper reporter, a magazine editor, and a professor of English. She was the director of the Institute for the Study of History, Life, and Culture of Black People at Jackson State College in Mississippi. Her awards include the Yale Series of Younger Poets Award for For My People *(1942) and a Fulbright Fellowship. She has published several more volumes of poetry, including* Ballad of the Free *(1966),* Prophets for a New Day *(1970),* October Journey *(1973), and* This is My Century: New and Collected Poems *(1989). For her novel* Jubilee, *published in 1966 she received the Houghton Mifflin Literary Fellowship. She has written several critical works, including* Richard Wright, Daemonic Genius: A Portrait of the Man, A Critical Look at His Work *(1988), and* How I Wrote Jubilee and Other Essays on Life and Literature *(1990).*

"I Want to Write" was first published in For My People *in 1942. The poem creates a visionary world of black identity, and with it Margaret Walker establishes herself as a spokesperson for her people.*

I Want to Write

I want to write
I want to write the songs of my people.
I want to hear them singing melodies in the dark.
I want to catch the last floating strains from their sob-torn throats.
I want to frame their dreams into words; their souls into notes.
I want to catch their sunshine laughter in a bowl;
fling dark hands to a darker sky
and fill them full of stars
then crush and mix such lights till they become
a mirrored pool of brilliance in the dawn.

INTERVIEW

The Art of Not Forgetting: An Interview with Judith Ortiz Cofer

by Marilyn Kallet

JUDITH ORTIZ COFER

"The Art of Not Forgetting: An Interview with Judith Ortiz Cofer," was first recorded by Marilyn Kallet on November 9, 1993, and was completed in May 1994. Cofer had come to Knoxville as Distinguished Writer-in-Residence, a program funded by an NEA Audience Development Grant received by the University of Tennessee. During her residency, she gave several readings and taught classes at Oak Ridge High School. The rhythm of Cofer's speaking is fast and packed with ideas — though she lives in Georgia, her rhythm in English resembles that of spoken Spanish and of metropolitan New Jersey. (For more on Cofer's background, *see page 31.)*

The interview with Judith Ortiz Cofer was published in Prairie Schooner *(1994).*

MK: The concept of not forgetting plays a central part in your work and aesthetics. Why is not forgetting so important to you as a writer?

JOC: It's a complex concept for me. Many people of my parents' generation felt that if we assimilated, if we learned to live within the culture, it would be easier for us. I can see that as an economic survival technique, but as an artist I discovered that assimilation is exactly what destroys the artistic — to blend so well that you forget what makes you unique. When I started to write I really thought — like most English majors and graduate students — that I had to abstract all my ideas to be able to communicate the large concepts. I found out that what I really needed to communicate were the basics in our culture. Language and memory became important, because I realized that memory was the treasure in my backyard. My education had allowed me to become perceptive enough to be able to use memory plus imagination, to transform remembering into art. Not forgetting is a spiritual matter with me. It connects me to the reality of my life. As long as I understand that I will continue to produce art. One falls into the error of forgetting basic concepts like language and its power to affect reality. The language one speaks at home shapes the original reality and then one learns other versions of that to survive in the world. As a poet I have to be able to tell the difference, to transmit that. In a poem like "The Latin Deli" I don't just put in Spanish words as decoration. They are used to transmit a special kind of reality, to communicate to my English-speaking reader, to say, "Yes, this is a different reality, but you can understand it by paying close attention."

MK: So you are inviting the reader in?

JOC: Right. I don't use language to alienate. I use it to try to bridge, so that when I write a poem I don't send my reader to the dictionary. Rather I'm saying, "Read closely, it will become clear to you." What we speak and how we say things shapes the way we see the world.

MK: When you were little, was Spanish spoken at home?

JOC: Absolutely, especially since my mother was the one who was with us in the house all the time. She spoke nothing but Spanish. Our apartments were a microcosm of her *casa*. This is where she listened to her Spanish-language records, where the Spanish-language newspaper came in, and her books. She encouraged us to succeed in the outside world, but that was not her reality.

MK: How old were you when you first moved to Paterson?

JOC: The first time I was two, but then my father left on an extended tour with the navy, and we went back to Puerto Rico. Then directly after that he was transferred to the Roosevelt Roads Navy Base in Puerto Rico. We spent a couple of years in Paterson and then I attended first and second grade in Puerto Rico. The first time that I came back to Paterson to enter the world of school I was already in the third grade. By that time Spanish had become my first language again and there was the culture shock of going into the classroom. So you can understand how I trace my obsession with language back to that early time when I had to determine what language would serve me best.

MK: You were trying to figure out where you belonged, and where to find a sense of belonging.

JOC: Yes. I have an essay about that in *Silent Dancing*, about the teacher not understanding my needs. I decided at an early age that language was my best defense.

MK: And books?

JOC: They were not only a refuge but a guide. What people could not tell me or would not tell me I would find in books.

MK: Was your father bilingual?

JOC: Fully. He spoke textbook English. He was a perfectionist and he insisted on the correct pronunciation. I remember clearly one time when he had come to pick me up at catechism. One of my friends, a Puerto Rican, said *tousand* instead of *thousand*. He was too kind to correct her but later he said, "I want you to know that the word is *thousand*." He made me repeat it and I thought that

he was just being pushy. I finally understood that he felt that he would be treated better if he spoke well and he transmitted that to us.
MK: Language was a passport to . . . ?
JOC: The usual immigrant idea that if you speak intelligently people will treat you with respect. He was of that mind. Even though he was very authoritarian and the military shaped him, he understood that I needed books, and he encouraged me in that area and bought me books. In fact, he was the one who told my mother not to push me to cook if I didn't want to, that that was something *I* wasn't going to need. That was the most liberated decision he ever made in the sense that he thought my intelligence could take me farther than he had gone. He was the one who emphasized the importance of education. He insisted that my brother and I keep up with our studies no matter how unstable our lives were. He facilitated my move into the literary life by encouraging me to read voraciously, to think of education as empowering.
MK: Do you remember which books you were looking at, which ones influenced you at the beginning?
JOC: In fact I do. I have an essay called "The Paterson Public Library" coming out in my new book, *The Latin Deli.* In it, I talk about how nothing prevented me from going to the library. I was allowed a certain amount of time to go on Saturday mornings. There was a girl who hated me because the teacher used to humiliate her by making me tutor her in spelling. She lived on the way to the library and she had promised to beat me up. I remember fearing this girl — she was twice as big as I was. I guess I wanted books more than to save my life because she did carry through with her threat. That hour or so that I was given to go and get books was my best time. The library was impressive to a little girl. I don't know what it would look like now and I have resisted going back because at that time I felt like I was in one of those paintings of philosophers and their disciples sitting on the steps of a great temple. I would approach this magnificent library which was incongruously placed in the worst neighborhood you can imagine where this Greek temple arose from chaos with its lions and its columns.

I had a pink card which meant for a long time I could only check out children's books. So I started reading the world's fairy tales and folk tales at one end of the children's room and worked my way to the other. I experienced a sense of discovery when I found out that the Cinderella story appears in Africa and China, and that heroines didn't have to have pink skin and gold hair, that sometimes they had braided kinky hair and sometimes they had Asian features. That reassured me in my reality that the world was populated by people as different-looking as I thought I was.
MK: Did you identify with Cinderella?
JOC: Not so much with Cinderella as with the woman rising out of her condition and situation in life. I had decided at an early age that I wouldn't get married, mainly because my model for marriage was the passive wife and the

domineering husband — not so much in my grandmother's time but in the next generation. The fifties generation of my mother was a lot more traditional than the old women I knew as I child. . . . I wasn't looking for the prince, I was looking for how in the world was I going to be more than just a housewife, how could I leave Paterson and do other things. The fairy tales allowed me to see that sometimes by the use of wit and intelligence a girl could leave her allotted place in the ashes and come out into the sunlight! We didn't live in dire poverty, we were better off than most of the people in my neighborhood because my father had a military career. But I did not want a typical life for myself, I wanted to be a teacher. I wanted to get out into the wider world.

MK: It seems like writing has been a way into adventure. You have written eloquently about the atmosphere of women's lives as you were growing up. You mentioned earlier that you wanted to write more about your father.

JOC: I do, mainly because he was absent during my childhood. He was a man who came home every six months or so and spent some time with us. Because of the navy, most frequently he was home during the weekends and the rest of the time he was away. So I didn't really get to know him except that he usually made the final decisions. He was a quiet man, and year by year became more quiet and more depressed. I understood that this was not the life he had *chosen*. He had *accepted* his life. He would have really been a completely different kind of man had he been able to explore his potential. He was very intelligent and military life stifled him. And yet he looked around him and saw his friends who were factory workers and others imprisoned by the economy and their own lack of skills, so he stayed in the navy and became more and more withdrawn. I can only imagine his loneliness on a ship full of people who did not speak his native language far away from his family. So I never got to know my real father. I knew only what he became. And then he died. And so I need to explore that and yet have resisted doing so. First of all I have to explore my life as a woman and I know how to do that. I have the language, the avenues, the models. At some point I will begin to write about my father with some maturity and more hindsight.

MK: In terms of your gift for storytelling, does some of that come from your father as well as your mother and grandmother?

JOC: He wasn't a talker. He was a silent man and he directed our lives through silence. My mother's people owned land and were farmers, and they have a basic joy for life that seems to go with lives connected to the seasons and the earth. I didn't learn storytelling from my father so much as discipline. He knew exactly what he needed to do and he did it. I'm not the stoic that he was, however.

MK: Then the storytelling ability comes from your mother?

JOC: Yes, from my mother's mother. In my baby years I stayed close to my father's mother, but after that it was Mamá, my mother's mother, who was really the grandmother in my life. And she is a joyful storyteller. Hardships to her have been hurdles. She overcomes one and goes to the next, she doesn't dwell on them. I come from a tradition where the women tell stories. I trace the storyteller's impulse to the months I spent at my Mamá's house, listening to the women communicate and teach through their powerful narratives.

MK: What were you learning from them?

JOC: In "Casa," from *Silent Dancing,* I describe a scene where in the late afternoon the women gathered to tell stories and gossip and commiserate with each other while the men were at work and the boys were playing baseball. The girls learned by listening to the women. The women did not censor their speech. We listened to birthing stories, to marital problems. In some cases I assumed that the women were talking for our benefit, so that we would understand that a woman's life was hard. I started listening to them with the natural curiosity of a young girl to learn about the facts of life, and there was a simple pleasure in hearing them talk. Later when I started delving into my memories to find material for my work, these stories the women told became the triggers for early poems and later for the novels and the essays in *Silent Dancing.* The deeper I probed with the hindsight of an adult woman, the more I understood the subtext, which was lessons in life for a woman. In my work I try to shed light on what were at one time simply amusing little stories which I have now chosen to interpret as the handing-down of knowledge.

MK: In "Casa" language becomes a place; I can see you sitting there in the late afternoon.

JOC: Wasn't it Milosz who said that "language is the only homeland"? I believe that. The women spoke in Spanish of course, and I have to translate that into English. Something *is* lost. What people say to one another under intimate circumstances can never fully survive translation. There's a lot of nonverbal communication going on, many shared intimacies. The only way I can regain the power of the original storytelling is not to be a slave to the factual story, but rather to present it as drama, with me as the witness or audience. I try to give back to the women's voices the original power that they had for me as a child by using the techniques of the poet and fiction writer.

MK: Who are the writers who have most influenced your writing?

JOC: That's always a hard one for me to answer because I have done such eclectic reading. I am an English teacher and my background is in American literature. If any writers excited me during my early years in college it was Faulkner and Eudora Welty and Flannery O'Connor and the southern writers who used language with such delight. It's not that their themes were delightful, but that they really took language and went with it. They ignited something in my own storytelling impulse. I was definitely not influenced by the minimalists, for example, and the restrained language-users. It was interesting to me later when I did read Gabriel García Márquez, Manuel Puig, Mario Vargas Llosa, Isabel Allende, and other Latin American storytellers that they had a lot in common with the southern writers. They use language with what Márquez calls "plenitude." Language to them is a feast. Later I found out that there was a direct link between Faulkner and Márquez, that Márquez considers Faulkner his primary influence. So it comes full circle.

I have to admit also that as a child I read everything I could find, from Harlequin-style Spanish romances to the encyclopedia. I think my writing finally became a blend between my formal education and my eclectic reading in both English and Spanish.

MK: Which poets have influenced you most?

JOC: I've been an avid reader of poetry for many years. While I was in graduate school I read the "standard" poets. The first poet who gave me that "jolt," that shock of recognition, who made me feel that she was speaking directly to me, was Denise Levertov. After I looked up her poetry I seriously began to think of writing poetry myself.

MK: What was it about her work that impressed you?

JOC: It was both the control and the flexibility. She was speaking with emotion about certain subjects that were close to her, but she kept a certain control. The lines were naturally flowing and yet they seemed to have a reason for being. Later I read some of her essays about the lines. She was very conscious of what she was doing without being self-conscious. By studying Levertov's poetry I realized the art and craft involved in writing poetry, as well as the emotional release and self-discovery involved.

MK: Do you remember the first time you consciously thought of yourself as a writer?

JOC: I didn't consciously think of myself as a writer when I was writing my thesis, that's for sure! [*Laughter.*] As you know, I wasn't really able to give my own creative writing any time until after I finished graduate school. I did get married at nineteen and I did have a child at twenty-one and continued to go to school. All of my waking hours were involved in trying to keep my world from becoming chaos.

When I finished school I went to work for a wonderful woman named Betty Owen, who was the head of the English Department at Broward Community College in Hollywood, Florida. She was the first person to whom I showed my poetry, and she told me, "Send it out!" She became my reader and mentor. In 1978 when Betty Owen was saying "you can write," and occasionally a poem would get accepted, I began to think of myself as a writer. Then writing became so much a part of my life that I can hardly remember a time when I didn't write.

MK: Do you think of yourself as a poet at heart?

JOC: I do. I like that term better than any other. I remember when my novel came out I had a couple of poetry friends say, half-kiddingly, "I see you've sold out!" I felt horrible. It was like being accused of abandoning a child. But I have never stopped writing poetry. When I get up in the morning and I have two hours to write, I still give the first hour to poetry. I'm always working on a new poem. . . . I consider myself primarily a poet.

MK: How do you decide which genre to pursue, or does the work itself make that decision for you?

JOC: The work itself sometimes makes a double decision. Right now I'm working on a short story based on the character in "The Latin Deli" [a poem]. The direction is based on the strength of my obsession. If I write a poem and the subject continues to intrigue me, and I need to explore it in a more ample way, it might become an essay, a short story, or even a novel. I now have twenty pages of a story called "Corazon's Cafe." In this story, the woman from my poem has a husband who has just died and she is considering closing their grocery store. This woman intrigued me and I wanted to explore her character in more depth.

I recently wrote an essay called "The Story of My Body" for an anthology. . . . It's about how walking around in this body has affected my life. About how not being tall, being a "shrimp," and unathletic has influenced my individual reality. When I started writing it I knew that it couldn't be a poem, it couldn't be anything but a very structured essay which I divided into skin color, size, and physical appearance and the relativity of these to my sense of self. To my mother I'm tall, because she's 4'11". To everyone else, I'm short.

MK: Physical appearance does affect our reality, but it's not something we talk about.

JOC: I resisted writing about it. . . . And then I started thinking about how having been the last chosen for sports at school inspired my best secret stories. . . . I fantasized about being Wonder Woman and scooping up all of the P.E. teachers and putting them on a barren asteroid where they would perish because they had no inner resources. I didn't realize how much I disliked them until I wrote that! I needed to say this in an essay. An essay is an attempt to explore ideas. A poem is an attempt to concentrate ideas into their essential core.

Basically, the decision about genre is made when I sit down and decide the parameters of what I'm writing. Some fit very nicely into the poem because I see them as images. Others require language to be ample and generous.

MK: Storytelling unifies various genres you work with.

JOC: And obsessions! I have obsessions that are explored in different ways and genres.

MK: What are they?

JOC: Language as identity and as the mechanism for defining our world is something that I think about a lot. How saying one thing in a particular way is completely different than saying the same thing in another way. The relationships that women create, the intricate patterns that we weave out of affection and family loyalties, and how those have changed and shifted in a cosmic way from my grandmother's time to my own. And absences, absences leave a very real space people must fill. . . . These are some ideas that pop up in any work that I do, and I predict that whatever I do these ideas will always concern me.

MK: What are you working on now?

JOC: I am trying to finish *The Latin Deli.* I'm working on the title story based on the poem "The Latin Deli."

MK: Is there anything else you would like to say?

JOC: At universities, students are very concerned with becoming writers. They should also understand that writing is a vocation — more so than a profession, that when you commit yourself to it it is like a religious calling. It's not just about a public life or the publishing market. The power of the artist comes from being disciplined and comes through the creation of the work. Many new writers want to know, "*If* I write this, who will publish it?" I say to them, "Just write it!" The work is the important thing. Creation is the main reward. It's great to have the work published, but the process itself is what I need in my life.

Family Album

Family Album

◎ ◎ ◎

THE READINGS IN THIS SECTION OF *Worlds in Our Words* focus on connections between family members, though we intend for the word *family* to be construed as widely as possible, so that it enlarges, as a widening ripple moves outward in water, to include members of the community as family, plus members of various races, creeds, and cultures, and not only the human race but the animal world as well.

Some of the themes sounded by these selections are, not surprisingly, ancient ones concerning the power and fascination of family life and family love. There is the inevitable disappointment and failure of family life, too. Adults struggle to be role models, and children learn what to accept — or perhaps reject — of those role models. Inevitably there are family stories, handed down like heirlooms, wrought by voices and words. All of them amount to a rich celebration of family life in all its shades and tones.

The fiction selections of "Family Album" examine a wide variety of connections, from mother and daughter (Tereze Glück) to grandmother and granddaughter (Mary Hood and Paule Marshall). Pamela Walker's "Good Shabbos" shows us the power of love across family lines as a sympathetic neighbor, who is both Jewish and widowed, invites over a young Gentile for Sabbath to comfort her in a time of pain.

In rhythmical prose that evokes the hot sun and the "blue and green drift of sea" at a Mexican beach, Tereze Glück's "Yellow Light" summons a portrait of the fierce, complicated love between mother and daughter. Told from the daughter's point of view — the young daughter who worships her mother even as she knows how inappropriate and dangerous this mother can be — this is a story about closeness and desire, about homesickness for being "back together again, one body, one skin."

Mary Hood's "How Far She Went" and Paule Marshall's "To Da-duh, In Memoriam" pair granddaughters with their grandmothers. Hood's story is told from the point of view of a reluctant grandmother suddenly trying to live with a rebellious teenage granddaughter, a teenager the grandmother both needs and resents. Here we are shown the power of claiming one's connection to others. It is not automatic, even with blood relatives; it takes commitment and will. The power of making such a commitment is fierce and cauterizing: maybe old hurts can indeed be put to rest. From another standpoint, Marshall examines the granddaughter's view as she journeys to Barbados and meets the cranky elderly grandmother who must compare Barbados and New York City (the girl's home) in an ongoing competition. Even after the grandmother's passing, the girl remembers and celebrates this tough spirit who named fruit, trees, and flowers in the lush Barbados landscape.

The nonfiction selections in this section focus on family as well, though sometimes the family members are long gone. After death, it is imagination and storytelling that will help make the connections. We see the importance of storytelling in families; it keeps a link between past and present, the dead and the living, and important moral lessons are learned. Joy Harjo's personal essay "Family Album" offers a meditation on family and on the interaction of family history with American history, as well as an invocation of a timeless circle of relatives. At the outset, Harjo is traveling to Tallahassee grounds in northeastern Oklahoma with her friends. The car is filled with stories, the air filled with the noises of crickets and grasses and trees. She is on her way to the green corn ceremony, a dance for the continuity and renewal of the earth and the people. Her cousin John has given her two photographs of her family that help to spur her memories. Juxtaposed with historical events and the stories of individual members of her family — some of whom became wealthy when oil was found on their land in Oklahoma — are those ceremonies that join relatives in the tribal dancing of memories "larger than mere human memory."

A pairing of two pieces shows the living writer coming to grips with someone gone: In "A Walk with My Father" Pat Mora goes on a vivid spirit-journey with her father through an outdoor market, and in "Dear Mama" Sonia Sanchez writes a letter to the mother she lost when she was six years old. Mora feels the essence of "sweet sorrow" as she steps past stalls with her father, heeding his instruction, "*Fíjate, fíjate!*" (Notice, notice!). We join her in such noticing. And Sanchez realizes, as did Harjo, that we gather strength from our ancestors. The most painful of the nonfiction pieces is undoubtedly Maxine Hong Kingston's "No Name Woman," in which she describes the harrowing punishment a community inflicts on a woman who commits adultery. Claiming ancestry cannot always be pretty, yet Kingston refuses to turn from this outcast and ghost.

Wendy Wasserstein's one-act play *Tender Offer* gives us a glimpse of the father/daughter nexus and its importance. In this drama set in a dance studio, a young girl practices dance steps in a leotard and waits for her father. Soon the audience realizes that he has broken a promise and missed her recital. When he arrives, talking the language of business, of "tender offers" and "bids on the table," the girl's disappointment is heightened and he is remorseful. If daughters have missed out on connections, fathers have as well, and Wasserstein depicts the father as rounded, dynamic, open to change. Can he make up for the missed recital? Can the father and daughter find language comfortable for both? *Tender Offer* is surprisingly encouraging in its outcome.

The poetry selections in "Family Album" also show the range of possibilities available when we speak of "family" connections: here we have mother and daughter (Toi Derricotte, "Touching/Not Touching: My Mother"), son and mother (Tess Gallagher, "Each Bird Walking"), daughter and father (Sharon Olds, "The Race"), mother and newborn child (Olds, "Bathing the New Born"), and a mother and children separated by divorce (Minnie Bruce Pratt, "Down the Little Cahaba"). The speaker in Toi Derricotte's poem is fascinated by her mother and her mother's nakedness. The link of flesh serves as a source of wonder, identity, and attraction. Tess Gallagher's poem "Each Bird Walking" describes a poignant moment between lovers, a moment of shared stories that mitigates loss. The speaker's lover describes washing his ill mother (compare with Sharon Olds' "Bathing the New Born"). Here family history is dramatized and brought to life. As the speaker says, "On our lips that morning, the tart juice / of the mothers. . . ." In "Germinal," Linda Hogan celebrates "all things saved and growing," reminding us of our connection to the earth. This respect for older forms of life and this kinship with them is not merely theoretical in Hogan's work, but instinctive and visceral. Listening deeply, the poet hears the growth of roots and eggs "drumming / like old women / and blood stirring in the neck." "Elk Song" thanks the animals that provide food, praises the power and beauty of elk and of "gone elk," the spirit of animals who inhabited the earth before cities: "they are drumming / back the woodland," summoning "days we were equal / and strong." For the poet, who is Chickasaw by birth, all living things exist as one body.

Sharon Olds' poems "Bathing the New Born" and "The Race" show both ends of the spectrum of family life. In the first, the speaker (as parent) bathes her child and gazes in wonder and awe upon the helpless, tender life. In the second, the speaker describes a harrowing journey to be at the bedside of her dying father. He is as helpless now as the infant — the old cycle of the life of humans. Minnie Bruce Pratt's "Down the Little Cahaba" describes a seemingly idyllic moment of a mother and two sons floating in August on a river. Family history intrudes, though, as the speaker remembers when she lost her sons through divorce. In the present, as in the past, she still feels the sharp physical connection with her sons: "*I can never forget you. You moved inside me.*" In "Bentshen Licht" Rochelle Ratner describes her grandmother in a moment of religious observance. The sensory details sharpen the moment's insight, highlighting the paradox of connection and separation.

Ellen Bryant Voigt in "Visiting the Graves" will cause readers to think of Joy Harjo's "Family Album" as it stresses the link, across time, with those who preceded us. Cathy Song's "Picture Bride" will remind readers of Maxine Hong Kingston's work, as Song questions what her "sister" might be like, the one who stayed, the one who remained in another country.

Finally, Marilyn Kallet's interview with Linda Hogan rounds out the selections in "Family Album" as Hogan speaks of her global and earthly home. Teachers for Hogan are not simply family members, human families, but the "animals and seasons" that swirl around us, whose spirits we share as we move and live under the sun and moon. Hogan stresses that many of our problems stem from "lack of healthy relationship with the land, with self, with creation and the creative spirit."

◎ TEREZE GLÜCK

Tereze Glück was born in 1945 and grew up in Woodmere, Long Island. She is a graduate of Vassar College. Her collection of stories, May You Live in Interesting Times, *won the 1995 Iowa Short Fiction Award. She has received a grant from the National Endowment for the Arts and has been a fellow at the Virginia Center for the Creative Arts, Ragdale, and Ucross. Her stories have been published in the* North American Review, Antioch Review, *and the* Gettysburg Review *among others. Glück lives in New York City, where she works for a multinational corporation.*

Tereze Glück wrote "Yellow Light" in 1983. She comments: "I think everything is a story, if it can only be put through some crucible, and be made to yield up its light. When I write, I have to discover *something, see something I haven't seen before. I'm not interested in writing something that's all worked out ahead of time, that's just a laying out of old news, an arranging of finished thoughts. I guess I'm talking about* insight*" (letter to M. Kallet, 1996).*

Yellow Light

We lay by the water's edge, the blue and green drift of sea creeping towards us. My mother wore a bathing suit the colour of an orange. Later I knew it for what it was, a risky colour, a young colour, and even then I suspected. My mother had a connection to colour, was how she put it, and thought that even the blue of the water was hers. She thought she could do anything she wanted: put a whole body of colours together, and she liked to do just that. In hot weather she favoured pastels. I like pale colours, she said, bleached colours. Colours called — she said them aloud to me — peach, aqua, shell, mint, seafoam, banana. Banana yellow is a very particular shade of yellow, she told me. A very pale yellow.

We were in Mexico, lying on the sand beach, where men walked barefoot along the dark wet sand by the water's edge, selling their wares. My mother bought me a silver ring with a turquoise in the centre, and three bracelets for herself. Behind us was the curved arc of hotels, their gardens of bougainvillea, hibiscus, jacaranda. My mother, who loved the names of things, told me these.

"I'm feeling better," she said. "I'm recovering."

She had come here to recover, I wasn't sure from what but I had an idea. Recovery meant sun. She said the sun was a restorative. Already I knew her ways: how she would lie there, grains of sand sticking to her shining body. The sun reflected in her flat parts: her thighs, her chest, sometimes the flat of her cheek. Lying beside her I thought of her body as terrain, and these were the plains, the prairies, that glistened in the sun. It wasn't the suntan she was after; I'd overheard her explaining that to friends one summer at our house on the lake. It was the sensation, the burning itself. She said it bleached her brain and that was all to the good.

I knew if I lay there beside her long enough she would tell me something. I always knew when she was telling me things that were marginal, that she probably shouldn't be telling me. Usually it was about men, or love, or my father, but it might be her ideas about life: things she took for wisdom and thought she could hand on to me. At last she had a captive audience. She'd start in. "That Gordon," she says. "He broke my heart." I put my hands to my ears. "Don't tell *me*," I say; "I'm your child." Don't tell me, I'd say, even then, at seven, eight, nine.

"Oh, my poor Poppy!" she said, and laughed. "Poor old thing!" She had as many nicknames for me as she had colours or daydreams. She didn't have plans but she had plenty of daydreams. She scorned plans and I often would hear her, usually driving in the car with one of her friends and us, the children, in the back seat, complain of this or that person and his plans. "As if they had any control!" she said, and from the back seat I remember the shake of her head, the flyaway hair. People with plans were one of her complaints. She said they reproached her. "Sometimes I wish I could clear everybody off the planet," she said. "But then who'd drive," I said; because she didn't know how to drive and we relied on other people to get around. In the city it didn't matter, we walked or took taxis; but elsewhere we either went with friends or we didn't go.

Here's the sun.

So long as there's sun, my mother says, I make no demands of the universe.

Meanwhile I'm burning. My mother rubs lotion on my body, clears the hair away from my face and with her finger beneath my chin, arches my head upwards. "You have your father's skin," she says. "English skin." My father is, in addition to being English, tall, pale and bony. She says my body is his as well and that I walk just like him.

With her finger she's rubbing lotion on my cheeks, my nose. "Promise me something," she says.

"I promise," I say.

"But you don't know what yet!" she says.

"I promise anyway."

"Promise you'll never leave me," she says.

I was a knowing child. I watch her, swear I can see her skin mixing its colours, agitating and darkening before my very eyes, alive with cells. "Remember," I say, full of genius so vivid I can feel it jump in my skin — "Remember when I was inside your body?"

She turns her face toward me, glistening with amber oil. "Oh Poppy!" she says, clapping her hands, smiling her smile. "I remember!"

Sometimes I swear too that I do remember: dark, a mire as thick and smooth as velvet, the heartbeat. My mother often repeated a story to me, one which I myself recall. At three or four how I said to her: where did I used to be? and she said: inside me. I was silent a moment, and then said: I'm sorry I had to be born because now I have to be outside.

I will say this for myself: I always knew what my mother wanted, and I gave it to her.

Clouds are coming; she'll mind.

I steel myself, my heart, willing them away. She'll ignore them a while, strain towards cheer. "I have a theory," she says. "I fool the sun: When it's cloudy I lie out, grease myself up, just as if the sun were out. And the sun sees me, and it thinks — oh — I must be out, people are lying in me!"

She thought she could will anything: the sun to come out, the clouds to disperse, a man to love her.

In this at least she was right: she willed me. She said so. "Here you are," she'd say. " — here you are; I did it! I made you be here!"

"Come on, sun!" my mother said.

She told me how she had travelled along the coast of Portugal when she was young, how she and a friend had flung themselves onto the sand, even though it was April and still cool, and had flung their arms out to the side and said, "Bake me, sol!"

The sky was spotty anyway, even with her tricks: part cloud, holes in the clouds and moments of sun. I could see her thinking, how that the clouds were out and there was no direct heat from the sun to ward off thought. "About these men," she said. "I don't know what it is I do wrong. What is it I do wrong?"

In a few minutes the sun was out again and my mother said she had no business telling me half the things she did, but that was the way she was, and that was how it was going to be.

My mother, in Mexico, at family reunions in Amagansett, by the green lake in Connecticut, keeps watch for a cloudless sky. "I want azure," she says. "I want turquoise."

"Little peach," she says to me. "Little bear. It's good to have so many names. The Chinese have a saying: a well-loved child has many names. I don't know where I heard it. Maybe I made it up. But it's true."

We look into each other's eyes. Her pupils in the bright sun are tiny. Her eyes are a nameless colour, khaki, she says, the colour of army tanks. " 'Oh, your eyes are the colour of army tanks!' " she mocks.

She sighs, her eyes looking up now, a watchful hunter, hunting for light. When it comes, unequivocal, that untarnished sun, it refracts off the shine of her skin, encasing me in a double warmth: its own, and hers.

Ever since I was a child, she says, this is what I've hankered after. My first broken heart. My father took me to Bermuda where I nursed my broken heart in the sun. I burned myself rightly there. We rented a boat with white sails and I lay on the bow, where the wind and sun both got me. In the morning my face was as puffed up as a melon and they had to give me pills to bring it down. Who could recollect a heart, broken or otherwise, under such a scorch, such searing?

My mother told me amazing things. There is a perfume, she said, by which I mean odour, not one you wear, which belongs with this landscape, although it is not here. She stopped then. With me at least she could be mysterious. But I did not care to prompt her. "The fragrance I have in mind," she said, "is oranges. I will tell you about the first time I smelled orange trees in bloom. It was in Seville, in the south of Spain." I knew the word, Spain, and that it was a country, but that was all.

She told me that in this city, Seville, the streets were made of cobblestone, and you could hear the horses' hooves on the cobbled roads, that their hooves echoed on the stone. "I remember all that," she said, "but primarily it was a place you could smell — overpowering, that perfume, pungent, stifling — I mean the smell of oranges."

"Oranges," I repeat, trying to imagine their smell. "The colour," I say, "of your bathing suit."

She props herself up on an elbow, I can see where the white skin meets, turns, brown. She's smiling at me. "You are a brilliant child," she says. "You are an ingenious person. And that's what I think."

She dives into the turquoise water and I watch her orange bathing suit and her shining skin send off light. I watch her the way a child watches its mother. She kicks up water like a fish, one of those flying kinds of fish, and then she turns and looks at me and I look right back. She walks toward me through the water and I stand there and let her. The light is in her eyes but I can see her fine.

And so it goes, each of us trying to surprise the other. The day proceeds and soon the sky begins to darken, until in the argument of light, the brilliant yellow concedes to gray. That day, my mother had so much sun on her I thought she'd become sun, herself. That day, and every day before it, and after, we seduced one another, until, by evening, in the clearer light of dusk, we were back together again, one body, one skin.

◎ *MARY HOOD*

Mary Hood was born in 1946 in Brunswick, Georgia. She earned a B.A. at Georgia State University in Atlanta. Her awards include the Flannery O'Connor Award for short fiction and the Southern Review*/Louisiana State University Short Fiction Award, both given in 1984, for* How Far She Went *(short stories) and the Townsend Prize for Fiction, in 1988, for her second book,* And Venus Is Blue *(a novella and short stories).*

"How Far She Went" is the title story from Mary Hood's first book of short stories. In some sense it might be considered the classic "generation gap" story as a teenage girl and her grandmother have a difficult summer together. It is also a powerful story of loss, forgiveness, and love reclaimed (or perhaps simply "claimed") at last—a necessary bond in an atmosphere of male violence.

How Far She Went

They had quarreled all morning, squalled all summer about the incidentals: how tight the girl's cut-off jeans were, the "Every Inch a Woman" T-shirt, her choice of music and how loud she played it, her practiced inattention, her sullen look. Her granny wrung out the last boiled dishcloth, pinched it to the line, giving the basin a sling and a slap, the water flying out in a scalding arc onto the Queen Anne's lace by the path, never mind if it bloomed, that didn't make it worth anything except to chiggers, but the girl would cut it by the everlasting armload and cherish it in the old churn, going to that much trouble for a weed but not bending once — unbegged — to pick the nearest bean; she was sulking now. Bored. Displaced.

"And what do you think happens to a chigger if nobody ever walks by his weed?" her granny asked, heading for the house with that sidelong uneager unanswered glance, hoping for what? The surprise gift of a smile? Nothing. The woman shook her head and said it. "Nothing." The door slammed behind her. Let it.

"I hate it here!" the girl yelled then. She picked up a stick and broke it and threw the pieces — one from each hand — at the laundry drying in the noon. Missed. Missed.

Then she turned on her bare, haughty heel and set off high-shouldered into the heat, quick but not far, not far enough — no road was *that* long — only as far as she dared. At the gate, a rusty chain swinging between two lichened posts, she stopped, then backed up the raw drive to make a run at the barrier, lofting, clearing it clean, her long hair wild in the sun. Triumphant, she looked back at the house where she caught at the dark window her granny's face in its perpetual eclipse of disappointment, old at fifty. She stepped back, but the girl saw her.

"You don't know me!" the girl shouted, chin high, and ran till her ribs ached.

As she rested in the rattling shade of the willows, the little dog found her. He could be counted on. He barked all the way, and squealed when she pulled the burr from his ear. They started back to the house for lunch. By then the mailman had long come and gone in the old ruts, leaving the one letter folded now to fit the woman's apron pocket.

If bad news darkened her granny's face, the girl ignored it. Didn't talk at all, another of her distancings, her defiances. So it was as they ate that the woman summarized, "Your daddy wants you to cash in the plane ticket and buy you something. School clothes. For here."

Pale, the girl stared, defenseless only an instant before blurting out, "You're lying."

The woman had to stretch across the table to leave her handprint on that blank cheek. She said, not caring if it stung or not, "He's been planning it since he sent you here."

"I could turn this whole house over, dump it! Leave you slobbering over that stinking jealous dog in the dust!" The girl trembled with the vision, with the strength it gave her. It made her laugh. "Scatter the Holy Bible like confetti and ravel the crochet into miles of stupid string! I could! I will! I won't stay here!" But she didn't move, not until her tears rose to meet her color, and then to escape the shame of minding so much she fled. Just headed away, blind. It didn't matter, this time, how far she went.

The woman set her thoughts against fretting over their bickering, just went on unalarmed with chores, clearing off after the uneaten meal, bringing in the laundry, scattering corn for the chickens, ladling manure tea onto the porch flowers. She listened though. She always had been a listener. It gave her a cocked look. She forgot why she had gone into the girl's empty room, that ungirlish, tenuous lodging place with its bleak order, its ready suitcases never unpacked, the narrow bed, the contested radio on the windowsill. The woman drew the cracked shade down between the radio and the August sun. There wasn't anything else to do.

It was after six when she tied on her rough oxfords and walked down the drive and dropped the gate chain and headed back to the creosoted shed where she kept her tools. She took a hoe for snakes, a rake, shears to trim the grass where it grew, and seed in her pocket to scatter where it never had grown at all. She put the tools and her gloves and the bucket in the trunk of the old Chevy, its prime and rust like an Appaloosa's spots through the chalky white finish. She left the trunk open and the tool handles sticking out. She wasn't going far.

The heat of the day had broken, but the air was thick, sultry, weighted with honeysuckle in second bloom and the Nu-Grape scent of kudzu. The maple and poplar leaves turned over, quaking, silver. There wouldn't be any rain. She told the dog to stay, but he knew a trick. He stowed away when she turned her back, leaped right into the trunk with the tools, then gave himself away with exultant barks. Hearing him, her court jester, she stopped the car and welcomed him into the front seat beside her. Then they went on. Not a mile from her gate she turned onto the blue gravel of the cemetery lane, hauled the gearshift into reverse to whoa them, and got out to take the idle walk down to her buried hopes, bending all along to rout out a handful of weeds from between the markers of old acquaintance. She stood there and read, slow. The dog whined at her hem; she picked him up and rested her chin on his head, then he wriggled and whined to run free, contrary and restless as a child.

The crows called strong and bold MOM! MOM! A trick of the ear to hear it like that. She knew it was the crows, but still she looked around. No one called her that now. She was done with that. And what was it worth anyway? It all came to this: solitary weeding. The sinful fumble of flesh, the fear, the listening for a return that never came, the shamed waiting, the unanswered prayers, the perjury on the certificate — hadn't she lain there weary of the whole lie and it only beginning? and a voice telling her, "Here's your baby, here's your girl," and the swaddled package meaning no more to her than an extra anything, something store-bought, something she could take back for a refund.

"Tie her to the fence and give her a bale of hay," she had murmured, drugged, and they teased her, excused her for such a welcoming, blaming the anesthesia, but it went deeper than that; *she* knew, and the *baby* knew: there was no love in the begetting. That was the secret, unforgivable, that not another good thing could ever make up for, where all the bad had come from, like a visitation, a punishment. She knew that was why Sylvie had been wild, had gone to earth so early, and before dying had made this child in sudden wedlock, a child who would be just like her, would carry the hurting on into another generation. A matter of time. No use raising her hand. But she *had* raised her hand. Still wore on its palm the memory of the sting of the collision with the girl's cheek; had she broken her jaw? Her heart? Of course not. She said it aloud: "Takes more than that."

She went to work then, doing what she could with her old tools. She pecked the clay on Sylvie's grave, new-looking, unhealed after years. She tried again, scattering seeds from her pocket, every last possible one of them. Off in the west she could hear the pulpwood cutters sawing through another acre across the lake. Nearer, there was the racket of motorcycles laboring cross-country, insect-like, distracting.

She took her bucket to the well and hung it on the pump. She had half filled it when the bikers roared up, right down the blue gravel, straight at her. She let the bucket overflow, staring. On the back of one of the machines was the girl. Sylvie's girl! Her bare arms wrapped around the shirtless man riding between her thighs. They were first. The second biker rode alone. She studied their strangers' faces as they circled her. They were the enemy, all of them. Laughing. The girl was laughing too, laughing like her mama did. Out in the middle of nowhere the girl had found these two men, some moth-musk about her drawing them (too soon!) to what? She shouted it: "What in God's — " They roared off without answering her, and the bucket of water tipped over, spilling its stain blood-dark on the red dust.

The dog went wild barking, leaping after them, snapping at the tires, and there was no calling him down. The bikers made a wide circuit of the churchyard, then roared straight across the graves, leaping the ditch and landing upright on the road again, heading off toward the reservoir.

Furious, she ran to her car, past the barking dog, this time leaving him behind, driving after them, horn blowing nonstop, to get back what was not theirs. She drove after them knowing what they did not know, that all the roads beyond that point dead-ended. She surprised them, swinging the Impala across their path, cutting them off; let them hit it! They stopped. She got out, breathing hard, and said, when she could, "She's underage." Just that. And put out her claiming hand with an authority that made the girl's arms drop from the man's insolent waist and her legs tremble.

"I was just riding," the girl said, not looking up.

Behind them the sun was heading on toward down. The long shadows of the pines drifted back and forth in the same breeze that puffed the distant sails on the lake. Dead limbs creaked and clashed overhead like the antlers of locked and furious beasts.

"Sheeeut," the lone rider said. "I told you." He braced with his muddy boot and leaned out from his machine to spit. The man the girl had been riding with had the invading sort of eyes the woman had spent her lifetime bolting doors against. She met him now, face to face.

"Right there, missy," her granny said, pointing behind her to the car.

The girl slid off the motorcycle and stood halfway between her choices. She started slightly at the poosh! as he popped another top and chugged the beer in one uptilting of his head. His eyes never left the woman's. When he was through, he tossed the can high, flipping it end over end. Before it hit the ground he had his pistol out and, firing once, winged it into the lake.

"Freaking lucky shot," the other one grudged.

"I don't need luck," he said. He sighted down the barrel of the gun at the woman's head. "POW!" he yelled, and when she recoiled, he laughed. He swung around to the girl; he kept aiming the gun, here, there, high, low, all around. "Y'all settle it," he said, with a shrug.

The girl had to understand him then, had to know him, had to know better. But still she hesitated. He kept looking at her, then away.

"She's fifteen," her granny said. "You can go to jail."

"You can go to hell," he said.

"Probably will," her granny told him. "I'll save you a seat by the fire." She took the girl by the arm and drew her to the car; she backed up, swung around, and headed out the road toward the churchyard for her tools and dog. The whole way the girl said nothing, just hunched against the far door, staring hard-eyed out at the pines going past.

The woman finished watering the seed in, and collected her tools. As she worked, she muttered, "It's your own kin buried here, you might have the decency to glance this way one time . . ." The girl was finger-tweezing her eyebrows in the side mirror. She didn't look around as the dog and the woman got in. Her granny shifted hard, sending the tools clattering in the trunk.

When they came to the main road, there were the men. Watching for them. Waiting for them. They kicked their machines into life and followed, close, bumping them, slapping the old fenders, yelling. The girl gave a wild glance around at the one by her door and said, "Gran'ma?" and as he drew his pistol, "Gran'ma!" just as the gun nosed into the open window. She frantically cranked the glass up between her and the weapon, and her granny, seeing, spat, "Fool!" She never had been one to pray for peace or rain. She stamped the accelerator right to the floor.

The motorcycles caught up. Now she braked, hard, and swerved off the road into an alley between the pines, not even wide enough for the school bus, just a fire scrape that came out a quarter mile from her own house, if she could get that far. She slewed on the pine straw, then righted, tearing along the dark tunnel through the woods. She had for the time being bested them; they were left behind. She was winning. Then she hit the wallow where the tadpoles were already five weeks old. The Chevy plowed in and stalled. When she got it cranked again, they were stuck. The tires spattered mud three feet up the near trunks as she tried to spin them out, to rock them out. Useless. "Get out and run!" she cried, but the trees were too close on the passenger side. The girl couldn't open her door. She wasted precious time having to crawl out under the steering wheel. The woman waited but the dog ran on.

They struggled through the dusky woods, their pace slowed by the thick straw and vines. Overhead, in the last light, the martins were reeling free and sure after their prey.

"Why? Why?" the girl gasped, as they lunged down the old deer trail. Behind them they could hear shots, and glass breaking as the men came to the bogged car. The woman kept on running, swatting their way clear through the shoulder-high weeds. They could see the Greer cottage, and made for it. But it was ivied-over, padlocked, the woodpile dry-rotting under its tarp, the electric meterbox empty on the pole. No help there.

The dog, excited, trotted on, yelping, his lips white-flecked. He scented the lake and headed that way, urging them on with thirsty yips. On the clay shore, treeless, deserted, at the utter limit of land, they stood defenseless, listening to the men coming on, between them and home. The woman pressed her hands to her mouth, stifling her cough. She was exhausted. She couldn't think.

"We can get under!" the girl cried suddenly, and pointed toward the Greers' dock, gap-planked, its walkway grounded on the mud. They splashed out to it, wading in, the woman grabbing up the telltale, tattletale dog in her arms. They waded out to the far end and ducked under. There was room between the foam floats for them to crouch neck-deep.

The dog wouldn't hush, even then; never had yet, and there wasn't time to teach him. When the woman realized that, she did what she had to do. She grabbed him whimpering; held him; held him under till the struggle ceased and the bubbles rose silver from his fur. They crouched there then, the two of them, submerged to the shoulders, feet unsteady on the slimed lake bed. They listened. The sky went from rose to ocher to violet in the cracks over their heads. The motorcycles had stopped now. In the silence there was the glissando of locusts, the dry crunch of boots on the flinty beach, their low mantalk drifting as they prowled back and forth. One of them struck a match.

" — they in these woods we could burn 'em out."

The wind carried their voices away into the pines. Some few words eddied back.

" — lippy old smartass do a little work on her knees besides praying — "

Laughter. It echoed off the deserted house. They were getting closer.

One of them strode directly out to the dock, walked on the planks over their heads. They could look up and see his boot soles. He was the one with the gun. He slapped a mosquito on his bare back and cursed. The carp, roused by the troubling of the waters, came nosing around the dock, guzzling and snorting. The girl and her granny held still, so still. The man fired his pistol into the shadows, and a wounded fish thrashed, dying. The man knelt and reached for it, chuffing out his beery breath. He belched. He pawed the lake for the dead fish, cursing as it floated out of reach. He shot it again, firing at it till it sank and the gun was empty. Cursed that too. He stood then and unzipped and relieved himself of some of the beer. They had to listen to that. To know that about him. To endure that, unprotesting.

Back and forth on shore the other one ranged, restless. He lit another cigarette. He coughed. He called, "Hey! They got away, man, that's all. Don't get your shorts in a wad. Let's go."

"Yeah." He finished. He zipped. He stumped back across the planks and leaped to shore, leaving the dock tilting amid widening ripples. Underneath, they waited.

The bike cranked. The other ratcheted, ratcheted, then coughed, caught, roared. They circled, cut deep ruts, slung gravel, and went. Their roaring died away and away. Crickets resumed and a near frog bic-bic-bicked.

Under the dock, they waited a little longer to be sure. Then they ducked below the water, scraped out from under the pontoon, and came up into free air, slogging toward shore. It had seemed warm enough in the water. Now they shivered. It was almost night. One streak of light still stood reflected on the darkening lake, drew itself thinner, narrowing into a final cancellation of day. A plane winked its way west.

The girl was trembling. She ran her hands down her arms and legs, shedding water like a garment. She sighed, almost a sob. The woman held the dog in her arms; she dropped to her knees upon the random stones and murmured, private, haggard, "Oh, honey," three times, maybe all three times for the dog, maybe once for each of them. The girl waited, watching. Her granny rocked the dog like a baby, like a dead child, rocked slower and slower and was still.

"I'm sorry," the girl said then, avoiding the dog's inert, empty eye.

"It was him or you," her granny said, finally, looking up. Looking her over. "Did they mess with you? With your britches? Did they?"

"No!" Then, quieter, "No, ma'am."

When the woman tried to stand up she staggered, lightheaded, clumsy with the freight of the dog. "No, ma'am," she echoed, fending off the girl's "Let me." And she said again, "It was him or you. I know that. I'm not going to rub your face in it." They saw each other as well as they could in that failing light, in any light.

The woman started toward home, saying, "Around here, we bear our own burdens." She led the way along the weedy shortcuts. The twilight bleached the dead limbs of the pines to bone. Insects sang in the thickets silencing at their oncoming.

"We'll see about the car in the morning," the woman said. She bore her armful toward her own moth-ridden dusk-to-dawn security light with that country grace she had always had when the earth was reliably progressing underfoot. The girl walked close behind her, exactly where *she* walked, matching her pace, matching her stride, close enough to put her hand forth (if the need arose) and touch her granny's back where the faded voile was clinging damp, the merest gauze between their wounds.

◎ *PAULE MARSHALL*

"To Da-duh, In Memoriam" originally appeared in the West Indian magazine New World *in 1967. It has since been reprinted in several anthologies and in Marshall's collection* Reena and Other Stories *(1983). See Paule Marshall's own preface for comments about the autobiographic connections of this memoir. For more information on Marshall,* *see page 46.*

To Da-duh, In Memoriam

This is the most autobiographical of the stories, a reminiscence largely of a visit I paid to my grandmother (whose nickname was Da-duh) on the island of Barbados when I was nine. Ours was a complex relationship — close, affectionate yet rivalrous. During the year I spent with her a subtle kind of power struggle went on between us. It was as if we both knew, at a level beyond words, that I had come into the world not only to love her and to continue her line but to take her very life in order that I might live.

Years later, when I got around to writing the story, I tried giving the contest I had sensed between us a wider meaning. I wanted the basic theme of youth and old age to suggest rivalries, dichotomies of a cultural and political nature, having to do with the relationship of western civilization and the Third World.

Apart from this story, Da-duh also appears in one form or another in my other work as well. She's the old hairdresser, Mrs. Thompson, in Brown Girl, Brownstones, *who offers Selina total, unquestioning love. She's Leesy Walkes and the silent cook, Carrington, "whose great breast . . . had been used it seemed to suckle the world" in* The Chosen Place, the Timeless People. *She's Aunt Vi in "Reena" and Medford, the old family retainer in "British Guiana" from* Soul Clap Hands and Sing. *And she's Avey Johnson's Great-aunt Cuney in* Praisesong for the Widow. *Da-duh turns up everywhere.*

She's an ancestor figure, symbolic for me of the long line of black women and men — African and New World — who made my being possible, and whose spirit I believe continues to animate my life and work. I wish to acknowledge and celebrate them. I am, in a word, an unabashed ancestor worshipper.

> ". . . Oh Nana! all of you is not involved in this evil business Death,
> Nor all of us in life."
>
> — *From "At My Grandmother's Grave," by* LEBERT BETHUNE

I did not see her at first I remember. For not only was it dark inside the crowded disembarkation shed in spite of the daylight flooding in from outside, but standing there waiting for her with my mother and sister I was still somewhat blinded from the sheen of tropical sunlight on the water of the bay which we had just crossed in the landing boat, leaving behind us the ship that had brought us from New York lying in the offing. Besides, being only nine years of age at the time and knowing nothing of islands I was busy attending to the alien sights and sounds of Barbados, the unfamiliar smells.

I did not see her, but I was alerted to her approach by my mother's hand which suddenly tightened around mine, and looking up I traced her gaze through the gloom in the shed until I finally made out the small, purposeful, painfully erect figure of the old woman headed our way.

Her face was drowned in the shadow of an ugly rolled-brim brown felt hat, but the details of her slight body and of the struggle taking place within it were clear enough — an intense, unrelenting struggle between her back which was beginning to bend ever so slightly under the weight of her eighty-odd years and the rest of her which sought to deny those years and hold that back straight, keep it in line. Moving swiftly toward us (so swiftly it seemed she did not intend stopping when she reached us but would sweep past us out the doorway which opened onto the sea and like Christ walk upon the water!), she was caught between the sunlight at her end of the building and the darkness inside — and for a moment she appeared to contain them both: the light in the long severe old-fashioned white dress she wore which brought the sense of a past that was still alive into our bustling present and in the snatch of white at her eye; the darkness in her black high-top shoes and in her face which was visible now that she was closer.

It was as stark and fleshless as a death mask, that face. The maggots might have already done their work, leaving only the framework of bone beneath the ruined skin and deep wells at the temple and jaw. But her eyes were alive, unnervingly so for one so old, with a sharp light that flicked out of the dim clouded depths like a lizard's tongue to snap up all in her view. Those eyes betrayed a child's curiosity about the world, and I wondered vaguely seeing them, and seeing the way the bodice of her ancient dress had collapsed in on her flat chest (what had happened to her breasts?), whether she might not be some kind of child at the same time that she was a woman, with fourteen children, my mother included, to prove it. Perhaps she was both, both child and woman, darkness and light, past and present, life and death — all the opposites contained and reconciled in her.

"My Da-duh," my mother said formally and stepped forward. The name sounded like thunder fading softly in the distance.

"Child," Da-duh said, and her tone, her quick scrutiny of my mother, the brief embrace in which they appeared to shy from each other rather than touch, wiped out the fifteen years my mother had been away and restored the old relationship. My mother, who was such a formidable figure in my eyes, had suddenly with a word been reduced to my status.

"Yes, God is good," Da-duh said with a nod that was like a tic. "He has spared me to see my child again."

We were led forward then, apologetically because not only did Da-duh prefer boys but she also liked her grandchildren to be "white," that is, fair-skinned; and we had, I was to discover, a number of cousins, the outside children of white estate managers and the like, who qualified. We, though, were as black as she.

My sister being the oldest was presented first. "This one takes after the father," my mother said and waited to be reproved.

Frowning, Da-duh tilted my sister's face toward the light. But her frown soon gave way to a grudging smile, for my sister with her large mild eyes and little broad winged nose, with our father's high-cheeked Barbadian cast to her face, was pretty.

"She's goin' be lucky," Da-duh said and patted her once on the cheek. "Any girl child that takes after the father does be lucky."

She turned then to me. But oddly enough she did not touch me. Instead leaning close, she peered hard at me, and then quickly drew back. I thought I saw her hand start up as though to shield her eyes. It was almost as if she saw not only me, a thin truculent child who it was said took after no one but myself, but something in me which for some reason she found disturbing, even threatening. We looked silently at each other for a long time there in the noisy shed, our gaze locked. She was the first to look away.

"But Adry," she said to my mother and her laugh was cracked, thin, apprehensive. "Where did you get this one here with this fierce look?"

"We don't know where she came out of, my Da-duh," my mother said, laughing also. Even I smiled to myself. After all I had won the encounter. Da-duh had recognized my small strength — and this was all I ever asked of the adults in my life then.

"Come, soul," Da-duh said and took my hand. "You must be one of those New York terrors you hear so much about."

She led us, me at her side and my sister and mother behind, out of the shed into the sunlight that was like a bright driving summer rain and over to a group of people clustered beside a decrepit lorry. They were our relatives, most of them from St. Andrews although Da-duh herself lived in St. Thomas, the women wearing bright print dresses, the colors vivid against their darkness, the men rusty black suits that encased them like strait-jackets. Da-duh, holding fast to my hand, became my anchor as they circled round us like a nervous sea, exclaiming, touching us with their calloused hands, embracing us shyly. They laughed in awed bursts: "But look Adry got big-big children!" / "And see the nice things they wearing, wrist watch and all!" / "I tell you, Adry has done all right for sheself in New York. . . ."

Da-duh, ashamed at their wonder, embarrassed for them, admonished them the while. "But oh Christ," she said, "why you all got to get on like you never saw people from 'Away' before? You would think New York is the only place in the world to hear wunna. That's why I don't like to go any place with you St. Andrews people, you know. You all ain't been colonized."

We were in the back of the lorry finally, packed in among the barrels of ham, flour, cornmeal and rice and the trunks of clothes that my mother had brought as gifts. We made our way slowly through Bridgetown's clogged streets, part of a funereal procession of cars and open-sided buses, bicycles and donkey carts. The dim little limestone shops and offices along the way marched with us, at the same mournful pace, toward the same grave ceremony — as did the people, the women balancing huge baskets on top their heads as if they were no more than hats they wore to shade them from the sun. Looking over the edge of the lorry I watched as their feet slurred the dust. I listened, and their voices, raw and loud and dissonant in the heat, seemed to be grappling with each other high overhead.

Da-duh sat on a trunk in our midst, a monarch amid her court. She still held my hand, but it was different now. I had suddenly become her anchor, for I felt her fear of the lorry with its asthmatic motor (a fear and distrust, I later learned, she held of all machines) beating like a pulse in her rough palm.

As soon as we left Bridgetown behind though, she relaxed, and while the others around us talked she gazed at the canes standing tall on either side of the winding marl road. "C'dear," she said softly to herself after a time. "The canes this side are pretty enough."

They were too much for me. I thought of them as giant weeds that had overrun the island, leaving scarcely any room for the small tottering houses of sunbleached pine we passed or the people, dark streaks as our lorry hurtled by. I suddenly feared that we were journeying, unaware that we were, toward some dangerous place where the canes, grown as high and thick as a forest, would close in on us and run us through with their stiletto blades. I longed then for the familiar: for the street in Brooklyn where I lived, for my father who had refused to accompany us ("Blowing out good money on foolishness," he had said of the trip), for a game of tag with my friends under the chestnut tree outside our aging brownstone house.

"Yes, but wait till you see St. Thomas canes," Da-duh was saying to me. "They's canes father, bo," she gave a proud arrogant nod. "Tomorrow, God willing, I goin' take you out in the ground and show them to you."

True to her word Da-duh took me with her the following day out into the ground. It was a fairly large plot adjoining her weathered board and shingle house and consisting of a small orchard, a good-sized canepiece and behind the canes, where the land sloped abruptly down, a gully. She had purchased it with Panama money sent her by her eldest son, my uncle Joseph, who had died working on the canal. We entered the ground along a trail no wider than her body and as devious and complex as her reasons for showing me her land. Da-duh strode briskly ahead, her slight form filled out this morning by the layers of sacking petticoats she wore under her working dress to protect her against the damp. A fresh white cloth, elaborately arranged around her head, added to her height and lent her a vain, almost roguish air.

Her pace slowed once we reached the orchard, and glancing back at me occasionally over her shoulder, she pointed out the various trees.

"This here is a breadfruit," she said. "That one yonder is a papaw. Here's a guava. This is a mango. I know you don't have anything like these in New York. Here's a sugar apple." (The fruit looked more like artichokes than apples to me.) "This one bears limes. . . ." She went on for some time, intoning the names of the trees as though they were those of her gods. Finally, turning to me, she said, "I know you don't have anything this nice where you come from." Then, as I hesitated: "I said I know you don't have anything this nice where you come from. . . ."

"No," I said and my world did seem suddenly lacking.

Da-duh nodded and passed on. The orchard ended and we were on the narrow cart road that led through the canepiece, the canes clashing like swords above my cowering head. Again she turned and her thin muscular arms spread wide, her dim gaze embracing the small field of canes, she said — and her voice almost broke under the weight of her pride, "Tell me, have you got anything like these in that place where you were born?"

"No."

"I din' think so. I bet you don't even know that these canes here and the sugar you eat is one and the same thing. That they does throw the canes into some damn machine at the factory and squeeze out all the little life in them to make sugar for you all so in New York to eat. I bet you don't know that."

"I've got two cavities and I'm not allowed to eat a lot of sugar."

But Da-duh didn't hear me. She had turned with an inexplicably angry motion and was making her way rapidly out of the canes and down the slope at the edge of the field which led to the gully below. Following her apprehensively down the incline amid a stand of banana plants whose leaves flapped like elephants ears in the wind, I found myself in the middle of a small tropical wood — a place dense and damp and gloomy and tremulous with the fitful play of light and shadow as the leaves high above moved against the sun that was almost hidden from view. It was a violent place, the tangled foliage fighting each other for a chance at the sunlight, the branches of the trees locked in what seemed an immemorial struggle, one both necessary and inevitable. But despite the violence, it was pleasant, almost peaceful in the gully, and beneath the thick undergrowth the earth smelled like spring.

This time Da-duh didn't even bother to ask her usual question, but simply turned and waited for me to speak.

"No," I said, my head bowed. "We don't have anything like this in New York."

"Ah," she cried, her triumph complete. "I din' think so. Why, I've heard that's a place where you can walk till you near drop and never see a tree."

"We've got a chestnut tree in front of our house," I said.

"Does it bear?" She waited. "I ask you, does it bear?"

"Not anymore," I murmured. "It used to, but not anymore."

She gave the nod that was like a nervous twitch. "You see," she said. "Nothing can bear there." Then, secure behind her scorn, she added, "But tell me, what's this snow like that you hear so much about?"

Looking up, I studied her closely, sensing my chance, and then I told her, describing at length and with as much drama as I could summon not only what snow in the city was like, but what it would be like here, in her perennial summer kingdom.

". . . And you see all these trees you got here," I said. "Well, they'd be bare. No leaves, no fruit, nothing. They'd be covered in snow. You see your canes. They'd be buried under tons of snow. The snow would be higher than your head, higher than your house, and you wouldn't be able to come down into this here gully because it would be snowed under. . . ."

She searched my face for the lie, still scornful but intrigued. "What a thing, huh?" she said finally, whispering it softly to herself.

"And when it snows you couldn't dress like you are now," I said. "Oh no, you'd freeze to death. You'd have to wear a hat and gloves and galoshes and ear muffs so your ears wouldn't freeze and drop off, and a heavy coat. I've got a Shirley Temple coat with fur on the collar. I can dance. You wanna see?"

Before she could answer I began, with a dance called the Truck which was popular back then in the 1930's. My right forefinger waving, I trucked around the nearby trees and around Da-duh's awed and rigid form. After the Truck I did the Suzy-Q, my lean hips swishing, my sneakers sidling zigzag over the ground. "I can sing," I said and did so, starting with "I'm Gonna Sit Right Down and Write Myself a Letter," then without pausing, "Tea For Two," and ending with "I Found a Million Dollar Baby in a Five and Ten Cent Store."

For long moments afterwards Da-duh stared at me as if I were a creature from Mars, an emissary from some world she did not know but which intrigued her and whose power she both felt and feared. Yet something about my performance must have pleased her, because bending down she slowly lifted her long skirt and then, one by one, the layers of petticoats until she came to a drawstring purse dangling at the end of a long strip of cloth tied round her waist. Opening the purse she handed me a penny. "Here," she said half-smiling against her will. "Take this to buy yourself a sweet at the shop up the road. There's nothing to be done with you, soul."

From then on, whenever I wasn't taken to visit relatives, I accompanied Da-duh out into the ground, and alone with her amid the canes or down in the gully I told her about New York. It always began with some slighting remark on her part: "I know they don't have anything this nice where you come from," or "Tell me, I hear those foolish people in New York does do such and such. . . ." But as I answered, recreating my towering world of steel and concrete and machines for her, building the city out of words, I would feel her give way. I came to know the signs of her surrender: the total stillness that would come over her little hard dry form, the probing gaze that like a surgeon's knife sought to cut through my skull to get at the images there, to see if I were lying; above all, her fear, a fear nameless and profound, the same one I had felt beating in the palm of her hand that day in the lorry.

Over the weeks I told her about refrigerators, radios, gas stoves, elevators, trolley cars, wringer washing machines, movies, airplanes, the cyclone at Coney Island, subways, toasters, electric lights: "At night, see, all you have to do is flip this little switch on the wall and all the lights in the house go on. Just like that. Like magic. It's like turning on the sun at night."

"But tell me," she said to me once with a faint mocking smile, "do the white people have all these things too or it's only the people looking like us?"

I laughed. "What d'ya mean," I said. "The white people have even better." Then: "I beat up a white girl in my class last term."

"Beating up white people!" Her tone was incredulous.

"How you mean!" I said, using an expression of hers. "She called me a name."

For some reason Da-duh could not quite get over this and repeated in the same hushed, shocked voice, "Beating up white people now! Oh, the lord, the world's changing up so I can scarce recognize it anymore."

One morning toward the end of our stay, Da-duh led me into a part of the gully that we had never visited before, an area darker and more thickly overgrown than the rest, almost impenetrable. There in a small clearing amid the dense bush, she stopped before an incredibly tall royal palm which rose cleanly out of the ground, and drawing the eye up with it, soared high above the trees around it into the sky. It appeared to be touching the blue dome of sky, to be flaunting its dark crown of fronds right in the blinding white face of the late morning sun.

Da-duh watched me a long time before she spoke, and then she said, very quietly, "All right, now, tell me if you've got anything this tall in that place you're from."

I almost wished, seeing her face, that I could have said no.

"Yes," I said. "We've got buildings hundreds of times this tall in New York. There's one called the Empire State building that's the tallest in the world. My class visited it last year and I went all the way to the top. It's got over a hundred floors. I can't describe how tall it is. Wait a minute. What's the name of that hill I went to visit the other day, where they have the police station?"

"You mean Bissex?"

"Yes, Bissex. Well, the Empire State Building is way taller than that."

"You're lying now!" she shouted, trembling with rage. Her hand lifted to strike me.

"No, I'm not," I said. "It really is, if you don't believe me I'll send you a picture postcard of it soon as I get back home so you can see for yourself. But it's way taller than Bissex."

All the fight went out of her at that. The hand poised to strike me fell limp to her side, and as she stared at me, seeing not me but the building that was taller than the highest hill she knew, the small stubborn light in her eyes (it was the same amber at the flame in the kerosene lamp she lit at dusk) began to fail. Finally, with a vague gesture that even in the midst of her defeat still tried to dismiss me and my world, she turned and started back through the gully, walking slowly, her steps groping and uncertain, as if she were suddenly no longer sure of the way, while I followed triumphant yet strangely saddened behind.

The next morning I found her dressed for our morning walk but stretched out on the Berbice chair in the tiny drawing room where she sometimes napped during the afternoon heat, her face turned to the window beside her. She appeared thinner and suddenly indescribably old.

"My Da-duh," I said.

"Yes, nuh," she said. Her voice was listless and the face she slowly turned my way was, now that I think back on it, like a Benin mask, the features drawn and almost distorted by an ancient abstract sorrow.

"Don't you feel well?" I asked.

"Girl, I don't know."

"My Da-duh, I goin' boil you some bush tea," my aunt, Da-duh's youngest child, who lived with her, called from the shed roof kitchen.

"Who tell you I need bush tea?" she cried, her voice assuming for a moment its old authority. "You can't even rest nowadays without some malicious person looking for you to be dead. Come girl," she motioned me to a place beside her on the old-fashioned lounge chair, "give us a tune."

I sang for her until breakfast at eleven, all my brash irreverent Tin Pan Alley songs, and then just before noon we went out into the ground. But it was a short, dispirited walk. Da-duh didn't even notice that the mangoes were beginning to ripen and would have to be picked before the village boys got to them. And when she paused occasionally and looked out across the canes or up at her trees it wasn't as if she were seeing them but something else. Some huge, monolithic shape had imposed itself, it seemed, between her and the land, obstructing her vision. Returning to the house she slept the entire afternoon on the Berbice chair.

She remained like this until we left, languishing away the mornings on the chair at the window gazing out at the land as if it were already doomed; then, at noon, taking the brief stroll with me through the ground during which she seldom spoke, and afterwards returning home to sleep till almost dusk sometimes.

On the day of our departure she put on the austere, ankle length white dress, the black shoes and brown felt hat (her town clothes she called them), but she did not go with us to town. She saw us off on the road outside her house and in the midst of my mother's tearful protracted farewell, she leaned down and whispered in my ear, "Girl, you're not to forget now to send me the picture of that building, you hear."

By the time I mailed her the large colored picture postcard of the Empire State building she was dead. She died during the famous '37 strike which began shortly after we left. On the day of her death England sent planes flying low over the island in a show of force — so low, according to my aunt's letter, that the downdraft from them shook the ripened mangoes from the trees in Da-duh's orchard. Frightened, everyone in the village fled into the canes. Except Da-duh. She remained in the house at the window so my aunt said, watching as the planes came swooping and screaming like monstrous birds down over the village, over her house, rattling her trees and flattening the young canes in her field. It must have seemed to her lying there that they did not intend pulling out of their dive, but like the hard-back beetles which hurled themselves with suicidal force against the walls of the house at night, those menacing silver shapes would hurl themselves in an ecstasy of self-immolation onto the land, destroying it utterly.

When the planes finally left and the villagers returned they found her dead on the Berbice chair at the window.

She died and I lived, but always, to this day even, within the shadow of her death. For a brief period after I was grown I went to live alone, like one doing penance, in a loft above a noisy factory in downtown New York and there painted seas of sugar-cane and huge swirling Van Gogh suns and palm trees striding like brightly-plumed Tutsi warriors across a tropical landscape, while the thunderous tread of the machines downstairs jarred the floor beneath my easel, mocking my efforts.

◎ *PAMELA WALKER*

Pamela Walker was born in 1948 in Iowa. She received an M.F.A. in fiction from the Writers Workshop in Iowa, and she also has an M.Ed. in learning disabilities from Bank Street College. With two other women, Walker opened the Bronx Dance Academy, a New York City public school of choice in which academics is integrated with the arts. Her publications include a novel, Twyla, *and short fiction that has appeared in the* Hawaii Review *and* Iowa Woman.

Walker writes: "'Good Shabbos,' written in 1988, is based on real events and inspired by a collection of Isaac Bashevis Singer's stories, which a friend Mireille gave me when I was in hospital after my first miscarriage. `Good Shabbos' is my first successful New York story, speaking to the urban diversity I love which keeps me rooted to concrete. It memorializes the life of my neighbor who died the following Passover" (letter to M. Kallet, 1996).

Good Shabbos

for Mireille

The winter day fell charcoal beyond the bare windows as Megan curled up on the sofa, an old wool blanket across her lap, five stacks of blue-books beside her. The week was done, another first semester ended. As quietly as dusk crept into the room, Megan marked a decade teaching English at Brewster Day Academy in Riverdale. Her companion of those years, a cocker spaniel she called Moon, snuggled against her thigh.

Megan felt content with the simple niche she had carved for herself in the city. She never longed for glamour; an afternoon in the hush of the Public Library's reading room was greater luxury than any she imagined as a girl aching to leave the Plains. When Megan met Jeff at the wedding of mutual friends, both had lived single for years. Jeff left his apartment in a fashionable brownstone for Megan's spacious quarters of faded elegance in a prewar building further uptown. He brought his cats, they set up home and became a family.

The head of Megan's department delivered the blue-books that morning. For the only time in her years at Brewster, Megan had not proctored midyears. She spent the week recuperating from a miscarriage. Though she felt well enough by Wednesday to make the trip to Riverdale, she could not face her colleagues' sadness. Even Jane Newton, the chisel-faced English department head, was softened at Megan's door, handing over the exam booklets.

"I was so sorry to hear your news." Jane touched Megan's hand. "You can't give up."

"We won't. We're hopeful, really."

"It happened to me when my girl was three, and it was such a disappointment." Megan never knew Jane had a daughter. "But I became pregnant again. Of course, I was scared to death, but it was good and our son was born."

"I'm glad."

"I'm sure you'll be successful."

"I'm sure too. Thanks, Jane." Often this past week, Megan found herself assuring others of hope she had not mastered.

Megan chose her best class to begin with, her brightest freshmen's essays on *The Scarlet Letter*, the tale with which she wooed her freshmen every fall. Slipping the rubber band over her wrist and resting the booklets against her knees, she hoped for a jewel, a line, a phrase so true she thought the student must be possessed to feel such depth.

Megan thought of Hester Prynne, her strength, her youth, her arrogance — that haughty smile as she emerged from prison, the A emblazoned on her dress. She stood alone against the world beneath the austere sun. Megan envied Hester, child clutched at her breast, upon the scaffold. The infant blinked, twisting from the vivid light, its cheeks flushed pink as the fragile blossoms of a wild rose bush. Megan's jewel was lost. In the deep night of the hospital as she eased off the gurney to the bed, Megan saw the tiny body cradled in her blood, its back a perfect curve at peace. She wondered had it been a girl like little Pearl.

When the bell rang, three hard, insistent blasts, Megan knew it was the Rabbi's wife whose habit it had become to hurry next door for Megan to solve her daily crises when her door would not unlock or if she needed parsnips from the Korean stand. Megan put aside the blue-books and padded in stockinged feet to the door. Her dog tick-tacked across the hardwood floor, ears perked, a quizzical rumble in her throat.

Mrs. Goldstein stood in the hall holding a bottle of kosher grape juice. A shock of gray hair sprang from beneath her stiff brown wig like Sister Superior's white hairline revealed below her wimple, a sight laced with the fear and excitement of a world forbidden to Megan as a schoolgirl. The Rabbi's wife wore a dark timeless dress of good wool.

"Mrs. Goldstein, how are you?"

Though everyone called Mrs. Goldstein the Rabbi's wife, in fact she was his widow. The Rabbi had been dead six months. Now Mrs. Goldstein brought bottles of seltzer and borscht next door for Megan to open as the Rabbi had done for her when he was alive. Mrs. Goldstein looked up at Megan, a grin out of place on her wizened face. She bobbed her head like Megan's Grandma Quinlan, who died back home the year that Megan had come East.

"Open?"

"Sure." The bottle sighed as Megan uncapped it.

"Come," the rebbetzin tugged at Megan's arm, "and bring your doggie."

Moon slipped out and ran ahead. Megan left her door unlatched and followed through the chilly hall. The Goldsteins' apartment had been painted before the Rabbi died. Its walls glistened under bright foyer lights. Mrs. Goldstein led Megan into the kitchen where a small sterling tumbler sat on the plain table, solitary in its beauty, etched with dainty filigree.

"Pour." Mrs. Goldstein gestured from the bottle to the tumbler. "To the top — the top!" she insisted when Megan stopped an inch below the rim.

Mrs. Goldstein picked up the brimming cup with both hands and carried it close to her bosom into the living room. Head bowed like an altar boy following the gaspy cadence of an organ, she did not spill a drop but set it on the table beside a shiny platter where two thin slices of chocolate roll lay head to head. Megan and her dog were invited for Shabbos, the Jewish Sabbath. Megan wondered if Mrs. Goldstein had intended from the start to make the invitation, the uncapped juice her ploy, or had she cut the cake and placed it with such care upon the serving plate for someone else? A woman from the synagogue perhaps had taken ill.

Silver candlesticks stood upon the dining table draped in white, the cloth embossed with swirls and flower baskets like Megan's multitude of linens, her Irish legacy along with handmade lace, doilies and hankies and antimacassars, starched stiff and wrapped with lavender. The etchings on the candlesticks matched those on the sterling cup. Slender candles sputtered, the frantic flames reflected in the windows, six flamencos dancing against the night.

The Rabbi's chair had been moved from the head of the table where he used to stand to say prayers and cut the challah bread which lay untouched beneath a blue velvet cloth, edges trimmed in braid, Hebrew symbols in its center, the golden threads as rich and sensuous as Hester Prynne's scarlet letter. Megan stood at the right hand of the Rabbi's wife as she mumbled a Jewish blessing over the chalice, then drank from it.

"Eat." Mrs. Goldstein jiggled the platter.

Megan broke off a nibble. The cake left a dry lump in her throat, but she did not dare sip from the sacred juice.

"Sit."

Megan sat on the chair's edge, crossing her leg and pointing her toes; a stretch buzzed up her shin bone. Moon sniffed the baseboards. Her collar tags rang like bells on a child's shoes.

"Ai, God," Mrs. Goldstein lamented, lowering her frail body onto the chair. She wore tie shoes with a chunky heel, the type the old women on Megan's Irish side had worn.

Grandma and her sisters were buried in those shoes. Mrs. Goldstein's thick calves hinted at the larger woman she once was. In pictures she showed

Megan, she stood beside her solemn husband in his Amish coat and flat-brimmed hat. She was not tall but strong with broad shoulders and the ample hips of one who had borne children, though Mrs. Goldstein was barren from the war. Her full, healthy face in the snapshots belied the years she and the Rabbi had survived beneath a Catholic farmer's hog barn.

"Ai, God, what is my life without the Rabbi?"

"I know, I know," Megan cooed her refrain to Mrs. Goldstein's sorrow.

"My nephew say, 'What you think? The Rabbi live forever?' I say, 'I never think.' " Mrs. Goldstein pursed her lips and shrugged. " 'Woman with your brain,' my nephew say, 'you are naive.' I say, 'Who should think, the Rabbi first? It's me, I have the heart.' " She touched her breast.

"We never know."

"They say it's God's way."

"Yes, they do."

"Have more." Mrs. Goldstein pushed the cake closer.

"Oh, that's okay, you have some." Megan pushed the platter back.

Mrs. Goldstein made a face. She had no stomach for the cake — for any food. "Where's your doggie? Give the doggie."

"Moon," Megan called and Moon came eagerly, knowing she would have a treat. "You want to give it to her?" Sometimes Mrs. Goldstein liked to feed the dog.

"No, no, you. You give." Mrs. Goldstein watched and smiled and bobbed her head. "More." She touched the plate when Megan stopped. Moon sat rapt, her black eyes wet, a hopeful twitter in her nose. "He is so smart. He want more. His eye say so."

"No, that's plenty for her."

The dog heard "no" and made a nest, circling twice before curling up on Megan's feet, her body warm and reassuring.

"A genius, your doggie. Now he know it gone. Wise eye, your doggie." Megan worried on Moon's eyes, grown cloudy with the passing years. "You know brassieres?" Mrs. Goldstein jolted Megan.

"Brassieres?"

"Yes, brassieres."

"Well, yes, I know brassieres."

"So then you see." With one deft move, Mrs. Goldstein popped hidden snaps and let her dress fall to her waist. She stood revealed in a new white bra from chest to below the midriff. "The Town Shop, you know the Town Shop?"

"Yes, I know the Town Shop."

Megan squirmed as though she were partaking of a sacrilegious act to see the Rabbi's wife disrobed.

"She say it good, but it no good."

"Mrs. Goldstein, it's fine. It's beautiful."

"Fine?" Mrs. Goldstein looked down her bodice, pulling the bra tight.

"Yes, just fine."

The old woman pulled her dress back over her shoulders. The front lay open, a pink rosette peeking from between her breasts.

"Mrs. Goldstein, do you have to go to synagogue tonight?"

"Pft," Mrs. Goldstein dismissed the thought. "I don't go to shul, not tonight, not tomorrow."

"Oh, that's good."

Megan relaxed against the chair's padded back. If Mrs. Goldstein was not going out, if she expected no one else, what difference did it make if she sat half-dressed at home?

"No, no, you must see." Mrs. Goldstein grew agitated. Her feet clopped the floor and she slipped out of her dress as smoothly as before, turning sideways where her breast protruded like a lump of rising dough, then backwards. "Look, look. See?"

The last two hooks of Mrs. Goldstein's bra were not closed. Megan pulled but the fabric resisted.

"Oh, you're right, Mrs. Goldstein, it's too tight."

"Now, you know."

"Yes, I do."

"She say it good, but it no good."

"No, it's too tight."

"I take it back."

Mrs. Goldstein reached behind, unhooked her bra and slid out, more facile than a young girl in gym class. Her breasts were long and tubular, meaty breasts that had lost their fat. Irish women started small and ended up with nothing. Grandma Quinlan hid beneath a pink chemise, even as she slept. On Megan's German side, the women kept full busts in age. Megan's breasts were young, firm though small. Someday she would be old with a flat Irish chest like Grandma Quinlan. Mrs. Goldstein handed her folded bra to Megan, which she set beside the platter on the table, while Mrs. Goldstein stood naked and made no move to cover herself.

"Let me help you, Mrs. Goldstein."

Megan lifted the garment and the old woman slid her shoulders in. Her skin was soft and cool. She plopped on her chair and her broad feet popped off the floor with new vitality. Snapping her dress, she bobbed her head, victorious that she was right and those who thought she lost her sense were wrong. The candles had grown smaller. They flickered orange and yellow.

"You tell her?" Mrs. Goldstein asked coyly.

"Tell her?"

Megan feared Mrs. Goldstein foresaw them walking to the Town Shop first thing Monday morning to exchange the crumpled bra.

"Write it. She believe you."

"The woman at the Town Shop?"

"Yes."

"You want me to write a note about the bra?"

Mrs. Goldstein nodded, a mirthful glint in her gray eyes.

"Oh, sure. Do you have a pen and piece of paper?"

"Yes, yes. For you I get it in the kitchen."

Megan had her doubts the shop would want the bra. The threads had sprung along one stay. Yet Mrs. Goldstein could not see the damage, and she believed quite urgently that a neighbor's note would put an end to her predicament. She returned, handing Megan a pen and pad.

Megan wrote quickly but legibly:

Please let Mrs. Goldstein return this bra.

It is too tight. Thank you.

her neighbor,

Megan Schaefer

"Now, it's done."

Easing onto her chair, Mrs. Goldstein held the pad and read with narrowed eyes. Her hands were wide and worn, the fingers marred by bulbous knuckles like Megan's peasant hands.

"Good. Thank you."

"You're welcome."

Mrs. Goldstein set the note aside with an air of finality. Sinking further in the chair, arms limp in her lap, she seemed to grow smaller. The green velvet back rose regally above her head like a mosque topped by a smooth wood ball. Her shoulders drooped from the relief of reaching safety for another night. Megan would go home and put up dinner soon.

"You must have baby."

"Oh, we will."

"Try again."

"We will. They make you wait."

"Oh, the doctor make you wait?"

"Yes."

"One child and you are not alone. You are not too old."

"No, not yet."

"If you cannot have, adopt."

"We will."

"Ai God, I should listen to the Rabbi. The Rabbi say adopt. I say no."

"Why, Mrs. Goldstein?"

The old woman shirked as if she would forget the reasons of her youth.

Her rheumy eyes steady, Mrs. Goldstein pulled up her shoulders with some kind of pride or maybe defiance for that which led her to deny the only man she ever knew, though she was left to doubly mourn. Megan thought of her own pungent odor in the hospital, an acrid sweat of fear and death. She lay in bed and smelled beneath her arms the strange, strong odor of her loss.

"Mrs. Goldstein, I have to be going."

"Your husband will be home."

"Yes."

"You must go."

"Yes."

"He is good husband, your husband."

"Yes, he is."

"Always friendly."

"Always."

Megan followed Moon into the kitchen, sweeping the dog into the crook of her arm.

"And you good neighbor, the best."

"Oh, that's okay." They were at the door. "You have a nice evening, Mrs. Goldstein."

"And you. With your husband."

"We will."

Moon sat in Megan's arm like a baby, eyes full of wonder on Mrs. Goldstein's wrinkled face.

"You good doggie." Mrs. Goldstein petted Moon's nose, gentle though tentative. She and the Rabbi had been scared of the dog. Now the deep crow's-feet crinkled around her eyes. "I like your doggie." Moon licked Mrs. Goldstein's thumb.

"And she likes you." Megan backed into the hall. "Good night."

"Thank you." Mrs. Goldstein stood at her door, the foyer brilliant behind her. She murmured, "You good neighbor," and she smiled a sly smile of the secret they shared, forming a kiss on her lips as Megan's grandmas never did, not the German, not the Irish, cold women bred of harsh winters and hard work, women who could turn away from a child's kiss.

The rebbetzin's door closed and the lock engaged as Megan hurried on tiptoes to her apartment, the cold of the tiles penetrating her thick socks, Moon's weight solid in her arms. Shouldering open the door, she kissed the dog's head and set her tenderly on the rug. Moon took Megan's love in stride, shaking her body and stretching, then toddling to the kitchen to slurp from her water bowl. The lamp cast a warm glow over Megan's sofa spot, the rumpled plaid blanket, blue-books fanned over leather, beckoning her to read and believe in her students' words. Jeffrey would be home soon.

◎ *JOY HARJO*

Joy Harjo's "Family Album" first appeared in The Progressive *in 1992. The essay includes two photographs of Harjo's family that she reflects upon in her writing. Family, place, and spirit are connected in Harjo's memory and in her language. (For more on Harjo, see page 65.)*

Family Album

For my cousin John Jacobs, 1918–1991, who will always be with me.

I felt as if I had prepared for the green corn ceremony my whole life. It's nothing I can explain in print; besides, no explanation would fit in the English language. All I can say is that it is central to the mythic construct of the Muscogee people (otherwise known as "Creek"), a rite of resonant renewal, of forgiveness.

The drive to Tallahassee grounds in northeastern Oklahoma with my friends Helen and Jim Burgess and Susan Williams was filled with stories. Stories here are as thick as the insects singing. We were part of the ongoing story of the people. Helen and I had made a promise to take part together in a ceremony that ensures the survival of the people, a link in the epic story of grace. The trees and tall reedlike grasses resounded with singing.

There's nothing quite like it anywhere else I've been, and I've traveled widely. The most similar landscape is in Miskito country in northeastern Nicaragua. I thought I was home once again as I walked with the Miskito people who had suffered terrible destruction of their homeland from both sides of the war. The insects singing provided a matrix of complex harmonies which shift cells in the body that shape imagination. I imagine a similar insect language in a place I've dreamed in west Africa. In summer in Oklahoma it's as if insects shape the world by songs. Their collective punctuation helps the growing corn remember the climb to the sun.

Our first stop on the way to the grounds was Holdenville to visit one of my favorite older cousins and his wife, John and Carol Jacobs. They would meet us later at the grounds. We traded gifts and stories, ate a perfectly fried meal at the Dairy Queen, one of the few restaurants open in a town hit hard by economic depression. I always enjoy visiting and feasting with these, my favorite relatives, and I feel at home in their house, a refuge surrounded with peacocks, dogs, and well-loved cats, guarded by giant beneficent spirits disguised as trees.

Across the road an oil well pumps relentlessly. When I was a child in Oklahoma, the monster insect bodies of the pumping wells terrified me. I would duck down in the car until we passed. Everyone thought it was funny. I was

called high-strung and imaginative. I imagined the collapse of the world, as if the wells were giant insects without songs, pumping blood from the body of Earth. I wasn't far off from the truth.

My cousin John, who was more like a beloved uncle, gave me two photographs he had culled for me from family albums. I had never before seen my great-grandparents on my father's side in photographs; this was the first time. I held them in my hand as reverberations of memory astounded me beyond language. I believe stories are encoded in the DNA spiral and call each cell into perfect position. Sound tempered with emotion and meaning propels the spiral beyond three dimensions.

I recognized myself in this photograph. I saw my sister, my brothers, my son and daughter. My father lived once again at the wheel of a car, my father who favored Cadillacs and Lincolns, cars he was not always able to afford but sacrificed to own because he was compelled by the luxury of well-made vehicles, sung to by the hum of a finely constructed motor. He made sure his cars were well-greased and perfectly tuned. That was his favorite music.

I was not surprised, yet I was shocked, to recognize something I always knew. The images of my great-grandmother Katie Menawe, my great-grandfather Marsie Harjo, my grandmother Naomi, my aunts Lois and Mary, and my uncle Joe were always inside me, as if I were a soul catcher made of a crystal formed from blood. I had heard the names, the stories, and perhaps it was because of the truth of those stories and what the names conveyed that the images had formed, had propelled me into the world. My grandchildren and great-grandchildren will see a magnification of themselves in their grandparents. It's implicit in the way we continue, the same as corn plants, the same as stars or the cascades of insects singing in summer. The old mystery of division and multiplication will always lead us to the root.

I think of my Aunt Lois's admonishments about photographs. She said a photograph can steal your soul. I believe it's true, for an imprint remains behind, forever locked in paper and chemicals. Perhaps the family will always be touring somewhere close to the border, dressed in their Sunday best, acutely aware of the soul stealer that Marsie Harjo hired to photograph them, steadying his tripod to the right of the road. Who's to say they didn't want something left to mark time in that intimate space, a place they could be in forever as a family, the world drenched in sienna?

Nothing would ever be the same again. The family is ever present, as is the photographer, unnamed except for his visual arrangement. I wonder whether he was surprised to see rich Indians.

Both of my great-grandparents' parents were part of the terrible walk of the Muscogee Nation from Alabama to Indian territory, where they were settled on land bordered by what is now Tulsa on the north, the place where my brothers, sister, and I were born. The people were promised that if they made this move they would be left alone by the U.S. Government, which claimed it needed the tribal homelands for expansion. But within a few years white settlers were once again crowding Indian lands, and in 1887 the Dawes Act, sometimes better known as the Allotment Act, was made law.

This act undermined one of the principles that had always kept the people together: that land was communal property which could not be owned. With the Dawes Act, private ownership of land was forced on the people. Land that supposedly belonged in perpetuity to the tribe was divided into plots, allotted to individuals. What was "left over" was opened for white settlement. But this did not content the settlers who proceeded by new laws, other kinds of trickery, and raw force to take over allotments belonging to the Muscogee and other tribes.

On December 1, 1905, oil was struck in Glenpool, Oklahoma. This was one of the richest pools of oil discovered in Oklahoma, which at its height produced forty million barrels annually. Marsie Harjo's allotted land was here. He was soon a rich man, as were many other Indian people whose allotted land lay over lakes of oil. This intensified the land grab. Many tribal members were swindled of their land, killed for money. It's a struggle that is still played out in the late Twentieth Century.

Oil money explains the long elegant car Marsie Harjo poses in with his family. In the stories I've been told, he always loved Hudsons. This may or may not be a Hudson. The family was raised in luxury. My grandmother Naomi and my aunt Lois both received their B.F.A. degrees in art and were able to take expensive vacations at a time when many people in this country were suffering economic deprivation. They also had an African-American maid, whose name was Susie. I've tried to find out more about her. I do know she lived with the family for many years and made the best ice cream.

There is an irony here because Marsie Harjo was also half or nearly half African-American. Another irony is the racism directed toward African-Americans and African blood in recent years by a tribe whose members originally accepted Africans and often welcomed them as relatives. Humanity was respected above color or ownership. The acceptance of African-American slavery came with the embrace of European-American cultural values. It was then we also began to hate ourselves for our darkness. It's all connected; this attitude towards ownership of land has everything to do with how human beings are treated, with the attitude toward all living things.

There are many ironies in this vision of the family of my great-grandparents, which is my family — a vision that explodes the myth of being Indian in this country for non-Indian and Indian alike. I wonder at the interpretation of the image of this Muscogee family in a car only the wealthy could own by another Muscogee person, or by another tribal person, or by a non-Indian anywhere in this land. This image challenges the popular culture's image of "Indian," an image that fits no tribe or person. I mean to question those accepted images, images that have limited us to cardboard cut-out figures, without blood, tears, or laughter.

There were many photographs of this family. I recently sent my cousin Donna Jo Harjo a photograph of her father Joe as a child of about five. He was dressed in a finely made suit and driving a child's-size scale model of a car. She's never lived in this kind of elegance. She lives on her salary as a sorter for a conglomerate nut-and-dried-fruit company in northern California. She has a love for animals, especially cats. Our clan is the Tiger Clan. She also is a great lover of horses. I wonder at this proliferation of photographs and think of the diminishment of the family in numbers to this present generation.

One of the photographs is a straight-on shot of my great-grandparents and two Seminole men dressed traditionally. The Seminoles in their turbans are in stark contrast to my grandparents, especially to Marsie Harjo, who is stately and somewhat stiff with the fear of God in his elegant whiteman's clothes, his homburg hat.

He was quite an advanced thinker and I imagine he repressed what he foresaw for the Muscogee people. I don't think anyone would have believed him. He was a preacher, a Creek Baptist minister. He represents a counterforce to traditional Muscogee culture and embodies a side of the split in our tribe since Christianity, since the people were influenced by the values of European culture. The dividing lines are the same several hundred years later.

My great-grandfather was in Stuart, Florida, to "save" the Seminole people, as he did every winter. He bought a plantation there and, because he hated pineapples, he had every one of the plants dug up and destroyed. Another story I've often heard says he also owned an alligator farm. I went to Stuart last spring on my way to Miami and could find no trace of the mission or the plantation anywhere in the suburban mix of concrete, glass, and advertisements. I had only memories that are easier to reach in a dimension that is as alive and living as the three dimensions we know with our five senses.

My great-grandmother Katie Menawe is much more hidden in this photograph. She is not in the driver's seat, and not next to the driver but in the very back of the car, behind her four children. Yet she quietly presides over everything as she guards her soul from the intrusive camera. I have the sense that Marsie boldly entered the Twentieth Century ahead of everyone else, while Katie reluctantly followed. I doubt she ever resolved the split in her heart. I don't know too much about her. She and her siblings were orphaned. They were schooled and boarded for some time at Eufaula Indian School. I don't know how old she was when she married Marsie Harjo. Her sister Ella, a noted beauty queen, was my cousin John's mother.

The name Menawe is one of those names in the Muscogee tribe that is charged with memory of rebellion, with strength in the face of terrible destruction. Tecumseh came looking for Menawe when he was building his great alliance of nations in the 1800s. Menawe was one of the leaders of the Red Stick War, an armed struggle against the U.S. Government and Andrew Jackson's demand for western settlement of the Muscogee tribes. The fighting forces were made up of Creeks, Seminoles, and Africans. Not many survived the struggle.

The Seminoles successfully resisted colonization by hiding in the Floridian swamps. They beat the United States forces who were aided by other tribes, including other Creeks who were promised land and homes for their help. The promises were like other promises from the U.S. Government. For their assistance, the Indian troops were forced to walk to Indian Territory like everyone else, to what later became the state of Oklahoma.

Menawe stayed in Alabama. He was soon forced west, but not before he joined with Jackson's forces to round up Seminoles for the move to Oklahoma. My cousin John said Menawe died on the trail. I know that he died of a broken heart. I have a McKenney Hall print of Menawe, an original hand-colored lithograph dated 1848. Katie has the eyes and composure of this man who was her father.

By going to Tallahassee grounds to join in traditional tribal ceremony, I was taking my place in the circle of relatives. I was one more link in the concatenation of ancestors. Close behind me are my son and daughter, behind them my granddaughter. Next to me, interlocking the pattern, are my cousins, my aunts and uncles. We dance together in this place of knowing beyond the physical dimensions of space, much denser than the chemicals and paper of photographs. It is larger than mere human memory, than any destruction we have walked through to come to this ground of memory.

Time can never be stopped; rather, it is poised to make a leap into knowing or a field of questions. I understood this as we stompdanced in the middle of the night, as the stars whirred in the same pattern overhead, as they had been when Katie, Marsie, and the children lived beneath them. I heard time resume as the insects took up their singing once more to guide us through memory. The old Hudson heads to the east of the border of the photograph. For the Muscogee, East is the place of origins, the place the People emerged from so many hundreds of years ago. It is also a place of return.

◎ *MAXINE HONG KINGSTON*

Maxine Hong Kingston was born in 1940 in Stockton, California. She received her B.A. from the University of California at Berkeley. Kingston taught high school until the late 1970s and then became a visiting associate professor of English at the University of Hawaii in Honolulu. Awards for her work include the National Book Critics Circle Award in 1976 for The Woman Warrior *and the American Book Award in 1981 for* China Men. *Her books include* The Woman Warrior: Memoirs of a Girlhood Among Ghosts *(1976),* China Men *(1980),* Hawaii One Summer *(1987), and* Tripmaster Monkey: His Fake Book *(1988).*

"No Name Woman" is a section from Kingston's memoir The Woman Warrior. *The worst punishment an individual in a culture can receive is never to have one's name spoken again. For a woman who committed adultery in China, such would be*

the punishment. Here Kingston reclaims this woman as an ancestor, refusing to leave her in the watery realm of "ghosts."

No Name Woman

"You must not tell anyone," my mother said, "what I am about to tell you. In China your father had a sister who killed herself. She jumped into the family well. We say that your father has all brothers because it is as if she had never been born.

"In 1924 just a few days after our village celebrated seventeen hurry-up weddings — to make sure that every young man who went 'out on the road' would responsibly come home — your father and his brothers and your grandfather and his brothers and your aunt's new husband sailed for America, the Gold Mountain. It was your grandfather's last trip. Those lucky enough to get contracts waved good-bye from the decks. They fed and guarded the stowaways and helped them off in Cuba, New York, Bali, Hawaii. 'We'll meet in California next year,' they said. All of them sent money home.

"I remember looking at your aunt one day when she and I were dressing; I had not noticed before that she had such a protruding melon of a stomach. But I did not think, 'She's pregnant,' until she began to look like other pregnant women, her shirt pulling and the white tops of her black pants showing. She could not have been pregnant, you see, because her husband had been gone for years. No one said anything. We did not discuss it. In early summer she was ready to have the child, long after the time when it could have been possible.

"The village had also been counting. On the night the baby was to be born the villagers raided our house. Some were crying. Like a great saw, teeth strung with lights, files of people walked zigzag across our land, tearing the rice. Their lanterns doubled in the disturbed black water, which drained away through the broken bunds. As the villagers closed in, we could see that some of them, probably men and women we knew well, wore white masks. The people with long hair hung it over their faces. Women with short hair made it stand up on end. Some had tied white bands around their foreheads, arms, and legs.

"At first they threw mud and rocks at the house. Then they threw eggs and began slaughtering our stock. We could hear the animals scream their deaths — the roosters, the pigs, a last great roar from the ox. Familiar wild heads flared in our night windows; the villagers encircled us. Some of the faces stopped to peer at us, their eyes rushing like searchlights. The hands flattened against the panes, framed heads, and left red prints.

"The villagers broke in the front and the back doors at the same time, even though we had not locked the doors against them. Their knives dripped with the blood of our animals. They smeared blood on the doors and walls. One woman swung a chicken, whose throat she had slit, splattering blood in red arcs about her. We stood together in the middle of our house, in the family hall with the pictures and tables of the ancestors around us, and looked straight ahead.

"At that time the house had only two wings. When the men came back, we would build two more to enclose our courtyard and a third one to begin a second courtyard. The villagers pushed through both wings, even your grandparents' rooms, to find your aunt's, which was also mine until the men returned. From this room a new wing for one of the younger families would grow. They ripped up her clothes and shoes and broke her combs, grinding them underfoot. They tore her work from the loom. They scattered the cooking fire and rolled the new weaving in it. We could hear them in the kitchen breaking our bowls and banging the pots. They overturned the great waist-high earthenware jugs; duck eggs, pickled fruits, vegetables burst out and mixed in acrid torrents. The old woman from the next field swept a broom through the air and loosed the spirits-of-the-broom over our heads. 'Pig.' 'Ghost.' 'Pig,' they sobbed and scolded while they ruined our house.

"When they left, they took sugar and oranges to bless themselves. They cut pieces from the dead animals. Some of them took bowls that were not broken and clothes that were not torn. Afterward we swept up the rice and sewed it back up into sacks. But the smells from the spilled preserves lasted. Your aunt gave birth in the pigsty that night. The next morning when I went for the water, I found her and the baby plugging up the family well.

"Don't let your father know that I told you. He denies her. Now that you have started to menstruate, what happened to her could happen to you. Don't humiliate us. You wouldn't like to be forgotten as if you had never been born. The villagers are watchful."

Whenever she had to warn us about life, my mother told stories that ran like this one, a story to grow up on. She tested our strength to establish realities. Those in the emigrant generations who could not reassert brute survival died young and far from home. Those of us in the first American generations have had to figure out how the invisible world the emigrants built around our childhoods fit in solid America.

The emigrants confused the gods by diverting their curses, misleading them with crooked streets and false names. They must try to confuse their offspring as well, who, I suppose, threaten them in similar ways — always trying to get things straight, always trying to name the unspeakable. The Chinese I know hide their names; sojourners take new names when their lives change and guard their real names with silence.

Chinese-Americans, when you try to understand what things in you are Chinese, how do you separate what is peculiar to childhood, to poverty, insanities, one family, your mother who marked your growing with stories, from what is Chinese? What is Chinese tradition and what is the movies?

If I want to learn what clothes my aunt wore, whether flashy or ordinary, I would have to begin, "Remember Father's drowned-in-the-well sister?" I cannot ask that. My mother has told me once and for all the useful parts. She will add nothing unless powered by Necessity, a riverbank that guides her life. She plants vegetable gardens rather than lawns; she carries the odd-shaped tomatoes home from the fields and eats food left for the gods.

Whenever we did frivolous things, we used up energy; we flew high kites. We children came up off the ground over the melting cones our parents brought home from work and the American movie on New Year's Day — *Oh, You Beautiful Doll* with Betty Grable one year, and *She Wore a Yellow Ribbon* with John Wayne another year. After the one carnival ride each, we paid in guilt; our tired father counted his change on the dark walk home.

Adultery is extravagance. Could people who hatch their own chicks and eat the embryos and the heads for delicacies and boil the feet in vinegar for party food, leaving only the gravel, eating even the gizzard lining — could such people engender a prodigal aunt? To be a woman, to have a daughter in starvation time was a waste enough. My aunt could not have been the lone romantic who gave up everything for sex. Women in the old China did not choose. Some man had commanded her to lie with him and be his secret evil. I wonder whether he masked himself when he joined the raid on her family.

Perhaps she encountered him in the fields or on the mountain where the daughters-in-law collected fuel. Or perhaps he first noticed her in the marketplace. He was not a stranger because the village housed no strangers. She had to have dealings with him other than sex. Perhaps he worked an adjoining field, or he sold her the cloth for the dress she sewed and wore. His demand must have surprised, then terrified her. She obeyed him; she always did as she was told.

When the family found a young man in the next village to be her husband, she stood tractably beside the best rooster, his proxy, and promised before they met that she would be his forever. She was lucky that he was her age and she would be the first wife, an advantage secure now. The night she first saw him, he had sex with her. Then he left for America. She had almost forgotten what he looked like. When she tried to envision him, she only saw the black and white face in the group photograph the men had had taken before leaving.

The other man was not, after all, much different from her husband. They both gave orders: she followed. "If you tell your family, I'll beat you. I'll kill you. Be here again next week." No one talked sex, ever. And she might have separated the rapes from the rest of living if only she did not have to buy her oil from him or gather wood in the same forest. I want her fear to have lasted just as long as rape lasted so that the fear could have been contained. No drawn-out fear. But women at sex hazarded birth and hence lifetimes. The fear did not stop but permeated everywhere. She told the man, "I think I'm pregnant." He organized the raid against her.

On nights when my mother and father talked about their life back home, sometimes they mentioned an "outcast table" whose business they still seemed to be settling, their voices tight. In a commensal tradition, where food is precious, the powerful older people made wrongdoers eat alone. Instead of letting them start separate new lives like the Japanese, who could become samurais and geishas, the Chinese family, faces averted but eyes glowering sideways, hung on to the offenders and fed them leftovers. My aunt must have lived in the same house as my parents and eaten at an outcast table. My mother spoke about the raid as if she had seen it, when she and my aunt, a daughter-in-law to a different household, should not have been living together at all. Daughters-in-law lived with their husbands' parents, not their own; a synonym for marriage in Chinese is "taking a daughter-in-law." Her husband's parents could have sold her, mortgaged her, stoned her. But they had sent her back to her own mother and father, a mysterious act hinting at disgraces not told me. Perhaps they had thrown her out to deflect the avengers.

She was the only daughter; her four brothers went with her father, husband, and uncles "out on the road" and for some years became western men. When the goods were divided among the family, three of the brothers took land, and the youngest, my father, chose an education. After my grandparents gave their daughter away to her husband's family, they had dispensed all the adventure and all the property. They expected her alone to keep the traditional ways, which her brothers, now among the barbarians, could fumble without detection. The heavy, deep-rooted women were to maintain the past against the flood, safe for returning. But the rare urge west had fixed upon our family, and so my aunt crossed boundaries not delineated in space.

The work of preservation demands that the feelings playing about in one's guts not be turned into action. Just watch their passing like cherry blossoms. But perhaps my aunt, my forerunner, caught in a slow life, let dreams grow and fade and after some months or years went toward what persisted. Fear at the enormities of the forbidden kept her desires delicate, wire and bone. She looked at a man because she liked the way the hair was tucked behind his ears, or she liked the question-mark line of a long torso curving at the shoulder and straight at the hip. For warm eyes or a soft voice or a slow walk — that's all — a few hairs, a line, a brightness, a sound, a pace, she gave up family. She offered us up for a charm that vanished with tiredness, a pigtail that didn't toss when the wind died. Why, the wrong lighting could erase the dearest thing about him.

It could very well have been, however, that my aunt did not take subtle enjoyment of her friend, but, a wild woman, kept rollicking company. Imagining her free with sex doesn't fit, though. I don't know any women like that, or men either. Unless I see her life branching into mine, she gives me no ancestral help.

To sustain her being in love, she often worked at herself in the mirror, guessing at the colors and shapes that would interest him, changing them frequently in order to hit on the right combination. She wanted him to look back.

On a farm near the sea, a woman who tended her appearance reaped a reputation for eccentricity. All the married women blunt-cut their hair in flaps about their ears or pulled it back in tight buns. No nonsense. Neither style blew easily into heart-catching tangles. And at their weddings they displayed themselves in their long hair for the last time. "It brushed the backs of my knees," my mother tells me. "It was braided, and even so, it brushed the backs of my knees."

At the mirror my aunt combed individuality into her bob. A bun could have been contrived to escape into black streamers blowing in the wind or in quiet wisps about her face, but only the older women in our picture album wear buns. She brushed her hair back from her forehead, tucking the flaps behind her ears. She looped a piece of thread, knotted into a circle between her index fingers and thumbs, and ran the double strand across her forehead. When she closed her fingers as if she were making a pair of shadow geese bite, the string twisted together catching the little hairs. Then she pulled the thread away from her skin, ripping the hairs out neatly, her eyes watering from the needles of pain. Opening her fingers, she cleaned the thread, then rolled it along her hairline and the tops of her eyebrows. My mother did the same to me and my sisters and herself. I used to believe that the expression "caught by the short hairs" meant a captive held with a depilatory string. It especially hurt at the temples, but my mother said we were lucky we didn't have to have our feet bound when we were seven. Sisters used to sit on their beds and cry together, she said, as their mothers or their slaves removed the bandages for a few minutes each night and let the blood gush back into their veins. I hope that the man my aunt loved appreciated a smooth brow, that he wasn't just a tits-and-ass man.

Once my aunt found a freckle on her chin, at a spot that the almanac said predestined her for unhappiness. She dug it out with a hot needle and washed the wound with peroxide.

More attention to her looks than these pullings of hairs and pickings at spots would have caused gossip among the villagers. They owned work clothes and good clothes, and they wore good clothes for feasting the new seasons. But since a woman combing her hair hexes beginnings, my aunt rarely found an occasion to look her best. Women looked like great sea snails — the corded wood, babies, and laundry they carried were the whorls on their backs. The Chinese did not admire a bent back; goddesses and warriors stood straight. Still there must have been a marvelous freeing of beauty when a worker laid down her burden and stretched and arched.

Such commonplace loveliness, however, was not enough for my aunt. She dreamed of a lover for the fifteen days of New Year's, the time for families to exchange visits, money, and food. She plied her secret comb. And sure enough she cursed the year, the family, the village, and herself.

Even as her hair lured her imminent lover, many other men looked at her. Uncles, cousins, nephews, brothers would have looked, too, had they been home between journeys. Perhaps they had already been restraining their curiosity and they left, fearful that their glances, like a field of nesting birds, might be startled and caught. Poverty hurt, and that was their first reason for leaving. But another, final reason for leaving the crowded house was the never-said.

She may have been unusually beloved, the precious only daughter, spoiled and mirror gazing because of the affection the family lavished on her. When her husband left they welcomed the chance to take her back from the in-laws; she could live like the little daughter for just a while longer. There are stories that my grandfather was different from other people, "crazy ever since the little Jap bayoneted him in the head." He used to put his naked penis on the dinner table, laughing. And one day he brought home a baby girl, wrapped up inside his brown western-style greatcoat. He had traded one of his sons, probably my father, the youngest, for her. My grandmother made him trade back. When he finally got a daughter of his own, he doted on her. They must have all loved her, except perhaps my father, the only brother who never went back to China, having once been traded for a girl.

Brothers and sisters, newly men and women, had to efface their sexual color and present plain miens. Disturbing hair and eyes, a smile like no other threatened the ideal of five generations living under one roof. To focus blurs, people shouted face to face and yelled from room to room. The immigrants I know have loud voices, unmodulated to American tones even after years away from the village where they called their friendships out across the fields. I have not been able to stop my mother's screams in public libraries or over telephones. Walking erect (knees straight, toes pointed forward, not pigeon-toed, which is Chinese-feminine) and speaking in an inaudible voice, I have tried to turn myself American-feminine. Chinese communication was loud, public. Only sick people had to whisper. But at the dinner table, where the family members came nearest one another, no one could talk, not the outcasts nor any eaters. Every word that falls from the mouth is a coin lost. Silently they gave and accepted food with both hands. A preoccupied child who took his bowl with one hand got a sideways glare. A complete moment of total attention is due everyone alike. Children and lovers have no singularity here, but my aunt used a secret voice, a separate attentiveness.

She kept the man's name to herself throughout her labor and dying; she did not accuse him that he be punished with her. To save her inseminator's name she gave silent birth.

He may have been somebody in her own household, but intercourse with a man outside the family would have been no less abhorrent. All the village were kinsmen, and the titles shouted in loud country voices never let kinship be forgotten. Any man within visiting distance would have been neutralized as a lover — "brother," "younger brother," "older brother" — one hundred and fifteen relationship titles. Parents researched birth charts probably not so much to assure good fortune as to circumvent incest in a population that has but one hundred surnames. Everybody has eight million relatives. How useless then sexual mannerisms, how dangerous.

As if it came from an atavism deeper than fear, I used to add "brother" silently to boys' names. It hexed the boys, who would or would not ask me to dance, and made them less scary and as familiar and deserving of benevolence as girls.

But, of course, I hexed myself also — no dates. I should have stood up, both arms waving, and shouted out across libraries, "Hey, you! Love me back." I had no idea, though, how to make attraction selective, how to control its direction and magnitude. If I made myself American-pretty so that the five or six Chinese boys in the class fell in love with me, everyone else — the Caucasian, Negro, and Japanese boys — would too. Sisterliness, dignified and honorable, made much more sense.

Attraction eludes control so stubbornly that whole societies designed to organize relationships among people cannot keep order, not even when they bind people to one another from childhood and raise them together. Among the very poor and the wealthy, brothers married their adopted sisters, like doves. Our family allowed some romance, paying adult brides' prices and providing dowries so that their sons and daughters could marry strangers. Marriage promises to turn strangers into friendly relatives — a nation of siblings.

In the village structure, spirits shimmered among the live creatures, balanced and held in equilibrium by time and land. But one human being flaring up into violence could open up a black hole, a maelstrom that pulled in the sky. The frightened villagers, who depended on one another to maintain the real, went to my aunt to show her a personal, physical representation of the break she had made in the "roundness." Misallying couples snapped off the future, which was to be embodied in true offspring. The villagers punished her for acting as if she could have a private life, secret and apart from them.

If my aunt had betrayed the family at a time of large grain yields and peace, when many boys were born, and wings were being built on many houses, perhaps she might have escaped such severe punishment. But the men — hungry, greedy, tired of planting in dry soil, cuckolded — had had to leave the village in order to send food-money home. There were ghost plagues, bandit plagues, wars with the Japanese, floods. My Chinese brother and sister had died of an unknown sickness. Adultery, perhaps only a mistake during good times, became a crime when the village needed food.

The round moon cakes and round doorways, the round tables of graduated size that fit one roundness inside another, round windows and rice bowls

— these talismen had lost their power to warn this family of the law: a family must be whole, faithfully keeping the descent line by having sons to feed the old and the dead, who in turn look after the family. The villagers came to show my aunt and her lover-in-hiding a broken house. The villagers were speeding up the circling of events because she was too shortsighted to see that her infidelity had already harmed the village, that waves of consequences would return unpredictably, sometimes in disguise, as now, to hurt her. This roundness had to be made coin-sized so that she would see its circumference: punish her at the birth of her baby. Awaken her to the inexorable. People who refused fatalism because they could invent small resources insisted on culpability. Deny accidents and wrest fault from the stars.

After the villagers left, their lanterns now scattering in various directions toward home, the family broke their silence and cursed her. "Aiaa, we're going to die. Death is coming. Death is coming. Look what you've done. You've killed us. Ghost! Dead ghost! Ghost! You've never been born." She ran out into the fields, far enough from the house so that she could no longer hear their voices, and pressed herself against the earth, her own land no more. When she felt the birth coming, she thought that she had been hurt. Her body seized together. "They've hurt me too much," she thought. "This is gall, and it will kill me." Her forehead and knees against the earth, her body convulsed and then released her onto her back. The black well of sky and stars went out and out and out forever; her body and her complexity seemed to disappear. She was one of the stars, a bright dot in blackness, without home, without a companion, in eternal cold and silence. An agoraphobia rose in her, speeding higher and higher, bigger and bigger; she would not be able to contain it; there would be no end to fear.

Flayed, unprotected against space, she felt pain return, focusing her body. This pain chilled her — a cold, steady kind of surface pain. Inside, spasmodically, the other pain, the pain of the child, heated her. For hours she lay on the ground, alternately body and space. Sometimes a vision of normal comfort obliterated reality: she saw the family in the evening gambling at the dinner table, the young people massaging their elders' backs. She saw them congratulating one another, high joy on the mornings the rice shoots came up. When these pictures burst, the stars drew yet further apart. Black space opened.

She got to her feet to fight better and remembered that old-fashioned women gave birth in their pigsties to fool the jealous, pain-dealing gods, who do not snatch piglets. Before the next spasms could stop her, she ran to the pigsty, each step a rushing out into emptiness. She climbed over the fence and knelt in the dirt. It was good to have a fence enclosing her, a tribal person alone.

Laboring, this woman who had carried her child as a foreign growth that sickened her every day, expelled it at last. She reached down to touch the hot, wet, moving mass, surely smaller than anything human, and could feel that it was human after all — fingers, toes, nails, nose. She pulled it up on to her belly, and it lay curled there, butt in the air, feet precisely tucked one under the other. She opened her loose shirt and buttoned the child inside. After resting, it squirmed and thrashed and she pushed it up to her breast. It turned its head this way and that until it found her nipple. There, it made little snuffling noises. She clenched her teeth at its preciousness, lovely as a young calf, a piglet, a little dog.

She may have gone to the pigsty as a last act of responsibility: she would protect this child as she had protected its father. It would look after her soul, leaving supplies on her grave. But how would this tiny child without family find her grave when there would be no marker for her anywhere, neither in the earth nor the family hall? No one would give her a family hall name. She had taken the child with her into the wastes. At its birth the two of them had felt the same raw pain of separation, a wound that only the family pressing tight could close. A child with no descent line would not soften her life but only trail after her, ghostlike, begging her to give it purpose. At dawn the villagers on their way to the fields would stand around the fence and look.

Full of milk, the little ghost slept. When it awoke, she hardened her breasts against the milk that crying loosens. Toward morning she picked up the baby and walked to the well.

Carrying the baby to the well shows loving. Otherwise abandon it. Turn its face into the mud. Mothers who love their children take them along. It was probably a girl; there is some hope of forgiveness for boys.

"Don't tell anyone you had an aunt. Your father does not want to hear her name. She has never been born." I have believed that sex was unspeakable and words so strong and fathers so frail that "aunt" would do my father mysterious harm. I have thought that my family, having settled among immigrants who had also been their neighbors in the ancestral land, needed to clean their name, and a wrong word would incite the kinspeople even here. But there is more to this silence: they want me to participate in her punishment. And I have.

In the twenty years since I heard this story I have not asked for details nor said my aunt's name; I do not know it. People who can comfort the dead can also chase after them to hurt them further — a reverse ancestor worship. The real punishment was not the raid swiftly inflicted by the villagers, but the family's deliberately forgetting her. Her betrayal so maddened them, they saw to it that she would suffer forever, even after death. Always hungry, always needing, she would have to beg food from other ghosts, snatch and steal it from those whose living descendants give them gifts. She would have to fight the ghosts massed at crossroads for the buns a few thoughtful citizens leave to decoy her away from village and home so that the ancestral spirits could feast unharassed. At peace, they could act like gods, not ghosts, their descent lines providing them with paper suits and dresses, spirit money, paper houses, paper automobiles, chicken, meat, and rice into eternity — essences delivered up in smoke and flames, steam and incense rising from each rice bowl. In an attempt to make the Chinese care for people outside the family, Chairman Mao encourages us now to give our paper replicas to the spirits of outstanding soldiers and workers, no matter whose ancestors they may be. My aunt remains forever hungry. Goods are not distributed evenly among the dead.

My aunt haunts me — her ghost drawn to me because now, after fifty years of neglect, I alone devote pages of paper to her, though not origamied into houses and clothes. I do not think she always means me well. I am telling on her, and she was a spite suicide, drowning herself in the drinking water. The Chinese are always very frightened of the drowned one, whose weeping ghost, wet hair hanging and skin bloated, waits silently by the water to pull down a substitute.

◎ *PAT MORA*

Pat Mora was born in El Paso, Texas, in 1942 and currently lives in Ohio. She is the author of several children's books, including A Birthday Basket for Tia, Pablo's Tree, *and* Tomas and the Library Lady, *and three volumes of poetry,* Chants *(1984),* Borders *(1986), and* Communion *(1991). Her first collection of essays,* Napantla: Essays from the Land in the Middle, *was published in 1993. Her new poetry manuscript is titled* A Mexican Quartet: Talk Show Interviews with Coatlique the Aztec Goddess, Malinche the Maligned, The Virgin of Guadalupe, *and* La Llorona: The Wailer. *She received a Kellogg National Fellowship in 1986. She has worked to preserve her Latina heritage as an educator and museum curator, as well as through her writings.*

"A Walk with My Father" appears in Prairie Schooner's *1994 special issue of Latino/Latina literature. Four days after his death, the narrator's father takes a walk with her through a California marketplace, making enthusiastic comments about the produce, naming all the herbs and flowers at his daughter's request. Skillfully Mora weaves Spanish and English in this celebration of father and daughter. "A Walk with My Father" makes it clear that Mora is above all a poet — for the writing is lyrical and focuses on the richness of bilingualism as a way of seeing the world.*

A Walk with My Father

Four days after my father died, he took a walk with me. We had last walked together three months before on a sunny, May morning. He had only been able to circle one block by then, his legs so weak after the steady fading away for two years of his body and mind, his slow disappearance.

On that last arm-in-arm walk we had stopped often to admire the flowers that flourish so effortlessly in California, luxurious hibiscus, imperious birds-of-paradise; blooms that require greenhouse care in the El Paso, the desert city that was once our home. Our special favorite had always been bougainvillea. "It grows even in alleys here," he said in years past. "*Ven,* come and see."

So we had stopped that May day to admire the orange, red, gold, and watermelon pink blooms festooning a modest white fence. "*Mira no mas.* Just look at that," he said, but his old delight was disappearing. Weariness was detaching him from this earth.

My father had little time to dwell on words. We've never been sure if he finished high school, and precise names of trees or fish or flowers were vague in his mind, interesting but unessential labeling for his savoring of nature's inventiveness.

The days between my father's death and the burial were pleasant on the surface, days of reminiscing with my mother and siblings, laughing to suppress the grief. Internally, I held my breath, fearing the inevitable moment beneath the pepper tree in the cemetery garden he and Mother had chosen. Mornings I'd slip out alone for a walk. At least, I thought I was alone.

One such day, I set off to see the ocean, hoping that the sight of that century-old repetition of waves would comfort me. En route, I discovered a weekly produce market, urban-style. I have reveled in fruit and vegetable markets of all shapes and sizes since I was small and went to markets with my family across the Rio Grande in Juárez.

As I approach the vendors this day calling out their morning greetings to one another, I think of the baskets of technicolor potatoes in Peru, of the gleaming candied fruits and vegetables in Mexico — green figs stuffed with coconut, rich brown sweet potatoes, oranges crusty with dried syrup. And I begin to hear my father's voice enjoying this meandering from stall to stall with me.

"*¡Mira todos los chinitos!*" he says, "Look at all the Chinese," as he studies the faces of Asian merchants busy bringing out their white, green, and purple vegetables. Like many Mexicans, my father is fond of the diminutive, *ito,* an ending he uses when observing any ethnic group including Whites. "*Pobres güeritos,*" he might say, "Poor anglos," watching their awkward attempts to dance salsa music, their frequent inability to display emotions, his use of the diminutive conveying his general affection for most humans, his compassion at their antics, his awareness that every group has its difficulties.

"What are those?" I ask a vendor, pen in hand wanting us to hear the names of the Chinese produce, to find comfort in specificity, even if my father might be lost admiring the shapes or lines of leafy and gleaming vegetables.

"Chinese okra, white squash, bitter melon."

Bitter indeed, I think, bitter to contemplate life without the huge physical presence that had been my father, his six-foot, two-hundred-and-ten-pound incarnation on this earth that had vanished before our eyes; the mind that had been able to make sense of the country of his birth and the country of his life, that in the end lost its way in some internal labyrinth where we could not follow.

The concreteness, physicality, of the market flowers and produce provides a link to pleasures my father and I share. I hear the personal pride he takes in California's abundance.

"Mira no mas, honey," he says. "Just look at the size of those strawberries!" I roll limes, lemons, grapefruits, and oranges in my hands. We smell the syrupy peaches.

We marvel at the flower stalls and chuckle at the wealthy yuppies carrying home huge bouquets, "conspicuous consumption," to their carefully appointed apartments. He smiles and shakes his head as I press for the names of things, as I tell him, "They say the little orange suns are straw flowers; the trumpets, foxglove; those are caspia, stargazers, phlox, bells of Ireland."

We stop at the snapdragons, remembering the scrawny versions we watered in our backyard in Texas. My father had bought the piece of land that became our home in place of taking my mother on a honeymoon, a decision she frowned on. How often each of the four children stood holding a hose through the years trying to tempt roses or larkspur or snapdragons to survive in that hard dirt below that glaring sun. My father remembers only successes. Perhaps he was always too busy working, grinding lenses day and night at his optical company, to consider just how difficult life was in that border town. Little flourished with ease, whether a plant or a business, particularly a business owned by a Mexican or Mexican American. "I have a map of Mexico on my face," he said to me late in his life, momentarily admitting the prejudice he had encountered.

We linger at the honeys — wildflower, orange blossom, sage, melon, star thistle, eucalyptus. "Let's get a bottle," he says. "Sometimes your mother gets a cough. Remember, just put a bit on the tip of your tongue, that or glycerine. You'll stop coughing." When I entered the room in which he died, there it was, a bottle of glycerine by his bed.

We leave the market for a bit and walk down to the ocean, another sight we both loved. Gone is the casual stroll along the palisades. Street people sleep on benches and under shrubs, reach out their smudged hands. The white statue of Santa Monica, hands folded, eyes closed, reminds me that my father's body has been wrapped in white, also so still, before the frame we knew was zipped into a shroud, all black.

We walk back to the market. The sun is bright, and more shoppers are arriving, women with shopping bags looking for bargains. I fumble in my purse for another pen. Since my father died, every pen I use runs out of ink. I want to write down the names, always the names, of the fresh herbs, names sweet on the tongue, lemon basil, baby dill, the green scents a counter to the concrete in which I live. He studies the cartons of sprouts and sunflower greens.

"*Para los conejos,*" he says laughing, rabbit food.

"What did I tell you?" my father says, walking toward a sign that says JOJOBA. My father always had what he called "million dollar ideas." He would read an article in a newspaper or magazine and decide how he, or we, could make a fortune. Not that any of us ever did. Another of his favorite phrases was "very scientific," and articles about jojoba through the years had combined scientific and financial possibilities for him. He had told any of us who'd sit and listen about the growing of jojoba, the oil that could be extracted, the money to be made. And now here it is, proof, a stand with jojoba seeds, products, brochures, and a woman ready also to talk endlessly about this marvelous plant. I listen briefly to humor my father but am relieved that the saleswoman is oblivious of his enthusiasm.

"*Mira todos los mexicanitos,*" he says, noticing the faces that resemble his own, the sound of Spanish.

"*Buenos días,*" a woman calls out to us.

"*Buenos días,*" I answer for us both. "*Cómo está señora?*"

"*Trabajando para mantener esta familiota grande que tengo. Esto nunca se acaba,*" she says, stating what my father understood to well, the constant need to work to support a large family.

"*You* did it, Daddy," I say, "supported the four of us, and Mother, grandmother and my aunt."

"No big deal," he says. "I liked it." And he begins examining the multicolored chiles, orange, green, yellow, red; the jalapeño, torito, serrano. He wants to buy some, knowing his purchases always drive my mother crazy. He laughs at his ability "to get her goat" after fifty-four years.

"I'll tell her that I'll show her how to cook," he says, and I laugh with him at my mother's predictable flaring at that phrase.

Our walk is sweet sorrow. The big man, that buffer between the world and me, has vanished. He was a gentle man who never lifted a hand except to help a person up, and yet who always talked of being ready to knock out any threat or intruder. As a boy, he sold newspapers and learned to sneak into boxing matches free by carrying his papers under one arm, saying "Press" casually when he walked by the ticket taker. What did they think of that dark-skinned boy out alone at night, sitting on his papers to be able to watch his gloved heroes?

He boxed a little when he was young, but his delight in watching "the fights" didn't end until his mind got lost in that labyrinth of words and memories. He admired the clever and powerful fighter and prided himself on being ever ready to take on anyone, even in his seventies. "Just let me at them," he would say of invisible muggers or thieves, and many a time my mother had to shake him awake since he was swinging punches in his dreams. He was a bull of a man, a gentle bull, but with a bull's heart.

I hear Spanish at another stand and my father follows me to eavesdrop. A couple in their late sixties, who could be my father's relatives from their facial features, are chatting with a couple from Spain, comparing growing seasons and harvests. The California grower boasts, "*Cinco cosechas al año,*" five harvests a year. We smile to hear the global aspect of his work with the soil.

"*Semillas de Amsterdam,*" he says with pride, the secret of the delicate carrots he sells, seeds from Amsterdam.

My father and I walk toward the apartment where he and my mother have lived for the last thirty years. Music is in the air, swirling up from a sax.

"*Fijate, fijate en el pie,*" my father says as always, insistently wanting me to notice something, this time the tapping of a black man's foot as he plays. My father always loved music, dancing, rhythm. We both hear the unsung phrase, "Don't come around much anymore," which says it all — my fear that his voice, my father's voice inside me, will also fade, that I will cease to hear his sound, his words, his faith in me and his admonishings, his urgings to me, "*fijate, fijate,*" notice, notice.

SONIA SANCHEZ

Sonia Sanchez was born in Birmingham, Alabama, in 1934. She moved to New York at the age of nine and was educated at Hunter College (B.A.) and New York University, where she studied with Louise Bogan. While she taught at San Francisco State University, Sanchez played a significant role in establishing the first black studies program in the country. She is the author of thirteen books. Her collection Homegirls and Handgrenades *(1984) won the American Book Award in 1985. She has received awards from the National Endowment for the Arts and from the Pennsylvania Coalition of 100 Black Women. Sonia Sanchez has also received the Governor's Award for Excellence in the Humanities (1988), the Peace and Freedom Award for Excellence in the Humanities (1968), and the Peace and Freedom Award from the Women's International League (1988). She holds the Laura Carnell Chair in English at Temple University.*

Sonia Sanchez's "Dear Mama" is from Under a Soprano Sky, *published by Africa World Press in 1989. In a Christmas letter, the author expresses her deepest feelings to her mother, who died when she was six. She lets her mother know that "My first real poem was about you Mama and death." She acknowledges the strength, music, and being that connect her to her mother and a "long line of Black people holding each other up against silence."*

Dear Mama

It is Christmas eve and the year is passing away with calloused feet. My father, your son, and I decorate the night with words. Sit ceremoniously in human song. Watch our blue sapphire words eclipse the night. We have come to this simplicity from afar.

He stirs, pulls from his pocket a faded picture of you. Black-woman. Sitting in frigid peace. All of your biography preserved in your face. And my eyes draw up short as he says, "her name was Elizabeth but we used to call her Lizzie." And I hold your picture in my hands. But I know your name by heart. It's Mama. I hold you in my hands and let time pass over my face: "Let my baby be. She ain't like the others. She rough. She'll stumble on gentleness later on."

Ah Mama. Gentleness ain't never been no stranger to my genes. But I did like the roughness of running and swallowing the wind, diving in rivers I could barely swim, jumping from second story windows into a saving backyard bush. I did love you for loving me so hard until I slid inside your veins and sailed your blood to an uncrucified shore.

And I remember Saturday afternoons at our house. The old sister deaconesses sitting in sacred pain. Black cadavers burning with lost aromas. And I crawled behind the couch and listened to breaths I had never breathed. Tasted their enormous martyrdom. Lives spent on so many things. Heard their laughter at Sister Smith's latest performance in church — her purse sailing toward Brother Thomas's head again. And I hugged the laughter round my knees. Draped it round my shoulder like a Spanish shawl.

And history began once again. I received it and let it circulate in my blood. I learned on those Saturday afternoons about women rooted in themselves, raising themselves in dark America, discharging their pain without ever stopping. I learned about women fighting men back when they hit them: "Don't never let no mens hit you mo than once girl." I learned about "womens waking up they mens" in the night with pans of hot grease and the compromises reached after the smell of hot grease had penetrated their sleepy brains. I learned about loose women walking their abandoned walk down front in church, crossing their legs instead of their hands to God. And I crept into my eyes. Alone with my daydreams of being woman. Adult. Powerful. Loving. Like them. Allowing nobody to rule me if I didn't want to be.

And when they left. When those old bodies had gathered up their sovereign smells. After they had kissed and packed up beans snapped and cakes cooked and laughter bagged. After they had called out their last goodbyes, I crawled out of my place. Surveyed the room. Then walked over to the couch where some had sat for hours and bent my head and smelled their evening smells. I screamed out loud, "oooweeee! Ain't that stinky!" and I laughed laughter from a thousand corridors. And you turned Mama, closed the door, chased me round the room until I crawled into a corner where your large body could not reach me. But your laughter pierced the little alcove where I sat laughing at the night. And your humming sprinkled my small space. Your humming about your Jesus and how one day he was gonna take you home . . .

Because you died when I was six Mama, I never laughed like that again. Because you died without warning Mama, my sister and I moved from family to stepmother to friend of the family. I never felt your warmth again.

But I knew corners and alcoves and closets where I was pushed when some mad woman went out of control. Where I sat for days while some woman raved in rhymes about unwanted children. And work. And not enough money. Or love. And I sat out my childhood with stutters and poems gathered in my head like some winter storm. And the poems erased the stutters and pain. And the words loved me and I loved them in return.

My first real poem was about you Mama and death. My first real poem recited an alphabet of spit splattering a white bus driver's face after he tried to push cousin Lucille off a bus and she left Birmingham under the cover of darkness. Forever. My first real poem was about your Charleswhite arms holding me up against death.

My life flows from you Mama. My style comes from a long line of Louises who picked me up in the night to keep me from wetting the bed. A long line of Sarahs who fed me and my sister and fourteen other children from watery soups and beans and a lot of imagination. A long line of Lizzies who made me understand love. Sharing. Holding a child up to the stars. Holding your tribe in a grip of love. A long line of Black people holding each other up against silence.

I still hear your humming Mama. The color of your song calls me home. The color of your words saying, "Let her be. She got a right to be different. She gonna stumble on herself one of these days. Just let the child be."

And I be, Mama.

◎ *WENDY WASSERSTEIN*

Wendy Wasserstein was born in 1950 in Brooklyn, New York. She received a B.A. from Mt. Holyoke College, an M.A. from City College in New York, and an M.F.A. from Yale University. While a student at Yale Drama School, she wrote her first off-Broadway play, Uncommon Women and Others *(1977). Wasserstein is the author of nine plays, including* Isn't It Romantic *(1981),* Tender Offer *(1983), and* The Heidi Chronicles *(1988), which was awarded the Pulitzer Price for drama. She has also written screenplays for television.*

Tender Offer *is published in an issue of Daniel Halpern's journal* Antaeus *devoted to one-act plays. The volume celebrates "the play as an act of 'recorded' literature . . . to be read at leisure."* Tender Offer *was first produced off-off-Broadway at the Ensemble Studio Theatre in 1983. Wasserstein, who told the* New York Times *that in her college years "I always thought in terms of getting by on being funny," here provides a poignant glimpse of a father-daughter relationship.*

Tender Offer

[*A girl of around nine is alone in a dance studio. She is dressed in traditional leotards and tights. She begins singing to herself, "Nothing Could Be Finer Than to Be in Carolina." She maps out a dance routine, including parts for the chorus. She builds to a finale. A man, Paul, around thirty-five, walks in. He has a sweet, though distant, demeanor. As he walks in, Lisa notices him and stops.*]

PAUL: You don't have to stop, sweetheart.

LISA: That's okay.

PAUL: Looked very good.

LISA: Thanks.

PAUL: Don't I get a kiss hello?

LISA: Sure.

PAUL: [*Embraces her.*] Hi, Tiger.

LISA: Hi, Dad.

PAUL: I'm sorry I'm late.

LISA: That's okay.

PAUL: How'd it go?

LISA: Good.

PAUL: Just good?

LISA: Pretty good.

PAUL: "Pretty good." You mean you got a lot of applause or "pretty good" you could have done better.

LISA: Well, Courtney Palumbo's mother thought I was pretty good. But you know the part in the middle when everybody's supposed to freeze and the big girl comes out. Well, I think I moved a little bit.

PAUL: I thought what you were doing looked very good.

LISA: Daddy, that's not what I was doing. That was tap-dancing. I made that up.

PAUL: Oh. Well it looked good. Kind of sexy.

LISA: Yuch!

PAUL: What do you mean "yuch"?

LISA: Just yuch!

PAUL: You don't want to be sexy?

LISA: I don't care.

PAUL: Let's go, Tiger. I promised your mother I'd get you home in time for dinner.

LISA: I can't find my leg warmers.

PAUL: You can't find your what?

LISA: Leg warmers. I can't go home till I find my leg warmers.

PAUL: I don't see you looking for them.

LISA: I was waiting for you.

PAUL: Oh.

LISA: Daddy.

PAUL: What?

LISA: Nothing.

PAUL: Where do you think you left them?

LISA: Somewhere around here. I can't remember.

PAUL: Well, try to remember, Lisa. We don't have all night.

LISA: I told you. I think somewhere around here.

PAUL: I don't see them. Let's go home now. You'll call the dancing school tomorrow.

LISA: Daddy, I can't go home till I find them. Miss Judy says it's not professional to leave things.

PAUL: Who's Miss Judy?

LISA: She's my ballet teacher. She once danced the lead in *Swan Lake,* and she was a June Taylor dancer.

PAUL: Well, then, I'm sure she'll understand about the leg warmers.

LISA: Daddy, Miss Judy wanted to know why you were late today.

PAUL: Hmmmmmmmm?

LISA: Why were you late?

PAUL: I was in a meeting. Business. I'm sorry.

LISA: Why did you tell Mommy you'd come instead of her if you knew you had business?

PAUL: Honey, something just came up. I thought I'd be able to be here. I was looking forward to it.

LISA: I wish you wouldn't make appointments to see me.

PAUL: Hmmmmmmm.

LISA: You shouldn't make appointments to see me unless you know you're going to come.

PAUL: Of course I'm going to come.

LISA: No, you're not. Talia Robbins told me she's much happier living without her father in the house. Her father used to come home late and go to sleep early.

PAUL: Lisa, stop it. Let's go.

LISA: I can't find my leg warmers.

PAUL: Forget your leg warmers.

LISA: Daddy.

PAUL: What is it?

LISA: I saw this show on television, I think it was WPIX Channel 11. Well, the father was crying about his daughter.

PAUL: Why was he crying? Was she sick?

LISA: No. She was at school. And he was at business. And he just missed her, so he started to cry.

PAUL: What was the name of this show?

LISA: I don't know. I came in in the middle.

PAUL: Well, Lisa, I certainly would cry if you were sick or far away, but I know that you're well and you're home. So no reason to get maudlin.

LISA: What's maudlin?

PAUL: Sentimental, soppy. Frequently used by children who make things up to get attention.

LISA: I am sick! I am sick! I have Hodgkin's disease and a bad itch on my leg.

PAUL: What do you mean you have Hodgkin's disease? Don't say things like that.

LISA: Swoosie Kurtz, she had Hodgkin's disease on a TV movie last year, but she got better and now she's on *Love Sidney.*

PAUL: Who is Swoosie Kurtz?

LISA: She's an actress named after an airplane. I saw her on *Live at Five.*

PAUL: You watch too much television; you should do your homework. Now, put your coat on.

LISA: Daddy, I really do have a bad itch on my leg. Would you scratch it?

PAUL: Lisa, you're procrastinating.

LISA: Why do you use words I don't understand? I hate it. You're like Daria Feldman's mother. She always talks in Yiddish to her husband so Daria won't understand.

PAUL: Procrastinating is not Yiddish.

LISA: Well, I don't know what it is.

PAUL: Procrastinating means you don't want to go about your business.

LISA: I don't go to business. I go to school.

PAUL: What I mean is you want to hang around here until you and I are late for dinner and your mother's angry and it's too late for you to do your homework.

LISA: I do not.

PAUL: Well, it sure looks that way. Now put your coat on and let's go.

LISA: Daddy.

PAUL: Honey, I'm tired. Really, later.

LISA: Why don't you want to talk to me?

PAUL: I do want to talk to you. I promise when we get home we'll have a nice talk.

LISA: No, we won't. You'll read the paper and fall asleep in front of the news.

PAUL: Honey, we'll talk on the weekend, I promise. Aren't I taking you to the theater this weekend? Let me look. [*He takes out appointment book.*] Yes. Sunday. *Joseph and the Amazing Technicolor Raincoat* with Lisa. Okay, Tiger?

LISA: Sure. It's Dreamcoat.

PAUL: What?

LISA: Nothing. I think I see my leg warmers. [*She goes to pick them up, and an odd-looking trophy.*]

PAUL: What's that?

LISA: It's stupid. I was second best at the dance recital, so they gave me this thing. It's stupid.

PAUL: Lisa.

LISA: What?

PAUL: What did you want to talk about?

LISA: Nothing.

PAUL: Was it about my missing your recital? I'm really sorry, Tiger. I would have liked to have been here.

LISA: That's okay.

PAUL: Honest?

LISA: Daddy, you're procrastinating.

PAUL: I'm procrastinating. Sit down. Let's talk. So. How's school?

LISA: Fine.

PAUL: You like it?

LISA: Yup.

PAUL: You looking forward to camp this summer?

LISA: Yup.

PAUL: Is Daria Feldman going back?

LISA: Nope.

PAUL: Why not?

LISA: I don't know. We can go home now. Honest, my foot doesn't itch anymore.

PAUL: Lisa, you know what you do in business when it seems like there's nothing left to say? That's when you really start talking. Put a bid on the table.

LISA: What's a bid?

PAUL: You tell me what you want and I'll tell you what I've got to offer. Like Monopoly. You want Boardwalk, but I'm only willing to give you the Railroads. Now, because you are my daughter I'd throw in Water Works and Electricity. Understand, Tiger?

LISA: No. I don't like board games. You know, Daddy, we could get Space Invaders for our home for thirty-five dollars. In fact, we could get an Osborne System for two thousand. Daria Feldman's parents . . .

PAUL: Daria Feldman's parents refuse to talk to Daria, so they bought a computer to keep Daria busy so they won't have to speak in Yiddish. Daria will probably grow up to be a homicidal maniac lesbian prostitute.

LISA: I know what that word prostitute means.

PAUL: Good. [*Pause.*] You still haven't told me about school. Do you still like your teacher?

LISA: She's okay.

PAUL: Lisa, if we're talking try to answer me.

LISA: I am answering you. Can we go home now, please?

PAUL: Damn it, Lisa, if you want to talk to me . . . Talk to me!

LISA: I can't wait till I'm old enough so I can make my own money and never have to see you again. Maybe I'll become a prostitute.

PAUL: Young lady, that's enough.

LISA: I hate you, Daddy! I hate you! [*She throws her trophy into the trash bin.*]

PAUL: What'd you do that for?

LISA: It's stupid.

PAUL: Maybe I wanted it.

LISA: What for?

PAUL: Maybe I wanted to put it where I keep your dinosaur and the picture you made of Mrs. Kimbel with the chicken pox.

LISA: You got mad at me when I made that picture. You told me I had to respect Mrs. Kimbel because she was my teacher.

PAUL: That's true. But she wasn't my teacher. I liked her better with the chicken pox. [*Pause.*] Lisa, I'm sorry. I was very wrong to miss your recital, and you don't have to become a prostitute. That's not the type of profession Miss Judy has in mind for you.

LISA: [*Mumbles.*] No.

PAUL: No. [*Pause.*] So Talia Robbins is really happy her father moved out?

LISA: Talia Robbins picks open the eighth-grade lockers during gym period. But she did that before her father moved out.

PAUL: You can't always judge someone by what they do or what they don't do. Sometimes you come home from dancing school and run upstairs and shut the door, and when I finally get to talk to you, everything is "okay" or "fine." Yup or nope?

LISA: Yup.

PAUL: Sometimes, a lot of times, I come home and fall asleep in front of the television. So you and I spend a lot of time being a little scared of each other. Maybe?

LISA: Maybe.

PAUL: Tell you what. I'll make you a tender offer.

LISA: What?

PAUL: I'll make you a tender offer. That's when one company publishes in the newspaper that they want to buy another company. And the company that publishes is called the Black Knight because they want to gobble up the poor little company. So the poor little company needs to be rescued. And then a White Knight comes along and makes a bigger and better offer so the shareholders won't have to tender shares to the Big Black Knight. You with me?

LISA: Sort of.

PAUL: I'll make you a tender offer like the White Knight. But I don't want to own you. I just want to make a much better offer. Okay?

LISA: [*Sort of understanding.*] Okay. [*Pause. They sit for a moment.*] Sort of, Daddy, what do you think about? I mean, like when you're quiet what do you think about?

PAUL: Oh, business usually. If I think I made a mistake or if I think I'm doing okay. Sometimes I think about what I'll be doing five years from now and if it's what I hoped it would be five years ago. Sometimes I think about what your life will be like, if Mount Saint Helen's will erupt again. What you'll become if you'll study penmanship or word processing. If you speak kindly of me to your psychiatrist when you are in graduate school. And how the hell I'll pay for your graduate school. And sometimes I try and think what it was I thought about when I was your age.

LISA: Do you ever look out your window at the clouds and try to see which kinds of shapes they are? Like one time, honest, I saw the head of Walter Cronkite in a flower vase. Really! Like look don't those kinda look like if you turn it upside down, two big elbows or two elephant trunks dancing?

PAUL: Actually still looks like Walter Cronkite in a flower vase to me. But look up a little. See the one that's still moving? That sorta looks like a whale on a thimble.

LISA: Where?

PAUL: Look up. To your right.

LISA: I don't see it. Where?

PAUL: The other way.

LISA: Oh, yeah! There's the head and there's the stomach. Yeah! [*Lisa picks up her trophy.*] Hey, Daddy.

PAUL: Hey, Lisa.

LISA: You can have this thing if you want it. But you have to put it like this, because if you put it like that it is gross.

PAUL: You know what I'd like? So I can tell people who come into my office why I have this gross stupid thing on my shelf, I'd like it if you could show me your dance recital.

LISA: Now?

PAUL: We've got time. Mother said she won't be home till late.

LISA: Well, Daddy, during a lot of it I freeze and the big girl in front dances.

PAUL: Well, how 'bout the number you were doing when I walked in?

LISA: Well, see, I have parts for a lot of people in that one, too.

PAUL: I'll dance the other parts.

LISA: You can't dance.

PAUL: Young lady, I played Yvette Mimimeux in a *Hasty Pudding Show.*

LISA: Who's Yvette Mimimeux?

PAUL: Watch more television. You'll find out. [*Paul stands up.*] So I'm ready. [*He begins singing.*] "Nothing could be finer than to be in Carolina."

LISA: Now I go. In the morning. And now you go. Dum-da.

PAUL: [*Obviously not a tap dancer.*] Da-da-dum.

LISA: [*Whines.*] Daddy!

PAUL: [*Mimics her.*] Lisa! Nothing could be finer . . .

LISA: That looks dumb.

PAUL: Oh, yeah? You think they do this better in *The Amazing Minkcoat?* No way! Now you go — da da da dum.

LISA: Da da da dum.

PAUL: If I had Aladdin's lamp for only a day, I'd make a wish. . . .

LISA: Daddy, that's maudlin!

PAUL: I know it's maudlin. And here's what I'd say:

LISA and PAUL: I'd say that "nothing could be finer than to be in Carolina in the mooooooooooornin.' "

◎ *LUCILLE CLIFTON*

Lucille Clifton was born in 1936 in Depew, New York, and was educated at Fredonia State College and Howard University. Clifton's first works were published in 1969 when she was the mother of six children all under the age of ten. A prolific poet, children's author, and screenplay writer, she has twice been nominated for a Pulitzer Prize, and she won an Emmy Award from the American Academy of Television Arts and Sciences. In 1992, she won the Shelley Memorial Award from the Poetry Society of America. Her latest volume of poems is Book of Light *(1993). Clifton is the former poet laureate of Maryland and is now distinguished professor of humanities at St. Mary's College in Maryland.*

"daughters" is the third poem in the opening section of Lucille Clifton's The Book of Light, *titled "reflection." These are spare and luminous poems tracing connections between generations, between men and women, among members of the black community, past and present. "daughters" specifically celebrates the lineage of magical, powerful women in Clifton's family. This poem is addressed to the spirit of Clifton's great-grandmother, whose "oddness" influences even the "gaudy girls" who are their descendants.*

daughters

woman who shines at the head
of my grandmother's bed,
brilliant woman, i like to think
you whispered into her ear
instructions. i like to think
you are the oddness in us,
you are the arrow
that pierced our plain skin
and made us fancy women;
my wild witch gran, my magic mama,
and even these gaudy girls.
i like to think you gave us
extraordinary power and to
protect us, you become the name
we were cautioned to forget.
it is enough,
you must have murmured,
to remember that i was
and that you are. woman, i am
lucille, which stands for light,
daughter of thelma, daughter
of georgia, daughter of
dazzling you.

◎ *TOI DERRICOTTE*

Toi Derricotte was born in 1941 in Detroit, Michigan. She received a B.A. from Wayne State University and an M.A. from New York University. Her work has been recognized with grants from the National Endowment for the Arts (1985 and 1990) and with the Lucille Medwick Memorial Award from the Poetry Society of America (1985). She is a teacher and professor of creative writing and minority literature, and she has been the featured poet in readings at more than one hundred theaters, museums, bookstores, and libraries. Derricotte has published three volumes of poetry, most recently Captivity, *published in 1989.*

"Touching/Not Touching: My Mother" is from Derricotte's most recent book of poetry, Captivity. *The title's slash mark reveals the poem's tension: how close can we come to those we love? After childbirth, after growing into adulthood, the speaker confronts her mother as an equal, and yet still as a child.*

Touching / Not Touching: My Mother

I

That first night in the hotel bedroom,
when the lights go out,
she is already sleeping (that woman who has always
claimed sleeplessness), inside her quiet breathing
like a long red gown. How can she
sleep? My heart beats as if I am alone,
for the first time, with a lover or a beast.
Will I hate her drooping mouth,
her old woman rattle? Once I nearly
suffocated on her breast. Now I can almost
touch the other side of my life.

II

Undressing
in the dark,
looking,
not looking,
we parade before each other,
old proud peacocks, in our stretch marks
with hanging butts. We are equals. No
more do I need to wear her high heels to step
inside the body of a woman.
Her beauty and strangeness no longer seduce
me out of myself. I show my good side, my
long back, strong mean legs, my thinness that
came from learning to hold back
from taking what's not mine. No more
a thief for love. She takes off her
bra, facing me, and I see those gorgeous
globes, soft, creamy,
high; my mouth waters.
how will I resist
crawling in beside her, putting
my hand for warmth under
her thin night dress?

◎ TESS GALLAGHER

Tess Gallagher was born in 1943. A poet, short story writer, and essayist, she lives and writes in Sky House, the house she designed and built in her birthplace, Port Angeles, Washington. She received a B.A. and an M.A. from the University of Washington, and an M.F.A. from the University of Iowa. Gallagher's most recent books of poetry are Portable Kisses Expanded *(1994),* My Black Horse: New and Selected Poems *(1995), and* Portable Kisses *(1996, Great Britain). Her translation of the Romanian poet Liliana Ursu's* The Sky Behind the Forest, *with the author and Adam Sorkin, will be published in 1996. She is working on short stories to be published in 1997. Gallagher wrote the introduction to* All of Us: The Collected Poems of Raymond Carver, *to be released in Great Britain later this year. Her other books include the poetry* Moon Crossing Bridge *(1992),* Amplitude: New and Selected Poems *(1987),* Under Stars *(1978), and* Instructions to the Double *(1976, reprint 1994); the short stories* The Lover of Horses *(1992); and her collected essays,* A Concert of Tenses *(1986). Tess Gallagher holds the Edward F. Arnold Visiting Professor of English at Whitman College during 1996–1997.*

"Each Bird Walking" is from Gallagher's Amplitude: New and Selected Poems. *The author notes that "The poem itself was probably drafted in 1980, from experiences that preceded that date." Though we have included this poem in the section "Family Album," it would also have been appropriate in "Finding Words" and "Transformations," for storytelling is a way of translating loss into meaning.*

Each Bird Walking

Not while, but long after he had told me,
I thought of him, washing his mother, his
bending over the bed and taking back
the covers. There was a basin of water
and he dipped a washrag in and
out of the basin, the rag
dripping a little onto the sheet as he
turned from the bedside to the nightstand
and back, there being no place

on her body he shouldn't touch because
he had to and she helped him, moving
the little she could, lifting so he could
wipe under her arms, a dipping motion
in the hollow. Then working up from

the feet, around the ankles, over the
knees. And this last, opening
her thighs and running the rag firmly
and with the cleaning thought
up through her crotch, between the lips,
over the V of thin hairs —

as though he were a mother
who had the excuse of cleaning to touch
with love and indifference
the secret parts of her child, to graze
the sleepy sexlessness in its waiting
to find out what to do for the sake
of the body, for the sake of what only
the body can do for itself.

So his hand, softly at the place
of his birth-light. And she, eyes deepened
and closed in the dim room.
And because he told me her death as
important to his being with her,
I could love him another way. Not
of the body alone, or of its making,
but carried in the white spires of trembling
until what spirit, what breath we were
was shaken from us. Small then,
the word *holy*.

He turned her on her stomach
and washed the blades of her shoulders, the
small of her back. "That's good," she said,
"that's enough."

On our lips that morning, the tart juice
of the mothers, so strong in remembrance, no
asking, no giving, and what you said, this
being the end of our loving, so as not to hurt
the closer one to you, made me look
to see what was left of us
with our sex taken away. "Tell me," I said,
"something I can't forget." Then the story of
your mother, and when you finished
I said, "That's good, that's enough."

◎ LINDA HOGAN

Linda Hogan was born in Denver, Colorado, in 1947 and is a member of the Chickasaw Nation. A graduate of the University of Colorado, she has published six books of poetry, including Seeing Through the Sun, *which won the 1986 American Book Award,* Savings *(1988), and* The Book of Medicines *(1993). She is the author of two books of stories,* The Big Woman *(1987) and* That Horse, *1985. Her first novel,* Mean Spirit *(1990), won the Oklahoma Book Award, the Mountains and Plains Booksellers Award, and the Colorado Book Award and was a finalist for both the National Book Critics Circle Award and for the Pulitzer Prize. Her new novel,* Solar Storms *(1995), has also met with critical acclaim. The recipient of many grants and awards including fellowships from the Guggenheim Foundation, the National Endowment for the Arts, the Minnesota State Arts Board, the Lannon Award, and the Five Civilized Tribes Museum Playwriting Award, Hogan is a professor at the University of Colorado. She has also served on the National Endowment for the Arts poetry panel. Hogan is a dedicated volunteer in wildlife rehabilitation and a writer for* Nature Conservancy.

"Germinal" is the first poem in Hogan's Savings. *It sets the tone for a book that sings the connectedness of all things. The strong two-beat lines ("drumming"; "the older world") emphasize the physicality and the intimacy of the poet's engagement with the earth and drive the poem rhythmically, like a pulse, downward to the roots.*

"Elk Song" is also from Savings. *It is a poem of thanksgiving, of reciprocity, and of kinship with all animals.*

Germinal

Downstairs, things are growing.
Down stairs to the cellar
guinea eggs have quickened
and grapes have turned to wine.
Lye is burning through its tub
near potatoes with pale shoots,
and the molds are dividing
in jellies beneath wax,
that underworld
beneath the house with its bad family,
that world below
drumming
like old women
and blood stirring in the neck,

and her strenuous effort to catch the plane that will enable her to see her father while he is still alive. This poem packed with feeling also helps us to hear idiomatic speech and the rapid tempo of contemporary urban life.

Bathing the New Born

I love with a fearful love to remember the
first baths I gave this boy —
my second child, so my hands knew what to do,
I laid the tiny torso along my
left forearm, nape of the noodle
neck in the crook of my elbow, hips
tiny as a bird's hips against my wrist, and the
thigh the thickness of a thick pencil held
loosely in the loop of my thumb and forefinger, the
sign that means perfect. I'd soap him slowly, the
long thin cold feet, the
scrotum tight and wrinkled as a rosy
shell so new it was flexible yet, the
miniature underweight athlete's chest, the
gummy furze of the scalp. If I got him too
soapy he'd get so slippery he'd
slide in my grip like an armful of white
buttered noodles, but I'd hold him not too tight,
I knew I was so good for him, and I'd
talk to him the whole time, I'd
tell him about his wonderful body
and the wonderful soap, the whole world made of love,
and he'd look up at me, one week old,
his eyes still wide and apprehensive of his
new life. I love that time
when you croon and croon to them, you can see the
calm slowly entering them, you can
feel it in your anchoring hand, the
small necklace of the spine against the
muscle of your forearm, you feel the fear
leaving their bodies, he lay in the blue
oval plastic baby tub and
looked at me in wonder and began to
move his silky limbs at will in the water.

The Race

When I got to the airport I rushed up to the desk
and they told me the flight was cancelled. The doctors had
said my father would not live through the night
and the flight was cancelled. A young man with a
dark blond mustache told me
another airline had a non-stop
leaving in seven minutes — see that
elevator over there well go
down to the first floor, make a right you'll
see a yellow bus, get off at the
second Pan Am terminal — I
ran, I who have no sense of direction
raced exactly where he'd told me, like a fish
slipping upstream deftly against the
flow of the river. I jumped off that bus with my
heavy bags and ran, the bags
wagged me from side to side as if to
prove I was under the claims of the material, I
ran up to a man with a white flower on his breast,
I who always go to the end of the line, I said
Help me. He looked at my ticket, he said make a
left and then a right go up the moving stairs and then
run. I raced up the moving stairs
two at a time, at the top I saw the
long hollow corridor and
then I took a deep breath, I said
goodbye to my body, goodbye to comfort, I
used my legs and heart as if I would
gladly use them up for this, to
touch him again in this life. I ran and the
big heavy dark bags
banged me, wheeled and swam around me like
planets in wild orbits — I have seen
pictures of women running down roads with their
belongings tied in black scarves
grasped in their fists, running under serious
gray historical skies — I blessed my
long legs he gave me, my strong
heart I abandoned to its own purpose, I
ran to Gate 17 and they were
just lifting the thick white

lozenge of the door to fit it into the
socket of the plane. Like the man who is not
too rich, I turned to the side and
slipped through the needle's eye, and then I
walked down the aisle toward my father. The jet was
full and people's hair was shining, they were
smiling, the interior of the plane was filled with a
mist of gold endorphin light,
I wept as people weep when they enter heaven,
in massive relief. We lifted up
gently from one tip of the continent and
did not stop until we set down lightly on the
other edge, I walked into his room and
watched his chest rise slowly and
sink again, all night
I watched him breathe.

◎ *MINNIE BRUCE PRATT*

Minnie Bruce Pratt was born in Selma, Alabama, in 1946. She received a B.A. from the University of Alabama with honors in English and a Ph.D. from the University of North Carolina at Chapel Hill. Pratt began to write when her ten-year marriage ended in a fight to retain custody of her two sons. She is the founding member of LIPS, a lesbian-feminist action group. Pratt has published three volumes of poetry: Sound of One Fork *(1981),* Crime Against Nature *(1990) and* We Say We Love Each Other *(1992). Among numerous national awards, she has been the recipient of the Lamont Poetry Award. She teaches at George Washington University and the University of Maryland at College Park.*

"Down the Little Cahaba," from Crime Against Nature, *reflects on the struggles that lesbian women face in a homophobic culture. In this case the poet deals with the loss of custody of her children.*

Down the Little Cahaba

Soundless sun, the river.   Home in August
we float down the Little Cahaba, the three of us,
rubber inner tubes, hot laps, in water so slow
we hear the rapids moving upstream toward us,
the whispers coming loud.   Then the river bends,

the standing water at the lip, hover, hover,
the moment before orgasm, before the head emerges,
then over suddenly, and sound rushing
back from my ears.   The youngest caught in the rapids:
half-grown, he hasn't lived with me in years,
yet his head submerged at a scrape of rock pushes
pain through me, a streak inside my thighs,
vagina to knee.   Swept to the outside curve,
the boys climb upstream to plunge down again.

I stand at the mud bank to pick up
shells, river mussels with iridescent inner skin,
with riverine scars from once-close flesh.

Years back, at the beach, with piles of shells
in our laps, with the first final separation on us,
one asked: *How do we know you won't forget us?*

I told them how they had moved in my womb: each
distinct, the impatient older, the steady younger.
I said: *I can never forget you.   You moved inside me.*

I meant: *The sound of your blood crossed into mine.*

◎ ROCHELLE RATNER

Rochelle Ratner was born in 1948 and grew up in Atlantic City, New Jersey. She is the author of thirteen collections of poetry, the most recent being Someday Songs *(1992). Ratner has also published two novels,* Bobby's Girl *(1986) and* The Lion's Share *(1991). Her critical book on women writers,* Trying to Understand What It Means to Be a Feminist, *was published in 1984. Ratner lives in New York City, where she is executive editor of* American Book Review *and poetry editor of the Zionist/Socialist quarterly* Israel Horizons.

Ratner writes: "'Bentshen Licht' (literally "bless night") was written in the late 1970s, a period during which I was exploring not traditional Judaism, but the imagery I recalled from home and family. The portrait of the woman with a dishtowel over her head is a very clear memory I have of my grandmother: though she wasn't religious, she went to synagogue on the High Holidays and lit candles every Friday. The youthful voice would be my own. The "second soul" is an image from Kabbalah in which man receives a second soul on the Sabbath, but I'm borrowing it here to describe our very special bonding."

Bentshen Licht

A dishtowel
blue at the edges
is draped on her head
but even so
her eyes close

shut the dark in

the fresh linen smell
clears her nostrils

weightless fingers
pause over the flame
to be warmed

Dear Lord
let her not see
till the blessing's over

a youthful voice
under her own
rushes through the words
sing-song

this Sabbath
no longer just a bride
but a mother also

turns to watch her daughter

feels the second soul
        growing away from her.

◎ *CATHY SONG*

Cathy Song was born in Honolulu, Hawaii, in 1955. She received her B.A. from Wellesley College and an M.A. in creative writing from Boston University. She is the author of two books of poems, Picture Bride, *winner of the Yale Series of Younger Poets in 1982, and* Frameless Windows, Squares of Light *(1988). Song's work is strongly influenced by her affinity with visual artists Georgia O'Keeffe and Kitagawa Uta-*

maro, a nineteenth-century Japanese printmaker. There is also an undercurrent of music in all her work, a hint of the melancholy shakuhachi *— a Japanese wind instrument that Song heard in her childhood. She teaches creative writing in mainland universities in Hawaii and has been a role model for new generations of writers there.*

"Picture Bride" is the title poem of Song's award-winning 1982 collection. Opening the first section, "Black Iris," sets the tone for the book — gentle and intimate — as Song tries to imagine her grandmother's journey from Korea to Hawaii as a young "catalogue bride." The lines move gracefully, lightly, spanning cultures and generations. The late Richard Hugo, who chose this book as winner of the Yale series, said of Song's poetry: "She often reminds a loud, indifferent, hard world of what truly matters to the human spirit."

Picture Bride

She was a year younger
than I,
twenty-three when she left Korea.
Did she simply close
the door of her father's house
and walk away. And
was it a long way
through the tailor shops of Pusan
to the wharf where the boat
waited to take her to an island
whose name she had
only recently learned,
on whose shore
a man waited,
turning her photograph
to the light when the lanterns
in the camp outside
Waialua Sugar Mill were lit
and the inside of his room
grew luminous
from the wings of moths
migrating out of the cane stalks?
What things did my grandmother
take with her? And when
she arrived to look
into the face of the stranger
who was her husband,

thirteen years older than she,
did she politely untie
the silk bow of her jacket,
her tent-shaped dress
filling with the dry wind
that blew from the surrounding fields
where the men were burning the cane?

◎ *ELLEN BRYANT VOIGT*

Ellen Bryant Voigt was born in 1943 in Danville, Virginia. Her educational background includes a B.A. from Converse College and an M.F.A. from the University of Iowa. Besides being a writer, Voigt is a professional pianist and a professor and visiting faculty member at Warren Wilson College. Awards for her work include grants from the Vermont Council on the Arts (1974–1975); a grant from the National Endowment for the Arts (1976–1977); and a Guggenheim Foundation fellowship (1978–1979). She also received the Emily Clark Balch award from the Virginia Quarterly Review *in 1987. Voigt has published five books of poetry, including* The Lotus Flowers *(1988),* Two Trees *(1992), and* Kyrie: Poems *(1995). Her most recent book is a collection of essays,* Poets Teaching Poets: Self and World *(1996).*

"Visiting the Graves" first appeared in the literary magazine Ploughshares *and is printed in* The Lotus Flowers. *The ritual activity the poem describes soon tires the speaker's children, weary of "trying / to climb a tree of bones."*

Visiting the Graves

All day we travel from bed to bed, our children
clutching homemade bouquets
of tulips and jonquils, hyacinth,
handfuls of yellow salad from the fields.
In Pittsylvania County our dead face east,
my great-grandfather and his sons facing
what is now a stranger's farm.
One great-uncle chose a separate hill,
an absence in the only photograph.
Under the big oak, we fumble for his name
and the names of sisters scattered like coins.
But here is my father, near the stone

we watched him weep beside for twenty years.
And my mother beside him, the greenest slab of grass.
By horse, it was hours to Franklin County,
to Liberty Christian Church where her mother lies.
The children squabble in the car, roll on the velvet
slope of the churchyard, pout or laugh as we point out
the gap in the mountain where *her* mother's grave
is underwater, the lake lapping the house, the house
still standing like a tooth. We tell them how
we picked huckleberries from the yard,
tell them what a huckleberry is, but the oldest
can't keep straight who's still alive, the smallest
wants her flowers back — who can blame them,
this far from home, tired of trying
to climb a tree of bones. They fall asleep
halfway down the road, and we fall silent, too,
who were taught to remember and return,
my sister is driving, I'm in the back,
the sky before us a broken field of cloud.

INTERVIEW

Imagining a Wider Community: An Interview with Linda Hogan

by Marilyn Kallet

LINDA HOGAN

Marilyn Kallet's interview with Linda Hogan took place on April 7, 1993 at Hogan's hotel, while she was getting ready to leave Knoxville, Tennessee, and go home to Colorado. She had been to Knoxville as part of an NEA Audience Development grant. Since the interview, Hogan's novel Solar Storms *has been published to outstanding reviews. The novel embodies Hogan's concern for the interconnectedness of all beings, a vision expressed here.* *(For more on Hogan, see page 146.)*

MK: You mentioned earlier that taking walks with lots of space surrounding you helps you to think about time. Would you say more about how geography affects your thinking and writing?

LH: We're all affected by place whether we realize it or not. For one thing, all our stories—creation stories, myths, oral traditions—are, in part, about storied land. Stories live in the land. They "take place" in context with all the rest. Our daily lives are linked to place. One of the problems with the dominant culture is that it wants to escape this connection. As Rachel Rosenthal said in a recent performance, people use intellect and science as a tool so they won't have to dirty their hands with matter. For indigenous people, the link between the person and the land is a connecting point, not only with ordinary, daily life, but with the cosmos. It is about relationship. And relationship is the most central part of our lives, our being, not only relationship with other people, but with all things. I believe a lot of neuroses have to do with a lack of healthy relationship with the land, with self, with creation and the creative spirit.

MK: Where is "home" for you?

LH: Home was always, in my heart, Oklahoma. I can feel even now the stillness of the land, the smell of it. But I've lived a long time in Colorado, so I believe it is home too. Especially since I know the stories there, the land, the animals, and the people in our community. But I am thinking that home is larger than this. As the earth has grown smaller and we know its fragility, it is important for us now to expand our view of home to a larger space, a global community, and to think of land, ocean, mountains, desert, as home. And we need to extend our sense of community to include animals and other forms of life.

MK: You write about the power of language. Did you begin your work as a poet, and then move to fiction?

LH: Yes, I did begin as a poet. And I love poetry. It feels like magic.

MK: How and why did you begin to include fiction in your writings?

LH: I had to learn how to write fiction because I had a story to tell that couldn't be told in poetry. I've had to be flexible all along about form—I've had to find a way to do what needs to be done, spoken. That's why I use both fiction and poetry. Poetry is incredible to work on. It's more quiet, more slow, more feeling, more in the world of being than fiction. Fiction is more linear. The writer has to juggle complex intellectual elements such as plot and character development, so fiction didn't—at first—feel as good to work on. But I'm starting to really like it. I also think if you're a poet, that's training for *any* other kind of writing, because with poetry you have to think about language in such a concentrated way.

Working at a university I've made the observation that many student writers write for the sake of writing. They are really writing for other writers, not to tell a necessary story, not out of urgency and need. I have keenly felt that writing must be more than that, that it must have a power to enter the world, to begin to change the stories people live by, to open that story into something larger, into something that helps us know how to live. This means that we have to expand not only our work but our ideas about audience. It wouldn't bother me to have academics reject my work if somebody read it and it changed their attitude about deforestation, for example. I think I began to write out of a desire to make change in the world, searching for language that would help me speak my innermost hopes and ways. Writing was something of a foreign language I learned to be fluent in so that I could communicate emotions and what I knew was important—an ethical way of thinking about the world—communicate what racism is and what it does to people.

MK: When did you start writing?

LH: In my late twenties. I started late.

MK: For many of us who came up in the sixties the issue of how to integrate poetry and politics is important. Can you say more about that?

LH: It's complex. I'm not good at being arrested and put in jail. That's not the way for me. For me, trying to have integrity in my life means writing what I think is essential and important.

MK: Who were your most important teachers?

LH: I don't know that I've had human teachers. My teachers really have been animals and seasons. There have been people I've admired and listened to. But

I've never had a mentor or somebody reading over my words and giving me feedback. I'd love to have that now—but now I'm so old everybody thinks *I* should be doing that!

MK: Who do you like to read?

LH: Marguerite Duras—I found her book *The North China Lover* to be extraordinary in its spareness and its ability to make vivid a particular place, a family, the land and the relationships. Also I love Pablo Neruda, I used to read him all the time. I'm very interested in Latin American writers. I like to read translations. I'm interested in some of the contemporary European writers. Also Meridel Le Sueur is wonderful. She is still, in my view, a consummate artist, one of the best, most important American writers.

Being a creative writer one has to keep reading in all the other fields. It's cross-discipline work. Writers can become too closed in. I've been on panels where people talk about how poetry saves lives. That's such a narrow point of view. Poetry might save the writer's soul or help other people in some way, but it's not bread. It doesn't disarm armies. We become so narrow we forget the larger picture. Reading philosophy, natural history, and natural science is very important to keep us open as writers.

I'm really interested in the work of Vicki Hearne, who wrote *Adam's Task*. And there's Linda Tellington-Jones in New Mexico, who has started a new way of working with horses which is gentle. Several years ago I used to go out to a ranch in Parker, Colorado, where an ex-jockey—a very tough woman—and an ex-rodeo clown were working with a gentle technique of dealing with horses. It was so effective it made me wonder why it took so long to use this method. You could see the horses breathe a sigh of relief! Of course back in the old days they used to beat them with two-by-fours to get them to do what they wanted. A horse really was broken, literally. Was it Kundera who said our worst human failings show in the horrifying way we treat animals?

MK: Would you tell us about the script you worked on last year?

LH: I worked on a script for Turner Broadcasting. Scott Momaday really liked *Mean Spirit*, and he recommended me for this production. It was an interesting project. My section of the work concerned certain historical events from 1492 to 1900. I wrote a narrative, which afterward was changed so much that it didn't seem like my work. I found that painful, since they added pages and pages on Pocahontas and John Smith which I hadn't written. They cut some of what was political and changed it from a narrative about history to first-person — people speaking about "I" as Indian, "you" as non-Indian — which separates people enough to keep change from happening. And I now hear they've gone to another production company altogether, so I'm trying to get my work back. But in terms of the writing it was a great experience for me to work on something that covered that much material. I had to do a lot of research. I had a researcher, and we worked together really well. Looking at what happened in that 500 years on this continent and writing it all at once over last summer I realized the *immensity* of what happened. After initial contact every tribe averaged 90 percent loss of population, often more. The 10 percent who were left had to deal with the violence against them, epidemics, and politics designed to starve them. I hadn't really understood how *purposeful* the Americans were in trying to eradicate Indian people, in their genocide.

MK: What will become of the script?

LH: It was supposed to be aired this year in November. However the man at the production company, Don Olmeyer, got a job heading NBC. Then the script went back into the Turner pool. I'm hoping that the change to yet another production company will be an advantage and allow me to change the script back to the way I wrote it. It's a three-part TV series.

MK: What new work are you comfortable talking about?

LH: I have a new book of poems just out, *The Book of Medicines.* I'm working on a new novel. I'm also working on an article for an anthology to be put out by the Nature Conservancy called *The Last Great Places* anthology. To me it's a dream come true that I would get to write for *Nature Conservancy.* I would love to do the kind of work where you travel and look at what's going on with the land and the animals and then write about it.

The novel I'm working on is set in the North and is partly about adoption and partly about the James Bay development project, Hydro-Quebec. The novel focuses on adoption because it has been such a significant factor in Indian communities. In the middle 1960s nearly every child born in Pine Ridge was removed from their mother and family. In 1978, when the American Indian Religious Freedom Act was passed, the Indian Child Welfare Act was also passed. This permitted native parents to keep children and specified that Indian foster families were needed for those the parents could not care for. Because of the large number of children lost from their communities, I wanted to write about what happens when a person returns, to find out who they came from. I am an adoptive mother, and wanted to write about the issues on this subject, the needs of children, the pain.

As to the James Bay part of the book, this project is so unbelievable in its conception that I felt it had to be addressed. Hydro-Quebec has drowned rivers, diverted rivers, destroyed land, and has been changing the salinity in Hudson Bay and James Bay. The Beluga whales are nearly extinct. Rotting vegetation has released mercury into the environment so the people are becoming ill, the fish are poisoned. It affects an area as large as the state of California. It's unthinkable. It's displacing people who have lived there for longer than ten thousand years. It has destroyed the habitat for migrating birds. It has killed at least one herd of ten thousand caribou. These kinds of crimes can't be permitted any longer, and I see fiction as a way of calling attention to them. Not only that, but I think protest and legal actions lack the emotions, the feelings of the people, and story is a way to touch the heart. It often carries a weight that the grey language of law lacks.

MK: You mentioned that you were having a hard time with it. Why?

LH: Yes, I am having a hard time with it. Because it is so important to me. Because I had a failed adoption and still have the pain of that experience, the writing brings me face to face with the pain. And because I feel the urgency of writing about James Bay. On a more superficial level, I simply have less time than I need to write. This seems true of women my age group, we have overworked, we are tired, too much is asked of us, and we have been kind enough to try to give what has been asked.

MK: What's a work day like for you at home?

LH: I like to begin the day with writing, when my mind is fresh. I overdose on caffeine and then get down to work on a good writing day. But I also have much office work. Writing becomes a business. I often spend five hours a day working on nonwriting chores associated with writing. Given the best of writing days, I work until lunch, go for a walk, then work a few more hours in the afternoon.

The exciting thing about writing is how it happens, how a story takes on life, begins to move in its own direction, surprises the writer with its growing. When it's working, time passes quickly, the characters speak inside your inner ear, the scenes are there just needing words. When it's working, the story shows you a new way to live, it offers a writer wisdom one would never have without it.

Histories

Histories

◎ ◎ ◎

LITERATURE CAN GIVE LIFE TO THOSE collective memories we term *history* and *culture*, embodying tradition and the present in characters who enable us to see ourselves and others more clearly. In the following selections women writers tell us how they and their people have lived, suffered, and survived to pass on their stories. "Remember the things they told us," Luci Tapahonso reminds us, for in the voices of the ancestors there are lessons.

Walking between cultures is a fact of life for the writers included here. Most of the following selections depict a meeting between or a collision of cultures. Several bear witness to abuses of power, to crimes committed by one culture against another. Our collective memories depend on writers to narrate or sing our histories in a way that holds meaning for us.

Elizabeth Cook-Lynn's story "A Visit from Reverend Tileston" opens with a portrait of the quiet dignity of *the People*, an extended family of Dakotapi (Dakota) living in the bend of the Missouri River in 1935. Juxtaposed against the silent hard work of the adults and the laughing of the children comes the Reverend Tileston and his flock of smiling do-gooders. The women of the Family are willing to bend down and pray with him until his histrionics ruin their day's work — then his part in their story is over.

In Sharon Niederman's "A Gift for Languages," Dr. de la Torre, a professor of comparative literature, has spent her adult life trying to escape from her family, especially her Yiddish grandmother. In her stylishness and her career achievements she seems to have made the break. But a death brings out grief that takes her back to ancient Jewish ritual.

In Tillie Olsen's "O Yes," told in the rhythms of gospel, of poetry, we hear a familiar story: children of different races may play together, but as they grow older cultural and class divisions become pernicious. Healing does not occur between the two girls, Carol and Parialee. On the contrary, their junior high school crowds "sort them out," entrenching race and class differences.

The excerpt from Toni Morrison's *Beloved* gives us the account of the birth of Denver, the child of Sethe, a runaway slave. Denver tells this story to Beloved and to the reader with a voice committed to the adventure of freedom and storytelling.

"The Shawl" by Cynthia Ozick tears at us, its characters are so vulnerable. We learn how Rosa's breast dries up in the concentration camp, how her shawl protects the infant Magda, and how it becomes a tattered reminder of loss, a comforter where no comfort can be found.

The essays in this section deepen our understanding of many cultures in America. Amy Ling's personal essay depicts immigration from a child's point of view. Arriving in New York Harbor in 1945, her little brother asks, "Whose America is it? Theirs or ours?" Though Amy Ling has experienced being an outsider, her scholarship on Asian-American writers has widened the scope of literature.

Adrienne Rich's essay "History stops for no one" is both an introduction to the work of Irena Klepfisz and a meditation on multicultural aesthetics. Rich asserts that "the relationship to more than one culture, nonassimilating in spirit and therefore living amid contradictions, is a constant act of self-creation." Klepfisz's work deserves our attention as a "paradigm of this poetry of cultural re-creation." As a child, Klepfisz escaped the Nazis by fleeing Poland with her mother. She lost her home, her culture, and the possibility of a future writing Yiddish literature. "Beginning with almost total loss," Rich tells us, Klepfisz has had to re-create herself "as Jew, woman, and writer."

For Luci Tapahonso, Navajo tradition provides vitality and stability. Her "The Kaw River Rushes Westward" is a reflection on Navajo attitudes toward language and culture. English and Navajo are proudly interwoven in her family life and in her work. Poetry, storytelling, song, and prayer are at the heart of her culture.

Momoko Iko's play *Gold Watch* breaks the silences surrounding the internment of the Japanese living in America in 1942. The play helps us to understand the personal impact of this event — the internment of 120,000 people — by dramatizing the terrible effects of removal on an ordinary family in the Pacific Northwest.

In Lucille Clifton's work humor helps to relieve the tensions brought about by cultural differences. Her poem "them and us" pokes fun at the mainstream nostalgia for Elvis. White people may hold to the myth that talent can persuade death to give way; African Americans are less naive.

The subject of slavery becomes personal and vivid in Patricia Clark's "Bill of Sale." In the midst of a carefree outing in East Tennessee the narrator comes across a bill of sale, dated 1862, documenting the sale of a young woman named Liza. Despite the sunny day the evil of slavery is uncomfortably close at hand.

In Toi Derricotte's sustained poem "A Note on My Son's Face" the narrator suffers mixed emotions as she admires the "gold head" of her grandson.

She is reminded of how critical she was of her own son, whose "face was too dark, / nose too broad, mouth too wide." Self-hatred, soaked up from the society at large, instills poison.

Joyce Carol Thomas's "Brown Honey in Broomwheat Tea" also traces connections beween generations, mingling themes of love, identity, and caution. The young narrator in this lyric recounts the beautiful names and qualities her parents have blessed her with. This child is learning self-love, and yet the knowing parents must also teach a warning to "children kissed long by the sun."

Colleeen McElroy's "For My Children" traces ancestry to provide her children with a fully shaped image of who they are. Before "shackles and slaves and a bill of rights," the poet calls up Bilad as-Sudan, Watusi shadows and Dahomey doors, Burundi warriors, Seminole ancestry, Ashanti mysteries and rituals. The poem of ancestry is laced with music.

Rita Dove's "Crab-Boil" recalls from a child's point of view the shame of segregated beaches. The narrator and her aunt have gone crabbing, venturing beyond the littered "colored-only shore." She remembers her young fear that her family would be chased back, and deeper fears surface, of being killed like the crabs. In the end the hungry girl eats the crabs and defers to her aunt: "After all, she *has* / grown old in the South."

Irena Klepfisz's "Warsaw, 1983: *Umschlagplatz* (place of deportation to concentration camps) recounts her return to Treblinka. She has to remind herself that she lives "on another continent," that it is 1983, and that she is a visitor. Helping us to imagine her history and that of other refugees, Klepfisz chronicles the terrible march across Poland in the first autobiographical section of her poem "*Bashert*."

In its spare lines, "Family Tree" by Linda Pastan also evokes the Nazi death camps. The poem asks, "How many leaves / has death undone already." Pastan compares fallen leaves to "burned out stars." The poem insists on the responsibility of memory, on breaking silences and "telling again // and again / the long story / of smoke."

Silence itself is a prison cell, Janice Mirikitani reminds us in "Prisons of Silence." The poem remembers the internment of the Japanese in California during World War II, a memory of "abandoned homes, confiscated land, / loyalty oaths, barbed wire prisons." This poem tears down silences, opening cells of rage and healing.

The children in Pat Mora's poem "La Migra" are playing "Border Patrol." The "pretend" border guard does not speak Spanish, and possesses boots, handcuffs, "Oh, and a gun." But the other child, the "captured Mexican maid," is not alone. She hears many others singing in Spanish about the desert's sweet water. It is the patrol guard who will have to run when his jeep gets a flat in the desert.

Wendy Rose's "I Expected My Skin and My Blood to Ripen" haunts the page in the voice of a Sioux mother slaughtered at Wounded Knee, her babies murdered, her clothes stripped off with her frozen skin to become a museum exhibit. Rose's voice is alive with sorrow and rage and protest, as the poetry documents greed and genocide in America.

In Luci Tapahonso's "Shjáá Áko Dahjiníłeh / Remember the Things They Told Us," tradition offers continuity and hope. By continuing the tradition of prayers at dawn, the Navajo people continue their connection to the holy people. Each child embodies the creation myth; in prayers, songs, and stories they are reminded of their powerful relatives in nature.

In an interview, Colleen J. McElroy identifies and condemns "a bondage of color" in the United States: "There is a great fear that if we allow a culture of diversity, we'll have to look at our cultural history in all its tawdriness and denial." In her writings she focuses on black women "in a personal way," writing about individuals and not stereotypes, ripping away "at least part of the bondage of racism."

◎ *ELIZABETH COOK-LYNN*

Elizabeth Cook-Lynn was born in 1930 in Fort Thompson, South Dakota. A member of the Crow Creek Sioux tribe, she was raised on the reservation. She was strongly influenced by her grandparents, who were among the first to write in the Sioux language. She has published the multigenre The Badger Said This *(1977),* Seek the House of Relatives *(poetry, 1983),* The Power of Horses and Other Stories *(1990), and* From the River's Edge *(a novel, 1991). Cook-Lynn founded* Wicazo Sa Review: A Journal of Native American Studies *in 1985. She is professor emeritus of English and Native American studies at Eastern Washington University.*

"A Visit from Reverend Tileston" is from The Power of Horses and Other Stories. *All of the stories in the book portray the enduring culture of the Dakotapi of the Upper Plains. Cook-Lynn writes in a restrained and understated manner of life in Sioux Country, at times using satire to underscore intrusions upon a traditional way of life.*

A Visit from Reverend Tileston

Fifty miles from the nearest town of any size, deep in the bend of the Missouri River, where the *Dakotapi* had made history for generations, lived the Family: Father, a firstborn son whose eyes bore the immutable and unspoken agony of his generation, handsome and strong, a cattleman not so much from choice as from necessity; Mother, a fine quill artist, small-boned and stout, a woman with one crooked elbow caused by a childhood accident, a good cook, accomplished at the piano, guitar, and harmonica, talents she had learned at the government boarding school; Uncle, the Mother's younger brother, a truck driver sometimes, a drunk increasingly often, whenever those inexplicable waves of grief washed over him; Grandmother, Grandfather, and five children ranging in age from three to fifteen years. Uncle's son often lived with the Family, as did the Grandmother's half sister and her husband and their two granddaughters. The Family was part of a small community which had reassembled itself at this place after the violent diaspora and displacement which was endured by this ancient tribe for several generations, the Family all the more closely knit because of this tragedy of recent history as well as the more practical problem of long distances to the few sparse surrounding towns settled a hundred years before by whites anxious to possess land and become rich. The year was 1935, and this was a place where strangers, though alien and undesirable, even called *to'ka*, were largely unthreatening and often ignored, and where strange events were witnessed with inexplicable but characteristic tolerance.

From the graveled road which followed the course of the river, the small, three-room frame house in which the Family now lived, built by the U.S. government for Bureau of Indian Affairs employees in early reservation days and abandoned in later times, looked strangely remote and ageless. It seemed to stare listlessly toward the river's loop, and in winter its long-windowed eyes would be the first to catch a glimpse of the landing of the Canada geese on the cold shores of the whitened, timeless river. It turned its back on the ludicrously inexpedient pyramid-shaped, steel-roofed icehouse, which had once afforded Bureau employees from the East the luxury of iced drinks in the summer as they came to this blistering Dakotah prairie to work "in the Indian service." The icehouse was abandoned now, also, too big and deep to be of any use to the Family except for the summer drying of the pounded meat and berry patties, *wasna*, which would be laid out upon its roof in the sun. During this drying process the children would be set to fanning the flies away with long willows, a task which held their attention a surprisingly brief time. Bored, they would run off in pursuit of more imaginative pastimes, only to be called back as soon as Grandmother discovered their absence.

Also at the rear of the house was a large *tipi*, the color of smoke at the top, streaked with rain, lined with cowhides, comfortable, shaded in late afternoon by the lone pine tree which was, itself, a stranger to the hot Plains country of the Dakotah, itself a survivor of the days when Bureau employees lived there. The children imagined that the tree was brought there by a medicine man and was used in his cures, but it was not a cedar, just a scraggly pine tree which had barely survived hard times. There was a tall hand pump set in the middle of the yard, where Grandmother would kneel to wash the paunch during butchering times, and also a corral set some distance away in the tall pasture grass at the foot of a small rise in the prairie landscape. A huge mound of earth covered a man-made cave, which was complete with wooden steps and a slanting door that had to be picked up and drawn aside. A very large bull snake often found refuge from the blistering sun under one of the wooden steps, stretching himself full-length in the soft, cool, black earth.

Just beyond the cave was a small, white outdoor toilet, another survivor of former times, a product of imaginative Public Health Service officials who set about dotting Indian reservations with these white man's conveniences during the early part of the century. Across the road from the house a gray stuccoed Catholic church, Saint Anne's, sat with a closed, tight-lipped visage, as though shielding itself from the violent summer prairie storms which came intermittently, pounding the gravel and the stucco, flattening the prairie grass. To the rear of the church lay the remains of the ancestors in a cemetery which, years later, was said to be occupied by a den of rattlesnakes.

In summer evenings, the air was often still and quiet, heavy with moisture. After a late meal, the quiet deepened. The only sound was Grandmother's soft footsteps as she went back and forth to the kitchen, carrying dishes from the table. Her ankle-length black dress hid her bowed legs, and her head was covered, always, with a black scarf, her long white braids lying on her breast. Every now and then she stopped to wipe her smooth face with a white cloth, breathlessly.

"Grandmother, we should cook outside tomorrow," said the Youngest Daughter, disheveled and hot, bearing a load too heavy for her to the kitchen.

The Mother simply sat, one arm outstretched on the table, the crooked one fanning her face and hair with a handkerchief. For her it had been a long day, as she and her sister had spent the afternoon picking wild plums and buffalo berries along the river.

As the evening came on, the children could be heard outside, running and chasing one another around the house and yard, trying to touch each other on the back, stretching away, laughing, now and again falling and crashing into the bushes near the pump. The dogs barked loudly. It was a game the boys never seemed to tire of, even as the sun started to glow in the west and Uncle went outside to begin his nightly summer ritual of starting a smoke-fire, a smudge, to keep the mosquitoes away for the evening.

"Hoksila kin tuktel un he?" muttered Uncle as he looked around for one of his nephews to help him gather firewood. "He's never around when you need him."

"Go get some of that wood over there by the back porch." He directed his voice toward the hapless Youngest Daughter, who wrinkled up her nose but went, dutifully, to get the wood. Uncle bent down on one knee to place the sticks and dead leaves just right to produce a heavy smoke. He carefully touched a match to the soft underbrush, and as the smoke rose, he watched, one thumb hooked in his belt. In a few moments smoke filled the air, and members of the Family began to gather for the evening.

They might even see man-being-carried in the sky, thought Uncle, and then he could tell a story if the children felt like listening and could stay awake long enough for the stars to show themselves clearly.

When he straightened up, he was surprised to see a small black sedan some distance down the road, making its way slowly toward them. He kept his eyes on the road to see if he could recognize in the dusk who it was. He stepped up on the porch and lit a cigarette, the match illuminating the fine, delicate bones of his deeply pocked, scarred face.

Holding the match close for a moment, Uncle said, to no one in particular, "A car's coming."

Cars were rarely seen here on this country road this late in the evening.

As Uncle stood watching, he heard church music, faint at first, and later blaring, and he realized after a few long moments that it was coming from the loudspeaker positioned on top of the sedan.

"On-ward Christian so-o-o-l-diers," sang the recorded voices of an entire church choir into the quiet evening light as the car came slowly into the river's bend, "with the cross of J-e-e-e-sus going on before."

Uncle stood with the cigarette in his mouth, his hands in his pockets, as his brother-in-law came out of the house and sat down on the porch step with a cup of coffee. They watched the car approach and listened to the music, now blaring loud enough to get the attention of the children, who stopped running and stood gazing at the strange-looking vehicle.

They stood, transfixed, as the car approached slowly and came to a stop. The loudspeaker fell silent as the driver of the sedan parked the car on the side of the road near the mailbox and, with great cheer, stepped from the car, waving and smiling. He was a man of about forty with a broad, freckled face. He was perspiring heavily, and he made his way down the short path from the road to the house. Behind him came two women dressed in blue-and-white flowered dresses, brown stockings, and flat brown shoes; their faces, like pale round melons, were fixed with broad smiles. They all carried black leather-bound Bibles, the kind with red-tipped pages.

"Boy, it's hot!" said the fortyish, freckled man as he held out his hand in greeting. The Father did not look at him, nor did he get up. He put the cup to his lips and sipped coffee quietly, ignoring the intrusion with sullen indifference. Uncle kept his hands in his pockets, and with his tongue he shifted his cigarette to the other side of his mouth.

Ignoring what was clearly a personal affront by the two men on the steps, the freckled man said, "Say, that's a good trash-burning operation there," turning to the children standing beside the smudge. The children looked first at the smudge and then back at the perspiring man, and, silently, they shook hands with him. Grasping the unwilling hand of the Youngest Daughter, standing a few feet away, the man, in a loud voice, asked, "Is your mommy home, honey?" Nearly overcome with embarrassment, she said, "Yeah, she's in there," and gestured toward the door.

"Well," the man said as he turned and walked up the steps slowly, avoiding the Father and the Uncle still mutely positioned there, "we've come a long way with the message of hope and love we've got right here," and he patted the black leather-bound book he carried. As he tapped on the screen door, the Mother appeared, and the freckled man quickly opened the door, stepped inside, and held it open for the two smiling women who accompanied him to squeeze inside and in front of him.

"I'm Sister Bernice," began the plumper of the two women, "and this is Sister Kate . . .?" Her voice trailed off as if she had asked a question. When there was no response, she turned to the freckled man, and putting her hand on his elbow, she said, "And we're here with Reverend Tileston."

Taking a deep breath, the Reverend said to the Mother in his kindliest voice, "Ma-a'aam, we'd like to pray with you," and there in the middle of the room, he knelt and began paging through his Bible, motioning for the women to join him as he knelt. His two companions quickly dropped to their knees, and the plump one said to the Mother, "Please pray with us, sister," and the Mother, after a brief, uncertain moment, also knelt. Espying the Grandmother and her half sister peering at them curiously from the kitchen doorway, the Reverend quickly got up and led them to the middle of the room, saying, "Come on with us, Granny, pray with us," and the two old women, too, with great effort, got to their knees. The Youngest Daughter, having followed the astonishing trio into the house, stood beside her grandmother and looked expectantly at the perspiring freckled man as he fell to reading from the leather-bound book:

> "With ALL our energy we ought to lead back
> ALL men to our most MER-ci-ful Re-DEEmer,"

he read. His voice rose:

> "He is the Divine Cons-o-o-oler of the afflicted";

Youngest Daughter hung her head, copying the attitude of the visitors.

> "To rulers and subjects alike He teaches lessons of true holiness,"

the Reverend sucked in air:

> "unimpeachable justice, and,"

he breathed again:

> "generous charity."

The Reverend's voice seemed to fill the cramped little room, and Sisters Bernice and Kate, eyes tightly closed, murmured, "Amen," louder and louder with each breath the minister took.

Youngest Daughter glanced first at her Mother, then her Grandmothers, who were kneeling shoulder to shoulder, faces impassive, eyes cast to the floor. Then, the Reverend closed the book, raised his arms, and recited from memory, Proverbs:

"Hear O children, a father's instruction," he shouted. "Be attentive, that you may gain understanding! Yea, excellent advice I give you; my teaching do not forsake."

One of the dogs, hunching itself close to the screen door, began to whine.

The Reverend continued to shout: "When I was my father's child, frail, yet the darling of my mother, he taught me, and said to me: 'Let your heart hold fast my words! Keep my commands, do not forget; go not astray from the words of my mouth.' "

His arms fell and his voice softened as he uttered the last phrase, opened his eyes, and looked, unseeing, at the little girl, his gaze moist and glittering. The dog's whine became more persistent, his tone now pitched higher to match the Reverend's, and he began to push his nose against the screen door, causing it to squeak loudly.

The Reverend Tileston looked into the passive faces of the Mother and the Grandmothers, and as he said, "The beginning of wisdom is: get wisdom; at the cost of ALL-L-L-L you have," his arm swung dangerously close to the unfortunate dog, who flattened his ears and pushed himself closer to the door.

"Get understanding," Reverend Tileston urged. "Forsake her not and she will preserve you; love her, and she will safeguard you; extol her, and she will exalt you; she will bring you honors if you embrace her; she will put on your head a graceful diadem; a glorious crown will she bestow upon you."

The words seemed to roll from his tongue, and Youngest Daughter imagined shining crowns placed upon the heads of her Mother and her Grandmothers, still kneeling stiffly and impassively. She was thrilled with the sound of the English words, though she knew she didn't comprehend their meaning. It was like the times when Felix Middle Tent, the well-known Dakotah orator, made his speeches at the tribal council meetings she sometimes attended with her father, when he used his most eloquent and esoteric Dakotah vocabulary, oftentimes derisively referred to by Uncle as "jawbreakers."

As the Reverend's hefty arm again swept the room, the whining dog lurched backward and fell against a large pail of buffalo berries which Mother had left on the porch that late afternoon. Terrified, the dog leapt into the second pail of plums, scattering them wildly, then he dashed under the porch, where he set up a mournful howl. The boys, who had been listening at the side window, fled into the bushes, laughing and screaming.

The Mother and Grandmothers, surprised and shocked at this turn of events but bent upon retrieving the day's pickings, swept past the astonished, speechless minister, shouting abuse at the now thoroughly miserable dog, and the screen door slammed behind them. Younger Daughter was left looking into the disappointed faces of the Reverend and his companions. She smiled.

Forced by these circumstances to admit that the spiritual moment was lost, the Reverend Tileston got to his feet and ushered Sisters Bernice and Kate out of the house, carefully picking a path through the berries covering the porch. He was relieved that the Father and Uncle were nowhere to be seen, and he turned at the last step and made a final effort, saying, "Meditate, Mothers, on the Scriptures, have knowledge of them, for they are the food which sustains men during times of strife."

The women, engrossed in saving the berries, didn't hear him.

His final proselytizing gesture, the attempted distribution of printed pamphlets, was also ignored.

Their composure now completely shattered, the trio which bore God's Word into this obscure bend in the river found its way, falteringly, to the sedan, switched on the loudspeaker, and drove slowly away.

Youngest Daughter looked after them as they ventured deeper into the curve along the river, and the faint echo of "with the cross of Jee-e-sus . . ." rang in her ears. After a moment she went to find Uncle, who would tell her a story about the star people and how the four blanket carriers once helped him find his way home from a long and difficult journey.

She hoped that the Reverend knew about the blanket carriers.

◎ SHARON NIEDERMAN

Sharon Niederman grew up in New Jersey. Over the last two decades she has earned her living by doing every kind of writing imaginable, from ghostwriting textbooks to being managing editor of a fan magazine. She received her M.A. from the University of Colorado, then settled in New Mexico. From 1990 to 1993 she was arts editor of the Santa Fe Reporter, *and she currently teaches at the University of New Mexico in Albuquerque. She is the editor of* Shaking Eve's Tree: Short Stories of Jewish Women *(1990) and* A Quilt of Words: Women's Diaries, Letters and Original Accounts of Life in the Southwest, 1860–1969 *(1988), and she coedited* New Mexico Poetry Renaissance *(1994). Both* A Quilt *and* Poetry Renaissance *have received Border Regional Library Association's Southwest Book Award. Sharon Neiderman is currently working on a novel based on the lives of ranching women in rural New Mexico.*

"A Gift for Languages" was one of Niederman's first stories, written in 1986. It appears in Shaking Eve's Tree. *In this story, Dr. Rosalind de la Torre — "born Rosalie Zelnick" — finds herself torn out of her pretensions and out of her desire to be assimilated by the death of a beloved professor. Instinctively she rends her designer*

clothing the way her Yiddish grandmother might have torn her peasant dress in "the old country" of her Polish village.

A Gift for Languages

I

Dr. de laTorre loved her work. Hazy mornings, strolling from her brown shingle cottage on Hilegas to her office on campus, she immersed herself in scents of eucalyptus and good coffee, the Mediterranean softness of the air, and the sense of engaged, passionate life being lived on the streets of Berkeley. Unlike so many others who had come of age in the 1960's, she didn't feel she had to prove her right to exist by trying to fix the world. She knew she deserved everything she had.

She hadn't always been Dr. Rosalind de la Torre. Born Rosalie Zelnick, she'd kept her ex-husband's name. His Buenos Aires family had called her Rosalinda; she had shortened it to Rosalind.

This morning she took more than her usual care dressing. She knew she'd be on display at the Comparative Literature Department meeting this afternoon when she gave her evaluation of the new curriculum proposals. Brainy women had a special obligation to look particularly chic and sexy, she believed, and she prided herself on never looking like a teacher or a librarian. Rosalind favored pure, intense colors — clear red, royal blue, black — in interesting textures and styles that looked trendy, and at the same time as though they would always be fashionable. She cultivated her appearance of elegant, expensive simplicity as carefully as she cultivated her taste in films, food and music.

From her well-organized closet she chose a fuchsia sweater dress with a hemline well above her knees, patterned black stockings and little Italian boots. She'd purchased her underwear in Paris. The outfit would catch her colleagues slightly off guard, giving her the bit of extra space she needed to evaluate her interactions and stay ahead. Being the youngest in the department to hold her position — assistant professor at thirty-two — she constantly faced the judgments of people who wanted to stop her before she got started. There was definitely an art to being just provocative enough. Always a good student, she'd mastered this art as thoroughly as any of her languages.

Rosalind loved the peace she found in the early morning. As she moved about her house, she again admired each lovingly selected object and furnishing. She dearly wanted her home to be a reflection of her unique and excellent taste. Although she knew good things, money wasn't the real factor here. Even before she'd earned a decent living, she'd bought things she loved. Really special things weren't easy to find, and she'd learned to regret missed opportunities. Her house was eclectic, comfortable, and, she thought, quite perfect. Brass arc lamps coexisted harmoniously with leather chairs, a burgundy cut-velvet sofa, muted old carpets, oak tables, lacquer chests and stained-glass windows. Cream-colored walls provided a warm background for her art and photographs.

She still reveled in having an entire place just to herself. With a fireplace. After all those years of sharing a bedroom with Grandma in that claustrophobic Bronx apartment, she still hungered for privacy. Back then, Grandma got the bed; she slept on a cot. She was never alone. At night, Grandma snored terribly and woke Rosie to help her to the bathroom. When Grandma bathed, Rosie helped her out of the tub and dried the enormous wrinkled brown body. So many tasks, repeated over and over, but they never seemed to help. Grandma was just sick, and she never got any better. "How are you today?" Rosie would ask when she gave Grandma her medicine in the morning. "What's the good of complaining?" was the answer each day. With her parents working all day in their dry-cleaning store, Rosie always worried something terrible might happen to Grandma. Then again, she half hoped something might. She didn't know which was worse — the smells or the superstitions.

Over and over, Grandma told her the stories that made up her life, half in English, half in Yiddish. How she left her Polish village at fourteen and never saw her mother again. How she came to this country in steerage, sick for days. Lived on the lower East Side with her mean, grudging uncle and worked in the sweatshops, picking fuzz from bolts of cloth. Sundays weren't so bad. Then she and her girlfriends got all dolled up and strolled down Second Avenue or maybe went to Coney Island.

When she was sixteen, she met Grandpa, a second cousin, at a family wedding. "I waited four years for him," Grandma told her. "Then, the night before my wedding, his sister, your Tante Sophie, came to me and begged me not to marry him. 'He's no good,' she told me. 'He'll ruin your life. He runs around, can't save his money.' Was she right about the money! He never was an easy man to live with."

Rosie never knew how she came to understand Yiddish; she seemed just to know what the words meant. Later, German came easily to her in high school. Thank you, Grandma, she thought. Poor Grandma never learned to read, except for the racing forms. Just sat in front of the television until she died.

Meanwhile, her parents fought. About everything. "Your mother," yelled Rosie's father, "is driving me crazy. And in my own home yet!" But the apartment was cheaper than a nursing home.

Out of rebellion and hope, her parents had been leftists. All that remained of their youthful idealism was their disbelief in God. Their atheism tortured Grandma, who mouthed prayers morning, noon and night and invoked God continually. Oh God, help me. Oh God, save me. Oh God, you didn't hear that.

Oh God oh God Oh God. She lit her candles, Shabbes and Yahrtzeit, muttering her prayers alone.

Naturally, Rosie read a lot. Library books were free, and reading didn't bother anybody. Jane Austen, George Eliot, the Brontës, then Dostoevsky and Tolstoy. "Always got your nose in a book," was her father's customary greeting.

Well, she'd made it pay. A smart girl, hadn't they always said so? Her father saved his first kind words for when she won the Regents scholarship at sixteen. "Good girl, Rosie," he said, ruffling her hair. "We're real proud of you." He sounded like he meant it. Then he retreated behind his newspaper. Of course he was pleased. Now it wouldn't cost him a cent to educate her.

So she escaped to Buffalo. That was her biggest achievement. Bigger than the *cum laude* degree. Bigger than the garduate fellowship, and even bigger than the Fulbright. All she'd ever really wanted to do was to create a life different from theirs. And she'd certainly done that, she thought, looking around her domain with satisfaction. She owed them nothing. She'd done it all on her own.

When Joachim (who sat next to her in Seventeenth Century literature, smoked a pipe, and was definitely dark and handsome) asked her to marry him, she welcomed the change to get even further away. They sailed out of San Francisco for Argentina, and no one saw her off. His family doted on her, called her "La Flaca" (the thin one), waited four years for her to become pregnant. Her mother-in-law, Paolina, oversaw Rosalinda's housekeeping; exhibited her at countless family dinners, organized shopping expeditions with Joachim's sisters and summers at Mar del Plata. She had no life of her own. While Joachim worked in the family import-export business, she spent afternoons at the movies. In Buenos Aires, she learned that freedom and empty time were not the same thing at all. One afternoon, she saw *Hiroshima, Mon Amour*, and the intense longing and grief the movie aroused broke the daze of her boredom and isolation. She knew she had to leave. She returned to New York, taking one suitcase and her perfect Spanish.

Days, she typed at an office in the city; nights she slept at her parents' apartment, in her own bed. Her high school girlfriend, Terri, came in from Berkeley for a visit. Rosalind had to finish her degree. Why not California? She started packing the day her acceptance came in the mail. From the moment she arrived, Berkeley felt like home. Now it felt like her true love: the place she was faithful to, would cross oceans for, that always welcomed her, that she knew so well, that held pleasures and discoveries for her always.

2

If he hadn't called her name in the café, Rosalind wouldn't have noticed Dr. Hoffmann. She stopped in for brioches to take to the office when she ran into him, sitting alone, wearing his émigré beret and reading his *New York Times*. His appearance chilled her. How small he looked, shrunken, like Picasso or Sartre when they were very old men; his face so deeply lined, the flesh pulled tightly around the bones, revealing the very structure of his skull.

"Rosalind, my dear, how beautiful you're looking this morning," he said in his charming accent, smiling and taking her hand in both of his. She hadn't seen him all semester, though he'd never mention the lapse. He seemed so openly happy to see her, she blushed. Since his wife, Alicia, died the previous year, she'd drifted apart from her mentor. His neediness at this time made her uncomfortable. She told herself that trying to see him through this lonely period would only use her up.

But now, looking into his kind, intelligent face, she wondered how much of the need was his; how much hers. She hated seeing how badly he'd aged. He couldn't be near eighty yet, she thought. Ten years gone now since she'd first been his student — his prize — then his assistant, typing and editing his manuscripts on archetypes in world literature. Nothing in her life equaled the excitement she'd felt over her first conversations with the eminent Dr. Karel Hoffmann. He'd been the first to recognize her potential, not just to accept her but to believe in her ability to make a real contribution. She hadn't seriously thought of getting her Ph.D. until Dr. Hoffmann insisted she go on, and helped her find the fellowship.

He and Alicia had lost everyone when they fled Germany. Rosalind fit easily into the design of their family life, joining them for holiday dinners, helping them entertain, or just staying for supper to continue working with Dr. Hoffmann into the evening. In their refined world, filled with artifacts illuminated in niches like saints — pre-Columbian carved jade, an enameled Fabergé music box, a Japanese cherrywood bowl from the hands of a Living National Treasure — plus Bokhara carpets and the best wine and music (Alicia played Bach so beautifully on their Steinway), Rosalind became the person she'd always wanted to be. She felt she had entered the warmly lit home you spend your life walking past on the street, wishing you could go inside.

But she couldn't stop just now. She was in a hurry to meet Brian Miller, a student from European Classics, to discuss his term paper. Brian was very bright, in a class of not very exciting students, and, she had to admit, very attractive. Quickly, she made a plan to go to the opera with Dr. Hoffmann Sunday afternoon. They'd catch up then.

3

Brian Miller, age twenty-two, senior in business administration from Crescent City, just below the Oregon border, waited for her — his six-foot frame leaning against her office door. Brian had sufficient irregularities about his looks to save him from anonymous, athletic wholesomeness. Rosalind noticed in particular the tiny gap between his two front teeth and the thick dark brows emphasizing the amused expression in his light-brown eyes. Outwardly ignoring the deliberate way he sized her up, she actually applauded this little show of audacity from one of his generation — this new breed with its intelligence neatly channeled into material striving, its grim predictability, and its lack of curiosity.

Rosalind, always in command in front of a class but not unfriendly, had often been party to confessions, both intended and oblique, during the intimacy of office hours. Precisely because of the respect her manner and scholarship inspired, this generation trusted her with its heartbreak and confusion. She, in turn, translated their appeals into practical suggestions for improvement. The exposure did not alter their mutual sense of propriety. On the fingers of one hand, she could name the students who had, in ten years, ever moved inside the circle of discrimination she inscribed around herself.

Now this Brian sat across from her, his arrogance intriguing as well as annoying. He sketched out his ideas for his term paper. She knew perfectly well he'd never have enrolled in the class were it not a requirement for graduation. He was the sort who only wanted to get through school so he could get out there and make as much money as he could the fastest way possible. When he finished speaking, he looked at her with a frankness that had nothing to do with library research, sending her a direct sexual charge. So much for the world of the intellect.

"What do you think of it?" he asked, showing his lopsided grin.

"I think you'll do very well," she replied, the air thick with double entendres.

"But don't you have any suggestions?" he wanted to know. He had to be aware of the game that had been set in motion. She wondered: How long had he intended to approach her? How much class time did he spend calculating the right approach? There was no law against imagination and no way to control your students' thoughts. Her behavior, however, was impeccable. She could afford to let this play out a bit. A little flirtation, like a little Belgian chocolate, could help get you through the semester.

"I can't think of anything to add to what you've put together," she said. "But if I do get any interesting ideas, I'll let you know." She gave him a smile he could interpret any way he chose and turned to her papers.

4

When Dr. Hoffmann entered her silver Saab Sunday afternoon, Rosalind was struck by his frailty. His movements had become slower and more cautious than she remembered, as if his batteries were losing their charge, and she registered with dismay the grayish cast of his complexion. Rosalind rejected the flash of panic she felt and turned her thoughts to practical matters. Was he getting proper medical attention to get him through this period of rundown? Vitamin B shots could do wonders. Did he need a temporary housekeeper? Would he call her if she could help him find someone?

Of course she wanted to take care of him, comfort him — but how could she just drop everything? She was impossibly busy, as always. As they drove across the Bay Bridge in the misty sunlight, Rosalind chattered about her classes, plans for her publications and new books she'd discovered, avoiding the silence of unasked questions.

In the years they'd attended musical events together, the San Francisco Opera had always been their favorite setting. In its fin-de-siècle opulence, they returned together to the world gone by, which was no less vivid for their sharing it in imagination rather than memory. When she took Dr. Hoffmann's arm and walked up these steps, life became for Rosalind perfectly civilized and elegant, as delicious as the exquisite Sacher torte one would savor with excellent company at the Café Voltaire.

But today, the professor tottered heavily at her side. Discreetly, she helped him up the steps. Inside the high-ceilinged lobby, he bought her a red rose, and tears burned her eyes as she pinned the flower to her black velvet jacket. She averted her head and started toward their seats.

This afternoon, the spectacle and finery of *Così fan tutte* failed to hold her attention. The image of Brian Miller returned as it had all week — lanky, relaxed, assured — just damn sexy. She could no longer meet his eyes in class. His eyes drank her in as she lectured, paced, and turned to write on the blackboard. His attention excited her and inspired her performance. No matter that her cleverness was mainly wasted on those dull undergraduates. She took pleasure in recalling how Brian lingered outside the door after class. She'd simply outwaited him until he finally sauntered off.

Of course, these little reveries were just whimsy. She could tune him out any time she chose. Pretty visions of Brian alternated with Rosalind's worries about Dr. Hoffmann, whose breathing beside her sounded irregular. She wondered if they ought to cancel their customary supper at Jack's and head straight back across the bay.

As she helped Dr. Hoffmann back to the car, he lost his balance, stumbled and took a bad fall. Seeing him crumpled on the sidewalk, Rosalind gathered all her resources and willed herself to remain calm. She focused on the task at hand. With effort, she raised him to his feet. He was shaken and badly bruised; clearly, their night on the town was impossible. Not wanting him to see her fright, she tried her best to keep up a soothing conversation on the way home. Undeniably, something was seriously wrong, and she drove like a demon. When she got him into his house and turned on the lights, he looked too sick to leave alone.

"Can I make you some soup?" she asked, as she looked for blankets to wrap him in and pillows to prop him up on the sofa.

"Fix yourself something, Rosalind," he said. "But don't let me keep you."

She brought out a tray with mugs of consommé and toast.

"Shall I call your doctor?" she asked.

"That won't be necessary."

"Really, Dr. Hoffmann, if you don't mind my saying . . ."

"Please don't concern yourself, my dear."

In the end she won, and it was a good thing she'd insisted. Dr. Duncan checked him into the hospital "for tests."

When Rosalind finally returned home from the Medical Center, it was after nine. Wound too tight to sleep or concentrate on work, she thought of a hot bath with soothing mineral salts, clouds of steam. Instead, without pausing to think, she went to the phone and dialed Brian's number.

"Hello?" he answered in his slow, level voice.

"Hello, Brian," she said, with a lilt he'd never heard in the classroom.

He took a beat. "Dr. de la Torre?" he asked.

She gave him a pretext that seemed reasonable for them both. "I was just going over your outline, and there are some parts I think we ought to discuss."

He understood her immediately, as she'd known he would. "Is this a convenient time for you?" he wanted to know.

"Tonight is fine," she said.

He was at her door in half an hour. She offered him a Courvoisier and poured one for herself. Within the hour, they were in bed together, no questions asked. She had chosen well. This boy knew a great deal; at moments, she swore he knew everything. A slow, accurate, and unself-conscious lover, his attention to her cost him no sacrifice. He left around two A.M., and she finally fell asleep, too exhausted to think. Except that in the few seconds before she dropped off, she again saw Dr. Hoffmann's face as he lay on the sidewalk.

5

Barely present, Rosalind sat at Dr. Hoffmann's hospital bedside, wondering how soon she could respectably leave. Seeing him completely helpless, barely able to speak or move, tubes in his nose and arms attaching him to machines, she couldn't help thinking: Why not just have it over with? Although the stroke had left him paralyzed, she knew he still recognized her. She had loved this man as much as she'd ever loved anyone, but at this crucial time she just felt weary and numb. There was no fitting way to say goodbye. She refused to imagine the void his passing would leave in her life and in the world.

She gazed at the green treetops outside the window and thought of the afternoon ahead with Brian. Her body responded with an involuntary shock of pleasure. Brian's healthy, uncomplicated maleness short-circuited her analytic mind and lit up her sensations. With him, she didn't have to think. She only felt. While he was not what she'd term a grand passion, she had to admit he'd become her compulsion. She constantly craved the pleasure he willingly provided. Yet his offhandedness went counter to the urgency she felt with him.

She knew nothing more about him now than when they'd started last month. She couldn't help wondering: Did he have a girlfriend? A sweet bubblehead back home? Or a campus trust-funder from Ohio? In bed and out, she worked at trying to get him as obsessed with her as she was with him, but he behaved as casually as if she were just another experience of many. Still, she insisted to herself, Brian was "safe." Only a student, ten years younger, he was a prime example of a generation that replaced content with form. At least he was smart enough to behave. He arrived and left on time, and he always called when he said he would.

Rosalind had gone to his apartment only once. He lived in a way she'd left far behind and had no desire to revisit, with his cheap wall posters, empty refrigerator, ugly throws over uglier chairs, loud, unfamiliar rock music blaring through the walls, and, pervading all this, the smell of stale beer. By contrast, her own sandalwood-scented sheets, down pillows, and firm queen-sized mattress made their encounters — which began in the fading late-afternoon light and ended in darkness — far more pleasant and private.

Despite her nonstop desire for Brian, Rosalind refused to make the mistake of believing she was in love with him. Falling in love was the worst thing that could happen to a woman. Hadn't she seen this disaster repeated often enough? No matter how gifted or accomplished the woman — and Berkeley was full of brilliant, beautiful women — love provided a socially condoned route to self-destruction. Love automatically took precedence over work, money, reputation, ambition — the entire professional life that a woman had struggled so hard and honorably to create. Love succeeded where the world had failed to knock you out of the game. The fact of physical need couldn't be helped, but why pretty it up? Rosalind knew better than to believe love would improve her life.

Dr. Hoffmann seemed to be asleep. She bent and kissed his parchment forehead and left the room, each tap of her kidskin pumps reverberating along the corridor. Now she could go home and get ready for Brian.

6

Rosalind didn't cry at Dr. Hoffmann's funeral or at his memorial service. She ached with her frozen grief. Nothing to be said, nothing to be done. She could only sit alone in a dark room. The image of Brian failed to magnetize her thoughts.

Finally the tears began. A relief. Then came panic so overwhelming and unexpected that she ran to the bathroom, vomiting. She locked the doors, unplugged the phone and sat on the floor, hugging her knees and swaying from side to side.

Wanting to scream, then hearing a broken howl unlike any sound she'd ever produced, she remembered the mourning rituals of her ancient European great-aunts. All her life, she'd tried to shut out their hysterical keening. Now she even smelled them: mothballs and Evening in Paris.

Rosalind knew what to do. She found candles and matches. She went to the closet, grabbed her I. Magnin black silk dress, made a half dozen gashes with her scissors and dressed herself in mourning. Then she took her beautiful pastel sheets, ripped them down the middle and covered every mirror in the house. *So the departing soul doesn't startle itself.*

Now she knew. She wasn't smarter or stronger or better. She had only reinterpreted her grandmother's immigrant endurance for her own purposes. She would rather die than be like her wheezing, kvetching grandmother. She would rather die *than be Jewish like her grandmother:* worn out, despised, prevented from freely choosing a life; resigned to feeding only on crumbs, crumbs that wouldn't be missed and devouring them quickly when no one was looking. Though Rosalind had fed on the finest delicacies, an abundance of delectable imports arrayed on white linen in a summer garden, still she hungered.

◎ *TILLIE OLSEN*

Tillie Olsen was born on a farm in or near Omaha in 1912 or 1913. She left high school during the depression and is self-educated. Tell Me a Riddle *(stories, 1961; 1994) won the Rea Award for the Short Story; her published fiction also includes* Yonnondio: From the Thirties *(1974; 1984).* Silences *(1978), Olsen's groundbreaking essays on the tragic silences in writers' lives, remains a classic in feminist studies. Olsen composed* Mother to Daughter, Daughter to Mother: A Feminist Press Daybook and Reader *(1984), and with her daughter, Julie Olsen Edwards, published* Mothers and Daughters: That Special Quality — An Exploration in Photographs *(1987; 1995). She has received the O. Henry Award (for "Tell Me a Riddle"), a Guggenheim Foundation Fellowship, and grants from the Ford Foundation and the National Endowment for the Arts. She holds six honorary degrees, and has taught at Amherst College, Stanford University, M.I.T., and the University of Massachusetts, and was a Fellow of the Radcliffe Institute. Her Literary Award from the American Academy and Institute of Arts and Letters was "for very nearly constituting a new form of fiction."*

"O Yes" is one of the four stories that compose Tell Me a Riddle. *It first appeared in* Prairie Schooner *as "Baptism" (1956). The rhythmical prose conveys both the poetry of the characters' consciousness and the social environment in which they live. As John Leonard says in his introduction, "Memory, history, prophecy, and poetry converge."*

O Yes

for Margaret Heaton, who always taught

1

They are the only white people there, sitting in the dimness of the Negro church that had once been a corner store, and all through the bubbling, swelling, seething of before the services, twelve-year-old Carol clenches tight her mother's hand, the other resting lightly on her friend, Parialee Phillips, for whose baptism she has come.

The white-gloved ushers hurry up and down the aisle, beckoning people to their seats. A jostle of people. To the chairs angled to the left for the youth choir, to the chairs angled to the right for the ladies' choir, even up to the platform, where behind the place for the dignitaries and the mixed choir, the new baptismal tank gleams — and as if pouring into it from the ceiling, the blue-painted River of Jordan, God standing in the waters, embracing a brown man in a leopard skin and pointing to the letters of gold:

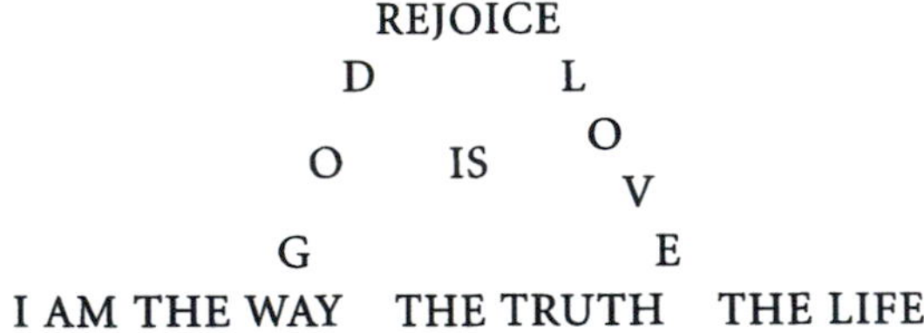

At the clear window, the crucified Christ embroidered on the starched white curtain leaps in the wind of the sudden singing. And the choirs march in. Robes of wine, of blue, of red.

"We stands and sings too," says Parialee's mother, Alva, to Helen; though already Parialee has pulled Carol up. Singing, little Lucinda Phillips fluffs out her many petticoats; singing, little Bubbie bounces up and down on his heels.

Any day now I'll reach that land of freedom,
Yes, o yes
Any day now, know that promised land

The youth choir claps and taps to accent the swing of it. Beginning to tap, Carol stiffens. "Parry, look. Somebody from school."

"Once more once," says Parialee, in the new way she likes to talk now.

"Eddie Garlin's up there. He's in my math."

"Couple cats from Franklin Jr. chirps in the choir. No harm or alarm."

Anxiously Carol scans the faces to see who else she might know, who else might know her, but looks quickly down to Lucinda's wide skirts, for it seems Eddie looks back at her, sullen or troubled, though it is hard to tell, faced as she is into the window of curtained sunblaze.

I know my robe will fit me well
I tried it on at the gates of hell

If it were a record she would play it over and over, Carol thought, to untwine the intertwined voices, to search how the many rhythms rock apart and yet are one glad rhythm.

When I get to heaven gonna sing and shout
Nobody be able to turn me out

"That's Mr. Chairback Evans going to invocate," Lucinda leans across Parry to explain. "He don't invoke good like Momma."

"Shhhh."

"Momma's the only lady in the church that invocates. She made the prayer last week. (Last month, Lucy.) I made the children's 'nouncement last time. (That was way back Thanksgiving.) And Bubbie's 'nounced too. Lots of times."

"Lucy-inda. SIT!"

Bible study announcements and mixed-choir practice announcements and Teen Age Hearts meeting announcements.

If Eddie said something to her about being there, worried Carol, if he talked to her right in front of somebody at school.

Messengers of Faith announcements and Mamboettes announcement and Committee for the Musical Tea.

Parry's arm so warm. Not realizing, starting up the old game from grade school, drumming a rhythm on the other's arm to see if the song could be guessed. "Parry, guess."

But Parry is pondering the platform.

The baptismal tank? "Parry, are you scared . . . the baptizing?"

"This cat? No." Shaking her head so slow and scornful, the barrette in her hair, sun fired, strikes a long rail of light. And still ponders the platform.

New Strangers Baptist Church invites you and Canaan Fair Singers announcements and Battle of Song and Cosmopolites meet. "Oh Lord, I couldn't find no ease," a solo. The ladies' choir:

O what you say seekers, o what you say seekers,
Will you never turn back no more?

The mixed choir sings:

> *Ezekiel saw that wheel of time*
> *Every spoke was of humankind . . .*

And the slim worn man in the pin-stripe suit starts his sermon On the Nature of God. How God is long-suffering. Oh, how long he has suffered. Calling the roll of the mighty nations, that rose and fell and now are dust for grinding the face of Man.

O voice of drowsiness and dream to which Carol does not need to listen. As long ago. Parry warm beside her too, as it used to be, there in the classroom at Mann Elementary, and the feel of drenched in sun and dimness and dream. Smell and sound of the chalk wearing itself away to nothing, rustle of books, drumming tattoo of Parry's fingers on her arm: *Guess.*

And as the preacher's voice spins happy and free, it is the used-to-be playyard. Tag. Thump of the volley ball. Ecstasy of the jump rope. Parry, do pepper. Carol, do pepper. Parry's bettern Carol, Carol's bettern Parry. . . .

Did someone scream?

It seemed someone screamed — but all were sitting as before, though the sun no longer blared through the windows. She tried to see up where Eddie was, but the ushers were standing at the head of the aisle now, the ladies in white dresses like nurses or waitresses wear, the men holding their white-gloved hands up so one could see their palms.

"And God is Powerful," the preacher was chanting. "Nothing for him to scoop out the oceans and pat up the mountains. Nothing for him to scoop up the miry clay and create man. Man, I said, create Man."

The lady in front of her moaned *"Oh yes"* and others were moaning *"Oh yes."*

"And when the earth mourned the Lord said, Weep not, for all will be returned to you, every dust, every atom. And the tired dust settles back, goes back. Until that Judgment Day. That great day."

"Oh yes."

The ushers were giving out fans. Carol reached for one and Parry said: "What *you* need one for?" but she took it anyway.

"You think Satchmo can blow; you think Muggsy can blow; you think Dizzy can blow?" He was straining to an imaginary trumpet now, his head far back and his voice coming out like a trumpet.

"Oh Parry, he's so good."

"Well. Jelly jelly."

"Nothing to Gabriel on the great getting-up morning. And the horn wakes up Adam, and Adam runs to wake up Eve, and Eve moans; Just one more minute, let me sleep, and Adam yells, Great Day, woman, don't you know it's the Great Day?"

"Great Day, Great Day," the mixed choir behind the preacher rejoices:

When our cares are past
when we're home at last . . .

"And Eve runs to wake up Cain." Running round the platform, stooping and shaking imaginary sleepers, "and Cain runs to wake up Abel." Looping, scalloping his voice — "Grea-aaa-aat Daaaay." All the choirs thundering:

Great Day
When the battle's fought
And the victory's won

Exultant spirals of sound. And Carol caught into it (Eddie forgotten, the game forgotten) chanting with Lucy and Bubbie: *"Great Day."*

"Ohhhhhhhhhh," his voice like a trumpet again, "the re-unioning. Ohhhhhhhhh, the rejoicing. After the ages immemorial of longing."

Somone *was* screaming. And an awful thrumming sound with it, like feet and hands thrashing around, like a giant jumping of a rope.

"Great Day." And no one stirred or stared as the ushers brought a little woman out into the aisle, screaming and shaking, just a little shrunk-up woman not much taller than Carol, the biggest thing about her her swollen hands and the cascades of tears wearing her face.

The shaking inside Carol too. Turning and trembling to ask: "What . . . that lady?" But Parry still ponders the platform; little Lucy loops the chain of her bracelet round and round; and Bubbie sits placidly, dreamily. Alva Phillips is up fanning a lady in front of her; two lady ushers are fanning other people Carol cannot see. And her mother, her mother looks in a sleep.

Yes. He raised up the dead from the grave. He made old death behave.

Yes. Yes. From all over, hushed. *O Yes*

He was your mother's rock. Your father's mighty tower. And he gave us a little baby. A little baby to love.

I am so glad

Yes, your friend, when you're friendless. Your father when you're fatherless. Way maker. Door opener.

Yes

When it seems you can't go on any longer, he's there. You can, he says, you can.

Yes

And that burden you been carrying — ohhhhh that burden — not for always will it be. No, not for always.

Stay with me, Lord

I will put my Word in you and it is power. I will put my Truth in you and it is power.

O Yes

Out of your suffering I will make you to stand as a stone. A tried stone. Hewn out of the mountains of ages eternal.

Ohhhhhhhhhhh. Out of the mire I will lift your feet. Your tired feet from so much wandering. From so much work and wear and hard times.

Yes

From so much journeying — and never the promised land. And I'll wash them in the well your tears made. And I'll shod them in the gospel of peace, and of feeling good. Ohhhhhhhhh.

O Yes.

Behind Carol, a trembling wavering scream. Then the thrashing. Up above, the singing:

They taken my blessed Jesus and flogged him to the woods
And they made him hew out his cross and they dragged him to Calvary

Shout brother, Shout shout shout. He never cried a word.

Powerful throbbing voices. Calling and answering to each other.

They taken my blessed Jesus and whipped him up the hill
With a knotty whip and a raggedy thorn he never cried a word
Shout, sister. Shout shout shout. He never cried a word.

Go tell the people the Saviour has risen
Has risen from the dead and will live forevermore
And won't have to die no more.
Halleloo.
Shout, brother, shout
We won't have to die no more!

A single exultant lunge of shriek. Then the thrashing. All around a clapping. Shouts with it. The piano whipping, whipping air to a froth. Singing now.

I once was lost who now am found
Was blind who now can see

On Carol's fan, a little Jesus walked on wondrously blue waters to where bearded disciples spread nets out of a fishing boat. If she studied the fan — became it — it might make a wall around her. If she could make what was happening (*what* was happening?) into a record small and round to listen to far and far as if into a seashell — the stamp and rills and spirals all tiny (but never any screaming).

wade wade in the water

Jordan's water is chilly and wild
I've got to get home to the other side
God's going to trouble the waters

The music leaps and prowls. Ladders of screamings. Drumming feet of ushers running. And still little Lucy fluffs her skirts, loops the chain on her bracelet; still Bubbie sits and rocks dreamily; and only eyes turn for an instant to the aisle as if nothing were happening. "Mother, let's go home," Carol begs, but her mother holds her so tight. Alva Phillips, strong Alva, rocking too and chanting, *O Yes*. No, do not look.

Wade,
Sea of trouble all mingled with fire
Come on my brethren it's time to go higher
Wade wade

The voices in great humming waves, slow, slow (when did it become the humming?), everyone swaying with it too, moving like in slow waves and singing, and up where Eddie is, a new cry, wild and open, "O help me, Jesus," and when Carol opens her eyes she closes them again, quick, but still can see the new known face from school (not Eddie), the thrashing, writhing body struggling against the ushers with the look of grave and loving support on their faces, and hear the torn, tearing cry: "Don't take me away, life everlasting don't take me away."

And now the rhinestones in Parry's hair glitter wicked; the white hands of the ushers, fanning, foam in the air; the blue-painted waters of Jordan swell and thunder; Christ spirals on his cross in the window — and she is drowned under the sluice of the slow singing and the sway.

So high up and forgotten the waves and the world, so stirless the deep cool green and the wrecks of what had been. Here now Hostess Foods, where Alva Phillips works her nights — but different from that time Alva had taken them through before work, for it is all sunken under water, the creaking loading platform where they had left the night behind; the closet room where Alva's swaddles of sweaters, boots, and cap hung, the long hall lined with pickle barrels, the sharp freezer door swinging open.

Bubbles of breath that swell. A gulp of numbing air. She swims into the chill room where the huge wheels of cheese stand, and Alva swims too, deftly oiling each machine: slicers and wedgers and the convey, that at her touch start to roll and grind. The light of day blazes up and Alva is holding a cup, saying: Drink this, baby.

"DRINK IT." Her mother's voice and the numbing air demanding her to pay attention. Up through the waters and into the car.

"That's right, lambie, now lie back." Her mother's lap.

"Mother."

"Shhhhh. You almost fainted, lambie."

Alva's voice. "You gonna be all right, Carol . . . Lucy, I'm telling you for the last time, you and Buford get back into that church. Carol is *fine*."

"Lucyinda, if I had all your petticoats I could float." Crying. "Why didn't you let me wear my full skirt with the petticoats, Mother."

"Shhhhh, lamb." Smoothing her cheek. "Just breathe, take long deep breaths."

". . . How you doing now, you little ol' consolation prize?" It is Parry, but she does not come in the car or reach to Carol through the open window: "No need to cuss and fuss. You going to be sharp as a tack, Jack."

Answering automatically: "And cool as a fool."

Quick, they look at each other.

"Parry, we have to go home now, don't we, Mother? I almost fainted, didn't I, Mother? . . . Parry, I'm sorry I got sick and have to miss your baptism."

"Don't feel sorry. I'll feel better you not there to watch. It was our mommas wanted you to be there, not me."

"Parry!" Three voices.

"Maybe I'll come over to play kickball after. If you feeling better. Maybe. Or bring the pogo." Old shared joys in her voice. "Or any little thing."

In just a whisper: "Or any little thing. Parry. Good-bye, Parry."

And why does Alva have to talk now?

"You all right? You breathin' deep like your momma said? Was it too close 'n hot in there? Did something scare you, Carrie?"

Shaking her head to lie, "No."

"I blames myself for not paying attention. You not used to people letting go that way. Lucy and Bubbie, Parialee, they used to it. They been coming since they lap babies."

"Alva, that's all right. Alva. Mrs. Phillips."

"You *was* scared. Carol, it's something to study about. You'll feel better if you understand."

Trying not to listen.

"You not used to hearing what people keeps inside, Carol. You know how music can make you feel things? Glad or sad or like you can't sit still? That was religion music, Carol."

"I have to breathe deep, Mother said."

"Not everybody feels religion the same way. Some it's in their mouth, but some it's like a hope in their blood, their bones. And they singing songs every word that's real to them, Carol, every word out of their own life. And the preaching finding lodgment in their hearts."

The screaming was tuning up in her ears again, high above Alva's patient voice and the waves lapping and fretting.

"Maybe somebody's had a hard week, Carol, and they locked up with it. Maybe a lot of hard weeks bearing down."

"Mother, my head hurts."

"And they're home, Carol, church is home. Maybe the only place they can feel how they feel and maybe let it come out. So they can go on. And it's all right."

"Please, Alva. Mother, tell Alva my head hurts."

"Get Happy, we call it, and most it's a good feeling, Carol. When you got all that locked up inside you."

"Tell her we have to go home. It's all right, Alva. Please, Mother. Say good-bye. Good-bye."

When I was carrying Parry and her father left me, and I fifteen years old, one thousand miles away from home, sin-sick and never really believing, as still I don't believe all, scorning, for what have it done to help, waiting there in the clinic and maybe sleeping, a voice called: Alva, Alva. So mournful and so sweet: Alva. Fear not, I have loved you from the foundation of the universe. And a little small child tugged on my dress. He was carrying a parade stick, on the end of it a star that outshined the sun. Follow me, he said. And the real sun went down and he hidden his stick. How dark it was, how dark. I could feel the darkness with my hands. And when I could see, I screamed. Dump trucks run, dumping bodies in hell, and a convey line run, never ceasing with souls, weary ones having to stamp and shove them along, and the air like fire. Oh I never want to hear such screaming. Then the little child jumped on a motorbike making a path no bigger than my little finger. But first he greased my feet with the hands of my momma when I was a knee baby. They shined like the sun was on them. Eyes he placed all around my head, and as I journeyed upward after him, it seemed I heard a mourning: "Mama Mama you must help carry the world." The rise and fall of nations I saw. And the voice called again Alva Alva, and I flew into a world of light, multitudes singing, Free, free, I am so glad.

2

Helen began to cry, telling her husband about it.

"You and Alva ought to have your heads examined, taking her there cold like that," Len said. "All right, wreck my best handkerchief. Anyway, now that she's had a bath, her Sunday dinner. . . ."

"And been fussed over," seventeen-year-old Jeannie put in.

"She seems good as new. Now *you* forget it, Helen."

"I can't. Something . . . deep happened. If only I or Alva had told her what it would be like. . . . But I didn't realize."

You don't realize a lot of things, Mother, Jeannie said, but not aloud.

"So Alva talked about it after instead of before. Maybe it meant more that way."

"Oh Len, she didn't listen."

"You don't know if she did or not. Or what there was in the experience for her. . . ."

Enough to pull that kid apart two ways even more, Jeannie said, but still not aloud.

"I was so glad she and Parry were going someplace together again. Now that'll be between them too. Len, they really need, miss each other. What happened in a few months? When I think of how close they were, the hours of makebelieve and dressup and playing ball and collecting. . . ."

"Grow up, Mother." Jeannie's voice was harsh. "Parialee's collecting something else now. Like her own crowd. Like jivetalk and rhythmandblues. Like teachers who treat her like a dummy and white kids who treat her like dirt; boys who think she's really something and chicks who. . . ."

"Jeannie, I know. It hurts."

"Well, maybe it hurts Parry too. Maybe. At least she's got a crowd. Just don't let it hurt Carol though, 'cause there's nothing she can do about it. That's all through, her and Parialee Phillips, put away with their paper dolls."

"No, Jeannie, no."

"It's like Ginger and me. Remember Ginger, my best friend in Horace Mann. But you hardly noticed when it happened to us, did you . . . because she was white? Yes, Ginger, who's got two kids now, who quit school year before last. Parry's never going to finish either. What's she got to do with Carrie any more? They're going different places. Different places, different crowds. And they're sorting. . . ."

"Now wait, Jeannie. Parry's just as bright, just as capable."

"They're in junior high, Mother. Don't you know about junior high? How they sort? And it's all where you're going. Yes and Parry's colored and Carrie's white. And you have to watch everything, what you wear and how you wear it and who you eat lunch with and how much homework you do and how you act to the teacher and what you laugh at. . . . And run with your crowd."

"It's that final?" asked Len. "Don't you think kids like Carol and Parry can show it doesn't *have* to be that way?"

"They can't. They can't. They don't let you."

"No need to shout," he said mildly. "And who do you mean by 'they' and what do you mean by 'sorting'?"

How they sort. A foreboding of comprehension whirled within Helen. What was it Carol had told her of the Welcome Assembly the first day in junior high? The models showing How to Dress and How Not to Dress and half the girls in their loved new clothes watching their counterparts up on the stage — *their* straight skirt, their sweater, their earrings, lipstick, hairdo — "How Not to Dress," "a bad reputation for your school." It was nowhere in Carol's description, yet picturing it now, it seemed to Helen that a mute cry of violated dignity hung in the air. Later there had been a story of going to another Low 7 homeroom on an errand and seeing a teacher trying to wipe the forbidden lipstick off a girl who was fighting back and cursing. Helen could hear Carol's frightened, self-righteous tones: ". . . and I hope they expel her; she's the kind that gives Franklin Jr. a bad rep; she doesn't care about anything and always gets into fights." Yet there was nothing in these incidents to touch the heavy comprehension that waited. . . . Homework, the wonderings those times Jeannie and Carol needed help: "What if there's no one at home to give the help, and the teachers with their two hundred and forty kids a day can't or don't or the kids don't ask and they fall hopelessly behind, what then?" — but this too was unrelated. And what had it been that time about Parry? "Mother, Melanie and Sharon won't go if they know Parry's coming." Then of course you'll go with Parry, she's been your friend longer, she had answered, but where was it they were going and what had finally happened? Len, my head hurts, she felt like saying, in Carol's voice in the car, but Len's eyes were grave on Jeannie who was saying passionately:

"If you think it's so goddamn important why do we have to live here where it's for real; why don't we move to Ivy like Betsy (yes, I know, money), where it's the deal to be buddies, in school anyway, three coloured kids and their father's a doctor or judge or something big wheel and one always gets elected President or head song girl or something to prove oh how we're democratic. . . . What do you want of that poor kid anyway? Make up your mind. Stay friends with Parry — but be one of the kids. Sure. Be a brain — but not a square. Rise on up, college prep, but don't get separated. Yes, stay one of the kids but. . . ."

"Jeannie. You're not talking about Carol at all, are you, Jeannie? Say it again. I wasn't listening. I was trying to think."

"She will not say it again," Len said firmly, "you look about ready to pull a Carol. One a day's our quota. And you, Jeannie, we'd better cool it. Too much to talk about for one session. . . . Here, come to the window and watch the Carol and Parry you're both all worked up about."

In the wind and the shimmering sunset light, half the children of the block are playing down the street. Leaping, bouncing, hallooing, tugging the kites of spring. In the old synchronized understanding, Carol and Parry kick, catch, kick, catch. And now Parry jumps on her pogo stick (the last time), Carol shadowing her, and Bubbie, arching his body in a semicircle of joy, bounding after them, high, higher, higher.

And the months go by and supposedly it is forgotten, except for the now and then when, self-important, Carol will say: I really truly did nearly faint, didn't I, Mother, that time I went to church with Parry?

And now seldom Parry and Carol walk the hill together. Melanie's mother drives by to pick up Carol, and the several times Helen has suggested Parry, too, Carol is quick to explain: "She's already left" or "She isn't ready; she'll make us late."

And after school? Carol is off to club or skating or library or someone's house, and Parry can stay for kickball only on the rare afternoons when she does not have to hurry home where Lucy, Bubbie, and the cousins wait to be cared for, now Alva works the four to twelve-thirty shift.

No more the bending together over the homework. All semester the teachers have been different, and rarely Parry brings her books home, for where is there space or time and what is the sense? And the phone never rings with: what you going to wear tomorrow, are you bringing your lunch, or come on over, let's design some clothes for the Katy Keane comic-book contest. And Parry never drops by with Alva for Saturday snack to or from grocery shopping.

And the months go by and the sorting goes on and seemingly it is over until that morning when Helen must stay home from work, so swollen and feverish is Carol with mumps.

The afternoon before, Parry had come by, skimming up the stairs, spilling books and binders on the bed: Hey frail, lookahere and wail, your momma askin for homework, what she got against YOU? . . . looking quickly once then not looking again and talking fast. . . . Hey, you bloomed. You gonna be your own pumpkin, hallowe'en? Your momma know yet it's mu-umps? And lumps. Momma says: no distress, she'll be by tomorrow morning see do you need anything while your momma's to work. . . . (Singing: *whole lotta shakin goin on.*) All your 'signments is inside; Miss Rockface says the teachers to write 'em cause I mightn't get it right all right.

But did not tell: Does your mother work for Carol's mother? Oh, you're neighbors! Very well, I'll send along a monitor to open Carol's locker but you're only to take these things I'm writing down, nothing else. Now say after me: Miss Campbell is trusting me to be a good responsible girl. And go right to Carol's house. After school. Not stop anywhere on the way. Not lose anything. And only take. What's written on the list.

You really gonna mess with that book stuff? Sign on *mine* says do-not-open-until-eX-mas. . . . That Mrs. Fernandez doll she didn't send nothin, she was the only, says feel better and read a book to report if you feel like and I'm the most for takin care for you; she's my most, wish I could get her but she only teaches 'celerated. . . . Flicking the old read books on the shelf but not opening to mock-declaim as once she used to . . . Vicky, Eddie's g.f. in Rockface office, she's on suspended for sure, yellin to Rockface: you bitchkitty don't you give me no more bad shit. That Vicky she can sure sling-ating-ring it. Staring out the window as if the tree not there in which they had hid out and rocked so often. . . . For sure. (*Keep mo-o-vin.*) Got me a new pink top and lilac skirt. Look sharp with this purple? Cinching in the wide belt as if delighted with what newly swelled above and swelled below. Wear it Saturday night to Sweet's, Modernaires Sounds of Joy, Leroy and Ginny and me goin if Momma'll stay home. IF. (*Shake my baby shake*). How come old folks still likes to party? Huh? Asking of Rembrandt's weary old face looking from the wall. How come (softly) you long-gone you. Touching her face to his quickly, lightly. NEXT mumps is your buddybud Melanie's turn to tote your stuff. *I'm* gettin the hoovus goovus. Hey you so unneat, don't care what you bed with. Removing the books and binders, ranging them on the dresser one by one, marking lipstick faces — bemused or mocking or amazed — on each paper jacket. Better. Fluffing out smoothing the quilt with exaggerated energy. Any little thing I can get, cause I gotta blow. Tossing up and catching their year-ago, arm-in-arm graduation picture, replacing it deftly, upside down, into its mirror crevice. Joe. Bring you joy juice or fizz water or kickapoo? Adding a frown line to one bookface. Twanging the paper fishkite, the Japanese windbell overhead, setting the mobile they had once made of painted eggshells and decorated straws to twirling and rocking. And is gone.

She talked to the lipstick faces after, in her fever, tried to stand on her head to match the picture, twirled and twanged with the violent overhead.

Sleeping at last after the disordered night. Having surrounded herself with the furnishings of that world of childhood she no sooner learned to live in comfortably, then had to leave.

The dollhouse stands there to arrange and rearrange; the shell and picture card collections to re-sort and remember; the population of dolls given away to little sister, borrowed back, propped all around to dress and undress and caress.

She has thrown off her nightgown because of the fever, and her just budding breast is exposed where she reaches to hold the floppy plush dog that had been her childhood pillow.

Not for anything would Helen have disturbed her. Except that in the unaccustomedness of a morning at home, in the bruised restlessness after the sleepless night, she clicks on the radio — and the storm of singing whirls into the room:

. . . sea of trouble all mingled with fire
Come on my brethern we've got to go higher
Wade, wade. . . .

And Carol runs down the stairs, shrieking and shrieking. "Turn it off, Mother, turn it off." Hurling herself at the dial and wrenching it so it comes off in her hand.

"Ohhhhh," choked and convulsive, while Helen tries to hold her, to quiet.

"Mother, why did they sing and scream like that?"

"At Parry's church?"

"Yes." Rocking and strangling the cries. "I hear it all the time." Clinging and beseeching. ". . . What was it, Mother? Why?"

Emotion, Helen thought of explaining, *a characteristic of the religion of all oppressed peoples, yes your very own great-grandparents* — thought of saying. And discarded.

Aren't you now, haven't you had feelings in yourself so strong they had to come out some way? ("what howls restrained by decorum") — thought of saying. And discarded.

Repeat Alva: *hope . . . every word out of their own life. A place to let go. And church is home.* And discarded.

The special history of the Negro people — history? — just you try living what must be lived every day — thought of saying. And discarded.

And said nothing.

And said nothing.

And soothed and held.

"Mother, a lot of the teachers and kids don't like Parry when they don't even know what she's like. Just because . . ." Rocking again, convulsive and shamed. "And I'm not really her friend any more."

No news. Betrayal and shame. Who betrayed? Whose shame? Brought herself to say aloud: "But may be friends again. As Alva and I are."

The sobbing a whisper. "That girl Vicky who got that way when I fainted, she's in school. She's the one keeps wearing the lipstick and they wipe it off and she's always in trouble and now maybe she's expelled. Mother."

"Yes, lambie."

"She acts so awful outside but I remember how she was in church and whenever I see her now I have to wonder. And hear . . . like I'm her, Mother, like I'm her." Clinging and trembling. "Oh why do I have to feel it's happening to me too?

"Mother, I want to forget about it all, and not care, — like Melanie. Why can't I forget? Oh why is it like it is and why do I have to care?"

Caressing, quieting.

Thinking: *caring asks doing. It is a long baptism into the seas of humankind, my daughter. Better immersion than to live untouched. . . . Yet how will you sustain?*

Why is it like it is?

Sheltering her daughter close, mourning the illusion of the embrace.

And why do I have to care?

While in her, her own need leapt and plunged for the place of strength that was not — where one could scream or sorrow while all knew and accepted, and gloved and loving hands waited to support and understand.

◎ *TONI MORRISON*

Toni Morrison was born in 1931 in Lorain, Ohio. She received a B.A. from Howard University and an M.A. from Cornell University. She is the Robert F. Goheen Professor in the Council of the Humanities at Princeton University. She is trustee of the National Humanities Center as well as cochair of the Schomburg Commission for the Preservation of Black Culture. Morrison's many awards include a National Book Award nomination and an Ohioana Book Award for Sula *(1974); a National Book Critics Circle Award and an American Academy and Institute of Arts & Letters Award for* Song of Solomon *(1977); and a National Book Award nomination, a National Book Critics Circle Award nomination, the Robert F. Kennedy Award, and a Pulitzer Prize for fiction for* Beloved *(1988). She won the Nobel Prize for literature in 1993. Her other novels include* The Bluest Eye *(1970) and* Tar Baby *(1981); she has also written a play,* Dreaming Emmett.

The following excerpt from Morrison's novel Beloved *recounts the birth of Denver, the child of Sethe, and is here told by Denver to Beloved. Sethe was a runaway slave in Ohio, and she was unable to go further in her escape due to severely swollen feet and a terrible beating to her back. She encounters a white indentured servant, Amy Denver, a runaway herself, who has "good hands" and who ministers to Sethe. Heading to the river together, Sethe goes into labor and Amy helps her through childbirth. Beloved is the embodiment, or ghost, of one of Sethe's children killed by her in an effort to prevent white owners from taking her into slavery.*

The Birth of Denver

"Tell me," Beloved said. "Tell me how Sethe made you in the boat."

"She never told me all of it," said Denver.

"Tell me."

Denver climbed up on the bed and folded her arms under her apron. She had not been in the tree room once since Beloved sat on their stump after the carnival, and had not remembered that she hadn't gone there until this very desperate moment. Nothing was out there that this sister-girl did not provide in abundance: a racing heart, dreaminess, society, danger, beauty. She swallowed twice to prepare for the telling, to construct out of the strings she had heard all her life a net to hold Beloved.

"She had good hands, she said. The whitegirl, she said, had thin little arms but good hands. She saw that right away, she said. Hair enough for five heads and good hands, she said. I guess the hands made her think she could do it: get us both across the river. But the mouth was what kept her from being scared. She said there ain't nothing to go by with whitepeople. You don't know how they'll jump. Say one thing, do another. But if you looked at the mouth sometimes you could tell by that. She said this girl talked a storm, but there wasn't no meanness around her mouth. She took Ma'am to that lean-to and rubbed her feet for her, so that was one thing. And Ma'am believed she wasn't going to turn her over. You could get money if you turned a runaway over, and she wasn't sure this girl Amy didn't need money more than anything, especially since all she talked about was getting hold of some velvet."

"What's velvet?"

"It's a cloth, kind of deep and soft."

"Go ahead."

"Anyway, she rubbed Ma'am's feet back to life, and she cried, she said, from how it hurt. But it made her think she could make it on over to where Grandma Baby Suggs was and . . ."

"Who is that?"

"I just said it. My grandmother."

"Is that Sethe's mother?"

"No. My father's mother."

"Go ahead."

"That's where the others was. My brothers and . . . the baby girl. She sent them on before to wait for her at Grandma Baby's. So she had to put up with everything to get there. And this here girl Amy helped."

Denver stopped and sighed. This was the part of the story she loved. She was coming to it now, and she loved it because it was all about herself; but she hated it too because it made her feel like a bill was owing somewhere and she, Denver, had to pay it. But who she owed or what to pay it with eluded her. Now, watching Beloved's alert and hungry face, how she took in every word, asking questions about the color of things and their size, her downright craving to know, Denver began to see what she was saying and not just to hear it: there is this nineteen-year-old slave girl — a year older than herself — walking through the dark woods to get to her children who are far away. She is tired, scared maybe, and maybe even lost. Most of all she is by herself and inside her is another baby she has to think about too. Behind her dogs, perhaps; guns probably; and certainly mossy teeth. She is not so afraid at night because she is the color of it, but in the day every sound is a shot or a tracker's quiet step.

Denver was seeing it now and feeling it — through Beloved. Feeling how it must have felt to her mother. Seeing how it must have looked. And the more fine points she made, the more detail she provided, the more Beloved liked it. So she anticipated the questions by giving blood to the scraps her mother and grandmother had told her — and a heartbeat. The monologue became, in fact, a duet as they lay down together, Denver nursing Beloved's interest like a lover whose pleasure was to overfeed the loved. The dark quilt with two orange patches was there with them because Beloved wanted it near her when she slept. It was smelling like grass and feeling like hands — the unrested hands of busy women: dry, warm, prickly. Denver spoke, Beloved listened, and the two did the best they could to create what really happened, how it really was, something only Sethe knew because she alone had the mind for it and the time afterward to shape it: the quality of Amy's voice, her breath like burning wood. The quick-change weather up in those hills — cool at night, hot in the day, sudden fog. How recklessly she behaved with this whitegirl — a recklessness born of desperation and encouraged by Amy's fugitive eyes and her tenderhearted mouth.

"You ain't got no business walking round these hills, miss."

"Looka here who's talking. I got more business here'n you got. They catch you they cut your head off. Ain't nobody after me but I know somebody after you." Amy pressed her fingers into the soles of the slavewoman's feet. "Whose baby that?"

Sethe did not answer.

"You don't even know. Come here, Jesus," Amy sighed and shook her head. "Hurt?"

"A touch."

"Good for you. More it hurt more better it is. Can't nothing heal without pain, you know. What you wiggling for?"

Sethe raised up on her elbows. Lying on her back so long had raised a ruckus between her shoulder blades. The fire in her feet and the fire on her back made her sweat.

"My back hurt me," she said.

"Your back? Gal, you a mess. Turn over here and let me see."

In an effort so great it made her sick to her stomach, Sethe turned onto her right side. Amy unfastened the back of her dress and said, "Come here, Jesus," when she saw. Sethe guessed it must be bad because after that call to Jesus Amy didn't speak for a while. In the silence of an Amy struck dumb for a change, Sethe felt the fingers of those good hands lightly touch her back. She could hear her breathing but still the whitegirl said nothing. Sethe could not move. She couldn't lie on her stomach or her back, and to keep on her side meant pressure on her screaming feet. Amy spoke at last in her dreamwalker's voice.

"It's a tree, Lu. A chokecherry tree. See, here's the trunk — it's red and split wide open, full of sap, and this here's the parting for the branches. You got a mighty lot of branches. Leaves, too, look like, and dern if these ain't blossoms. Tiny little cherry blossoms, just as white. Your back got a whole tree on it. In bloom. What God have in mind, I wonder. I had me some whippings, but I don't remember nothing like this. Mr. Buddy had a right evil hand too. Whip you for looking at him straight. Sure would. I looked right at him one time and he hauled off and threw the poker at me. Guess he knew what I was a-thinking."

Sethe groaned and Amy cut her reverie short — long enough to shift Sethe's feet so the weight, resting on leaf-covered stones, was above the ankles.

"That better? Lord what a way to die. You gonna die in here, you know. Ain't no way out of it. Thank your Maker I come along so's you wouldn't have to die outside in them weeds. Snake come along he bite you. Bear eat you up. Maybe you should of stayed where you was, Lu. I can see by your back why you didn't ha ha. Whoever planted that tree beat Mr. Buddy by a mile. Glad I ain't you. Well, spiderwebs is 'bout all I can do for you. What's in here ain't enough. I'll look outside. Could use moss, but sometimes bugs and things is in it. Maybe I ought to break them blossoms open. Get that pus to running, you think? Wonder what God had in mind. You must of did something. Don't run off nowhere now."

Sethe could hear her humming away in the bushes as she hunted spider-webs. A humming she concentrated on because as soon as Amy ducked out the baby began to stretch. Good question, she was thinking. What did He have in mind? Amy had left the back of Sethe's dress open and now a tail of wind hit it, taking the pain down a step. A relief that let her feel the lesser pain of her sore tongue. Amy returned with two palmfuls of web, which she cleaned of prey and then draped on Sethe's back, saying it was like stringing a tree for Christmas.

"We got a old nigger girl come by our place. She don't know nothing. Sews stuff for Mrs. Buddy — real fine lace but can't barely stick two words together. She don't know nothing, just like you. You don't know a thing. End up dead, that's what. Not me. I'm a get to Boston and get myself some velvet. Carmine. You don't even know about that, do you? Now you never will. Bet you never even sleep with the sun in your face. I did it a couple of times. Most times I'm feeding stock before light and don't get to sleep till way after dark comes. But I was in the back of the wagon once and fell asleep. Sleeping with the sun in your face is the best old feeling. Two times I did it. Once when I was little. Didn't no-body bother me then. Next time, in back of the wagon, it happened again and doggone if the chickens didn't get loose. Mr. Buddy whipped my tail. Kentucky ain't no good place to be in. Boston's the place to be in. That's where my mother was before she was give to Mr. Buddy. Joe Nathan said Mr. Buddy is my daddy but I don't believe that, you?"

Sethe told her she didn't believe Mr Buddy was her daddy.

"You know your daddy, do you?"

"No," said Sethe.

"Neither me. All I know is it ain't him." She stood up then, having finished her repair work, and weaving about the lean-to, her slow-moving eyes pale in the sun that lit her hair, she sang:

"When the busy day is done
And my weary little one

Rocketh gently to and fro;
When the night winds softly blow,
And the crickets in the glen
Chirp and chirp and chirp again;
Where 'pon the haunted green
Fairies dance around their queen,
Then from yonder misty skies
Cometh Lady Button Eyes."

Suddenly she stopped weaving and rocking and sat down, her skinny arms wrapped around her knees, her good good hands cupping her elbows. Her slow-moving eyes stopped and peered into the dirt at her feet. "That's my mama's song. She taught me it."

"Through the muck and mist and gloam
To our quiet cozy home,
Where to singing sweet and low
Rocks a cradle to and fro.
Where the clock's dull monotone
Telleth of the day that's done,
Where the moonbeams hover o'er
Playthings sleeping on the floor,
Where my weary wee one lies
Cometh Lady Button Eyes.

"Layeth she her hands upon
My dear weary little one,
And those white hands overspread
Like a veil the curly head,
Seem to fondle and caress
Every little silken tress.
Then she smooths the eyelids down
Over those two eyes of brown
In such soothing tender wise
Cometh Lady Button Eyes."

Amy sat quietly after her song, then repeated the last line before she stood, left the lean-to and walked off a little ways to lean against a young ash. When she came back the sun was in the valley below and they were way above it in blue Kentucky light.

"You ain't dead yet, Lu? Lu?"

"Not yet."

"Make you a bet. You make it through the night, you make it all the way." Amy rearranged the leaves for comfort and knelt down to massage the swollen feet again. "Give these one more real good rub," she said, and when Sethe sucked air through her teeth, she said, "Shut up. You got to keep your mouth shut."

Careful of her tongue, Sethe bit down on her lips and let the good hands go to work to the tune of "So bees, sing soft and bees, sing low." Afterward, Amy moved to the other side of the lean-to where, seated, she lowered her head toward her shoulder and braided her hair, saying, "Don't up and die on me in the night, you hear? I don't want to see your ugly black face hankering over me. If you do die, just go on off somewhere where I can't see you, hear?"

"I hear," said Sethe. "I'll do what I can, miss."

Sethe never expected to see another thing in this world, so when she felt toes prodding her hip it took a while to come out of a sleep she thought was death. She sat up, stiff and shivery, while Amy looked in on her juicy back.

"Looks like the devil," said Amy. "But you made it through. Come down here, Jesus, Lu made it through. That's because of me. I'm good at sick things. Can you walk, you think?"

"I have to let my water some kind of way."

"Let's see you walk on em."

It was not good, but it was possible, so Sethe limped, holding on first to Amy, then to a sapling.

"Was me did it. I'm good at sick things ain't I?"

"Yeah," said Sethe, "you good."

"We got to get off this here hill. Come on. I'll take you down to the river. That ought to suit you. Me, I'm going to the Pike. Take me straight to Boston. What's that all over your dress?

"Milk."

"You one mess."

Sethe looked down at her stomach and touched it. The baby was dead. She had not died in the night, but the baby had. If that was the case, then there was no stopping now. She would get that milk to her baby girl if she had to swim.

"Ain't you hungry?" Amy asked her.

"I ain't nothing but in a hurry, miss."

"Whoa. Slow down. Want some shoes?"

"Say what?"

"I figured how," said Amy and so she had. She tore two pieces from Sethe's shawl, filled them with leaves and tied them over her feet, chattering all the while.

"How old are you, Lu? I been bleeding for four years but I ain't having nobody's baby. Won't catch me sweating milk cause . . ."

"I know," said Sethe. "You going to Boston."

At noon they saw it; then they were near enough to hear it. By late afternoon they could drink from it if they wanted to. Four stars were visible by the time they found, not a riverboat to stow Sethe away on, or a ferryman willing to take on a fugitive passenger — nothing like that — but a whole boat to steal. It had one oar, lots of holes and two bird nests.

"There you go, Lu. Jesus looking at you."

Sethe was looking at one mile of dark water, which would have to be split with one oar in a useless boat against a current dedicated to the Mississippi hundreds of miles away. It looked like home to her, and the baby (not dead in the least) must have thought so too. As soon as Sethe got close to the river her own water broke loose to join it. The break, followed by the redundant announcement of labor, arched her back.

"What you doing that for?" asked Amy. "Ain't you got a brain in your head? Stop that right now. I said stop it, Lu. You the dumbest thing on this here earth. Lu! Lu!"

Sethe couldn't think of anywhere to go but in. She waited for the sweet beat that followed the blast of pain. On her knees again, she crawled into the boat. It waddled under her and she had just enough time to brace her leaf-bag feet on the bench when another rip took her breath away. Panting under four summer stars, she threw her legs over the sides, because here come the head, as Amy informed her as though she did not know it — as though the rip was a breakup of walnut logs in the brace, or of lightning's jagged tear through a leather sky.

It was stuck. Face up and drowning in its mother's blood. Amy stopped begging Jesus and began to curse His daddy.

"Push!" screamed Amy.

"Pull," whispered Sethe.

And the strong hands went to work a fourth time, none too soon, for river water, seeping through any hole it chose, was spreading over Sethe's hips. She reached one arm back and grabbed the robe while Amy fairly clawed at the head. When a foot rose from the river bed and kicked the bottom of the boat and Sethe's behind, she knew it was done and permitted herself a short faint. Coming to, she heard no cries, just Amy's encouraging coos. Nothing happened for so long they both believed they had lost it. Sethe arched suddenly and the afterbirth shot out. Then the baby whimpered and Sethe looked. Twenty inches of cord hung from its belly and it trembled in the cooling evening air. Amy wrapped her skirt around it and the wet sticky women clambered ashore to see what, indeed, God had in mind.

Spores of bluefern growing in the hollows along the riverbank float toward the water in silver-blue lines hard to see unless you are in or near them, lying right at the river's edge when the sunshots are low and drained. Often they are mistook for insects — but they are seeds in which the whole generation sleeps confident of a future. And for a moment it is easy to believe each one has one — will become all of what is contained in the spore: will live out its days as planned. This moment of certainty lasts no longer than that; longer, perhaps, than the spore itself.

On a riverbank in the cool of a summer evening two women struggled under a shower of silvery blue. They never expected to see each other again in this world and at the moment couldn't care less. But there on a summer night surrounded by bluefern they did something together appropriately and well. A pateroller passing would have sniggered to see two throw-away people, two lawless outlaws — a slave and a barefoot whitewoman with unpinned hair — wrapping a ten-minute-old baby in the rags they wore. But no pateroller came and no peacher. The water sucked and swallowed itself beneath them. There was nothing to disturb them at their work. So they did it appropriately and well.

Twilight came on and Amy said she had to go; that she wouldn't be caught dead in daylight on a busy river with a runaway. After rinsing her hands and face in the river, she stood and looked down at the baby wrapped and tied to Sethe's chest.

"She's never gonna know who I am. You gonna tell her? Who brought her into this here world?" She lifted her chin, looked off into the place where the sun used to be. "You better tell her. You hear? Say Miss Amy Denver. Of Boston."

Sethe felt herself falling into a sleep she knew would be deep. On the lip of it, just before going under, she thought, "That's pretty. Denver. Real pretty."

◎ *CYNTHIA OZICK*

Cynthia Ozick was born in 1928. Her works include Trust, The Cannibal Galaxy, *and* The Messiah of Stockholm *(1987), novels;* The Pagan Rabbi and Other Stories *(1971),* Bloodshed and Three Novellas *(1976; 1995),* Levitation: Five Fictions *(1982; 1995), and* The Shawl *(1989), collections of short fiction;* Art and Ardor: Essays *(1983),* Metaphor and Memory: Essays *(1989), and* What Henry James Knew and Other Essays on Writers *(1993). She has also written a play,* Angel. *Ozick has received the Academy of Arts Award for Literature, two O. Henry First Prizes for Short Story, and fellowships from the Guggenheim Foundation and the National Endowment for the Arts.*

"The Shawl" is the title story of Ozick's 1989 volume of short fiction. Here Ozick brings her gift for stylistics to the unspeakable, to a story of how the Nazi concentration camps dehumanized people, in this case a woman and her child. "The Shawl" is one of the few works of fiction to evoke the horror of the camps from within, and in so doing creates an impact equal to the nonfiction writings of survivors such as Eli Weisel and Primo Levi.

The Shawl

Stella, cold, cold, the coldness of hell. How they walked on the roads together, Rosa with Magda curled up between sore breasts, Magda wound up in the shawl. Sometimes Stella carried Magda. But she was jealous of Magda. A thin girl of fourteen, too small, with thin breasts of her own, Stella wanted to be wrapped in a shawl, hidden away, asleep, rocked by the march, a baby, a round infant in arms. Magda took Rosa's nipple, and Rosa never stopped walking, a walking cradle. There was not enough milk; sometimes Magda sucked air; then she screamed. Stella was ravenous. Her knees were tumors on sticks, her elbows chicken bones.

Rosa did not feel hunger; she felt light, not like someone walking but like someone in a faint, in trance, arrested in a fit, someone who is already a floating angel, alert and seeing everything, but in the air, not there, not touching the road. As if teetering on the tips of her fingernails. She looked into Magda's face through a gap in the shawl: a squirrel in a nest, safe, no one could reach her inside the little house of the shawl's windings. The face, very round, a pocket mirror of a face: but it was not Rosa's bleak complexion, dark like cholera, it was another kind of face altogether, eyes blue as air, smooth feathers of hair nearly as yellow as the Star sewn into Rosa's coat. You could think she was one of *their* babies.

Rosa, floating, dreamed of giving Magda away in one of the villages. She could leave the line for a minute and push Magda into the hands of any woman on the side of the road. But if she moved out of line they might shoot. And even if she fled the line for half a second and pushed the shawl-bundle at a stranger, would the woman take it? She might be surprised, or afraid; she might drop the shawl, and Magda would fall out and strike her head and die. The little round head. Such a good child, she gave up screaming, and sucked now only for the taste of the drying nipple itself. The neat grip of the tiny gums. One mite of a tooth tip sticking up in the bottom gum, how shining, an elfin tombstone of white marble gleaming there. Without complaining, Magda relinquished Rosa's teats, first the left, then the right; both were cracked, not a sniff of milk. The duct-crevice extinct, a dead volcano, blind eye, chill hole, so Magda took the corner of the shawl and milked it instead. She sucked and sucked, flooding the threads with wetness. The shawl's good flavor, milk of linen.

It was a magic shawl, it could nourish an infant for three days and three nights. Magda did not die, she stayed alive, although very quiet. A peculiar smell, of cinnamon and almonds, lifted out of her mouth. She held her eyes open every moment, forgetting how to blink or nap, and Rosa and sometimes Stella studied their blueness. On the road they raised one burden of a leg after another and studied Magda's face. "Aryan," Stella said, in a voice grown as thin as a string; and Rosa thought how Stella gazed at Magda like a young cannibal. And the time that Stella said "Aryan," it sounded to Rosa as if Stella had really said "Let us devour her."

But Magda lived to walk. She lived that long, but she did not walk very well, partly because she was only fifteen months old, and partly because the spindles of her legs could not hold up her fat belly. It was fat with air, full and round. Rosa gave almost all her food to Magda, Stella gave nothing; Stella was ravenous, a growing child herself, but not growing much. Stella did not menstruate. Rosa did not menstruate. Rosa was ravenous, but also not; she learned from Magda how to drink the taste of a finger in one's mouth. They were in a place without pity, all pity was annihilated in Rosa, she looked at Stella's bones without pity. She was sure that Stella was waiting for Magda to die so she could put her teeth into the little thighs.

Rosa knew Magda was going to die very soon; she should have been dead already, but she had been buried away deep inside the magic shawl, mistaken there for the shivering mound of Rosa's breasts; Rosa clung to the shawl as if it covered only herself. No one took it away from her. Magda was mute. She never cried. Rosa hid her in the barracks, under the shawl, but she knew that one day someone would inform; or one day someone, not even Stella, would steal Magda to eat her. When Magda began to walk, Rosa knew that Magda was going to die very soon, something would happen. She was afraid to fall asleep; she slept with the weight of her thigh on Magda's body; she was afraid she would smother Magda under her thigh. The weight of Rosa was becoming less and less; Rosa and Stella were slowly turning into air.

Magda was quiet, but her eyes were horribly alive, like blue tigers. She watched. Sometimes she laughed — it seemed a laugh, but how could it be? Magda had never seen anyone laugh. Still, Magda laughed at her shawl when the wind blew its corners, the bad wind with pieces of black in it, that made Stella's and Rosa's eyes tear. Magda's eyes were always clear and tearless. She watched like a tiger. She guarded her shawl. No one could touch it; only Rosa could touch it. Stella was not allowed. The shawl was Magda's own baby, her pet, her little sister. She tangled herself up in it and sucked on one of the corners when she wanted to be very still.

Then Stella took the shawl away and made Magda die.

Afterward Stella said: "I was cold."

And afterward she was always cold, always. The cold went into her heart: Rosa saw that Stella's heart was cold. Magda flopped onward with her little pencil legs scribbling this way and that, in search of the shawl; the pencils faltered at the barracks opening, where the light began. Rosa saw and pursued. But already Magda was in the square outside the barracks, in the jolly light. It was the roll-call arena. Every morning Rosa had to conceal Magda under the shawl against a wall of the barracks and go out and stand in the arena with Stella and hundreds of others, sometimes for hours, and Magda, deserted, was quiet under the shawl, sucking on her corner. Every day Magda was silent, and so she did not die. Rosa saw that today Magda was going to die, and at the same time a fearful joy ran in Rosa's two palms, her fingers were on fire, she was astonished, febrile: Magda, in the sunlight, swaying on her pencil legs, was howling. Ever since the drying up of Rosa's nipples, ever since Magda's last scream on the road, Magda had been devoid of any syllable; Magda was a mute. Rosa believed that something had gone wrong with her vocal cords, with her windpipe, with the cave of her larynx; Magda was defective, without a voice; perhaps she was deaf; there might be something amiss with her intelligence; Magda was dumb. Even the laugh that came when the ash-stippled wind made a clown out of Magda's shawl was only the air-blown showing of her teeth. Even when the lice, head lice and body lice, crazed her so that she became as wild as one of the big rats that plundered the barracks at daybreak looking for carrion, she rubbed and scratched and kicked and bit and rolled without a whimper. But now Magda's mouth was spilling a long viscous rope of clamor.

"Maaaa — "

It was the first noise Magda had ever sent out from her throat since the drying up of Rosa's nipples.

"Maaaa . . . aaa!"

Again! Magda was wavering in the perilous sunlight of the arena, scribbling on such pitiful little bent shins. Rosa saw. She saw that Magda was grieving for the loss of her shawl, she saw that Magda was going to die. A tide of commands hammered in Rosa's nipples: Fetch, get, bring! But she did not know which to go after first, Magda or the shawl. If she jumped out into the arena to snatch Magda up, the howling would not stop, because Magda would still not have the shawl; but if she ran back into the barracks to find the shawl, and if she found it, and if she came after Magda holding it and shaking it, then she would get Magda back, Magda would put the shawl in her mouth and turn dumb again.

Rosa entered the dark. It was easy to discover the shawl. Stella was heaped under it, asleep in her thin bones. Rosa tore the shawl free and flew — she could fly, she was only air — into the arena. The sunheat murmured of another life, of butterflies in summer. The light was placid, mellow. On the other side of the steel fence, far away, there were green meadows speckled with dandelions and deep-colored violets; beyond them, even farther, innocent tiger lilies, tall, lifting their orange bonnets. In the barracks they spoke of "flowers," of "rain": excrement, thick turd-braids, and the slow stinking maroon waterfall that slunk down from the upper bunks, the stink mixed with a bitter fatty floating smoke that greased Rosa's skin. She stood for an instant at the margin of the arena. Sometimes the electricity inside the fence would seem to hum; even Stella said it was only an imagining, but Rosa heard real sounds in the wire: grainy sad voices. The farther she was from the fence, the more clearly the voices crowded at her. The lamenting voices strummed so convincingly, so passionately, it was impossible to suspect them of being phantoms. The voices told her to hold up the shawl, high; the voices told her to shake it, to whip with it, to unfurl it like a flag. Rosa lifted, shook, whipped, unfurled. Far off, very far, Magda leaned across her air-fed belly, reaching out with the rods of her arms. She was high up, elevated, riding someone's shoulder. But the shoulder that carried Magda was not coming toward Rosa and the shawl, it was drifting away, the speck of Magda was moving more and more into the smoky distance. Above the shoulder a helmet glinted. The light tapped the helmet and sparkled it into a goblet. Below the helmet a black body like a domino and a pair of black boots hurled themselves in the direction of the electrified fence. The electric voices began to chatter wildly. "Maamaa, maaamaaa," they all hummed together. How far Magda was from Rosa now, across the whole square, past a dozen barracks, all the way on the other side! She was no bigger than a moth.

All at once Magda was swimming through the air. The whole of Magda traveled through loftiness. She looked like a butterfly touching a silver vine. And the moment Magda's feathered round head and her pencil legs and balloonish belly and zigzag arms splashed against the fence, the steel voices went mad in their growling, urging Rosa to run and run to the spot where Magda had fallen from her flight against the electrified fence; but of course Rosa did not obey them. She only stood, because if she ran they would shoot, and if she tried to pick up the sticks of Magda's body they would shoot, and if she let the wolf's screech ascending now through the ladder of her skeleton break out, they would shoot; so she took Magda's shawl and filled her own mouth with it, stuffed it in and stuffed it in, until she was swallowing up the wolf's screech and tasting the cinnamon and almond depth of Magda's saliva; and Rosa drank Magda's shawl until it dried.

◎ *AMY LING*

Amy Ling was born in 1939 in Beijing. She was educated at Queens College and received her M.A. from the University of California at Davis and her Ph.D. from New York University. Ling is director of Asian-American Studies at the University of Wisconsin at Madison. She has published Chinamerican Reflections *(poetry, 1984) and a breakthrough book of scholarship,* Between Worlds: Women Writers of Chinese Ancestry *(1990). Amy Ling has coedited several volumes of Asian-American literature, most recently* Reading the Literature of Asian America *(1992) with Shirley Lim. She is on the editorial board of the Oxford Companion to American Women's Writing.*

"Whose America Is It?" first appeared in Weber Studies *in 1995. This personal essay opens with a portrait of Ling's family on the U.S.S.* General Stewart *in 1994. Reflecting back on her little brother's question — "Whose America is it?" — Ling comments: "What is my work in Asian-American literature today but an effort to make a home, a comfortable place, for myself in this still too often hostile land."*

Whose America Is It?

It was a grey November morning, 1945, as the army troop transport U.S.S. *General Stewart* neared its destination, its decks crowded with American soldiers and nurses, and a handful of Chinese and Indian immigrants, mostly mothers and small children. From Calcutta, India, through the Suez Canal, the Mediterranean, across the wide, rough, gray-green Atlantic Ocean, it had been four long weeks at sea. My three-year-old brother and I stood with our mother at the rail, caught up in the excitement. We'd been scrubbed and brushed; mother had dressed him in woolen shorts, a navy blue jacket; me in a red woolen dress that she had knitted, and she tied a big plaid ribbon in my hair. Mother herself wore a red Chinese dress with a daisy trim — red the color of celebration and joy. We stared in awe as the giant green lady with the torch and book slid past us, and the jagged skyline of New York City grew larger and larger, gradually looming over us.

"These are the tallest buildings in the world," mother explained.

"Whose America is it? Theirs or ours?" my brother asked suddenly.

"Theirs," mother answered.

Tears streamed down his chubby cheeks. "Then they'll throw me into the ocean."

Mother tried to reassure him that this wouldn't happen. We had reached America; the land of the free; the country where everyone was treated equally; the land that belonged to Grandma Traub, her adopted mother, who would take care of us; the land where Daddy had been working for a year buying furniture and preparing an apartment for us. We were the fortunate few who had connections. We were able to leave a war-torn China where food was scarce, bombs were dropping, people were dying. America was the Beautiful Country; that was its name. It was the land of wealth and opportunity. No need for tears. This was a time to celebrate.

But now, with hindsight, I realize my brother was wise beyond his years, for how did President Bush greet the Haitians crossing the waters between their island and Florida in 1992? How did President Clinton receive the Chinese passengers on the *Golden Enterprise* trying to land in July 1993? The 9 August 1993 cover of *Newsweek* announced that 60% of people in the United States population believe that "immigration is bad for the country." And where do I stand on this complex issue? How can I say we must close the door to others like me longing to take part in the American Dream? How can I agree with Garrett Hardin's cold and logical "lifeboat ethics"? On the other hand, now that I'm on this side of the "golden door," wouldn't I lose if the door were open to everyone? The world has too many "tired" and "poor," innumerable "masses yearning to breathe free." We would no longer be a country of wealth, opportunity, and open spaces if everyone were to come in. But then is it morally right for a few nations to hold so much of the world's wealth? On the other hand, I must admit that I feel relieved and lucky (and guilty) to have been on the U.S.S. *General Stewart* in 1945 rather than the *Golden Enterprise* in 1993.

What is my work in Asian American literature today but an effort to make a home, a comfortable place, for myself in this still too often hostile land. The educational policy in the United States when I was growing up was totally homogenizing and assimilationist. The prevailing national self-concept was Israel Zangwill's metaphor of the large melting pot, where all the peoples of the world would be mixed together and come out WASP, celebrating Columbus Day and Thanksgiving from the Pilgrims' point of view; Memorial and Veteran's Day and the Fourth of July, waving the red, white and blue. I was not supposed to notice that in the three decades of my developing and maturing years, the United States fought three wars in Asia against people that looked like me: in the Forties against the Japanese, in the Fifties against Koreans and Communist Chinese, and in the Sixties against Vietnamese, Cambodians and Laotians. It's extremely difficult and totally confusing to feel American and to look like the enemy, to think myself at home and be asked where I come from, to be a professor of literature and complimented on my good English. As Maxine Hong Kingston has written, "I learned to make my mind large, as the universe is large, so that there is room for paradoxes." (When people compliment Maxine on good English, her response is a gentle but pointed, "Thanks. So's yours.")

As a child, though I did not take conscious note of the larger political scene and how I did or did not fit into it, I couldn't help but notice that in the land of the redwhiteandblue the redyellowandbrown were generally relegated to inferior positions. No matter how enthusiastically we waved the flag, our skin color, eye shape, hair texture and facial features did not change. Nor did our positions in the hierarchy based on skin color and race. Being "yellow" was perhaps not as bad as being "brown" or "black," but, without a doubt, it was not as good as being "white." There was some acknowledgment of the venerable age of Chinese culture and the high level of craftsmanship and attention to detail in the *objets d'art* that came from that part of the world, but, as I imbibed from the general atmosphere and from frequent remarks, Chinese people were so funny looking. Why didn't they open their eyes more? How could they see out of such slits? Their noses were so flat; they couldn't hold up glasses. And they did everything in such an upside down way: imagine having your last name come first, reading a book from the back to the front, writing up and down on a page instead of from side to side, having soup at the end of the meal! All these inversions could only be explained by the fact that these creatures came from the underbelly of the globe.

When I was growing up, being any color but white and from any culture but WASP meant you were of an inferior order with no right to enter certain places, like country clubs and Ivy League schools. For peoples of color to buy a house in certain neighborhoods in the 1950s was either impossible or, as happened to one Chinese American family in New York shortly before we purchased our house in Queens, was to risk being stoned. We were all taught that white was right and beautiful, and obviously, everything else was wrong and ugly. Being a good student, I believed what I was taught, even if it meant self-rejection and self-denial.

I grew up on a diet of Mother Goose nursery rhymes and European fairy tales, wishing I could be a blue-eyed princess with long blond hair. Since our first four years were spent in Allentown, Pennsylvania, and Mexico, Missouri — small towns where we were the only Chinese family — I never saw another Asian face apart from my own and those of my family. I became so self-estranged that I'd sometimes do a double-take when passing a mirror, wondering who that Chinese girl was that I caught out of the corner of my eye. I couldn't even say the word "Chinese," much less be one. The only Old World connection I held on to was Chinese food, which I continued to enjoy and to eat with chopsticks. Otherwise, I was perversely pleased to be ignorant of things Chinese and was surprised when people wished me a happy Chinese New Year. How superficial to judge a book by its cover, I thought. Just because I have Chinese facial features doesn't mean I know anything about China or Chinese customs. I'm American!

Moving from all of Andrew Lang's rainbow collection of fairy tales, and every dog and horse novel in the library, I discovered a "kindred spirit" in L. M. Montgomery's *Anne of Green Gables* and savored all the volumes of Anne's story, feeling great pangs of loss at coming to the end. Here was a home for me even if it was on Prince Edward Island in Canada. I enjoyed all of Louisa May Alcott's work, never noticing, as Maxine Hong Kingston has noted, how Alcott put down the Chinese. What did they have to do with me or I with them? Having a nose for English classics, or was it because my mother had been an English major?, I came upon Jane Austen at about age twelve and was electrified. Through her novels I experienced a luminous world of verbal wit and grace, of social complexities, but ultimate harmony and happy endings. I pressed *Pride and Prejudice* on all my friends and was puzzled when their response was less than enthusiastic. I couldn't understand why my ninth grade English teacher was impressed by my having read all of Jane Austen; what was extraordinary about that? But I was pleased, in my senior year, at age sixteen, to be informed that I had received the highest grade in my high school on the New York State Four-Year English Regents examination.

So it seemed natural that I would be an English major in college and go on to graduate school. After much soul-searching, I disregarded my father's warning that no one would ever hire a Chinese English teacher. I disobeyed his request that I train to be a kindergarten teacher because his kindergarten teacher had been the most influential person in his life. I didn't think anything of being the only Asian person in my English classes; after all, there were only a handful of us in the entire college, and so one couldn't expect to see Asian Americans in every discipline. Besides, the professors always knew my name long before everyone else's.

I was awed by the vistas opened to me through the literature I was assigned: Beowulf presented a primitive, dark, ancient world that yet could speak to me; Chaucer's Canterbury pilgrims were delightful in their vitality; and Shakespeare was a brave new world to explore and marvel at. I thought of this great body of literature as the torch of classics and culture that I, the honored and proud torch-bearer / teacher would pass on to the next generation. For the Ph.D. I wanted to enlarge my reading beyond England so I wrote a dissertation in Comparative Literature on the painter in the lives and works of William Thackeray, Emile Zola and Henry James. Poetry, literature and the artistic sensibility were for me the Olympian heights. I could think of nothing nobler to devote my life and my energies to.

Then Civil Rights and the Women's Liberation Movements struck me like a bolt of lightning, rousing me from what I now realized had been a dormant state. Why indeed had Blacks and women been denied equal status in this society? Of course, Black is beautiful and so are yellow and brown and red. I looked at the torch I was bearing and began to wonder how I fit into the picture: why wasn't one writer of color part of this torch? Was it possible, as my professors and colleagues argued, that nothing really worthwhile had ever been written by any person of color? If it had been, they argued, then, like cream, it would have risen to the top and we'd certainly all know about it. I was learning now that what had risen to the top was determined by who was doing the lifting. It made good sense. Books didn't rise like cream. Some are promoted; others are ignored. Investigating for myself, and also taking advantage of the groundbreaking work beginning to be done by other scholars, I discovered that there were powerful books written by women and peoples of color: Ralph Ellison's *Invisible Man*, Zora Neale Hurston's *Their Eyes Were Watching God*, John Okada's *No-No Boy*, Hanama Tasaki's *Long the Imperial Way*, Carlos Bulosan's *America Is in the Heart*— to name only a few. The trouble was not that no one from a racial American minority had written any good books, but that no scholar, since they were almost exclusively white and male, cared about what "those people" had written. Or perhaps, since these texts were written out of multicultural contexts, they were classified as "ethnography" or "anthropology" and not considered "literature." Maxine Hong Kingston's second book, *China Men*, was so classified by the Library of Congress, and *Imagining America*, a collection of multicultural short stories Wesley Brown and I coedited, was reviewed in *The Nation* by Robert Fogarty as "social reportage" and "anthropology"; he was surprised to discover that a few of the stories "are more textured and have all the style and complexity of a 'best' story" (593).

Thus, when presented with the task of writing a book to maintain my university teaching post, I faced a fork in the road. Should I rework my dissertation, as most people did, or start a new project altogether? The world already had shelves and shelves of books, many critical "loose, baggy monsters" on Thackeray, James, and Zola. What I had to say added nothing to the hundred-year-old discussion among the experts. What was infinitely more attractive to me was the opportunity to explore a question I needed answered for myself: what have Chinese American women like me written in English and published in the United States? Like Toni Morrison, I decided to write the book I wanted to read.

I began with the only handful of writers that had been uncovered by Asian American literature anthologizers: Kai-yu Hsu, Frank Chin et. al., and David Hsin-fu Wand. By the time I finished my project, ten years later, I had collected nearly forty names, and this list was limited to women prose writers of only one Asian ancestry. As an undergraduate I had once toyed with the idea of being an archeologist, but was discouraged by my anthropology professor who asked if I really wanted to spend my life digging in the hot sun unlikely ever to uncover anything so exciting as Troy. Literary archeology, I discovered, was less exhausting and equally exhilarating, for each writer uncovered was to me a delight.

Contrary to what I had been told, there were Chinese American women writers out there, writing in English. Despite Chinese custom that left wives back in China to care for their husband's parents, despite U.S. immigration laws that tried to keep them out of this country, women writers of Chinese ancestry managed to have a history one hundred years in length. That was a remarkably long period since the Chinese men themselves had only been here for one hundred and fifty years. Each writer I uncovered affirmed me, made me less of an anomaly; each seemed a gift. Not all of them turned out to be accomplished writers by today's standards, but in some cases, such as the Eaton sisters, their life stories were as fascinating as the stories they wrote. In many ways, I found myself mirrored in Mai-mai Sze's *Echo of a Cry,* Chuang Hua's *Crossings,* and Lin Tai-yi's *The Eavesdropper.* Like me, these were cosmopolitan immigrants from China; like me, some were also painters who had lived in France; and all, like me, shuttled constantly — physically and psychologically — between worlds; the western world of their present and the Asian world of their past. To discover these women's writings, to research their lives, to organize this disparate and unwieldy group, to publicize and disseminate their work — here was my real home, the intellectual and psychological place exactly suited to me.

When I began this project, the reaction of my colleagues in a traditional English Department of a large Eastern state university made me feel I had stepped off the face of the earth and exiled myself far from the known, civilized world and into "terra incognita where dwelt monsters" (Westfall 359). A friend told me I was a trailblazer, but blazing a trail to a place no one else wanted to go. In the mid 1980s, in the academic winnowing process called tenure, I was told I was chaff after twelve years of being wheat (or was it rice?). One colleague tried to comfort me by telling me that our university did not need any Chinese experts because there weren't any Chinese students in the English department (decidedly rice). I asked him how many sixteenth-century Englishmen we had. My poetry was lambasted by a professor who admitted he did not know anything about "Chinese" poetry, but he didn't think much of "this stuff." He hadn't seemed to notice that I was writing in English, nor did he find any contradiction in his confession to ignorance of the genre and his readiness to pass a negative judgment. Most candidates had five outside letters evaluating their work; for me, the chair solicited eight. All were favorable, but none were brought into the discussion. One colleague risked his own position by breaking the "confidentiality" of the tenure meeting and thus helping me prepare a grievance; still others were brave enough to step forward to testify on my behalf.

Those were the dark years when my emotional, mental, and spiritual distress took the form of physical illness. I was hospitalized and operated on for an obstructed bowel; my intestines had literally become tied in knots. I was repeatedly afflicted with bronchitis, trying to cough up all the junk in my lungs. The night before the grievance hearings began, I went to bed tremendously anxious about the next day's events. Having to face my chair and colleagues and accuse them of racial bias was a frightening prospect. Was I making a huge mistake? Would I be forever blackballed from the profession, now that I had begun to find my place? That night, I had a dream that I shall never forget.

I dreamt I was handed a sword and told to go on stage to perform with the other sword dancer. I protested that I had not rehearsed and didn't know what to do. I was given no choice, but pushed onto the stage. I had seen the Chinese sword dance performed several times, once by my own stepmother, and it was an exciting show of flashing swordplay. But to my horror, this was no choreographed display; these swords were heavy and sharp, and the other dancer was trying to decapitate me. Going into this ordeal with no training, no preparation, I would certainly lose my head, but I fought my best. Having taken fencing in college, I parried and thrust, and somehow my sword was always in the right place at the right time. After what seemed an interminable period, the music and the attack came to an end. Scarcely believing that my head was still intact, I stepped down from the platform. But no sooner had I taken my seat than they brought me the sword again and required me to return to the stage for another bout. Aghast, I remounted the steps like the condemned going to the guillotine. But once again, as if my sword had a life of its own and were wielded by some other force, I escaped unscathed.

I awoke feeling tremendously relieved and comforted. Someone had lifted a boulder from my chest and reassured me. Was it the spirit of Hua Mulan, the Woman Warrior, whom I knew through Maxine's book? Or was it the spirit of a woman warrior deep within me, a force in my own subconscious — my conviction that I had Right on my side and need not worry. I just had to be strong, to go through the ordeal without breaking down, and everything would be all right.

Needless to say, I won the grievance. But since the entire process was the university's way of policing itself, my victory consisted of another three-year contract and going through the same crucifixion, being evaluated by the same colleagues again in three years. I returned to work, a marked woman, snubbed by colleagues who glanced away uneasily or scowled when we crossed paths in the mailroom or in the halls. Even my friends seemed uncomfortable to be seen with me.

Over the years, I had compiled a thick folder of rejection letters from publishers who did "not see a place for my book in their lists," or who told me to go to the "natural audience" for such a text, presumably China or perhaps Chinatown. At a National Women's Studies Association conference, however, I met Gloria Bowles, editor of the *Athene Series* at Pergamon Press, who asked to see my manuscript on Chinese American women writers and was enthusiastic about having it in her list under the imprint of her Oxford-based press. And suddenly, the world took a dizzying one hundred and eighty degree turn. Since then, I've had the unusual and gratifying experience of finding myself respected and feted as a pioneer. Before giving a lecture as part of the interview process two years ago at my present university, I received the most glowing introduction I'd ever heard. I couldn't believe my ears. Was it really me that this young stranger was talking about? I can't remember any of the particulars. I only remember being totally incredulous and overwhelmed. He was not alone; others were of the same opinion. In fact, by a unanimous vote, the English Department offered me a tenured position in their department and the directorship of a new program in Asian American Studies.

I have not changed, nor has my work, but by some mysterious alchemy, the world around me is now a more hospitable place. Suddenly, it seems many people are interested in exploring the trail I've blazed. I receive letters and phone calls from these people every day: publishers want to bring more multicultural materials into their texts; compilers of encyclopedias and reference books want articles on the writers I've discovered; directors of College Race and Gender Centers invite me to their campuses to speak; graduate students from various parts of the world want me to direct their dissertations, and most gratifyingly, a Chinese scholar has recently asked permission to translate my book into Chinese. Her translation will provide me a way of going "home" again.

I am grateful for all this flattering attention, but I am also alarmed by what seems to be a rising reactionary wave of attacks against multiculturalism, against the "politically correct" attitude by those who feel that something fundamentally "American" is being threatened by admitting the voices of the redyellowandbrowns. "Why don't you go back where you came from?" we're hearing again. When I recently asked some teenagers playing hockey on the public tennis court to allow my children, husband, and me to play tennis there, one muttered under his breath, "I thought we'd nuked them all." The conservative intellectual response is, "ethnic studies will lead to the lowering of standards," to the "disuniting of America" and the "Balkanization of the U.S." Lynne Cheney dismissed ethnic studies as "victim studies." Pat Buchanan had a frightening amount of time and cheers at the 1992 Republican Convention.

The fears that multiculturalism is "disuniting" America and "lowering standards" are voiced by those who have not read the multicultural texts that I know and love. The advice of the muse of Sir Philip Sidney's Astrophel four hundred years ago still holds true: "Look in thy heart and write." When we follow this advice, we will, of course, be speaking about the specificities of our own lives, but at the same time, paradoxically, we will be speaking for others. Sky Lee's *Disappearing Moon Café* is ostensibly about three generations of a Chinese Canadian family, but in telling the stories of the men and women whose lives were twisted and thwarted to uphold the convention of the "purity" of a patrilineal descent, Lee speaks to and for everyone about the relationship between sacrifice, "ideals," and conventions. She makes us think more deeply about these concepts and reconsider them in the special light she has cast on them. Joy Kogawa's beautiful novel, *Obasan*, tells of the quest of one Japanese Canadian woman for her mother, who disappeared when the protagonist was a young child, but the narrative is more fundamentally about the exploration of two different responses to pain: speaking out and remaining silent. Which response is more effective, which indicates greater strength? There are many such texts. Students have told me at the end of the semester that the books in my Asian American Women Writers course were the best they have read in four years as English majors.

Far from being an indicator of the demise of western civilization, multicultural literature is the affirmation of the most fundamental principle of a democracy: to give all people an equal voice. Why is it considered "normal" for me, a Chinese American female, to study Chaucer, Shakespeare and Milton, but a "political act," and a subversive one at that, for me to say that we would all benefit from reading Maxine Hong Kingston and Wesley Brown? If ours is a democracy, why are certain voices dominant and others ignored? Isn't everyone's story potentially equally engaging, equally informative, equally moving? The legacy of the Civil Rights and Women's Movements is simply the recognition that no single perspective can express the "Human Condition" or take the "Universal" stance, but that we each have our own particular histories, our individual perspectives, and that all of these, different as they may be, express the "human condition" in all its complexity. Each voice is valid and valuable. And the more open we are to listening to these diverse voices, the more enriched and enlarged our own lives will be. When we all learn to respect voices different from our own, then each of us can realize that "wherever we happen to be standing, why, that spot belongs to us as much as any other spot" (Kingston 107). And, at long last, we can all be at home in this global village called Earth.

WORKS CITED

Brown, Wesley and Amy Ling, eds. *Imagining America: Multicultural Stories from the Promised Land.* New York: Persea Books, 1991.

Brown, Wesley. *Darktown Strutters.* New York: Cane Hill Press, 1994.

Bulosan, Carlos. *America Is in the Heart.* 1943. Seattle: U of Washington Press, 1981.

Ellison, Ralph. *Invisible Man.* 1947. New York: Signet, 1952.

Fogarty, Robert. "Collectors' Items." *The Nation,* November 16, 1992.

Hua, Chuang. *Crossings.* 1968. Boston: Northeastern University Press, 1986.

Hurston, Zora Neale. *Their Eyes Were Watching God.* 1937. Urbana: U of Illinois Press, 1978.

Kingston, Maxine Hong. *The Woman Warrior.* 1976. New York: Vintage International, 1989.

Kogawa, Joy. *Obasan.* 1982. New York: Anchor, 1993.

Lee, Sky. *Disappearing Moon Café.* Seattle: Seal Press, 1990.

Lin, Tai-yi. *The Eavesdropper.* Cleveland: World, 1959.

Ling, Amy. *Between Worlds: Women Writers of Chinese Ancestry.* (New York: Pergamon Press, 1990; now at Teachers College Press).

Okada, John. *No-No Boy.* 1957. Seattle: U of Washington Press, 1979.

Sze, Mai-mai. *Echo of a Cry. A Story Which Began in China.* New York: Harcourt Brace, 1945.

Sidney, Sir Philip. *Astrophel and Stella,* 1591, 1598.

Tasaki, Hanama. *Long the Imperial Way.* Boston: Houghton Mifflin, 1950.

Westfall, Suzanne R. "Ping Chong's Terra In/Cognita: Monsters on Stage." Shirley Lim and Amy Ling, eds. *Reading the Literature of Asian America.* Philadelphia: Temple UP, 1992.

◎ *ADRIENNE RICH*

*Adrienne Rich, born in Baltimore in 1929, is one of the foremost feminist poets and essayists in America. She attended Radcliffe College in 1951, the same year Auden chose her first book of poems for the Yale Younger Poets Series. Over the next forty years she published more than fifteen books of poems, three collections of essays and speeches, and a feminist study of motherhood. Her honors include two Guggenheim Fellowships, the Fellowship of the Academy of American Poets, the Lenore Marshall/*Nation *Prize, the Fund for Human Dignity Award of the National Gay Task Force, the Common Wealth Award in Literature, the Lambda Book Award, and* *the* Los Angeles Times *Book Prize for Poetry. In 1974, when* Diving into the Wreck *received the National Book Award, Rich refused to accept the award as an individual but accepted it jointly with Audre Lorde and Alice Walker, two other nominees, "in the name of all the women whose voices have gone and still go unheard in a patriarchal world."*

The title of Rich's essay "History stops for no one" is taken from the poem "Warsaw, 1983: Umschlagplatz" *by Irena Klepfisz. A Jewish writer who fled Poland as a child, Klepfisz writes of her return to Warsaw in 1983. An earlier version of Rich's essay introduces Klepfisz'* Notes from the Mother Tongue: Poems Selected and New, 1971–1990, *published in 1990. The essay appears in Rich's* What is Found There: Notebooks on Poetry and Politics *(1993).*

"History stops for no one"

It was not natural. And she was the first. . . .

A poet can read. A poet can write.

A poet is African in Africa, or Irish in Ireland, or French on the left bank of Paris, or white in Wisconsin. A poet writes in her own language. A poet writes of her own people, her own history, her own vision, her own room, her own house where she sits at her own table quietly placing one word after another word until she builds a line and a movement and an image and a meaning that somersaults all of these into the singing, the absolutely individual voice of the poet: at liberty. A poet is somebody free. A poet is someone at home.

How should there be Black poets in America?

— JUNE JORDAN, "The Difficult Miracle
of Black Poetry in America"

Zi shemt zikh/She is ashamed

Zi shemt zikh.

She has forgotten
alts fargesn

forgotten it all.

Whom can I speak to?
she wonders. . . .

Mit vemen
ken ikh redn?
Whom can I speak to?

di meysim farshteyen
mir afile nit

even the ghosts
do not understand me. . . .

In der femd

among strangers

iz hir heym

is her home.

— IRENA KLEPFISZ, "*Di rayze aheym/*
The Journey Home"

To have as birthright a poetic tradition that everyone around you recognizes and respects is one kind of privilege. At very least, it lets you know what you hold in your hands, as person and artist. Like a strong parent who both teaches and browbeats, can be learned from, stormed away from, forgiven, but whose influence can never be denied. Like a family from which, even in separation, you bring away certain gestures, tones, ways of looking: something taken for granted, perhaps felt as constriction, nonetheless a source, a point of departure.

Until recently, North American poetry has largely been the province of people who possessed — or took on through education — a literary family tree beginning with the King James Bible, the Greek and Latin classics, branching into the Renaissances of Europe and England, and transported to the colonies by the colonizers as part of their civilizing mission to the wilderness. On that mission, they violently disrupted the original poetry of this continent, inseparable as it was and is from Indian life. In the determination to destroy tribal life, poetry had to be desecrated. Later, the descendants of the desecraters collected, transcribed, and printed surviving Indian songs and chants as artifacts of a "vanishing" people. Only in the late twentieth century, a renaissance of American Indian culture has produced a new, written, poetic literature expressive of indigenous people who, in the words of the poet Chrystos, are emphatically "Not Vanishing."

Africans carried poetry in contraband memory across the Middle Passage to create in slavery the "Sorrow Songs." A young girl in slavery in Boston, Phillis Wheatley, mastered Anglo-American metrics and conventions to become, after Anne Bradstreet, the second woman (and the first Black) poet published in this country. African-American poets have had to invent and synthesize a language in which to be both African and American, to "write . . . towards the personal truth" of being African-American and create a poetics of that experience. They have above all created a musical language, jazz, which has incalculably affected the national poetic language.

Such writers — men and women of color, poets born to a language other than English, lesbian and gay poets, poets writing in the upsurge of the women's poetry movement of the past twenty years — have not started in cultural poverty even though their cultures have been ruptured and misprized. The relationship to more than one culture, nonassimilating in spirit and therefore living amid contradictions, is a constant act of self-creation. I see the life of North American poetry at the end of the century as a pulsing, racing convergence of tributaries — regional, ethnic, racial, social, sexual — that, rising from lost or long-blocked springs, intersect and infuse each other while reaching back to the strengths of their origins. (A metaphor, perhaps, for a future society of which poetry, in its present suspect social conditions, is the precursor.)

One paradigm of this poetry of cultural re-creation is the work of Irena Klepfisz. It begins with a devastating exterior event: the destruction of European Jewry in the Nazi period through the genocide known as the Holocaust or, in Yiddish, *der khurbn*. "The Yiddish word was important, for, unlike the term Holocaust, it resonated with *yidishe geshikte,* Jewish history, linking the events of World War II with *der erste und tsveyster khurbn,* the First and Second Destruction (of the Temple)." Born in 1941 in the Warsaw Ghetto, this poet is unequivocally rooted in the matrix of history. Beginning with almost total loss — of family, community, culture, country, and language — she has taken up the task of re-creating herself as Jew, woman, and writer by facing and learning to articulate that destruction. If she had stopped there, had become only the author of her early poems and of "*Bashert,*" her work would have claimed a unique place in the poetry that necessarily, and stubbornly, came after Auschwitz.

But Klepfisz goes further, not by way of leaving behind *der khurbn* — an impossibility for any Jew or any other person who wants to understand living in the twentieth century — but by searching, through her poetry, for what is possible in a world where *this* was possible. Most poets emerge with existence itself as a given (though not always with literacy as a given, literature as a given). This poet cannot:

> during the war
> germans were known
> to pick up infants
> by their feet
> swing them through the air
> and smash their heads
> against plaster walls
>
> somehow
> i managed
> to escape that fate.

Lines like graffiti on a wall. The consciousness that, precisely, existence itself is not to be taken for granted will impel her journey.

What does it mean to be a Holocaust survivor or a child of survivors? The question has haunted Jewish life worldwide since 1945 — through denial and silence, through amnesia and mythologizing, through a search for resonance. Certainly in the United States it has had its own reverberations and failures of resonance. For Klepfisz this is not just a question of present meaning, but of lost, irreplaceable resources, cultural and emotional riches destroyed or scattered before she could know them. The question for her is, then, also what it can mean to grow up as a Jew in the United States in the years after *der khurbn*; to grow into a Jewish woman, single, childless, a lesbian, an artist from a community of survivors who see their great hope for meaning in a new generation of Jewish children. What is allowed, what is available, to the poet located in these ways?

Before *der khurbn*, Yiddish poetry — the tradition Klepfisz might, "under other circumstances," have possessed as a continuing heritage — was largely writen by men yet in the language called *mame-loshen* or "mother tongue": vivid, emotionally vibrant, vernacular, as opposed to Hebrew, the language of scholarship and religious study, reserved for men only. Yiddish was a people's language, a women's language, the language of the Ashkenazic Jewish diaspora. The women poets of this tradition (many of them still untranslated, so that we have but a few names: Celia Dropkin, Anna Margolin, Kadia Molodowsky, Fradel Schtok, Malka Tussman among them) were known as more sexually frank than the men; but even of them the Anglophone reader knows only what's translated. It's a dead end to try to imagine what might have become of Yiddish poetry — or of Klepfisz as a poet — in a different history. The only history is the one we know, however imperfectly — that a great Western cultural movement was exterminated not only under the Nazis, but under Stalinism. Being "Western" didn't save this movement. And, to the present day, many Europeans of both East and West, many Americans of both North and South are unaware of, or indifferent to, this.

The great flowering of Yiddish literature took place in the late nineteenth and early twentieth centuries along with the rise of Jewish secularism and the Jewish labor and socialist movements. Out of these traditions, history uprooted Irena Klepfisz, depositing her into a community of survivors in New York.

In a time when speculative biography has been displacing serious writing about poets and poetry, I touch on this poet's personal history with some reluctance and only because it seems to me inseparable from a serious reading of her work. We have seen an obsession with intimate details, scandals, the clinical or trivializing reduction of artists' lives. The biographies of poets are commodities. It is also true that when a poet who is not male (or white) writes from direct experience, this poetry is subsumed as mere documentary or polemicizing. If I speak here, then, of experiences from which Klepfisz's poetry has been precipitated, it's because historical necessity has made her the kind of poet she is: neither a "universal" nor a "private" stance has been her luxury.

The ghettos of the Nazi period were part of a deliberate plan to destroy the Jewish people in their entirety. Throughout Poland, thousands of Jews were forced to retreat into increasingly densely populated areas enclosed by walls and barbed wire. By 1940 nearly half a million Jews were locked, compressed, within the Warsaw Ghetto; by 1941, the year of Klepfisz's birth, the penalty for attempting to escape was death. Of course, they were all under sentence of death: 83,000 Jews died from hunger and disease within twenty months in the Warsaw Ghetto alone. The ghettos were holding pens for Jews destined for forced labor camps and ultimate destruction — bases for selective deportation.

Throughout the ghettos Jews organized armed resistance movements. In Warsaw they constructed tunnels leading to the sewer system for escape and for bringing in arms and explosives. In street-to-street and under-street fighting the Jews held out. In April 1943 the Nazis decided to subdue the ghetto with an air attack. In this battle Michal Klepfisz, the poet's father, was killed. Because her mother had blue eyes and spoke fluent Polish, she and her child were able to pass and were hidden by Polish peasants. Polish became Klepfisz's first language. They emigrated after the war to Sweden, then to the United States when Klepfisz was eight years old, where she learned English in school while living in a world of spoken Yiddish: a world of people who had carried the remains of their culture to another continent — in their memories, in old snapshots and documents, archives rescued from conflagration, reconstituted institutions. And, not least, Klepfisz's mother, as a presence in her poems, embodies continuity, endurance, and the oral tradition's access to the lost.

The shattering of a culture is the shattering not only of artistic and political webs, but of the webs of family and community within which these are first nurtured and transmitted. Two long early poems, unpublished till 1990, delineate the search for what has most intimately been lost: the father-hero-martyr-deserter, whose absence becomes enormous presence:

> These two:
> widow and half-orphan
> survived and now resided
> in a three-room apartment
> with an ivy-covered fire escape
> which at night
> clutched like a skeleton
> at the child's bedroom wall . . .

The missing one
was surely
the most
        important
link . . .

And when the two crowded
into the kitchen at night
he would press himself between them
pushing, thrusting, forcing them to remember,
even though he had made his decision,
had chosen his own way . . .
he would press himself between them
hero and betrayer
legend and deserter —
so when they sat down to eat
they could taste his ashes.

But the search is also for all "those whom I would have known / had circumstances been different." *Had circumstances been different:* a terse, matter-of-fact phrase behind which lies all the unprovable: history reversed or unwinding differently, the possibility of having lived "an ordinary life," the life of "common things, gestures and events" that Klepfisz invokes elsewhere, to have become not the child survivor lighting candles "for all the children / who have perished," but a child playing with other children, in Jewish Warsaw, in the *yidishe svive,* in a home peopled with parents, extended family, worker-intellectuals.

But because "history stops for no one," Klepfisz has gone on to write poetry of uncompromising complexity, clothed in apparently simply, even spare, language — simple and bare as the stage of a theater in which strict economies of means release a powerful concentrate of feeling.

There is extraordinary vitality in Klepfisz's early poems on women in the Holocaust. Images and voices rush. They floodlight a neglected dimension of the resistance to genocide: the survival strategies, the visceral responses, of women. They burn and bristle with urgency, contained within a disciplined and crafted poetics.

when they took us   to the shower   i saw
the rebitsin   her sagging breasts   sparse
pubic hairs   i knew   and remembered
the old rebe   and turned   my eyes away
i could still hear   her advice   a woman
with a husband   a scholar

when they turned on the gas i smelled
it first coming at me pressed myself
hard to the wall crying rebitsin rebitsin
i am here with you and the advice you gave me
i screamed into the wall as the blood burst from
my lungs cracking her nails in women's flesh i watched
her capsize beneath me my blood in her mouth i screamed

when they dragged my body into the oven i burned
slowly at first i could smell my own flesh and could
hear them grunt with the weight of the rebitsin
and they flung her on top of me and i could smell
her hair burning against my stomach

when i pressed through the chimney
it was sunny and clear my smoke
was distinct i rose quiet left her
beneath

"death camp" is a poem of death so alive that its smoke remains in our nostrils. As in other Klepfisz poems, control of tone and image allow the wild and desperate quality of experience to be heard. In "perspectives on the second world war," a "terror" — the woman hiding with her child, her hallucinating prescience of worse possibilities — is juxtaposed with a point later in time when to speak of such things would be "too impolite" in detached "conversations over brandy." These poems engage physical and moral immediacy in ways that make them continuingly urgent. In them, Klepfisz takes the considerable risk of trying to bear witness to this part of her history without compromise and without melodrama. She succeeds because she is a poet, not only a witness.

"*Bashert*" (Yiddish for "fated," "predestined") is a poem unlike any other I can think of in North America, including Jewish-American, poetry. It delineates not only the survivor experience (in the skin of the mother "passing" as gentile with her young daughter), but what happens after survival — the life that seems to go on but cannot persevere; the life that does go on, struggling with a vast alienation, in a state of "equidistance from two continents," trying to fathom her place as a Jew in the larger American gentile world, first as a student.

> walking home alone at midnight. The university seems an island ungrounded. Most of its surrounding streets have been emptied. On some, all evidence of previous life removed except for occasional fringes of rubbish that reveal vague outlines that hint at things that were. On others,

> old buildings still stand, though these are hollow like caves, once of use and then abandoned. . . . Everything is waiting for the emptiness to close in on itself, for the emptiness to be filled in, for the emptiness to be swallowed and forgotten.

A landscape that might be some blasted Jewish ghetto of postwar Europe but is actually the edges of a Black ghetto surrounding an elite American university:

> I see the rubble of this unbombed landscape, see that the city, like the rest of this alien country, is not simply a geographic place, but a time zone, an era in which I, by my very presence in it, am rooted. No one simply passes through. History keeps unfolding and demanding a response. A life obliterated around me, of those I barely noticed. A life unmarked, unrecorded. A silent mass migration. Relocation. Common rubble in the streets.

This is not the mass-marketed immigrant experience. The poem is not about finding safety, freedom, a better life in America. It stares down the American myth that if you are just hardworking, virtuous, motivated, tenacious enough, the dream of freedom, security, and happiness can be realized. In its rhythmic, relentless, almost choral double dedication, it invokes the random and various shapes of death and survival. "*Bashert*" mourns the dead and the survivor alike, defying such ideas as that the fittest survive or that victims "choose" their destiny. Moving between poetry and blocks of prose in a poem where everything is made concrete and there are no cloudy generalities or abstract pronouncements, Klepfisz has written one of the great "borderland" poems — poems that emerge from the consciousness of being of no one geography, time zone, or culture, of moving inwardly as well as outwardly between continents, landmasses, eras of history; or, as Chicana poet Gloria Anzaldúa expresses it, in "a constant state of mental nepantilism, an Aztec word meaning *torn between ways.*" A consciousness that cannot be, and refuses to be, assimilated. A consciousness that tries to claim all its legacies: courage, endurance, vision, fierceness of human will, and also the underside of oppression, the distortions that quarantine and violent deracination inflict on the heart. When I say that "*Bashert*" is a poem unlike any other, I mean this through and through: in its form, in its verse and prose rhythms, in its insistence on memory without nostalgia, its refusal to let go.

And yet, as the poetry of this continent has become increasingly a poetry written by the displaced, by American Indians moving between the cities and the reservations, by African-Americans, Caribbean-Americans, by the children of the internment camps for Japanese-Americans in World War II, by the children of Angel Island and the Chinese Revolution, by Mexican-Americans and Chicanos with roots on both sides of the border, by political exiles from Latin America, "*Bashert*" takes its place (as does Klepfisz's poetry as a whole) in a multicultural literature of discontinuity, migration, and difference. Much of this new literary flowering is also lesbian or gay, feminist, and working class.

Displacement invents its poetics out of a mixture of traditions and styles, out of the struggle to name what has been unnameable in the dominant European traditions. (Yiddish itself has been disparaged by the privileging of Hebrew on the one hand and English on the other.) It is often a bilingual poetry, incorporating patois and languages other than English, not in allusion to Western or Asian high culture, as in Modernist poems of the 1920s and after, but because bilingualism is both created by the experience of being migrant, immigrant, displaced, and expressive of the divisions as well as the resources of difference. Klepfisz's bilingual poems do not — and this is significant — drop Yiddish phrases in a cosy evocation of an idealized past, embodied in *bubbe* and *zayde*, or as a kind of Jewish seasoning on an American tongue. Poems such as "*Di rayze aheym* / The Journey Home," "*Etlekhe verter oyf mame-loshen* / A few words in the mother tongue," or "Fradel Schtok" painfully explore the world of a writer located not only between landscapes, but also between languages; the words of the mother tongue are handled and savored with extreme delicacy, as a precious yet also tenuous legacy. In "Fradel Schtok" we enter the mind of a poet trying to change languages, far more internally rupturing than the change of countries. We meet Fradel Schtok at the moment when she feels her native language fading. "*Di rayze aheym,*" in deceptively simple and brief phrases, transposes *How shall I sing the Lord's song in a strange land?* — that ancient Jewish lament — into *How shall I remember, how shall I speak, in the language of an alien culture?* There is a paradox here: Klepfisz uses the Anglo-American language with enormous sensitivity, consciousness, and art. But these qualities emerge not from a triumphant linguistic posture, but precisely from her refusal to pretend that it is the language of choice or the supremely expressive language.

In white North America, poetry has been set apart from the practical arts, from political meaning, and also from "entertainment" and the accumulation of wealth — thus, pushed to the margins of life. Klepfisz, inheriting an entwined European-Jewish-Socialist-Bundist political tradition and a Yiddish cultural tradition, naturally refuses such "enclosures." In particular, the refusal to segregate art from daily life and work is a pressing concern for her. And surely the Holocaust itself — as well as the tradition of *yidishkayt* — demands a renewed vision of what art — poetry, in this instance — stands for and against. Theodor Adorno's drastic statement that "after Auschwitz, to write a poem is barbaric" has to be severely parsed. If taken at face value, it would mean a further desolation even than we have already had to face. Adorno, a German Jew who lived for many years as a refugee in the United States, may have forgotten the ancient role of poetry in keeping memory and spiritual community alive. On the other hand, his remark might be pondered by all poets who too fluently find language for what they have not yet absorbed, who see human suffering as "material." Klepfisz's art resists such temptations, both through the force and beauty of her work, and by the ways in which she demands accountability of art.

Survivorhood isn't a stasis; the survivor isn't an artifact, despite efforts perhaps to reify or contain her, give her the lines we think she ought to speak. Klepfisz's poems are the work of a woman who feels, acts, and creates in living time: a feminist, a lesbian, an activist in the women's movement for many years, an essayist and editor as well as a poet. She writes sometimes from cities where a window box, a potted plant, a zoo, an aboretum become "mnemonic devices" for the natural world and "water is a rare sight . . . but it can / be reached"; sometimes from a countryside or a shoreline where

> she'd never before been forced to distinguish
> herself from trees   or sand and sea   and it became ob
> vious that when it came to rocks   she could never prove
> her own distinctness.

From the urban plant that sensualizes the apartment where two women make love, or the fiercely generative tangle of narcissus roots in a glass jar, to a garden of wildflowers transplanted with uneven success to the "inhospitable soil" of a former garage, the sudden wildness of a city cat transplanted to the country, living things are charged in these poems by a fresh and totally unsentimental consciousness. There is a tough and searching empathy; the poet is not outside of nature, looking in: she is observant and participant, a different yet kindred being who instinctively responds to growth, deprivation, persistence, wildness, tameness.

Klepfisz is also one of those artists who, within and by means of her art, explores the material conditions by which the imaginative impulse, which belongs to no gender, race, or class, can be realized or obstructed. "Contexts" places the child's passion for words alongside the seamstress-mother's recognition of how bread must be put on the table; the poet-proofreader along with the aging blind scholar for whom she works; the worker going home wearily by subway with the beggar working the car. "Work Sonnets" depict the crushing of dreamlife and imagination in those who, because of class, race, and gender, get written off by capitalism and its need for robots: they are not expected to dream. But the woman clerical worker who finally speaks in the poem has a dreamlife, if a buried one, and has evolved her own strategies for survival, calculating closely her participation in the system — and even, ironically, in the poem. These poems are political to the core without a single hortatory line. Like their author, they do not take their existence for granted.

Later poems examine the pain and necessity of a Jew who identifies with the Palestinians under Israeli occupation. From the Warsaw Ghetto resistance to the *intifada* her trajectory is clear:

> All of us part.   You move off   in a separate
> direction. The rest of us return
> to the other Jerusalem.   It is night.
> I still hear your voice.   It is in the air
> now   with everything else   except sharper
> clearer.   I think of your relatives
> your uncles and aunts   I see the familiar
> battered suitcases   cartons with strings
> stuffed pillowcases
> children sitting on people's shoulders
> children running to keep up . . .
>
> . . . If I forget thee
> Oh Jerusalem   Jerusalem   Hebron
> Ramallah   Nablus   Qattana . . .
> . . . may I forget
> my own past   my pain
> the depth of my sorrows.

Throughout, this poetry asks fundamental questions about the uses of history. That it does so from a rootedness in Jewish history, an unassimilated location, is one part of its strength. But history alone doesn't confer this strength; the poet's continuing labor with Jewish meaning does. The other part, of course, is the integrity of its poetics. A Klepfisz poem lives amid complex tensions even when its texture may appear transparent. There is a voice, sometimes voices, in these poems that can often best be heard by reading aloud. Her sense of phrase, of line, of the shift of tone is almost flawless. But perfection is not what Irena Klepfisz is after. A tension among many forces — language, speechlessness, memory, politics, irony, compassion, hunger for what is lost, hunger for a justice still to be made — makes this poetry crucial to the new unfoldings of history that we begin, in the 1990s, to imagine.

◎ *LUCI TAPAHONSO*

Luci Tapahonso was born in Shiprock, New Mexico, in 1953. She is a member of the Navajo Nation. She received a B.A. and an M.A. from the University of New Mexico. While a student, Tapahonso was encouraged to write by Leslie Marmon Silko, and her first book, One More Shiprock Night, *was published in 1981. Her other books of poetry include* A Breeze Swept Through *and, most recently,* Sáanii Dahataał / The Women Are Singing *(1993). Tapahonso's first language is Navajo; she interweaves Navajo and English in her writings and in her life. She has been named one of the Top Women of the Navajo Nation and has received a New Mexico Eminent Scholar Award and an Outstanding Native American Award. Tapahonso has also been named an Influential Professor at the University of Kansas.*

"The Kaw River Rushes Westward" is a preface to Sáanii Dahataał / The Women Are Singing. *Tapahonso follows the "deep" and "loud" Kaw river back to her home state of New Mexico. Tapahonso's stories stem from her Navajo origins and are only complete when she is accompanying them with the Navajo songs that cannot be written down.*

The Kaw River Rushes Westward

North of our home in Lawrence, Kansas, the Kaw River flows wide and brown. When I first saw this river, I was surprised at how deep and how loud it is. Its banks are lined with thick groves of trees. In comparison, the San Juan and Rio Grande rivers in New Mexico are clear and shallow. One fall we drove home to Shiprock, New Mexico, about 1300 miles away. Our route took us across Kansas, into Colorado, and then down into northwestern New Mexico. It was such a contrast to see the wide fierce water change to the quiet shallow San Juan in New Mexico. The terrain in Kansas is mostly rolling hills and flat plains, and as the rivers changed, the landscape did also, ranging from steep canyons, mountain gorges, and finally emptying out into the Rio Grande riverbed. This flowed into the San Juan, which is a mile south of my parents' home. The night we arrived in Shiprock I was very much aware that the river nearby was quiet, reflecting the dark sky and stars above. Alongside this river are huge, old cottonwoods; willows and tamarack brushes are tucked along the sandy cliffs.

We drove into the yard late at night and my parents were awake, waiting for us. After we ate a long-awaited meal of mutton stew and náneeskaadí, tortillas, we went to bed. It was dark and quiet in the house of my childhood. My daughter and I talked quietly awhile before we fell asleep. In the darkness, we heard the faint songs of the Yeis, the grandfathers of the holy people, and the low, even rhythm of the drum. They had been dancing and singing for six days and nights already. From across the river valley, the songs drifted into our last waking moments, into our dreams. While we slept, they sang, praying and giving thanks for the harvest, for our return and the hundreds of others who returned home that weekend for the fall festivities. The Yeis danced for all of us — they danced in their fatigue, they danced in our tired dreams. They sang for us until their voices were hardly more than a whisper. Around three the next morning, they stopped to rest.

In the morning, we woke refreshed and happy. The morning air was clear and crisp with a harvest chill, and there across the blue valley stood Shiprock, a deep purple monolith. I drank coffee outside, watched the dogs act silly, and then I caught up on news of what had happened since my last trip. While we ate breakfast, my father watched news, the table radio played Navajo and English songs alternately, my mother told me a little story about when she was four or five years old, I braided my daughter's hair, and two of my sisters came over to visit. This is the familiar comfort I felt as a child, and it is the same for my children. The songs the Yeibicheii sang, that the radio played, and that my mother hummed as she cooked are a part of our memories, of our names, and of our laughter. The stories I heard that weekend were not very different from the stories I heard as a child. They involved my family's memories, something that happened last week, and maybe news of high school friends. Sometimes they were told entirely in Navajo and other times in a mixture of Navajo and English.

There is such a love of stories among Navajo people that it seems each time a group of more than two gather, the dialogue eventually evolves into sharing stories and memories, laughing, and teasing. To be included in this is a distinct way of showing affection and appreciation for each other. So it is true that daily conversations strengthen us as do the old stories of our ancestors that have been told since the beginning of the Navajo time.

Just as the rivers we followed home evolved from the huge, wide Missouri River to the shallow water in the San Juan riverbed, the place of my birth is the source of the writing presented here. This work ranges from stories I heard as a child, to stories that were told by relatives, friends, or colleagues, and to other poems and stories that are based on actual events. Most of the pieces originated in Navajo, either orally or in thought, and the English translation appears here. I have retained the first person narrative in most of the stories because it is the stronger voice and truer to the person who told the story originally. Many of these poems and stories have a song that accompanies the work. Because these songs are in Navajo, a written version is not possible. When I read these in public, the song is also a part of the reading. This is very much a consideration as I am translating and writing — the fact that the written version must stand on its own, even though I know that it is the song which makes it complete.

The combination of song, prayer, and poetry is a natural form of expression for many Navajo people. A person who is able to "talk beautifully" is well thought of and considered wealthy. To know stories, remember stories, and to retell them well is to have been "raised right"; the family of such an individual is also held in high esteem. The value of the spoken word is not diminished, even with the influences of television, radio, and video. Indeed, it seems to have enriched the verbal dexterity of colloquial language, as for instance, in the names given to objects for which a Navajo word does not exist, such as "béésh nitséskees" or "thinking metal" for computers and "chidí bijéí" or "the car's heart" for a car battery.

I feel fortunate to have access to two, sometimes three languages, to have been taught the "correct" ways to use these languages, and to have the support of my family and relatives. Like many Navajos, I was taught that the way one talks and conducts oneself is a direct reflection of the people who raised her or him. People are known then by their use of language.

It is with this perspective that I share the following stories, poetry, and prayers. Once my oldest brother said about my nálí, my paternal grandmother, who died decades ago: "She was a walking storybook. She was full of wisdom." Like many other relatives, she had a profound understanding of the function of language. This writing, then, is not "mine," but a collection of many voices that range from centuries ago and continue into the future.

For many people in my situation, residing away from my homeland, writing is the means for returning, rejuvenation, and for restoring our spirits to the state of "hohzo," or beauty, which is the basis of Navajo philosophy. It is a small part of the "real thing," and it is utilitarian, but as Navajo culture changes, we adapt accordingly.

I view this book as a gift from my mother and father, both of whom embody the essence of Navajo elders — patience, wisdom, humor, and courage. It is a collaboration of sorts with my sisters and brothers, my extended family, and my friends. I especially appreciate the tremendous support of my daughters and my husband. Their thoughts, humor, and encouragement sustain me and all I undertake. Ahéhee'.

◎ *MOMOKO IKO*

Momoko Iko was born in 1940 in Wapato, Washington. When she was two her family was evacuated to the Portland Assembly Center, and then to Heart Mountain, Wyoming, two of the ten internment camps established by the Department of Justice. Early memories of this time provide a realistic atmosphere for Iko's play Gold Watch. *Iko began writing when she attended Northern Illinois University. She completed her degree in English at the University of Illinois. Initially she wrote personal memoirs, then fiction, and turned to writing drama in 1968. Lorraine Hansberry's* A Raisin in the Sun *showed Iko the political possibilities of theater. Iko is one of the pioneers in Asian-American theater.*

Gold Watch *takes place on the Northwest coast between the fall of 1941 and the late spring of 1942, in the days preceding internment, and shows the upheaval in one family caused by Executive Order 9066, which allowed for the wholesale removal of the Japanese from the western United States on the basis of "military necessity." Directed by C. Bernard Jackson, the play was premiered at the Inner City Cultural Center, Los Angeles, in 1972.*

Gold Watch

Time and Place: The play takes place in the Pacific Northwest on the Murakami truck farm and in the Japanese Christian community's church. The time is the fall of 1941 to the late spring of 1942.

CHARACTERS

MASARU (MASU) MURAKAMI a man in his forties, lean, hard-muscled, wiry. His face is weathered and dark tanned, his hands, roughened. He is a farmer who uses his body when he talks and is given to mimicry, expansive gestures. MASU wears long-sleeved shirts (worn Pendletons) over undershirts, work boots, khakis, and a beat-up porkpie hat.

KIMIKO MURAKAMI a woman in her early thirties, with a body that moves as lithely as a girl's, but quietly. She is pale, and in contrast to Murakami, her face looks older. She is invariably gracious but proud. KIMIKO wears cotton housedresses with cardigans, aprons, and slippers, and at Christmas, a homemade, unfrilly party dress with midheel party shoes.

TADAO MURAKAMI boy of fourteen, skinny, well coordinated. His movements are quiet and unobtrusive but there is an underlying intensity or concentration. TADAO has overalls and work shoes for farm; shirts with sweater vest, cord pants, and winter jacket. He has a good Sunday suit, which he wears in Christmas scene.

CHIEKO MURAKAMI a four-year-old, full of play and affection, direct in her expressions of feeling. CHIEKO wears cord bib pants, blouses, cardigan, and a frilly homemade velvet dress at Christmas with Mary Jane shoes.

TANAKA also in his forties, owns the only Japanese tradestore in the area. He tends to scurry along, duck his head before speaking, and is formal in manners. With MASU, he is more direct — a naturally courteous man. TANAKA always wears conservative but contemporary suits and hats.

SETSUKO TANAKA Tanaka's wife, a blooming woman who likes to gossip and visit. Basically, she is a blunt but decent human being. She dresses nicely for any occasion, midheels, gloves, hats, and winter coat.

HIROSHI TANAKA a slim, erect young man of nineteen who through a rigid posture masks his youthful idealism and pain. He wears a conservative suit or Japanese school uniform and cap of the times.

REVEREND SUGANO a well-meaning man of the church. Dress accordingly.

JAPANESE COMMUNITY PEOPLE mostly farmers and wives. Most are in their thirties to forties; some younger, some older. Dress accordingly.

THREE NIGHTRAIDERS three white men dressed as farmers or country people. Dress accordingly.

ACT ONE

[*Time: Dawn, Labor Day weekend, 1941*

The interior of the Murakami two-room house: one room serves as a kitchen, dining and living area: wooden table and four unmatched chairs, potbellied stove and stack of kindling and Japanese newspapers beside; small laundry tub sink with one faucet jutting from wall; a wooden icebox next to sink; upturned vegetable crates — papered and flour sack curtained — lined with jars of peaches, pears, cherries, corn, eggplant, tomatoes, mushrooms, etc; dishes, pots, pans, glasses, cups, rice bowls are organized on all available flat surfaces and shelves above sink; under the sink are a wooden vat of Tsukemono (pickled vegetables) and bottles of homemade sake. In living area is an overstuffed chair and hassock, rough handcrafted table and bookcase, kerosene lamps, a faded carpet at door and curtainless windows. The second room is divided into two bedrooms by a heavy curtain strung across the middle and short curtains separating bedrooms from living area. In the parents' section: a brass double bed covered by a handmade Japanese futon; nice dresser of wood inlay on top of which is a Japanese lacquer box for gloves, hankies, jewelry (Kimiko's special things), brush, comb, and mirror. The children's section: cots and orange crate shelves personalized by Tadao and Chieko. Chieko has a girlish homemade quilt on her bed.

On Rise: Kimiko gets out of metal frame bed, goes into the kitchen and dishes out rice, misoshiru (soup), puts some tsukemono on plate, goes back to bedroom to wake up Masu.]

KIMIKO [*getting dressed, pinning back hair*]: *Okinasai,* Masu. *Okinasai, neh.* [*Casually*] The bank man, maybe he will give us more time to pay back the loan . . .

MASU: "Pay back croptime" . . . "pay back croptime!" The crops are in. Everybody gets paid back.

KIMIKO: But, Masu, there will be nothing left over. Chieko needs shoes for school. If she has to wear Tadao's old work shoes again . . . you know what a fuss she made last year. I promised.

MASU: How much did you make from the people who drive by?

KIMIKO: Eighty dollars.

MASU: You have enough!

KIMIKO: Until next year?

MASU: Pay everyone back! Pay for everything you buy today. Next week, we start again. "Pay back croptime." "Pay back croptime."

KIMIKO: Tadao needs a new pair of pants for school — corduroy — from store. He needs money for school and

MASU [*shoving it aside*]: Aaah! I've got work to do.

[*Masu jumps out of bed, goes into the kitchen, grabs an egg, cracks it over his rice and eats breakfast. Kimiko is trying to decide whether to approach him again. In the time she decides and enters kitchen area, Masu leaves. Lights fade and rise on front porch — dinnertime — same day. Masu entering house, turns and seeks Kimiko, Chieko, and Tanaka returning from shopping.*]

MASU: Hoh! Tane, you're just in time for some sake before supper.

CHIEKO [*running up*]: Papa, see all the good stuff we bought . . .

KIMIKO [*cutting in*]: *Atokara . . .*

[*Kimiko skirts direct confrontation with Masu, carrying in some purchases, shooing Chieko into the house. Tanaka comes onto steps carrying groceries and a visible bolt of cloth.*]

MASU [*putting down melons*]: Sonofabitch! What have you got there?

He eyes the bolt of cloth elaborately.

TANAKA [*embarrassed, trying to change the subject*]: Melons! This late?

MASU: Found them . . . clearing the field. Still good.

[*His good humor at seeing Tanaka disappears as he continues to eye the cloth.*]

What's new in town?

TANAKA: It gets chillier every year. Let's go inside. [*Opening door for Masu.*] I didn't mean to bother your dinner. How are they? We could sell some at the store?

[*The two men enter house.*]

MASU: Kimi! Get Tanaka sake!

[*Kimiko gets the sake cups and pitcher and gets the bottle from the corner. Masu goes to the sink to wash up. Tanaka gives Kimiko the cloth. Kimiko, a quick look at Masu, takes the cloth into the bedroom. She returns, fills porcelain pitcher with sake and heats it in a pan of hot water on stove top. Masu, washing, takes large handfuls of water from the tap and splashes his face and arms. He makes smacking sounds with his hands against his face and body.*]

CHIEKO: Papa, look at my new shoes — Mary Janes!

[*Kimiko tries to shut up Chieko with gestures. Masu grabs a towel hanging from a nail, and goes into the bedroom to change his shirt. Tanaka and Kimiko exchange glances as Masu enters bedroom.*]

KIMIKO: *Sa!* Sit down, Tanaka-san. Make yourself comfortable.

[*Kimiko takes pitcher of sake from pan and pours some sake into the cup beside Tanaka. She leaves the pitcher by his cup. Masu comes out from the bedroom in zori slippers and a fresh change. He sits down across from Tanaka, slapping his thighs as he does. He takes the pitcher and pours himself a drink, raises his cup, "kam-pai" and drinks. Then he pours another cup and settles into his seat, ready for a chat. He offers Tanaka another cupful.*]

TANAKA [*refusing by putting his hand in front of the sake cup*]: No, no more — just one to warm up . . . have to get back for dinner too.

MASU [*laughing*]: Tanaka-san, you come here, you ask how are the crops . . . you have one sake and now you are leaving. For a visit, it's too short. If it is business, it hasn't been stated.

TANAKA: You know, Setsuko. I must get going.

MASU: Besides that, you forgot your bundle. Your large parcel. Kimi, get Tanaka-san his parcel.

KIMIKO [*preparing dinner, stiffens*]: Masu, I paid for it.

MASU [*knowing she's lying*]: Kimi, get Tanaka-san his parcel.

TANAKA: Tanaka-san, Tanaka-san, we are not strangers, Masu.

KIMIKO: Masu, think about the children.

MASU: Kimi . . .

[*Masu ignores her and goes to get the cloth.*]

KIMIKO: Masu, please . . .

TANAKA: Masu, listen, don't be stupid. This has got nothing to do with pride. Do you hear — nothing.

[*Masu hands him the bolt. Tanaka won't take it.*]

KIMIKO [*disgusted and angry*]: Your pride, your pride. Is that all there is?

[*Masu goes to door, exits onto porch and slams the bolt across the porch rail and walks away. Tanaka exits to porch. He sighs like a man who has witnessed this scene too often to expect any different and yet is always expecting a change to occur. Kimiko comes onto porch and takes the cloth in with her. Masu watches her.*]

MASU: Why does she have to do it like this?

TANAKA: You're too stubborn, a stupid mule.

MASU: Sometimes I want to put a blanket over my shoulders and move on again.

[*Tanaka offers Masu a cigarette. Masu takes one, hunkers down, they light up.*]

TANAKA: What else could she do?
MASU: Was I asking you?
TANAKA: Don't talk so loud within my hearing!

[*Tanaka joins him and the two continue to smoke. Tanaka gets out his case and offers Masu another. He refuses. Tanaka looks for an opening.*]

If you were just a little bit more sensible, Masu. You know you have credit with me.

MASU: Still? Is that so? I still do?

TANAKA: Masu . . .

MASU [*jumping up*]: To pay you off, all I need is a rainbow, stretching from waaay over there . . . to right here. And I will need that rainbow five years running.

TANAKA: You exaggerate. It's not your fault the crops brought in so little, but it's not Kimiko's either — not the children's. Why should they suffer?

MASU: You are "sensible," Tane.

TANAKA [*bitterness creeping into his voice*]: Listen, *bozu-san*, in Japan, we would not be friends, true? But this is America, Masu. You don't owe me. Take the cloth.

MASU [*uncomfortable . . . rises, slaps his thighs*]: All right! Next year, you will have the best vegetables in the valley. Come warm up before you go.

TANAKA: No, the wife.

[They walk to porch.]

MASU [*indicating missing bolt of cloth*]: Kimi is a practical woman.
TANAKA: Then listen to her sometimes.
MASU [*laughing*]: I can't. Life is sad enough.

[*The men say goodbye. Tanaka exits. Masu lingers on the porch and enters house. Kimiko looks up sharply at Masu's entry.*]

KIMIKO: Chieko . . . dinnertime!
MASU: Tadao. Tadao!
KIMIKO: He's not home yet. He said he was going to play foo-to-bal-lu.
MASU: Foo-to-bal-lu? What is that?

[*Chieko enters with book and goes to Masu, climbs on his lap, wanting him to read to her. He attacks the book warily, trying to read but he can't — the book is in English. Tadao enters, carrying school books.*]

MASU: You're late for dinner!
TADAO: Sorry.

[*Tadao takes his seat at the table, relaxed.*]

MASU: Playing footobalu?

TADAO [*looking swiftly at Kimiko*]: Huh, yeah.

[*Kimiko keeps dishing out food.*]

MASU: What is foo-to-bal-lu?

CHIEKO [*unmindful of others*]: Papa, read to me after dinner? Okey-dokey?

MASU: Your brother will read to you. [*To Tadao.*] What is foo-to-bal-lu?

TADAO [*full of himself but apprehensive*]: Well there's eleven guys on each side, and. It's a game where you . . .

MASU [*gesturing*]: With a footo and a balu?

TADAO [*laughing but upset*]: Yeah, Papa, with a foot and a ball.

[*Masu uncertain now. Fact? Jest? Putdown? He does not know what football is, so he shrugs it off and grunts. He begins eating. He wolfs down rice. Chieko begins to copy him and gets gentle reprimand from Kimiko. Kimiko clears the table. Chieko renews her attempt to get her father to read to her. His embarrassment is getting him angry. He sends her away. She sits on the chair and tries to read the book. Tadao helps to clear table.*]

TADAO [*to Kimi*]: The shoes cost more than you gave me.

[*Kimi indicating Tadao should ask father. Tadao refuses. Kimi goes to bedroom and gets her purse. She returns. Masu is reading Japanese papers and drinking sake.*]

TADAO: He won't let me work off the shoes, Mama.

KIMIKO: Talk to Papa.

TADAO: He won't understand.

KIMIKO: You do it. Take this blank check.

[*She presses blank check and bank note on Tadao and leaves. Tadao is angry but he goes to the table and sits down, clears his throat. Masu looks up.*]

TADAO [*placing in front of Masu the note, then check*]: You have to sign these. Fertilizer and stuff and this . . .

[*Masu responds with grunts, expressions, then takes the check, looks at it.*]

MASU: For what?

TADAO: I need some money for school stuff.

MASU [*cutting in*]: How much?

TADAO: It won't be much, Papa.

MASU: *So-ca?* How much?

TADAO: I put some money down on some football shoes.

MASU [*tired of hearing about football*]: Foo-to-bal-lu shoes?

TADAO: All the guys have them.

MASU [*getting angry*]: You need special shoes for a game? For this foot-to-ballu? Make your own!

TADAO: You can't do that . . . I never got the bike . . .

MASU [*waves it off abruptly*]: We have food . . . we have a house . . . we have clothes because of Tanaka . . . but no money.

[*Chieko comes up to Masu, disgusted.*]

CHIEKO: I can't read this!

TADAO [*low but determined*]: I want those shoes, Papa.

[*Masu hears but doesn't respond. He indicates to Tadao to read the book, takes the note and signs it, but leaves the check unsigned on table. Tadao notices this, and in anger goes to bedroom. Chieko takes book and follows, pushing it on Tadao. Kimiko enters and sets up table to cut material from homemade patterns made out of newspaper. Masu moves to soft chair.*]

TADAO [*from behind the curtain reading "The Boy Who Drew Cats"*]: That night, he goes to this haunted house, on a dare . . . and even though he tries to be brave, he's scared.

CHIEKO: *She's* scared. When Mama reads me the story, the little boy is a little girl like me.

TADAO: Who's reading this story, anyway?

CHIEKO: You are, maddy-cat!

TADAO: All right. He tries to sleep but he can't sleep, thinking about the evil rat. He finds a corner, and he gets his blanket and mat, and tries to go to sleep again.

KIMIKO [*cutting material around pattern she's made*]: I can make you a shirt. You could use a new shirt for *Kenjinkai* and *Senryu.*

[*Masu does not respond.*]

KIMIKO [*trying a new approach*]: It's left-over material, you know. Put a curtain on the window. That will be nice. Then you could move the cloth aside and look at the sky.

MASU [*turning to newspaper*]: I can see the sky without a curtain. The emperor and his warlords are at it again.

KIMIKO: Don't tell me. I don't want to hear about such horrible things.

MASU: Why not? Don't you have a samurai up your family tree somewhere?

KIMIKO: Don't talk so vulgar.

MASU: Look around here: farmers, fishermen, peasants. That's what we were! That's what we are! Still we crawl around, sniff at holes. Hoh, Samurai! *Doko desuka! Bushido* was never ours! Sonofabitchcocksaccas.

KIMIKO: Masu!

MASU: All right, all right. Shimizu had trouble in town?

KIMIKO: Haruko-san was so afraid. Said the men were drunk.

MASU: Shimizu is always a samurai when he's drunk.

KIMIKO [*taking up some mending*]: Tadao wants those football shoes so much, Masu.

MASU: You don't let up, do you?

KIMIKO: Beginning spring I will be out there all day with you. We'll have more money. A good year is due. I can do it.

MASU: That's no good, you keep losing babies on me that way.

[*Kimiko falls silent and becomes very still. Masu, rising, tries to placate her.*]

You're not as strong as you look. Come on, let's go to bed.

KIMIKO [*continues darning the sock*]: You go. I have things to finish up.

MASU: Leave it. Let's go to bed.

KIMIKO [*flaring up*]: This isn't Japan! This is America! When are you going to understand that!

MASU [*mimicking*]: This isn't Japan. This is America! I know. I know! What do you want, *obahan?* You want me to go around with a wooden bowl? Would that make me more American? Tanaka's a friend. What friend makes you feel like a beggar? What friend? Your son is ashamed of me. You make him ashamed of me, and me, I make him hate me. I would rather have that!

KIMIKO [*rising abruptly, upsetting her darning*]: Let's go to bed. Come on, let's go!

[*Masu waves her away. Kimiko goes to the sink and begins sorting the dishes to be washed. She is still angry. Tadao enters. He has on a light jacket. He's going out.*]

KIMIKO [*sharp, transferring anger to son*]: Where are you going?

TADAO: Out.

KIMIKO [*frightened re: Shimizu*]: It's too late . . . go study.

TADAO [*exiting through door*]: I finished.

[*Kimiko looking to Masu to stop Tadao.*]

MASU: This is America.

KIMIKO: Let's go to bed.

[*Kimiko goes into bedroom, Masu following. Tadao, on porch, takes out a cigarette from a hiding place, lights it and continues to exit offstage. Lights fade to black and rise on:*]

[Pearl Harbor Interim — *Roosevelt's declaration of war re: the attack on Pearl Harbor.*]

[*Lights fade up on the Murakami home. Kimiko is busy trying to get ready for party. Chieko enters with Masu dragging in an evergreen.*]

CHIEKO [*excited*]: Papa got three trees, but this is the best one, huh, Papa?

TADAO [*entering from bedroom, dressed in white shirt, tie*]: What's the others for?

MASU: For our cheap friends.

[*Tadao helps set up the tree in the stand. Masu is happy.*]

CHIEKO [*pestering*]: Now, Mama, now. Let's decorate now. Please, pop the popcorn.

KIMIKO: Later, after the party.

CHIEKO: Aw, Mama, please.

[*Kimiko relents and begins popping corn, shaking pan so as not to burn the corn.*]

CHIEKO: You take so long!

KIMIKO [*indicating popcorn and cranberry strings already made*]: So impatient. Start putting those on the tree.

CHIEKO: Help me, Taddie! Don't be a maddy cat.

[*Tadao and Chieko begin decorating tree but Tadao is also too slow for Chieko; she runs back to Kimiko, urging her to be faster.*]

KIMIKO: Stop that, pes-ky child, and don't eat "popu cornu," string it. [*As Masu grabs her, being playful.*] Masu, you're going to change your clothes, *neh?*

MASU: No! Don't I look good enough?

KIMIKO [*as Masu lifts her off ground*]: Stop it, stop it, Masu. What will the children think?

MASU: They will think their mama and papa did have a reason to get married, hey, Kimi?

[*He released her, but is still playful. For the first time, some of her softness and gayness shows.*]

CHIEKO [*to Tadao, who is decorating the tree*]: You okey-dokey, Taddie?

TADAO: Just string the popcorn.

[*Chieko sits and strings popcorn and cranberries, every so often sneaking popcorn into her mouth. Masu and Kimiko help decorate.*]

KIMIKO: Why did you get so many trees? What are they for?

MASU [*expansive, mimicking*]: One's for Tane. He likes the whole idea, but he needs an excuse. The other's for Jiro Yamada, that *kechinbo.* I saw him on the way to the pass, and I offered him a ride. I thought he might want to get a tree too. He gets on his high tone. "I'm Buddhist. I don't observe 'Cu-rissu-chan' holidays!" he says. That man, Kimi, didn't even know he was Buddhist until he came to this country. "I'm surprised, shocked at you, Murakami-san!" he says, "you, who almost became a Buddhist monk." "Yamada-san," I say, "only a real Buddhist could appreciate 'Cu-ri-su-ma-su' as I do." Kimi, what do you think? I take a tree to him, present it with a short lecture about Buddhist acceptance, and give him the hand of Buddha!

KIMIKO [*laughing*]: Oh Masu, no. You can't do that. That would be terrible.

MASU: Why not? The sonofabitchcocksacca.

CHIEKO: Papa, Taddie says to put up the star.

MASU: *Atokara.*

CHIEKO [*shoving tin star into his hand*]: Aw, papa.

KIMIKO [*helping him onto chair*]: Come on, *jichan*, put up the star.

[*Masu, still expansive, clowning, gets on a chair, puts up the star, and gets down.*]

MASU [*surveying tree and getting sake and cup*]: Bi-u-ti-ful!

[*He starts to go outside, gestures to Tadao to go join him.*]

Tadao!

CHIEKO: Where are you going?

[*Tadao indicates it's none of her business. Masu indicates they are going outside.*]

Don't forget to tell Santa Claus I want a Shirley Temple doll, Papa.

MASU: *So-ca?*

[*Kimiko shushes Chieko and she continues to decorate tree with Chieko while Masu and Tadao exit to porch.*]

MASU: About Mama's present.

TADAO: Can I have some, Papa?

MASU: Sure, sure.

[*He fills his own cup and gives it to Tadao. He laughs nervously. He is not quite sure how to handle this situation.*]

MASU: Women with women — men with men. About Mama's present, sa, Tane will bring the "gasu." *Atokara*, you go and turn on the fire and . . .

TADAO [*breaking in*]: Okay, Papa, can we talk?

MASU [*sitting*]: Sure.

TADAO: Papa, I've been thinking . . .

TANAKA [*off stage*]: Masu! Hop-pi Cu-ris-su-ma-su!

MASU [*standing to greet Tanaka*]: Hoh, Tane . . . Hop-pi Cu-ris-su-ma-su! [*To Tadao.*] Later.

[*Tanaka, Setsuko, and Hiroshi enter. They are carrying presents and food. Ad lib greetings, bowing, etc.*]

MASU [*giving Tanaka a cup of sake*]: This Hiroshi? Big . . . nineteen?

TADAO: Hi Hiro, how you been?

[*Hiroshi, stiff, nods brusquely.*]

MASU [*alerting family*]: Mama! Chieko! [*To Tanakas.*] Come in, come in!

[*All entering. Setsuko and Kimiko exchange greetings. Setsuko puts down food wrapped in furoshiki and pulls out Christmas-wrapped gifts from a bag.*]

CHIEKO: Oh goodie, presents.
KIMIKO: Hush!
SETSUKO: Nothing really, but children should have some presents.
KIMIKO: Always so very kind.
CHIEKO [*shaking one gift*]: What's in here?
KIMIKO: Never mind — put them under the tree.

[*Everyone being good hosts or good guests. Hiroshi takes sake offered him by Masu but moves away from group.*]

MASU [*to Tanaka*]: Four years, sa, a long time . . . a boy can change in four years.

SETSUKO: Not Hiroshi. What do you think we sent him back for? Not just to be high tone. Good thing, too. Stay around here, just become another dirt farmer [*Cutting herself off.*]. Anyway, no monkey business for him over there. American children: No respect, no self-control, flighty . . . head in the clouds. Kimiko-san, you understand, *neh*?

KIMIKO [*all graciousness*]: Maybe too much radio, *neh*. Hiroshi's turned into a handsome young man. Everything all right now?

SETSUKO: Fine. I told those FBI, I'm American born. Before you close us down, go close that dimestore across the street too. Germans own it. They closed us for a week anyway. I don't care.

KIMIKO: You were very bold.

SETSUKO [*with a who-needs-them attitude*]: Some wholesalers won't sell to us anymore. Hiroshi is a good son and once we find him a sensible wife . . .

[*Kimi demurs and begins setting out dishes of food.*]

SETSUKO [*helping Kimiko*]: You still using these old cups? Why don't you write home and have them send you some new ones.

KIMIKO: They're special to me. They were my mother's. I thought this Christmas should be extra special.

SETSUKO [*not so much snide as tactless*]: Don't look special to me. Are you still working on the embroidery? If you need more thread, we have it. We can't sell it anyway now.

KIMIKO [*distaste covered*]: No . . . I don't need it, but thank you, *neh*.

TANAKA [*shuffling Hana cards*]: Masu,what do you think? Will Japan advance this far? Pearl Harbor is Pearl Harbor . . . they make it very hard on us.

TANAKA [*re: Hiroshi*]: He says the bombing was in retaliation for the embargoes.

HIROSHI [*an observer of this holiday scene*]: Last year scrap steel . . . before that, oil. Japan is slowly being starved to death. The United States is jealous of Japan. I told the dumb FBI . . .

TANAKA [*cutting in*]: Idiot! It took all my talking to make them understand he's a stupid, hot-headed boy.

MASU: What did he say?

TANAKA: Nothing! Just acting arrogant with them, that's all.

[*Hiroshi is visibly annoyed.*]

MASU [*tasting dishes, showing great relish, kidding with women*]: Not bad, not bad.

SETSUKO: What do you mean, not bad!

MASU: I don't see what I want.

SETSUKO: And what is that?

MASU: [*improvises lewd, sexual remark in Japanese*]

SETSUKO [*in Japanese*]: Oh, you bad boy!

TANAKA [*trying to get Hana game started*]: Come on, sit down. Hiroshi!

HIROSHI [*coming to table*]: It had to be the embargoes. Japan was slowly being starved to death.

MASU [*lacking solemnness*]: *Sa!* Certain death to possible starvation?

HIROSHI: The Imperial Way cannot be defeated. It is the only way! Still, I wasn't prepared for Pearl Harbor. I believe Pearl Harbor was Japan's way of letting America know that she must be respected. What are these white countries screaming about anyway? We, I mean, Japan, does in Asia only what white people do all over the world. Asia belongs to yellow people. The bitter struggle is with China. Who will lead the yellow people of Asia?

TANAKA [*dealing out cards*]: Shut up, you young fool. War is no game!

MASU [*looking at his cards*]: Asia belongs to yellow people, or yellow rulers?

HIROSHI: Japan's rulers think only of their people.

MASU: That is what the ruling class always say. Who starts?

HIROSHI: Are you questioning the sincerity of the Japanese government?

MASU: Questioning? No, all governments lie.

SETSUKO: Masu, you're Japanese, don't forget.

TANAKA [*beginning play*]: I'll start.

HIROSHI: How can you be so blinded. Look what they do to us — arrest us with no reason. I'm an American citizen but . . .

MASU [*cutting in*]: To think, Tane, you sent him over there to be educated — curious the process of education.

TANAKA: [*shrugs off, and slaps down card*]

SETSUKO: He went to one of the best common schools in Tokyo.

MASU: I'm sure he did.

SETSUKO: They produce more leaders . . .

MASU [*cutting in*]: I'm sure they do. [*To Hiroshi.*] One minute you are for Japan and, then, you are an outraged American.

HIROSHI: You, Murakami-san, you don't get angry?

MASU: I'm always angry — that's why it never shows.

TANAKA [*to Hiroshi*]: Your turn. Play!

HIROSHI [*catching card*]: Philosophical thoughts are useless at a time like this.

MASU [*slapping down and catching card*]: And war is useful? Yes, I suppose it is useful. Forget what your teachers have taught you — what do you feel?

HIROSHI [*struggling with real feelings*]: I'm disillusioned with this country . . . I feel we have no future here.

MASU: You may be right.

HIROSHI [*finding rote words*]: Manchuria is important to Japan. We are entitled to our territorial integrity. China must now swallow us up.

MASU [*beginning to take Hiroshi seriously*]: Territorial integrity . . . who taught you such clever words?

HIROSHI: Murakami-san, you question integrity for yellow people?

MASU: No, but what has integrity to do with the rape of China?

HIROSHI [*used to rote answers*]: The Chinese will smother us to death. They are worthless swine anyway.

MASU [*no longer any hint of joking*]: Then we must be worthless swine, too. They have been our teachers for centuries.

HIROSHI [*outraged and puzzled*]: The Chinese?

MASU: Yes, the Chinese. You have no doubts about the Imperial Way?

HIROSHI [*indicating parents*]: Of course not. I wanted to stay on but they forced me to come back here. But I'll get back.

TANAKA [*cutting in*]: *Bakatare.* Don't talk idiot-talk!

[*Hiroshi leaves table.*]

TANAKA [*angry*]: All the time talking about things we can't control. Setsuko, come play!

TADAO [*approaching Hiroshi*]: What's Japan like?

HIROSHI: The Imperial Way, how can I explain it? You know what is happening? Them — they don't understand.

[*Setsuko is too busy to play. Tanaka throws his cards in, disgusted. Masu pours him another sake.*]

MASU: Drink up.

HIROSHI [*indicating Masu and Tanaka*]: They are simple men, behind the times. Japan was fated to rule Asia.

TADAO: Yeah, sure, but if a guy went to Tokyo, what would it be like for him? What do you do at school?

HIROSHI: We have drills and economics, history. I am fluent in Japanese now. You grow up to be a man fast.

TADAO: That sounds okay! Do they teach you how to fly? I'm interested in airplanes — the Messerschmitt, the Zero, the Grumman Wildcat, the Spitfire — I got drawings of them all — I can recognize them too.

TANAKA: What do you think, Masu, could he be right? Why do the FBI pick on me? I love this country.

MASU: Who knows? The sonofabitchcocksaccas are full of themselves. *Kuso de ippai.*

TANAKA: These are serious times.

MASU: I won't deny that, Tane. [*Turning to Hiroshi.*] Such confidence in the Imperial Way. You would join the Imperial Army?

HIROSHI: Of course. If they'd have me.

TANAKA [*cutting in*]: *Nani? Bakamono neh? Nan ya yutterun no?*

MASU: If he wants to, he will . . .

TANAKA: Stupid wild talk! He will not go back!

MASU: How will you stop him?

TANAKA: I am his father! [*Under.*] Don't encourage him.

MASU [*tiring of the subject*]: Come on, we have business. Tadao, give Hiroshi more sake. Anyone so certain he is a man needs more sake.

[*Masu indicates to Kimi he's going out for a smoke. In house, the party continues with ad lib conversations, re airplanes, food, etc. Masu and Tanaka move to offstage truck and return with Kimi's present as lights rise on bath house. Tanaka and Masu struggle to set gas heater under tub, placing tanks of gas and air. They stop, survey their work. Tanaka lights a cigarette.*]

TANAKA: Turn that handle there.

MASU: Is this all there is to it? I could make one myself.

TANAKA: Quit complaining.

[*Masu lights a match, warily tries to light the burner. The flames flare up and make him rear back. Tanaka offers Masu a cigarette.*]

MASU [*accepts and lights it off the burner*]: You think she will be happy with a present like this?

TANAKA: What a question! Of course. No pumping. No lugging pails.

MASU: I don't know. If I were a woman . . .

TANAKA [*cutting in*]: Take my word.

MASU: Still, not very pretty. A fine piece of silk for a dress. She might like that better.

TANAKA: What does she need silk for?

MASU: True, this costs more in the long run. Having to buy gas and air. Think of that! Buying air!

TANAKA: Take my word, it will make her very happy.

MASU: Hah, you're right. If you say so, you're right. You two understand each other much better than I do. You should have married her.

TANAKA: Don't talk stupid!

MASU: She would be much happier.

TANAKA: I have a wife.

MASU [*teasing*]: We will trade. How about that? Would you like that?

TANAKA: Maybe it was a foolish expense at a time like this.

MASU: *Hoh?* What do you mean?

TANAKA: Only that the future is uncertain. When the FBI questioned me, I told them I trusted Uncle Sam but they didn't believe me.

MASU: That was a bad night?

TANAKA: They were so well-prepared . . . picked us up that very Sunday. I never thanked you for looking after Setsuko.

MASU: Forget it.

TANAKA: They said Hiroshi came back from Japan to spy. I explain and explain: I personally love America but still want my son to have a good Japanese education. They let us go but they didn't believe me. I hear in the cities, they keep you in jail.

MASU [*back to burner*]: *So ca?* Think of it . . . fast hot water. Not so solemn, Tane, it's cu-ri-su-ma-su. Don't let them stop you from living. *Hoh,* I have a present for you.

TANAKA: So?

[*Masu goes offstage, Tanaka following as lights fade in bath house, rise on house, Kimiko and Setsuko moving toward door.*]

KIMIKO: Oh and, again, thank you for the *han-pan,* the *mochi-gashi,* the smoked salmon. All such delicacies. Masu will enjoy them so much.

SETSUKO: Nothing, it means so little to us, but . . .

KIMIKO [*finishing train of thought*]: The children will be so happy.

SETSUKO [*re: popcorn balls*]: What are these called again?

KIMIKO: "Pop-pu-cor-nu-ball-tsu." Chieko wanted to make them. And thank you again for . . .

SETSUKO [*cutting in*]: So pretty and cheap to make. Oh it's nothing, nothing.

[*Masu and Tanaka enter. Masu has tree in hand.*]

MASU: Such a formal man you are, Tane. Do you know something, you only laugh when you are embarrassed or apologizing for something.

[*The boys come out. The women are on the porch.*]

No time to get you drunk.

[*Masu stands up tree and presents it to Tanaka, formally.*]

Hop-pi Curisumasu, Tane!

TANAKA [*visibly touched*]: Yes . . . Hop-pi Curisumasu to you. Make sure to come for New Year. The best Japanese food anywhere.

[*Tanaka hands the tree to Hiroshi.*]

KIMIKO: *Domo arigato gozaimasu. O-tsukai sama desu.*

[*Goodbyes again. Tanakas exit. Family goes into house.*]

CHIEKO: They're gone, they're gone — goody!
KIMIKO: Chiecha, mustn't say such things.
CHIEKO: Come on Taddie, let's eat the *mochi!*
KIMIKO: Not tonight . . .
MASU [*surveying tree*]: Let her. A fine tree, a fine tree!
CHIEKO [*at tree, picking up a big present*]: Taddie, do you think this is big enough for a Shirley Temple doll?
KIMIKO: Santa Claus hasn't come yet.
MASU: Tadao, what do you think? Should we take a Cu-ri-su-ma-su bath?
TADAO: Yeah, come on, Mom, let's take a bath.
KIMIKO: Tomorrow, *neh?*
MASU: You and me, Chie-po. We'll take a bath then.

[*Masu and Chieko prepare for bath. Kimiko is cleaning up.*]

KIMIKO: It will take all night. You should have told me sooner. There is no water, nothing.
TADAO: Papa and me will do the work.
KIMIKO: All right! It will be a cold bath! It will take all night to heat the water.
TADAO: No, it won't. I'll do it.

[*Tadao exits. Masu begins to dance, showing Chieko as they move. Chieko tries but becomes impatient and wants to be swung instead.*]

CHIEKO: No, no, on your shoulders Papa . . . on your shoulders . . .

[*Masu grimaces, acts like a weary old man and swings Chieko on his shoulders and does a slow bon odori. She does not like it.*]

No, no, run — run, Papa!

[*Masu gives her a mock disgusted look and she laughs. Masu switches dance to horse, back to dance.*]

Faster . . . faster . . .

[*Kimiko enters anywhere in this sequence. She is dressed in a yukata, has a towel hanging from her neck, and carries a bar of soap. She begins to follow in the dance. Tadeo comes back in zori and pants, carrying Masu's change. They slip winter jackets over their shoulders as they exit to bath. Lights fade and rise on bath house.*

Actors are nude and in place in an old wooden Japanese-style tub with an aluminum corrugated roof siding. Kimiko slowly sinks in, Tadao climbing in, until they are in tub. Masu standing in bath, holding Chieko who is resisting.]

CHIEKO: It's too hot, papa!

TADAO: Japanese baths are supposed to be too hot, dummy.

CHIEKO: Dummy you too.

MASU [*putting Chieko on edge and slipping in tub himself*]: Enough!

KIMIKO: What a fine present, Masu. A hot bath makes everything better, *neh?*

TADAO: Mama is a good faker.

MASU: You knew?

TADAO: She always knows. When did you find out?

KIMIKO [*playful and teasing*]: I didn't know for certain. Just like when Tanaka-san and Papa smoke . . .

[*Kimiko showing the way Masu smokes.*]

Men always think we women are fooled! But . . . that's our secret, *neh* Chiechan? Besides, when the two of you conspire, everyone knows!

CHIEKO: Papa, it's too hot!

KIMIKO: This is wonderful . . . wonderful.

TADAO: Japanese always take hot baths, right Papa?

MASU: [*grunts in agreement, to Tadao*]

[*He grabs Chieko and dumps her quickly in and out of tub's hot water, she screaming.*]

You are Japanese, Chieko.

[*Lights fade down and up — short time passing. Everyone languid. Masu drinking sake.*]

MASU: Time to scrub!

[*Chieko protests as Masu lifts her out of tub and soaps her down with Japanese hitchime. She wants to get back into tub now and Masu follows her. He then sinks deeper into water and putting towel on his head, stretches out and starts singing a Japanese tune. He begins to flirt with Kimiko. She responds to him. He scoots deeper into the water and pinches her. She jumps and yelps.*]

KIMIKO: Masu, the children!

MASU: It's Cu-risu-masu . . . Kimi . . . for your own Je-su-us Cur-ri-su-to sake, let them see us happy.

[*Lights fade slowly and rise slowly as family gets out of tub, dresses, and comes back to house.*]

KIMIKO: *Sa,* time to go to sleep, Chiechan.
CHIEKO: I don't want to go to sleep.
KIMIKO: Chiechan . . .
CHIEKO: I don't want to. Why does Taddie get to stay up?
TADAO: Go on, po-head.
CHIEKO: Papa, I don't want to . . .
KIMIKO [*cut in*]: Now be good or Santa Claus won't bring you anything.
MASU: Don't say that. So, po-po, you don't want to go to sleep?
CHIEKO [*delaying bedtime*]: Sing my song, Papa, I'll help you.
MASU: Will you go to sleep then?
CHIEKO: Maybe . . .

[*Masu sings the song, "Chie, Chie, po, po, Chie, po po, suzume no gakko, sensei wa," etc. getting faster toward the end.*]

MASU: Now, will you go to sleep?
CHIEKO [*taking Masu's hand*]: You come with me.
MASU: You're a big girl. Mama will sleep with you.
CHIEKO: I don't want her. I want you.
MASU: Chie.
CHIEKO: I hate you, Papa.
KIMIKO: Chiechan. Mustn't say such things.
CHIEKO: Taddie said so. I can too. Taddie says you're a dirty Jap.

[*Masu looks at Tadao. Tadao glares at Chieko and exits. Chieko does not understand what she has said and is surprised at how serious everyone has gotten. She knows she did something bad. Masu takes her in his arms again.*]

MASU: Chie-po, wasn't it nice today?
CHIEKO: [*agrees*]
MASU: Don't you wish this nice day could go on and on into tomorrow and tomorrow night?
CHIEKO: [*agrees*]
MASU: Then you have to do your part. You have to sleep. Will you?
CHIEKO: Yes, Papa. [*Chieko gets up to go, returning to Masu.*] Papa, good night.
MASU: Good night, Chie-po.

[*Chieko goes with Kimiko to bed. Masu gets sake, grabs jacket and goes out. He opens door to find Tadao sitting on porch. He stands, considering his son.*]

TADAO: She's lying, Papa.
MASU: Is that so? You didn't say that? Sure you didn't.

[*Masu takes a drink. Offers some to Tadao. Tadao refuses.*]

The years go by so fast. I don't feel any different, but you . . . sometimes, I forget, you are not a boy anymore. I enjoyed myself this morning — when we filled the tub. You did most of the work.

TADAO: Mama got a bang out of it.

MASU [*continuing his train of thought*]: And I realized that the reason I was enjoying myself so much was that we haven't been like that for a long time. Years, I guess. That's strange, Tadao, to think, years.

TADAO: Papa . . . do you ever think about going back to Japan?

MASU: No . . . why?

TADAO: Nothing, doesn't matter.

MASU: Tell me.

TADAO: I hate it here.

MASU: Hiroshi has impressed you.

TADAO: You think you know so much, Papa.

MASU: I wasn't making light of what you said. It's getting worse at school?

TADAO: It's rough in town, at school, everywhere, but that's not it, Papa. Hiroshi just makes sense to me. We weren't . . . you weren't poor in Japan, were you?

MASU: *Sa* . . .

TADAO: Mama says you come from a good family . . . that you were going to be a priest . . . a Buddhist monk. Why did you come here?

MASU: You have grown up . . . right here, in this house and I didn't even notice it. I was the black sheep of my family. Everyone who comes here is the black sheep of their family . . . their class . . . their country. They were not wanted where they were. Strange, the only people who are not black sheep are black people.

TADAO [*annoyed his father is getting off point*]: Papa!

MASU: It's true. Before I married your mama, I worked on a ship. I worked with some black men, and they told me. Their fathers didn't want to come here. Slave traders brought them.

TADAO: Papa! I'm not interested in niggers! Not now!

MASU [*dealing with a new word*]: "Ni-gas?"

TADAO: Black men.

MASU: *So ca* . . . is that it?

TADAO: What?

MASU: On the boat, sometimes, I hear white men say "nigas," but I didn't understand. You say it, now, I understand!

TADAO [*frustrated*]: Papa, sometimes you act like — like you came from Mars — like you don't know anything!

MASU [*cutting in*]: I know well enough! I know enough. How do you know, Tadao? There are no black men around here. We are all "ni-gas." Everyone here! Tanaka-san and men like him came here because men like my father, my brothers, said: "You don't want to starve? Go somewhere else then, but don't bother us! So Tanaka came here and he stopped starving but he can't forget — he can't forget he was a "ni-ga" in Japan and he wants to forget. He wants to forget very bad. So he does to other men what my father and brothers did to him. He thinks that will stop making him a "ni-ga," but that won't do it!

TADAO: If we go back to Japan, it'll be better. Papa, you never think about other people's feelings. If you loved Mama . . .

MASU [*cutting in*]: I don't know, Tadao. Your mama is a good mother, not much of a wife — but a good mother. She's had a lot to bear. Sometimes she is so good, so fine, but most of the time it is hard to find the woman in her. You smoke? [*Tadao indicates no.*] Neither do I. You are right, Tadao. In Japan, I would have been a different man. I might not have married. And you . . . you wouldn't be here to worry about such things. I'd be a good man, but no husband at all. Here the problems are different.

[*Masu moves around, debating with himself.*]

[*Decided.*] I wanted to be a monk. When I was fourteen, I entered under a master. When I was seventeen, I decided I didn't want to be a monk, and I was sent to Hawaii to stay with an uncle. My uncle was like my father so, when I could, I came here. I worked as a lumberjack. Then I worked the fishing boats . . . up the Columbia River. The salmon jump. They jump high! They leap like the soft arch of a rainbow. They glisten but their color does not disturb the eye. At the lower reaches of the river, where the spawning salmon begin their struggle upstream, they are lovely and full of wonder. They are not weary yet, not desperate to be born again. Their time is still immense and boundless . . .

TADAO: It's different now. It's not just the white trash. It's everybody.

MASU [*pulling out his watch*]: You like this watch? One day, I'll give it to you. You like it?

TADAO: Yeah. Was it your father's?

MASU [*laughing*]: No, I bought it in a pawnshop, off the wharf in Seattle. It's pure gold . . . see, pure gold. When you were six, Mama took you back to Japan, you remember?

TADAO: Sort of. I think I liked it there.

MASU: Because it was different.

TADAO: Why stay where you're not wanted.

MASU: Do you know why I stayed here? I was freer. I could see what it was like to be a lumberjack, a fisherman, and anything else that came my way. Try it out and forget it. Put a blanket on my shoulder and go where I wanted. This land was wide and boundless once. Every act still had no name, and every piece of land and sky was not spoken for. It's different for you. You were born here, and so, when other people tell you that you don't belong, it must hurt. That didn't hurt me. I knew I didn't come from this land. I knew what I came from. It can't be helped. We were born, Tadao, to different times, so our lives are different, must be different, if we are to survive.

TADAO: I want to go back, Papa, I hate it here.

MASU: It will be hard in Japan.

TADAO [*cutting in*]: Hiro's going back! He says the war will be over in six months. He says we belong there!

MASU [*considering the possibility*]: Mama has relatives in Japan. You can be my present to my father. I could talk to Tane . . . he likes to see me in debt to him.

TADAO: Papa, let's try it. If it doesn't work, we'll come back here.

MASU: It's too bad you had to grow up so fast, Tadao. You're still very young.

TADAO: I understand a lot of stuff you don't.

MASU: So, Hiroshi says the war will end in six months . . . he sounds like the American generals, doesn't he? I must be getting old, Tadao. I want you to understand me. It's late. One more drink apiece.

[*Drinks, offers Tadao one, which Tadao accepts.*]

TADAO: You're going to talk to Mr. Tanaka then?

MASU: What? Yes . . . I will. But think this over, Tadao. Some decisions you can't go back on.

TADAO: I don't care about that. We belong there. When we all go back . . .

MASU [*cutting in*]: What? You, maybe you. Not me!

TADAO: But you said . . .

MASU: You wanted this man-to-man, now you have it. You, maybe Mama and Chie, you can go back, but not me. I can't go back! I can't go back.

[*Masu exits to packing house. Tadao goes into house. Lights fade and rise. Masu sits at kitchen table, his sumie brush and stone at hand and he writes in Japanese.*]

MASU: I am sorry about football shoes. Take this watch instead. In Japan, if you go, it will be more useful.

MASU: [*looking over his notes, says in Japanese the same thing*]

[*Masu places the watch and message under the tree, and exits. Tadao enters, has some handcrafted gifts. He notices the watch, checks back toward the bedroom, takes the watch and note, tries to read the Japanese by the tree light, moves to chair, tries to read the note as lights fade to black.*]

[*End of Act One.*]

[*During intermission, more war news and forties music.*]

ACT TWO

[*Time: Late spring, 1942*

At entrance to church basement where there is a table / lectern in front and American flag. Chairs are set up for meeting. Setsuko, Tanaka, and Reverend Sugano wait for Masu.]

SETSUKO: They put sugar in Shimizu's tractor — why does he have to go around saying: *Yat-ta-do! Yat-ta-do!*

[*Masu enters.*]

REVEREND SUGANO: Stupid, plain stupid, talking out of turn.

SETSUKO: And they broke in Kagawa's tool shed.

TANAKA: *Chikisho!*

REVEREND SUGANO: Now, Tanaka-san, keep your head.

MASU: What did they say?

TANAKA: We have six days.

MASU: Six days . . . how? How are vegetables to be ripe, picked, crated, and sold in six days?

TANAKA: Other communities had two days . . .

MASU: Answer the question! Did you negotiate? I thought it was agreed; if we planted, we would harvest.

TANAKA: Masu, I tried. Some things can't be helped.

MASU: Don't say it, Tane!

TANAKA: It's been hard for all of us . . . you know that!

REVEREND SUGANO: It's not Tanaka-san's fault. The rules keep changing every day. No one is sure from day to day.

MASU: I heard that, General George Armstrong Custer! Military necessity! First it was evacuate, go inland. Then, no one can leave without army permission. We would be allowed to stay, work our farms, be protected from the scavengers. They're toying with our lives, Tane.

TANAKA: The reverend is right. We must go along.

REVEREND SUGANO: That's why we wanted to talk to you before the meeting. People listen to you.

MASU [*ignoring Sugano*]: Go along?

REVEREND SUGANO: Murakami-san, things are confused. Everything is terrible. These are bad times. His own son still wants to leave home, go back to Japan, join the Imperial Army. It is worse for you and the other farmers, but there must be someone to keep a level mind.

TANAKA: I'll store your equipment with my merchandise. The government has storage depots.

MASU: Store goods? Who will ever buy them? Mice? Listen to me, Tane . . . listen to one who is not sane, so level-minded. In insane times, listen to me.

REVEREND SUGANO: Murakami-san, this is not a year's crop.

MASU: I know that!
REVEREND SUGANO: The more mature the grain, the lower the head hangs.
MASU [*under*]: *Kusokue.*
TANAKA: Masu, go along.
MASU [*to Tanaka*]: So you are listening to him again. [*To Reverend Sugano.*] Proverbs are the answers of dead men!

[*Masu leaves.*]

TANAKA: Masu, reconsider!

[*Lights fade and rise on church basement — before dusk — same day. People of community begin to enter the church meeting hall. The theater itself can be considered the hall, with the actors at strategic points in the audience. Crowd enters from different entrances in groups and scatters. Enter group A: M.1, M.2, M.3, W.1 (wife of M.3) and W.2.*]

MAN 1: Did you hear about Kagawa?
MAN 2: Worse than the Shimizus?
MAN 1: He went into that bar after the sign went up, and they beat him up.
MAN 2: He and Shimizu were always pushy. The nail that sticks its head up, gets pounded down.

[*Man 4 enters to join group A.*]

MAN 4: That *yat-ta-do* fool. Shimizu deserved what he got!
MAN 1: Shame . . . how can anyone say that?
MAN 4: He should have watched his tongue.
MAN 3: The seed store wouldn't refund our money.
MAN 2: I don't believe that. They have been good to me.
WOMAN 1: If Kagawa-san had a wife, everything would be different.

[*Group B: W.3, W.4 enter.*]

WOMAN 2: Well, what do you think? They say we'll have to leave.
WOMAN 3: No . . . No!
WOMAN 2: I hear in California . . .
WOMAN 3 [*cutting in*]: Rumors . . . just rumors . . .
MAN 4 [*to woman 2*]: I said so. Your husband should have sold early like me. It's your own fault.

[*Man 4 moves to another part of hall.*]

WOMAN 4: My children blame Japan. They say Japan makes trouble for us.

[*Group C: Mr. and Mrs. Shimizu enter. Mrs. goes toward women, Mr. toward men.*]

MRS. SHIMIZU [*crying*]: Burning down our shed, putting sugar in our tractor. Why are there such terrible men? What did we do?

WOMAN 2: Now, now, don't blame yourself . . . God will punish them.
MRS. SHIMIZU: But what will we do?

[*Enter Kagawa, reassures Mrs. Shimizu and goes with her to Mr. Shimizu. Leaves her with Mr. Shimizu and Setsuko and goes to side of hall.*]

REVEREND SUGANO [*at table*]: Please, please, sit down . . . please.

[*Some community members seat themselves, others stand, or lean against posts.*]

Members of this community and church. We face trying days ahead, and we must look to our inner resources to help guide us now. Let us have a silent prayer. [*Ad libbing prayer.*] Now, I have to tell you, we will have to leave here and go into camps.

[*A confusion of reactions. Hiroshi enters.*]

SHIMIZU: They're going to take us to the mountains and shoot us.
SETSUKO: Don't be silly.

[*Goes off to join group D: M.5, M.6 and W.5 (wife of M.6), M.7.*]

MAN 5: They say they built camps out where no one can see them.
MAN 6: That's what I heard.
WOMAN 4 [*to no one in particular*]: They're going to put us in camps?
MAN 7: What are the Buddhists going to do?
WOMAN 5: Jiro Yamada went to Utah. I told you we should have gone inland when we had a chance.
MAN 6: Leave me alone.

[*Group remix: Setsuko, M.7, W.5, W.2, M.5.*]

SETSUKO: Don't cry.
WOMAN 5: They're going to shoot us!
SETSUKO: No, no, rumors! Irresponsible rumors!
MAN 5: They put some city people in buses with red flags and curtains pulled down so nobody could see inside. Tell me what that means!
SETSUKO: To protect us. So the *hakujins* can't see us and get mad.
WIFE 5: Oh, no! Right after Pearl Harbor, they take away my brother in Seattle. His wife ask and ask, but they don't tell her nothing.
REVEREND SUGANO: Please, please, as long as we cooperate, we have nothing to worry about. Let Tanaka-san explain to us the way we will get ready.

[*Sugano sits down.*]

TANAKA [*going to table / lectern*]: Yes, now, if we all stay calm, everything will be all right.
MAN 7: What are they doing at the temple?
MAN 1: It must be bad. Tanaka-san is not smiling.

TANAKA: The official name of the order is: Civilian Exclusion Order 9066.
KAGAWA: Get on with it!

[*Agreement by others.*]

TANAKA: What it says is that we must all register and report in at Portland Assembly Center six days from now. There we will learn exactly where we are to go.

[*A confusion of reactions by community members. Some are loud, some are heard only by people close by.*]

MAN 6: What? Six days.
WOMAN 4: This is terrible . . . terrible.
WOMAN 3: They can't mean that.
MAN 1: They don't mean it . . . they don't mean it.
MAN 7 [*to no one in particular*]: What do the Buddhists say?
MAN 3: What about our crops?
WOMAN 2: What does it mean?
TANAKA: Please . . . please . . . now, let us have some order.
MAN 7: Yes, let him talk.
KAGAWA: What about the crops? Didn't they say we could harvest . . .
TANAKA [*cutting in*]: No, no. What the government man said was that in his personal opinion, we could harvest what we planted. He did not promise . . .
MAN 3 [*cutting in*]: But he said so. He's an important army man, isn't he?
MRS. SHIMIZU: I told you not to seed.
MR. SHIMIZU: They're going to take us away in buses too and kill us.
MRS. SHIMIZU [*starting to cry*]: Don't say that . . .
WOMAN 1: Please, don't cry.
MAN 7 [*very loud*]: What are the Buddhists going to do?
REVEREND SUGANO [*scurrying up to podium*]: They are going to cooperate the same as us. We had a meeting.
KAGAWA: Does that mean we let the crops rot in the ground?
TANAKA: The government man made it very clear. He said if he were in our position, he would . . .
MASU [*cutting in*]: He was never in our position. He never will be!
REVEREND SUGANO: Murakami-san, you speak out of turn.
MASU: And you, Preacher, you are not even useful in the pulpit.
WOMAN 5: What did Murakami-san say?
WOMAN 3: It's disgraceful . . . he has no shame. Why is he yelling? He never could farm — he has nothing to lose.
MR. SHIMIZU: So?
MAN 3: He's never been a good farmer, you know that.
MR. SHIMIZU: He's no farmer but he's telling the truth now.
MASU: They lied to us.

TANAKA: You know there are few established procedures. You know when he said . . .

KAGAWA [*cutting in*]: By all means, of course, you can harvest your crops . . .

TANAKA [*cutting in*]: Please, let me finish . . .

MASU [*cutting in*]: Round-eyed words, Tanaka! They mean nothing!

TANAKA [*ignoring Masu*]: The curfew comes soon. We must get clear in our minds how to proceed in the next few days. If we understand what we are to do, there will be no trouble. First of all, we must get together all important papers: birth certificates, passports, entrance registration . . .

MASU [*cutting in*]: First of all, crate what we can and sell what we can . . .

TANAKA [*cutting in*]: No! It's more important now to get ourselves ready! Pick out what you love best; I have been told, we can take only what we can carry. We will need blankets and . . .

MASU [*cutting in*]: We will stay and tend our crops and we will harvest them.

MRS. SHIMIZU: Yes. Yes. They promised us.

TANAKA: No! No promises were made.

MASU: Only self-righteous threats.

REVEREND SUGANO [*placating*]: Murakami-san, we can talk later.

MASU: About what, Preacher!

WOMAN 1: He's only saying the truth.

WOMAN 4: It's shameless.

TANAKA: No, Murakami-san. If we do not follow the army's orders, they will show us no mercy.

KAGAWA [*to Masu*]: What will you do?

MASU: I will tend my crops and pick them. If they keep me from the fields, I will sit on my front porch and wait until they come get me.

MR. SHIMIZU: That's no answer. What is the Japanese Consul doing to protect us?

TANAKA [*pleading*]: Masu, this is an emergency. Your pride is of no concern here.

MASU: Untended fields are an emergency. Unpicked cucumbers and asparagus and radishes and tomatoes and melons are an emergency. We seeded, cut out the irrigation ditches, weeded; we worked hard in good faith. And now, they say: One week. I say: Go to the bottom of hell.

REVEREND SUGANO: You are talking about material, worldly things. We are talking about our lives.

MASU [*to community*]: So am I! You know the Shimizus. Like the rest of us farmers, both of them get up before dawn and work until there is no light. We take time and patience making caps out of wax paper, and we go out and place these wax paper caps over every melon plant. Do we do that to become rich? Why grow melons? Why work stubborn land? Because that careful labor is the only way to make melons grow, and that is our lives. Now a government puts out a price book . . .

MAN 5 [*cutting in*]: Two dollars an acre for unharvested crops — the dogs!

MASU [*continuing*]: And vultures circle . . .

MAN 6 [*cutting in*]: Some *hakujin* had the nerve to offer me twenty dollars for my tractor. Twenty dollars!

MAN 2: I got almost book price for my tractor.

MASU: They barter our lives cheap and, Tanaka, you want us to agree to that?

MAN 3: I told you they weren't going to let us stay.

TANAKA [*fighting back*]: There are old people to consider. There are children. Our families, our safety, our reputations — these are what are important. Not your stupid pride.

MASU [*to community*]: Dogs, let loose, destroyed Shimizu's equipment, burned down his shed. This order is more of the same. If we say no, they will have to stop playing with our lives.

REVEREND SUGANO: His way will lead only to disaster.

MASU: And your way, Preacher, will destroy a people.

TANAKA: Masu, you have a responsibility to the rest of us.

MASU: So do you! Don't sacrifice us to your fears!

HIROSHI: Murakami-san, leave these old women, come back to Japan with me.

TANAKA: Arrogant men who put their own honor above all else have no place here. There are larger loyalties.

MASU: *Bakayaro!* Do you understand me so little?

TANAKA [*to community*]: Bah . . . well, I am certain about my loyalties. I am loyal to the land that fed us. I am loyal to the land that put a roof over my head for the first time in my life. I am loyal to . . .

HIROSHI [*cutting in*]: Tell us, old woman!

MASU: Hiroshi, quiet!

TANAKA [*angered*]: I am loyal to the land that let me live. We are not going to sacrifice ourselves for your filthy honor.

MASU: But you sacrifice us to those who want to destroy us.

TANAKA: If you don't like the smell of the stables, hold your nose or get out!

MASU: Stables don't offend me. They are occupied by honest animals.

TANAKA: Arrogance like yours must be destroyed!

MASU [*exiting*]: Dead men, ever and always, dead men.

HIROSHI: Murakami-san, wait!

[*Masu gestures, shove it. Lights fade to black and rise on Murakami house — early evening — same day.*]

MASU [*on porch, yelling at Tadao and Chieko, who are outside*]: Tadao, go check the water. Take Chiechan with you!

[*Masu enters the house. He slams his hat on the table. Kimiko, flustered, worried, harried, trying to set up table for food.*]

MASU: A land of cocksaccas! They talk about freedom but they hate and fear it.

KIMIKO: Nightriders shot up Shimizu's place.

MASU: I heard at the meeting.

KIMIKO: And the packing shed burned down and they put sugar and sand in all the machines.

MASU: I said I heard!

KIMIKO [*fearing the worst*]: Masu, what happened at the meeting?

MASU: They will be good Japanese peasants and listen to their leaders. A minister who could not serve the needs of a flea . . .

KIMIKO [*cutting in*]: What about the crops? Will we be able to harvest them? The tractor, the pickup?

MASU [*continuing*]: . . . and a merchant who sells us death.

KIMIKO [*cutting in sharply*]: Masu! What was decided!

MASU: Six days from now we will meet at the church and go to Portland. At Portland, they will let us know where the sheep are to be taken. We will be shipped at night so we do not disturb the sleep of the "decent" people. That doesn't frighten you, Kimi? No! Of course not. You can have your minister hold your hand! [*Kimiko does not take bait.*] Kimi, this time, it will take more than quick wits to save us.

KIMIKO: Masu, some things cannot be helped . . .

MASU [*upsetting the table*]: That's all everyone says!

[*Kimiko scurries to gather up the dishes, which infuriates Masu. He grabs her, she struggles; he holds onto her until he is calmer.*]

Storms, yes. Storms cannot be helped . . . and weather and seas and stubborn land. Have you ever been at sea during a storm?

KIMIKO: [*indicating no*]

MASU [*continuing*]: The thunder fills up the entire sky, no small portion of it. The fright is awesome. The waves pound high and threaten to grab you up and plunge you back into its depths. And on land, out there, in the fields, the lightning streaks from horizon to horizon and the rain pounds down. There is so much energy, you cannot believe in it. But it is there, demanding that you remember what you left: the earth, the sea. That I understand. To that I can say, *shikataganai.* But men, not men. They don't impress me the same way. Cocksaccas, sonofabitchcocksaccas.

KIMIKO [*anxious, cutting in*]: The house, the crops, the equipment? I know we don't have much but if we go into the camps . . . if we go without anything at all . . . afterwards, what will happen, afterwards.

MASU: Afterwards? Afterwards. Do you know why I left the temple? Because even Buddha described my perfect state as one when everything vital and necessary in me is gone. Gone, in one wave of a hand.

KIMIKO: Six days . . . they can't mean we must be ready so soon.

MASU: Why not? An emergency is an emergency and in an emergency, life can be ignored.

KIMIKO: What can we take with us?

MASU: We're not going.

KIMIKO: Talke sense! Masu, talk sense!

TADAO [*entering from porch where he's stood listening*]: Didn't you hear? We're not going. We're going back to Japan. Aren't we, Papa? Aren't we?

[*Masu grabs his hat, tips over his chair in a rush to get away from Tadao and exits. Tadao looks to his mother for an answer. Kimiko picks up the scattered dishes. Lights fade to black and rise on dimly lit kitchen area — very late that night. Masu is stumbling about in the dark, trying to get a bottle of sake opened. He is drunk. Kimiko, hearing the clatter, enters and tries to get him to come to bed. He is cut up and obviously got the worst of a fight.*]

KIMIKO: No more, Masu, no more, please.

MASU: Go back to bed, Kimi. Leave me alone.

[*She tries to grab the bottle and he rears away.*]

You sonofabitch woman, get away from me.

KIMIKO: Tadao! [*Tadao enters.*]

MASU: Leave him out of this!

[*They struggle. Masu has a knife that he was using to open the sake bottle. He is unaware of this but it is the knife that activates Tadao. He barges in and flings the two apart. Masu falls to the floor, bottle in hand, knife in hand. Kimiko tries to help him but she is brushed aside.*]

MASU [*to Tadao*]: You have always stood with her against me. Maybe she needs it.

[*He crawls on all fours to the table and gets up and plops down on a chair, trying to open the bottle again.*]

Any woman who lets two children die for every one she manages to keep alive needs something.

TADAO: Shut up, Papa! Shut up!

KIMIKO [*low, intense*]: And why did they die? Tell him. Tell him why. Because you could not afford a doctor. Because you could not afford not having me in the fields. Tell him!Tell Tadao!

TADAO: Shut up, Mama! Please shut up!

KIMIKO: You should have become a monk. It would have been better for both of us.

MASU [*sometimes angry, sometimes ironic*]: Always a pack! Always someone to support you! Isn't that right, *kusobaba!* Turning Tadao against me, probably turning Chieko right now.

[*Drops the knife, falls on all fours looking for it, crawling around the floor again.*]

After being with you, Tanaka sneaks around me like a sniffing cat. [*He sniffs at Kimiko's dress.*] Tanaka, a friend? What friend makes you feel like a beggar?

KIMIKO [*quiet and deadly*]: You men run the world. That's the price you pay.

MASU: You, Tanaka, *bakayaro* Cu-ri-su-chan minister, this country, made for each other! [*Mimicking.*] I hate war, don't talk about it and it will go away, and your Je-sus Cu-risto will save you.

TADAO: We're not going back to Japan, are we, Papa?

[*Masu, now turning toward Tadao.*]

MASU [*again switching ironic/angry*]: No! We're not going back to Japan. No, we're not going back to Japan. So go comfort your mother. Go on! What are you waiting for?

[*Tadao crosses to Kimiko. Masu tries to get on chair, manages or doesn't.*]

That's right. That's right. I went into one of those No Ja-pu! bars. I knew. I knew, before I went, there was nothing there I wanted. But my son, my cocksacca son, dying to get in. Mad and dying. When they say no, he wants to run away to Japan. [*Mimicking.*] "Oh, Papa . . . why stay where you're not wanted."

[*Wringing his hands, implying his son is a woman, Masu gets out of the chair, knife falls to the floor, and makes a lurch at his son to say "dir-le Jap."*]

Does he fight back? Oh, no . . . he's ashamed and his father is a dir-le Jap!

TADAO [*moving away*]: That's right. That's right. You talk so big. But you can't do anything. Nothing but get drunk. Get drunk and nothing else. If it wasn't for you, if it wasn't for you

[*He sees the knife, picks it up, and he points it at his father, which infuriates Masu.*]

MASU: Put that down. Put that knife down!

TADAO: Stay away from me, Papa, I'll kill you. I'll do it, I will . . .

MASU [*calm*]: He would . . . he's your son. [*Moving in on Tadao.*] Sonofabitchcocksacca.

[*Chieko enters, rubbing her eyes, not sure of what's happening but whimpering.*]

TADAO [*dropping knife*]: Stop crying. I'm sick of it.

MASU [*gentle, turning toward daughter*]: Chieko . . .

TADAO [*getting gold watch and tossing it on table*]: I'm not going to need this.

[*Tadao exits as lights fade to black and rise on Murakami home — day before departure. The room is bare of everyday clutter. The moving out process — vis-*

ible with clothes and articles in piles, a few packed boxes here and there. Soft armchair sits amidst the emptiness. Next to it, a packed orange crate. Tadao enters house. Kimiko is packing.]

KIMIKO: Did Chieko cry?

TADAO: One of the ladies gave her some candy and there's lots of kids at the church. She calmed down and started playing with them. I told her we'd be there tomorrow.

KIMIKO: Good. [*They start packing.*] I wish you would tell Papa you are sorry. We all said things we are ashamed of, didn't we?

TADAO: [*not responding*]

KIMIKO [*indicating handmade end table*]: Papa's left the watch over there ever since that night. You could have taken it back and nothing would have been said.

TADAO: Why are you sticking up for him now?

KIMIKO [*exasperation*]: Tadao! Why do you have to be so stubborn, like your father?

TADAO: I'm nothing like him.

KIMIKO: Don't say such things! You only bring bad things on yourself. It will be hard enough! You know that. You know how Papa says if we don't all hold together now, we might as well be dead. Well, he is right in that. He has been running around, trying to get everything done. He's trying to make up. You must do your part.

TADAO: I'm helping you.

KIMIKO: Papa left the watch for you for three days and you did not even touch it.

TADAO: I don't want it, Mama. Can't you understand? I don't want it.

[*Kimiko, worn out, tired, ready to cry.*]

Don't Mama . . .

KIMIKO: Papa and I made up . . . patched things over.

TADAO: You should have left him long ago.

KIMIKO: And gone where? Tell me?

TADAO: Anywhere! We would have been all right.

KIMIKO: That is not true, Tadao, that is just not true. You don't have to say you are sorry. If you work with him, he will know. He is doing all this because he feels so bad.

TADAO: He's doing all this because he's a big number one zero nothing!

KIMIKO: I will not listen!

[*She begins to pack furiously, slamming things around, pounding clothes into boxes, shooting angry looks at her son. As she packs, she suddenly comes across a faded, delicately colored kimono and fancy Japanese slippers, high, very small. She looks at the shoes, makes a gesture of comparison, her feet now, the shoes. Slowly, she slips back through time and although she is talking to Tadao, she is talking to herself, remembering. There are many abrupt swings of mood as she lives out her past — young, shy, playful, angry, thrilled, pleased with herself, totally open. Eventually, she returns to present and focuses on "now."*]

KIMIKO: When your Papa came back from America, his uncle and my older sister decided he should marry. He was over thirty, so he accepted the idea. I never liked my sister. I know I shouldn't say that, but I never did. She was so proper and so bossy . . . and pretty. So pretty. She was always trying to run my life! And she thought my idea of going to college was silly and improper, but I was smarter than her. I graduated common school and passed all the examinations. Then I found out they were going to marry me off to him, I was so angry! I thought my sister had talked everyone into it, Mama, Papa, my relatives, for spite. So I couldn't go to college. Then I met your papa. He was nothing like his uncle, my sister's husband. He was generous, and he loved to make people laugh and be happy. They called him the great *yancha:* lazy, good-for-nothing, but loved. Maybe a little crazy, too. In Japan, men are very arrogant. They don't think twice telling a woman she is ugly. Can't cook. Can't dance. Can't serve properly. Can't keep up a proper home . . . whatever. But your Papa, not once, not even to the others, did he talk badly of me. I was told to leave the room so they could discuss the marriage arrangements. His uncle, Mama told me afterward, said: Well, she is very clumsy for her age. And Masu, your Papa, said: But I think she might smile in bed. Do you? he asked my sister. Oh, he made her squirm. Well, Kimi-chan, Mama said, it was not the proper thing for him to say, but she liked him, said he would be just right for me. After the wedding, at the party, my sister was here, there, fluttering about, scolding me . . . don't touch your hair so! Sit straight! Be graceful! And I made this face to your father, and he understood. He said to her, right out loud, in front of everyone: "Get away from here — you're not my wife!" Such consternation! My sister was outraged. Then Masu expected me to come back with him. Me, with you in me. My sister didn't like that. But I think the sea air did me good. You were the healthiest of my babies. Tadao, Papa forgave you. When are you going to forgive him?

TADAO: [*not answering*]

KIMIKO [*back to now*]: If you don't do it now . . . one day it will be too late . . . and you will never have the right to ask your son to forgive you.

TADAO: I won't need to.

KIMIKO: That's what your father thought.

[*Lights fade to black and rise on front porch — almost dawn. Masu, talking to himself, inventorying the farm.*]

MASU: Hidalgo will see the crops through harvest: split the profit. Pickup:

Goodrich. The bank will hold the tractor. Sell it for me. Who knows. Still need the pickup. He can collect it at the church. Damn! have to go tell him. Maybe we can take it to Portland. He can get it there . . . no . . . maybe . . .

[*He hears noises off in the packing shed and goes to investigate.*]

Cocksacca! . . . get away from there!

[*One nightraider runs upstage, Masu in pursuit, two raiders behind him, crates being thrown, two of the men get some kind of grip on him — one trying to find opening to hit him with butt of rifle. Tadao and Kimiko, hearing commotion, enter to porch. Tadao charges from porch, gets man with rifle. Man throws Tadao off, finds his opening, smashes Masu in the head. Tadao scrambling to feet, grabs shotgun. Man lets go in a panic to leave. Masu lying still. Tadao falls to packing shed ground and begins shooting at fleeing men.*]

TADAO [*shooting*]: Sonofabitchcocksuckers! Sonofabitchcocksaccas!

[*Kimiko is trying to pull Masu to house. She gives up, tears cloth from robe and tries to wipe away blood.*]

KIMIKO: Is this better, Masu? Tadao, hurry, please hurry. *Okinasai*, Masu. *Okinasai.*

[*Tadao joins mother at body. She is still in midst of emergency; he is spent out.*]

TADAO: He's not going to wake up. He's dead.
KIMIKO: Help me, help me carry him to the house. Clean off the blood.
TADAO: Why? He's dead.
KIMIKO: Go get Tanaka-san!
TADAO: He's dead, Mama — that's the truth.

[*He falls down on his knees and begins scrambling over the body, searching the pockets for the gold watch. Kimiko is shocked. She cannot believe what she is seeing.*]

KIMIKO: Have some respect!
TADAO [*gold watch in hand*]: It's mine. He gave it to me, remember.
KIMIKO: Lucky, Masu, always lucky.
TADAO [*grabbing body of Masu*]: Him?! Lucky?! Get up, you sonofabitchcocksacca! You goddamned sonofabitch Jap cocksucker, get up!
KIMIKO [*soft to Masu*]: Truth? What is this true to? To you? Is this what is true in you? Didn't you know that dreams are for night and the quiet after love? Didn't you know? *Okinasai* Masu, *neh?* On a clean bed . . . on clean sheets . . . [*Suddenly attacking Tadao.*] Stupid boy! Do you think he would want Chieko to see him like this . . . Or you or me . . . what is this true to?

[*She rises and goes to edge of packing shed to maintain composure. Tadao takes *the watch, talking softly to his father, wanting to tell him he does love and respect him.*]

TADAO: It's too late, Papa. It's just too late now.

[*Picks up shotgun and strides away.*]

KIMIKO [*calling him back*]: Tadao!

[*No response. She returns to body of Masu.*]

Okinasai, Masu. Wake up. It's morning time.

The End

LUCILLE CLIFTON

"them and us" is from Lucille Clifton's The Book of Light *(see page 141). Most of the poems in this collection emphasize connection and kinship. But this poem would laugh out loud if it could, gently mocking "them" and the cultural mentality that "insists on elvis." This poem exults in rhythms, and though it speaks of differences it also connects people of color to their rock 'n' roll heroes and to life rather than to nostalgia.*

them and us

something in their psyche insists on elvis
slouching into markets, his great collar
high around his great head, his sideburns
extravagant, elvis, still swiveling those
negro hips. something needs to know

that even death, the most faithful manager
can be persuaded to give way
before real talent, that it is possible
to triumph forever on a timeless stage
surrounded by lovers giving the kid a hand.

we have so many gone. history
has taught us much about fame and its
inevitable tomorrow. we ride the subways
home from the picture show, sure about
death and elvis, but watching for marvin gaye.

◎ PATRICIA CLARK

Patricia Clark was born in 1951 in Tacoma, Washington. She received a B.A. from the University of Washington, an M.F.A. from the University of Montana, and a Ph.D. from the University of Houston. Clark is currently an associate professor of English at Grand Valley State University in Grand Rapids, Michigan. Awards for her work include the Lucille Medwick Memorial Award from the Poetry Society of America (1989) and fellowships at the Bread Loaf Writers Conference and the MacDowell Colony. Her poems have appeared in The New Criterion, New England Review/Bread Loaf Quarterly, North American Review, Pennsylvania Review, Seattle Review, Black Warrior Review, Nebraska Review, Widener Review, *and* Iowa Woman.

The main issue in "Bill of Sale" is the realization that history needs to be tangible before we can quite believe it. Here the speaker confronts herself with some shame upon realizing that until now she has not understood fully the real import of slavery in the United States.

Bill of Sale *(Lenoir Museum)*

I've known this all along,
                                        or so I keep insisting
to quiet the troubling thoughts
that won't be still.
                                        A piece of paper
dated 1862 in a nearby county
records that for twenty-five hundred dollars
a young woman named Liza
        was sold as a slave.

A minute ago we were outside laughing
in the Tennessee sunlight,
        planning a picnic
beside the Clinch River where grass
lures people to lie down and drift.

Now a shadow, the darkness of history
uncomfortably close at hand.
        I feel stupid and thick
in my body, unable to believe anything
until I see it with my eyes.

And I see the farmhands and the owners,
red dirt stuck to their boots, and their faces —
        not grotesque, but ordinar —
and the wagons waiting, horses chewing,

and a black woman, her face hidden,
a breeze kicking up dust
        around her bare feet.

◎ TOI DERRICOTTE

"A Note on My Son's Face" is from Captivity, *Toi Dericotte's third book of poems. Her golden-headed grandchild reminds her of the negative feelings she had about her son's darker skin. Confronting societal prejudices that she has unwillingly absorbed, the poet asks: "How can we wake / from a dream / we are born into . . . . // how can we ask forgiveness?" (For more on Derricotte, see page 142.)*

A Note on My Son's Face

I

Tonight, I look, thunderstruck
at the gold head of my grandchild.
Almost asleep, he buries his feet
between my thighs;
his little straw eyes
close in the near dark.
I smell the warmth of his raw
slightly foul breath, the new death
waiting to rot inside him.
Our breaths equalize our beartbeats;
every muscle of the chest uncoils,
the arm bones loosen in the nest
of nerves. I think of the peace
of walking through the house,
pointing to the name of this, the name of that,
an educator of a new man.

Mother. Grandmother. Wise
Snake-woman who will show the way;
Spider-woman whose black tentacles
hold him precious. Or will tear off his head,
her teeth over the little husband,
the small fist clotted in trust at her breast.

This morning, looking at the face of his father,
I remembered how, an infant, his face was too dark,
nose too broad, mouth too wide.
I did not look in that mirror
and see the face that could save me
from my own darkness.
Did he, looking in my eye, see
what I turned from:
my own dark grandmother
bending over gladioli in the field,
her shaking black hand defenseless
at the shining cock of flower?

I wanted that face to die,
to be reborn in the face of a white child.

I wanted the soul to stay the same,
for I loved to death,
to damnation and God-death,
the soul that broke out of me.
I crowed: My Son! My Beautiful!
But when I peeked in the basket,
I saw the face of a black man.

Did I bend over his nose
and straighten it with my fingers
like a vine growing the wrong way?
Did he feel my hand in malice?

Generations we prayed and fucked
for this light child,
the shining god of the second coming;
we bow down in shame
and carry the children of the past
in our wallets, begging forgiveness.

II

A picture in a book,
a lynching.
The bland faces of men who watch
a Christ go up in flames, smiling,
as if he were a hooked
fish, a felled antelope, some
wild thing tied to boards and burned.
His charring body
gives off light — a halo
burns out of him.
His face scorched featureless;
the hair matted to the scalp
like feathers.
One man stands with his hand on his hip,
another with his arm
slung over the shoulder of a friend,
as if this moment were large enough
to hold affection.

III

How can we wake
from a dream
we are born into,
that shines around us,
the terrible bright air?

Having awakened,
having seen our own bloody hands,
how can we ask forgiveness,
bring before our children the real
monster of their nightmares?

The worst is true.
Everything you did not want to know.

RITA DOVE

Rita Dove was born in 1952 in Akron, Ohio. Dove traveled to Germany on a Fulbright scholarship and then earned an M.F.A. in creative writing from the University of Iowa. She is the first African American and the youngest person to hold the position of Poet Laureate of the United States. Her many published works include novels, poetry, and a verse-play, The Darker Face of the Earth *(1994). Dove's* Thomas and Beulah *(poetry, 1986) won the Pulitzer Prize. Her most recent volume is* Mother Love: Poems *(1995). Dove is a professor of creative writing at the University of Virginia.*

"Crab-Boil" is from Grace Notes *(1989). The poem is dated "Ft. Myers, 1962." The narrator remembers "the sky / above the forbidden beach" where she and her aunt went crabbing. Public accommodation laws in the South were put into effect on a state-by-state basis, with only some parks open to blacks by 1959. "Crab-Boil" was written with a light touch, but it holds a memory of fear and defiance.*

Crab-Boil

(*Ft. Myers, 1962*)

Why do I remember the sky
above the forbidden beach,
why only blue and the scratch,
shell on tin, of their distress?
The rest

imagination supplies:
bucket and angry pink beseeching
claws. Why does Aunt Helen
laugh before saying "Look at that —

a bunch of niggers, not
a-one get out 'fore the others pull him
back." I don't believe her —

just as I don't believe *they* won't come
and chase us back to the colored-only shore
crisp with litter and broken glass.

"When do we kill them?"
"Kill 'em? Hell, the water does *that.*
They don't feel a thing . . . no nervous system."

I decide to believe this: I'm hungry.
Dismantled, they're merely exotic,
a blushing meat. After all, she *has*
grown old in the South. If
we're kicked out now, I'm ready.

◎ *IRENA KLEPFISZ*

Irena Klepfisz was born in Warsaw, Poland, in 1941. She and her mother escaped Poland disguised as Polish peasants, and they emigrated to the United States in 1949. Klepfisz was educated at City College, New York, and at the University of Chicago. A Jewish lesbian-feminist, she was a founder of Conditions *magazine, and was one of the earliest writers to explore ethnicity. She is the author of* Keeper of Accounts *(1982) and* Different Enclosures: Poetry and Prose of Irena Klepfisz, *and she coedited* The Tribe of Dina: A Jewish Women's Anthology. *She is a consultant on Yiddish language to* Bridges. *Recent books are* Dreams of an Insomniac: Jewish Feminist Essays, Speeches and Diatribes, *and* A Few Words in the Mother Tongue: Poems Selected and New, 1971–1990, *(both 1990), the latter the source of these selections.*

In "Warsaw, 1983: Umschlagplatz*" the poet returns as an adult to the place where Polish and Yiddish plaques read "they go from here to Treblinka." The concentration camp is located only fifty miles from Warsaw. By July 11, 1945, when the Soviet army entered Warsaw, 800,000 Jewish men, women, and children had been put to death there.*

"1. Poland: My mother is walking down a road" is taken from Klepfisz's "Bashert" *(Yiddish for "fated"). An autobiographical prose-poem, this personal epic moves across cultures and years, and shifts genres as it unfolds. In "History stops for no one," Adrienne Rich rightly calls this "one of the great 'borderland' poems — poems that emerge from the consciousness of being of no one geography, time zone, or culture. . . ." The consciousness that creates this poem insists on remembering all the aspects of its heritage, even the most shattering.*

Warsaw, 1983: Umschlagplatz

In Treblinke bin ikh nit geven.
I was never in Treblinka.

— *H. LEIVIK*

No horrors this time.
It's 1983.   June.   Summer.

Warsaw is tense   but over *Solidarność*
over amnesty.

A small white brick wall.
Two plaques in Polish   and Yiddish
to the effect   that from here
zaynen zey geforn kayn Treblinke.
Two stubby candles on either side
neither burning.   The guide
lights one with a lighter.
The wind blows it out.

A gas station pumping gas
right behind.   A building on
one side.   Perhaps   from that time
efsher an eydes.   Maybe it saw.
And there are tracks
I think.

I do not cry.   What's to cry
about?   An ordinary street.
People   going about
their business forty years later
tense about amnesty.

This street might have been my home.
This street might have been the beginning
of my journey to death.
I must remember:
it was neither.

I live on another continent.
It is 1983.   I am now a visitor.
History stops for no one.

1. Poland: *My mother is walking down a road.*

My mother is walking down a road. Somewhere in Poland. Walking towards an unnamed town for some kind of permit. She is carrying her Aryan identity papers. She has left me with an old peasant who is willing to say she is my grandmother.

She is walking down a road. Her terror in leaving me behind, in risking the separation is swallowed now, like all other feelings. But as she walks, she pictures me waving from the dusty yard, imagines herself suddenly picked up, the identity papers challenged. And even if she were to survive that, would she ever find me later? She tastes the terror in her mouth again. She swallows.

I am over three years old, corn silk blond and blue eyed like any Polish child. There is terrible suffering among the peasants. Starvation. And like so many others, I am ill. Perhaps dying. I have bad lungs. Fever. An ugly ear infection that oozes pus. None of these symptoms are disappearing.

The night before, my mother feeds me watery soup and then sits and listens while I say my prayers to the Holy Mother, Mother of God. I ask her, just as the nuns taught me, to help us all: me, my mother, the old woman. And then catching myself, learning to use memory, I ask the Mother of God to help my father. The Polish words slip easily from my lips. My mother is satisfied. The peasant has perhaps heard and is reassured. My mother has found her to be kind, but knows that she is suspicious of strangers.

My mother is sick. Goiter. Malnutrition. Vitamin deficiencies. She has skin sores which she cannot cure. For months now she has been living in complete isolation, with no point of reference outside of herself. She has been her own sole advisor, companion, comforter. Almost everyone of her world is dead: three sisters, nephews, and nieces, her mother, her husband, her in-laws. All gone. Even the remnants of the resistance, those few left after the uprising, have dispersed into the Polish countryside. She is more alone than she could have ever imagined. Only she knows her real name and she is perhaps dying. She is thirty years old.

I am over three years old. I have no consciousness of our danger, our separateness from the others. I have no awareness that we are playing a part. I only know that I have a special name, that I have been named for the Goddess of Peace. And each night, I sleep secure in that knowledge. And when I wet my bed, my mother places me on her belly and lies on the stain. She fears the old woman and hopes her body's warmth will dry the sheet before dawn.

My mother is walking down a road. Another woman joins her. My mother sees through the deception, but she has promised herself that never, under any circumstances, will she take that risk. So she swallows her hunger for contact and trust and instead talks about the sick child left behind and lies about the husband in the labor camp.

Someone is walking towards them. A large, strange woman with wild red hair. They try not to look at her too closely, to seem overly curious. But as they pass her, my mother feels something move inside her. The movement grows and grows till it is an explosion of yearning that she cannot contain. She stops, orders her companion to continue without her. And then she turns.

The woman with the red hair has also stopped and turned. She is grotesque, bloated with hunger, almost savage in her rags. She and my mother move towards each other. Cautiously, deliberately, they probe past the hunger, the swollen flesh, the infected skin, the rags. Slowly, they begin to pierce five years of encrusted history. And slowly, there is perception and recognition.

In this wilderness of occupied Poland, in this vast emptiness where no one can be trusted, my mother has suddenly, bizarrely, met one of my father's teachers. A family friend. Another Jew.

They do not cry, but weep as they chronicle the dead and count the living. Then they rush to me. To the woman I am a familiar sight. She calculates that I will not live out the week, but comments only on my striking resemblance to my father. She says she has contacts. She leaves. One night a package of food is delivered anonymously. We eat. We begin to bridge the gap towards life. We survive.

◎ COLLEEN J. McELROY

*Colleen J. McElroy was born in 1935 in St. Louis, Missouri. Her degrees are from Harris Teachers College, Kansas State University, and the University of Washington. Most recently she has been a professor of English and director of the creative writing program at the University of Washington. Awards for her work include grants from the National Endowment for the Arts, the Matrix Women of Achievement Award, a Fulbright fellowship, a Rockefeller fellowship, and a Jessie Ball DuPont Distinguished Black Scholar Residency. McElroy has written a textbook (*Speech and Language Development of the PreschoolChild: A Survey, *1972);* Jesus and Fat Tuesday and Other Short Stories *(1987); and eight volumes of poetry, most recently* What Madness Brought Me Here: New and Selected Poems, 1968–1990.

"For My Children" is from McElroy's second book of poetry, Music from Home:

Selected Poems *(1976). The speaker celebrates personal memories and the enlargement, too, of her growing consciousness of racial history. In an interview* *(see page 288)**, McElroy recounts an incident in college in Munich when one of her professors prodded her with the question "What are you?" He wanted her to know her roots. Since that time, McElroy has searched beyond the superficial for answers about her ancestors.*

For My Children

I have stored up tales for you, my children
  My favorite children, my only children;
Of shackles and slaves and a bill of rights.
But skin of honey and beauty of ebony begins
  In the land called Bilad as-Sudan,
So I search for a heritage beyond St. Louis.

My memory floats down a long narrow hall,
  A calabash of history.
Grandpa stood high in Watusi shadows
In this land of yearly rituals for alabaster beauty;
Where effigies of my ancestors are captured
  In Beatle tunes,
And crowns never touch Bantu heads.

My past is a slender dancer reflected briefly
  Like a leopard in fingers of fire.
The future of Dahomey is a house of 16 doors,
The totem of the Burundi counts 17 warriors —
  In reverse generations.
While I cling to one stray Seminole.

My thoughts grow thin in the urge to travel
  Beyond Grandma's tale
Of why cat fur is for kitten britches;
Past the wrought-iron rail of first stairs
  In baby white shoes,
To Ashanti mysteries and rituals.

Back in the narrow hallway of my childhood,
  I cradled my knees
In limbs as smooth and long as the neck of a bud vase,
I began this ancestral search that you children yield now
  In profile and bust
By common invention, in being and belonging.

The line of your cheeks recalls Ibo melodies
  As surely as oboe and flute.
The sun dances a honey and cocoa duet on your faces.
I see smiles that mirror schoolboy smiles
  In the land called Bilad as-Sudan;
I see the link between the Mississippi and the Congo.

◎ *JANICE MIRIKITANI*

Janice Mirikitani was born in Skykomish, Washington, and now lives and works in San Francisco. Poet, choreographer, editor, and community activist, she is a Nisei (second-generation Japanese American). Her parents emigrated from Nagano-Ken, Japan. She is the author of two books: Awake in the River *(1987), and* Shedding Silence *(1978). She has edited several anthologies, including* Making Waves: An Asian Women's Anthology.

"Prisons of Silence," which first appeared in Shedding Silence, *was performed by the Asian American Dance Collective in 1983 at the Repertory Concert. The poem takes on "the country of betrayal," the United States, which emprisoned 120,000 Japanese people living on the West Coast during World War II.*

Prisons of Silence

1

The strongest prisons are built
with walls of silence.

2

Morning light falls between us
like a wall.
We have laid beside each other
as we have for years.
Before the war, when life
would clamor through our windows,
we woke joyfully to the work.

I keep those moments
like a living silent seed.

After day's work, I would
smell the damp soil in his hands,
his hands that felt the outlines
of my body in the velvet
night of summers.

I hold his warm hands to this
cold wall of flesh
as I have for years.

3

Jap!
Filthy Jap!

Who lives within me?

Abandoned homes, confiscated land,
loyalty oaths, barbed wire prisons
in a strange wasteland.

Go home, Jap!
Where is home?
A country of betrayal.
No one speaks to us.

We would not speak to each other.

We are accused.

Hands in our hair,
hands that spread our legs
and searched our thighs for secret weapons,
hands that knit barbed wire
to cripple our flight.

Giant hot hands flung me,
fluttering, speechless into
barbed wire, thorns in a broken wing.

The strongest prisons are built
with walls of silence.

4

I watched him depart that day
from the tedious wall of wire,

the humps of barracks,
handsome in his uniform.

I would look each day for letters
from a wall of time,
waiting for approach of my deliverance
from a wall of dust.

I do not remember
reading about his death
only the wall of wind
that encased me, as I turned my head.

5

U.S. Japs hailed as heroes!

I do not know the face of this country
it is inhabited by strangers
who call me obscene names.

Jap. Go home.
Where is home?

I am alone wandering
in this desert.

Where is home?
Who lives within me?

A stranger with a knife in her tongue
and broken wing,
mad from separations and losses cruel
as hunger.

Walls suffocate her as a tomb,
encasing history.

6

I have kept myself contained
within these walls shaped to my body
and buried my rage.
I rebuilt my life
like a wall, unquestioning.
Obeyed their laws . . . their laws.

7

All persons of Japanese ancestry
    filthy jap.
Both alien and non-alien
    japs are enemy aliens.
To be incarcerated
    for their own good
A military necessity
    The army to handle only the japs
Where is home?
A country of betrayal.

8

This wall of silence crumbles
from the bigness of their crimes.
This silent wall
crushed by living memory.

He awakens from the tomb
I have made for myself
and unearths my rage.

I must speak.

9

He faces me in this small
room of myself.
I find the windows
where light escapes.

From this cell of history
this mute grave,
we birth our rage.

We heal our tongues.

We listen to ourselves

    Korematsu, Hirabayashi, Yasui.

We ignite the syllables of our names.

We give testimony.

e bigness of our sounds freed
:lapping hands,
; for reparations.

We give testimony.

Our noise is dangerous.

10

We beat our hands
like wings healed.
We soar
from these walls of silence.

◎ *PAT MORA*

"La Migra," which first appeared in Ms. *in 1993, has been anthologized in* Unsettling America: An Anthology of Contemporary Multicultural Poetry *(1994).* La migra *is the term used along the United States–Mexico border for the Border Patrol.* Agua dulce brota aqui, aqui, aqui *means "sweet water gushes here, here, here."* *(For more on Mora, see page 128.)*

La Migra

I

Let's play *La Migra*
I'll be the Border Patrol.
You be the Mexican maid.
I get the badge and sunglasses.
You can hide and run,
but you can't get away
because I have a jeep.
I can take you wherever
I want, but don't ask
questions because
I don't speak Spanish.
I can touch you wherever

I want but don't complain
too much because I've got
boots and kick — if I have to,
and I have handcuffs.
Oh, and a gun.
Get ready, get set, run.

II

Let's play *La Migra*
You be the Border Patrol.
I'll be the Mexican woman.
Your jeep has a flat,
and you have been spotted
by the sun.
All you have is heavy: hat,
glasses, badge, shoes, gun.
I know this desert,
where to rest,
where to drink.
Oh, I am not alone.
You hear us singing
and laughing with the wind,
Agua dulce brota aquí,
aquí, aquí, but since you
can't speak Spanish,
you do not understand.
Get ready.

◎ LINDA PASTAN

Linda Pastan was born in New York City in 1932. She was educated at Radcliffe College (B.A.) and Brandeis University (M.A.). Pastan has published nine volumes of poetry, the most recent of which are An Early Afterlife *(1995), and* Heroes in Disguise *(1991). She has received the Dylan Thomas Award, the Di Castagnola Award, The Bess Hokin Prize of* Poetry *Magazine, and the Maurice English Award. She has also received fellowships from the National Endowment for the Arts and from the Maryland Arts Council. Pastan is the Poet Laureate of Maryland.*

Pastan's "Family Tree" appears in The Imperfect Paradise *(1989), and makes use of the metaphor of the family tree to compare the loss of human life and the scattering and burning of leaves. Though the metaphor is organic, the images are sinister, evoking the deaths of millions in the concentration camps. Yet the music of the poem is quiet, understated, in the spare lines and tercets created by Pastan.*

Family Tree

How many leaves
has death undone already
poplar   maple   oak

raked into funeral pyres
and burned
gathered
in empty sacks
and dragged away
larch   linden   birch

leaves like the maps
of small countries
I will never visit

palm-shaped leaves
whose life lines
have run out?

How many leaves
in the long autumn retreat
their brown uniforms crisp

has the wind
taken away
or scattered

like drying shells
at the edge
of a grassy surf

cherry   sumac   elm
tear-shaped or
burned out stars

while the trunks
of the trees grow fat
and the branches shake?

I stand on a New Year's day
unwilling to drink
to a year

that will bring me
one new life
but take another back

and I count
the leaves
walnut   ash

the chorus
of silent throats
telling again
and again
the long story
of smoke.

◎ *WENDY ROSE*

Wendy Rose was born in California in 1948, of Hopi/Miwok and Scotch ancestry. She is the author of nine volumes of poetry, including Lost Copper *(1980),* What Happened When the Hopi Hit New York, The Halfbreed Chronicles *(1985),* Bone Dance: New and Selected Poems, 1965–1993, *and* Now Poof She is Gone *(1994). She has held positions with the Women's Literature Project of Oxford University Press, the Smithsonian Native Writers' Series, the MLA Commission on Languages and Literature of the Americas, and the Coordinating Council of Literary Magazines. She is coordinator of American Indian studies at Fresno College, where she also teaches.*

"I Expected My Skin and My Blood to Ripen" first appeared in Lost Copper *and has been included in* Bone Dance. *The poem's language is accessible and understated in its personal testimony about genocide. The sorrow in the poem is made real and palpable through its horrifying details.*

I Expected My Skin and My Blood to Ripen

When the blizzard subsided four days later [after the massacre in 1890 at Wounded Knee], a burial party was sent . . . a long trench was dug. Many of the bodies were stripped by whites who went out in order to get the Ghost shirts and other accoutrements the Indians wore . . . the frozen bodies were thrown into the trench stiff and naked . . . only a handful of items remain in private hands . . . exposure to snow has stiffened the leggings and moccasins, and all the objects show the effects of age and long use . . . [items pictured for sale] moccasins $140; hide scraper $350; buckskin shirt $1200; womens' leggings $275; bone breastplate $1000 . . .

— *Kenneth Canfield's* 1977 *Plains Indian Art Auction Catalog*

I expected my skin and my blood
to ripen, not be ripped from my bones;
like fallen fruit I am peeled, tasted,
discarded. My seeds open
and have no future.
Now there has been no past.
My own body gave up the beads,
my own hands gave the babies away
to be strung on bayonets,
to be counted one by one
like rosary stones and then
tossed to the side of life
as if the pain of their birthing
had never been.
My feet were frozen to the leather,
pried apart, left behind — bits of flesh
on the moccasins, bits of paper deerhide
on the bones. My back was stripped
of its cover, its quilling intact,
was torn, was taken away.
My leggings were taken like in a rape
and shriveled to the size
of stick figures
like they had never felt the push
of my strong woman's body
walking in the hills.
It was my own baby
whose cradleboard I held —
would've put her in my mouth like a snake
if I could, would've turned her into a bush
or rock if there'd been magic enough
to work such changes. Not enough magic
to stop the bullets, not enough magic

to stop the scientists, not enough magic
to stop the money.

◎ *JOYCE CAROL THOMAS*

Joyce Carol Thomas was born in Oklahoma in 1938. Her family migrated to California when she was ten and there she earned a B.A. from San Jose University and an M.A. from Stanford University. Some of her early books of poems are Bittersweet *(1973),* Blessing *(1975), and* Inside the Rainbow *(1982). Her first novel,* Marked by Fire *(1982), won both the National Book Award and the American Book Award. Her collection of poems for all ages,* Brown Honey in Broomwheat Tea *(1993), won a Coretta Scott King Award, and a companion volume,* Gingerbread Days, *was published in 1995. She adapted her recent novel* When the Nightingale Sings *into a musical, and another musical,* Abyssinia, *based on* Marked by Fire, *has had record-breaking productions at the North Shore Music Theatre in Massachusetts (1995). Thomas is professor of English at the University of Tennessee.*

"Brown Honey in Broomwheat Tea" is the title poem of Joyce Carol Thomas' book of poems for all ages, illustrated by Floyd Cooper (1993). Originally called "Black Child," the poem appeared in 1981 in a chapbook by that title. The poem was written during the time when children were being murdered in Atlanta. In that context the poem's quiet warning is meant literally. Yet even in 1996, cautions for children of color are still necessary. The emphasis in Thomas's work, however, is on the positive. As she wrote to us for this anthology: "One of the finest places to practice my art is in giving hope and joy to the young."

Brown Honey in Broomwheat Tea

My mother says I am
Brown honey in broomwheat tea
My father calls me the sweetwater of his days
Yet they warn
There are those who
Have brewed a
Bitter potion for
Children kissed long by the sun
Therefore I approach

The cup slowly
But first I ask
Who has set this table

◎ *LUCI TAPAHONSO*

"Shą́ą́ Áko Dahjiníłeh / Remember the Things They Told Us" is from Tapahonso's collection Sáanii Dahataał / The Women Are Singing *(1993). This lovely prose-poem links the wisdom and sacred power of the past with the Navajo people of the present.* *(For more on Tapahonso, see page 229.)*

Shą́ą́ Áko Dahjiníłeh
Remember the Things They Told Us

1

Before this world existed, the holy people made themselves visible
by becoming the clouds, sun, moon, trees, bodies of water, thunder,
rain, snow, and other aspects of this world we live in. That way,
they said, we would never be alone. So it is possible to talk to them
and pray, no matter where we are and how we feel. Biyázhí daniidlį́,
we are their little ones.

2

Since the beginning, the people have gone outdoors at dawn to pray.
The morning light, adinídíín, represents knowledge and mental awareness.
With the dawn come the holy ones who bring blessings and daily gifts,
because they are grateful when we remember them.

3

When you were born and took your first breath, different colors
and different kinds of wind entered through your fingertips
and the whorl on top of your head. Within us, as we breathe,
are the light breezes that cool a summer afternoon,
within us the tumbling winds that precede rain,
within us sheets of hard-thundering rain,
within us dust-filled layers of wind that sweep in from the mountains,

within us gentle night flutters that lull us to sleep.
To see this, blow on your hand now.
Each sound we make evokes the power of these winds
and we are, at once, gentle and powerful.

4

Think about good things when preparing meals. It is much more than
physical nourishment. The way the cook (or cooks) think and feel become
a part of the meal. Food that is prepared with careful thought,
contentment, and good memories tastes so good and nurtures the mind
and spirit, as well as the body. Once my mother chased me out of the kitchen
because it is disheartening to think of eating something cooked
by an angry person.

5

Be careful not to let your children sit or play on tables or countertops.
Not only is it bad manners, but they might have to get married
far sooner than you would ever want.

6

Don't cut your own hair or anyone else's after dark. There are things
that come with the darkness that we have no control over. It's not
clear why this rule exists, but so far no one is willing to become
the example of what happens to someone who doesn't abide by it.

INTERVIEW

Against a Bondage of Color: An Interview with Colleen J. McElroy

by Patricia Clark

COLLEEN J. McELROY

The interview with Colleen J. McElroy, "Against a Bondage of Color," was conducted in Seattle, Washington, by Patricia Clark on September 1, 1991. McElroy has had an interesting career — from speech pathologist to poet and college professor. Though McElroy's work is remarkable for its exuberance, she is passionate and serious about America's denial of its past concerning race, its culture history "in all its tawdriness and denial."

PC: Many people might wonder how you got to poetry from speech pathology, though to others it might seem a fairly natural progression. Will you talk about that a bit?

CJM: As a speech pathologist, I dealt with neurologically impaired patients. And I was concerned with language. Most of my patients had the mechanism, the physiology of speech, they just didn't have the connections.

PC: And what was your job then?

CJM: To retrain them; to retrain them to find language.

PC: Did you start writing poems when you were working as a speech pathologist?

CJM: No, it was much later. It was after going to poetry readings and listening to poets. I said, "I can do that." I started writing very late, you know. I was in my mid-thirties before I put pen to paper — as a poet.

PC: Yes, and you had already written a book, right? One on speech acquisition?

CJM: Yes, and I'd done reports for governmental agencies.

PC: Had you already been a talk show host?

CJM: Yes, that too.

PC: And you were writing at that job, too?

CJM: Yes. I really had a writing background, but I had not done anything in terms of poetry. So when my work was accepted by John Gardner what he got was an outpouring of poems. I was really trying to catch up. There would be times when I'd write four poems in a day.

PC: Feeling that fire to catch up somehow?

CJM: Yes. I just had so many poems I needed to write.

PC: I wonder if you would recommend that in some ways.

CJM: Oh, I don't know if I would recommend that in any way! [*Laughter.*]

PC: Well, there are a lot of students today who know early on they want to specialize in creative writing, and they take a lot of writing workshops. I just wonder if there aren't some pluses to having other kinds of experiences.

CJM: Oh, I think almost every poet I know has had something else. Poets who I really admire —

PC: Who are you thinking of?

CJM: Oh, I'm thinking of Denise Levertov, who has spent most of her adult life as a poet but who has been so involved in other kinds of things, especially political organizations or movements. I'm thinking of Al Young, who was a musician. I think that the ability to see the poem, the possibility of the poem, means having a set of experiences that will prove useful. When you start to write, you inevitably bump into things that you would not otherwise if you focused only on the subject.

PC: It's interesting to me how often in the poems you're writing about your family, you're the outcast. You're going back, but you're never quite "of them."

CJM: Yes, although there are times when my mother wants me to be.

PC: Is that partly distance? Partly becoming the poet, the writer, the recorder of things?

CJM: No, I can never remember when I didn't want to leave home. The sense of travel, movement, has always been there. I just can't remember when there wasn't a need to leave there [St. Louis in the 1950s].

PC: Do you think that's a healthy desire?

CJM: It has been for me. I don't know what I would have been otherwise. I have no idea what I would be.

PC: Perhaps you would be one of your cousins?

CJM: Maybe. One of the essays I just finished writing is called "Going Home." These are poetic memoirs, so they have some of the rhythms of poems though they're written in prose. They're fragmentary, and in them I say "these things come to me in bits and pieces so that's how I will write them." And one of the pieces that keeps coming back is "Why do you have to go to all those places?" And the response is "Because they're there." My way of seeing myself, my way of seeing the world has changed drastically because of travel. I don't know how I would have survived without it.

PC: I see. It seems as though, too, in some of the poems where you're traveling, you deal with being black in a way that's perhaps just not possible when dealing with it in the American landscape. Is that right?

CJM: Right. Because here it is a question of color, a bondage of color, but in other places, color is not always the key issue. A refrain from the poetic memoir I recently finished reads: "They want to know what you are and when they ask, they don't want to know your color."

PC: That's just not a concern?

CJM: They can see that.

PC: So what does "What are you?" mean to them: occupation?

CJM: No. It means, "What are your roots?" Or: "How do you account for the accumulation of what you are?"

PC: What an interesting difference of questions.

CJM: Yes. The first time I was asked was in a history class in Germany. I gave the professor several answers, none of which he could accept. I told him I was a Negro, that I was an American. He said, "I don't want to know where you live, I want to know what you are. Don't come back until you can tell me what you are because how can you possibly study someone else's history when you don't know your own?"

PC: How old were you when that happened?

CJM: I was in college in Munich.

PC: So did you find out before you went back to class?

CJM: Yes, and I had to do a lot of searching. And a lot of it was speculation at that time. Getting in touch with my mother, getting in touch with people back in the States. Really bugging people, and finally finding a source which happened to be my favorite aunt. And she gave me what she knew, which was fragmented, but it was enough to begin to piece together things. She is one who has not been bullied by class or caste.

PC: It rolls off her?

CJM: No, but she knows how to handle it. This is my red-haired, green-eyed aunt. And she's learned how to deal with things in her way.

PC: Was she a role model for you?

CJM: Yes.

PC: More than your mother, say?

CJM: Well, my mother and I have a particular and peculiar relationship but my aunt Jennie was the one to encourage me to travel. She said, "You're so brave going out there; I wish I could."

PC: Probably a lot of her unfulfilled dreams in you?

CJM: Right.

PC: Does your family love your work, read your work?

CJM: My mother took her poem to church.

PC: The poem called "Ruth"? What a terrific poem!

CJM: I had sent her the book [*Queen of the Ebony Isles*], and I was real nervous about sending the book because the poem was in it. And a couple of months later I called and in the course of conversation said "Did you get the book?" And she said "Yeah, I got the book." And I said "What did you think?" And she said, “Well, I took one of the poems to church.” And I said “Well?” And she said, “I don’t know — they seemed to like it.”

PC: Was that a backhanded compliment or what? [*Laughter.*]

CJM: And then my father got on the phone and said, “She took her poem; she didn’t take mine!” So I knew which one she’d taken.

PC: Which was his? The fishing poem?

CJM: No. “My Father’s Wars.”

PC: Did he like it?

CJM: Oh I think so. But they don’t talk about it [my work]; they want to know if I have another book coming out. And they want the book. They’ve gone past the point of “What are you doing?” They know what I’m doing. And when my mother got *Cardboard Pines* — she’s having vision problems [double cataracts] — but she’s slowly going through it. And she said, “Where did you get all that stuff?”

PC: There seems to be quite a renaissance of black writing going on in the United States.

CJM: I suppose.

PC: Would you use the word *renaissance?* Or do you think the writing has been there and just hasn’t received attention?

CJM: Of course, I think it’s been there. The only time I feel I can teach a course in black literature is when I decide to do, say, the major writers of the Harlem Renaissance. Then I know I have *x* number of writers, but if you’re going to teach anything that spans numbers of years, you’re considering a multitude of writers.

PC: What do you think of the recent multicultural discussions? And then the resultant backlash about political correctness?

CJM: Well, I think this country suffers from what I call a bondage of color — and as long as that bondage exists there’s going to be a fight. It’s a given. . . . There is a great fear that if we allow a culture of diversity, we’ll have to look at our cultural history in all its tawdriness and denial. Despite its existence, this country doesn’t acknowledge its bondage of color, markers to note any struggles over issues of race. When I travel abroad, I find markers, monuments to cultural heroes who have died in the struggle for representation. Markers such as, how many people died in this revolution and what this hero stands for. You can’t find that in this country. You cannot go into the South and find markers that say “*X* number of slaves died on this spot in the rebellion of such and so.” But if you go into Yugoslavia or Romania or Malaysia you find towns where they have such markers.

PC: America’s into a lot of denial.

CJM: Yes. And I think the reaction “Why do we have to be politically correct?” is another manifestation of that denial.

PC: Well, I guess part of the argument with universities is that these are places committed to free speech — and if someone says something we find repugnant, well, we have to tolerate that. You think it’s bull?

CJM: I think it's bull. I think it's all a part of denial. I think that if there was a degree of political honesty in this country, we may very well be on the brink of revolution. But it would be much more honest than the current dishonest focus on the First Amendment, in part. Because the amendment itself supports denial. Racism is self-evident.

PC: Aren't we afraid to examine it?

CJM: Yes. Because when we do, it's painful. It's the horror of our history.

PC: Do you think of yourself as a black writer, or an African American writer? Or as a woman writer?

CJM: Do I have to choose? If so: all. All of those things. I'm Popeye; "I yam what I yam."

PC: And they're concurrent in your head?

CJM: All the way. I can't nor do I want to separate them.

PC: Would you talk a bit about your writing habits?

CJM: I go through different notebooks or journals. And I write down lines, something I remember. I finally received as a gift a voice-activated tape recorder to put in my car because of my terror of going off the road, a clear and present danger. I'd be in the car and then the line would come to me.

PC: You mean you were trying to write, going 65 m.p.h.?

CJM: Yes. I have a famous story or an infamous story, of being on the freeway and pulling off to the shoulder to write. A state patrolman came up and tapped on the window and I turned and snarled, "Get away, I'm writing!" Mostly I'm ruminating, and in the process of ruminating I hear something. An example is my poem "Never Depend on a Shoo-in Candidate," where the first lines go: "the prince was a boob who couldn't remember the broad's face / his only clue was a shoe / and then the struggle to remember which foot. . . ." I got those lines and realized "I know that!" For me, poetry has often been a discovery of what I know.

PC: So starting with those Cinderella lines — do you know where you're going in the poem? Or is that something you work out as you go along?

CJM: I don't always know where I'm going. Fortunately that was a first line; usually what I get is the last line.

PC: Do you try and write on any kind of schedule?

CJM: Only when I'm teaching and I'm forced into some kind of schedule, ragged though it may be. And that's usually because I only have *x* number of days off.

PC: Has the voice-activated tape in the car been helpful?

CJM: It is, when I put it in there. If I can remember.

PC: Do you find that driving is good for writing?

CJM: Yes, somewhat. What I encourage my students to do is to find that time where they're most actively creative. For me, it's just as I'm falling asleep or just when I'm waking up. So I put a notebook beside the bed.

PC: Do you like to have a certain kind?

CJM: Yes. There's this thing I found at the paint store — it looks like a brush except it's a notepad. It has a little hole in the handle so I can hang it up. It's wonderful! And because it was hanging it never got onto the cluttered table. I could reach for it when I was half-asleep. But that's what I need, and I need to be able to get it without having to wake up entirely. To stay in the state of "twilight sleep."

PC: How much of the poem might you write then? Or when would you go back to it?

CJM: It depends on the poem. "Song of a Woman Who Knew Too Much" is one of my prose poems. That one was written in a kind of "twilight sleep." I had been trying to write that mythical poem for a long time and I wasn't getting anywhere. Then I went to eight and a half hours of Fellini movies — and when you say, "Would you advise people to do that?" — no! — but that's how I got the poem started. Then finally I got into bed and wrote a little more. From my handwriting you can see how my body was asleep. I mean, you can barely make out the words.

PC: Hearing about your writing process makes me wonder, you teach in a creative writing program: can you teach people how to be poets?

CJM: No, but I can teach them techniques. I can teach them how to read, how to be careful readers, I can teach them something about the music of language because as thinkers we don't consciously make language musical. I constantly reinforce the fact that there's an underlying musical quality to language. That really makes a difference between the poet and the nonpoet. So when you see some people who think that poetry's easy, simple — it's because they're not aware of what goes into it.

PC: It seems as though it's more usual for a successful poet to write good prose and good fiction than the reverse.

CJM: Yes, it will be much more the case that the poet will do well in that direction and the fiction writer will have a more difficult time. Something has to happen, something in the music, in the way you approach language.

PC: Maybe compression, too?

CJM: Yes, compression is part of it. I'm thinking of it in terms of dance. It's the difference between samba and modern ballet. And they're both dances. But the samba has tight little rotating movements and modern ballet just goes in great leaps. And what happens is that most people think that poetry is only the samba, or only ballet. Poetry is both.

PC: And you're saying that great leaps are the heart of poetry?

CJM: Yes. Ballet dancers make that leap of faith [*Gesticulates*]. The body and gravity cooperate. Poetic language is also like the samba, that tight little twist and turn of rhythmical patterns. Sometimes you do have to use samba rhythms but more often than not you're making leaps because otherwise . . . how else would you make those metaphors work?

PC: But how you can tell your students how to have that happen to them?

CJM: Well, what they have to do is practice leaps. They just have to make a lot of dumb statements before those wonderful ones.

PC: In other words, a beginning writer is going to fall flat on her face?

CJM: A lot! Gravity fails you. You say, "What was that?" It is a question, though, of taking the chance. You have to be willing to take chances without being conscious of taking those chances. You need to make the poem look easy, especially when it's complicated. You can't look over your shoulder, and you can't look down. I use the metaphor of the water-strider, the bug that skips right over the top of the water. If you skip over the top of the water, you can make it. But don't look down.

PC: Isn't that quite a paradox, though, that aspect of creativity? We say to our students, "Be wild, be creative, but don't think about it, loosen up."

CJM: Yes, it's very hard, because we have so structured our lives around doing it right.

PC: And doing it with the intellectual side of the brain, which is not really where poems are coming from. Do you worry at all about what the current poetry fashion is?

CJM: Well, I've never fit it! So no, not really.

PC: Are you optimistic about the future?

CJM: I used to think, if I could take one student from the beginning of his or her academic career to the end of that career with a sense of "I have learned something if not but one thing" then I have accomplished what I set out to do. And I expected at that time I could do that with several students. Now I say, "If I can get one student to ask one question" then I've done it. When I get them to start asking questions, then I've done it. All I can do is say, "Look at it! Examine it! Don't accept anything at face value." Which has become a part of my poetry and my writing.

PC: I remember Phillip Levine saying that, finally, every poem is a political poem. Do you believe that?

CJM: Well, I do have a message, I think, but the message is less of an organization than it is of the culture. The very fact that I focus on black women in a personal way means that I've ripped away at least part of the bondage of racism. I write about individuals, not everyone under some stereotyped blob of color. And to go back, for a moment, to the question of fashion — I don't have to worry about whether my writing fits a fashion or if I'm considered to be a certain kind of writer. Writing is simply what I do.

Transformations

Transformations

◎ ◎ ◎

THE POINT OF THE COMPASS AROUND which all the readings in this section turn is change. Who is changed? Often, the main character or the protagonist of a story, the narrator of a nonfiction piece, or the speaker of a poem. What is changed? Perhaps a way of looking at the world or at others.

Transformation is as important in being human as it is in the art of writing. Before pen touches paper (or computer keyboard taps out words), one's experience is being altered by the words one chooses in which to express it. Sylvia Watanabe identifies the key role of the fiction writer as one of transformation, and it is one of the oldest of processes: to make the familiar strange and the strange familiar. We are altered by each experience, and we make ourselves new over time.

The readings can be grouped thematically. One theme of "Transformations" is that of using the power of imagination to transform an unacceptable or painful circumstance. Tremendous power is unleashed in the process, as if fission has occurred. Another theme (overlapping with imagination) is the transformation of the self through experience to become a "new" person: stronger and sadly wiser. A third theme is the use of language, especially in the making of metaphor and in storytelling, as a way of transforming one's experience of the natural world. A final theme is transformative healing through love, through contact with nature.

Grace Paley's story "A Conversation with My Father" describes an encounter between a storytelling daughter and her bedridden, 86-year-old father. At his insistence for a story, she relates a city tale that doesn't please him — so she tries out different versions as he listens. The father and daughter see the world differently; he keeps arguing against a character's "fated" end, and the daughter keeps insisting on the power of change, the power of other possible endings for the woman in her story.

Mariflo Stephens's story "Waltzing into Heaven" is a powerful demonstration of the transformative power of friendship and learning to effect healing in the life of Iris, a teenaged orphan. It takes time, but through a teacher's patience and skill, Iris learns about her own power and control.

Another view of suffering and healing comes in "Born Again" by Joyce Madelon Winslow. The main character rejects the usual response to cancer patients ("You're so brave") and dramatizes how knowledge of death and confrontation with it transform our living. Winslow's story reads at times like a poem, so skillfully, precisely and rhythmically is language used — it cuts through any waste of words the way the recognition of our mortality will cut away pretenses.

In "Emma," Eileen Joy summons up the imaginary country of Merula, where the narrator, a baker, works his transformations on pie crust with blackbirds as the filling. It is especially in his obsession for a beautiful woman, however, that the baker exemplifies transformation. Ironically the woman in question has run away from the plot of Flaubert's *Madame Bovary.* The baker's questions concern the art of fiction itself. "How many times can a person start over, reinvent himself? Anything is possible."

In the nonfiction section, Naomi Wolf sketches the horror of eating disorders in "Hunger," showing the power of a distorted body image and the damaging changes it can work on a woman's body. Wolf urges that women transform their thinking and escape what is essentially "a political idealogy." Barbara Noreen Dinnerstein's moving personal essay about three generations of women in her family, "*Bubbie,* Mommy, Weight Watchers and Me," reinforces the impact of Wolf's observations. Like many first-generation Americans, "*Bubbie,*" grandmother, shows her love through food. But the second-generation mother, obsessed with weight and image, threatens the healthy and loving bond between granddaughter and grandmother. The essay carries the narrator's inspiring transformation: "I am proud to look the way I do. I am a strong proud Jewish woman from peasant stock."

Hilda Raz's personal essay, "Junk," resembles a journal, a place where the author transforms suffering and pain into meaning. This writing is built in fragments, the way a quilt might be pieced together, the way a life might be put back together after a breast has been removed, after the stitches heal.

In "Where People Know Me," Sylvia Watanabe writes movingly of the illness of her mother. Watanabe faces, besides her mother's decline, her own alienation from her Hawaii relatives by a life far away in Michigan and also her grandmother's move to a nursing home. By the end of her memoir, we sense Watanabe to be on the brink of transformation as she faces her mother's fate. She writes, " . . . I feel as if I've plunged into a pool of icy water." Surely that "icy water" hints at the cold knowledge of mortality and death, of our own solitary final journeys. The self is continually transformed by the experience of living.

The drama selection for "Transformations" is an absurdist play by Rosalyn Drexler called *Room 17C* that, in a sense, is a transformation itself of some characters readers will likely be familiar with: Willy and Linda Loman from Miller's *Death of a Salesman* and Gregor Samsa from Kafka's "The Metamorphosis" meet here. In this selection it is the cockroach who is most able to deal with life's surprising changes and transformations.

In poetry, Paula Gunn Allen's "Weed" shows the paradoxical effects of nature on the growth of a weed: sun and water, both essential, are also brutal in their strength. Still, this hardy weed thrives, "growing, / tall in the heat and bright" — an example of transformation through photosynthesis.

"Betrayal" by Patricia Clark and "Dusk" by Kathryn Stripling Byer both focus the eyes of a female speaker on father figures. Clark's poem shows the girl struggling to forget and forgive her father's harsh and unfair punishment by a transformative reaching toward imagination; Byer feels the loss of the father though she acknowledges that he gave her the great gift of transforming nature through naming its beauty.

"Red Poppy" by Tess Gallagher makes links with the fiction of Joyce Madelon Winslow ("Born Again") and the nonfiction of Hilda Raz ("Junk") and Sylvia Watanabe ("Where People Know Me"). Death focuses the mind on a bedside, a room in a hospital— and both imagination and love are transforming powers that provide solace. In Gallagher's poems about the illness and dying of her husband Raymond Carver, she shows us how poetry maps the impossible: the poet talks past death through love.

"The Undertaking," Louise Glück's short poem, describes a transformative moment when the self finds the "darkness" of life lifting and fear giving way to joy and luck. If it's spring in the natural world, so it is too for the self at this wondrous, unexpected time.

Naming is a powerful exercise of transformation. Joy Harjo's poem acknowledges that gift in its title: "For Anna Mae Pictou Aquash, Whose Spirit Is Present Here and in the Dappled Stars (for we remember the story and must tell it again so we may all live)." The murder of a young activist Native woman in South Dakota, the desecration of her body by the FBI, and her burial in an unmarked grave outrage the poet — who now renames and reclaims Anna Mae Pictou Aquash. The poem cannot save this young woman, but it serves as the "turning around of the enemy's language" through love.

Linda Hogan's "Geodes" is similar to Gluck's poem in its description of "crystals of light / growing in the dark . . . ." As a rock is split, its treasure is revealed but the reader is intimately aware that dark and light are bound together: "all the life growing / in the broken heart of things."

LuAnn Keener's poem "The Hummingbirds" uses the words "a natural alchemy" to describe the epiphanic process her speaker goes through out of "the sodden melancholy of self" to some higher state. Nature in the form of birds, bodies like "bright shuttles," bring her a renewed sense of wonder and transcendence.

Denise Levertov uses the Greek myth of the fabulous musician in her poem "A Tree Telling of Orpheus." The poem's speaker is a tree and she sees Orpheus himself as a kind of tree, with his "two / moving stems, the short trunk, the two / arm-branches . . . each with five leafless twigs at their ends. . . ." The burden he carries is a musical instrument which he begins to play. The transformation begins here as the speaker senses the notes as water that moistens her roots "deep under earth." But Orpheus continues and begins to sing. Finally his words are powerful enough that those hearing actually uproot themselves to follow him, though it causes them much wrenching and tearing asunder. His transformative music and lyrics lead them to an "ancient grove" where they wait, and perhaps are still waiting, with the memory of the experience felt deep within the rings of their cortex.

Thylias Moss tells stories of the natural world and sees imaginatively with a jitterbug language of vitality. Her poem "Tornados" turns the violent storm twirls into "roulette wheel[s]" and "perfect nappy curl[s]." Intensity and dynamism are hallmarks of her language. Melissa Range's poem "Lot's Wife" completes the poetry section with a look at a transformative moment in biblical lore. The speaker evokes Lot's wife, woman without a name, who is finally given voice; the speaker recounts the story from her unique point of view.

An interview with writer Sylvia Watanabe closes out "Transformations." Watanabe describes how the Hawaiian landscape of her youth has been transformed by development and wealth. Her interest in the collision of cultures, represented by interesting individuals, is revealed in "Where People Know Me" as well as in her "Talking to the Dead" (in the section titled "Spirit and Song"). As Watanabe's mother changes before her eyes as someone ill with cancer, Watanabe finds herself perhaps transformed as well. The initiation into the chilling world of terminal illness finds Watanabe keeping close to her husband yet also being "born" into cold, new knowledge.

◎ GRACE PALEY

Grace Paley was born in 1922 in New York, New York. Paley studied at Hunter College and New York University, though she never received a degree. She has taught at Columbia University and Syracuse University, and she has been a longtime faculty member of Sarah Lawrence College in Bronxville, New York. Awards for her work include a Guggenheim fellowship, a National Institute of Arts and Letters Award for short story writing, and a nomination for the PEN Faulkner Award for Fiction for Later the Same Day *(1986). She published two earlier volumes of stories:* The Little Disturbances of Man *(1959) and* Enormous Changes at the Last Minute *(1974).*

"A Conversation with My Father" is from Enormous Changes at the Last

Minute. *The narrator of the story clearly stakes out her belief in the transformative power of words, of language, of storytelling. If she cannot convince her father, perhaps she can convince the reader instead, especially those of us who grew up on the magic of "Once upon a time. . . ."*

A Conversation with My Father

My father is eighty-six years old and in bed. His heart, that bloody motor, is equally old and will not do certain jobs anymore. It still floods his head with brainy light. But it won't let his legs carry the weight of his body around the house. Despite my metaphors, this muscle failure is not due to his old heart, he says, but to a potassium shortage. Sitting on one pillow, leaning on three, he offers last-minute advice and makes a request.

"I would like you to write a simple story just once more," he says, "the kind Maupassant wrote, or Chekhov, the kind you used to write. Just recognizable people and then write down what happened to them next."

I say, "Yes, why not? That's possible." I want to please him, though I don't remember writing that way. I *would* like to try to tell such a story, if he means the kind that begins: "There was a woman . . ." followed by plot, the absolute line between two points which I've always despised. Not for literary reasons, but because it takes all hope away. Everyone, real or invented, deserves the open destiny of life.

Finally I thought of a story that had been happening for a couple of years right across the street. I wrote it down, then read it aloud, "Pa," I said, "how about this? Do you mean something like this?"

> Once in my time there was a woman and she had a son. They lived nicely, in a small apartment in Manhattan. This boy at about fifteen became a junkie, which is not unusual in our neighborhood. In order to maintain her close friendship with him, she became a junkie too. She said it was part of the youth culture, with which she felt very much at home. After a while, for a number of reasons, the boy gave it all up and left the city and his mother in disgust. Hopeless and alone, she grieved. We all visit her.

"O.K., Pa, that's it," I said, "an unadorned and miserable tale."

"But that's not what I mean," my father said. "You misunderstood me on purpose. You know there's a lot more to it. You know that. You left everything out. Turgenev wouldn't do that. Chekhov wouldn't do that. There are in fact Russian writers you never heard of, you don't have an inkling of, as good as anyone, who can write a plain ordinary story, who would not leave out what you have left out. I object not to facts but to people sitting in trees talking senselessly, voices from who knows where . . ."

"Forget that one, Pa, what have I left out now? In this one?"

"Her looks, for instance."

"Oh. Quite handsome, I think. Yes."

"Her hair?"

"Dark, with heavy braids, as though she were a girl or a foreigner."

"What were her parents like, her stock? That she became such a person. It's interesting, you know."

"From out of town. Professional people. The first to be divorced in their country. How's that? Enough?" I asked.

"With you, it's all a joke," he said, "What about the boy's father? Why didn't you mention him? Who was he? Or was the boy born out of wedlock?"

"Yes," I said. "He was born out of wedlock."

"For godsakes, doesn't anyone in your stories get married? Doesn't anyone have the time to run down to City Hall before they jump into bed?"

"No," I said. "In real life, yes. But in my stories, no."

"Why do you answer me like that?"

"Oh, Pa, this is a simple story about a smart woman who came to N.Y.C. full of interest love trust excitement very up-to-date, and about her son, what a hard time she had in this world. Married or not, it's of small consequence."

"It is of great consequence," he said.

"O.K.," I said.

"O.K. O.K. yourself," he said, "but listen. I believe you that she's good-looking, but I don't think she was so smart."

"That's true," I said. "Actually that's the trouble with stories. People start out fantastic. You think they're extraordinary, but it turns out as the work goes along, they're just average with a good education. Sometimes the other way around, the person's a kind of dumb innocent, but he outwits you and you can't even think of an ending good enough."

"What do you do then?" he asked. He had been a doctor for a couple of decades and then an artist for a couple of decades and he's still interested in details, craft, technique.

"Well, you just have to let the story lie around till some agreement can be reached between you and the stubborn hero."

"Aren't you talking silly, now?" he asked. "Start again," he said. "It so happens I'm going out this evening. Tell the story again. See what you can do this time."

"O.K.," I said. "But it's not a five-minute job." Second attempt:

> Once, across the street from us, there was a fine handsome woman, our neighbor. She had a son whom she loved because she'd known him since birth (in helpless chubby infancy, and in the wrestling, hugging ages, seven to ten, as well as earlier and later). This boy, when he fell into the fist of adolescence, became a junkie. He was not a hopeless one. He was in

fact hopeful, an ideologue and successful converter. With his busy brilliance, he wrote persuasive articles for his high-school newspaper. Seeking a wider audience, using important connections, he drummed into Lower Manhattan newsstand distribution a periodical called *Oh! Golden Horse!*

In order to keep him from feeling guilty (because guilt is the stony heart of nine-tenths of all clinically diagnosed cancers in America today, she said), and because she had always believed in giving bad habits room at home where one could keep an eye on them, she too became a junkie. Her kitchen was famous for a while—a center for intellectual addicts who knew what they were doing. A few felt artistic like Coleridge and others were scientific and revolutionary like Leary. Although she was often high herself, good mothering reflexes remained, and she saw to it that there was lots of orange juice around and honey and milk and vitamin pills. However, she never cooked anything but chili, and that no more than once a week. She explained, when we talked to her, seriously, with neighborly concern, that it was her part in the youth culture and she would rather be with the young, it was an honor, than with her own generation.

One week, while nodding through an Antonioni film, this boy was severely jabbed by the elbow of a stern and proselytizing girl, sitting beside him. She offered immediate apricots and nuts for his sugar level, spoke to him sharply, and took him home.

She had heard of him and his work and she herself published, edited, and wrote a competitive journal called *Man Does Live by Bread Alone*. In the organic heat of her continuous presence he could not help but become interested once more in his muscles, his arteries and nerve connections. In fact he began to love them, treasure them, praise them with funny little songs in *Man Does Live* . . .

the fingers of my flesh transcend
my transcendental soul
the tightness in my shoulders end
my teeth have made me whole

To the mouth of his head (that glory of will and determination) he brought hard apples, nuts, wheat germ, and soybean oil. He said to his old friends, From now on, I guess I'll keep my wits about me. I'm going on the natch. He said he was about to begin a spiritual deep-breathing journey. How about you too, Mom? he asked kindly.

His conversation was so radiant, splendid, that neighborhood kids his age began to say that he had never been a real addict at all, only a journalist along for the smell of the story. The mother tried several times to give up what had become without her son and his friends a lonely habit. This effort only brought it to supportable levels. The boy and his girl took their electronic mimeograph and moved to the bushy edge of another borough. They were very strict. They said they would not see her again until she had been off drugs for sixty days.

At home alone in the evening, weeping, the mother read and reread the seven issues of *Oh! Golden Horse!* They seemed to her as truthful as ever. We often crossed the street to visit and console. But if we mentioned any of our children who were at college or in the hospital or dropouts at home, she would cry out, My baby! My baby! and burst into terrible, face-scarring, time-consuming tears. The End.

First my father was silent, then he said, "Number One: You have a nice sense of humor. Number Two: I see you can't tell a plain story. So don't waste time." Then he said sadly, "Number Three: I suppose that means she was alone, she was left like that, his mother. Alone. Probably sick?"

I said, "Yes."

"Poor woman. Poor girl, to be born in a time of fools, to live among fools. The end. The end. You were right to put that down. The end."

I didn't want to argue, but I had to say, "Well, it is not necessarily the end, Pa."

"Yes," he said, "what a tragedy. The end of a person."

"No, Pa," I begged him. "It doesn't have to be. She's only about forty. She could be a hundred different things in this world as time goes on. A teacher or a social worker. An ex-junkie! Sometimes it's better than having a master's in education."

"Jokes," he said. "As a writer that's your main trouble. You don't want to recognize it. Tragedy! Plain tragedy! Historical tragedy! No hope. The end."

"Oh, Pa," I said. "She could change."

"In your own life, too, you have to look it in the face." He took a couple of nitroglycerin. "Turn to five," he said, pointing to the dial on the oxygen tank. He inserted the tubes into his nostrils and breathed deep. He closed his eyes and said, "No."

I had promised the family to always let him have the last word when arguing, but in this case I had a different responsibility. That woman lives across the street. She's my knowledge and my invention. I'm sorry for her. I'm not going to leave her there in that house crying. (Actually neither would Life, which unlike me has no pity.)

Therefore: She did change. Of course her son never came home again. But right now, she's the receptionist in a storefront community clinic in the East Village. Most of the customers are young people, some old friends. The head doctor has said to her, "If we only had three people in this clinic with your experiences . . ."

"The doctor said that?" My father took the oxygen tubes out of his nostrils and said, "Jokes. Jokes again."

"No, Pa, it could really happen that way, it's a funny world nowadays."

"No," he said. "Truth first. She will slide back. A person must have character. She does not."

"No, Pa," I said. "That's it. She's got a job. Forget it. She's in that storefront working."

"How long will it be?" he asked. "Tragedy! You too. When will you look it in the face?"

◎ *MARIFLO STEPHENS*

Mariflo Stephens was born in Virginia in 1950. She received her M.F.A. from the University of Virginia. She has worked as a reporter on the Florida Times Union *and the* Bergen Record. *Stephens now hosts a regular literary program on public radio, and she has recently completed her first novel,* The Lady with the Alligator Purse. *Her stories and articles have appeared in various publications including the* Washington Post, *the* Charlottesville Observer, *and* Virginia Quarterly Review. *She has been an editor at Iris magazine for several years, and she recently edited and published an anthology of poems,* Some Say Tomato *(1993).*

Stephens wrote "Waltzing into Heaven" in 1988: "I was fantasizing about a teenage girl . . . seen on a horse farm. I knew that I wanted to write about a teenaged orphan who would be transformed from victim to victor by learning to ride and love a horse. The horse's name, ole Glory, is a play on the flag of the United States, where one in four females will fall victim to sexual assault. When the story was published by Iowa Woman, *the editor commented that although she was deluged with stories about sexual abuse, this was the only one to represent a healing."*

Waltzing into Heaven

Iris has ole Glory between her knees. Glory's hooves beat a steady ka-fallop, ka-fallop that resonates in the empty barn. She circles the ring once, twice, three times under the skylight, by the tack room, past the open barn door. Iris lets the smell of sawdust, horseflesh and saddlesoap fill her face. She rubbed the saddle down the night before with a translucent bar of saddlesoap she kept in a box under her bed and the scent of the soap stayed in her hands all night long. All night she dreamed of ole Glory and of today. In the single bed with the institutional maple headboard and scratchy sheets, she tossed, doubling the sheets around her body until, in sleep, she felt gripped as if by a vise. She jerked awake; found herself clammy, suddenly afraid. It was familiar. Iris waited for dawn, sitting up in bed with her arms around her knees. She waited for something else, too — for what passed through her in the night to disappear completely with the morning. It is something she can't name aloud. To herself she calls it the shadow, for that is how it feels to her: a dark, gritty thing looming; coming up behind or beside her or in front of her. It's connected to her in a manner so intimate she can barely get away from it. She feels it trail after her night and day. When this shadow comes too close, Iris flings herself forward in time. *Fast-forward your mind.* She thinks of nothing then, nothing but riding Glory and how she'll welcome the raw morning air and the fresh taste of it in her mouth. Today it will be mid-morning before she's far enough away from that gritty dark thing.

Glory breaks her stride for a beat, then two, then three as Iris leans forward gently to coax her into a canter. The horse paws the sawdust and arches her long neck. Iris runs her hand along Glory's velvet coat. There now, there. The canter is smooth; Glory rocks Iris the way a wave might move an anchored boat. Everthere, everthere, swaying to an unfathomed rhythm, something writ in the moon. Glory will circle the ring a good two or three times before something might cause her to miss a beat and lose her gait. Glory can keep her canter; not all the schooling horses can. All Iris has to do is shift her weight to her left and Glory's right-thrusting hoof will take the lead. Iris sees Crigger, the barn cat, eye the ring, trying to cross without getting stomped. Iris knows Glory is used to this but Crigger is fussy, more skittish than the horses, and if Crigger darts, jewel-eyed in the morning dim of the stable ring, Glory might break her gait. So Iris straightens in the saddle and relaxes her fingers on the reins. Easy now. Iris has been taught a light touch.

At first she'd tried to befriend Crigger. On her first day at the stable, Iris reeled from the odor of manure and another smell she came to know as horseflesh. The horses seemed huge and they frightened her senseless. Even Glory. When Glory blew her dark nostrils, Iris froze at the whinny, braced herself for the stampede she'd seen on television westerns. Then she tried to meet the horse's eyes but they seemed too far away, straining as if trying to focus on something out of reach. Iris bent down to the yellow cat in the sawdust. "Kitty, here kitty." She liked animals but not large ones. Large animals meant bad things, fenced pastures and mad bulls.

She hadn't meant to choose anything to do with horses. But the rules at Girls Home dictated one activity or "recreation" per year. "Teenaged orphans," the ancient-looking rules read, "must choose one outside recreation each year." All the girls there were teenagers now. The only other choice for Iris was baton twirling, which entailed joining a group called the "Twirlettes" and performing at all sorts of functions while wearing Vaseline on your teeth so you couldn't stop smiling. Horses it was. But a kitten, a kitten she could keep in her pocket and hold up to her nose, even this yellow one in the barn. "Here kitty, come here kitty."

"Oh, no, not a barn cat. Never molly-coddle a barn cat." Murt was striding toward Iris, ready to whisk the cat away with her riding crop.

Iris put her head down. She felt scolded. And this ruddy-faced woman frightened her.

Murt thought Iris wouldn't last five minutes. She'd seen other girls from Girls Home and some from the Rehab Center who couldn't get used to the horses. But those two places paid the bills for her riding school and Murt had to try with this girl.

"That cat's not used to gentlein'. Gentlein' will ruin that kind of animal. That kind, but not this," she told Iris, walking over to the stalls, putting a hand out to the first horse.

Murt could not have said why she opened the stall door with a flick of her hand, let the new gelding out with no lead rope or bridle, just a halter. She thought she'd whistle him around the ring. Two months with Murt and he knew her whistle.

But Blaze, the new gelding, began to rear and paw the air. Murt held both arms out to the horse in supplication. She jerked her head behind her to the corner of the barn. There was Iris. Her arms over her head like positioned air-raid victims, Iris crouched in the sawdust, covering Crigger with her palms. There was something about the bend in the child's neck, something practiced. It triggered in Murt an insight she felt only with her animals. She whistled Blaze back into the stall, kept her eyes on Iris. That pose, arms over head, convinced her that this one was injured. It was the injured little birds who took care of big homely Murt and her large, hungry horses.

"Get on up, little bird. That horse won't hurt you." Murt led Iris into the tack room. She showed her the chart of the stalls, the horses' names, and the saddles and bridles hanging on the wall. Iris touched them with one finger.

This morning Iris sucks the fragrant air in through her teeth and Glory picks up her walk. Tiny particles of sawdust coat her eyelashes, the hair on her forearms. Iris is passing the stable windows now and the sun stiffens her face, draws her eyes to the center of the ring. Soon the ring will be filled with riding students. Iris will control some of the horses on the lead rope and let them circle her, turning the rope over her head like she's seen Murt do. Some of the students will be scared and she wants to keep eye contact with them, doesn't want to turn her body with the lead rope.

Most of the students have already begun treating Iris the way they treat Murt. Iris knows which students hold the reins too tightly and which ones dig their heels absent-mindedly into their mount's belly. And she knows the ways each horse confuses the signals. "Easy Shephard," is all she has to say when

Shephard starts to reel. Iris likes helping the students but this is not why she longs for this time in the ring, why she lathers the saddle at night with closed eyes, letting her head fall back with the memory of the ring, the horse's back.

Now Glory's starting a trot, and Iris posts with a rhythm as steady as breathing and just as easy. Sometimes it happens with a trot, sometimes a canter. When it happens, when she's found it, Iris and Glory are one. They have no shape, no weight; they are part of the air, the pungent stable, the earth. Iris is without physical boundaries, without thought. Nothing bad has ever happened to her and there's nothing she has to forget. Glory is waltzing her into heaven and the grace of their dance is so intense that the beauty of it lifts them off the ground. They are headed into the eye of the sun, straight up through the skylight. And then slowly, softly, a recognition returns and Iris feels her body on Glory's back. She notices the strands of mane between her fingers. There's a piece of her long bang in her eye. Iris lands back into the ring where Crigger might dart, where Murt might step out from the tack room or the field, coming through the open barn door. Back to where the shadow might fall from a diagonal light in the barn's ceiling.

The barn's lumber is still new. Some of it is so green it can be peeled away in strings and the smell of it is still in the air. The construction of the barn, the actuality of it, still surprises Murt and sometimes stops her in the middle of some small task like hanging up a bridle. She could be looping the leather straps over a nail hanger in the tack room, folding the reins so they'll lie flat and won't tangle, and the simple motion of it — lifting the reins over a nail — will stop her for a second. The fact of her riding school having come into being at all will catch her. Her mouth will gape, "I wanted it and I got it." A surprise still too full of shock to please her.

Her wish for it had been like a hollow breath. But out of this invisibility came the raw lumber, the frame, then the shape of a barn, then the school itself. The administrator of the Rehab Center showed her the special steel-lined helmets for the brain-damaged students, asked her to sign something, then wrote her a check.

Murt never thought she'd be able to make a go of it. There weren't that many people in the whole country who thought riding was anything to learn, much less pay for. When Murt was growing up, even the smallest farmer kept a cow-pony to scour the fields. Keeping horses was commonplace. Murt remembers, and at times still dreams of it, an evening when her father sat smoking by the woodstove and the talk turned from trading horses to children. When Murt's name came up, her father shook his head. "The world's got no use, no use whatsoever for a homely woman." She'd felt the sting sear through her back to her chest.

After she married Joe Mooney and worked at his filling station, Joe told his partner, Murt's folks, anyone who'd listen, how Murt could work like a man; how it was Murt who had the idea to start a feed store out of the back of the station. It had paid off. Murt loaded feed by herself onto the backs of flatbed trucks and talked horses, horses, horses to those coming for the special grains she ordered. And if Joe climbed on top her less and less often, making her spread her legs like a forked road, she was glad of it. When she saw orange smears on his clothes from somebody's makeup, she was gladder still. Someone got a postcard from him that had been mailed from a dog track. For a few months after he left, she still smelled him in the house.

Murt watches Iris circle Glory around the ring. "Bring her on in, little bird, and groom her. Fifteen minutes."

Iris nods her head and Murt watches her lean closer to the horse's neck, gently tightening the reins by bringing her fists to her chest. The horse slows.

Murt can't hear what Iris is saying. Iris's mouth is moving like a puppet's, animated. Iris talks to the horse while she swings her leg over its rump to dismount. She talks soothingly as if she's trying to ease the separation. Iris catches the reins under Glory's neck and leads her to the stalls, near where Murt is standing, watching her. Iris rises on tiptoe and nuzzles Glory's nose, soft and salmon-colored.

Murt is thinking how Iris has changed, how this lively, sure-footed girl leading Glory is as different as night and day from the Iris she first met, the girl who hid in a corner of the barn and hugged herself. Too, Murt can't help thinking how much Iris has helped her. At first all she could consider was the irony of it. Her hurt back, that excuse for laziness her father had used — bad back, epidemic among certain segments of the rural poor. And then Iris, the scared, slight girl who always had a piece of her bangs in her eyes, being the one to pick up the pitchfork and say, "Look here, I can do it." She jabbed the pitchfork into the straw, flinging the manure behind her like she'd done it every day of her life, her thin arms suddenly steel. "Look here," she said again and toed the bailing twine around the hay, split it, and tossed the clean straw into the stalls. "What else needs doing besides freshening the stalls?"

"Feed," Murt had groaned, answering from a cot set up in the tack room, not really expecting the girl to do anything else. Then Murt saw Iris's shadow carrying two buckets of feed in either hand.

For the first whole day she laid on the cot like something frozen. Her legs stayed split apart, the way they'd fallen when she eased herself down. Once she felt Iris breathe on her face. The second day, Iris pulled her up, her thin arms under Murt's shoulders. They set up a hot-plate and a coffee pot in the tack room.

One side of the tack room is lined with rows of dark bridles and lead ropes coiled and hanging on nails. The leather smells strong enough to think of tasting it. On the opposite wall are rows of bright ribbons — red for second place, there are many of these; some yellow third place ribbons, and a few blue ribbons. There is a brass plaque on the connecting wall which faces the doorway and a framed piece of embroidery hangs above it. The plaque catches light and is hard to read, but Iris lingers a moment, anchoring a heavy saddle on its wooden arm, and reads: "4-H Champion for Equitation, 1961, Miss Myrtle Halifax." Champion, she thinks. She reads the embroidered hanging, too: "If you pick up a horse every day of your life for every day of its life, you can always carry it."

A year ago Iris couldn't imagine owning something like that, something handmade and personal, but pretty and new looking. What Iris owned, in one of the boxes under her bed, were the dance costumes her mother had worn long ago. They were satiny but faded. Then this Christmas when Iris opened one of her few presents, one was a similar framed piece Murt had embroidered, a chestnut horse, with "I'd rather be riding" stitched in red. Girls Home won't allow anything on the walls but they let Iris hang the frame on her door and even the meanest girls respect that.

"Ten minutes till the first class," Murt says and holds her hand wordlessly out the tack room doorway. Iris hangs Glory's bridle over Murt's wrist.

Iris feels like a rubber band, she's ridden so long this morning, and Murt has let her go till the very last minute. She says, "Maybe we could start class with a grooming lesson. I could rub Glory down."

"Okay, but when I bring in the other horses, check their hooves first."

Iris turns to go back to Glory's stall but she stops short, skids in the sawdust. Murt has hung up Glory's bridle inside and stands in the tack room doorway again, holding out a large oval brush. Iris guessed it right. She knows she'll have to rub Glory down, then pick the hooves. She holds one hand behind her like a ballet dancer in an arabesque and Murt drops the brush in her palm. Iris is sweaty and breathless but not tired. Never tired of being here at the barn. Lucky, that was it. She had been unlucky all her life until that one day when she knew she'd found something and she saw a way to keep it. When Murt laid on the little bed in the tack room, Iris saw that look in her eye. Like the shadow. She sometimes called it the all-alone look and she saw it in people and felt it herself. It was a kind of blind staring that she couldn't stop. It was because of that darkness in Murt's eye that Iris said "Look here," and grabbed the pitchfork and started to work.

This morning they work in tandem. It hadn't been easy to convince the headmistress of Girls Home to let Iris come to work for Murt. While Murt sat in the headmistress's office, Iris was already crying with disappointment in her room, stuffing part of a sheet in her mouth to muffle the sound the way she'd always done in foster homes. But Murt opened the door, ignored the tears, and said, "We've done it," and then imitated the headmistress so well that even Iris had to laugh. All kids in places like this, Iris told Murt, learn to mock.

"We have regulations, this home is operated by the Order of the Eastern

Star," Murt mimicked. "I told her, 'I'm going to pay Iris. Tell that to the Eastern Star. She'll have money and a skill when she turns eighteen.' "

"Oh, that was it. They've had a lot of trouble this year with the eighteen-year-olds."

Girls Home can't legally keep the girls after they turn eighteen, and though the Eastern Star supplies them with a letter of recommendation and a list of job possibilities, most girls don't follow up. This year one girl was ordered back by the court after she'd been convicted for shoplifting nail polish. Someone in the court system found out she'd faked an ID, not to buy beer but to get out of Girls Home. Iris can't understand this. She thinks Girls Home is nice. Though when they brought her there in that long car at night, she felt alarmed at the darkness of the country she'd come to. Something about the long curving driveway that led uphill to the L-shaped building seemed ominous. "Fast-forward your mind," she told herself.

At each curve of the driveway Iris had leaned her forearm into the cool stub of the absent door handle in the police car. "There are no door handles in the back seat," the matron said, "sorry." Iris had gazed at the lawn lanterns that dotted the driveway's edge like steady fireflies. She imagined that where she was being taken so far out in the country that it was like going to the edge of a cliff. She stared into the black in front of her. The small driveway lights made half-moons in the grass. Iris could feel the rough fabric of the policematron's jacket beside her.

"Yessiree," the policematron said. "You are a lucky girl. This place's run by the Order of the Eastern Star and they're mighty picky who they take in. You wouldn't have gotten in if you hadn't been an abuse case. I don't think so, at least. Got any relatives who're Masons or anything?"

"I don't know," Iris answered.

In Iris's world she knew to look away from whatever might be offered up as kindness from whatever authority might be temporarily in charge of her. It might be a policematron, a foster mother, a social worker or a teacher. It might not even be kindness. It might be something else. Whatever it was, it would not last. It would not follow her, dog her. Only what she called the shadow did that. The shadow won over kindness, won over almost everything except sleep, except a sudden wash of forgetting that came out of nowhere as a mercy.

"Here it is," the policematron said, holding the door open for Iris, carrying her boxes tied with string. Iris always felt she was too big, took up too much room, and she climbed clumsily out of the police car, losing her footing in the gravel. She didn't know if she should say "Thank you" or not, but was led away before she could think on it. Three more of the lawn lanterns sat in front of a large sign which read: "Order of the Eastern Star — A Home for Girls."

Iris had conjured up a vision of a tiny blue star in a far corner somewhere ever since she first heard the name — Order of the Eastern Star. For a wild moment in the police station, she believed in fairy godmothers and guardian angels again; for however harsh the woman had seemed, this destination was the end of a long and confusing space of time through which Iris moved heavily, in a numb trance.

The string of people in authority — the teachers, social workers, foster parents, the string that had landscaped her life since her mother had died — had broken in two the day Nell the janitor at the high school found her out of gym class. Iris was hiding in the locker room's bathroom stall because she had to do the thing that kept her in the numb trance. Nell could see it: could see Iris was too big and didn't fit into the clothes someone else had owned first.

Iris thought Nell had probably never owned many new clothes either when she was a teenager; when she was "coming up," the black woman called it. But it was Nell who noticed her feet flat along one side of the toilet. The janitor followed a trail of garnet-colored blood from the drain in the corridor between the showers and the bathroom stalls. Wearing Chinese slippers with holes cut out for corns, Nell padded into the room where Iris sat. She saw her feet first. And when Nell got the gym teacher and the principal all together in the principal's office, she was so riled up she made the gym teacher call the school counselor and Iris's foster mother. Nell herself got those pasty-faced people together and said, "Somebody has to *see* to this chile."

At first, Iris thought Nell wasn't on her side to call all the people in that way. Iris had finally told her about the trance; how she had to wear the black bathing suit bottoms all the time even when they made purple marks along the tops of her thighs; how she kept her legs together, how finally she couldn't wear a Kotex pad or put in a tampon because that would break the trance and she couldn't open up her legs for anything, not after that smelly man had slipped his hands in there. He had crowded her and crowded her and pushed at her and hurt her but then she found that the bathing suit bottoms would keep that bad feeling away, would keep away the echo of that bad thing. That bad thing that seemed to keep on happening to her.

Iris comes out of the tack room carrying a tool that first looked to her like a bottle opener. It's a pick for the horses' hooves. She loves the look of it now, and how expert she is at holding it. When she's hard at work, bending over a hoof, she feels completely there. "This work," she told Murt, "is what keeps me from flying apart."

Murt nodded her head. Murt does not know who or what has injured her little bird, but she knows Iris has been healed somehow by this horse barn, this shaft of light from the skylight, something. Now Murt is leading two horses, a pair of reins in each hand, from the field to the barn. She will tether them in their stalls so Iris can get at their hooves.

Iris hears the van from Girls Home coming toward the barn. She'll have two students from here and three from the Rehab Center, one whose handicap is labeled "severe." This afternoon she'll freshen the stalls with straw and clean the tack room. She won't take a saddle home to lather tonight. But if she's not too tired, she'll ride Glory bareback out of the barn and into the field to graze. She might ride Blaze and Shephard out, too. When she gets to Girls Home, some of the girls will still be in their Twirlette costumes, the silver fringe up around their hips pointing down in a V at the crotch. They'll tease her about her horsey smell. Sometimes they snort and toe the floor. Whatever they do she'll ignore them. She'll glide down the hall to the showers, feeling the slight soreness in her limbs from her day's work. She knows that when she steps from the shower, her arms and legs glistening, she'll be really, finally clean. And before she faces the uncertain terrors that await her in dreams, she'll step out with her towel in front of her, taking one long and two short paces in her bare feet. One, two-three, one, two-three; then bow, then waltz right into heaven.

Murt's eyes stayed on Iris, on her narrow hips, the turn of her calf as she lifted her leg to climb into the van. Girl, girl, Murt thought, watching the van rumble down the gravel driveway, and closed her name into her heart like a fist.

JOYCE MADELON WINSLOW

Joyce Madelon Winslow, who lives in Washington, D.C., is a journalist and public relations consultant. She has been writing short stories for twenty years. Her first story, "Benjamin Burning," won the Avery Hopwood Award for major fiction at the University of Michigan. Her second story won the PEN/Syndicated Fiction Project award, and her third story garnered her an NEA grant. She has won first place in the National Press Club fiction contest twice. In the last three years she has won nine national contests. "Born Again" won the Raymond Carver Fiction Contest in 1993.

Winslow's mother died of cancer at forty-nine, and Winslow wrote this story during four "magical" hours on the anniversary of her mother's death, her yarzeit, trying to finish it by midnight on the night of that day.

Born Again

In Loving Memory of Reisa I. Winslow
Written at The MacDowell Colony
with the encouragement of Tillie Olsen

There was, of course, something very different about me and some people could sense it though they didn't know what it was. I was determined I wasn't going to tell anyone anymore. I'd gotten tired of seeing their faces open wide as fundamentalists rapt on their preacher when they took it in. Then, like they'd lost faith, they'd go slightly blank, as though it didn't make a difference. But, secret out, they and I both knew the world had divided into Us and Them. We — Us — knew we were mortal. They didn't have to know they were mortal. I dearly wished I could be born again.

Some days, looking out the big picture window of the house in New Hampshire, I wondered how anything could manage to live. Sheaths of ice coated every branch of the tall spruce, every green needle was fanned out in ice so that when the bitter wind blew the spruce fans clinked like wind chimes. I watched the chickadees hop from branch to branch trying to get a foothold and failing, sliding halfway down a thin ice-coated limb like it was a water slide, and trying again and again. It was funny on my side of the window, desperate on theirs.

I'd never thought how hard it was for the birds in winter until sickness made my life a winter. Then I seemed to be able to see the pain in everything. The air escaping logs when they caught in the fireplace sounded less like whistling and more like a wheezing for breath. Fire lifted pages of my books in the fireplace, turned the pages one by one and consumed them like the Last Voracious Reader. That's how I thought. In finalities. I was angry so I burned the books.

Other days I could not imagine not living. That's when, if I felt well enough and it wasn't a chemo week, I went to parties. Then I wore a blonde wig because the chemo had defoliated me. No hair anywhere. I felt like a cross between Anne Frank and a porno movie. A punk babe who had waxed and shaved herself to get into a string bikini.

One day I got creative and set up the camera on timer. Stripped and lay on the living room rug naked, in the same position as my baby picture, stretched out full length in crawl position, upper body arched like a salamander pointing its head toward sun, supported on fingers splayed like lizard feet, enormous eyes in a bald head, alert, chest forward, innocent nipples. Only now one nipple and a concave scar where the other breast had been.

I thought the picture would be interesting, placed next to the baby picture. A Diane Arbus Before and After series. Portrait of the young woman as baby, crawling into the world, oblivious to her own mortality. Portrait of the young woman at 36, scarred with Knowledge, maybe close to death, who can't imagine dying.

The third and final picture of the series would be Death, which I imagined as a skeleton. My skeleton, the skull grinning the grotesque leer of women in de Kooning paintings, like women in the throes of ecstasy or pain. So, in a kind of gallows humor which I was entitled to have, I dressed as a skeleton for the Halloween party. That I would be wearing a wig would be seen as normal at Halloween. A skeleton in a blonde wig. Very funny.

* * *

Maybe I chose the skeleton because the soft black print leotard on which the luminous bones were imprinted was easy to get on. My own bones hurt. While I was dressing I remembered when they injected me with radioactive dye that made my bones light up from the inside. You had to wait for hours in the waiting room while your blood took the dye throughout your body, while it dyed the bones from the marrow out, from the heart out, really. You could have a cup of coffee in the cafeteria, read *The New York Times* in your work clothes and expensive blonde wig that looked better than your real hair, and no one suspected as they smiled at you, and found you attractive and passed you the cream, still smiling, that your bones were glowing in the dark. Then you sauntered back into the waiting room and they called you. Without even taking your clothes off, they leaned you face down on a body-sized camera lens and you could watch the computer glow green as they scanned you. You could wonder, terrified, were those purple dots cancer? Or the red clustered in your ankles, is that why they hurt? Was the cancer already eating you cell by cell? Was it lining your bones like poison sap?

The young Black girl, bored at the machine, said only you'd have to ask your doctor, she wasn't allowed to interpret what you were seeing. You understand. You might get hysterical. She wasn't trained to handle that. You watched her face for the next two hours of the bone-by-bone scan for some clue as she marked things down that corresponded to those clusters of colors and you prayed, please, don't let the cancer be red. Don't let it be purple. The girl left the room and then came back. The doctor could see you one week from today.

Which was more horrible? Waiting and waiting for the answer? Or having the week finally go by when time had become precious? "The bones are clean," the doctor said. He never explained the colors. I was so relieved I didn't ask. "Your ankles probably hurt because of your boots," he said. "People have to get used to boots weighing them down all over again, every winter. A lot of things will happen to you and they'll have nothing to do with cancer."

I figured I would not be the only skeleton at the party. And all but one person would be wearing a wig. Not that it mattered anymore, but the quality of the wig was the status marker in the support group. One short, plump woman wore a cheap wig with plastic curls and a seam that showed around the top of her forehead. I wondered if she wore it because she was stupid, or simply had no fashion sense, or whether she needed the world to know she was brave. That's what people said if you gave the secret away. "You're so brave."

The funny thing is, none of us were. We did it because we had no choice. There's nothing heroic about surviving. You do it because you're scared of dying. It would have been brave to refuse chemotherapy, to kiss mortality on the lips, to give up hope and accept the inevitable. It would be brave to let oneself die with grace and art and small rituals. To die at least as magnificently as a bull in a ring.

Instead, every four weeks for nine months I sat in the chemo chair pretending I was a prize fighter. First the whiff of the green Naugahyde, then the smell of alcohol, then the too-tight pressure of rubber tied around my upper arm. The nurse slapped and slapped the inside of my wrist to make a vein stand up, any vein not already fatally collapsed like a tire with too many puncture holes.

I pretended the slapping was warm-up for the fight. I imagined a crowd cheering, placing bets. In the blue bathrobe and blonde hair, weighing 110 pounds, I flung the robe open to reveal a shapely body in gold-sequined leotard, a body that looked like it had looked just months before when men had stopped me on the beach and asked my name. The crowd would rise to their feet and I'd be in my corner, next to the water bucket, getting punched on the shoulder, getting told to keep my head down, and they'd put the teeth in my mouth and the bell would ring.

Then the nurse would bring over the tray with three huge syringes of poison and the throw-up pan and I'd be riding wave after wave of nausea, and then I'd throw up, and the nurse would fan me, like a trainer. Get up, get up, get back in the ring. Fight. I'd close my eyes and see a field of blackness and the nausea would roll over me again and I'd feel like I was under water and could see the surface but not get to it and I'd try to battle up to the top. The nausea would roll over me again and I'd be losing consciousness, feel something course through my vein and the intense burning of it would rouse me. I was wearing boxing gloves, I was swimming against nauseating currents in boxing gloves, punching, punching, trying to connect, trying to feel the thud, the snap of a punch, but feeling only waves rolling me backwards, nauseous, choking, unable to breathe. I'd come to again and the trainer would be yelling my name. The crowd, the water, was roaring, and I had to get up, I couldn't lose consciousness, I couldn't lose myself. I was crying. I could feel the warmth of the tears and hear the fighter in the next green chair and the next, all hooked up to IVs, all fighting for their lives every fourth week. They were saying, "eat some ice cream, drink some ginger ale," and I was ashamed I was crying.

"You're so brave," people said. During chemo I looked at my hands, clenched the way they might be inside boxing gloves. I smelled like vomit and some stranger was cleaning my face and asking wouldn't I like more Atavan, with Atavan you threw up and didn't remember it the next day. You didn't remember, or only half-remembered, anything that happened to you when you were on Atavan. That was the problem. There wasn't time enough not to remember a whole day.

I dated a guy while I was on chemo and bald and in the blonde wig. I even danced with him cheek to cheek. He never suspected. I timed the dates, telling him that the week I was on chemo I was out of town on a journalistic assignment. That was perfectly plausible. I was often out of town on assignments when I had been well. My by-line had been a constant in the newspaper.

He didn't suspect even though chemo had made me thinner and yellower. People who knew me before saw me as too thin. People who hadn't known me just saw me as thin. As for the yellower part, I could camouflage that with makeup. And the blonde wig really was gorgeous. I just looked a little too elegant. Men who didn't know me thought I was rich and were delighted to discover it hadn't spoiled me.

"You're so down to earth," they said. "You're so easy to get along with" by which they meant I listened to them. Really listened. Not because they were so interesting but because I didn't have the energy, sometimes, to talk. "You're pretty," they said, and went to stroke my hair. Then I said something witty that forced me to throw my head back with laughter, out of their reach. It's hard to play in the big leagues when you're bald.

The guy I dated while I was on chemo was an artist. That's what he wanted me to believe. He hadn't painted a picture in years. He worked as a Top Secret Clearance paste-up artist at a graphics division of the government. He told me he'd designed the lettering style for the word "patriot" in Patriot Missile without knowing what it was. When he saw pictures of the weapon in the newspaper during the Persian Gulf war he said, "My God, those are my letters." That was about as interesting as his job, or his life, had ever been.

I didn't mind that he exaggerated when he said he was an artist. When you face mortality you get real tolerant. I'd also learned that people often talked half in reality, half in wishes. When you figured out which were wishes you saw through to the soul. His wish to be an artist, to be creative, was sweet.

We laughed a lot and listened to his 1940s record collection and cooked for each other. We dressed in vintage clothes and went swing dancing, when I could. The blonde wig fit into the forties just fine. The music, the clothes, even the Art Deco plates he served food on put me in another era, out of my body, out of my fear. Months went by and it was about time to get intimate. I didn't want to scare him away. I liked his company. One night we talked and talked on the couch, first sitting apart, and then his hand massaging my feet, in his lap, and then he was kissing me, and the wig slipped.

There wasn't much to hide at that point and I told him. To my amazement he didn't run, or change his face around, or tell me I was brave. He cried. Then he made love to me. I felt like a freak, scarred and bald and thin. He told me I had a beautiful face and a beautiful body and the scar was not terrible and the hair would come back. I lay there like rigor mortis had set in. He did his best to arouse me, then petted my head and held me all night. For the first time in a long time I felt safe. Then he called and told me he thought he could love me too much. He didn't have the strength. Call him if I got scared and needed to talk late at night, sometime. He was sorry he wasn't brave, goodbye.

Putting on the skeleton costume wasn't really like putting on a costume. It seemed like wearing the truth. I'd thought other women would come as skeletons and I was right. Seven of the women in the support group came as skeletons. Two were scarecrows. One came as a fundamentalist preacher in long black coat and wide-brimmed hat, with a Gideon Bible tucked under her arm. "I was going to be a judge," she said, "and wear my son's black graduation gown . . ." and then her voice trailed off. When she thought of that costume she'd forgotten for the moment she might not be alive to see his graduation. This was October and that would be June.

Donna, the leader of the group, hadn't arrived yet with the key so we all stood outside the gray stone church: seven skeletons, two scarecrows and a fundamentalist preacher. We laughed at how we must look to other people, but it was Halloween and the world was in costume. It's just that underneath ours we were even more grotesque, missing breasts and ovaries and glands and section of bone and marrow and red blood. We tabulated it once: as a group we'd lost almost enough body parts to make another person.

Interesting how much you can lose and still feel female. Life is wet, I'd determined. Chemo made it dry. It dried saliva, my esophagus, stomach and bladder linings, and the slippery juices of passion. It stopped menstruation cold. I had to sign away that part. I'd never have to use birth control again.

Chemo couldn't distinguish between what made me female and what was cancer. It killed everything fast-growing. Besides hair and skin and ovary eggs it killed all the in and out avenues, the Champs Elysees of my body. I could draw pictures of how I configured inside from the pain. That's why I cried in the boxing ring. For 36 hours following chemo every cell I owned experienced Hiroshima. Then came two weeks of fatigue so profound I could not remember why I had shuffled from the bedroom to the kitchen, too tired to care, too tired to hope. Between the two of them, the cancer and chemo wrecked a lot that was female. So I got the wig done once a week. A girl's got her pride.

Tonight was going to be festive. A party, not a session where everyone cried and secretly prayed for the extra 36 months you were supposed to survive if you put in time at a support group. In truth, it was not always supportive. We competed for tragedy, mine worse than yours. I'm going in for another procedure. Oh yeah, well, my father died, I got mugged and my blood count went down.

Donna, our cheerful group leader, had brought a chocolate cake from her freezer. It was half-eaten, especially the half that was chocolate. She'd also brought candy corns with all the white tips bitten off. She made coffee with caffeine, as though we could drink it, and she kept tossing her hair. It was brown, long, and real. She was years out of chemo. She didn't tell us why she'd brought chewed-up refreshments. I was just glad to have them. No one else brought any. Judy had a boom box and Caroline contributed a fistful of candles. We'd all thought of wine.

It was Friday night, the church was empty, the street the church was on was pretty deserted, so we turned the music up loud, turned the lights off, lit the candles and drank. Then we danced the Electric Slide. Every couple of minutes one of us got winded and fell into one of the too-small chairs in the church classroom, but for the better part of half an hour, at least seven of us, luminous bones flailing, wigged skulls grinning, danced in unison in a line wiggling our hips *electric*, breathing *electric* with the music.

"Did you finish your kitchen curtains?" I asked Moira. She was holding up the ends of the long preacher's coat and yelling *"boola, boola, electric,"* and twirling around.

"Yeah, they look nice. I wanted them up before the Cat Scan."

"When is it?"

"Monday."

"They're not going to find anything," I said. I meant anything bad. I slipped a bony arm underneath my costume, over the good breast.

"It doesn't matter," she said, "it's already in the brain. *Electric.*"

"An old man swam up to me in the pool yesterday," I told her as we rocked front, wiggled back. "He said he used to ride a bike ten miles a day—*electric*—till he had a stroke last year. He told me, 'It's hard growing old, too.' "

"Let's get some wine," Moira said. She grabbed me and twirled us both to the teacher's desk where the cake and candycorns were piled unceremoniously right onto the wood. Donna had not brought napkins or plates or plastic glasses for the wine. Moira pushed the brim of her preacher's hat back. "My head itches."

"Let's switch wigs," I said. "Just for the hell of it." We uncorked two bottles and laughed.

"I decided today what I'd wear to the funeral," Moira said. She chugged on her bottle of wine.

"Whose funeral?"

"Mine. Art loves my pink dress. I thought If I'm going to be lying next to him in perpetuity I may as well wear something he likes." We laughed and chugged to the count of ten, wiping our mouths on our sleeves.

"You're lucky you're married," I said. "The only hugs I get these days are in the support group and, frankly, you girls are not my type."

"What about Vincent?"

"I told him. Sudden death syndrome."

"I'll drink to that," Moira said. She raised the Gideon Bible. "To sudden death."

I had a bony arm across her shoulders. We danced some more, holding our bottles and chugging on the "boola boola" parts, like it was a magic word.

"Have you decided where to go for vacation?" Moira asked.

"I have to avoid summer this year with radiation, so I thought I'd go to Santa Fe in December, between chemos."

"Eat at Rancho de Mayo, they have great sopapillas. Or they did 20 years ago. Art and I honeymooned there."

That's how we talked. Like Death was real. And like the whole world could happen to us, that this day was like any other, only a holiday, and that this was not a party for the doomed, though we had come after sitting in radiated caverns like trolls while the Radiation Technician left the room, while the mechanical table to which we were strapped rotated and lasers hidden in all four walls sighted and fired. The table rotated again. A shadow of the good breast climbed the wall, rose onto the ceiling like a sun with a nipple, rose in the sky like a huge shadow of what I had lost, a Metro Goldwyn Mayer production of My Left Breast. Every day, for nine weeks, they radiated. Outside, blinking in the sunlight, I had to keep the entire chest and neck area covered. Sunshine could throw the burn over the edge.

I looked at Moira in her fundamentalist preacher's outfit, her hat pushed back, her wig pushed back, Moira belting down booze like a fallen angel, and wished ferociously I could be Born Again. I determined that with my own skeleton hands I'd shove death back, give death an eye blacker than skull sockets pecked out by crows.

Let's get out of here, I said to Moira. The dancing had splintered into small groups of skeletons discussing symptoms.

"Where?"

"Anywhere. It beats The Layaway Plan." That was Moira's and my code word for the group. "Let's go dance in the sanctuary, raise hell. No one will be there."

"Raise hell in church?" She hiccupped and dabbed wine off the Gideon Bible with the sleeve of her preacher's coat.

"What are they going to do, kill us?" I elbowed her. We fell into each other and knocked our bottles together.

"Or give us a life sentence?" she hooted. We slugged back more wine.

"Or force us to teach choir boys sex?" I leered. Leers look great when you're luminous.

Like naughty schoolchildren we left the classroom, giggling. We held bottles and the Bible and candles. The church was pitch black. The candles lit our way down a long, narrow corridor with pointed, Gothic windows guarded by strange stone gargoyles. Candles held up to these creatures slanted macabre shadows across the cold slate floor. We steadied ourselves on the rough stone walls, our bottles clinking against unexpected sharp angles. Where the massive stone changed to smooth granite I saw two huge, arched oak doors bearing brass angel wings and pull rings big as the circumference of a neck. I stuck the candle in my wine bottle and with my good arm pulled the heavy wooden door open.

We entered a sanctuary intended to replicate the horrible grandeur of Medieval English churches. By candlelight we could see the newel post in the narthex. It was carved wood, a life-sized head of St. Ambrose. He smiled under my hand. The portico opened to a vast, vaulted space holding twelve granite pillars. They soared so high our heads rested on our backs to see their tops. At the apex: stained glass windows illuminated by moonlight. And a single great wrought iron chandelier with tiny electric candles casting dim, yellowish light. The windows glimmered with ruby-winged seraphim, flaming suns, amethyst stars of heavenly zeal.

Awed into silence we walked down the central aisle of dark, carved wooden chairs, past row upon row. Hundreds of chairs, each holding a hymnal on its woven hemp seat, a purple velvet cushion on the floor beneath. Our shoes clattered on the even slate squares. Moira's preacher's coat swished as we made our way, an eerie processional, my skeleton glowing in the half darkness following the fundamentalist preacher, both of us holding candles, lighting the path to the first row of chairs.

We sat down directly in front of the octagonal wooden lectern carved with roses and fleurs-de-lis, draped in purple velvet. Behind the lectern hung a bronze crucifix and the hymnal board, displaying the numbers of four hymns from last week.

"Do you believe in God?" Moira whispered.

"No, but I pray a lot."

We looked at each other and swigged our wine.

"I think I'm going to die soon," Moira said.

"How can you say that?"

"People are leaving me like rats on a sinking ship. They sense something."

I looked at her. It was hard to believe she was going to die soon. She looked wonderful. Moira had refused the medications that would slow the growth of her tumor but bloat face and body beyond recognition. I knew from group she had radium implanted in her skull. I thought Moira was brave.

"I love you," she said. She put her arms around me.

"We're not leaving yet," I straightened her preacher's hat. Hugs and "I love yous" were how we ended each group. I needed this night to be different. I needed to be giddy like everyone else on Halloween.

"We're rising from the grave," I said to her. "Thump that bible, Madam. Raise thy voice." I took a deep breath and hollered: "Claim thy space." We listened to that echo off the cold, gray granite. "Save me, Father," I yelled.

"Father, ather, ather," it echoed.

I stood, climbed three steps to the altar, faced the burnished gold candlesticks tall as me and yelled. "Save me. Save me. Save me. By what miracle do we escape destruction?" My voice reverberated throughout the church. I stuck my candle into one of the two candleholders and looked at Moira. She climbed the steps of the altar, stuck her candle into the other holder, hitched up the preacher's coat, clutched the Bible and her bottle and stepped up onto the ancient Spanish pew overlooking the congregation.

"Careful," I reached out an arm, saw my bones flicker in the candlelight.

"Gather thy hair into a cemetery under sacred stones," her voice echoed down the aisles. "Hide thy locks in the cracks of walls and boards. Thou will need them at thy resurrection."

I marvelled at her wobbly manner on top of the pew — a combination of drunkenness and the dignity of God.

"What does that mean — about the hair?" I took a swig.

"I've been reading about the soul. Old English superstition says it can leave you when you're sleeping, dreaming, without you even knowing it. Absence of soul is what makes you die. Aborigines believe their priests can see a wayward soul when it hides in hair. The soul looks to them like a tiny human being. Ordinary mortals just see it as a lock of hair. If you return the wayward soul back into a sick person, she gets well. Where did you put your hair?"

"It pretty much came out in the shower. I scooped it out of the drain and tossed it."

"I put some of mine into lockets for the girls," she began to cry.

"Save me!" I implored, trying to get her back into the holiday spirit. "By what miracle do we escape destruction?"

"Tie a strip of cloth around thy waist to hold onto thy shadow," she climbed down from the pew. "Thy soul can escape through thy shadow. Ghosts of the dead come to lure out thy soul, leaving thee to die." She hitched her belt tighter.

We sat for a minute, drinking, and noticed the organ directly opposite the pew. Silver pipes rose from floor to ceiling. Moira pumped the pedals. I pressed a white key. A bell chimed. I played a chord. The rich harmony resounded throughout the stone-gray church, softening it. Harking back to seventh grade piano lessons I filled the church with bells: Moonlight Sonata, Barcarole, Volga Boatmen.

Moira laughed — a wonderful sound. To the rhythm of Volga Boatmen she intoned: "Thy soul resides in blood. Thy soul is sucked out through blood. Turn away from mirrors lest your soul be seen and caught." She held up a hand to silence my playing. "Cover all thy mirrors in the sickhouse lest souls reflected in the mirrors take flight. Cover all thy mirrors in thy house after a death for whosoever sees himself in the mirror first, after a death, shall die himself. Horror! Horror! Horror!"

I emphasized that with three chords in rapid succession. Moira looked at me in horror and appreciation.

"By what miracle," I pounded chords in the bass, "do we escape destruction?"

"Bring me black stones," Moira commanded. "Small, to pin down the soul that wants escape from its shadow. But stand not on my shadow lest thee kill my soul for to obscure shadow-soul is to bury its owner." She screamed, "We're standing in each other's shadows."

We both screamed and ran to the other side of the altar. The church fell silent, cold, blurry. Lights flickered in my eyes. The floor seemed uneven. It was. We were standing on the lip of a crypt. Raised cement seams ran around its perimeter. They were striated like a fork run through icing. Every so often a small triad of homemade cement leaves broke the line.

"They stand for eternity," Moira whispered. We knelt on the cold stone floor.

"*Charles Payne Cheney, 27.*
Willa Halsel Cheney, 21.
Mary Lynn Cheney, 23.
Pray for their souls."

"They're younger than us," we ran our hands over the raised stone letters. An empty wine bottle clattered down three steps.

"This is where I'll be when I'm dead," Moira said. "They'll lay me out up here. And this is the view I'll have."

I looked out at the disciplined rows of chairs. In the dark they looked like people holding hymnals in their laps. Behind them glowed a round rose window.

"What will you wear?" Moira asked.

"To your funeral?"

"No. Yours."

"Moira, for heaven's sakes! Nothing that has to be dry-cleaned."

"You prepared for everything but what you'd wear? You who are so vain?"

"Stop it. I don't know what I'm going to wear tomorrow."

I'd dreamt it once, though, during the eighth month of chemo, when I couldn't imagine more pain. It was the one outfit that made me look good no matter how thin I got: a red silk suit with tiny black hearts, clubs and spades. I never wore the dress again, couldn't even touch it to throw it away. It hung in my closet like evil.

"Tell me what you're wearing," Moira demanded. "I might not be here to see it." Her voice was desperate.

"Come on, we're drunk," I reached across the crypt to kiss her.

"Dead drunk, and still," she raised her bottle to her lips, shook it empty, "dying. Ha! I was going to say 'drinking,' but there's no more left."

That's when I saw it. Picture number three in the series. I suddenly saw myself dead. Not a skeleton with a grinning skull. It was me lying in the coffin. Me, in my red silk suit with the tiny black hearts and spades, matching belt fastened around my waist, my black patent heels shined. Red lipstick, too much rouge, and the blonde wig. Me, dead. I was not beautiful like some leaf that thrust out its best colors just before it fell. I was yellow and waxed and fixed.

I started to cry. I was shivering. "I've got to get out of here," I stood up, ran down three altar steps, ran down the long aisle toward the rose window, ran past St. Ambrose on the newel post, out the heavy oak door, down the narrow long corridor by moonlight, only by moonlight, holding the walls of stone this one, then that one till the stone gave way to carpet, ran past classrooms and out the door to the street.

I could see my breath in the cold night air. I stripped off the skeleton costume, pulled it down over my arms, down to the waist. Pulled the black turtleneck sweater over my head, off came the wig. I rubbed both my arms, I could feel them and my bare chest, numb on one side from cut nerves, but I could feel the other side. I was not in a red silk dress inside a coffin. I was not a waxy, yellow cadaver. Nothing was different, I glowed white in the moonlight. I wasn't dead, I was still skin. I was bones.

◎ EILEEN JOY

Eileen Joy was born in 1962 in Washington, D.C., and was raised in Arlington, Virginia. She received her M.F.A. from Virginia Commonwealth University and has published fiction and poetry in New Virginia Review, The Sun, Short Fiction by Women, *and* Chick-Lit: Postfeminist Fiction. *She has received a fellowship for a residency at the Virginia Center for the Creative Arts. She is currently pursuing a Ph.D. in medieval literature at the University of Tennessee.*

"I have never been satisfied with the ending of Flaubert's Madame Bovary,*" writes Joy. "Suicide always seems too harsh a punishment for Emma. Why should authors always have the last word? To me, Emma Bovary, as a literary creation, lives always in a domain uninhabited by Flaubert himself. Still, she is trapped within the time and place he constructed for her. . . . I wrote 'Emma' as a kind of answer to the question: How would Emma have rewritten the ending to her story, if given the chance?" (letter to M. Kallet, 1996).*

Emma

History has many skins, layer upon layer of fragile papyrus, a thick apocrypha of facts and fictions, strands of white hair, cups full of brown teeth and jewelry gone green with rust. If our skin becomes dust and dust persists through all of our calamities, then I'm as eternal as air, sitting on the prow of the ship that sails to Byzantium, a twinkle in my eye. My bones might rot in the hull of the earth, but I hope that is a part of me that will settle on the wing of a gull and I will survive, yes, I will survive in spite of everything. It is love, the star in my palm, that will get me through, shake me out of time, make me like the seed plucked out of the poppy, small and hard, tasteless, eternal.

As of now I'm still alive, still tormented by fleshy possibilities. I may be old, a bachelor, my white knees turned wobbly, my hands shaky from too much wanting, my heart gaunt and unused, wheezy, but I'm not ready for my shroud. I'm still capable of walking down our long, narrow alleys, knocking on doors with the brass knob of my cane, grinding my teeth in the middle of the night. If at my age time is a rare currency, perhaps I've squandered it spending every day pining for Emma, the woman who lives across from me, but I am tired of prudence, of thriftiness.

The country I live in is small, named after my great great-grandfather, Merula, which is also my name. My family lost favor when I was a child, but the new Merula didn't have time for nurturing old grudges — there were too many fresh vendettas, and bullets were scarce. When the turmoil was over we weren't exiled or lined up against a basement wall. We were appointed the official State Bakers, perhaps a kind of humiliation, and now I carry that tradition forward, waking at six every morning to lay blackbirds into pie crusts, beaks and all.

Blackbird pie is a national delicacy, a sweet crunchy tart, and there is some status in bringing things to their final sugary rest. I don't have to wait in line for bread like everyone else. My vodka is made from the finest grains. Tailors stitch my suits. But I am not a man inclined to snobbery. I make the pies and cakes myself. I spend most of my time in storms of flour and salt and my nails are blanched a pale yellow color. On the door of my shop is a brass knocker in the shape of a dove which must be grasped around the breast, but no one thinks to knock when they come to visit. I'm a public servant, after all.

If you were to seek me out, a small formality, your gloved hand around the gold bird knocking very gently, perhaps urgently, would please me. I am a lonely man, and I often wish someone would seek me out. They say we are a country of the dispossessed, but in fact we are, most of us, quite possessed by one thing or another, quite beguiled by grim-faced men who often interrupt our dreams, come into our houses, uninvited, wearing black uniforms and carrying guns. Personally, I find myself possessed by a foreign woman who wears men's trousers and smokes French cigars. She lives across from me and her name, her beautiful name, is Emma.

During Nehora, which is our siesta, I sit on my terrace reading my maps, hoping I'll see her. It has been almost two weeks since I've last caught sight of her and I'm craving a glimpse of her long black hair and her crooked nose. Maps are my distraction. Only yesterday I learned "sierra" means mountains. We have no mountains here, no hills covered with olive trees or steep, sandy cliffs. I have never been anywhere but this hot stretch of beach, nor have I seen any sea except the green one which surrounds us, but I want to know how the world is fitted together, the ways in which it groans and cracks, where God's fingers have pressed down into it.

I have a regular correspondence with the Royal Geographic Society and they have sent me a number of their traveler's maps. Currently I am studying "The Land of the Maya," an ancient kingdom, its bones and crockery embedded in the Yucatan Peninsula, a body of land which swells into the Caribbean sea like a cancer. Guatemala and Honduras lie beneath it, crumpled pieces of brown land. Everywhere, indicated by small black triangles on the map, there are piles of stones testifying to something not so apparent, something less visible and terribly old.

Here in Merula we have no ancient civilizations over which we have to carefully cover our tracks. If there are pyramids in Mexico, one should not be too smug, for there is surely something in the grass there as well, some residue of Aztec breath grown heavy with time. Nothing is truly dead in this world. Even the blackbirds I shoot and bake into pies occasionally cause the Prime Minister and others indigestion. Sometimes I am blamed for including too much nutmeg in the recipe, but my ingredients never vary, only the birds, which come in all shapes and sizes.

They will sometimes fly over my bungalow in groups at night, taunting me with their throaty mourning. They know I am a man of ritual. I will only pick up my gun on Sunday mornings to shoot them. In this way, I give them a fighting chance. I am a man of honor, but once I killed a blackbird with my bare hands, and it was a terrible thing to have to do, but I couldn't help myself.

It has been two weeks now, two weeks since Emma has allowed me to touch her luminous ebony hair. We had an appointment once, every Wednesday for the first hour after midnight, the time when Emma said she felt most alive. She would sit on her terrace and I would stand behind her in my evening coat, brushing her hair into the warm wind. It was too long for her to manage all by herself. I would brush it until the sparks fell out like rain, tiny constellations of light dancing between us, then turning to ash, and the black sea would be humming behind us.

The joy I felt then was excruciating, almost painful, for that was all Emma allowed me, the brushing of her hair. My fingertips would be numb with desire, with electricity. Afterwards Emma would pour us a black market scotch into a heavy crystal tumbler and we would lean against the cool stucco plaster of her house, passing the glass back and forth and looking for some chance of life in the stars. Emma called me her companion, her *compagnon,* but I was never invited inside, no, that would be unseemly, she once told me.

Perhaps if you had walked by at one of those times, one of those Wednesdays, and you had looked up, you would have thought there had recently been some fight, some disagreement between us. The silence would have been overwhelming, but it was the silence of two people who had told each other everything. It was the calm of two people who had reached a comfortable agreement, though at times, old and bereft as I am, I suppose I yearned for more.

There was a time when Emma and I had talked from dusk until dawn, when I would tell her everything about Merula and she would tell me her own personal history, how she had come to Merula alone from a country with grass and convents and a medieval past, how she had left behind a shattered life, a trail of men who probably thought her dead, her escape had been so perfect.

I told her how our island had started: sand and wind and blackbirds covering the beaches like blankets of flies. There were so many blackbirds they outnumbered everything, even us. There was a time when the birds were sacred. Their songs, low and mournful, were considered holy, but there were years of drought, shrunken fruit, and poisoned water. We were hungry and the birds seemed indifferent to us. They were sweet meat posing as prophecy. Now they are a delicacy, a piquant dessert, and it seems there are so many of them we will never be without this luxury of eating blackbirds, of licking from our fingers the remains of the first inhabitants of this place. This is what I told her.

Since I spent most of my childhood in political uncertainty and have spent most of my adult life with crusts and birds, a woman like Emma was a discovery for me. Anyone could see she was not from Merula. She is much too tall to be one of us and her skin is too close to her bones, almost transparent. Our sun is not good for her, but she would frequently take in the night air in defiance of curfew. This is how we first met.

I was contemplating Canis Major one evening through my bedroom window when I saw her descending the steps of her terrace. It was too windy for star-gazing. My windows were rattling, and there was clattering in my cupboards. I couldn't believe anyone would be so ill-advised as to venture out after the prescribed hour. I didn't know someone had moved into the empty house across the street from me, let alone someone so beautiful and gaunt, and so pale-looking. I rushed outside, not even thinking. I know I must have startled her at first because she backed away from me.

"You're the baker," she said. "We're neighbors," she said, as if she were repeating herself, as if I did not understand her clearly.

"What are you *doing?*" I asked her, perhaps too urgently.

"I live here."

"Yes, *so?*" I said to her.

"I'm going for a walk," she told me, "What do you *want?*"

She was confused. I convinced her to go back to her house, that if she had to be outside we could sit on her balcony. It wasn't safe for anyone to walk anywhere, not after eight. Even to just sit at the door of your house, idly staring, is considered a threat in this place. But we could sit outside for a short while, I told her, I am a man of public office, after all, my family has a history here, we could talk. If someone were to walk by, I told her, an officer or *gendarme,* I'll simply lean over the balcony and say, "Good evening, brother!" He'll see who I am and pass on.

She was distracted, but she agreed in the end. She told me she didn't know what she had been thinking, or why she had started down the street as if she were in another place. I suppose, now, she knew exactly where she was going. She's a master of subterfuge, of mixed signals.

Nevertheless she took my advice, we ascended the steps of her terrace and we became friends. We were like drinking acquaintances who play cards once a week and exchange sly gossip. Emma appointed me guardian of her hair; she was my confessor. I have committed no sins that I am aware of, but there are little things that happen in a day, things I need to tell someone, how various cats perch on my windowsill in the afternoons, eyeing my ovens and greedily licking their lips, how a blackbird, in rigor mortis, might extend a wing, tentatively, over the edge of my chopping block. I fell in love, perhaps out of pity for a woman whose reputation had been maligned in another place. This was a tragedy I understood intimately.

In her own country Emma had been sadly misunderstood. She was born in a place where houses are built at the foot of brown hills, overlooking nothing, where trees are miserly and hide the sun. She was educated in a convent and was severely punished for trying to assert herself there. Her husband was a doctor who had worshipped her, who had tried to please her, but he hadn't understood her sensual nature. He had never comprehended her need to always hear the clicking of horses' hooves on the pavement outside her window, to hear the strains of an opera while making love, to feel that love could burn holes in her hands. She had acquired lovers, with disastrous results. She had burned, but she had also turned to ice.

Emma would tell me the most intimate details of her affairs, how she had been desperate for a grand passion, how she faked her suicide in order to get away from all the monotonous men, ate black poison and survived its inky death, watched her husband hover over her, sick with despair, and despised him for it. She told me she understood perfectly if I felt I had to fall in love with her, but she wanted me to know that she couldn't accommodate me. Emma liked to refer to herself as "one of the disappeared."

Once she told me, "Making love to me would be like making love to a dead woman."

I don't believe her. Emma's movements are slow, first she would speak, then gesture what she meant, but there was something about her which was not from the side of the dead. Underneath her white skin is a mass of veins, small branches of blue ice, a frozen life that begs to be revived.

All my life I've buried things, stripped birds of their skins, scraped out hearts and lungs for puddings—one resurrection was all I wanted, some atonement. It couldn't be a woman from Merula, a woman who ate my pies, who didn't understand how to properly hold a fork, how to chew and swallow gracefully. Emma seemed to understand this, to understand my hesitation when it came to the women of my island. In our conversations, when we used to drink and talk and not just drink, we kept nothing from each other. But Emma told me she was not willing to be revived, not by anyone.

Emma once said to me, "Think of me as an indifferent tourist."

Another time she said to me, "Men are bastards."

But Emma let me brush her hair, she pressed glasses of scotch into my hands, and I was dizzy from these things, almost grateful, but a man my age is impatient. Perhaps I shouldn't have caused so much grief between us, but she had taken that bird in and given it comfort. She said it had just flown into her window one day and perched on the back of a chair, acting as if it wanted to stay. I suppose I was jealous.

And there is another matter, another woman, young, a woman with brown skin and green eyes like mine, something else Emma has taken in and given succor — the butcher's wife, Xenobia, thrown out by the butcher one day last month, they say for acting sullen, and no one knew where she had gone to. So Emma had taken in Xenobia, had let a blackbird fly in her window, but I was to stay on the terrace. I was to keep my respectful distance. She says she will never forgive me, that men are always cruel when they can't have what they want.

"I think you really wanted to strangle me," she told me, only her gown on, three buttons undone, shocked at seeing me there, Xenobia lying behind her, the sheets thrown off the bed, the moon illuminating the arch of Xenobia's oiled back, the curve of her neck.

I wish Emma understood, a woman won't take in a man, then takes in a woman, takes in a bird, feeds it and strokes its beak. In my mind there was an inequity. An old man like me, never married, cannot easily shake the image of two women intertwined, an inarticulate moan disturbing the serenity of the dark evening.

"Who are you kidding?" Emma had said to me, defiantly, holding what was dead and broken against her breast. "I've seen the way you eye the soldiers when they gather on the corner."

In the Land of the Maya, in Kohunlich, there is a stucco-covered pyramid. Stone idols, women carved out of limestone, surround it. There is no other information on the map. I am forced to imagine the rest, the brown grass, the missing ears and noses, cans and broken glass, graffiti — the trash of history. I imagine the faces of the idols as broad, their features worn down in the wind, but their lips remaining full with defiance.

I had only meant to show Emma the Hunger Moon, the full moon of February. It wasn't our regular night, I know, but I didn't think Emma would mind. I had drunk some vodka, my head was light, I had only my robe on. I didn't think to knock. I hadn't thought Emma would mind the intrusion. A full moon is a happy occasion in Merula.

Didn't Emma know how much of a temptation it would be for me? When I saw its outline on her shoulder, I lost my composure. A man has to direct his anger at something. Even with its heart beating against my palm, I couldn't stop myself. When I felt its small bones crack under my fingers, the small rush of warm air, its last exhalation, on my face, I knew I had accomplished something: a finality, an end.

There is no undoing any of this, but if you could, try to imagine us, Emma and me, up ahead of you. See if you can't picture us leaning out of a window and sipping our scotch, smiling at some unknown friend passing by below, waving at the soldiers as if to say, carry on, we're behind you one hundred percent — an unrealized yet-to-be-written story without an end, or even a beginning. Nothing is irrevocable. We are only hinted at, suggested. We are only the faintest point of light on your retina, the slightest shadow of what's to come, citizens of a country not yet dreamed of. History hasn't claimed us. Not yet. How many times can a person start over, reinvent himself? Anything is possible.

◎ *NAOMI WOLF*

Naomi Wolf was born in San Francisco in 1963. She is a Yale graduate and a Rhodes Scholar. Her publications include The Beauty Myth: How Images of Beauty Are Used Against Women *(1991) and most recently* Fire with Fire: The New Female Power and How It Will Change the 21st Century *(1993). Currently living in Washington, D.C., she is a frequent lecturer and writer on women's issues.*

"Hunger," excerpted from The Beauty Myth, *explores the very real consequences (in the form of life-threatening eating disorders) for women trying to conform to societal images of "beauty." Wolf writes from personal experience, since she was an anorexic as a teenager. From the personal, Wolf moves to expose the economic forces that deny women psychological freedom.*

Hunger

> I saw the best minds of my generation destroyed by madness, starving. . . .
>
> — ALLEN GINSBERG, *"Howl"*

There is a disease spreading. It taps on the shoulder America's firstborn sons, its best and brightest. At its touch, they turn away from food. Their bones swell out from receding flesh. Shadows invade their faces. They walk slowly, with the effort of old men. A white spittle forms on their lips. They can swallow only pellets of bread, and a little thin milk. First tens, then hundreds, then thousands, until, among the most affluent families, one young son in five is stricken. Many are hospitalized, many die.

The boys of the ghetto die young, and America has lived with that. But these boys are the golden ones to whom the reins of the world are to be lightly tossed: the captain of the Princeton football team, the head of the Berkeley debating club, the editor of the *Harvard Crimson*. Then a quarter of the Dartmouth rugby team falls ill; then a third of the initiates of Yale's secret societies. The heirs, the cream, the fresh delegates to the nation's forum selectively waste away.

The American disease spreads eastward. It strikes young men at the Sorbonne, in London's Inns of Court, in the administration of The Hague, in the Bourse, in the offices of *Die Zeit*, in the universities of Edinburgh and Tübingen and Salamanca. They grow thin and still more thin. They can hardly speak aloud. They lose their libido, and can no longer make the effort to joke or argue. When they run or swim, they look appalling: buttocks collapsed, tailbones protruding, knees knocked together, ribs splayed in a shelf that stretches their papery skin. There is no medical reason.

The disease mutates again. Across America, it becomes apparent that for every well-born living skeleton there are at least three other young men, also bright lights, who do something just as strange. Once they have swallowed their steaks and Rhine wine, they hide away, to thrust their fingers down their throats and spew out all the nourishment in them. They wander back into Maury's or "21," shaking and pale. Eventually they arrange their lives so they can spend hours each day hunched over like that, their highly trained minds telescoped around two shameful holes: mouth, toilet; toilet, mouth.

Meanwhile, people are waiting for them to take up their places: assistantships at *The New York Times*, seats on the stock exchange, clerkships with federal judges. Speeches need to be written and briefs researched among the clangor of gavels and the whir of fax machines. What is happening to the fine young men, in their brush cuts and khaki trousers? It hurts to look at them. At the expense-account lunches, they hide their medallions of veal under lettuce leaves. Secretly they purge. They vomit after matriculation banquets and after tailgate parties at the Game. The men's room in the Oyster Bar reeks with it. One in five, on the campuses that speak their own names proudest.

How would America react to the mass self-immolation by hunger of its favorite sons? How would Eastern Europe absorb the export of such a disease? One would expect an emergency response: crisis task forces convened in congressional hearing rooms, unscheduled alumni meetings, the best experts money can hire, cover stories in newsmagazines, a flurry of editorials, blame and counterblame, bulletins, warnings, symptoms, updates; an epidemic blazoned in boldface red. The sons of privilege *are* the future; the future is committing suicide.

Of course, this is actually happening right now, only with a gender difference. The institutions that shelter and promote these diseases are hibernating. The public conscience is fast asleep. Young women are dying from institutional catatonia: four hundred dollars a term from the college endowment for the women's center to teach "self-help"; fifty to buy a noontime talk from a visiting clinician. The world is not coming to an end because the cherished child in five who "chooses" to die slowly is a girl. And she is merely doing too well what she is expected to do very well in the best of times.

Up to one tenth of all young American women, up to one fifth of women students in the United States, are locked into one-woman hunger camps. When they fall, there are no memorial services, no intervention through awareness programs, no formal message from their schools and colleges that the society prefers its young women to eat and thrive rather than sicken and die. Flags are not lowered in recognition of the fact that in every black-robed ceremonial marches a fifth column of death's-heads.

Virginia Woolf in *A Room of One's Own* had a vision that someday young women would have access to the rich forbidden libraries of the men's colleges, their sunken lawns, their vellum, the claret light. She believed that would give young women a mental freedom that must have seemed all the sweeter from where she imagined it: the wrong side of the beadle's staff that had driven her away from the library because she was female. Now young women have pushed past the staff that barred Woolf's way. Striding across the grassy quadrangles that she could only write about, they are halted by an immaterial barrier she did not foresee. Their minds are proving well able; their bodies self-destruct.

When she envisaged a future for young women in the universities, Woolf's prescience faltered only from insufficient cynicism. Without it one could hardly conceive of the modern solution of the recently all-male schools and colleges to the problem of women: They admitted their minds, and let their bodies go. Young women learned that they could not live inside those gates and also inside their bodies.

The weight-loss cult recruits women from an early age, and eating diseases are the cult's bequest. Anorexia and bulimia are female maladies: From 90 to 95 percent of anorexics and bulimics are women. America, which has the greatest number of women who have made it into the male sphere, also leads the world with female anorexia. Women's magazines report that there are up to a million American anorexics, but the American Anorexic and Bulimia Association states that anorexia and bulimia strike a million American women *every year;* 30,000, it reports, also become emetic abusers.

Each year, according to the association, 150,000 American women die of anorexia. If so, every twelve months there are 17,024 more deaths in the United States alone than the total number of deaths from AIDS tabulated by the World Health Organization in 177 countries and territories from the beginning of the epidemic until the end of 1988; if so, more die of anorexia in the United States each year than died in ten years of civil war in Beirut. Beirut has long been front-page news. As criminally neglectful as media coverage of the AIDS epidemic has been, it still dwarfs that of anorexia; so it appears that the bedrock question — why must Western women go hungry — is one too dangerous to ask even in the face of a death toll such as this.

Joan Jacobs Brumberg in *Fasting Girls: The Emergence of Anorexia Nervosa as a Modern Disease* puts the number of anorexics at 5 to 10 percent of all American girls and women. On some college campuses, she believes, one woman student in five is anorexic. The number of women with the disease has increased dramatically throughout the Western world starting twenty years ago. Dr. Charles A. Murkovsky of Gracie Square Hospital in New York City, an eating diseases specialist, says that 20 percent of American college women binge and purge on a regular basis. Kim Chernin of *The Hungry Self* suggests that at least half the women on campuses in the United States suffer at some time from bulimia or anorexia. Roberta Pollack Seid in *Never Too Thin* agrees with the 5- to 10-percent figure for anorexia among young American women, adding that up to six times that figure on campuses are bulimic. If we take the high end of the figures, it means that of ten young American women in college, two will be anorexic and six will be bulimic; only two will be well. The norm, then, for young, middle-class American women, is to be a sufferer from some form of the eating disease.

The disease is a deadly one. Brumberg reports that 5 to 15 percent of hospitalized anorexics die in treatment, giving the disease one of the highest fatality rates for a mental illness. *The New York Times* cites the same fatality rate. Researcher L.K.G. Hsu gives a death rate of up to 19 percent. Forty to 50 percent of anorexics never recover completely, a worse rate of recovery from starvation than the 66 percent recovery rate for famine victims hospitalized in the war-torn Netherlands in 1944–45.

The medical effects of anorexia include hypothermia, edema, hypotension, bradycardia (impaired heartbeat), lanugo (growth of body hair), infertility, and death. The medical effects of bulimia include dehydration, electrolyte imbalance, epileptic seizure, abnormal heart rhythm, and death. When the two are combined, they can result in tooth erosion, hiatal hernia, abraded esophagus, kidney failure, osteoporosis, and death. Medical literature is starting to report that babies and children underfed by weight-conscious mothers are suffering from stunted growth, delayed puberty, and failure to thrive.

It is spreading to other industrialized nations: The United Kingdom now has 3.5 million anorexics or bulimics (95 percent of them female), with 6,000 new cases yearly. Another study of adolescent British girls alone shows that 1 percent are now anorexic. According to the women's press, at least 50 percent of British women suffer from disordered eating. Hilde Bruch states that in the last generation, larger patient groups have been reported in publications in Russia, Australia, Sweden, and Italy as well as Great Britain and the United States. Sweden's rate is now 1 to 2 percent of teenage girls, with the same percentage of women over sixteen being bulimic. The rate for the Netherlands is 1 to 2 percent; of Italian teenagers also, 1 percent suffer from anorexia or bulimia

(95 percent of them female), a rise of 400 percent in ten years. That is just the beginning for Western Europe and Japan, since the figures resemble numbers for the United States ten years ago, and since the rate is rising, as it did in America, exponentially. The anorexic patient herself is *thinner* now than were previous generations of patients. Anorexia followed the familiar beauty myth pattern of movement: It began as a middle-class disease in the United States and has spread eastward as well as down the social ladder.

Some women's magazines report that 60 percent of American women have serious trouble eating. The majority of middle-class women in the United States, it appears, suffer a version of anorexia or bulimia; but if anorexia is defined as a compulsive fear of and fixation upon food, perhaps most Western women can be called, twenty years into the backlash, mental anorexics.

What happened? Why now? The first obvious clue is the progressive chiseling away of the Iron Maiden's body over this century of female emancipation, in reaction to it. Until seventy-five years ago in the male artistic tradition of the West, women's natural amplitude was their beauty; representations of the female nude reveled in women's lush fertility. Various distributions of sexual fat were emphasized according to fashion — big, ripe bellies from the fifteenth to the seventeenth centuries, plump faces and shoulders in the early nineteenth, progressively generous dimpled buttocks and thighs until the twentieth — but never, until women's emancipation entered law, this absolute negation of the female state that fashion historian Ann Hollander in *Seeing Through Clothes* characterizes, from the point of view of any age but our own, as "the look of sickness, the look of poverty, and the look of nervous exhaustion."

Dieting and thinness began to be female preoccupations when Western women received the vote around 1920; between 1918 and 1925, "the rapidity with which the new, linear form replaced the more curvaceous one is startling." In the regressive 1950s, women's natural fullness could be briefly enjoyed once more because their minds were occupied in domestic seclusion. But when women came en masse into male spheres, that pleasure had to be overridden by an urgent social expedient that would make women's bodies into the prisons that their homes no longer were.

A generation ago, the average model weighed 8 percent less than the average American woman, whereas today she weighs 23 percent less. Twiggy appeared in the pages of *Vogue* in 1965, simultaneous with the advent of the Pill, to cancel out its most radical implications. Like many beauty-myth symbols, she was double-edged, suggesting to women the freedom from the constraint of reproduction of earlier generations (since female fat is categorically understood by the subconscious as fertile sexuality), while reassuring men with her suggestion of female weakness, asexuality, and hunger. Her thinness, now commonplace, was shocking at that time; even *Vogue* introduced the model with anxiety: " 'Twiggy' is called Twiggy because she looks as though a strong gale would snap her in two and dash her to the ground . . . Twiggy is of such a meagre constitution that other models stare at her. Her legs look as though she has not had enough milk as a baby and her face has that expression one feels Londoners wore in the blitz." The fashion writer's language is revealing: Undernurtured, subject to being overpowered by a strong wind, her expression the daze of the besieged, what better symbol to reassure an establishment faced with women who were soon to march tens of thousands strong down Fifth Avenue?

In the twenty years after the start of the second wave of the women's movement, the weight of Miss Americas plummeted, and the average weight of Playboy Playmates dropped from 11 percent below the national average in 1970 to 17 percent below it in eight years. Model Aimee Liu in her autobiography claims that many models are anorexic; she herself continued to model as an anorexic. Of dancers, 38 percent show anorexic behavior. The average model, dancer, or actress is thinner than 95 percent of the female population. The Iron Maiden put the shape of a near skeleton and the texture of men's musculature where the shape and feel of a woman used to be, and the small elite corps of women whose bodies are used to reproduce the Iron Maiden often become diseased themselves in order to do so.

As a result, a 1985 survey says, 90 percent of respondents think they weigh too much. On any day, 25 percent of women are on diets, with 50 percent finishing, breaking, or starting one. This self-hatred was generated rapidly, coinciding with the women's movement: Between 1966 and 1969, two studies showed, the number of high school girls who thought they were too fat had risen from 50 to 80 percent. Though heiresses to the gains of the women's movement, their daughters are, in terms of this distress, no better off: In a recent study of high school girls, 53 percent were unhappy with their bodies by age thirteen; by age eighteen and over, 78 percent were dissatisfied. The hunger cult has on a major victory against women's fight for equality if the evidence of the 1984 *Glamour* survey of thirty-three thousand women is representative: 75 percent of those aged eighteen to thirty-five believed they were fat, while only 25 percent were medically overweight (the same percentage as men); 45 percent of the *underweight* women thought they were too fat. But more heartbreaking in terms of the way in which the myth is running to ground hopes for women's advancement and gratification, the *Glamour* respondents chose losing ten to fifteen pounds above success in work or in love as their most desired goal.

Those ten to fifteen pounds, which have become a fulcrum, if these figures are indicative, of most Western women's sense of self, are the medium of what I call the One Stone Solution. One stone, the British measurement of fourteen pounds, is roughly what stands between the 50 percent of women who are not overweight who believe they are and their ideal self. That one stone, once lost, puts these women well below the weight that is natural to them, and beautiful, if we saw with eyes unconstrained by the Iron Maiden. But the body quickly restores itself, and the cycle of gain and loss begins, with its train of torment and its risk of disease, becoming a fixation of the woman's consciousness. The inevitable cycles of failure ensured by the One Stone Solution create and continually reinforce in women our uniquely modern neurosis. This great weight-shift bestowed on women, just when we were free to begin to forget them, new versions of low self-esteem, loss of control, and sexual shame. It is a genuinely elegant fulfillment of a collective wish: By simply dropping the official weight one stone below most women's natural level, and redefining a woman's womanly shape as by definition "too fat," a wave of self-hatred swept over First World women, a reactionary psychology was perfected, and a major industry was born. It suavely countered the historical groundswell of female success with a mass conviction of female failure, a failure defined as implicit in womanhood itself.

The proof that the One Stone Solution is political lies in what women feel when they eat "too much": guilt. Why should guilt be the operative emotion, and female fat be a moral issue articulated with words like good and bad? If our culture's fixation on female fatness or thinness were about sex, it would be a private issue between a woman and her lover; if it were about health, between a woman and herself. Public debate would be far more hysterically focused on male fat than on female, since more men (40 percent) are medically overweight than women (32 percent) and too much fat is far more dangerous for men than for women. In fact, "there is very little evidence to support the claim that fatness causes poor health among women. . . . The results of recent studies have suggested that women may in fact live longer and be generally healthier if they weigh ten to fifteen percent *above* the life-insurance figures *and* they refrain from dieting," asserts *Radiance;* when poor health is correlated to fatness in women, it is due to chronic dieting and the emotional stress of self-hatred. The National Institutes of Health studies that linked obesity to heart disease and stroke were based on male subjects; when a study of females was finally published in 1990, it showed that weight made only a fraction of the difference for women that it made for men. The film *The Famine Within* cites a sixteen-country study that fails to correlate fatness to ill health. Female fat is not in itself unhealthy.

But female fat is the subject of public passion, and women feel guilty about female fat, because we implicitly recognize that under the myth, women's bodies are not our own but society's, and that thinness is not a private aesthetic, but hunger a social concession exacted by the community. A cultural fixation on female thinness is not an obsession about female beauty but an obsession about female obedience. Women's dieting has become what Yale psychologist Judith Rodin calls a "normative obsession," a never-ending passion play given international coverage out of all proportion to the health risks associated with obesity, and using emotive language that does not figure even in discussions of alcohol or tobacco abuse. The nations seize with compulsive attention on this melodrama because women and men understand that it is not about cholesterol or heart rate or the disruption of a line of tailoring, but about how much social freedom women are going to get away with or concede. The media's convulsive analysis of the endless saga of female fat and the battle to vanquish it are actually bulletins of the sex war: what women are gaining or losing in it, and how fast.

The great weight shift must be understood as one of the major historical developments of the century, a direct solution to the dangers posed by the women's movement and economic and reproductive freedom. Dieting is the most potent political sedative in women's history; a quietly mad population is a tractable one. Researchers S. C. Wooley and O. W. Wooley confirmed what most women know too well — that concern with weight leads to "a virtual collapse of self-esteem and sense of effectiveness." Researchers J. Polivy and C. P. Herman found that "prolonged and periodic calorie restriction" resulted in distinctive personality whose traits are "passivity, anxiety and emotionality."

It is those traits, and not thinness for its own sake, that the dominant culture wants to create in the private sense of self of recently liberated women in order to cancel out the dangers of their liberation.

Women's advances had begun to give them the opposite traits — high self-esteem, a sense of effectiveness, activity, courage, and clarity of mind. "Prolonged and periodic caloric restriction" is a means to take the teeth out of this revolution. The great weight shift and its One Stone Solution followed the rebirth of feminism so that women just reaching for power would become weak, preoccupied, and, as it evolved, mentally ill in useful ways and in astonishing proportions. To understand how the gaunt toughness of the Iron Maiden has managed spectacularly to roll back women's advances toward equality, we have to see that what is really at stake is not fashion or beauty or sex, but a struggle over political hegemony that has become — for women, who are often unaware of the real issues behind our predicament — one of life and death.

Theories abound to explain anorexia, bulimia, and the modern thinning of the feminine. Ann Hollander proposes that the shift from portraiture to moving images made thinness suggestive of motion and speed. Susie Orbach in *Fat Is a Feminist Issue* "reads" women's fat as a statement to the mother about separation and dependence; she sees in the mother "a terrible ambivalence about feeding and nurturing" her daughter. Kim Chernin in *The Obsession* gives a psychoanalytic reading of fear of fat as based on infantile rage against the all-powerful mother, and sees food as the primordial breast, the "lost world" of female abundance that we must recover "if we are to understand the heartland of our obsession with the female body. . . . We can understand how," Chernin writes, "in a frenzy of terror and dread, [a man] might be tempted to spin out fashionable images of [a woman] that tell her implicitly that she is unacceptable . . . when she is large." In *The Hungry Self*, Chernin interprets bulimia as a religious rite of passage. Joan Jacobs Brumberg sees food as a symbolic language, anorexia as a cry of confusion in a world of too many choices, and "the appetite as voice": "young women searching for an idiom in which to say things about themselves focused on food and styles of eating." Rudolph Bell in *Holy Anorexia* relates the disease to the religious impulses of medieval nuns, seeing starvation as purification.

Theories such as these are enlightening within a private context; but they do not go far enough. Women do not eat or starve only in a succession of private relationships, but within a public social order that has a material vested interest in their troubles with eating. Individual men don't "spin out fashionable images" (indeed, research keeps proving that they are warm to women's real shapes and unmoved by the Iron Maiden); multinational corporations do that. The many theories about women's food crises have stressed private psychology *to the neglect* of public policy, looking at women's shapes to see how they express a conflict about their society rather than looking at how their society makes use of a manufactured conflict with women's shapes. Many other theories have focused on women's reaction to the thin ideal, but have not asserted that the thin ideal is *proactive*, a preemptive strike.

We need to reexamine all the terms again, then, in the light of a public agenda. What, first, is food? Certainly, within the context of the intimate family, food is love, and memory, and language. But in the public realm, food is status and honor.

Food is the primal symbol of social worth. Whom a society values, it feeds well. The piled plate, the choicest cut, say: We think you're worth this much of the tribe's resources. Samoan women, who are held in high esteem, exaggerate how much they eat on feast days. Publicly apportioning food is about determining power relations, and sharing it is about cementing social equality: When men break bread together, or toast the queen, or slaughter for one another the fatted calf, they've become equals and then allies. The world *companion* comes from the Latin for "with" and "bread"—those who break bread together.

But under the beauty myth, now that all women's eating is a public issue, our portions testify to and reinforce our sense of social inferiority. If women cannot eat the same food as men, we cannot experience equal status in the community. As long as women are asked to bring a self-denying mentality to the communal table, it will never be round, men and women seated together; but the same traditional hierarchical dais, with a folding table for women at the foot.

In the current epidemic of rich Western women who cannot "choose" to eat, we see the continuation of an older, poorer tradition of women's relation to food. Modern Western female dieting descends from a long history. Women have always had to eat differently from men: less and worse. In Hellenistic Rome, reports classicist Sarah B. Pomeroy, boys were rationed sixteen measures of meal to twelve measures allotted to girls. In medieval France, according to historian John Boswell, women received two-thirds of the grain allocated to men. Throughout history, when there is only so much to eat, women get little, or none: A common explanation among anthropologists for female infanticide is that food shortage provokes it. According to UN publications, where hunger goes, women meet it first: In Bangladesh and Botswana, female infants die more frequently than male, and girls are more often malnourished, because they are given smaller portions. In Turkey, India, Pakistan, North Africa, and the Middle East, men get the lion's share of what food there is, regardless of women's caloric needs. "It is not the caloric value of work which is represented in the patterns of food consumption" of men in relation to women in North Africa, "nor is it a question of physiological needs. . . . Rather these patterns tend to guarantee priority rights to the 'important' members of society, that is, adult men." In Morocco, if women are guests, "they will swear they have eaten already" or that they are not hungry. "Small girls soon learn to offer their share to visitors, to refuse meat and deny hunger." A North African woman described by anthropologist Vanessa Mahler assured her fellow diners that "she preferred bones to meat." Men, however, Mahler reports, "are supposed to be exempt from facing scarcity which is shared out among women and children."

"Third World countries provide examples of undernourished female and well-nourished male children, where what food there is goes to the boys of the family," a UN report testifies. Two-thirds of women in Asia, half of all women in Africa, and a sixth of Latin American women are anemic — through lack of food. Fifty percent more Nepali women than men go blind from lack of food. Cross-culturally, men receive hot meals, more protein, and the first helpings of a dish, while women eat the cooling leftovers, often having to use deceit and cunning to get enough to eat. "Moreover, what food they do receive is consistently less nutritious."

This pattern is not restricted to the Third World: Most Western women alive today can recall versions of it at their mothers' or grandmothers' table: British miners' wives eating the grease-soaked bread left over after their husbands had eaten the meat; Italian and Jewish wives taking the part of the bird no one else would want.

These patterns of behavior are standard in the affluent West today, perpetuated by the culture of female caloric self-deprivation. A generation ago, the justification for this traditional apportioning shifted: Women still went without, ate leftovers, hoarded food, used deceit to get it — but blamed themselves. Our mothers still exiled themselves from the family circle that was eating cake with silver cutlery off Wedgwood china, and we would come upon them in the kitchen, furtively devouring the remains. The traditional pattern was cloaked in modern shame, but otherwise changed little. Weight control became its rationale once natural inferiority went out of fashion.

The affluent West is merely carrying on this traditional apportioning. Researchers found that parents in the United States urged boys to eat, regardless of their weight, while they did so with daughters only if they were relatively thin. In a sample of babies of both sexes, 99 percent of the boys were breast-fed, but only 66 percent of the girls, who were given 50 percent less time to feed. "Thus," writes Susie Orbach, "daughters are often fed less well, less attentively and less sensitively than they need." Women do not feel entitled to enough food because they have been taught to go with less than they need since birth, in a tradition passed down through an endless line of mothers; the public role of "honored guest" is new to us, and the culture is telling us through the ideology of caloric restriction that we are not welcome finally to occupy it.

What, then, is fat? Fat is portrayed in the literature of the myth as expendable female filth; virtually cancerous matter, an inert or treacherous infiltration into the body of nauseating bulk waste. The demonic characterizations of a simple body substance do not arise from its physical properties but from old-fashioned misogyny, for above all fat is female; it is the medium and regulator of female sexual characteristics.

Cross-culturally, from birth, girls have 10–15 percent more fat than boys. At puberty, male fat-to-muscle ratio decreases as the female ratio increases. The increased fat ratio in adolescent girls is the medium for sexual maturation and fertility. The average healthy twenty-year-old female is made of 28.7 percent body fat. By middle age, women cross-culturally are 38 percent body fat: This is, contrary to the rhetoric of the myth, "not unique to the industrialized advanced Western nations. They are norms characteristic of the female of the species." A moderately active woman's caloric needs, again in contradiction to a central tenet of the myth, are only 250 calories less than a moderately active man's (2,250 to 2,500), or two ounces of cheese. Weight gain with age is also normal cross-culturally for both sexes. The body is evidently programmed to weigh a certain amount, which weight the body defends.

Fat is sexual in women; Victorians called it affectionately their "silken layer." The leanness of the Iron Maiden impairs female sexuality. One-fifth of women who exercise to shape their bodies have menstrual irregularities and diminished fertility. The body of the model, remember, is 22 to 23 percent leaner than that of the average woman; the average woman wants to be as lean as the model; infertility and hormone imbalance are common among women whose fat-to-lean ratio falls below 22 percent. Hormonal imbalances promote ovarian and endometrial cancer and osteoporosis. Fat tissues store sex hormones, so low fat reserves are linked with weak estrogens and low levels of all the other important sex hormones, as well as with inactive ovaries. Rose E. Frisch in *Scientific American* refers to the fatness of Stone Age fertility figures, saying that "this historical linking of fatness and fertility actually makes biological sense" since fat regulates reproduction. Underweight women double their risk of low-birth-weight babies.

Fat is not just fertility in women, but desire. Researchers at Michael Reese Hospital in Chicago found that plumper women desired sex more often than thinner women. On scales of erotic excitability and readiness, they outscored thin women by a factor of almost two to one. To ask women to become unnaturally thin is to ask them to relinquish their sexuality: "Studies consistently show that with dietary deprivation, sexual interests dissipate." Subjects of one experiment stopped masturbating or having sexual fantasies at 1,700 calories a day, 500 more than the Beverly Hills Diet. Starvation affects the endocrine glands; amenorrhea and delayed puberty are common features in starving women and girls; starved men lose their libido and become impotent, sometimes developing breasts. Loyola University's Sexual Dysfunction Clinic reports that weight-loss disorders have a far worse effect on female sexuality than do weight-gaining disorders; the heavier women were eager for courtship and sex, while anorexics "were so concerned with their bodies that they had fewer sexual fantasies, fewer dates, and less desire for sex." The *New England Journal of Medicine* reports that intense exercisers lose interest in sex. Joan Jacobs Brumberg agrees that "clinical materials suggest an absence of sexual activity on the part of anorexics." Pleasure in sex, Mette Bergstrom writes, "is rare for a bulimic because of a strong body hatred." "The evidence seems to suggest," writes Roberta Pollack Seid, "and common sense would confirm, that a hungry, undernourished animal is less, not more, interested in the pleasures of the flesh."

What, finally, is dieting? "Dieting," and, in Great Britain, "slimming," are trivializing words for what is in fact self-inflicted semistarvation. In India, one of the poorest countries in the world, the very poorest women eat 1,400 calories a day, or 600 more than a Western woman on the Hilton Head Diet. "Quite simply," writes Seid, dieters "are reacting the way victims of semi-starvation react . . . semi-starvation, even if caused by self-imposed diets, produces startlingly similar effects on all human beings."

The range of repulsive and pathetic behaviors exhibited by women touched by food diseases is portrayed as quintessentially feminine, proof positive of women's irrationality (replacing the conviction of menstrual irrationality that had to be abandoned when women were needed for the full-time work force). In a classic study done at the University of Minnesota, thirty-six volunteers were placed on an extended low-calorie diet and "the psychological, behavioral and physical effects were carefully documented." The subjects were young and healthy, showing "high levels of ego strength, emotional stability, and good intellectual ability." They "began a six-month period . . . in which their food intake was reduced by half—a typical weight reduction technique for women.

"After losing approximately 25% of their original body weight, pervasive effects of semistarvation were seen." The subjects "became increasingly preoccupied with food and eating, to the extent that they ruminated obsessively about meals and food, collected recipes and cookbooks, and showed abnormal food rituals, such as excessively slow eating and hoarding of food related objects." Then, the majority "suffered some form of emotional disturbance as a result of semistarvation, including depression, hypochondriasis, hysteria, angry outbursts, and, in some cases, psychotic levels of disorganization." Then, they "lost their ability to function in work and social contexts, due to apathy, reduced energy and alertness, social isolation, and decreased sexual interest." Finally, "within weeks of reducing their food intake," they "reported relentless hunger, as well as powerful urges to break dietary rules. Some succumbed to eating binges, followed by vomiting and feelings of self-reproach. Ravenous hunger persisted, even following large meals during refeeding." Some of the subjects "found themselves eating continuously, while others engaged in uncontrollable cycles of gorging and vomiting." The volunteers "became terrified of going outside the experiment environment where they would be tempted by the foods they had agreed not to eat . . . when they did succumb, they made hysterical, half-crazed confessions." They became irritable, tense, fatigued, and full of vague complaints. "Like fugitives, [they] could not shed the feeling they were being shadowed by a sinister force." For some, doctors eventually had to prescribe tranquilizers.

The subjects were a group of completely normal healthy college men.

During the great famine that began in May 1940 during the German occupation of the Netherlands, the Dutch authorities maintained rations at between 600 and 1,600 calories a day, or what they characterized as the level of semistarvation. The worst sufferers were defined as starving when they had lost 25 percent of their body weight, and were given precious supplements. Photos taken of clothed starving Dutch women are striking for how preternaturally modern they look.

At 600–1,600 calories daily, the Dutch suffered semistarvation; the Diet Centers' diet is fixed at 1,600 calories. When they had lost 25 percent of their body weight, the Dutch were given crisis food supplementation. The average healthy woman has to lose almost exactly as much to fit the Iron Maiden. In the Lodz Ghetto in 1941, besieged Jews were allotted starvation rations of 500–1200 calories a day. At Treblinka, 900 calories was scientifically determined to be the minimum necessary to sustain human functioning. At "the nation's top weight-loss clinics," where "patients" are treated for up to a year, the rations are the same.

The psychological effects of self-inflicted semistarvation are identical to those of involuntary semistarvation. By 1980 more and more researchers were acknowledging the considerable emotional and physical consequences of chronic dieting, including "symptoms such as irritability, poor concentration, anxiety, depression, apathy, lability of mood, fatigue and social isolation." Magnus Pyke, describing the Dutch famine, writes that "starvation is known to affect people's minds and these people in Holland became mentally listless, apathetic and constantly obsessed with thoughts of food." Bruch notes that with involuntary progressive semistarvation, "there is a coarsening of emotions, sensitivity and other human traits." Robert Jay Lifton found that World War II victims of starvation "experienced feelings of guilt over having done something bad for which they are now being punished, and dreams and fantasies of food of every kind in limitless amounts." Starving destroys individuality; "anorexic patients," like others who starve, asserts Hilde Bruch, "exhibited remarkably uniform behavior and emotional patterns until they gained some weight." "Food deprivation," Roberta Pollack Seid sums it up, "triggers food obsessions for both physical and psychological reasons. . . . undernourishment produces lassitude, depression and irritability. Body metabolism slows down. . . . And hunger drives the hungry person to obsess about food." The psychological terror of hunger is cross-cultural: Orphans adopted from poor countries cannot control their compulsion to smuggle and hide food, sometimes even after living for years in a secure environment.

Authoritative evidence is mounting that eating diseases are caused mainly by dieting. Ilana Attie and J. Brooks-Gunn quote investigators who found "chronic, restrained eating" to "constitute a cumulative stress of such magnitude that dieting itself may be 'a sufficient condition for the development of anorexia nervosa or bulimia.'" Roberta Pollack Seid reaches the same conclusion. "Ironically, dieting . . . itself may provoke obsessive behaviour and binge-eating." It may indeed *cause* both eating disorders and obesity itself." Sustained caloric deprivation appears to be a severe shock to the body that it remembers with destructive consequences. Seid writes that "women's problems with food seem to stem . . . from their effort to get an ultra-lean body. . . . The only way 95% can get it is by putting themselves on deprivatory diets." Attie and Brooks-Gunn concur: "Much of the behavior thought to cause anorexia nervosa and bulimia may actually be a consequence of starvation. . . . The normal weight dieter who diets to look and feel thin also is vulnerable to disturbed emotional, cognitive and behavioral patterns by virtue of the constant stress of trying to stay below the body's 'natural' or biologically regulated weight." Dieting and fashionable thinness make women seriously unwell.

Now, if female fat is sexuality and reproductive power; if food is honor; if dieting is semistarvation; if women have to lose 23 percent of their body weight to fit the Iron Maiden and chronic psychological disruption sets in at a body weight loss of 25 percent; if semistarvation is physically and psychologically debilitating, and female strength, sexuality, and self-respect pose the threats explored earlier against the vested interests of society; if women's journalism is sponsored by a $33-billion industry whose capital is made out of the political fear of women; then we can understand why the Iron Maiden is so thin. The thin "ideal" is not beautiful aesthetically; she is beautiful as a political solution.

The compulsion to imitate her is not something trivial that women choose freely to do to ourselves. It is something serious being done to us to safeguard political power. Seen in this light, it is inconceivable that women would not have to be compelled to grow thin at this point in our history.

The ideology of semistarvation undoes feminism; what happens to women's bodies happens to our minds. If women's bodies are and have always been wrong whereas men's are right, then women are wrong and men are right. Where feminism taught women to put a higher value on ourselves, hunger teaches us how to erode our self-esteem. If a woman can be made to say, "I hate my fat thighs," it is a way she has been made to hate femaleness. The more financially independent, in control of events, educated and sexually autonomous women become in the world, the more impoverished, out of control, foolish, and sexually insecure we are asked to feel in our bodies.

Hunger makes women feel poor and think poor. A wealthy woman on a diet feels physically at the mercy of a scarcity economy; the rare woman who makes $100,000 a year has a bodily income of 1,000 calories a day. Hunger makes successful women feel like failures: An architect learns that her work crumbles; a politician who oversees a long-range vision is returned to the details, to add up every bite; a woman who can afford to travel can't "afford" rich foreign foods. It undermines each experience of control, economic security, and leadership that women have had only a generation to learn to enjoy. Those who were so recently freed to think beyond the basics are driven, with this psychology, back to the feminine mental yoke of economic dependence: fixation on getting sustenance and safety. Virginia Woolf believed that "one cannot think well, sleep well, love well is one has not dined well." "The lamp in the spine does not light on beef and prunes," she wrote, contrasting the dispiriting food of poverty, of the hard-pressed women's colleges with that of the rich men's colleges, the "soles sunk in a deep dish, over which the college cook has spread a counterpane of the whitest cream." Now that some women at last have achieved the equivalent of £500 a year and a room of their own, it is back once more to four ounces of boiled beef and three unsweetened prunes, and the unlit lamp.

The anorexic may begin her journey defiant, but from the point of view of a male-dominated society, she ends up as the perfect woman. She is weak, sexless, and voiceless, and can only with difficulty focus on a world beyond her plate. The woman has been killed off in her. She is almost not there. Seeing her like this, unwomaned, it makes crystalline sense that a half-conscious but virulent mass movement of the imagination created the vital lie of skeletal female beauty. A future in which industrialized nations are peopled with anorexia-driven women is one of few conceivable that would save the current distribution of wealth and power from the claims made on it by women's struggle for equality.

For theorists of anorexia to focus on the individual woman, even within her family, misses the tactical heart of this struggle. Economic and political retaliation against female appetite is far stronger at this point than family dynamics.

This can no longer be explained as a private issue. If suddenly 60 to 80 percent of college women can't eat, it's hard to believe that suddenly 60 to 80 percent of their families are dysfunctional in this particular way. There is a disease in the air; its cause was generated with intent; and young women are catching it.

Just as the thin Iron Maiden is not actually beautiful, anorexia, bulimia, even compulsive eating, symbolically understood, are not actually diseases. They *begin,* as Susie Orbach notes, as sane and mentally healthy responses to an insane social reality: that most women can feel good about themselves only in a state of permanent semistarvation. The anorexic refuses to let the official cycle master her: By starving, she masters it. A bulimic may recognize the madness of the hunger cult, its built-in defeat, its denial of pleasure. A mentally healthy person will resist having to choose between food and sexuality — sexuality being bought, today, by maintenance of the official body. By vomiting, she gets around the masochistic choice. Eating diseases are often interpreted as symptomatic of a neurotic need for control. But surely it is a sign of mental health to try to control something that is trying to control you, especially if you are a lone young woman and it is a massive industry fueled by the needs of an entire determined world order. Self-defense is the right plea when it comes to eating disasters; not insanity. Self-defense bears no stigma, whereas madness is a shame.

Victorian female hysteria, mysterious at the time, makes sense now that we see it in the light of the social pressures of sexual self-denial and incarceration in the home. Anorexia should be as simple to understand. What hysteria was to the nineteenth-century fetish of the asexual woman locked in the home, anorexia is to the late-twentieth-century fetish of the hungry woman.

Anorexia is spreading because it works. Not only does it solve the dilemma of the young woman faced with the hunger cult, it also protects her from street harassment and sexual coercion; construction workers leave walking skeletons alone. Having no fat means having no breasts, thighs, hips, or ass, which for once means not having asked for it. Women's magazines tell women they *can* control their bodies; but women's experiences of sexual harassment make them feel they *cannot* control what their bodies are said to provoke. Our culture gives a young woman only two dreams in which to imagine her body, like a coin with two faces: one pornographic, the other anorexic; the first for nighttime, the second for day — the one, supposedly, for men and the other for other women. She does not have the choice to refuse to toss it — nor, yet, to demand a better dream. The anorexic body is sexually safer to inhabit than the pornographic.

At the same time, it works for male-dominated institutions by processing women smoothly, unwomaned, into positions closer to power. It is "trickling down" to women of all social classes from elitist schools and universities because that is where women are getting too close to authority. There, it is emblematic of how hunger checkmates power in any woman's life: Hundreds of thousands of well-educated young women, living and studying at the fulcrum of cultural influence, are causing no trouble. The anorexic woman student, like the anti-Semitic Jew and the self-hating black, fits in. She is politically castrate, with exactly enough energy to do her schoolwork, neatly and completely, and to run around the indoor track in eternal circles. She has no energy to get angry or get organized, to chase sex, to yell through a bullhorn, asking for money for night buses or for women's studies programs or to know where all the women professors are. Administering a coed class half full of mentally anorexic women is an experience distinct from that of administering a class half full of healthy, confident young women. The woman in these women canceled out, it is closer to the administration of young men only, which was how things were comfortably managed before.

For women to stay at the official extreme of the weight spectrum requires 95 percent of us to infantilize or rigidify to some degree our mental lives. The beauty of thinness lies not in what it does to the body but to the mind, since *it is not female thinness that is prized, but female hunger, with thinness merely symptomatic.* Hunger attractively narrows the focus of a mind that has "let itself go." Babies cannot feed themselves; invalids and the orthodox require special diets. Dieting makes women think of ourselves as sick, religious babies. Only this new mystique could prove strong and deep-reaching enough to take on the work given up by domestic isolation and enforced chastity. "Natural" is a word that is rightly challenged. But if there is a most natural urge, it is to satisfy hunger. If there is a natural female shape, it is the one in which women are sexual and fertile and *not always thinking about it.* To maintain hunger where food is available, as Western women are doing, is to submit to a life state as unnatural as anything with which the species has come up yet. It is more bizarre than cannibalism.

Dieting is the essence of contemporary femininity. Denying oneself food is seen as good in a woman, bad in a man. For women, the Austin (Texas) Stress Clinic found, "dieting concern" was strongly related to "positive feminine traits"; for men, food restraint was related to "socially undesirable femininity." Where the feminine woman of the Feminine Mystique denied herself gratification in the world, the current successful and "mature" model of femininity submits to a life of self-denial in her body.

But this hallmark of enviable adjustment has as little innate validity as the earlier one. It too is based upon a vital lie. Where "immature" women in the 1950s wanted clitoral orgasms while "mature" ones passively yielded, today oral desire is interpreted in a similar sexual code. It is considered immature for women to eat heartily, since they're told they risk their sexuality; they are seen as mature if they starve, promised to win sexuality that way. In the 1970s, when clitoral pleasure was reclaimed, many women must have wondered how they had lived in an atmosphere that denied it. In the 1980s women were forced to deny their tongues and mouths and lips and bellies. In the 1990s, if women can reclaim the pleasure of appetite, we may wonder what possessed us during the long, mean, pointless years of hunger. Women's self-denial where food is concerned is represented today as good for her mate and even better for herself. Beyond the beauty myth, feminine hunger will look as obviously destructive to the well-being of women and their loved ones as their earlier enforced suffocation in the home looks to us from here.

Sex, food, and flesh; it is only political ideology — not health, not men's desires, not any law of loveliness — that keeps women from believing we can have all three. Young women believe what they have no memory to question, that they may not have sex, food, and flesh in any abundance; that those three terms cancel each other out.

◎ *BARBARA NOREEN DINNERSTEIN*

Barbara Noreen Dinnerstein was born in Newark, New Jersey in 1958. She is a Jewish lesbian writer "who happens to be deaf." She was living in San Francisco when she wrote "Bubbie, *Mommy, Weight Watchers and Me" in the 1980s.*

"Bubbie, *Mommy, Weight Watchers and Me," was included in Lesléa Newman's* Bubbe Meisehs by Shayneh Maidelahs: An Anthology of poetry by Jewish Granddaughters About Our Grandmothers" *(1989).* Bubbe Meisehs *translates as "grandmother stories," while* Shayneh Maidelahs *means "beautiful girls" — an affectionate term that bubbes would use toward their granddaughters. Other Yiddish and Hebrew words in this text translate as follows:* Shabbos *is the Sabbath,* hallah *is the traditional braided egg bread,* Zayde *is grandfather, and* mandle brot *and* lokshen kugel *mean almond cake and noodle pudding.* Mispochah *means family, including all relatives and ancestors,* Shaygetz *is an unflattering term for a non-Jewish man, and* knadles *are matzoh balls.*

Bubbie, *Mommy, Weight Watchers and Me*

The lady up in front was Rosalie, she used to be fat, *feh.* My mommy told me she was the lecture. I mean she showed us pictures of herself when she was fat. She told us to put a picture of ourselves on the 'fridgerator of us eating and looking really fat and ugly. She said remember what you look like. Remember how ugly you are. The picture Mommy picked out of me was one of me at *Bubbie*'s house.

It was *Rosh Hashana.* We were eating honey cake that *Bubbie* and I made. We spent the whole afternoon in the kitchen cooking and baking for when company came for *Shabbos. Bubbie* told me if she wanted to have a sweet New Year she had to eat sweet things, so she kept nibbling on my fingers. We baked a round *hallah* to hide under the towel for when *Zayde* came home. Then we would all sit at the big table and *Zayde* would say the prayers. *Bubbie,* Mommy and me would do the candles. Then we would eat. I even got to sneak a sip of my mom's wine.

In the picture I was sitting between *Bubbie* and Mommy. I don't think I looked ugly there, just happy. Why did she have to pick that picture to scotch tape on the refrigerator? My brother Leonard who always made fun of me saw that picture on the refrigerator. He drew a lot of flies all around me. Why did mom have to pick a picture of me at a time when I felt so warm and safe and let Leonard draw flies all around me?

Even things at *Bubbie*'s house changed. Mommy made *Bubbie* promise not to feed me anymore. No more egg creams, no more tea in a glass with a sugar cube between our teeth, no more *mandle brot* and no more *lokshen kugel* and no more honey cake. My *Bubbie* always told me I had the sweetest *tushy.* Rosalie called it your grotesque buttocks. My *tushy* didn't seem different to me, no matter what Rosalie called it.

Bubbie told me Rosalie used to be *mispochah* until she married "that *Shaygetz* Stanley." *Bubbie* told me Mommy was becoming too American. She said that Mommy was forgetting who her people were. I didn't understand, then. Mommy stopped calling me *knadle* and told *Bubbie* to speak English to me, no Yiddish. My *Bubbie* still called me her *shayneh maidel,* told me I had the best *tush* and still fed me. It became our secret.

Bubbie was proud, she'd say, "Never forget who you are, who your people are. You are from peasant stock, hardy, built to survive. We are not Americans, just like we were not Russians, we are travellers on a long road waiting to go home again. This diet stuff of your mother's is just another way to pretend we belong. Jews don't belong. Be proud, be strong, be who you are. Someday we will have a home, someday we will be able to look like Jews and be proud."

Next to my *Bubbie,* my Mommy was my best friend. Just like *Bubbie* and me, Mommy and I used to cook together and play together in the kitchen. She would tell me stories about growing up on the Lower East Side and about her *Bubbie* Bayla. I would tell her all my secrets and she would promise me they were safe. My Mommy made me laugh at her singing *Sunrise Sunset* and the *Boogie Woogie Bugle Boy* for the millionth time. She would dance all over the kitchen singing into the ladle like it was a microphone. Sometimes we laughed so hard we wet our pants.

When my Mommy lost all that weight, we stopped singing and talking and playing in the kitchen. She apologized to me for making me sick. I didn't understand what she meant. I thought all those things we did together were the best. She said she made me sick like her and that is why I had to go to Weight Watchers. She told me I had to think of the future, getting boyfriends and stuff. I didn't know how to tell her I didn't want boyfriends and stuff. I liked what we did.

To this day I don't understand what she was talking about, those moments with her were precious. I yearn for that time I spent in the kitchen with my mom and my *Bubbie,* warm and safe, braiding the *hallah,* mushing the *knadles,* licking the spoons, telling the secrets, making eat for the family, laughing and crying.

When my *Bubbie* died, before I threw my handful of dirt on her coffin to say goodbye, I promised her I would never forget who I am and where my people come from. I am proud to look the way I do. I am a strong proud Jewish woman from peasant stock.

◎ *HILDA RAZ*

Hilda Raz was born in Rochester, New York, and educated at Boston University. She has published two books of poetry, What Is Good *(1988) and* The Bone Dish *(1989), and her work has appeared in* Poetry After Modernism *(1991),* Touchstones: American Poets on a Favorite Poem, Poems for a Small Planet: Contemporary American Nature Poetry, The Scribners Book of American Nature Writing, The Confidence Woman, *and* The Whole Story: Editors on Fiction, *as well as in* Ploughshares *and many other journals. She is associate professor of English at the University of Nebraska, where she is editor of* Prairie Schooner, *now in its seventieth year of publication.*

"Junk" was published originally in The Confidence Woman *(essays, 1991). The essay tests the limits of language, and praises friendships without limits as well as marriage and doctors who know how to love. "Junk" shows us a writer's mind, a woman's mind, a human being at her most courageous and honest, and in this it resembles Winslow's "Born Again." Despite her justifiable anger at a society that gives so little money to research on breast cancer, the essay ends with a tone of renewal, not bitterness.*

Junk

What was it for if I cannot speak?

— CZESLAW MILOSZ

What is the source of our first suffering? It lies in the fact that we hesitated to speak. It was born in the moment when we accumulated silent things within us.

— GASTON BACHELARD

It is always what is under pressure in us, especially under pressure of concealment, that explodes in poetry.

— ADRIENNE RICH

> Question: You do keep a writer's notebook? Answer: I keep a notebook. . . . I keep everything in my notebook, though. I keep grocery lists in there. I try not to make it sacred. . . . Of course, it contains a lot of junk.
>
> — RITA DOVE TO STAN RUBIN, *The Post-Confessionals*

Junk: a word for the mess of confusing detail in our lives, as in (overheard), "I've got to make something out of this junk or get rid of it." Art: what we hope to make from our junk. Disguise: the boundary between junk and art.

* * *

This essay is an attempt to be faithful to some details of my life; to compact art with junk; to show how I press junk (process) into writing (product).

Credentials, or junk / product outline: two published books of poems; three marriages; twenty-seven publications in magazines; two children, one born with a hole near his heart; editor-in-chief of a major literary quarterly; child hurt in an auto accident; twenty-two residencies at universities and colleges. Father dead at fifty-seven, of cancer. Forty-seven public-school residencies. Mother and brother, suicides. Scholarships. Surgery. Fellowships. Cancer surgery. Boards of Directors and Boards of Governors. The societal privileges of education and job. The societal privations of being female.

The year I was born in Rochester, New York, Jewish kin in Europe were digging their graves or building shelters in attics of Gentile friends so they could, like Anne Frank (whose notebook Mother gave me on my fifteenth birthday), survive for a while in hiding. I grew up playing outdoors in the unfenced backyards of our neighbors, in summer stealing warm tomatoes and grass-chives from their gardens planted on the banks of the old Erie Canal bed. Trains ran at the bottom of these banks, and we crossed the tracks often — in winter tripping on hand-me-down ice skates, in summer juggling stick-and-string fishing poles. (Later the New York Interstate was built over the canal bed. Last summer I saw the concrete walls that keep eight lanes of traffic out of those backyards.) My mother knew I'd been stealing by the reek of onions on my breath; she monitored her children by pressing their bodies close. On my fourth birthday, my brother Jimmy, who was sixteen, left to fight with the infantry on the European front. Our parents had given permission. They believed he should fight *like heroes of old for our People.* Someone said these words at dinner. Also, he had graduated from high school and was too young for college. He left during my party. Our mother wept as she played "Happy Birthday" on the piano. She agreed with our father that he should go. His serial number was 12241744. Later his infantry division, the 42nd Blue and Grey, gave him a patch for his uniform, the figure of yin (blue) and yang (gray). Margo Cameron and Irene Wienans, Scots Presbyterian and Catholic respectively, my best friends and co-conspirators in vegetable crime, sorted birthday presents by shape and color and built a fortress. I am remembering as I write. No one then wrote anything down.

My first husband's Uncle Frank inherited a set of journals kept during a long lifetime by my first husband's grandfather, a sea captain. On our honeymoon we traveled to Beaufort, North Carolina, to claim the journals. Uncle Frank lived in an old house on the coast, and I, just eighteen, discovered both the southern beaches and the perils of inserting a diaphragm at night in an outhouse. The journals, ruined by rain, had been junked. My first husband was sad. For months before our wedding I had been reading in secret his grey board-bound journals to learn his mind. I supposed he had an equally passionate desire to discover the mind of his lost grandfather.

My brother came home when he was nineteen, refused a scholarship to MIT, and reclaimed his upstairs bedroom. He drove each day across town to the University of Rochester where he earned a B.S. and the Ph.D. in physics. He never talked or wrote about his experience of war. His letters from the front, lost now, had been descriptions of landscape. When he shot himself, he was forty. He knew he would never discover *even one building block of the universe.* Physics then was a young man's subject, so, at thirty-five, he became an academic dean. At the time of his death he was still consulting for Brookhaven and Argon National Laboratories, the only pacifist with Q clearance we knew. No one mentioned notebooks. Two years later our mother, frozen by Parkinson's disease, managed to drag a chair to the balcony of her apartment building, climb over the railing, jump, and die. Her junk was photo albums — pictures of Daddy robust and Daddy gaunt, two kids growing up, one photo of me balanced between Jimmy's arms on the handlebars of his huge bike, he was six-four, I'm smiling but I'm terrified, no pictures of my brother in uniform — and her clothes, household goods, and knitting. These things I brought to my house where they stay. If she kept notebooks, I missed them. Twelve poems hide my brother in my work. One, "Piecing," that begins "No woman in my family sews / but Nana jumped down a well / to save my mother, the sickly one / they say fell in . . . ," reaches for our mother.

In Janet Burroway's novel *Opening Nights* the male protagonist signals his emotional emancipation by hurling a tin box of his dead father's (a suicide) notebooks into the deep waters of a lake. These notebooks record every one of the increments of the deepening depression into which his father sank and drowned.

My first notebook, dated Thursday morning, October 4th, 1962, begins, "Mucus. No blood. Thursday night. Some effacement. Contractions mild, circa twenty seconds, *not* Braxton-Hicks." The child I produced is, for the moment, twenty-seven. His sister is twenty-four. I have not refrained from writing notebooks since, although only three of them begin with the body. When the children were small they begged me (or maybe I begged them, "listen to the part where you say *Batmaan;* listen to the part where you say "*My* do it!") to read out loud from my notebooks. We smiled over lists of their first words and snickered about my comments — at three months Sarah "flirts with her father." I blush as I write. Years of psychoanalysis in Boston have taught me less than the notebooks do when I have heart and stomach to read them. Gail Godwin says she annotates her notebooks. In recent years I have learned to annotate mine. They need comment. Some pages are nearly illegible, scrawled with left-hander's carelessness in the midst and haste of living. With luck, after my death, someone will care enough to browse through and find foolishness and cowardice — and the smarter commentary in the margins. The first notebook, called "John's," ends with this anecdote: his father, "John's dearest friend, was very angry last night when John refused to stop playing with the car's gearshift. He was taken up, finally, and put to bed in disgrace. All night he kept waking, yelling 'Daddy, Daddy, mad at Johnny our car switches.' He wouldn't be comforted. Next day, out for a drive, he said the whole story again. Car switches again and again. Daddy mad at Johnny."

Twenty years later the car John was driving, my car, slid into the gravel verge of the road to Surprise, Nebraska, flipped twice, and ripped open. John was not wearing a seat belt. A farmer found him, unconscious and not breathing, in the middle of a field. The rescue squad of Ulysses arrived just in time to put him on life support. A helicopter took him to the trauma center of Lincoln General Hospital, where, in the Intensive Care Unit, he lay still for a long time. When he woke up, he couldn't talk because he had a respirator tube in his throat. "Is this the worst from now on?" he managed to write days later on a pad of paper his father brought to the hospital. I framed the page. We're all — his father, his father's wife, his sister, his stepfather and I — all waiting to find out.

By thinking as if I were writing, I stayed far enough away from terror to help John live well through the months of his recovery. In plain fact, however, most of my words disappeared while I sat on a plane from Boston as an emergency passenger returning from an abbreviated vacation in Maine. I waited patiently to land while my nouns — son, heart, blood, spine — dissolved. Or maybe they left to provide space in my throat for air. By the time I reached Intensive Care, John's fat breathing tube had taken all the room in his throat, and I had nothing to say.

All language builds from silence: I listened hard in order to have something to write down — for his sake, for his sister's, for people still breathing in the world — so urgent was my need to catch what happened while I sat by John's bed holding his foot. The hiss of the respirator. Then I heard static on the car radio that seemed attached to the stoplights, interruptions of landscape I steered my borrowed car through to get to him each day. The arch-shaped tunnel the car cut in the August heat became a sound of tires pushing through asphalt on the way to the hospital, some hiss burned in air. The motor sound I pushed my foot and turned my wrists to meet. The elevator. The waiting room. Noise and its interruption. I had the call to bear witness to a world turned perfectly strange. *What Is Good*, my first book, draws its life from that call. Who can retrieve language? Who cares to? I was sitting up, lying down, waiting by the side of a body whose shape was familiar and strange, strange. My son without his words, with only the rise and fall of his chest, the vertical traces of the monitoring machines, the clicks and sighs as the pumps sucked out and pushed in air and fluid, into and out of his long body. I couldn't gather him up. He is six-four. The mechanical umbilicus was blue and inflexible. I must have remembered the other time he was attached to machines. He had been a child, his chest opened and closed with hundreds of stitches from surgery to mend his heart. Then I had no notebook. A nurse put her hands behind his small head, pulled him to a sitting position inside a plastic tent. I stood by the foot of that bed watching his eyes open, close. Tubes everywhere. "What is it *for* if I cannot speak?" Milosz asked in the silence. As I write these words, I think of the movie *Alien* and the genius that put together a monster from our worst fears for our bodies: loss of integrity of the chest wall, all boundaries of the body, and the loss of breath.

Everyone else in Intensive Care died. John talked without pause for three days after he was taken off the respirator, but it was music he wrote during his long recovery. He wrote down his first music. I cooked, served, worked, read aloud. I wrote a notebook that hid a book of poems. I wrote in order to give myself away. But of course you can't give yourself away, except to yourself, some exhausted body you'll become. Then you'll be glad you put up the tomatoes, froze the snips of chives, wrote down *some* version of what happened. Later you can sit in the sun on the retaining wall, built after the basement flooded, and feel the warm sheet over your cheekbones. You can read your own crabbed handwriting. Long before the accident, the children's father left our house. Later, when they were grown, the children left.

The notebook I write now says "Cancer" on its beige cover. A woman at work suggested I write about breast cancer because so many women have it. A man I know said, "Don't." A friend in New York told me in her tinny long-distance voice what her friend Diana Trilling said — don't write after illness. Wait. Is writing like acting-out? I can't wait.

"Yet why not say what happened?"— Robert Lowell was a famous man writing the poems in *Life Studies* in 1957 when he taught students at Boston University a different way to write poems. Anne Sexton and Sylvia Plath learned to loosen their tongues in his workshop and to loosen their poems. My father was dying. My English teacher was courting me, and I was sloughing off Arnie Gordon and Jerry Bufano, high-school boyfriends, in favor of an older man. I kept no notebook but I read one, my English teacher's — in secret, for love. As a member of Lowell's workshop I wrote a lot of poems; he thought my love lyrics were prayers to the sun. My English teacher gave me *A* after *A* for prose poems instead of papers, transferred me out of his Freshman Composition class, and proposed marriage with an old mine-cut diamond ring in a gum paper he tucked into my fist at the supermarket on Valentine's Day after I said I preferred my dormitory to his cold apartment. Boston. My coat was gray suede lined with a fur that smelled funny in wet weather, called mouton. Sheep.

Six months ago I gave up my breast to a surgeon in Lincoln, Nebraska, in order to live. Or so I believe, knowing full well research may show the sacrifice futile. One woman in nine has breast cancer. In one year more people die of breast cancer than have perished from AIDS since that epidemic began.

Research money is minimal when it's available. The National Cancer Institute budget increase for 1990 is less than the rate of inflation. True facts: My cancer measured three millimeters; was discovered in a routine mammogram, no lump to feel, would have taken two years to become a palpable lump; demonstrates the usefulness of mammography in saving women's lives. Or so I've been told. I've also been told early diagnosis prolongs life because the diagnosis is made two years earlier. Eight months ago an anthology of poems on the subject of breast cancer came to my office for review. I was flummoxed, poor innocent. Already some women have written poems about breast cancer. Some women editors have published them. Helene Davis's *Chemo-Poet* (Alice James Books) was published first in *Prairie Schooner,* the magazine I edit, because the poems are smart, funny and bitter, good work.

During my long recovery — surprise — I lost my language. Weakened by surgery the previous year, I had not regained strength after breast surgery when, a week out of the hospital, my running shoe caught a nail on the gazebo stair at the university arboretum and pitched me down. Poor ankle, how we hated your black and blue, your refusal to support me through deep trouble, your banal pain — harsher than my dramatic incision's. Too weak to walk the length of the house, too sad to read, no words to speak into the telephone, I managed twice a day to drag myself with the help of a walker to a car to drive it, blessed extension of my poor body, to a local coffee-house where I wrote page after page in my beige notebook — nonsense, junk about garbage, all modifiers and invective. Yards of bloody bandage.

Not long ago the poetry editor of a national magazine sent a card asking to see recent work. I sent off notebook-poems — fractured syntax and fury — and one formal poem written as thanks to a colleague who never allowed ten days to pass without a gift of books, flowers, bread from her kitchen, an hour's visit, a long, slow walk by my side. Her most recent gift is a green stone in the shape of a triangle she picked up from the ocean floor during a kayaking trip to Baja. I don't know about kayaking. But the strength in her arms I stretch for on my rowing machine each day. Her legs pump me along our city streets at a good clip now, faster than — really, really — I can go. I have so little strength. Words practiced in the notebook gave the shape of the stone to the poem. I gave her a copy she must have left on her dining room table. How many people gather at her table? Five people have mentioned the poem to me. Vanessa Bell's dining room table was painted to look like a breast, nurture for family, her sister Virginia Woolf and their friends: Bloomsbury.

I have lost a breast, and all the organs we carry inside our bodies to be called female, and before that, two families. To write these words I excavate some dump filled long ago. Soon I will begin to exercise for days of water kayaking with a friend from our shared youth. She has had the same hard diagnosis (her mother died from breast cancer), but she is strong and wiry, and together we hope to see the ocean that gave up the green stone. To convince her, I had to write about kayaks, women with bare breasts, strong arms, waves, a poem in the shape of the green stone.

Of George Sand's *Journal to Musset* Marie Jenney Howe wrote in 1928, "When George Sand was normal she did her work. Whenever she lost her poise she wrote a journal. . . . When her emotions upset her life she got rid of them in writing, and these outpourings testify how much inner rebellion the tremendous personality which was George Sand had to contend with, in order to do a man's work in the world." We know better now. We know inner rebellion is necessary for women to do any work in the world, and George Sand's work is women's work. These journals hold my attention. They chronicle a sexual obsession. Certainly the prose is fervid. How else should it be? It is her wit that is surprising. In the midst of suffering, "I lived through long weeks of terror and trembling," she writes. "I could not die, because we do not die of anguish, we live on. We continue to suffer.

"Then there is jealousy. . . . He spoke so admiringly of a certain woman that I would willingly have done her harm. That is as ugly as it is stupid. . . . May that woman aid him and console him, may she teach him to believe in love. . . . Alfred, I am going to write a book."

The notebook I write and glean for books make no distinction between junk and art. Next to a published poem, written here in ink with erasure and ellipses and recopied onto the facing page, is another better one — as yet untouched, uncopied, unrevised, waiting for my next dig. Nights of illness or pain are filled with silence I can't break, not even by bringing my pen to rest on the paper in my lap. "Darling, make a *list*," my mother says to me in her voice I no longer quite remember. "What is bad — this spasm, that stricture, the sound of our front door on its brass hinges — will stop only with your death. Too bad. Child, what is good? Make a list. Do it now. Death will wait." I do it.

Blessed mind. Often it offers the perfectly intact embroidered bathrobe with the worn-out part-synthetic slippers. I can remember, yes, yes, the first shower after childbirth, after surgery, the first shower after illness. I remember the outdoor shower at the beach cottage we rented one summer. We stood our children naked under that spigot and washed and washed sand from their tough brown bodies. Then we drank wine. What is good returns to you, a gift.

This spring is cold, too chilly to put out geraniums and begonia and fern. The plants in their peat coverings wait on the kitchen table blooming and blooming between pots of parsley, bleeding heart, lavender, and artemisia arboretum. Only the clematis is in the ground, better able to bear cold earth. Let it be safe from the rabbits. It's my birthday, I give myself the same gift this year as last, a week in the public schools with children who write down their hearts' news. This year I am driving back and forth in the strong car through the early spring countryside in order to spend each night with my husband. Other years I have spent my birthday evening in basement guest rooms of cordial strangers. One year in Milligan, Nebraska, I ate birthday dinner alone, a non-paying guest of the diner owner, who served me beef testicles, called prairie oysters. Gritty, tough, they were good. One year I read Joanna Russ's *How to Suppress Women's Writing.* That basement room was filled with the residue of four athletic sons, all grown and gone off. To get to the bathroom I had to straddle a fortress of football pads.

What does writing have to do with living? I earn my wages as an editor by reading stories and poems written from your lives, pockets of bacteria, art made from junk. A famous poet came to our university to interview for a job. When asked why she writes, she lifted her left arm, index finger extended, to her temple and said, "Bang."

"To keep from silence," she said.

When I was a young woman, I worked for the Planned Parenthood League of Massachusetts. I worked to pay for psychoanalysis. Each salary check I endorsed to Dr. Fineman, a student at the Boston Psychoanalytic Institute. I was on scholarship, reduced rates. Five days a week for the famous fifty-minute hour, for three years, I lay on his couch and spoke my mind, some junk. He rarely spoke; once he said, "Be careful. You're very angry." I went home and before the night was over I tore the curtains from the windows and began to write. Then I gave birth to a son. The Board of Directors of Planned Parenthood gave me a gift, a pair of red cashmere pants, size six. The child I delivered weighed almost nine pounds. After John's birth I was very sad and wanted to return him to Bonwit Teller with the pants. During the years before his birth, Planned Parenthood had helped repeal the blue laws in Massachusetts that made prescribing birth control illegal. We opened research clinics in order to provide the new birth control pill free to indigent women. Pregnant, primiparous, paid, and by now with the title Assistant Director, I counselled pregnant women. They were multiparous, often carrying their tenth, eleventh, twelfth child.

Years later, on vacation from my second marriage, I spent a couple of days with the man who became my third husband. I never turned a hair when my second husband sued my third husband for alienation of affections, with penalties of jail and/or $*100,000.* My third husband worked then for a bike shop. We learned my value was above rubies, maybe one ruby. But I am confusing junk and art. I was upset and confused. The evidence used in court was my notebook.

Today I record these birthday gifts — I have no choice — in the order in which they come:

— Sarah calls from Wisconsin to say that the Sora Rail is a bird, brown on top, grey underneath with a grey bib, the size of a fat grackle, whose habit it is to walk around in places anywhere grasses grow tall enough to cover its head. I imagine Sarah, who is shy, a museum preparator, walking everywhere in the world grass grows tall enough to hide her perfect face, her brilliant head, her strong and elegant body.

— I drop an earring on the kitchen floor and, in the blur, find it without my eyeglasses — there, sharp under my palm, first try as I fall to my knees.

— A possum crossing Highway 6, the first one I've seen alive although plenty of dead ones stick to these country roads.

— A meadowlark flying at the verge of the highway trailing six feet of bark ribbon.

— Five days teaching in the schools well finished, my first residency since surgery.

— A bird's nest (a warbler's?) the size of a teacup, on the sidewalk under the flowering redbud tree. I find it on my way to the mailbox. No eggs in it, or nearby — I looked.

— In the mailbox a package from Sarah, an iron wind-bell in the shape of a bird exactly the size to fit the nest.

— A three-inch blossom on the hibiscus I cut back to nubbins two days ago in an angry fit.

These days I am very angry. Nebraska's tornado winds have nothing on me. I cut up a pair of shorts with long, left-handed scissors, hide the shreds in the garbage. Exhausted from pruning back the old juniper hedges — branches as large around as my wrist — after what Mother called "a nice rest and a cup of tea," I attack the page. God knows what I write down. My dearest writer friend says she has begun again to keep a notebook. I ask if she confides to her pages the fury she feels as she ends her marriage of twenty-five years, cleans out their family junk. "Yes," she says. Oh friend, dig with your hair flying. "I would like to bury all the hating eyes," wrote Anne Sexton.

The porch swing of the warblers. John calls me on Tuesday to say Happy Mother's Day. I tell him about eight warblers, now, as we speak, in the birch tree, leaping at each other, waving their wings, shaking clouds of yellow pollen from the branch tips outside my third-floor office window, the dangly blossoms like earrings, all that roiling moving the room like a ship slipped from its moorings. "The porch swing of the warblers," John says from New York City. "I'm sorry I said you should come home to visit when I'm well, not wait until you feel guilty when I'm sick," I whisper. "I'm sorry I yelled at you on your birthday for never answering the phone," he whispers back. His new quintet is finished. The premiere performance is Sunday.

Andrews Hall has bugs everywhere, tiny black, long-bodied bugs with wings. Sarah would know what to call them. When the exterminator comes, I stay home.

For months I disconnect the telephone by our bed, I have nothing to say. I can push my fingers over these keys to make words. My fingers know words that have nothing to do with poison, with my cold breast, with either junk or art. They are false facts, pure disguise. You come into my office wearing your white shorts. You carry a canister with a long wand. Where bugs jump on the windowsills you place a puff of spray. A young woman with floating hair stops you with a hand on your shoulder. You lower your cheek to her hand, poor cheek of poison. You give her an apple. She takes a bite, puts the red shoulder of the apple down in a dish of paperclips on my desk. See, I am not here. I am home in bed recovering from cancer. I am letting my hair grow floaty.

You are recovering from surgery. Lucky, the doctor says, you are lucky I've given you back perfect shoulders, unscarred armpits. In the hospital for four days you lie in sun from your window, topless but for the wide ace bandage over the paper dressing like a strapless top, a good contrast with cotton shorts like men's underwear the hospital provides. Forties chic. You toast in the sun admiring your perfect shoulders, your unblemished, sweet armpit. I can almost lift my arm. I look like a girl at the beach.

Can you write during the days of recovering? You know the answer. My heart is empty. How will you fix the junk of recovery?

The fingers of the rain are tapping again.
I send out my heart's drum.
Blood stripe on the feathered tulip dissolves into wet.
All night a low thrumming.

Up, up the two-toned hosta
green from sopped earth.
Along your bruised ribs, cream bells.
Title? Recovery.

Watching TV together Easter Sunday with my husband's family, we see a story about a family of Jews kept hidden for two years in a basement hole not much deeper than a grave. Food lowered, their shit raised up, newspapers provided by the housewife who, never having read or bought newspapers for her family, asked the butcher to use newspaper to wrap fish — so clever she was with her own five children to save, and her life, and her husband's life — all lost if she were discovered. The man she rescued as a boy says to the interviewer, "She is not an ordinary person. Which ordinary person would risk the lives of her five children? Not *me*. Maybe my own life. Not an ordinary person. A saint." Yet she was ordinary, as maybe my husband's family would be ordinary, as maybe he is ordinary staying with me through such trouble. No one in the living room speaks. Do they notice me? My husband rarely speaks. He keeps no notebook.

Feminist psychologist Carol Gilligan writes about the female sense of ethical boundaries as fluid, our judgments made in the best interests of community, a sense women have of an extended self. Marcia Southwick describes physical boundaries that seem damaged by passion, a sense of self made liquid and vulnerable, in her poem "The Rain's Marriage":

> *Once,*
> *I was certain of the boundaries between my body*
> *and whatever it touched, as if*
> *touch itself were a way of defining exactly where* I
> *stopped*
> *and the rest of the world began.*
> *Then I lost the sense that I was hemmed in*
> *by skin. My body felt like something loaned to me —*
> *it might break, or dissolve to ashes,*
> *leaving me stranded*
> *. . . like rain falling into any shape that accepts*
> *it. . . .*

Art critic Arthur Danto attacks the "invidious distinction between the fine and the (merely) decorative arts . . . [and] so many divisions both hidden and obvious that define our attitudes toward the things of life" in his essay on "Furniture as Art" published in the *Nation* (23 April 1990). The collapsing of boundaries has become one tenet of a feminist aesthetic as well as a directive for formal experiment. Even the boundaries between the work of individual artists are being challenged by collaborators, Sandra Gilbert and Susan Gubar as critics; Gilbert and George as performance and visual artists; Judith Guest and Rebecca Hill as fiction writers; Olga Broumas and Jane Miller in *Black Holes, Black Stockings*, a book of poems; Tess Gallagher and Raymond Carver, poets and writers of fiction, at work together on his final book of poems.

Rita Dove says she tries not to think about what she's doing when she's writing in her notebook. I imagine she wants her life to dissolve into her work like a lozenge, life melting slowly into poem into drama into fiction. Where do we make the boundaries between life and art? The formal boundaries between notebook and essay and poem? Between anecdote and fictional or historical narrative? Where does sensation in my body leave off and the orgasm of my work begin? What artistic implications attend the alteration of the body's boundaries? What if my silhouette changes in a flash, two hours' time, fifteen minutes, nine months? What happens to my work if I lose, or seem to lose, parts of my body? If I am delivered of a child? How do we say the unspeakable? Millions murdered. Paralysis. How to cut through the anesthetic fog to the blade about its work?

During the biopsy I was awake, my head close to the laser scalpel, its smell of bitter smoke and flesh. A nurse held my hand. The tall surgeon tucked his tie into his shirt, military fashion, before we began. My brother at his ease was eating tsimmis, on leave in my memory. We were not on leave, that family of nurse, surgeon, and patient. Headphones fed me, slowly, slowly, the music my husband put on tape for the occasion. The surgeon nervous because I am not asleep. Let me know if I hurt you. You never hurt me.

From my journal: "At the video store tonight I see the man who took my breast and his wife. They are . . . friendly, yes, friendly, like peers. She calls me by name and when I look puzzled says her name, a well-known name in this state. In a separate part of the store he finds me alone, bends to me and asks, *sotto voce,* how I'm doing. I say I'm on my pins, back in the office, didn't teach my graduate seminar. He looks worried, says keep in touch. Let me know how you're doing. I come away in pain as from a meeting with an old lover after damage has been done. All evening I hurt. What in our lives as women has made us into actors in a single, reiterated drama of pain, loss, pain, and witness? Today I see my husband's body turn instantly to a woman he cares for, a woman who works with him, when she cries out in pain (a caught finger, pinched, and a broken nail). Everything in him reacts protectively. He checks his impulse to hurry but bends to her and trims off her nail as I leave the room. Natural enough. Just so did the surgeon bend to me two months ago. A big, handsome man, thin and cheerful. As he bends to me tonight — how *am* I? How I am: mixed, thank you for asking. Less pain. Less sadness. And you, Doctor Surgeon, who made my ribs ache and broke my skin and sewed it into the neat scar that crosses my chest like John's, how can I thank you who opened my body? 'Better, better,' I say. We discuss the vision of Bertolucci, the aroma of Kona coffee."

LeAnn and I have worked in the same office for two decades. She tells me today is Nicholas's ninth birthday. He insists on the same story again this year, how she lumbered to the garden to plant — "Tell me *what* you planted" — peas, green beans, lettuce — and then she had to stop, and then he was born. He wore a cap to keep his small head warm. "And then the garden froze?" he says every year at this point in the story. "Yes," LeAnn says. "And then we had to plant again after I came home?" "Yes," says LeAnn, "lettuce, peas, green beans, tomatoes, parsley, garlic, potatoes."

The catalogue is everywhere — book reviews, essays, poems — names Adam gave the things of the world to push down against silence. Sometimes silence seems female, Eve's way, her resistance to Adam's naming. My poem "She Speaks" tries to deconstruct the earth's labels, to return them to silence.

Fire in a house of women who have renounced their names becomes "an orange / presence in a circle of stones, / now like the sun, now the moon, / now flickering, now pausing, now going — soundlessly — up." Prolix, inefficient babble? When silence pushes hard I make my mother's list: possum, tulip, rain, uniform, bell, bandage, chive, tomato, blade — *house, bridge, fountain, gate* (Rilke *via* Maxine Kumin). "Was there a way of naming things that would not invent names, but mean names without naming them?" asked Gertrude Stein in "Poetry and Grammar," *Writings and Lectures 1909–1945*. This exactly is what I try.

I went dark before surgery holding my husband's hand. I woke up holding his hand. For six months, every night I hold myself against my husband's side and fall asleep. Every morning I place my palm against his palm before getting up. For six months, every step I take away from him is painful, pure terror. He is my anchor in this world that sweeps overboard families, children, my work, my body. I am crazy. These random entries from my notebook: "New Year's Eve, Sarah takes me by the hand to climb to the roof of State Security Savings Building where, under a giant bronze eagle, we see fireworks at midnight. We two. On the drive home in her car, she promises never, never to desert me. I feel bad. I go for a walk. John comes to me. I hold his arm. I am happy to be alive in this world. To sleep with Dale, whose flesh is warm. He clowns with his guitar and earphones and talks young. To see my strong children, alive, adult. To have shelter, food, a job. To have a new breast. To be literate. To see and hear, taste, smell, to touch. I have no control over any of the people I love. None. Over the future, theirs or mine. Tomorrow: rise, bathe, exercise. Who knows the rest?"

> A poem begins as a lump in the throat, a sense of wrong, a homesickness, a lovesickness. It is never a thought to begin with.
>
> — ROBERT FROST *in a letter to Louis Untermeyer, 1916*

Anthology means garland. A garland of poems by different authors. *Her Soul Beneath the Bone: Women's Poetry on Breast Cancer*, edited by Leatrice H. Lifshitz, published by the University of Illinois Press. These women have done the work. I have been well for weeks. In all tests no distant cancer has been found. The prognosis is excellent. My attention turns from my body, from my writing, from my works, from myself, back where it belongs: to you, your body, your writing, your work. This morning from the radio the voice of Ursula Hegi reading from her new book. Ursula Hegi at Bread Loaf, John Irving's Fellowship student. I am a visiting editor, here for the panel. It is raining. She comes to me to shout over the music in the Barn. We talk about her writing, mine, our children, about divorce, work. I ask her to send stories to my magazine. She does and we publish one. Now she is speaking on National Public Radio from Seattle, and in Lincoln, Nebraska, I am lying awake in the early morning light, listening to her story, my arms crossed over my old breast, my new breast.

From the notebook, 16 March, four months after surgery:

First the jaw goes, teeth and all
hinges, intricate slivers of bone.
Then silence. Then the brain pan
opens its lid, falls over
with the velocity of a hard-pitch
baseball, spit everywhere. Then nose
in comic relief pops off, a sound
like old bubblegum. What's left?
Light on trees, on sidewalks. Magnolia.

Into the null that clay head cries,
huge skull forced back against
scream's lift, pulled from the void
by Sarah's hands. It rests between glass shelves
on a bronze collar, jagged edges cut to hide
the scar from neck wrenched
out of gray earth; no torso, only sob
out of the gape of this head's loud mouth, and mine.

I conjure comfort with a table set with pottery
bowls, each open like my cupped hands for her
newborn head,
tomatoes resting there,
chives the color of amaryllis skin before the bud
breaks open, round bread,
and soup from cabbage and potatoes,
most homely food to nourish me
and a friend, mother of daughters both.
A spring feast. All I can do.

Six months after surgery to the day I return to my office and find it good. Twenty years of my work, often paid at minimum wage, seldom paid for hours I gave over to read manuscripts, have given me a title on my door: *EDITOR, PRAIRIE SCHOONER.* The door opens to my key. Light through the clean windows. The birch tree's flower earrings are hidden now by leaves. Manuscripts fill every bin in the library we keep for graduate students. My desk is covered with paper, stories to accept, reviews, poems, the living word. Your words, your junk and what you have made of it, make a shield in my mind. My life fades as yours grows vivid. Be here for me, writers. I sit at my desk and wait for your art.

◎ *SYLVIA WATANABE*

Sylvia Watanabe was born in 1952 on the Hawaiian island of Maui and now lives in Grand Rapids, Michigan. She earned a B.A. from the University of Hawaii and an M.A. from SUNY Binghamton. Awards for her work include a Japanese American Citizens League National Literary Award, a fellowship from the National Endowment for the Arts, and the O. Henry Award. Her first collection of stories, Talking to the Dead *(1992), was nominated for the PEN Faulkner Award. She is currently working on a novel.*

"Where People Know Me" first appeared in Between Friends: Writing Women Celebrate Friendship *(1994), edited by Mickey Pearlman. In an interview (see page 403), Watanabe discusses the deaths of her mother and her two grandmothers, saying, "I think that whenever a person loses someone who has been central to her development, in the way that these three women were to mine, it is almost as if some deep process of change begins to happen — to accommodate that loss. Maybe, like planting up the empty spaces in a garden, one begins turning physical absence into words."*

Where People Know Me

Late at night, long after the other residents in the senior care facility have gone to sleep, Big Grandma is wakeful. She cruises the hallways of the fourth floor wing in her electric wheelchair, making occasional forays — when the night staff at the nurses' station is not watchful — into the forbidden region of the elevators. On one occasion, she made it down to the ground floor, where security finally caught up to her, headed out the lobby doors, toward the parking lot. When they asked where she was going, she answered, in Japanese, "Where people know me."

This is what the Japanese-speaking night nurse reported to Aunt Tee, my mother's oldest sister, who tells my mother, who calls long-distance from Honolulu to tell me. Meanwhile, Aunt Tee has gotten in touch with Aunt Emma, now the second oldest since Aunt Dorothy's passing, and Emma is offended at not being notified — as "age etiquette" dictates — before my mother who is youngest, even though she, that is, Emma, hasn't spoken to Grandmother in years. Emma then complains to Dorothy's daughter who gets back to Tee's daughter who tells her mother, who phones my mother again and claims the whole thing is making it so she can't sleep nights. "You're the trained social worker," Aunt Tee says. "Why is Mama doing this to me?" It takes days more of burning up the city phone lines before family peace is restored. For a long time, this is what it meant to me to live in a place where people know you.

Here in Grand Rapids we've been having a week of record cold when my mother's call comes. The day's high was ten degrees, and the mercury's dropping as darkness falls. "You probably don't get many attempted escapes from the senior home there," my mother observes.

This is one of our private afternoon conversations, when Dad has gone to a meeting of his retirees' union and she has the house to herself. I can hear "Days of Our Lives" playing on the television in the background. The first time she called like this it was a few months after I left the Islands, nearly ten years ago. But even now I am obliged to remind her, out of the thriftiness she has taught me, that she is phoning long-distance in the middle of the day. I still relish that thrill of stolen pleasure when she replies, "Oh never mind," as if we are old girlfriends settling in for a good chat.

After the family news, she gives me the rundown on her Birthday Girls Lunch Club, her arthritis exercise group, and her General Electric cooking class. The cooking class, which has adopted the motto, "Encounter the good tastes of American cuisine," has moved on from ethnic desserts to ethnic salads. I am relieved to hear this since my waistline cannot tolerate many more encounters with the good tastes of Turkish baklava or Hungarian chocolate rum torte, which have been arriving with regularity by two-day priority mail.

It is hard to believe, laughing with her, that she's recently had cancer surgery. My father and I, who are much less resilient, are still recovering from the scare of almost losing her. But the doctors found the tumor early, and after a few months of recuperation, Mother has resumed her full social calendar. "It's like calling the sickness back to keep talking about it," she finally tells me, exasperated with being cross-examined about her latest medical checkup.

Now, before going off to prepare one of her ethnic desserts for a housewarming party, she fills me in on the neighborhood news. The Blums' divorced son has moved back in with them. The Shigetas are traveling in India. The ugly Labrador retriever puppy next door has turned out to be a rottweiler. "I know you're very busy," she segues, and before she says another word I know that someone will be requiring birthday greetings, congratulations, or get-well wishes.

After we hang up, I sit in my darkening kitchen and watch the lights come on in the surrounding houses. It occurs to me that it's been days since I've seen any of the people who live in them. I think of the old man who stopped by one afternoon the previous summer, while my husband, Bill, and I were unloading groceries from the car. As we exchanged pleasantries, it was clear that the man had something on his mind. "By the way, you didn't happen to be around this time a couple of days ago, did you?" he finally inquired. All around us, our neighbor's air conditioners were humming and their houses were tightly shuttered against the heat. Bill said he did not recall, then asked why. The man explained that his wife had been out walking alone when she'd fallen on the sidewalk across from our house. "Broke her wrist clean through," he continued. "And no one saw or heard a thing." After he'd gone, we realized that neither of us had caught his name.

This incident is still on my mind the next time I speak with my mother. "We'd have helped that woman if we'd seen her," I begin.

"Of course you would've," Mother answers.

"It's just that everyone around here keeps to themselves," I say. "Not like it is back home with everybody in each other's business. I can never work when I'm at home."

"I bet you get a lot of work done there." Her reply is without irony. "What are you writing now?"

I can't help laughing then. "Oh, about what it's like back home."

My next visit to the Islands is in late May, a few months after Big Grandma's near-escape. As soon as we arrive at my parents' house and unload the car, my mother starts reminding me to call people. "Don't forget to get in touch with Aunt Tee," she says. "And Aunt Emma — you know how she is. And your dad's sister Winnie has been phoning every day for a week . . . "

The following morning we drop by Emma's on our way to pick up Aunt Tee, who is going with us to visit Big Grandma. My mother worries about Emma, who has turned more and more reclusive in the last several years, since her husband died and her daughter has moved off the island. My aunt has developed a fear of prowlers, so she keeps all her windows fastened and her curtains drawn, even during the day. From the outside, it is impossible to tell that anyone is home, but my mother assures me that Emma hardly ventures out, unless accompanied either by herself or Tee. Aunt Emma has also had a locksmith install a deadbolt and a couple of additional locks on the living room door, and we can hear her undoing these as we stand on the front stoop, in the drizzle, with our cardboard boxes of homemade food.

After she lets us in, she disappears into the kitchen with the boxes, while we make our way through the stacks of newspapers and magazines lining the dim foyer to the cluttered living room. A reading lamp glows on the end table next to the couch and a game show is playing on TV.

"Oh, 'Hollywood Squares,'" my mother says. "I watch that sometimes."

"I never do. I just keep the sound on for the company." Aunt Emma has materialized in the doorway. Her gaunt face is framed by stiff gray curls, and she is wearing a pants outfit of bluish gray.

When we leave, we invite her to come with us, but she declines, as she always does. "You were always the favorite," she tells my mother. "Mama would never know that I was there."

* * *

The senior care facility, where Big Grandma is staying, occupies an entire wing of what was formerly called the Japanese Hospital and has now become one of the largest medical centers in the Islands. It was in the Japanese Hospital that my grandmother watched her twelve-year-old son, Masahiro, die of septicemia more than seventy years before. It is in another wing of the same hospital that my mother was operated on for pancreatic cancer.

As she, Aunt Tee, and I step out of the elevators, my aunt explains that the night staff has tried using medication, even physical restraint, to curtail Big Grandma's nocturnal activities. They have yet to overcome her determined resistance, which includes occasional episodes of biting. "They have confiscated her dentures," Aunt Tee says, barely able to contain her mortification. Now, if you bring any edibles for Big Grandma, you must go to the nurses' station and ask for her teeth. My aunt stops there to do so now, and also to drop off the loaves of mango bread she has baked. "Penance food," my mother whispers, as Aunt Tee distributes mango bread and expresses our thanks and apologies all around.

Big Grandma is sitting up in bed, dozing or pretending to doze, when we arrive at her room. Someone has dressed her in a baby-blue duster trimmed with lace, and braided her white hair with pink and yellow ribbons. It is a new look for my one-hundred-eight-year-old grandmother.

"Isn't that nice?" Aunt Tee says too brightly.

"Easter egg colors," my mother adds. They both have the same fixed smile on their faces — the same smile, I suddenly realize that is on mine. As we stand grimacing at my grandmother, I resist the impulse to reach over and pull the ribbons from her hair.

Big Grandma opens her eyes and lies back on the pillows, looking us over. Seeing that she has wakened, Mother gestures at me to approach, then says, "Look, look who's come to see you all the way from Michigan."

Big Grandma regards me blankly.

"It's Sylvia," my mother persists. "From Michigan."

"Where?" Big Grandma asks, turning her good ear toward us.

"Mee-shee-gen," Mother repeats, louder.

"Ah," Big Grandma replies. She glances around the room, then back at me, comprehension dawning on her face. "I was wondering where this was."

In my memory, she is always dressed in midnight blue. She wears black *tabis* and straw slippers on her feet. Her hair is neatly oiled and pulled away from her face into a knot that is held in place with brown plastic combs.

Her sense of fashion, if one could call it that, was not guided by vanity but by what she thought appropriate to who she was. Even in very early photographs, she wore dark colors, muted pinstripes and inconspicuous floral

prints, though the kimonos were eventually replaced by mama-san shifts with high collars and elbow-length sleeves. She seems always to have thought of herself as old. This is not to say that she was resigned to aging; for her it was not a process of defeat. She told me once, "You can't be freed until you're old. After I came to Hawaii, there were so many young men looking for a wife, I married your grandfather to get away from them. We had a good life. Then he died. Someone else wanted to marry me, but I'd already had one husband. I didn't need another."

It seemed curious to me that she should speak of freedom with such spirit, when she had more rules than anyone I ever knew. She had rules for what colors and styles to wear, and rules for when you took a bath or were served dinner (the oldest and youngest, which meant she and I, were always first), and rules for eating at table (take less than your fill, never leave a single grain of rice in your bowl, refuse the last piece of chicken). I recall, when I was six or seven, being seated at the dining table and instructed in the proper use of chopsticks. After she'd showed me how to hold them (thumb on the bottom, middle finger between, index finger on top), I was handed the pair and a bowl of Rice Krispies, then told to pick out the grains of cereal, one by one.

Big Grandma also had rules she never expected anyone else to follow, like her strict diet and exercise regimen, invented by a doctor in Japan. The diet, which allowed fish but no meat and touted the curative properties of icicle radishes, was taken in five small meals a day. The exercise regimen consisted of twenty repetitions each of thirty-seven different routines — including ones for every major organ in your body. Each morning, Big Grandma woke at five, performed her exercises, ate her first small meal of the day, and was out puttering around the yard by six. She took a half-hour nap after her midday meal, spent the afternoon on her quilting, and had her bath at four. In the evening, she performed her waking routing in reverse and was in bed before nine. On Saturdays she attended matinees at the Japanese movie theater in Chinatown, and on Sundays spent the morning at the Buddhist temple. From day to day there were small variations in her routine, but in general this was how she lived from as far back as I could remember, until she lost the use of her legs when she was past one hundred.

As a young child, until I was old enough to begin school, I spent a great deal of time in Big Grandma's company. Every weekday before work, my mother dropped me off at Aunt Tee's house, where my grandmother lived. By the time I arrived she was usually out in the yard. I'd sit under a big mango tree and eat my breakfast while she worked nearby. Often, she'd pick fresh fruit from the yard to accompany my milk and toast. Sometimes there were fresh lychees or pomegranates. "This is what silkworms eat," she'd say, giving me a handful of purple mulberries. In mango season she'd harvest the bright red and golden fruit from my aunt's tree. I'd help with the spotting, gazing up into the shady branches, and we'd pick mangoes until she'd gathered a whole fragrant apronful. Then we'd sit on the grass and eat them together, with Big Grandma saving all the peelings to put on the compost later.

Despite the strictness of her dietary regimen, I was quick to notice that it did not exclude experimentation. For years she listened to a talk radio program, broadcast over a local Japanese-language station, in which people would call in with their favorite (and usually bad-tasting) cures for everything from rheumatism to temporary amnesia. She took note of all the call-in remedies and if one particularly interested her, she had no reservations about trying it out on me. I was a sickly child, subject to allergies and "bronchial conditions." For a while, after I was diagnosed as anemic, she took to feeding me duck eggs. When I objected to their taste, she tried to disguise them in egg salad, a ploy which did not fool me one bit. To this day, I immediately get suspicious whenever I hear ads for turkey bacon, soy bean ice cream, or any other kind of undercover food which claims to be something it is not. But the worst things my grandmother gave me were the brownish-green drinks she concocted out of unconventional vegetables. Tonics of chives or aloe. Pureed mountain yams. The bitterest bitter melon tea. She'd pour some of whatever concoction she'd come up with into a large tumbler, so there'd be just about an inch of the stuff down there at the bottom, and she'd say, "See? You can polish that off with no trouble at all."

Big Grandma's quest to restore me to health also included visits to sundry healers and prayer ladies. I don't know how she heard of these people — perhaps from the radio or at church — but there was a tacit understanding between us not to mention our visits to anyone else. We'd wait until my aunt had gone to work, then we'd change into our going-out dresses and, hand in hand, set out for the bus stop on the corner. We visited a shiatsu specialist who treated your ailments with finger massage; an herbalist who made you inhale scented steam; and an acupuncturist nun who stuck you with needles or applied heated glass suction cups to strategic places on your back and chest. Big Grandma herself claimed that she had the power to perform *reiki,* that is, to heal with the energy flowing from her hands. I still recall her sitting up nights beside my childhood sickbed, the touch of her cool palms upon my forehead, while her lips moved silently, chanting prayers.

"Your grandmother and I were never friends," my mother remarks, after I tell her these memories.

When I ask why, Mother answers, "For one thing, she was never around." After Grandfather's death, Big Grandma had gone to work as a cook and live-in housekeeper for a wealthy businessman's family and was away for days at a time. Then my mother adds, "Besides, it would never have occurred to us to be friends. That wasn't how it was."

"So, how was it?" I persist.

She explains that children were bound to their parents by duty and gratitude. Then she smiles. "Isn't it a pity that all that's changed?"

Another time we are sitting out on the porch, sipping iced coffees, and she tells me, "When I was a girl, we always heard stories about fathers who signed their financial obligations over to their grown children, then headed back to Japan. In those days, children were so brainwashed to be dutiful, they'd work their whole lives to pay off those debts. Usually, the heaviest burden fell to the eldest."

I think of Aunt Tee and how she left school when she was fourteen to help support the family.

Mother continues, "Your grandmother taught us that nothing is stronger than the bond of obligation between a parent and a child. All of us felt it. But I couldn't help thinking, she'd cut those ties, hadn't she? And what about those fathers who dropped everything to go back to Japan?"

These are stories she'd told me many times, but now in the cool reflective light they cast, it chills me a little to remember what my grandmother described as the "freedom" that comes with growing old. It seems that widowhood had not simply freed her from the expectations of men. It had also freed her to create — out of that closed, tightly knit world she inhabited with her daughters — a female version of the old way she knew so well. I can't pretend to know how this came about, so I try to imagine how it was for her — a mother, alone, with four young daughters, and work always keeping her away from home.

Yet, even as we slip the ties that bind us to that old way, I can't help asking, when we are free of all this, what holds us then?

To which my mother answers, sighing, "Who knows?" Then adds, "Friendship maybe. A kind of love."

Whenever I am home, my mother cooks. On most mornings, when I come out into the kitchen she greets me with the question, "What would you like for dinner tonight?" By the time I sit down to my first cup of coffee she has already hung the laundry, swept and mopped the floors, and is taking a break, clipping recipes or coupons from the previous night's paper.

On other days I wake to the smell of baking. A few mornings before Easter, a wonderful yeasty fragrance fills the whole house, and when I emerge from my bedroom there are pans of sweet rolls cooling on every available surface in the living and dining rooms. Mother reminds me that they are having a bake sale for her General Electric cooking class. While she was at it, she decided to make extras to give away. None of it penance food.

She believes that everything to do with eating should be a pleasure, and she takes as much care in selecting the food she will cook as in its actual preparation. When I am visiting, she rousts me out of bed on Wednesday mornings way before six, so we can get down to the open market when the produce vendors are setting up. Afterward, I drive her to Chinatown, where she is acquainted with the specialties of every shop. She sniffs and pokes, quizzes the vendors about prices, and periodically offers me bits of cryptic advice, like, "buy fish whole," or "the sound of a pineapple tells you if it's sweet."

After my return to Grand Rapids, Mother and I continue to keep in frequent touch. On one occasion, she reports that Big Grandma has decided that she is visiting at her uncle's estate back in Japan. "The last time I saw her," Mother says, "she complained of what a long stay it's been. Then she looked around at her roommate and the other residents out in the hall, and whispered, 'I can't figure out what all these strangers are doing here.' "

During another call, my mother announces that she and my father are accepting our invitation to come out and see us the following spring. This will be their first visit in the five years since my husband and I moved to Michigan. She also says that she's been losing weight and may have to buy a whole new wardrobe for the trip. This cheerful declaration implies darker possibilities, but I refrain from delving into them. Instead, she volunteers that her doctor is keeping track of her progress and isn't concerned a single bit.

Every week she reports losing another pound or two, but her monthly checkups turn up nothing unusual. She's developed a bit of a backache, but both she and her doctor agree that is is an old muscle strain flaring up. I begin calling her several times a week to keep track of how she's doing, and she, surprisingly, seems to welcome my concern.

In March, when my father and mother arrive for their scheduled visit, I am nevertheless surprised by the change in her. She has gone from 110 pounds to less than ninety, and her clothes hang loosely on her small frame. Her hands tremble when she unbuttons her jacket or lifts her fork to eat, and she hardly eats — just tiny bites.

But she loves everything. Our little house. The crocuses blooming in the yard. The unpredictable March weather. She loves that it can be 70 degrees and sunny one day, and snowing the next. When it starts to snow, she grabs her coat and boots so she can be outside in it. She crunches wet snow into little balls and throws them at us when my father and I step out the door. I take pictures of the two of them — in the snow on the front walk, in the snow on the side of the house, and in the snow in the back yard. Mother takes naps in the afternoon but she is always up by dinner. She sits on a stool in the kitchen and watches while I cook. I teach her my recipes for *tabouli*, refried beans, and meatless marinara sauce. When we go to the market, she is enthusiastic over the strawberries and asparagus that have just come in season.

One day, my husband drives us all out to Lake Michigan. It is a forty-minute ride, and on the way over my mother begins to sing. I remember summer evenings back in the Islands, when it was too hot to stay inside, and she and I went for rides beside the sea. Then in the middle of telling me about some dance she'd been to when she was young, she'd start to sing, and I'd join in. We'd both sing, riding the night roads, all the way home.

A few weeks after my parents return to Honolulu, Mother takes to her bed. Her back is worse and she complains of "hunger pains." When I ask my father if she gets out at all, he replies that she doesn't, then adds that he is doing all the housework now. I ask if she ever cooks anymore, and when he hesitates, I realize that something is very wrong.

However, Mother refuses to give in to panic and insists that there is no reason for my return. Meanwhile, she goes from doctor to doctor and they turn up nothing. One performs an endoscopy and diagnoses gastritis. Another prescribes swimming therapy for her back condition. She regards all this as good news, but meanwhile the weight keeps slipping off her. "You have to feed her," I tell my father. "We have to fatten her up." To which he responds sadly, "She's lost her joy in food."

I begin making plans to fly back when he calls and says she's taken another turn for the worse. She has a fever and can't keep anything down. Before I hang up, she gets on the phone. The last words she ever says to me are, "I don't know what's wrong." That afternoon my father takes her to the emergency room and she is rushed into surgery, where the surgeon finds an abscess covering two thirds of her liver. He inserts a drainage tube then closes her up. "I've never seen anything like it," he tells my father.

I return to the Islands the next day. One of my cousins meets me at the airport. My mother is at the same hospital where she had surgery two years before, and when we arrive at the waiting room of the intensive care unit, my father and Aunt Tee are there. I put my arms around my father, who keeps saying, "We've been through this before, I just know she is going to get better."

The rules of the unit allow us to visit my mother in pairs for ten minutes, three times an hour, at twenty-minute intervals. My mother lies unconscious, with tubes running in and out of her body and a respirator to help her breathe. During one of the breaks between visits, I phone Bill in Michigan, and he says that he'll be with me soon.

Over the next few days there is no change. Aunt Tee drops by again. The Birthday Girls come. The ladies from the General Electric cooking class bring food for our vigil. The long hours are beginning to tell on my father, who decides to go home in the afternoons to take short naps.

One afternoon I am alone with Mother when Aunt Emma enters the room. I look around for Aunt Tee, but Emma has come alone.

"I rode the bus," she says, positioning herself on the other side of the bed.

After we exchange a bit more small talk, I run back to my mother and pick up where I'd left off. "Remember the time . . . " I say to her, listing things we've seen and done.

A few minutes go by this way, when Aunt Emma suddenly speaks up; she has been remembering, too. She leans close to Mother's pillow, and murmurs, "Remember when we were kids, and you got a new pair of shoes, and I didn't get any? Remember the lady at the corner store who gave you free ice cream that you never shared? Remember how you wanted to tag along wherever I went and how Mama beat me for not taking you?"

More days pass. Bill arrives. The doctors move Mother out of intensive care. It's not looking good, they say. The antibiotics aren't working, and the infection is in her blood.

In the new room we can be with Mother all the time. We stand by the bed, massaging her icy hands and feet. Her circulation is poor and her toes have turned black. Dad quits talking about miracle recoveries. One afternoon, while Bill is getting a cup of coffee and I am half-dozing in a chair across the room, I can hear my father talking to her. "It's okay, Betty," he is saying. "You can let go now. You can let go."

She doesn't let go, just yet. The blackness spreads upward from her toes to her legs. She is so full of fluids they are leaking from all the places where she has been stuck with syringes and IV needles. The fluids are causing her body to swell, and it has become impossible to find a pulse to take her blood pressure. Nevertheless, the lab technicians come by like clockwork to check her blood pressure and shoot her up with insulin, which immediately leaks back out. I finally ask for permission to have them stop this futile routine, and her doctors give it.

None of our friends or relatives come by anymore. There is a sign on the door that says *Visitors Limited to Immediate Family.* I sense that it is difficult for my father to be there; the air conditioning, the hours of sitting on a hard chair are bad for his arthritis, so I tell him that it's all right if he leaves early because we'll call if anything happens.

When the nurses come in to change the bedding, they instruct Bill and me to wear rubber gloves whenever we touch my mother. This is to safeguard against infection from the fluids leaking out of her. Periodically, someone comes in to vacuum out her mouth and throat with a suction device on the side of the bed. The necessity for doing this becomes more and more frequent, and finally, one of the nurses shows me how to do it. There is the smell of blood, perhaps of earth, around my mother's bed.

With just my husband there in the room with us, I sing to her. She lies in the same position she's been in, with her head turned to one side, and one leg slightly bent, as if she's dancing. I sing, "Sunset glow the day is over, let us all go home . . . " I close my eyes and imagine myself large, large enough to hold all of her, her dying, within me.

Bill and I have rented a room in the hospital where we can catch quick naps during the day or grab a few hours of sleep at night. The room is in the same wing as the senior care facility, a floor below my grandmother's. At one or two in the morning, after a day of sitting with my mother, he and I squeeze into the narrow, twin-size bed and, still in our street clothes, almost immediately fall asleep. We have slept less than an hour when we are wakened by banging at the door. We stumble to our feet, and I feel as if I've plunged into a pool of icy water. I am so cold my teeth are chattering and it is difficult to catch my breath. Bill steadies me, then opens the door. There are two nurses on the other side. They tell us, in a businesslike way, to go to my mother's room. As we follow them down the corridor, I think of Big Grandma somewhere upstairs, wakeful, among strangers.

◎ *ROSALYN DREXLER*

Rosalyn Drexler was born in 1926. Drexler has written novels, short fiction, and plays, and her work is included in numerous anthologies. Her most recent novel is Art Does Not Exist *(1992). She has also written six novels under the pseudonym of Julia Sorel. Drexler's three play collections are* The Line of Least Existence and Other Plays *(1967),* The Investigation and Hot Buttered Roll *(1969), and* Transients Welcome *(1984). She has received a Pollock-Krasner grant for visual arts, a play commission from the New York State Commission on the Arts, grants from the National Endowment for the Arts, and Obie Awards for* Transients Welcome, Writer's Opera, *and* Home Movies. *Drexler has taught at the Iowa Writers Workshop, at Oberlin College, and at several other major institutions. Most recently she has been a visiting professor of playwriting at Sarah Lawrence College.*

Room 17C appears in Transients Welcome. *It was first produced at the Omaha Magic Theatre in Omaha, Nebraska, in 1984. The play envisions an encounter between characters from Arthur Miller's* Death of a Salesman *and Franz Kafka's "The Metamorphosis."*

Room 17C

The bug in *Room 17C* does not have to be in bug costume; a well worn brown suit will suffice. The actor should, in his movement and delivery of lines, project a bug persona, i.e., an affinity for the corners of the room — crawling, scurrying in a nervous manner, flattening out, creeping upon, hanging from, hiding. He is *not* to be cute, but must engage our compassion and encourage the audience's recognition that they too are vulnerable and at one time or another have been "bugs" themselves. Perhaps a bug is someone who has given up one lifestyle for another; has chosen to retire from the "rat race," and therefore is regarded by others as the lowliest of the low: a bug. The bug is not sad; he accepts what he is. This frees his spirit. He does not have to be what he is not.

Linda Normal, the family wage earner, has taken up where her husband Willy left off after his retirement as a salesman. But her life is still not her own since her husband keeps phoning to check up on her. She has to harden herself. In some way she is still playing his "masochistic" game. Whatever she does pains him. He threatens her with his suicide, but it is she who will die in the line of duty, burned to a crisp with her "knock-em-dead" sports line.

Attracted to the spirited bug Sammy Gregor, Linda lets her hair down; she enjoys an unexpected romantic interlude involving intimate confessions, food, and dance. The situation is absurd, but should be played as realistically as possible. This can only heighten the absurdist elements while still retaining the realistic underpinnings of believable human drama. *The play is not Kafka goes to Disneyland!*

CHARACTERS

LINDA NORMAL	A TRAVELING SALESWOMAN
SAMMY GREGOR	A MAN-SIZED COCKROACH
BIFF NORMAL	MALE IN HIS EARLY TWENTIES; LINDA'S SON.

[*A hotel room: twin bed, dresser with mirror, chair, night-table. There is a phone on night-table.*

A suitcase is open on bed. It contains Linda's clothing and some samples of her sports line. A framed photograph is hidden in the lingerie.

There are two doors: one leading to the hall, the other to the bathroom.]

ACT 1

[*Hotel room. Bathroom door opens. Linda enters the room. She sits on bed and dials the phone.*]

LINDA: Hello, operator? I want to make a person-to-person call to Mr. Willy Normal. No, it is not a collect call. Charge it to my room. Thank you. [*She waits a few rings.*] Operator . . . operator . . . I'll try again later . . . Thank you.

[*She starts to unpack, carries a dress or two to the closet. Her back is to the bed.*

A large, man-sized cockroach crawls from under the bed. At first only his head is visible.

Linda hangs her dresses up. She turns around. At once she notices the cockroach observing her with his large, luminous eyes. She backs away in fright.]

LINDA: Oh!

COCKROACH: You seem to be a neat person. Ever leave food around?

LINDA: It talks! Wh-h, wh-h what do you want?

COCKROACH: I like it a few days old at least. Brings out the flavor; but I'll eat anything. My situation does not allow me to indulge a rather gourmet inclination.

LINDA: Either you crawl back into the woodwork or I call the front desk! They'll know what to do.

COCKROACH: That's a laugh. Exterminator comes once a month. That's it. Those of us who survive get carte blanche.

LINDA: You're loathsome.

COCKROACH: Loathsome and lonesome. I've learned to live with it. [*He crawls around room, gathering speed. He jumps on the bed and bounces.*] You'll like the bed. Lots of bounce. Once I got stuck on the ceiling. But then I plunked right down again. Lay on my back like this . . . [*He lies on bed, feet waving in air.*] It's a dangerous position for me to be in; however seeing things from above was worth it.

LINDA: Worth it? How?

COCKROACH: Changed my perspective. Running around the floor looking for shadows is a very alienating experience. I despised myself. Every time the lights went on I ran for my life. You can't imagine the terror. But rising above it, ah-h! Turned my life around. I've had my transcendental moment. [*He slowly edges toward Linda.*]

LINDA: Don't come any closer or I'll stomp you.

COCKROACH: No you won't. You don't want to have parts of me stuck to your nice new shoes: bits of brown wing, thick white ooze, broken legs thin as a stitch.

LINDA: Disgusting! I can smell you from here. I can smell every filthy place you've been.

COCKROACH: I think you're imagining it.

LINDA: Not likely; I have an exceptionally fine sense of smell.

COCKROACH: Well, I suppose I do possess an inherited characteristic odor. Can't argue with one's gene pool, can one?

LINDA: I'll give you that.

COCKROACH: I've been told by certain other transients that my smell reminds them of home.

LINDA: I pity you. [*She takes a deep breath at the window.*]

COCKROACH: Pity is bad, compassion is good.

LINDA: I don't really pity you. Why would I waste pity on your kind? Before long you'd be dependent on me.

COCKROACH: For what?

LINDA: Becoming sexy. You'd be all over me at night: a small bite here, a small bite there.

COCKROACH: Love nips don't last long; just enough pain to punctuate the pleasure.

LINDA: Keep me up itching all night — all the night long.

COCKROACH: Anything to make you notice me.

LINDA: You know, you remind me of my husband Willy, always playing on my sympathy. He is, rather he was a traveling salesman: a parasite selling things to people that they didn't need: hair brushes made of hog's bristles, clothing brushes, toothbrushes, every kind of brush — to get them hooked he'd give them, absolutely free, a vegetable brush — well he's retired now. Got a gold-plated watch to commemorate his masochism. Who cares any more.

COCKROACH: Not me.

LINDA: Me neither. I don't have time to cry. Not when I'm on the road. It's my turn now. Now it's me who attends to business: sales conferences, customer relations, quotas, beating the competition — then afterwards the easy camaraderie of smoke filled rooms, scotch and soda, things illicit, illusion swiftly followed by disillusion — So what if it all adds up to a big zip! So what if I've become what I most despise — a parasite. Doing something is better than doing nothing. Used to think things would change for the better. What a dope I was. They never will.

COCKROACH: Things *have* changed — for both of us.

LINDA: Don't link us together, please!

COCKROACH [*he edges toward Linda.*] : But I must.

LINDA: Stop where you are! Don't make another move toward me. This conversation is taking place only because I'm here, and you're here, and no one else is here.

COCKROACH: That's a lie. This conversation is taking place because I intrigue you. Because I'm a swell conversationalist. I aim to please, baby.

LINDA: You're nothing but a bug.

COCKROACH: Wrongo. In my former life I was a clerk. Brought home the paycheck. Supported father, mother, sister — they began to settle in — grew weak — lost weight — became parasitic — My ability to take care of things took away their reason for being. Minute I changed, ummm, took my present form and remained in my room listening, just listening, they came to life again; they wanted *me* to be dependent on *them*. You see before you a martyr.

LINDA: Are you telling me you *chose* to become a roach to save your family? I think not! I think you're a dreamer who grew his own shell to crawl into.

COCKROACH: Why I am the way I am hardly matters any more since I am never, ever changing back. This is it for me. Would you excuse me for a few seconds?

LINDA: Going somewhere?

COCKROACH: To the bathroom pipes. How I love a tropical climate. The pipes, the pipes they sing to me of moist mother love. The truth is that I was hatched from a nest of gritty black specks, splattered according to nature's maternal time clock upon a shiny brass pipe below a sink. Have you ever put your ear to a pipe? You can hear the ocean that way. You can even hear the sighs of baby alligators as they migrate, in all innocence, to a watery grave.

[*He crawls to the bathroom. Linda slams door. She leans on it.*]

LINDA: You can stay in there forever! Don't try to soften me up with sad stories. I've heard 'em all. Where are the good old happy stories? Where are the success stories? I want to laugh. I want to laugh dammit!

COCKROACH: You want to laugh? Oh, I'm sorry.

LINDA: Forget it.

COCKROACH: I'm ready to come out — Hey, don't think I'm trapped in here. Only human beings can be locked in. I have access. I can go underground. I know the way back.

LINDA: And I can leave any time I want to. I can vacate the premises. Check out.

COCKROACH: Because of a bug? How unsophisticated. By the way, what's your name? I might have to beg for mercy, or curse my fate. Supplication has better results when one directs it to a specific deity such as yourself.

LINDA: My name is Linda. Linda Normal. Start begging.

COCKROACH: I'm Sammy Gregor. You can call me Sammy.

LINDA: You're living on borrowed time Sammy.

COCKROACH: Say Linda — what if you have to use the john?

LINDA: Let me worry about that.

COCKROACH: You'll have to stop leaning on the door.

LINDA: I'm not leaning on the door.

COCKROACH: They always lean on the door. I don't have to use a door to get in or out.

LINDA: Don't you?!

COCKROACH: You're the prisoner Linda.

LINDA [*she barricades the door with a piece of furniture*]: Why don't you dummy up and listen to your pipes.

COCKROACH: Okay, but I have a tendency to sing alone.

LINDA: Sing. Chirp. Whatever. Who cares.

COCKROACH [*he sings*]:

BABY I'M IN A STRANGE SITUATION
CAN'T SAY I LIKE THIS NEW SENSATION
YOU'VE GOT ME WHERE YOU WANT ME
BEHIND CLOSED DOORS
WHAT YOU GONNA DO WITH ME NOW?

LINDA [*she dials phone. On phone*]: Hello, I want to make a person-to-person call to a Mr. William Normal . . . from Linda — thank you . . . Willy? It's me darling. Yes, I had a good trip down. Lonely? Already? Oh don't be such a sad sack Willy. Keep busy. Get off your butt. So what if the watch isn't digital. It's gold-plated isn't it? No I haven't even unpacked yet. Met an irresistible stranger in the elevator? Hardly. What? Talk louder I can't hear you Willy.

COCKROACH [*sings*]:

JUST WANT YOU TO KNOW ME
TO SHOW ME THE WILD SIDE
OF LOVE
DON'T LEAVE ME
RETRIEVE ME
FROM LIFE'S OLD GARBAGE PILE

LINDA [*into phone*]: No, nobody is here with me. It's the radio. What program? Oh — Oldies but Goodies. Don't worry. I won't get into trouble. I'M NOT YOU! Tony Bennett is not under my bed. Really, the voice you hear is on the radio. The RADIO! Please believe me. Oh stop blubbering. Yes darling I forgive you all of your transgressions, sexual and otherwise. Whatever. I know how hard it is to be normal when you're on the road. Even harder when your name is Willy Normal. Burden to bear Willy. We all have one. You were only looking for companionship not a soul mate. I hear you. Water under the bridge Willy. Dirty, filthy, bilge water under the bridge. Forget it. I've forgotten it. Where's your backbone dammit! Sit up straight Willy or no one'll know you're at the table.

COCKROACH [*sings*]:

BABY THIS IS THE PITS
DON'T DENY IT
I'M ALLOWED TO KNOCK IT,
'CAUSE I TRIED IT
YOU'VE GOT ME WHERE YOU WANT ME
RIGHT ON THE FLOOR
WHAT YOU GONNA DO WITH ME NOW?

LINDA: I know you tried your best. So you were fired; why suffer? Enjoy life Willy. I do. My new Spring line should knock 'em dead. They ain't never seen sportswear like this! . . . Why do you want to go and ruin my trip? . . . No, no, no! Don't kill yourself darling, it'd be anti-climactic. You hear me? Willy? Willy? Of course I love you. Here's a big kiss for you [*makes kissing sound*].

[*Hangs up phone.*]

Damn! He wants me to give him a reason to live, on the telephone! [*To Sammy.*] Hey Sammy, how ya doin' in there? Why don't you crawl down to the lobby and hide in a pile of newspapers?

[*Sammy enters from the bathroom. Linda does not see him.*]

COCKROACH: Already been down. Read the headlines. Nibbled on a crumb or two. Came back to share my life with you.

LINDA [*she backs away from him. Runs into the bathroom*]: Keep away from me.

COCKROACH: There is no sanctuary for you Linda.

LINDA: I don't want sanctuary. I want to pee.

COCKROACH [*he rummages through her luggage. He finds a pair of running trunks and puts them on. He runs in place*]: These running trunks are very comfortable. I'd like to place an order.

LINDA: What running trunks?

COCKROACH: Found 'em in your luggage.

LINDA: Stop whatever you're doing till I come out.

COCKROACH [*admires himself in mirror*]: I could model your line for you. Make you rich and famous.

LINDA: I'm not Walt Disney. Be a sport, pal, disappear.

[*She comes out of bathroom.*]

COCKROACH [*gliding to window*]: Look out there Linda. The world beckons. There's more to consider than you and me — there's preaching, pimping and prostitution — there's hunger, freezing, and destitution. There's daily despair and plenty to fear — and at night the crunch, crunch, crunch of rats and roaches on the prowl.

LINDA: Mr. Gregor you don't have to lecture me. I didn't create what's happening out there, and I can't change what's happening out there. Call me selfish if you want to, but I came here for two reasons: business and pleasure. The rest doesn't mean beans to me. Besides I'm shockproof by now; I've seen everything — I've seen you.

COCKROACH: I disgust you, don't I.

LINDA: Yeah, if you put it that way, yeah.

COCKROACH [*sits on bed*]: My sister wasn't disgusted by me. She accepted my transformation. Took care of me. Played her violin while I trembled in ecstasy. Then without warning, at the age of thirteen when she became a woman, she gave it up. Out she went to meet her friends. After that nobody paid any attention to me. It was as if I no longer existed. At night the door to my room was left open. In the half-light I could watch them all: sister bent over a book, mother intent on her sewing, father nodding half-asleep — a tender family scene with their backs to me. Always their backs to me. I wanted to kill myself, but I decided to check into a hotel instead.

LINDA: Just like Willy. Too sensitive to fight back. I'll bet you like scaring people with that bug-ugly look of yours. You wouldn't have it any other way.

COCKROACH [*removes the running trunks. He gets into bed*]: What other way can I have it?

LINDA [*picks up a shoe. Hides it behind her back*]: Get out of my bed! I said get out! I will not let you turn this trip into a Japanese horror film.

COCKROACH: Get in.

LINDA: Get out.

COCKROACH: I saw your photograph.

LINDA: Photograph?

COCKROACH: In your suitcase; face down at first, swaddled in silk lingerie. Hidden by you.

LINDA: It was wrapped for safety. Glass breaks when luggage is handled roughly.

COCKROACH: You did hide it.

LINDA: Why would I do that? It's a perfectly ordinary photograph.

COCKROACH: Not ordinary to me. I find it — *personal*! Hardly a flight of flies above the butter dish.

LINDA [*revealing an emotional involvement*]: Personal? You find it intimate? Revealing? Alright yes, it is personal! Yet holding a pose goes beyond the personal into the painful. Family photographs tell too much — dear Willy swooning at my feet for instance. I can't remember whether the photographer suggested it, or whether passion placed him there, underfoot. At any rate he was more than willing to be there, his body flattened, his head at a tilt as if waiting for some final blow. In his brown suit he resembled a bug, yes, a cockroach. Perhaps I am partial to cockroaches Sammy, have always wanted them in the picture. But you Sammy are my first real cockroach. I smelled you — remember? — the minute I entered this room.

COCKROACH [*at Linda's feet. Sings*]:

JUST WANT YOU TO USE ME
LINDA
I'M GETTIN' FEVERISH
WHY WON'T YOU ABUSE ME
LINDA
IGNORE MY EVERY WISH
REFUSE ME
ABHOR ME
I'M GETTIN' OFF ON THIS
LINDA BE MINE.

LINDA: You're so delicate, I might do you harm . . .

COCKROACH: How?

LINDA: By forcing you to stay within an embrace beyond roach endurance. What if . . .

COCKROACH: Yes?

LINDA: What if you can't withstand the poetry of a magic moment?

COCKROACH: Ah poetry, the deadly stranger in our midst. . . . Come to bed now.

LINDA [*Linda approaches. She beats him with her shoe*]: There's poetry in a shoe too.

COCKROACH: How cruel you are.

LINDA: Why are you bugging me?

COCKROACH: I have my bug destiny to fulfill. It's not me it's my gene pool. Oh darling let me rest in your unshaved armpit, crawl between your thighs, investigate your glistening tongue, bask in your passionate hot breath. Whatdya say?

[*Phone rings.*]

LINDA [*on phone*]: Yes? Who? Willy? Is anything wrong? You can't find the instant coffee? Look in the cabinet over the sink. It should be there. It always has been there, yes, beside the jar of teabags and the brown sugar.

COCKROACH [*crawls into Linda's lap*]: Sugar. I call my baby sugar . . .

LINDA [*gives a small cry. Brushes Cockroach off*]: Get off! — Not you Willy; a speck of dust. It's so dirty here in New York. What? You've lost sympathy with me? I've made my bed, and now I have to sleep in it? Why Willy, I do believe you're jealous of me. That must be it. You can't take it any more? Take what? No you're not useless, Willy. Talk to Biff. He's a good son. He loves you. Of course he respects you. We all respect you. Oh, I forgot to remind you to check the water heater. Pan has to be emptied. No, the hose does not lead directly to the gas line. Boy do you sound depressed! Yes I miss you. I even miss you when we're together. Just a joke Willy. Say, really wish you were here. Room is swell except for the roach problem. However, few more days and I'll be in your arms. What's a few days out of a marriage of twenty-five years hon? Yes, I love you too. Always have. Always will.

[*She hangs up.*]

[*to Sammy*]: I have to go downstairs, Ballroom D, sign up for my conference. If you're still here when I get back, you can kiss your feelers good-bye.

SAMMY: I understand the logic of this particular situation.

LINDA: Do you?

SAMMY: I am a utopian quester. You are utopia; however, I know when to back off.

LINDA: Let's hope so.

COCKROACH [*sings*]:

BABY I'M BEGGING FOR A FAVOR
CAN'T SAY I'VE EVER LICKED THIS FLAVOR

YOU'VE GOT ME WHERE YOU WANT ME
UNDER YOUR THUMB
WHATCHA GONNA DO WITH ME NOW-OW-OW?

LINDA: For someone who revels in dung and bird droppings you have a romantic nature. Still, don't be here when I get back.

[*She exits.*]

COCKROACH [*uses phone. Imitates Linda's voice*]: Room service? This is room 17C. I'd like to have an order sent up. Two hamburgers, one rare. Sauteed onions. Ketchup. Fries. A bottle of Moet-Chandon tres Sec. And a plate of chocolate-covered mints. I'll be in the shower, so please leave the tray outside the door. Thank you.

[*Hangs phone up.*]

[*He clears table in room. Brings glasses from the bathroom. Turns radio on: music. Knock on door. He waits a few seconds, then opens door and brings in the tray of food. He smells food. Examines the champagne label. Puts bottle back into ice-bucket.*]

Life can be so pleasant: a roof over one's head, food on the table, and a beautiful adversary in the grand ballroom.

LINDA [*she returns*]: Still here?

COCKROACH: I've taken the liberty of ordering a celebration feast.

LINDA: They take orders from a cockroach?

COCKROACH: From a voice on the phone.

LINDA [*examines champagne label*]: What's wrong with domestic?

COCKROACH: The downtrodden need more than bread and water.

LINDA: Hamburgers! I love hamburgers — hey is this food rotten enough for you?

COCKROACH: Nothing's rotten enough for me, but this'll have to do.

LINDA: I'm famished — so please don't crawl over my food or I'll throw up.

COCKROACH: My table manners are impeccable dear Linda. I haven't forgotten mother's linen tablecloths and polished silver; father's crystal goblets and precisely folded napkins — the centerpiece of flowers from our garden.

[*They seat themselves at table, on which the tray has been put.*]

LINDA [*while she eats*]: Thing is, concerning Willy and my son Biff — they haven't gotten along since Biff walked in on Willy when he was with some woman, somewhere — pass me the pickles — Thanks — Here, you have some too — Willy always tried to help the kid; introduced him to the district manager of his firm — set the kid up with his own route. Well Biff was gung-ho to start, arrived a day early, and that's when he found out his dad wasn't one-hundred percent perfect. Talk about men putting women on a pedestal! Biff had his dad living on Mount Everest. Poor kid, thought he had to take sides, defend me. I couldn't have cared less.

COCKROACH: You didn't care?

LINDA: Nothing I could do about it. His life is his life. All he talked about was how his life was slipping through his fingers. I said Willy, the time to start worrying is when your fingers start slipping through your fingers. Oh I was sorry for him: age creeping up, nothing to show for a lifetime of work. But I couldn't solve it for him — More ketchup? I'm a ketchup freak. Give me a piece of meat and I'll smother it in ketchup. Ummm. So what does the man want?

COCKROACH: Another chance maybe.

LINDA: At what?

COCKROACH: Going backwards instead of forwards.

LINDA: Why would anyone want to be young?

COCKROACH: The young have a future.

LINDA: The young want us dead so they can take over. Willy understands that, but he can't bear the thought of it. He's taken out insurance for Biff. Says if he can't take care of him properly when he's alive, he'll look after him when he's dead. He needs that boy's love more than anything in the world.

COCKROACH: Ah the sweetness and the sorrow — Damn! I think there's ground bone in the burger — almost broke my mandible.

LINDA: You have no regrets? I mean about your transformation — the loss of teeth, a life sans eyelids, sans ears, sans all the basic equipment you once had as a human being.

COCKROACH: Nope.

LINDA: I have regrets. I've spent most of my life with a man who doesn't love life. You, a bug, raise my spirits and make me feel that it is possible to be really happy — You would not cling to me — You have your life. I have mine. Did you say you knew the way back?

COCKROACH: I said I was a parasite.

LINDA: So you said — Let's open the champagne.

COCKROACH [*he opens the champagne. Pours it. Smells the cork. Swishes some champagne around in his mouth*]: Good. Good. Much better than vinegar. (*Glass raised.*) Cheers.

LINDA [*glass raised*]: Cheers!

[*They drink.*]

COCKROACH [*sings*]:

MADAM, I'M IN THE MOOD FOR A SEXY TANGO
OR SHALL WE DANCE THE LIGHT FANDANGO?

YOU MAKE MY HEART GO BINGO-BANGO
I'LL BET YOU TASTE JUST LIKE MANGO.

LINDA: Yes, let's dance. I'll close my eyes and pretend not to hear the urgent rustling of your crisp shell, the rush of wind as it tosses those useless wings of yours around me.

COCKROACH: Have no fear — Sammy's here.

[*He takes her in his arms. They dance.*]

Munch the painter, painted a woman dancing with death. He didn't trust women, but was irresistibly drawn to them. Strindberg too.

LINDA: True; victims of sexual dysfunction both of them. Skeletons have no right to yearn for flesh. Not in their condition — and yet . . .

COCKROACH: Yet what used to be, echoes in their bones.

LINDA: They need blood. Where do they get it?

COCKROACH: Painters from the paint tube. Writers from the pen.

LINDA: From the placenta, I think. Every man longs to be belly to belly with his past.

[*Dance ends. Roach goes to the bed.*]

COCKROACH: Yes. Come closer.

LINDA: You have nothing to lose.

COCKROACH: And everything to gain.

[*Linda approaches bed. Cockroach draws her down to him. He holds her there.*]

LINDA: Forgive me for believing there are creatures lower than myself. Let me go. Please.

[*There is a knock on door.*]

BIFF [*voice from hall*]: Mom? Are you in there? It's Biff, Mom.

LINDA [*to Sammy*]: Damn! It's my kid. Why the heck is he here? [*Calls.*] Biff?

BIFF: It's me mom.

LINDA: I'll be right there. [*To roach.*] Hide — get under the bed.

COCKROACH: NO.

LINDA: Please! If Biff sees us together it'll traumatize him.

BIFF: Mom!

LINDA: Coming.

COCKROACH: Let him in. You haven't done anything to be ashamed of.

[*Linda opens door. Biff enters. They embrace. Suddenly he sees the Cockroach.*]

BIFF: God! Who's the guy in the costume? — Oh no, you've been cheating on Dad. How could you do this to me?

LINDA: To you? What right do you have to come sneaking around here? I'm a grown woman with a life of her own.

COCKROACH [*to Biff*]: Name's Sammy Gregor. I'm a mutant. Anything else you wanna know?

LINDA: He's a friend — that's all.

BIFF: He's a stranger — He's stranger than that too.

COCKROACH: I'm not really a stranger. When I was smaller I lived in your house. You didn't notice me of course. I hugged the baseboards and slept wrapped in beds of dust. As I remember it you kept me alive, always dropping food on the floor. Thank you.

BIFF [*to Linda*]: No wonder Dad turned to other women. You stepped all over him. And now this — this insect! What does he have that Dad doesn't?

LINDA: Feelers! He has feelers. Looks aren't everything.

BIFF: Mother, you are the lowest of the low. You are below sea-level. You are a reef that harbors poisonous fish and other prickly denizens. Where it is darkest, coldest, timeless, you find pleasure. You have no temperature of your own but take on the icy temperature of bone-chilling currents. You do not care where you drift so long as there is movement. And you do not even notice that this movement is carrying you away from those who love you. Woman is a perilous craft, and crafty though she is, cannot avoid the rocks in her path, so ready is she to abandon herself to the elements — to wreck what has formerly had direction and buoyancy.

LINDA: I hadn't realized that I had raised a woman hater, Biff; and an excessively literary one to boot. Why don't you go commiserate with your admirable father? Time to renew old ties. You broke his heart. There's still time to mend it.

BIFF: I didn't hurt Dad, you did! That's why he wants to kill himself. He's all by himself, while you whore around with this, this night crawler!

LINDA: For what it's worth Biff, Mr. Gregor and I have not been intimate. We were just having some dinner together, and conversing on an elevated plane.

BIFF: Honest?

LINDA: Honest. Isn't that right Mr. Gregor?

COCKROACH: Yes; conversing on an elevated plane, not yet aloft.

BIFF: That's different. [*He goes to window.*] Hey — hey there's smoke coming out of the hotel. [*Sound of fire engines.*] Let's get out of here — C'mon!

[*The three of them run for the door. They exit. Phone rings. Linda reappears. She answers the phone.*]

LINDA: Willy? Real sneaky of you Willy [*coughs*] sending Biff to spy on me [*coughs*]. Today is your last day on earth? — Funny, it's mine too [*coughs*] —

Remember to put out the pilot light on the heater and the stove — the clothes dryer too — if the house blows up where will Biff live? And listen Willy, I've never loved you — You're as cold as yesterday's mashed potatoes. This evening I met someone, fell in love, and am about to die of smoke poisoning [*coughs*] — Tell me Willy, were all the lies worth it? [*coughs.*] Goodbye Will . . . [*She passes out on bed.*]

[*Cockroach enters.*]

COCKROACH: Linda where are you? Linda?

[*He finds her on bed. Examines her to see if she is alive. He walks to front of stage and addresses the audience.*]

Life my friends is surprisingly short. I can't understand why Linda would have turned back to answer the phone. Force of habit? Destiny? Unfortunately the irresistible distance from door to bed proved fatal. Linda has not survived. In death she lacks the livelier character of former times. I'd weep if I could. Take this dry rustling of my useless wings as a sign of sorrow. I am left. And I grieve. But I am always left. Or is it that I remain while others destroy themselves? I an insect, survive; I who crawl out of offal and debris. I an insect. A vermin. The lowliest of the low, stay. I do not invent change; I adapt to the natural order of things. Even mushroom clouds cannot divert my way of life. My lifestyle is as old as the ocean. Of course I lack imagination. Lucky for me. Linda had imagination. Imagination can accomplish the end of the world. Life is long enough for that. Well anyway — long live earth and all the creatures who live upon it — and now before I travel on, allow me to entertain you with that rousing, top of the charts roach anthem you have been waiting for. [*Sings: to the tune of America.*]

OH WOE IS ME
FOR MISERY
FOR BUGS OF LITTLE BRAIN
FOR PURPLE BRUISES INFAMY
AND LIFE'S UPROOTED PAIN
OH COCKAROACH
OH COCKAROACH
GOD HAS DISTASTE FOR THEE
YET HE DOES GOOD
AS WELL HE SHOULD
FOR ME, AND YOU, AND WE.

End of play

◎ PAULA GUNN ALLEN

Paula Gunn Allen, who is of Laguna Pueblo, Sioux, and Lebanese-Jewish heritage, was born in New Mexico in 1939. She is the author of The Woman Who Owned the Shadows *(a novel, 1983);* The Sacred Hoop: Recovering the Feminine in American Indian Tradition *(essays, 1986); eight volumes of poetry, the most recent of which is* Skins and Bones: Poems 1979–1987 *(1988); and* Grandmothers of the Light: A Medicine Woman's Sourcebook *(1991).* Spider Woman's Granddaughters: Traditional Tales and Contemporary Writing by Native American Women *(Allen, ed., 1989), won an American Book Award. Allen is a professor of Native American studies and ethnic studies at the University of California at Berkeley.*

"Weed is from Skins and Bones. *One of Allen's main interests is the use of Native American myth. Certainly there is a transformative power to myth and symbol. In her essay "Something Sacred Going On Out There: Myth and Vision in American Indian Literature," Allen writes that "Conscious and unconscious are united through the magic of symbolic progression so that the symbols can convey direct, rational meanings and stir indirect memories and insights that have not been raised to conscious articulation." The weed in "Weed" embodies this process, becoming more than a mere plant and taking on a mythic toughness as "She drank the rain for fuel."*

Weed

She stood, a weed tall in the sun.
She grew like that and went
over it again and again trying to be tall
trying not to die in the drying sun
the seeming turbulence of waiting
the sun so yellow
so still

There was nothing else to do. It was like that
in her day, and the sun who rose so bright
so full of fire reminded her of that.
It was the sun that did it; it was the rain.
She stood it all, and more:
the water pounding from the high rock face
of the mesas that made her yard
she knew where she was growing. Didn't
she know what sun will do, what happens to weeds
when their growing time's done? Didn't she care?

She got the sun into her, though.
The fire. She drank the rain for fuel.
She stood there in the day, growing,
trying to stand tall like a right weed would.

The drying was part of it.
The dying. Come from heat, the transformation
of fire. The rain helped because it understood
why she just stood there, growing,
tall in the heat and bright.

◎ *PATRICIA CLARK*

"Betrayal" first appeared in Poetry *magazine in June 1992. It is one of a series of poems Clark has written about her father, included in a manuscript of her poems called* Commencement. *The poems use memory as a way of understanding the past and focus on several important incidents between the speaker and her father. "Betrayal" shows the beginning of a child's separation from parents, in this case prompted by an incident where the child's veracity is questioned. There is pain here, but one consolation is the growth toward consciousness and another is the growth of imagination and, subsequently, art.* *(For more on Clark, see page 266.)*

Betrayal

For pencils, that's why he took off
his belt. Pencils I might have stolen.
Until I'd say so, this strap
laid against my flesh.

Across his knees, I studied
linoleum. When tears dripped down,
they gleamed against the kitchen dirt.
And a hardening, a peach pit
in my belly. Not believed!

My sisters smirked at me in bed.
I lay, wide-eyed, in the seamless dark.
From my gentle father, a hand

raised in anger. No comfort
from anyone else.

Now this space inside, admitting
no one. Rooms with light, high
windows. Already I was moving
my possessions in.

◎ KATHRYN STRIPLING BYER

Kathryn Stripling Byer grew up in southern Georgia. She received an M.F.A. from the University of North Carolina at Greensborough. Currently, Byer is poet-in-residence at Western Carolina University and visiting professor of English in the M.F.A. program at the University of North Carolina at Greensborough. Her first book, The Girl in the Midst of the Harvest *(1986), was published in the AWP Award Series by Texas Tech University Press. Her second volume,* Wildwood Flower *(1992), won the Lamont Prize from the Academy of American Poets. Byer has completed her third book of poems,* Black Shawl.

Of "Dusk," the poet has commented: "One of the first poems in which I heard my own voice beginning to emerge. Through it, I began to understand that one creates one's own story, or myth, by going back to the family story and finding a way forward by retelling that story from one's own point of view. Family history can be both confining and transforming. As Flannery O'Connor said, 'Our limitations are our gateways to reality,' and it was those gateways that fascinated me" (letter to M. Kallet, 1996).

Dusk

My father made the birds fly overhead
that afternoon in late fall when he lifted me
above the weeds as tall as I was then
into a wagon load of hay. There at the field's edge
while he whistled, restless in the cold,
I watched the shadows of the nearby pines
trail the woods like tattered clouds.

He brooded on the silent stalks
and never noticed me while all his wagons

turned toward home at dusk. Why do I still believe
I saw him standing by the sea of stubble
waving me goodbye until I reached the gatepost
where I sent his goodbye back across the weeds?

He disappeared into his ruined rows
with the dust that sifted through the dying light.
He left me reaping shadows for his hand until the branches
at the road's bend hid the field. That's when
the swallows rising from the roadside thicket
streaked the early darkness with their wings
before they turned and followed sunset out of sight.

I saw their feathers gleam like grain thrown on the wind.

◎ *TESS GALLAGHER*

"Red Poppy" is from Moon Crossing Bridge *(1992). This is a love poem whose fierceness both faces the dying and death of her husband, Raymond Carver, and under the pressure of grief skillfully transforms the literal event into metaphors "so the real gave way to / the more-than-real." The poet has noted that "'Red Poppy' was written probably in 1989, about February or March." Raymond Carver died at home on August 2, 1988. (For more on Gallagher, see page 144.)*

Red Poppy

That linkage of warnings sent a tremor through June
as if to prepare October in the hardest apples.
One week in late July we held hands
through the bars of his hospital bed. Our sleep
made a canopy over us and it seemed I heard
its durable roaring in the companion sleep
of what must have been our Bedouin god, and now
when the poppy lets go I know it is to lay bare
his thickly seeded black coach
at the pinnacle of dying.

My shaggy ponies heard the shallow snapping of silk
but grazed on down the hillside, their prayer flags
tearing at the void—what we

stared into, its cool flux
of blue and white. How just shaking at flies
they sprinkled the air with the soft unconscious praise
of bells braided into their manes. My life

simplified to "for him" and his thinned like an injection
wearing off so the real gave way to
the more-than-real, each moment's carmine
abundance, furl of reddest petals
lifted from the stalk and no hint of the black
hussar's hat at the center. By then his breathing stopped
so gradually I had to brush lips to know
an ending. Tasting then that plush of scarlet
which is the last of warmth, kissless kiss
he would have given. Mine to extend a lover's right past its radius,
to give and also most needfully, my gallant hussar,
to bend and take.

◎ *LOUISE GLÜCK*

Louise Glück was born in 1943 in New York, New York. She was educated at Sarah Lawrence College and Columbia University. A visiting faculty member at a number of universities, colleges, and writing programs, Glück has been a senior lecturer in English at Williams College since 1984. Awards for her work include a Rockefeller Foundation grant, National Endowment for the Arts grants, Guggenheim Memorial Fellowships, an award in literature from the American Academy and Institute of Arts and Letters, and a National Book Critics Circle Award for The Triumph of Achilles *(poetry, 1985). Glück has published seven volumes of poetry, most recently* The Wild Iris *(1992).*

"The Undertaking" appeared in Glück's second book of poetry, The House on Marshland *(1975). Glück was called "a new species of poet" in* The New York Times Book Review *on the appearance of this book, and her poems are famous for their spareness and their classical allusions.*

The Undertaking

The darkness lifts, imagine, in your lifetime.
There you are — cased in clean bark you drift
through weaving rushes, fields flooded with cotton.

You are free. The river films with lilies,
shrubs appear, shoots thicken into palm. And now
all fear gives way: the light
looks after you, you feel the waves' goodwill
as arms widen over the water; Love,

the key is turned. Extend yourself—
it is the Nile, the sun is shining,
everywhere you turn is luck.

◎ *JOY HARJO*

William Carlos Williams wrote that "it is difficult / to get the news from poems," and yet "men die miserably every day / for lack / of what is found there" ("Asphodel, That Greeny Flower"). Harjo's "For Anna Mae Pictou Aquash, Whose Spirit Is Present Here and in the Dappled Stars..." literally provides us with the news of an activist Micmac woman murdered on the Pine Ridge Reservation in 1976. Her people retrieved the body and buried her properly, and the poem provides its own memorial. This poem is included in In Mad Love and War (1990). (For more on Harjo,, see page 65.)

For Anna Mae Pictou Aquash, Whose Spirit Is Present Here and in the Dappled Stars (for we remember the story and must tell it again so we may all live)

Beneath a sky blurred with mist and wind,
I am amazed as I watch the violet
heads of crocuses erupt from the stiff earth
after dying for a season,
as I have watched my own dark head
appear each morning after entering
the next world
to come back to this one,
amazed.
It is the way in the natural world to understand the place
the ghost dancers named
after the heart/breaking destruction.

Anna Mae,
everything and nothing changes.
You are the shimmering young woman
who found her voice,
when you were warned to be silent, or have your body cut away
from you like an elegant weed.
You are the one whose spirit is present in the dappled stars.
(They prance and lope like colored horses who stay with us
through the streets of these steely cities. And I have seen them
nuzzling the frozen bodies of tattered drunks
on the corner.)
This morning when the last star is dimming
and the buses grind toward
the middle of the city, I know it is ten years since they buried you
the second time in Lakota, a language that could
free you.
I heard about it in Oklahoma, or New Mexico,
how the wind howled and pulled everything down
in a righteous anger.
(It was the women who told me) and we understood wordlessly
the ripe meaning of your murder.
As I understand ten years later after the slow changing
of the seasons
that we have just begun to touch
the dazzling whirlwind of our anger,
we have just begun to perceive the amazed world the ghost dancers
entered
crazily, beautifully.

In February 1976, an unidentified body of a young woman was found on the Pine Ridge Reservation in South Dakota. The official autopsy attributed death to exposure. The FBI agent present at the autopsy ordered her hands severed and sent to Washington for fingerprinting. John Trudell rightly called this mutilation an act of war. Her unnamed body was buried. When Anna Mae Aquash, a young Micmac woman who was an active American Indian Movement member, was discovered missing by her friends and relatives, a second autopsy was demanded. It was then discovered she had been killed by a bullet fired at close range to the back of her head. Her killer or killers have yet to be identified.

◎ *LINDA HOGAN*

"Geodes" is from Linda Hogan's Savings *(1988). The speaker sees people as geodes, shining inside, and those who have suffered and have been broken hold within treasures — life is "growing in the dark," meanings and stories are starting to form. A poem about transformations, this is also about the constancy of change, the constancy of songs and stories, which illuminate our lives.* *(For more on Hogan, see page 146.)*

Geodes

for freedom

We open
and there is that shining inside,
that light in the broken ones,
light in the woman unraveling threads
from grief's torn black cloth.
There's roaring light in the woman
holding seashells in her hand,
the one with red lava in her groin,
the woman with wild rice she harvested,
holy women
reading the world like a snake skin,
these women of earth's core
with amber earrings
who laugh and cry
in their brown shoes,
fight back in their jean jackets,
the woman
hugging a rag basket,
closing its open mouth
so it won't tell the story
of all the rags
and crystals of light
growing in the dark
and all the life growing
in the broken heart of things.

LUANN KEENER

LuAnn Keener was born in 1954 in Bonham, Texas. She has an M.F.A. in creative writing from the University of Arkansas and an M.A. in French from North Texas State University. Keener has published two volumes of poetry, the more recent being Color Documentary *(1994). A few of her numerous awards are the Irene Leach Poetry Prize, the Hackney Poetry Award, and the Chelsea Prize for Poetry. She is the founding editor of* Sulphur River, *a small poetry journal. Keener teaches at Virginia Polytechnic Institute and State University.*

" 'The Hummingbirds' is part of a new series of poems returning to the subject of my rural childhood in Texas. My relationship in those years with nature largely formed me, providing both the matrix of becoming and the metaphors for understanding. When the human world was confusing and painful, the outdoors was home. One of the most important themes of my work is the relationship between those two worlds and a revisioning of the natural world that honors our biological roots and the kinship to all life" (letter to M. Kallet, 1996).

The Hummingbirds

For two weeks each summer
the green bank of the trumpet vine
whirred with light, the hummingbirds
spinning on geometric tracks
precise as stars,
nectar fueled, out of reach
yet near and common as bees.
I took them for granted
like all of the furniture of childhood.
In rain once, I saw one sitting still
under the eve, familiar
as the sodden, melancholy self
I also belonged to.
But their bright shuttles flying in sunlight
opened a window in some turret
of my brain, where I knew
the world more storied than others guessed,
a natural alchemy that did not give out
in the chalk dust and hard bells
of elementary school, as my parents struggled,
as the arthritic farmhouse sifted
the past into our hair. A high transom

would not shut, through which live
rubies and emeralds came and went
on zodiacal errands of becoming.

◎ *DENISE LEVERTOV*

Denise Levertov was born in 1923 in England, where her Welsh mother educated her at home. Levertov moved to the United States in 1948. Over the last forty-five years she has created a poetic opus the hallmark of which is rhythmical inventiveness and integrity, visionary insight into the ordinary, and precision of imagery. Levertov has more than twenty books to her credit, including poetry, essays, and translations. Her most recent volumes are a memoir, Tesserae *(1995), and* Evening Train *(1992). Among numerous honors, Levertov was recently awarded the scholarship for distinguished poetic achievement by the Academy of American Poets.*

In 1968 "A Tree Telling of Orpheus" appeared in the premiere issue of Stone Brook, *and it also appears in* Relearning the Alphabet *(1981). In "A Tree Telling of Orpheus" Levertov writes lines that resemble dance in their movement and physicality. A mythic Thracian hero, Orpheus the singer was a prototype for the poet: he named things and thereby gave them being. Levertov traces Orpheus's most difficult journey, and in celebrating his story the poem itself becomes a lyrical inspiration.*

A Tree Telling of Orpheus

White dawn. Stillness.   When the rippling began
        I took it for sea-wind, coming to our valley with rumors
        of salt, of treeless horizons. But the white fog
didn't stir; the leaves of my brothers remained outstretched,
unmoving.
                Yet the rippling drew nearer — and then
my own outermost branches began to tingle, almost as if
fire had been lit below them, too close, and their twig-tips
were drying and curling.
                                Yet I was not afraid, only
                                deeply alert.
I was the first to see him, for I grew
                out on the pasture slope, beyond the forest.
He was a man, it seemed: the two
moving stems, the short trunk, the two
arm-branches, flexible, each with five leafless twigs at their ends,

and the head that's crowned by brown or gold grass,
bearing a face not like the beaked face of a bird,
more like a flower's.
He carried a burden made of
some cut branch bent while it was green,
strands of a vine tight-stretched across it. From this,
when he touched it, and from his voice,
which unlike the wind's voice had no need of our
leaves and branches to complete its sound,
came the ripple.
But it was now no longer a ripple (he had come near and
stopped in my first shadow) it was a wave that bathed me
as if rain
rose from below and around me
instead of falling.
And what I felt was no longer a dry tingling:
I seemed to be singing as he sang, I seemed to know
what the lark knows; all my sap
was mounting towards the sun that by now
had risen, the mist was rising, the grass
was drying, yet my roots felt music moisten them
deep under earth.
He came still closer, leaned on my trunk:
the bark thrilled like a leaf still-folded.
Music! There was no twig of me not
trembling with joy and fear.

Then as he sang
it was no longer sounds only that made the music:
he spoke, and as no tree listens I listened, and language
came into my roots
out of the earth,
into my bark
out of the air,
into the pores of my greenest shoots
gently as dew
and there was no word he sang but I knew its meaning.
He told of journeys,
of where sun and moon go while we stand in dark,
of an earth-journey he dreamed he would take some day
deeper than roots . . .
He told of the dreams of man, wars, passion, griefs,
and I, a tree, understood words — ah, it seemed

my thick bark would split like a sapling's that grew too fast in the spring
when a late frost wounds it.
Fire he sang,
that trees fear, and I, a tree, rejoiced in its flames.
New buds broke forth from me though it was full summer.
As though his lyre (now I knew its name)
were both frost and fire, its chords flamed
up to the crown of me.
I was seed again.
I was fern in the swamp.
I was coal.
And at the heart of my wood
(so close I was to becoming man or a god)
there was a kind of silence, a kind of sickness,
something akin to what men call boredom, something
(the poem descended a scale, a stream over stones)
that gives to a candle a coldness
in the midst of its burning, he said.

It was then,
when in the blaze of his power that reached me and changed me
I thought I should fall my length,
that the singer began
to leave me. Slowly
moved from my noon shadow
words leaping and dancing over his shoulders
back to me
rivery sweep of lyre-tones becoming
slowly again
ripple.

And I
in terror
but not in doubt of
what I must do
in anguish, in haste,
wrenched from the earth root after root,
the soil heaving and cracking, the moss tearing asunder —
and behind me the others: my brothers
forgotten since dawn. In the forest
they too had heard,
and were pulling their roots in pain
out of a thousand years' layers of dead leaves,
rolling the rocks away,

breaking themselves
out of their depths
You would have thought we would lose the sound of the lyre,
of the singing.
so dreadful the storm-sounds were, where there was no storm,
no wind but the rush of our
branches moving, our trunks breasting the air.
But the music!
The music reached us.
Clumsily,
stumbling over our own roots,
rustling our leaves in answer,
we moved, we followed.

All day we followed, up hill and down.
We learned to dance,
for he would stop, where the ground was flat, and words he said
taught us to leap and to wind in and out
around one another   in figures   the lyre's measure designed.
The singer
laughed till he wept to see us, he was so glad.
At sunset
we came to this place I stand in, this knoll
with its ancient grove that was bare grass then,
In the last light of that day his song became
farewell.
He stilled our longing.
He sang our sun-dried roots back into earth,
watered them: all-night rain of music so quiet
we could almost
not hear it in the
moonless dark.
By dawn he was gone.
We have stood here since,
in our new life.
We have waited.
He does not return.
It is said he made his earth-journey, and lost
what he sought.
It is said they felled him
and cut up his limbs for firewood.
And it is said
his head still sang and was swept out to sea singing.

Perhaps he will not return.
But what we have lived
comes back to us.
We see more.
We feel, as our rings increase,
something that lifts our branches, that stretches our furthest leaf-tips
further.
The wind, the birds,
do not sound poorer but clearer,
recalling our agony, and the way we danced.
The music!

THYLIAS MOSS

Thylias Moss was born in 1954 in Cleveland, Ohio, and received her B.A. from Oberlin College and her M.A. in English from the University of New Hampshire. Among Moss's awards are four grants from the Kenan Charitable Trust, an Artist's Fellowship from the Artist's Foundation of Massachusetts, a Pushcart Prize, the Witter Bynner Prize, the Deward Profile Performance Artist Award, and the Whiting Writer Award. Her volumes of poetry include Hosiery Seams on a Bowlegged Woman *(1983),* Pyramid of Bone *(1989),* At Redbones *(1990),* Rainbow Remnants in Rock Bottom Ghetto Sky *(1991), and* Small Congregations: New and Selected Poems *(1993).*

"Tornados," published in Rainbow Remnants in Rock Bottom Ghetto Sky, *displays the exhilarating, dynamic energy of all her poetry. The poet envies tornadoes, which "do black more justice" than she, though Moss too creates whirlwinds, writing poems both "tightly wound" and "spinning wildly."*

Tornados

Truth is, I envy them
not because they dance; I out jitterbug them
as I'm shuttled through and through legs
strong as looms, weaving time. They
do black more justice than I, frenzy
of conductor of philharmonic and electricity, hair
on end, result of the charge when horns and strings release
the pent up Beethoven and Mozart. Ions played

instead of notes. The movement
is not wrath, not hormone swarm because
I saw my first forming above the church a surrogate
steeple. The morning of my first baptism and
salvation already tangible, funnel for the spirit
coming into me without losing a drop, my black
guardian angel come to rescue me before all the words

get out, *I looked over Jordan and what did I see coming for
to carry me home. Regardez,* it all comes back, even the first
grade French, when the tornado stirs up the past, bewitched spoon
lost in its own spin, like a roulette wheel that won't
be steered, like the world. They drove me underground,
tornado watches and warnings, atomic bomb drills. Adult
storms so I had to leave the room. Truth is

the tornado is a perfect nappy curl, tightly wound,
spinning wildly when I try to tamper with its nature, shunning
the hot comb and pressing oil even though if absolutely straight
I'd have the longest hair in the world. Bouffant tornadic
crown taking the royal path on a trip to town, stroll down
Tornado Alley where it intersects Memory Lane. Smoky spirit-
clouds, shadows searching for what cast them.

◎ *MELISSA RANGE*

Melissa Range was born in 1973 in northeastern Tennessee. After receiving her B.A. in English from the University of Tennessee, she spent two months traveling through Botswana before returning to the United States to continue her education. Range lives in Norfolk, Virginia, where she is pursuing an M.F.A. in poetry at Old Dominion University.

" 'Lot's Wife,' written in the fall of 1994, is one of a series of poems focusing on Biblical characters, most of whom are women. I was reading the story of Sodom and Gomorra in Genesis; although I'd read it many times, this reading all I could think about was Lot's wife, how she had no name and no identity apart from the 'pillar of salt.' The poem is an attempt to forge an identity for this woman, to make her more than an accessory to her 'holy' husband, a blurb in Genesis, or a sermon illustrated" (letter to M. Kallet, 1996).

Lot's Wife

Genesis 19:12–26

Woman without a name
to record in the family history:
this silent daughter of many fathers
worked the light out of her eyes,
covered her hair, pressed her lips together,
and bore the children — the proud pain of boys
and the girls worthy of tears,
girls with destinies penciled out
in lines identical to her own.

When he grabbed her hand, pulled her out the door
before she'd had a chance
to snatch her mother's shawl from its peg,
she swallowed words again,
drifted after, not seeing or hearing him,
his desperate insistence old to her by now.
She knew the finality, the end of the home
that preserved her, the stable shack that kept her mind
from spinning out of her head,
its walls and floors all she had left of herself —
she, who'd been young once,
who'd tossed dreams into the air like babies,
waited for them to fall back into her hands.

She realized as she climbed, trailing behind —
she couldn't leave, wouldn't go with him
                                        into a new land.
She preferred fire, run, hell on earth
to one more night with him, one more day
mending his clothes without a *thank you,*
another slow year of watching her daughters
mature too quickly, grow into bondslaves.
She stopped, pivoted before the protestations
                                        reached her ears.
For a moment she saw the glory of flame,
felt the blaze on her skin,
heat stripping her with liberation.

Everyone knows the ending,
the crystallization into salt.

We shake our heads, saddened at her lack of faith.
Is it such a sin to love the only thing you have?
Sister of longing, I wish you rain and wind —
dissolve, soak into earth on the spot you are mother to,
fly up to God in free white particles.

INTERVIEW

Living Among Strangers: An Interview with Sylvia Watanabe

by Patricia Clark

SYLVIA WATANABE

Patricia Clark's interview with Sylvia Watanabe, was conducted on May 18, 1995 at Watanabe's home in Grand Rapids, Michigan. Talking to the Dead, *Watanabe's first book, is filled with the paradisal landscape of Hawaii and peopled with quirky individual characters who are filled with anxiety, longing, and love. One of Watanabe's main interests is in preserving a vanishing way of life by writing it into her stories. She is currently at work on a novel.*

PC: How did you come to be interested in writing?
SW: With a love of reading — I think almost anyone who writes would tell you that. . . . And with a love for "make pretend," as I used to call it, that began when I was very young. When I was growing up, my only sister was much older than me, and until I began going to school, I spent a lot of time either alone or in the company of adults. I didn't know what it was like to be around other children, and I made up for that lack with a very vivid fantasy life. My mother taught me to read before I started school, and from that time, I carried a book with me wherever I went. Another thing that I liked a lot was to draw pictures and tell stories about them as I drew.

PC: As you drew them, not later?
SW: Yeah, as I was drawing. I'd sit there with my crayons and a pad of drawing paper, just chattering away . . .
PC: Who was your audience?
SW: Myself [*Laughter.*] And it's still true! But I didn't really think of that. I was just lost in the world I was conjuring . . .
PC: Were there particular books that were a shaping influence?
SW: As a child? I read certain books over and over again. Graham, Milne, everything by Lewis Carroll. These were my favorites. By that time I had started school, so I read them every year, during the Christmas holidays. Carroll especially — who was so humorous and precise. I think I sensed intuitively, as children do, that every piece of the world he made fit perfectly into every other piece . . . you could lose yourself so easily. I also read Kipling and Alcott. And all my friends were reading the Nancy Drew mysteries, so I did too. Did you do that?
PC: No, not Nancy Drew, but the Bobbsey Twins.
SW: And then as I grew older, though not much older — in late elementary school, I discovered Victoria Holt and Phyllis Whitney and Daphne du Maurier. My bad taste was formed very early! — though those books seem much better than the formula romances now. My mother was a teacher and there was a library next to the school where she taught, and which I also attended. So after I finished my classes for the day, I used to walk over to the library to wait for her. I read everything, indiscriminately.
PC: Tell me some things, too, about where you grew up. I know it was in Hawaii, wasn't it? Which island and who was around in terms of family members?
SW: Well, let's see: When I was a child I spent a lot of summers on Maui, where I was born. My father's family is from there, and his parents stayed on in Makawao, a little village in the upcountry, when all their children moved to Honolulu. My grandparents had been in charge of a Japanese language school there, and they continued to live in the rickety little principal's cottage next door to the classroom building, even after the school closed down in the 50s.

They were also staunch "Presbygationalists" — my grandmother was Presbyterian, my grandfather Congregational — and had originally come from Japan to do missionary work among the Japanese plantation workers. My grandmother's stepfather had been a Presbyterian minister in Japan. She went with him when he traveled around the country, preaching at various churches, and she provided the organ accompaniment for the hymn singing. I used to think she could do anything. She was fluent in both Japanese and English — as was my grandfather. Because of their language skills, a lot of people in the Japanese community came to them for translations of official documents and to act as intermediaries with the legal system and such. My grandfather provided translation services for the Japanese consulate, and this among other things led to his internment during the Second World War.

PC: Where was he sent?

SW: To Lordsburg, New Mexico. I was surprised much later to find out that there were different sorts of internment facilities, and his was a prisoner of war camp, subject to the rules of the Geneva Convention.

PC: There wasn't the mass evacuation in Hawaii as there was on the West Coast . . .

SW: No, no. Out of 100,000 Japanese and Japanese Americans in the Islands, about 1200 or so were interned. Most of them community leaders.

PC: What about your mother's parents?

SW: My mother's father died when she was very young, and her mother wasn't interned or anything like that. They lived in Honolulu. I spent a lot of time with my mother's mother when I was very young, before I started school. In the mornings before work, my parents dropped me off at my grandmother's house and I spent the day with her. And for a while she came to live with us. She didn't know any English . . . but I always remember being able to communicate with her perfectly.

PC: Those were the main people, then, in your life? And it sounds like they had a large influence on you.

SW: They did, yeah. I guess that is why for a very long time I thought of older people as very powerful. The older women, in my family, especially.

PC: Do you think this is something cultural — that comes, perhaps, from Japanese culture?

SW: Very much. But it's a common view of the aged in a lot of so-called traditional cultures.

PC: This view of powerful elders comes up a lot in your stories. I mean you're aware of that, aren't you?

SW: Oh yeah . . . it was so deeply imprinted on me when I was young. But now, with the passing of my grandparents, there isn't anyone in my family to uphold that view. I guess it figures so prominently in my book of stories because even though I'd ceased to believe in the literal truth of that view, it continued to haunt me as a metaphor. Then too, in some ways, it was a very closed and hierarchic world my grandparents inhabited. My mother's mother for example, Big Grandma we called her . . . Big Grandma took me aside before I went away to graduate school — I was thirty at the time! — Anyway, she warned me to be sure and return from wherever I went. "You be sure and come back," she said. "Don't go to live among strangers."

PC: Well, I like that. I see the wisdom of that.

SW: Do you? I liked the idea too — of being part of a world where your place is already made for you, where relationships operate by certain rules, where you are surrounded by a kind of loving regard . . . but there isn't an outside support system to sustain this way of life. My grandmother lived to be 112, and she spent her last 12 years in a senior care home, living — as she always warned me not to do — among strangers.

PC: How do you think the landscape of the islands affected you? I often have the feeling when reading your stories of "no time," or of being in a hamlet somewhere.
SW: I think that the physical landscape has greatly influenced the temporality of that book. When I was growing up, it seemed as if time didn't pass because the island landscape is so green, always.
PC: A real paradise?
SW: Maybe, or the illusion of paradise. Here in Michigan, one has a sense of timelessness of another kind — you know, the seasonal cycle, the eternal return. But there is always a great difference, say, from one spring to the next . . . so you have a sense, as well, of a temporal progression; of being in time. You see this especially — out in the garden — with the way certain plants develop from year to year. In Hawaii, seasonal changes are so much subtler.
PC: I wonder if that would make you more attentive to seeing smaller differences?
SW: In some ways. There are just things you feel with your skin. If you live in a place where it is perpetually 85°, when it gets down to 70, you have to put on a sweater. It seems so funny now when I call my relatives back home, and they say, "We're freezing to death; it's been so unusually cold," and it's like 65.

And it's the same with distances — the island of Oahu, where I grew up, is maybe 80 miles around. I remember the first time, driving across country (in the States) with my husband, I'd get dizzy from all that space; the enormous scale of everything. When we were in Utah, I was at the wheel going through the mountains toward Salt Lake City — and it was so overwhelming, I felt as if I were going to evaporate any minute.
PC: I wonder then, if when you put the human figure into a landscape, say, yours in Hawaii versus the American West, whether the figure isn't always going to be more important in that landscape of smaller scale?
SW: Without sentimentalizing too much, there is something very embracing and easy about a place that's always warm and green. And so perhaps it is easier to feel as if you belong to a landscape like that. I think a lot of the feeling I have about the Hawaiian landscape has to do with Polynesian values about the land. There's a Hawaiian term for it, *aloha 'aina,* "the love of the land," which refers to one's rootedness to a place . . . a sense of belonging that is almost a feeling in your blood. A lot of people who live in the islands for any length of time end up feeling this and being changed by the experience of living there.
PC: Would you call it an environmental view of things?
SW: Yes — much like that of many Native American cultures, perhaps, though its influence in the present-day culture of the islands has been somewhat diluted. But there's something else — something you see in comparing the writing by Japanese Americans in Hawaii and those who've grown up in California — especially before the Second World War. In California, a lot of Japanese Americans were itinerant farmers who lived in the desert and kept

having to begin over and over again, as their leases came to an end, just trying to scratch a living from that hostile environment. In the work of writers like Hisaye Yamamoto and Wakako Yamauchi, you get a very strong sense of what it was like to live in constant struggle against the landscape you inhabit . . . which is, of course, a sort of metaphor for prevailing social conditions as well. Then the war happened, and the internment.

The natural landscape in Hawaii is, in contrast, so benign . . . And even if they did not have much political power before the war, Japanese and Japanese Americans constituted a much greater percentage of the island population than they did in California . . . and this sense of being part of a large and cohesive community may have influenced one's perception of one's environment.

PC: Are you saying all this makes a difference in psychology?

SW: . . . In one's sense of cultural identity, perhaps. In Hawaii there has always been a greater mixing of cultural and linguistic practices among different ethnic groups — though this is perhaps changing now. By bringing together so many immigrant groups, the plantation experience, as oppressive as it was, probably contributed to the breaking down of the traditional boundaries that separated the members of different ethnic groups. What subsequently developed in the islands was a kind of mixed, "creole" culture — to borrow the linguistic use of the term. The identification with that culture, which is not specifically Japanese or American colonial or Hawaiian, but a mixture of elements from all these traditions, as well as others — along with the strong feeling of attachment to the specific place where that mixed culture evolved — I think that is partly what distinguishes one's sense of identity as a Japanese American from Hawaii.

PC: I know that one issue recurring in your work is the collision of cultures (generational, ethnic, gender) and I'm wondering how you see this issue resolved in your fiction. Further, you have resolved it in more than one way, I'd guess (I'm thinking of stories such as "Anchorage" and "The Caves of Okinawa," which seem to end in very different ways) — how would you describe those different resolutions? This is such an important issue and one that affects people in real life — I wonder, do you hold out hope that fiction can teach us certain things about coping with life? Or does that seem too wildly optimistic to you?

SW: The cultural collision in "Anchorage" is resolved — if one can call it a resolution, maybe it is just a respite — through the prevailing of Little Grandma's point of view. She insists on the clear-sighted but loving acceptance of things as they are. On the other hand, in "Caves," Haru can never reach this place of rest and resists, up until the very end, accepting anything as it is. The resolution at the end of that story, where her will prevails, and her son returns to Vietnam, is also provisional at best. Maybe that's what I think that fiction can teach us — not what to be, or even where to stand, but to be more complexly aware.

PC: I'm also wondering about family and encouragement. Is writing something they encouraged you to do?
SW: My dad always wanted to be a writer, but he didn't pursue it. It wasn't a practical goal, and things were very hard during the thirties when he was in college. He was also very good in science, so he became an entomologist and went into public health.

But writing was in his family. His father was a scholar, and he was always scribbling away at something. I remember when he was in his 90s, he'd be locked away for hours at a time in his study, bent over a pad of rice paper with an ink brush in his hand.

I never came out and said I was going to be a writer. I just sort of sidled into it — you know, in case it didn't work.
PC: Gotcha. Yeah, plans for a graceful retreat. [*Laughter.*]
SW: So I started off teaching ESL, and then after that I moved into composition, and then I took a workshop in nonfiction forms so I could teach composition better, but in that workshop, I couldn't write anything but fiction.
PC: Well, how did that work?
SW: I found I just couldn't tell a straight story. Or maybe it was—that the narrative process, itself, changed everything.
PC: When you finally did sidle your way into writing fiction, then, and published stories, and then published your volume of short stories, what was the reaction of family members? Interest, fame?
SW: It was, "That's not us!" [*Laughter.*]
PC: Really!?
SW: And they were right — to some extent. Because characters in a story are and also are not drawn from real-life people — what did Stevens call it? The injection of the unreal into the real?

But, yes, my father was very happy — I was saddened that my mother could not have seen the book before she died. Her death and the publication of *Talking* happened around the same time.
PC: I remember when you came to Grand Valley State University's literary festival, you said something about the primary task of the fiction writer — that it was to make the familiar strange and the strange familiar. Could you talk about that powerful role of the writer as creator? And how you transform things in your work?
SW: Hmmm. . . . So that has come back to haunt me. I guess I meant a few different things, with regard to the role of the writer. In his essay "Imagination as Value," Stevens describes the imagination as the power to "perceive the normal in the abnormal, the opposite of chaos in chaos" — and I guess, at some abstract level, this is partly what I meant. Perhaps because of my own educational history — all my teachers were new critics, steeped in modernist aesthetics — I am very attracted to Stevens's notion of the transcendent, shaping power of

the imagination. This view also seemed in some way to align with my childhood propensity for "make pretend."

But, having grown up in what can only be described as the colonial culture of Hawaii — we were a colonial territory during my earliest childhood — anyway, growing up in that sort of culture made me very much aware of where this view of the imagination comes from. I suspect the modernist notion of "chaos" with its underlying view of the "primitive." Was it Isak Dinesen who described the Africans, among whom she lived, as "aspects of nature"? So I've tried, very consciously, to look to the culture in which I grew up for a narrative language. I'm intrigued by the process of how new, formerly "strange" cultural signifiers become introduced into our literary tradition . . . are made familiar.

And in drawing characters — that's where exploring the tension between the familiar and the strange is most fun for me. So that's a long-winded partial answer to your question . . .

PC: What do you mean — with regard to drawing characters?

SW: Well . . . I like to write about busybodies, for example — they're a pretty stock type of character — like Aunt Pearlie in "Anchorage" and "Talking to the Dead." But I always imagine that, as commonplace as a character like that might seem, she must also have some hidden places, odd little corners to explore. I'm interested in exploring those corners. I'd felt that I'd succeeded with Pearlie when one of my editors told me that she was just like a particular female relation of hers . . .

PC: Though members of your own family had denied any connection . . .

SW: Yeah, I knew I was writing about *somebody's* aunt!

PC: So you're saying that the transformative power was there to make your character accessible and believable to someone living in an entirely different cultural milieu — like New York City?

SW: But without consciously striving to do so. . . . I didn't sit down and say, Now, I am going to write a character who is accessible to someone in New York City.

PC: Do you think you know, too, when you're starting a story? Or do you have an image — maybe something quirky — and then you follow the string and ask, "What does this mean?"

SW: A lot of times, I start off with an image, or a bit of folklore, or a sensory impression. After my mother died, I was staying with my father, helping to clean up the house, and I was sometimes wakened at night by the sound of a radio, on very low volume, coming from the next room. In her last months, when she was in a great deal of pain, my mother had a habit of getting up and turning on the radio very low. But when I went to check things out, there would be no radio playing; it was perhaps my imagination filling the gap made by her absence. Or sometimes I'd walk into her room and smell the faint fragrance of incense. In Native Hawaiian belief, these sorts of inappropriate sensory impressions mean something . . . if you smell flowers when you are swimming out in the middle of the ocean, it is a portent of something. Anyway, I've gone off the point again . . . but these are the kinds of images that I start off with . . . and then in the process of making narrative sense of them, I incorporate bits of lore, this and that. I don't usually sit down and start writing until I have a frame in my head — which includes particular characters and a beginning and an end.

PC: Do you kind of know, then, "Oh my character's going to start in this situation and get to here, and end up here," somehow?

SW: And then in the process of sitting down and writing the story, you often find that that shifts and changes.

PC: And you're willing to alter that as you go along?

SW: Oh sure. Or the story often breaks into many strands so what you thought was the original ending would be one of the strands that breaks off.

PC: Do you consciously alter something that might have happened to you, and you say, "Well, this was a woman of this age and a man of that age, but I want to free myself of reality and I want to make it different"?

SW: Of course, yes.

PC: And I suppose you'd tell student writers to do that? Why?

SW: I guess it's that rule about writing what you *don't* know . . . or maybe . . . I might advise students to begin with what they know and take it where they don't know.

The stories in *Talking* are often read as autobiography, which I've never understood. Do you find that people read your poetry that way?

PC: I think they try to. And I wish they wouldn't. When I read your stories I don't read them autobiographically; I don't want to. I mean, I see little snippets of things and think, "Oh, that's something I've seen Sylvia do," but on the whole, the characters don't seem like you. I'm thinking of Yuri in "Talking to the Dead." She seems like a distinct person.

SW: Yeah, she's tall and I'm short. [*Laughter.*]

PC: Writers don't work in isolation — you mentioned that you lost your mother not too long ago, and also your very elderly grandmother. Did their deaths have an effect on your work? Could you describe that?

SW: When my grandmother died a year and a half ago, I realized that the three most important women in my life — she, my other grandmother, and my mother — were gone. I think that whenever a person loses someone who has been central to her development, in the way that these three women were to mine, it is almost as if some deep process of change begins to happen — to accommodate that loss. Maybe, like planting up the empty spaces in a garden, one begins turning physical absence into words. Through words, absence becomes presence. I wrote the story "Where People Know Me" not long after my mother's death.

PC: I get really caught up when I read your stories with the rhythm of the sentences. There's a polish to them, like the surface of a polished stone or agate. How do you do that, Sylvia?

SW: Well, I read them aloud . . . over and over again. As I'm reading a sentence, and a word doesn't quite fit — a rhythm doesn't seem right . . . I keep pressing at it, shifting order, trying other words—till it seems right.

PC: Have you also worked at varying sentence length? I notice a lot of sentence length variety: short, clipped sentences after a bunch of long ones. Characters who speak in short, clipped sentences; witty, clipped sentences.

SW: Maybe that's an aspect of the Japanese-Hawaiian culture. A lot wasn't said. You either knew or you didn't. "You listen to what I'm not saying," or "If you don't know what I'm not saying, I have nothing to say to you." [*Laughter.*]

PC: This also seems like a Jewish American tradition.

SW: I have an Italian American friend who grew up in Chicago. . . . From what she tells me about her family, I almost feel like I came from that family. She'll tell me they'll all be at the table, with one last piece of chicken on the serving dish, and everybody's dying for that piece of chicken, but the dish will just go from one person to the next . . . nobody'll touch that chicken.

PC: What do you think of the current multicultural rage or the backlash against it?

SW: I hope it's not just a rage. I wish the debate were less polarized . . . that less of it centered around jargon and terminology. The issue of political correctness, for example, seems to some extent like a red herring — chitchat about political etiquette — when bigger things are at stake. Recently, my husband and I taught a graduate fiction workshop in which a student submitted a draft of a story which depicted an all-white racial utopia which was under constant threat from a dark-skinned, mixed-blooded race. Needless to say, these "colored people" were primitive, inchoate, inscrutable, treacherous, and those weren't even their bad qualities! We had to ask ourselves, when we got that manuscript, whether to treat it like any other piece of fiction submitted to workshop — ignoring, in doing so, the insult and outrage with which we'd responded to the piece. And why exactly did we feel insulted? Because the poor student wasn't being politically correct? Or was there something else going on that needed to be addressed? We decided, of course, that we had to address the race issue. We had to address questions of audience — who did the writer expect to read this stuff? We had to talk about aesthetics and characterization — because in the area of characterization, aesthetics and one's attitudes about race do intersect. As Anne Stevenson puts it, "The way you say the world is what you get." But before we said one word about any of this, it turned out that the rest of the students in the workshop, without exception, had responded to the story as we had.

I couldn't help thinking how different things might have been if the student who'd written that piece had very early on — while his attitudes were still being formed — been exposed to a more varied and inclusive literary tradition. Maybe he would have been able to write about race and difference, among things, in a more complex way.

My own feeling about the multicultural movement is that it is still very much in evolution. We are evolving new models for imagining our polymorphous society — do we see ourselves as a mosaic or a tossed salad — do we use metallurgical metaphors or culinary ones? And how do we describe the increasing phenomenon of cultural hybridism? As a writer, I feel obliged to draw on all the traditions that have shaped my cultural identity. In "Imaginary Homelands," Salman Rushdie says of writers from immigrant traditions that we are unwilling to be excluded from any aspect of our heritage. And to be able to work at this place of intersection, where so many formerly disparate traditions come together, is what I believe to be the truly exciting possibility of the current multicultural "rage."

PC: Do you think of yourself as a woman writer?

SW: Yes, I do. That is a category — since one must always belong to a category — I feel most comfortable with. Partly because of its inclusiveness — because it doesn't elide difference in its universality. Most of the writers I admire now are women writers. And I think that some of the strongest writing is being produced by women. I'm thinking of Toni Morrison, Jamaica Kincaid, Alice Munro, Carol Shields, Hisaye Yamamoto, Margaret Drabble, Muriel Spark, Rachel Ingalls, among many, many others. And a list like this doesn't include the old girls — like O'Connor and Colette. A lot of these writers are incredible stylists. They've opened up the tradition and introduced new strategies, new characters, a new language.

PC: I wonder if it's because of how women have been discounted so long as writers, that they found just a kind of energy, opened a vein somehow. Struck gold, somehow.

SW: Women's culture . . . which has been submerged for a long time.

PC: Could you talk about your own struggles to forge an identity for yourself — both as a writer and as a person? I'm thinking about how complex that may be for you — with Japanese and Hawaiian roots, with being a woman, with living in very white Western Michigan?

SW: I thought a lot about this question and don't feel able to even begin to answer it . . . at this point in time. In a way, I hope that the other answers, as I've fleshed them out more completely in this interview, might provide some sort of indirect answer.

PC: Talk a little about film. I know that you've been involved in doing a screenplay of a story of yours for TV. What was that like? Would like to do more of it?

SW: It was very fun. I worked with my husband, Bill Osborn, on that project. He's very used to working by himself — writing has almost always been a completely solitary activity for him — so he might disagree with how much fun it actually was. But I'm used to joint projects from graduate school and other jobs I've had, so I enjoyed it. One of the most enjoyable things was when he'd get on a roll, then I'd pick it up, then he'd get an idea from what I'd written, and so on. We had two separate keyboards attached to the same computer, so our working style developed into a kind of conversation via the word processor.

PC: Do you worry about film taking away more readers?

SW: It is a worry for me which is mostly related to the disappointment I sometimes feel when I'm teaching freshman composition and I wonder where all the bad grammar is coming from. And not just bad grammar — but a general unease with written language. Because just the habit of reading would solve a lot of that. On the other hand, I am an incurable movie addict.

PC: Were you headed toward being a novelist all along, and you thought you'd practice on stories, or did you come to feel constrained, finally, by the form of short stories and want to have a bigger landscape to deal with?

SW: I always wanted to do both. It seemed like it would be a thrilling and dangerous thing to try and write a novel.

PC: And is it?

SW: Well, yeah, though I sometimes wonder how thrilling it is.

PC: Do you have the feeling, like a lot of writers, a superstitious thing that you ought not to talk about current work?

SW: I don't know if it's superstition, but it's almost as though the book trips me up so when I start to talk about it I immediately get tongue-tied. Anyway, it's sort of bad form, isn't it? To talk about what one hasn't yet written.

PC: How's it going? Are you far into it?

SW: About one-third.

PC: Do you have a title?

SW: Ummmm. Yes, I do, but I don't think I want to say it. It might change too.

PC: How about new projects? Or is that one you're going to finish first?

SW: The novel is the biggest priority right now. But I'm also working on an essay for another collection being edited by Mickey Pearlman. It's going to be a collection about the notion of home called something like "A Place Called Home."

PC: I know we share a mutual love of gardening. Do you think there's any effect on your writing life from the work of gardening? What effect?

SW: In both writing and gardening — if things are going well, you feel as if you've just opened up a window and flown through it to somewhere else. Actually, with gardening, you just have to open the back door and step outside. But in some seasons, especially in the spring and early summer, when the air smells a certain way, and the flowers are coming in — you step out that door, and it's like walking into a dream you just love being in. When I'm writing, and I get stuck, I go out and garden for several hours. Then the next day, I can write again. Sometimes the very same day. It's almost as if the garden itself becomes a kind of portal to find my way back into writing.

PC: Hmm. Interesting. So we're drawn outside after a morning at the desk partly, in a way, to solve something.

SW: And you become much more aware of sensory perceptions. Colors and smells. This perfect daffodil. These perfect tulips.
PC: Yes. As these are on Sylvia's table.
SW: It's such a satisfaction. The other night we harvested asparagus and fresh pea shoots, so for dinner we had a couple of stir fries with rice. And it was so satisfying to eat what we'd raised out of our own ground. My grandparents, you know, all of them were gardeners. My mom's mother especially. I remember her always having this impulse to plant something wherever she saw an empty spot in the garden.
PC: I wonder if that's what writers do. Fill up, articulate something about empty spaces.
SW: Yeah. I used to follow my grandmother around as she would work in the garden, planting up those empty spots . . . and sometimes, she'd pick something right out of the ground and eat it. She was intense and filled with pleasure. I learned a lot from watching her.

Working Life

Working Life

◎ ◎ ◎

For too long the realm of work, especially important work, has been seen as belonging only to men. The truth is that women have always bent their backs to a wide assortment of tasks, though they have not always been paid equally with their male counterparts. The selections in "Working Life" illustrate that women are engaged in a variety of work, creative as well as tedious, and that their work raises issues that resonate throughout their lives.

As various as the types of labor are the responses to it. Work may separate us from one another, or it may bring a sense of camaraderie. Work may bring pain in its unending tedium and the difficulty of breaking the cycle of poverty. Or work may begin as mere labor and lead us to knowledge and insight about ourselves, or become a kind of meditation that frees the imagination and the subconscious as it busies the hands. The hands in "Working Life" are women's hands — seen as they move over the keys of a word processor, as they slide an iron back and forth on clothes, as they reach to open a classroom's door, and as they perform a myriad of tasks in the home and on the job.

In Jamaica Kincaid's "Poor Visitor," the young narrator has done many tasks in her homeland of Antigua. However, she is facing her first job as an au pair, working far from home as an immigrant in New York City — a woman of nut-brown skin working for a white family. Though her employer family is kind to her, though they say she should regard them as family, she feels a great distance between them because of differences of race and class.

The narrator of the first part of this excerpt from Gloria Naylor's *Mama Day* has been seeking a job in New York for six months. By turns cynical and world-weary, humorous and crafty, Cocoa almost longs for the days of segregated job ads — "It would save me a whole lot of subway tokens." Clearly one issue that work reveals is the social and racial stratification of the country. (This will also surface as the main issue in Alice Childress's play *Florence.*)

Tillie Olsen's "I Stand Here Ironing" is justifiably well-known for its poignant depiction of a working-class woman who has tried to raise her daughter attentively despite upheaval and hardship. The narrator describes her daughter's childhood in language both poetic and heartbreaking. We see the cost of work in this child's too-early maturity and sadness, which the mother's sorrow cannot wish away.

The three nonfiction pieces included here form a set: the authors' subject is writing itself. Annie Dillard compares writing to apprenticeship in a trade. It takes courage to begin, for there is always a gap between grand conception and humble actuality, and it takes, also, backtracking and revision, as much throwing out as pushing forward. Maxine Kumin relishes the physical aspect of certain kinds of labor because "one set of self-imposed deadlines nurtures the other. . . ." Physical labor allows the mind to roam free and to meditate on all kinds of subjects. Natalie Goldberg narrates a tale of epiphany, of finding her vocation while teaching a class of sixth-graders. Feeling unqualified, she rashly quits her job shortly after signing a contract, trusting her gut instinct and thus showing others the way. Once she has decided to let go of her teaching job, she becomes an inspired teacher — and she gives each of the children a sweet memory.

Florence, Alice Childress's one-act play, is a brief but packed tale of work and dreams. It portrays race relations in America and the effect race has on one's expectations for work and for the future. Through conversations that take place at a train station in a small town in the South, the reader learns of strong-willed Florence who has gone to New York to be an actress. Florence's mother sets out to bring her daughter home, but reaches a turning point when she talks with the racist Mrs. Carter. When Mama realizes the uphill battle her daughter is waging, she becomes an activist for her daughter's career.

Poets, as well as fiction writers and dramatists, write of physical and mental work. Kate Braid writes of the way male construction workers at first taunt the "girl on the crew." Not only does the woman learn her job and keep up with the men, she surpasses them. Her efforts go beyond the normal into the heroic and the fantastic: "I bite off nails with my teeth." In "The Carpenter" by Kathryn Stripling Byer, similarly powerful work takes place as the speaker re-creates, through her writing, her grandfather's burned-out house — a necessary emotional labor of reconstruction. Barbara Crooker's vision of work is endless and brutal in "The Last Woman in America to Wash Diapers," but the task is palpable and clear, at least. In "The Tomato Packing Plant Line," Enid Shomer describes the physical labor of the assembly line, of weeding out the imperfect tomatoes, and her focus lingers on the young women now grown older who have not been able to hold on to their own "ripeness."

Laurie Blauner describes a different kind of labor: complex mental work. How often is work a means of escape? A means of transport to another place?

In "The Invention of Imagination," there is a Sisyphus-like repetition to work, the endless sharing of "the household of your heart."

In Frances McCue's tour-de-force "The Stenographer's Breakfast," with its long, confident lines, we find a satirical take on lawyers from the point of view of a legal secretary who takes dictation on all that transpires, a sassy control not found in the "non-dictated" world, the "alternative chaos."

Linda Hogan's "What Has Happened to These Working Hands?" is an incantation and a praise poem listing the work of women's hands throughout history, especially the work done by tribal women. Women have suffered and grieved in times of violence and war, but they have also learned to retrieve what is sustaining by returning to their cultural sources, digging up "buried songs." The repetition and rhythmical insistence of the lines reminds us that women and women's work endure. For Hogan, traditional ceremonies are a source of strength that her hands invoke here as a blessing. Affirmative, too, is Anita Skeen's vision of a teacher's labor. Weary and ready to give up the effort of teaching in a video culture, the teacher changes her mind when a student brings some writing of hers to share "like communion bread." Here is work as shared labor and shared emotion. Here is the power of connection through work.

In "Turtles" by Lois-Ann Yamanaka we meet a working-class teenager, Lucy, the narrator, who helps Bernie at his taxidermy shop in the small town of Pahala. When Bernie insists that they leave work to go and watch turtles hatching, Lucy rescues a baby turtle the way she herself might want to be rescued from her own impoverished and abusive home life.

It is fitting to end this gathering of poems with May Sarton's "The Work of Happiness." For over sixty years of writing, the "work of happiness" was writing itself, Sarton's deliberate, disciplined composing of her life.

Marilyn Kallet's interview with May Sarton took place at her home in York, Maine, when Sarton was seventy-nine years old. Though May Sarton was quite ill at the time, and never fully recovered, she did continue to write poetry and to keep a journal until her death in 1995.

◎ *JAMAICA KINCAID*

Jamaica Kincaid was born in 1949 in St. John's, Antigua, West Indies. She studied photography at the New School for Social Research in New York and attended Franconia College in New Hampshire. At seventeen Kincaid left Antigua for New York City. Kincaid is a staff writer for the New Yorker *and has lectured at Bennington Col-*

lege in Vermont. Awards for her work include the Morton Dauwen Zabel Award from the American Academy and Institute of Arts and Letters for At the Bottom of the River *(stories, 1992). In 1992 she received a Lila Wallace-*Reader's Digest *Fund annual writer's award. Besides her volume of short stories, Kincaid has published a children's book,* Annie, Gwen, Lilly, Pam and Tulip *(1989), and two novels, most recently* Lucy *(1990).*

Kincaid has often written about life on the Caribbean island of Antigua, where she was born. "Poor Visitor" describes the journey of a young woman from the islands to New York City to become an au pair *— a journey similar to one actually taken by Kincaid. Through her eyes we see America in a not-always-flattering new light. The uneasy tone of the story reveals the young woman's continued vulnerability and status as an outsider.*

Poor Visitor

It was my first day. I had come the night before, a gray-black and cold night before — as it was expected to be in the middle of January, though I didn't know that at the time — and I could not see anything clearly on the way in from the airport, even though there were lights everywhere. As we drove along, someone would single out to me a famous building, an important street, a park, a bridge that when built was thought to be a spectacle. In a daydream I used to have, all these places were points of happiness to me; all these places were lifeboats to my small drowning soul, for I would imagine myself entering and leaving them, and just that — entering and leaving over and over again — would see me though a bad feeling I did not have a name for. I only knew it felt a little like sadness. Now that I saw these places, they looked ordinary, dirty, worn down by so many people entering and leaving them in real life, and it occurred to me that I could not be the only person in the world for whom they were a fixture of fantasy. It was not my first bout with the disappointment of reality and it would not be my last. The undergarments that I wore were all new, bought for my journey, and as I sat in the car, twisting this way and that to get a good view of the sights before me, I was reminded of how uncomfortable the new can make you feel.

I got into an elevator, something I had never done before, and then I was in an apartment and seated at a table, eating food just taken from a refrigerator. In Antigua, where I came from, I had always lived in a house, and my house did not have a refrigerator in it. Everything I was experiencing — the ride in the elevator, being in an apartment, eating day-old food that had been stored in a refrigerator — was such a good idea that I could imagine I would grow used to it and like it very much, but at first it was all so new that I had to smile with my mouth turned down at the corners. I slept soundly that night, but it wasn't because I was happy and comfortable — quite the opposite; it was because I didn't want to take in anything else.

That morning, the morning of my first day, the morning that followed my first night, was a sunny morning. It was not the sort of bright sun-yellow making everything curl at the edges, almost in fright, that I was used to, but a pale-yellow sun, as if the sun had grown weak from trying too hard to shine; but still it was sunny, and that was nice and made me miss my home less. And so, seeing the sun, I got up and put on a dress, a gay dress made out of madras cloth — the same sort of dress that I would wear if I were at home and setting out for a day in the country. It was all wrong. The sun was shining but the air was cold. It was the middle of January, after all. But I did not know that the sun could shine and the air remain cold; no one had ever told me. What a feeling that was! How can I explain? Something I had always known — the way I knew my skin was the color brown of a nut rubbed repeatedly with a soft cloth, or the way I knew my own name — something I took completely for granted, "the sun is shining, the air is warm," was not so. I was no longer in a tropical zone, and this realization now entered my life like a flow of water dividing formerly dry and solid ground, creating two banks, one of which was my past — so familiar and predictable that even my unhappiness then made me happy now just to think of it — the other my future, a gray blank, an overcast seascape on which rain was falling and no boats were in sight. I was no longer in a tropical zone and I felt cold inside and out, the first time such a sensation had come over me.

In books I had read — from time to time, when the plot called for it — someone would suffer from homesickness. A person would leave a not very nice situation and go somewhere else, somewhere a lot better, and then long to go back where it was not very nice. How impatient I would become with such a person, for I would feel that I was in a not very nice situation myself, and how I wanted to go somewhere else. But now I, too, felt that I wanted to be back where I came from. I understood it, I knew where I stood there. If I had had to draw a picture of my future then, it would have been a large gray patch surrounded by black, blacker, blackest.

What a surprise this was to me, that I longed to be back in the place that I came from, that I longed to sleep in a bed I had outgrown, that I longed to be with people whose smallest, most natural gesture would call up in me such a rage that I longed to see them all dead at my feet. Oh, I had imagined that with my one swift act — leaving home and coming to this new place — I could leave behind me, as if it were an old garment never to be worn again, my sad thoughts, my sad feelings, and my discontent with life in general as it presented itself to me. In the past, the thought of being in my present situation had been a comfort, but now I did not even have this to look forward to and so I lay down on my bed and dreamt that I was eating a bowl of pink mullet and green figs cooked in coconut milk, and it had been cooked by my grandmother, which was why the taste of it pleased me so, for she was the person I liked best in all the world and those were the things I liked best to eat also.

The room in which I lay was a small room just off the kitchen — the maid's room. I was used to a small room, but this was a different sort of small room. The ceiling was very high and the walls went all the way up to the ceiling, enclosing the room like a box — a box in which cargo travelling a long way should be shipped. But I was not cargo. I was only an unhappy young woman living in a maid's room, and I was not even the maid. I was the young girl who watches over the children and goes to school at night. How nice everyone was to me, though, saying that I should regard them as my family and make myself at home. I believed them to be sincere, for I knew that such a thing would not be said to a member of their real family. After all, aren't family the people who become the millstone around your life's neck? On the last day I spent at home, my cousin — a girl I had known all my life, an unpleasant person even before her parents forced her to become a Seventh-Day Adventist — made a farewell present to me of her own Bible, and with it she made a little speech about God and goodness and blessings. Now it sat before me on a dresser, and I remembered how when we were children we would sit under my house and terrify and torment each other by reading out loud passages from the Book of Revelations, and I wondered if ever in my whole life a day would go by when these people I had left behind, my own family, would not appear before me in one way or another.

There was also a small radio on this dresser, and I had turned it on. At that moment, almost as if to sum up how I was feeling, a song came on some of the words of which were "Put yourself in my place, if only for a day; see if you can stand the awful emptiness inside." I sang these words to myself over and over, as if they were a lullaby, and I fell asleep again. This time I dreamt that I was holding in my hands one of my old cotton-flannel nightgowns, and it was printed with beautiful scenes of children playing with Christmas-tree decorations. The scenes printed on my nightgown were so real that I could actually hear the children laughing. I felt compelled to know where this nightgown came from, and I started to examine it furiously, looking for the label. I found it just where a label usually is, in the back, and it read "Made in Australia." I was awakened from this dream by the actual maid, a woman who had let me know right away, on meeting me, that she did not like me, and gave as her reason the way I talked. I thought it was because of something else, but I did not know what. As I opened my eyes, the word "Australia" stood between our faces, and I remembered then that Australia was settled as a prison for bad people, people so bad that they couldn't be put in a prison in their own country.

My waking hours soon took on a routine. I walked four small girls to their school, and when they returned at midday I gave them a lunch of soup from a tin, and sandwiches. In the afternoon, I read to them and played with them. When they were away, I studied my books, and at night I went to school. I was unhappy. I looked at a map. The Atlantic Ocean stood between me and the place I came from, but would it have made a difference if it had been a teacup of water? I could not go back.

Outside, always it was cold, and everyone said that it was the coldest winter they had ever experienced; but the way they said it made me think they said this every time winter came around. And I couldn't blame them for not really remembering each year how unpleasant, how unfriendly winter weather could be. The trees with their bare, still limbs looked dead, and as if someone had just placed them there and planned to come back and get them later; all the windows of the houses were shut tight, the way windows are shut up when a house will be empty for a long time; when people walked on the streets they did it quickly, as if they were doing something behind someone's back, as if they didn't want to draw attention to themselves, as if being out in the cold too long would cause them to dissolve. How I longed to see someone lingering on a corner, trying to draw my attention to him, trying to engage me in conversation, someone complaining to himself in a voice I could overhear about a god whose love and mercy fell on the just and the unjust.

I wrote home to say how lovely everything was, and I used flourishing words and phrases, as if I were living life in a greeting card — the kind that has a satin ribbon on it, and quilted hearts and roses, and is expected to be so precious to the person receiving it that the manufacturer has placed a leaf of plastic on the front to protect it. Everyone I wrote to said how nice it was to hear from me, how nice it was to know that I was doing well, that I was very much missed, and that they couldn't wait until the day came when I returned.

One day the maid who said she did not like me because of the way I talked told me that she was sure I could not dance. She said that I spoke like a nun, I walked like one also, and that everything about me was so pious it made her feel at once sick to her stomach and sick with pity just to look at me. And so, perhaps giving way to the latter feeling, she said that we should dance, even though she was quite sure I didn't know how. There was a little portable record-player in my room, the kind that when closed up looked like a ladies' vanity case, and she put on a record she had bought earlier that day. It was a song that was very popular at the time — three girls, not older than I was, singing in harmony and in a very insincere and artificial way about love and so on. It was very beautiful all the same, and it was beautiful because it was so insincere and artificial. She enjoyed this song, singing at the top of her voice, and she was a wonderful dancer — it amazed me to see the way in which she moved. I could not join her and I told her why: the melodies of her song were so shallow, and the words, to me, were meaningless. From her face, I could see she had only one feeling about me: how sick to her stomach I made her. And so I said that I knew songs, too, and I burst into a calypso about a girl who ran away to Port-au-Spain, Trinidad, and had a good time, with no regrets.

The household in which I lived was made up of a husband, a wife, and the four girl children. The husband and wife looked alike and their four children looked just like them. In photographs of themselves, which they placed all over the house, their six yellow-haired heads of various sizes were bunched as if they were a bouquet of flowers tied together by an unseen string. In the pictures, they smiled out at the world, giving the impression that they found everything in it unbearably wonderful. And it was not a farce, their smiles. From wherever they had gone, and they seemed to have been all over the world, they brought back some tiny memento, and they could each recite its history from its very beginning. Even when a little rain fell, they would admire the way it streaked through the blank air.

At dinner, when we sat down at the table — and did not have to say grace (such a relief; as if they believed in a God that did not have to be thanked every time you turned around) — they said such nice things to each other, and the children were so happy. They would spill their food, or not eat any of it at all, or make up rhymes about it that would end with the words "smelt bad." How they made me laugh, and I wondered what sort of parents I must have had, for even to think of such words in their presence I would have been scolded severely, and I vowed that if I ever had children I would make sure that the first words out of their mouths were bad ones.

It was at dinner one night not long after I began to live with them that they began to call me the Visitor. They said I seemed not to be a part of things, as if I didn't live in their house with them, as if they weren't like a family to me, as if I were just passing through, just saying one long Hallo!, and soon would be saying a quick Goodbye! So long! It was very nice! For look at the way I looked at them eating, Lewis said. Had I never seen anyone put a forkful of French-cut green beans in his mouth before? This made Mariah laugh, but almost everything Lewis said made Mariah happy, and so she would laugh. When I didn't laugh also, Lewis said, Poor Visitor, poor Visitor, over and over, a sympathetic tone to his voice, and then he told me a story about an uncle he had who had gone to Canada and raised monkeys, and of how after a while the uncle loved monkeys so much and was so used to being around them that he found actual human beings hard to take. He had told me this story about his uncle before, and while he was telling it to me this time I was remembering a dream I had had about them: Lewis was chasing me around the house. I wasn't wearing any clothes. The ground on which I was running was yellow, as if it had been paved with cornmeal. Lewis was chasing me around and around the house, and though he came close he could never catch up with me. Mariah stood at the open windows saying, Catch her, Lewis, catch her.

Eventually I fell down a hole, at the bottom of which were some silver and blue snakes.

When Lewis finished telling his story, I told them my dream. When I finished, they both fell silent. Then they looked at me and Mariah cleared her throat, but it was obvious from the way she did it that her throat did not need clearing at all. Their two yellow heads swam toward each other and, in unison, bobbed up and down. Lewis made a clucking noise, then said, Poor, poor Visitor. And Mariah said, Dr. Freud for Visitor. Then they laughed in a soft, kind way. I had meant by telling them my dream that I had taken them in, because only people who were very important to me had ever shown up in my dreams, and I could see that they already understood that.

GLORIA NAYLOR

Gloria Naylor was born in 1950 in Harlem. She graduated from Brooklyn College and earned an M.A. in Afro-American Studies from Yale. The Women of Brewster Place *(1982) received the American Book Award. Other novels include* Linden Hills *(1986),* Mama Day *(1989), and* Bailey's Cafe *(1992). Naylor has been awarded Guggenheim and NEA fellowships for her novels and the New York Foundation for the Arts Fellowship for her screenwriting. She balances her work as a writer and as president of One Way Productions, an independent production company she began in 1990, with her commitment to developing quality children's programming for stage, television, and film. Naylor has taught at George Washington University, Boston University, and Cornell University. In 1996 her volume* Children of the Night: Best Short Stories by Black Writers *will appear.*

The following excerpt is the first chapter of Naylor's Mama Day*. We meet Ophelia Day, or Cocoa, observing a man in a Third Avenue coffee shop; we follow her thoughts as she discovers that this is George, the interviewer in the office where she is seeking a job, and the man who will become her lover. Cocoa is the great-niece of Mama Day, the family matriarch who possesses second sight and whose psychic powers are tested by Cocoa. In alternating segments we are privvy to George's thoughts as well.*

from *Mama Day*

You were picking your teeth with a plastic straw — I know, I know, it wasn't really a straw, it was a coffee stirrer. But, George, let's be fair, there are two little openings in those things that you could possibly suck liquid through if you were desperate enough, so I think I'm justified in calling it a straw since dumps like that Third Avenue coffee shop had no shame in calling it a coffee stirrer, when the stuff they poured into your cup certainly didn't qualify as coffee. Everything about those types of places was a little more or less than they should have been. I was always thrown off balance: the stainless steel display cases were too clean, and did you ever notice that the cakes and pies inside of them never made crumbs when they were cut, and no juice ever dripped from the cantaloupes and honeydews? The Formica tabletops were a bit too slippery for your elbows, and the smell of those red vinyl seats — always red vinyl — seeped into the taste of your food, which came warm if it was a hot dish and warm if it was a cold dish. I swear to you, once I got warm pistachio ice cream and it was solid as a rock. Those places in New York were designed for assembly-line nutrition, and it worked — there was nothing in there to encourage you to linger. Especially when the bill came glued to the bottom of your dessert plate — who would want to ask for a second cup of coffee and have to sit there watching a big greasy thumbprint spread slowly over the "Thank You" printed on the back?

I suppose you had picked up the stirrer for your coffee because you'd already used the teaspoon for your soup. I saw the waitress bring you the Wednesday special, and that meant pea soup, which had to be attacked quickly before it lumped up. So not risking another twenty-minute wait for a soup spoon, you used your teaspoon, which left you without anything to use in your coffee when it came with the bill. And obviously you knew that our pleasant waitress's "Catch ya in a men-it, babe," doomed you to either your finger, a plastic stirrer, or coffee straight up. And you used plenty of sugar and milk. That guy knows the art of dining successfully on Third Avenue, I thought. When the lunch menu has nothing priced above six dollars, it's make do if you're gonna make it back to work without ulcers.

And there wasn't a doubt in my mind that you were going back to some office or somewhere definite after that meal. It wasn't just the short-sleeved blue shirt and tie; you ate with a certain ease and decisiveness that spelled *employed* with each forkful of their stringy roast beef. Six months of looking for a job had made me an expert at picking out the people who, like me, were hurrying up to wait — in somebody's outer anything for a chance to make it through their inner doors to prove that you could type two words a minute, or not drool on your blouse while answering difficult questions about your middle initial and date of birth.

By that August I had it down to a science, although the folks here would say that I was gifted with a bit of Mama Day's second sight. Second sight had nothing to do with it: in March of that year coats started coming off, and it was the kind of April that already had you dodging spit from the air conditioners along the side streets, so by midsummer I saw it all hanging out — those crisp butterflies along the avenues, their dresses still holding the sharp edges of cloth that had been under cool air all morning in some temperature-controlled box.

Or the briefcases that hung near some guy's thigh with a balance that said there was more in them than empty partitions and his gym shorts. And I guess being a woman, I could always tell hair: heads are held differently when they've been pampered every week, the necks massaged to relax tense muscles "so the layers will fall right, dear." The blonds in their Dutch-boy cuts, my counterparts in Jerri curls, those Asian women who had to do practically nothing to be gorgeous with theirs so they frizzed it or chopped it off, because then everybody knew they had the thirty-five dollars a week to keep it looking that way. Yeah, that group all had jobs. And it was definitely first sight on any evening rush-hour train: all those open-neck cotton shirts — always plaid or colored — with the dried sweat marks under the arms of riders who had the privilege of a seat before the northbound IRT hit midtown because those men had done their stint in the factories, warehouses, and loading docks farther down on Delancey or in East New York or Brooklyn.

But it took a little extra attention for the in-betweens: figuring out which briefcases that swung with the right weight held only pounds of résumés, or which Gucci appointment books had the classifieds neatly clipped out and taped onto the pages so you'd think she was expected wherever she was heading instead of just expected to wait. I have to admit, the appointment-book scam took a bit of originality and class. That type knew that a newspaper folded to the last section was a dead giveaway. And I don't know who the others were trying to fool by pretending to scan the headlines and editorial page before going to the classifieds and there finally creasing the paper and shifting it an inch or two closer to their faces. When all else failed, I was left with watching the way they walked — either too determined or too hesitantly through some revolving door on Sixth Avenue. Misery loves company, and that's exactly what I was searching for on the streets during that crushing August in New York. I out-and-out resented the phonies, and when I could pick one out I felt a little better about myself. At least I was being real: I didn't have a job, and I wanted one — badly. When your unemployment checks have a remaining life span that's shorter than a tsetse fly's, and you know that temp agencies are barely going to pay your rent, and all the doorways around Times Square are already taken by very determined-looking ladies, masquerades go right out the window. It's begging your friends for a new lead every other day, a newspaper folded straight to the classifieds, and a cup of herb tea and the house salad anywhere the bill will come in under two bucks with a table near the air conditioner.

While you finished your lunch and were trying to discreetly get the roast beef from between your teeth, I had twenty minutes before the next cattle call. I was to be in the herd slotted between one and three at the Andrews & Stein Engineering Company. And if my feet hadn't swollen because I'd slipped off my high heels under the table, I might have gone over and offered you one of the mint-flavored toothpicks I always carried around with me. I'd met quite a few guys in restaurants with my box of toothpicks: it was a foolproof way to start up a conversation once I'd checked out what they ordered and how they ate it. The way a man chews can tell you loads about the kind of lover he'll turn out to be. Don't laugh — meat is meat. And you had given those three slabs of roast beef a consideration they didn't deserve, so I actually played with the idea that you might be worth the pain of forcing on my shoes. You had nice teeth and strong, blunt fingers, and your nails were clean but, thank God, not manicured. I had been trying to figure out what you did for a living. The combination of a short-sleeved colored shirt and knit tie could mean anything from security guard to eccentric V.P. Regardless, anyone who preferred a plastic stirrer over that open saucer of toothpicks near the cash register, collecting flecks of ear wax and grease from a hundred rummaging fingernails, at least had common sense if not a high regard for the finer points of etiquette.

But when you walked past me, I let you and the idea go. My toothpicks had already gotten me two dates in the last month: one whole creep and a half creep. I could have gambled that my luck was getting progressively better and you'd only be a quarter creep. But even so, meeting a quarter creep in a Third Avenue coffee shop usually meant he'd figure that I would consider a free lecture on the mating habits of African violets at the Botanical Gardens and dinner at a Greek restaurant — red vinyl *booths* — a step up. That much this Southern girl had learned: there was a definite relationship between where you met some guy in New York and where he asked you out. Now, getting picked up in one of those booths at a Greek restaurant meant dinner at a mid-drawer ethnic: Mexican, Chinese, southern Italian, with real tablecloths but under glass shields, and probably Off-Broadway tickets. And if you hooked into someone at one of *those* restaurants, then it was out to top-drawer ethnic: northern Italian, French, Russian, or Continental, with waiters, not waitresses, and balcony seats on Broadway. East Side restaurants, Village jazz clubs, and orchestra seats at Lincoln Center were nights out with the pool you found available at Maxwell's Plum or any singles bar *above* Fifty-ninth Street on the East Side, and *below* Ninety-sixth on the West.

I'd never graduated to the bar scene because I didn't drink and refused to pay three-fifty for a club soda until the evening bore returns. Some of my friends said that you could run up an eighteen-dollar tab in no time that way, only to luck out with a pink quarter creep who figured that because you were a black woman it was down to mid-drawer ethnic for dinner the next week. And if he was a brown quarter creep, he had waited just before closing time to pick up the tab for your last drink. And if you didn't show the proper amount of gratitude for a hand on your thigh and an invitation to his third-floor walk-up into paradise, you got told in so many words that your bad attitude was the exact reason why he had come there looking for white girls in the first place.

I sound awful, don't I? Well, those were awful times for a single woman in that city of yours. There was something so desperate and sad about it all —

especially for my friends. You know, Selma kept going to those fancy singles bars, insisting that was the only way to meet "certain" black men. And she did meet them, those who certainly weren't looking for her. Then it was in Central Park, of all places, that she snagged this doctor. Not just any doctor, a Park Avenue neurosurgeon. After only three months he was hinting marriage, and she was shouting to us about a future of douching with Chanel No. 5, using laminated dollar bills for shower curtains — the whole bit. And the sad thing wasn't really how it turned out — I mean, as weird as it was when he finally told her that he was going to have a sex-change operation, but he was waiting for the right woman who was also willing to get one along with him, because he'd never dream of sleeping with another man — even after the operation; weirder — and much sadder — than all of that, George, was the fact that she debated seriously about following him to Denmark and doing it. So let me tell you, my toothpicks, as small a gesture as they were, helped me to stay on top of all that madness.

I finally left the coffee shop and felt whatever life that might have been revived in my linen suit and hair wilting away. How could it get so hot along Third Avenue when the buildings blocked out the sunlight? When I had come to New York seven years before that, I wondered about the need for such huge buildings. No one ever seemed to be in them for very long; everyone was out on the sidewalks, moving, moving, moving — and to where? My first month I was determined to find out. I followed a woman once: she had a beehive hairdo with rhinestone bobby pins along the side of her head that matched the rhinestones on her tinted cat-eyed glasses. Her thumbnails were the only ones polished, in a glossy lacquer on both hands, and they were so long they had curled under like hooks. I figured that she was so strange no one would ever notice me trailing her. We began on Fifty-third Street and Sixth Avenue near the Sheraton, moved west to Eighth Avenue before turning right, where she stopped at a Korean fruit stand, bought a kiwi, and walked along peeling the skin with her thumbnails. I lost her at Columbus Circle; she threw the peeled fruit uneaten into a trash can and took the escalator down into the subway. As she was going down, another woman was coming up the escalator with two bulging plastic bags. This one took me along Broadway up to where it meets Columbus Avenue at Sixty-third, and she sat down on one of those benches in the traffic median with her bags between her knees. She kept beating her heels against the sides and it sounded as if she had loose pots and pans in them. A really distinguished-looking guy with a tweed jacket and gray sideburns got up from the bench the moment she sat down, went into a flower shop across Columbus Avenue, came out empty-handed, and I followed him back downtown toward the Circle until we got to the entrance to Central Park. He slowed up, turned around, looked me straight in the face, and smiled. That's when I noticed that he had diaper pins holding his fly front together — you know, the kind they used to have with pink rabbit heads on them. I never thought anyone could beat my Central Park story until Selma met her neurosurgeon there. After that guy I gave up — I was exhausted by that time anyway. I hated to walk, almost as much as I hated the subways. There's something hypocritical about a city that keeps half of its population underground half of the time; you can start believing that there's much more space than there really is — to live, to work. And I had trouble doing both in spite of those endless classifieds in the Sunday *Times*. You know, there are more pages in just their Help Wanted section than in the telephone book here in Willow Springs. But it took me a while to figure out that New York racism moved underground like most of the people did.

Mama Day and Grandma had told me that there was a time when the want ads and housing listings in newspapers — even up north — were clearly marked colored or white. It must have been wonderfully easy to go job hunting then. You were spared a lot of legwork and headwork. And how I longed for those times, when I was busting my butt up and down the streets. I said as much at one of those parties Selma was always giving for her certain people. You would've thought I had announced that they were really drinking domestic wine, the place got that quiet. One of her certain people was so upset his voice shook. "You mean, you want to bring back segregation?" I looked at him like he was a fool — Where had it gone? I just wanted to bring the clarity about it back — it would save me a whole lot of subway tokens. What I was left to deal with were the ads labeled *Equal Opportunity Employer*, or nothing — which might as well have been labeled *Colored apply* or *Take your chances*. And if I wanted to limit myself to the sure bets, then it was an equal opportunity to be what, or earn what? That's where the headwork came in.

It's like the ad I was running down that afternoon: a one-incher in Monday's paper for an office manager. A long job description so there wasn't enough room to print Equal Opportunity Employer even if they were. They hadn't advertised Sunday, because I'd double-checked. They didn't want to get lost among the full and half columns the agencies ran. Obviously, a small operation. *Andrews & Stein Engineering Company:* it was half Jewish at least, so that said liberal — maybe. Or maybe they only wanted their own. I had never seen any Jewish people except on television until I arrived in New York. I had heard that they were clannish, and coming from Willow Springs I could identify with that. *Salary competitive:* that could mean anything, depending upon whether they were competing with Burger King or IBM. *Position begins September 1st:* that was the clincher, with all the other questions hanging in the balance. If I got the job, I could still go home for mid-August. Even if I didn't get it, I was going home. Mama Day and Grandma could forgive me for leaving Willow Springs, but not for staying away.

I got to the address and found exactly what I had feared. A six-floor office building — low-rent district, if you could call anything low in New York. Andrews & Stein was suite 511. The elevator, like the ancient marble foyer and maroon print carpeting on the fifth floor, was worn but carefully maintained. Dimly lit hallways to save on overhead, and painted walls that looked just a month short of needing a fresh coat. I could see that the whole building was being held together by some dedicated janitor who was probably near retirement. Oh, no, if these folks were going to hire me, it would be for peanuts. Operations renting space in a place like this shelled out decent salaries only for Mr. Stein's brainless niece, or Mr. Andrews's current lay. Well, you're here, Cocoa, I thought, go through the motions.

The cherry vanilla who buzzed me in the door was predictable, but there might still be reason for hope. When small, liberal establishments put a fudge cream behind their glass reception cages, there were rarely any more back in the offices. Sticking you out front let them sleep pretty good at night, thinking they'd put the ghost of Martin Luther King to rest. There were three other women there ahead of me, and one very very gay Oriental. God, those were rare — at least in my circles. The four of them already had clipboards and were filling out one-page applications — mimeographed. Cherry Vanilla was pleasant enough. She apologized for there being no more seats, and told me I had to wait until one of the clipboards was free unless I had something to write on. A small, small operation. But she wasn't pouring out that oily politeness that's normally used to slide you quietly out of any chance of getting the job. One of the women sitting there filling out an application was actually licorice. Her hair was in deep body waves with the sheen of patent leather, and close as I was, I couldn't tell where her hair ended and her skin began. And she had the body and courage to wear a Danskin top as tight as it was red. I guess that lady said, You're going to see me coming from a mile away, like it or not. I bet a lot of men did like it. If they were replacing Mr. Andrews's bimbo, she'd get the job. And the way she looked me up and down — dismissing my washed-out complexion and wilted linen suit — made me want to push out my pathetic chest, but that meant bringing in my nonexistent hips. Forget it, I thought, you're standing here with no tits, no ass, and no color. So console yourself with the fantasy that she's mixed up her addresses and is applying for the wrong job. Why else come to an interview in an outfit that would look better the wetter it got, unless you wanted to be a lifeguard? I could dismiss the other two women right away — milk shakes. One had her résumés typed on different shades of pastel paper and she was shifting through them, I guess trying to figure out which one matched the decor of the office. The other had forgotten her social security card and wanted to know if she should call home for the number. To be stupid enough not to memorize it was one thing, but not to know enough to sit there and shut up about it was beyond witless. I didn't care if Andrews & Stein was a front for the American Nazi party, she didn't have a chance. So the only serious contenders in that bunch were me, Patent Leather Hair, and the kumquat.

I inherited the clipboard from the one who'd forgotten her social security card, and she was in and out still babbling about that damn number before I had gotten down to Educational Background. Beyond high school there was just two years in business school in Atlanta — but I'd graduated at the top of my class. It was work experience that really counted for a job like this. This wasn't the type of place where you'd worry about moving up — all of those boxes and file cabinets crowded behind the receptionist's shoulder — it was simply a matter of moving around.

One job in seven years looked very good — with a fifty percent increase in salary. Duties: diverse, and more complex as I went along. The insurance company simply folded, that's all. If I'd stayed, I probably would have gone on to be an underwriter — but I was truly managing that office. Twelve secretaries, thirty-five salesmen, six adjusters, and one greedy president who didn't have the sense to avoid insuring half of the buildings in the South Bronx — even at triple premiums for fire and water damage. Those crooked landlords made a bundle, and every time I saw someone with a cigarette lighter, I cringed. I was down to Hobbies — which always annoyed me; what does your free time have to do with them? — when Patent Leather Hair was called in. She stood up the way women do knowing they look better when all of them is at last in view. I wondered what she had put down for extra-curricular activities. I sighed and crossed my legs. It was going to be a long wait. After twenty minutes Kumquat smiled over at me sympathetically — at least we both knew that he didn't have a possible ace in the hole anymore.

The intercom button on the receptionist's phone lit up, and when she got off she beckoned to the Oriental guy.

"Mr. Andrews is still interviewing, so Mr. Stein will have to see you. Just take your application to the second door on the left, Mr. Weisman."

He grinned at me again as I felt my linen suit losing its final bit of crispness under the low-voltage air conditioner. God, I wanted to go home — and I meant, home home. With all of Willow Springs's problems, you knew when you saw a catfish, you called it a catfish.

Well, Weisman was in and out pretty fast. I told myself for the thousandth time, Nothing about New York is ever going to surprise me anymore. Stein was probably anti-Semitic. It was another ten minutes and I was still sitting there and really starting to get ticked off. Couldn't Mr. Stein see me as well? No, she'd just put through a long-distance call from a client, but Mr. Andrews would be ready for me soon. I seriously doubted it. He was in there trying to convince Patent Leather that even though she thought she was applying for a position as a lifeguard, they could find room for someone with her potential. I didn't give her the satisfaction of my half-hour wait when she came flaming out — I was busily reading the wrapper on my pack of Trident, having ditched my newspaper before I came in. The thing was irreversibly creased at the classifieds, my bag was too small to hide it, and you never wanted to look that desperate at an interview. And there weren't even any old issues of *Popular Mechanics* or something in the waiting area — bottom drawer all the way.

I was finally buzzed into the inner sanctum, and without a shred of hope walked past the clutter of file cabinets through another door that opened into a deceptively large network of smaller offices. I entered the third on the left as I'd been instructed and there you were: blue shirt, knitted tie, nice teeth, and all. Feeling the box of mint toothpicks press against my thigh through the mesh bag as I sat down and crossed my legs, I smiled sincerely for the first time that day.

Until you walked into my office that afternoon, I would have never called myself a superstitious man. Far from it. To believe in fate or predestination means you have to believe there's a future, and I grew up without one. It was either that or not grow up at all. Our guardians at the Wallace P. Andrews Shelter for Boys were adamant about the fact that we learned to invest in ourselves alone. "Keep it in the now, fellas," Chip would say, chewing on his bottom right jaw and spitting as if he still had the plug of tobacco in there Mrs. Jackson refused to let him use in front of us. And I knew I'd hear her until the day I died. "Only the present has potential, *sir.*" I could see her even then, the way she'd jerk up the face, gripping the chin of some kid who was crying because his last foster home hadn't worked out, or because he was teased at school about not having a mother. She'd even reach up and clamp on to some muscled teenager who was trying to excuse a bad report card. I could still feel the ache in my bottom lip from the relentless grip of her thumb and forefinger pressed into the bone of my chin — "Only the present has potential, *sir.*"

They may not have been loving people, she and Chip — or when you think about it, even lovable. But they were devoted to their jobs if not to us individually. And Mrs. Jackson saw part of her job as making sure that that scraggly bunch of misfits — misfitted into somebody's game plan so we were thrown away — would at least hear themselves addressed with respect. There were so many boys and the faces kept changing, she was getting old and never remembered our individual names and didn't try to hide it. All of us were beneath poor, most of us were black or Puerto Rican, so it was very likely that this would be the first and last time in our lives anyone would call us "sir." And if talking to you and pinching the skin off your chin didn't work, she was not beneath enforcing those same words with a brown leather strap — a man's belt with the buckle removed. We always wondered where she'd gotten a man's belt. You could look at Mrs. Jackson and tell she'd never been a Mrs., the older boys would say. Or if she had snagged some poor slob a thousand years ago, he never could have gotten it up over her to need to undo his pants. But that was said only well out of her earshot after she had lashed one of them across the back or arms. She'd bring that belt down with a cold precision that was more frightening than the pain she was causing, and she'd bring it down for exactly ten strokes — one for each syllable: "Only the present has potential, *sir.*"

No boy was touched above the neck or below his waist in front. And she never, ever hit the ones — regardless of their behavior — who had come to

Wallace P. Andrews with fractured arms or cigarette burns on their groins. For those she'd take away dinner plus breakfast the next morning, and even lunch if she felt they warranted it. Bernie Sinclair passed out that way once, and when he woke up in the infirmary she was standing over him explaining that he had remained unconscious past the dinner he *still* would have been deprived of if he hadn't fainted.

Cruel? No, I would call it controlled. Bernie had spit in her face. And she never altered her expression, either when it happened during hygiene check or when she stood over him in the infirmary. Bernie had come to us with half of his teeth busted out, and he hated brushing the other half. She was going down the usual morning lineup for the boys under twelve, checking fingernails, behind ears, calling for the morning stretch (hands above head, legs spread, knees bent, and bounce) to detect unwashed armpits and crotches. Bernie wouldn't open his mouth for her and was getting his daily list of facts (she never lectured, she called it listing simple facts): if the remainder of his teeth rotted out from lack of personal care, then the dentist would have to fit him for a full plate instead of a partial plate. And it would take her twice as long to requisition twice the money that would then be needed from the state. That would lead him to spending twice as long being teased at school and restricted to a soft diet in the cafeteria. She said this like she did everything — slowly, clearly, and without emotion. For the second time she bent over and told him to open his mouth. He did, and sent a wad of spit against her right cheek. Even Joey Santiago cringed — all six feet and almost two hundred pounds of him. But Mrs. Jackson never blinked. She took out the embroidered handkerchief she kept in her rolled-up blouse sleeve and wiped her face as she listed another set of facts: she had asked him twice, she never asked any child to do anything more than twice — those were the rules at Wallace P. Andrews. No lunch, no dinner, and he still had his full share of duties. I guess that's why he passed out, no food under the hot sun and weeding our garden — that and fear of what she was really going to do to him for spitting on her. He was still new and didn't understand that she was going to do nothing at all.

Our rage didn't matter to her, our hurts or disappointments over what life had done to us. None of that was going to matter a damn in the outside world, so we might as well start learning it at Wallace P. Andrews. There were only rules and facts. Mrs. Jackson's world out there on Staten Island had rules that you could argue might not be fair, but they were consistent. And when they were broken we were guaranteed that, however she had to do it, we would be made to *feel* responsibility for our present actions — and our actions alone. And oddly enough, we understood that those punishments were an improvement upon our situations: before coming there, we had been beaten and starved just for being born.

And she was the only person on the staff allowed to touch us. Even Chip, who had the role of "good cop" to her "bad cop" — you needed a shoulder to cry on sometimes — could only recommend discipline. It must have been difficult with sixty boys, and I'd seen some kids really provoke a dorm director or workshop leader, and the guy would never lay a hand on them. They all knew her rules, and it was clear those men were afraid of her. And I could never figure it out, even with the rumor that was going around, which Joey Santiago swore by. Joey was a notorious liar, but he was the oldest guy there when I was growing up. And he said that some years back there was a dorm director who used to sneak into the rooms where we had the "rubber sheet jockeys" — kids under eight — and take them into the bathroom. After he was finished with them, they'd fall asleep on the toilet, where he'd make them sit until their rectums stopped bleeding. Mrs. Jackson and Chip came over one night, caught him at it, and she told the boys she was going to call the police. They took him back to the old stucco house she lived in on the grounds. The police car never came, but her basement lights stayed on. And Joey swore you could hear that man screaming throughout the entire night, although all of her windows were bolted down. It was loud enough to even wake up the older ones in the other dorms. That man was never seen again, and they knew better than to question Mrs. Jackson when she came over to pack up his things herself. And Chip had absolutely nothing to say about what had happened but "Keep it in the now, fellas" as he dug Mrs. Jackson a new rose garden the following morning. Every staff member and boy who came to Wallace P. Andrews heard that rumor and, one way or another, went over to see those roses in the corner of her garden. I can only tell you this, they were incredibly large and beautiful. And in the summer, when the evening breeze came from the east, their fragrance was strong enough to blanket your sleep.

Some thought that I was her favorite. I was one of the few who had grown up there through the nursery, and she couldn't punish me the way she did them, because I had a congenital heart condition. So she took away my books, knowing that I'd rather give up food or even have her use her strap. And once pleaded with her to do so, because I said I'd die if I had to wait a full week to find out how the Count of Monte Cristo escaped from prison. She said that was a fitting death for little boys who were caught cheating on their math exams. But fractions are hard, and I wanted a good grade at the end of the term. Ah, so I was worried about the *end* of the term? Well, she would now keep my books for two weeks. "Only the present has potential, *sir.*"

And the discipline she tailor-made for all of us said, like it or not, the present is *you.* And what else did we have but ourselves? We had a more than forgettable past and no future that was guaranteed. And she never let us pretend that anything else was the case as she'd often listed the facts of life: I am not your mother. I am paid to run this place. You have no mothers or fathers. This is not your home. And it is not a prison — it is a state shelter for boys. And it is not a dumping ground for delinquents, rejects, or somebody's garbage, because you are not delinquents, rejects, or garbage — you are boys. It is not a place to be tortured, exploited, or raped. It is a state shelter for boys.

Here you have a clean room, decent food, and clothing for each season because it is a shelter. There is a library in which you study for three hours after school — and you *will* go to school, because you are boys. When you are eighteen, the state says you are men. And when you are men you leave here to go where and do what you want. But you stay here until you are men.

Yes, those were the facts of life at Wallace P. Andrews. And those were her methods. And if any of the boys complained to the state inspectors about being punished, nothing was ever done. I guess at the bottom line, she saved them money. We grew and canned a lot of our own food, painted our own dorms, made most of the furniture, and even sewed curtains and bedspreads. And the ones she turned out weren't a burden on the state, either. I don't know of anyone who became a drug addict, petty thief, or a derelict. I guess it's because you grew up with absolutely no illusions about yourself or the world. Most of us went from there either to college or into a trade. No, it wasn't the kind of place that turned out many poets or artists — those who could draw became draftsmen, and the musicians were taught to tune pianos. If she erred in directing our careers, she erred on the side of caution. Sure, the arts were waiting for poor black kids who were encouraged to dream big, and so was death row.

Looking back, I can see how easy it would have been for her to let us just sit there and reach the right age to get out. It only takes time for a man to grow older, but how many of them grow up? And I couldn't have grown up if I had wasted my time crying about a family I wasn't given or believing in a future that I didn't have. When I left Wallace P. Andrews I had what I could see: my head and my two hands, and I had each day to do something with them. Each day, that's how I took it — each moment, sometimes, when the going got really rough. I may have knocked my head against the walls, figuring out how to buy food, supplies, and books, but I never knocked on wood. No rabbit's foot, no crucifixes — not even a lottery ticket. I couldn't afford the dollar or the dreams while I was working my way through Columbia. So until you walked into my office, everything I was — all the odds I had beat — was owed to my living fully in the now. How was I to reconcile the *fact* of seeing you the second time that day with the *feeling* I had had the first time? Not the feeling I told myself I had, but the one I really had.

You see, there was no way for me to deny that you were there in front of me and I couldn't deny any longer that I knew it would happen — you would be in my future. What had been captured — and dismissed — in a space too quickly for recorded time was now like a bizarre photograph that was developing in front of my face. I am passing you in the coffee shop, your head is bent over your folded newspaper, and small strands of your reddish-brown hair have come undone from the bobby pins and lie against the curve of your neck. The feeling is so strong it almost physically stops me: *I will see that neck again.* Not her, not the woman but the skin that's tinted from amber to cream as it stretches over the lean bone underneath. That is the feeling I actually had, while the feeling I quickly exchanged it with was: *I've seen this woman before.* That can be recorded; it took a split second. But a glance at the side of your high cheekbones, pointed chin, slender profile, and I knew I was mistaken. I hadn't even seen you sitting those three tables away during lunch. But I remembered your waitress well. The dark-brown arms, full breasts threatening to tear open the front of her uniform, the crease of her apron strings around a nonexistent waist that swung against a hip line that could only be called a promise of heaven on earth — her I had seen. And you had to have been there when she took your order and brought you whatever you were eating, and the fact is I never saw you. Not when I stood up, reached into my pocket for change, passed the two tables between us, and didn't see you then — until the neck bent over the newspaper. And it all could have been such a wonderful coincidence when you first walked into my office, a natural icebreaker for the interview, which I always hated, being forced to judge someone else. I could have brought up the final image of the weary slump, the open classifieds, and the shoes pulled off beneath the table. A woman looking for a job; we were looking for an office manager five blocks away. Afternoon interviews began at one o'clock, and it was twelve-forty-five. *And just imagine, Miss Day, when I passed you I said to myself, Wouldn't it be funny if I saw her again?* Except that it was terrifying when you sat down, and then ran your hand up the curve of your neck in a nervous mannerism, pushing up a few loose hairs and pushing me smack into a confrontation with fate. When you unconsciously did that, I must have looked as if someone had stuck a knife into my gut, because that's the way it felt.

You said, Call me George. And I thought, Oh God, this is going to be one of those let's-get-chummy-fast masquerades. Nine times out of ten, some clown giving you his first name is a sure bet he's not giving you the job. And they can comfort themselves because, after all, they went out of their way to be "nice." And in this case, you were stealing my thunder when the moment came for pulling out my toothpicks and reminding *Mr. Andrews* where I'd seen him before. But if we were George and Ophelia — chat, chat, chat — my mint toothpicks would just be added fuel to the fire that was sending this job up in smoke. These fudge-on-fudge interviews were always tricky anyway. You have the power freaks who wanted you to grovel at their importance. They figure if they don't get it from the other bonbons, it's sure not coming from anywhere else. Or there were the disciples of a free market with a Christ complex: they went to the Cross and rose without affirmative action, so you can, too. But our interview wasn't anything I could put my finger on. You just seemed downright scared of me and anxious to get me out of that office. And I knew the fastest way was this call-me-George business. I decided to fight fire with fire.

"And I'm used to answering to Cocoa. I guess we might as well start now because if I get the position and anyone here calls me Ophelia, I'll be so busy concentrating on my work, it won't register. I truly doubt I could have moved up as fast as I did at my last job — with a fifty percent increase in salary — if those twelve secretaries, thirty-five salesmen, and six adjusters in the office I was managing almost single-handedly had called me Ophelia. The way I see it, over half of the overtime I put in would have been spent trying to figure out who they were talking to."

There, I stuck that one to you. And you knew it, too, because you were finally smiling. And this time you took a real good look at my application.

"So you picked up this nickname at your last job — Omega Home Insurance?"

"No, I've had it from a child — in the South it's called a pet name. My grandmother and great-aunt gave it to me, the same women who put me through business school in Atlanta where I ended up graduating at the top of my class — A's in statistics, typing, bookkeeping. B plusses in — "

"That's fascinating. How do they decide on the pet name?"

"They just try to figure out what fits."

"So a child with skin the color of buttered cream gets called Cocoa. I can see how that fits."

I wanted to slap that smirk off your face. "It does if you understood my family and where I come from."

"Willow Springs, is it? That's in Georgia?"

"No, it's actually in no state. But that's a long story. And not to be rude, Mr. Andrews, but I really would like to talk about my credentials for working here. Where I was born and what name I was given were both beyond my control. But what *I* could do about my life, I've done well. And I'd like to spend the few minutes I have left of your time being judged on that."

Something happened to your face then. I had hit a raw nerve somewhere, and I cursed myself because I was sure I had succeeded in destroying the whole thing. It was little consolation knowing that I was going to be on your mind long after you kicked me out of your office.

"That's the only way I'd ever dream of judging anyone, Miss Day. And I meant it when I said call me George."

Great, I'd been demoted *up* to Miss Day. This man was really angry, and that George business again just clinched it, I guess. But then he did say *I meant it,* which means he knows about the whole charade and he's trying to reassure me that he's not angry about what I said. Ah, who can figure this shit out.

"And you can call me . . ." I was suddenly very tired — of you, of the whole game. "Just call me when you decide. I do need this job, and if you check out my references, you'll find that I'll be more than able to perform well."

"Fine. And this is the number where you can be reached?"

"Yes, but I'll be away for the next two weeks. If you don't mind, you could drop me a card, or I'll call when I get back since the job doesn't start until the first."

You frowned, but it came out the way it came out. Sure, he's thinking, how badly does someone need a job who's taking a vacation?

"But we'll be making our final decision after tomorrow. The person starts Monday."

"Your ad said the first."

"It did, but our current office manager told us this morning that she has to leave earlier than she had planned. And she'll have to break in her successor. This is a deceptively busy place and to have someone come in here cold — well, it wouldn't be fair to the new employee or to us. And we thought whoever got the position would probably appreciate starting work before September. I know how tight things are out there right now — most people have been looking for a long time."

Jesus, all we needed was the organ music and a slow fade to my receding back as the swirling sand of the rocky coastline began to spell out The End. Oh, yeah, if you aren't ready to start yesterday, there are a dozen who will be.

"I understand, and I wouldn't have wasted your time if I knew it was necessary to begin right away. I have to go home every August. It's never been a problem before because I had the same job for seven years. You see, my grandmother is eighty-three, and since we lost my cousin and her family last year, I'm the only grandchild left."

If you thought it was a cheap shot, sorry. At that point I was beyond caring.

"The whole family? That's really terrible — what happened?"

"Did you read about the fire in Linden Hills this past Christmas? Well, that was my cousin Willa and her husband and son. It upset us all a lot."

"I did read it. It was an awful, awful thing — and on Christmas of all days."

My God, the look in your eyes. You actually meant that. This would go down in Guinness as the strangest interview I'd ever been on.

"So you understand why I'm going back to Willow Springs."

"Of course I do. And you must understand why any qualified applicant would need to start Monday."

"Yes, I do."

We had sure become one understanding pair of folks by the time the lights in the theater came up and they pulled the curtain across the screen. We got up out of our seats and shook hands. Was it my imagination — did his fingers linger just a bit? Was it possible that since I was more than qualified, no one else would come along and they'd save . . . My heart sank when I got back to the reception area. I had to wade through a whole Baskin-Robbins on my way to the outside hall.

You had spunk, Ophelia, and that's what I admired in a woman. You were justified to come right out and tell me I was prying, and I hated myself all the while I was doing it. I had always valued my own privacy, and just because you were in a position where you had to answer questions that bordered on an invasion on yours made what I did all the more unfair. If it's any consolation, I didn't enjoy the sour aftertaste of abused power. But I was searching for some connection, some rational explanation. The only way I could sit through that interview was by lying to myself about what had really happened in that coffee shop: when I passed your bent neck, I stopped because I had seen you somewhere before, and I couldn't remember — that's all.

I had definitely seen your type before, and had even slept with some of them — those too bright, too jaded colored girls. There were a few at Columbia, but many more would come across the street from Barnard. They made no bones about their plans to hook into a man who — what was the expression then? — who was going somewhere. Well, after classes I went to work as a room-service waiter in the Hilton. It wasn't as glamorous as the work-study jobs in the library or dean's office, but it paid a lot better when you counted tips. During the slack periods my boss let me read, and I had Sundays off. But you see, that wasn't the right day. All the guys who were going somewhere had been able to take girls to the fraternity dances on Friday and Saturday nights where they could show off their brand-name clothes. They only needed a pair of jeans to go to the park with me, or to sit in my room and study. I was too serious, too dull. George doesn't know how to have fun, they'd say, he's so quiet. I suppose I was, but what could I honestly talk to them about? They would have thought I was crazy if I had told them that seeing them flow around me like dark jewels on campus was one of the most beautiful sights on earth.

Yes, I was one of the quiet ones who thought them beautiful, even with the polished iron webbing around their hearts. I understood exactly what they were protecting themselves against, and I was willing to help them shine that armor all the more, to be the shoulder they could cry on when it got too heavy — if they had only let me in. But they didn't want me then. And I was to meet them years later, at parties and dinners, when the iron had served them a bit too well. They were successful and they were alone: those guys who were going somewhere had by either inclination or lack of numbers left a good deal of them behind. They had stopped being frivolous, but they were hurt and suspicious. And maturity made me much more hesitant to take a chance on finding an opening into hearts like those. Often I had wanted to go over and shake some silk-clad shoulder who thought she was righteously justified in spreading the tired old gospel about not being able to meet good black men. She had met *me*. But I would have been too proud to remind her where.

Yeah, I knew your type well. And you sat there with your mind racing, trying to double-think me, so sure you had me and the game down pat. Give him what he wants. I fooled you, didn't I. All I wanted was for you to be yourself. And I wondered if it was too late, if seven years in New York had been just enough for you to lose that, like you were trying to lose your Southern accent. It amused me the way your tongue and lips were determined to clip along, and then your accent would find you in the spaces between two words — "talking about," "graduating at." In spite of yourself, the music would squeeze through at the ending of those verbs to tilt the following vowels up just half a key. That's why I wanted you to call me George. There isn't a Southerner alive who could bring that name in under two syllables. And for those brief seconds it allowed me to imagine you as you must have been: softer, slower — open. It conjured up images of jasmine-scented nights, warm biscuits and honey being brought to me on flowered china plates as you sat at my feet and rubbed your cheek against my knee. Go ahead and laugh, you have a perfect right. I had never been South, and you couldn't count the times I had spent in Miami at the Super Bowl — that city was a humid and pastel New York. So I had the same myths about Southern women that you did about Northern men. But it was a fact that when you said my name, you became yourself.

And it was also a fact that there was no way I was going to give you that job. And your firm plans about returning to Willow Springs helped to alleviate my guilt about that. We were going to turn other qualified people down — and it's never a matter of the most qualified, there's no such animal. It's either do they or don't they "fit." And where could I possibly place you? My life was already made at thirty-one. My engineering degree, the accelerating success of Andrews & Stein, proved beyond a shadow of a doubt that you got nothing from believing in crossed fingers, broken mirrors, spilled salt — a twist in your gut in the middle of a Third Avenue coffee shop. You either do or you don't. And you, Ophelia, were the don't. Don't get near a woman who has the power to turn your existence upside-down by simply running a hand up the back of her neck.

◎ *TILLIE OLSEN*

"I Stand Here Ironing," from Tillie Olsen's Tell Me a Riddle, *first appeared in* Pacific Spectator. *It was written between 1953–1954, and Olsen has said that it is not a coincidence that she considered this her first publishable story* (Silences, *1978, p. 19). Olsen knew only too well the difficulties of being a working-class mother, trying to manage multiple tasks without help. Few writers if any have evoked this conflict in working mother's lives as honestly and convincingly as Olsen.* *(For more on Olsen, see page 183.)*

I Stand Here Ironing

I stand here ironing, and what you asked me moves tormented back and forth with the iron.

"I wish you would manage the time to come in and talk with me about your daughter. I'm sure you can help me understand her. She's a youngster who needs help and whom I'm deeply interested in helping."

"Who needs help." Even if I came, what good would it do? You think because I am her mother I have a key, or that in some way you could use me as a key? She has lived for nineteen years. There is all that life that has happened outside of me, beyond me.

And when is there time to remember, to sift, to weigh, to estimate, to total? I will start and there will be an interruption and I will have to gather it all together again. Or I will become engulfed with all I did or did not do, with what should have been and what cannot be helped.

She was a beautiful baby. The first and only one of our five that was beautiful at birth. You do not guess how new and uneasy her tenancy in her now-loveliness. You did not know her all those years she was thought homely, or see her poring over her baby pictures, making me tell her over and over how beautiful she had been — and would be, I would tell her — and was now, to the seeing eye. But the seeing eyes were few or nonexistent. Including mine.

I nursed her. They feel that's important nowadays. I nursed all the children, but with her, with all the fierce rigidity of first motherhood, I did like the books then said. Though her cries battered me to trembling and my breasts ached with swollenness, I waited till the clock decreed.

Why do I put that first? I do not even know if it matters, or if it explains anything.

She was a beautiful baby. She blew shining bubbles of sound. She loved motion, loved light, loved color and music and textures. She would lie on the floor in her blue overalls patting the surface so hard in ecstasy her hands and feet would blur. She was a miracle to me, but when she was eight months old I had to leave her daytimes with the woman downstairs to whom she was no miracle at all, for I worked or looked for work and for Emily's father, who "could no longer endure" (he wrote in his good-bye note) "sharing want with us."

I was nineteen. It was the pre-relief, pre-WPA world of the depression. I would start running as soon as I got off the streetcar, running up the stairs, the place smelling sour, and awake or asleep to startle awake, when she saw me she would break into a clogged weeping that could not be comforted, a weeping I can hear yet.

After a while I found a job hashing at night so I could be with her days, and it was better. But it came to where I had to bring her to his family and leave her.

It took a long time to raise the money for her fare back. Then she got chicken pox and I had to wait longer. When she finally came, I hardly knew her, walking quick and nervous like her father, looking like her father, thin, and dressed in a shoddy red that yellowed her skin and glared at the pockmarks. All the baby loveliness gone.

She was two. Old enough for nursery school they said, and I did not know then what I know now — the fatigue of the long day, and the lacerations of group life in nurseries that are only parking places for children.

Except that it would have made no difference if I had known. It was the only place there was. It was the only way we could be together, the only way I could hold a job.

And even without knowing, I knew. I knew the teacher that was evil because all these years it has curdled into my memory, the little boy hunched in the corner, her rasp, "why aren't you outside, because Alvin hits you? that's no reason, go out, scaredy." I knew Emily hated it even if she did not clutch and implore "don't go Mommy" like the other children, mornings.

She always had a reason why we should stay home. Momma, you look sick, Momma. I feel sick. Momma, the teachers aren't there today, they're sick. Momma, we can't go, there was a fire there last night. Momma, it's a holiday today, no school, they told me.

But never a direct protest, never rebellion. I think of our others in their three-, four-year-oldness — the explosions, the tempers, the denunciations, the demands — and I feel suddenly ill. I put the iron down. What in me demanded that goodness in her? And what was the cost, the cost to her of such goodness?

The old man living in the back once said in his gentle way: "You should smile at Emily more when you look at her." What *was* in my face when I looked at her? I loved her. There were all the acts of love.

It was only with the others I remembered what he said, and it was the face of joy, and not of care or tightness or worry I turned to them — too late for Emily. She does not smile easily, let alone almost always as her brothers and sisters do. Her face is closed and sombre, but when she wants, how fluid. You must have seen it in her pantomimes, you spoke of her rare gift for comedy on the stage that rouses a laughter out of the audience so dear they applaud and applaud and do not want to let her go.

Where does it come from, that comedy? There was none of it in her when she came back to me that second time, after I had had to send her away again. She had a new daddy now to learn to love, and I think perhaps it was a better time.

Except when we left her alone nights, telling ourselves she was old enough.

"Can't you go some other time, Mommy, like tomorrow?" she would ask. "Will it be just a little while you'll be gone? Do you promise?"

The time we came back, the front door open, the clock on the floor in the hall. She rigid awake. "It wasn't just a little while. I didn't cry. Three times I called you, just three times, and then I ran downstairs to open the door so you could come faster. The clock talked loud. I threw it away, it scared me what it talked."

She said the clock talked loud again that night I went to the hospital to have Susan. She was delirious with the fever that comes before red measles, but she was fully conscious all the week I was gone and the week after we were home when she could not come near the new baby or me.

She did not get well. She stayed skeleton thin, not wanting to eat, and night after night she had nightmares. She would call for me, and I would rouse from exhaustion to sleepily call back: "You're all right, darling, go to sleep, it's just a dream," and if she still called, in a sterner voice, "now go to sleep, Emily, there's nothing to hurt you." Twice, only twice, when I had to get up for Susan anyhow, I went in to sit with her.

Now when it is too late (as if she would let me hold and comfort her like I do the others) I get up and go to her at once at her moan or restless stirring. "Are you awake, Emily? Can I get you something?" And the answer is always the same: "No, I'm all right, go back to sleep, Mother."

They persuaded me at the clinic to send her away to a convalescent home in the country where "she can have the kind of food and care you can't manage for her, and you'll be free to concentrate on the new baby." They still send children to that place. I see pictures on the society page of sleek young women planning affairs to raise money for it, or dancing at the affairs, or decorating Easter eggs or filling Christmas stockings for the children.

They never have a picture of the children so I do not know if the girls still wear those gigantic red bows and the ravaged looks on the every other Sunday when parents can come to visit "unless otherwise notified" — as we were notified the first six weeks.

Oh it is a handsome place, green lawns and tall trees and fluted flower beds. High up on the balconies of each cottage the children stand, the girls in their red bows and white dresses, the boys in white suits and giant red ties. The parents stand below shrieking up to be heard and the children shriek down to be heard, and between them the invisible wall "Not To Be Contaminated by Parental Germs or Physical Affection."

There was a tiny girl who always stood hand in hand with Emily. Her parents never came. One visit she was gone. "They moved her to Rose Cottage" Emily shouted in explanation. "They don't like you to love anybody here."

She wrote once a week, the labored writing of a seven-year-old. "I am fine. How is the baby. If I write my leter nicly I will have a star. Love." There never was a star. We wrote every other day, letters she could never hold or keep but only hear read — once. "We simply do not have room for children to keep any personal possessions," they patiently explained when we pieced one Sunday's shrieking together to plead how much it would mean to Emily, who loved so to keep things, to be allowed to keep her letters and cards.

Each visit she looked frailer. "She isn't eating," they told us.

(They had runny eggs for breakfast or mush with lumps, Emily said later, I'd hold it in my mouth and not swallow. Nothing ever tasted good, just when they had chicken.)

It took us eight months to get her released home, and only the fact that she gained back so little of her seven lost pounds convinced the social worker.

I used to try to hold and love her after she came back, but her body would stay stiff, and after a while she'd push away. She ate little. Food sickened her, and I think much of life too. Oh she had physical lightness and brightness, twinkling by on skates, bouncing like a ball up and down up and down over the jump rope, skimming over the hill; but these were momentary.

She fretted about her appearance, thin and dark and foreign-looking at a time when every little girl was supposed to look or thought she should look a chubby blonde replica of Shirley Temple. The doorbell sometimes rang for her, but no one seemed to come and play in the house or be a best friend. Maybe because we moved so much.

There was a boy she loved painfully through two school semesters. Months later she told me how she had taken pennies from my purse to buy him candy. "Licorice was his favorite and I brought him some every day, but he still liked Jennifer better'n me. Why, Mommy?" The kind of question for which there is no answer.

School was a worry to her. She was not glib or quick in a world where glibness and quickness were easily confused with ability to learn. To her overworked and exasperated teachers she was an overconscientious "slow learner" who kept trying to catch up and was absent entirely too often.

I let her be absent, though sometimes the illness was imaginary. How different from my now-strictness about attendance with the others. I wasn't working. We had a new baby, I was home anyhow. Sometimes, after Susan grew old enough, I would keep her home from school, too, to have them all together.

Mostly Emily had asthma, and her breathing, harsh and labored, would fill the house with a curiously tranquil sound. I would bring the two old dresser mirrors and her boxes of collections to her bed. She would select beads and single earrings, bottle tops and shells, dried flowers and pebbles, old postcards and scraps, all sorts of oddments; then she and Susan would play Kingdom, setting up landscapes and furniture, peopling them with action.

Those were the only times of peaceful companionship between her and Susan. I have edged away from it, that poisonous feeling between them, that terrible balancing of hurts and needs I had to do between the two, and did so badly, those earlier years.

Oh there are conflicts between the others too, each one human, needing, demanding, hurting, taking — but only between Emily and Susan, no, Emily toward Susan that corroding resentment. It seems so obvious on the surface, yet it is not obvious. Susan, the second child, Susan, golden- and curly-haired and chubby, quick and articulate and assured, everything in appearance and manner Emily was not; Susan, not able to resist Emily's precious things, losing or sometimes clumsily breaking them; Susan telling jokes and riddles to company for applause while Emily sat silent (to say to me later: that was *my* riddle, Mother, I told it to Susan); Susan, who for all the five years' difference in age was just a year behind Emily in developing physically.

I am glad for that slow physical development that widened the difference between her and her contemporaries, though she suffered over it. She was too vulnerable for that terrible world of youthful competition, of preening and parading, of constant measuring of yourself against every other, of envy, "If I had that copper hair," "If I had that skin. . . ." She tormented herself enough about not looking like the others, there was enough of the unsureness, the having to be conscious of words before you speak, the constant caring — what are they thinking of me? without having it all magnified by the merciless physical drives.

Ronnie is calling. He is wet and I change him. It is rare there is such a cry now. That time of motherhood is almost behind me when the ear is not one's own but must always be racked and listening for the child cry, the child call. We sit for a while and I hold him, looking out over the city spread in charcoal with its soft aisles of light. "*Shoogily,*" he breathes and curls closer. I carry him back to bed, asleep. *Shoogily.* A funny word, a family word, inherited from Emily, invented by her to say: *comfort.*

In this and other ways she leaves her seal, I say aloud. And startle at my saying it. What do I mean? What did I start to gather together, to try and make coherent? I was at the terrible, growing years. War years. I do not remember them well. I was working, there were four smaller ones now, there was not time for her. She had to help be a mother, and housekeeper, and shopper. She had to set her seal. Mornings of crisis and near hysteria trying to get lunches packed, hair combed, coats and shoes found, everyone to school or Child Care on time, the baby ready for transportation. And always the paper scribbled on by a smaller one, the book looked at by Susan then mislaid, the homework not done. Running out to that huge school where she was one, she was lost, she was a drop; suffering over the unpreparedness, stammering and unsure in her classes.

There was so little time left at night after the kids were bedded down. She would struggle over books, always eating (it was in those years she developed her enormous appetite that is legendary in our family) and I would be ironing, or preparing food for the next day, or writing V-mail to Bill, or tending the baby. Sometimes, to make me laugh, or out of her despair, she would imitate happenings or types at school.

I think I said once: "Why don't you do something like this in the school amateur show?" One morning she phoned me at work, hardly understandable through the weeping: "Mother, I did it. I won, I won; they gave me first prize; they clapped and clapped and wouldn't let me go."

Now suddenly she was Somebody, and as imprisoned in her difference as she had been in anonymity.

She began to be asked to perform at other high schools, even in colleges, then at city and statewide affairs. The first one we went to, I only recognized her that first moment when thin, shy, she almost drowned herself into the curtains. Then: Was this Emily? The control, the command, the convulsing and deadly clowning, the spell, then the roaring, stamping audience, unwilling to let this rare and precious laughter out of their lives.

Afterwards: You ought to do something about her with a gift like that — but without money or knowing how, what does one do? We have left it all to her, and the gift has as often eddied inside, clogged and clotted, as been used and growing.

She is coming. She runs up the stairs two at a time with her light graceful step, and I know she is happy tonight. Whatever it was that occasioned your call did not happen today.

"Aren't you ever going to finish the ironing, Mother? Whistler painted his mother in a rocker. I'd have to paint mine standing over an ironing board." This is one of her communicative nights and she tells me everything and nothing as she fixes herself a plate of food out of the icebox.

She is so lovely. Why did you want me to come in at all? Why were you concerned? She will find her way.

She starts up the stairs to bed. "Don't get me up with the rest in the morning." "But I thought you were having midterms." "Oh, those," she comes back in, kisses me, and says quite lightly, "in a couple of years when we'll all be atom-dead they won't matter a bit."

She has said it before. She *believes* it. But because I have been dredging the past, and all that compounds a human being is so heavy and meaningful in me, I cannot endure it tonight.

I will never total it all. I will never come in to say: She was a child seldom smiled at. Her father left me before she was a year old. I had to work her first six years when there was work, or I sent her home and to his relatives. There were years she had care she hated. She was dark and thin and foreign-looking in a world where the prestige went to blondeness and curly hair and dimples, she was slow where glibness was prized. She was a child of anxious, not proud, love. We were poor and could not afford for her the soil of easy growth. I was a young mother, I was a distracted mother. There were the other children pushing up, demanding. Her younger sister seemed all that she was not. There were years she did not want me to touch her. She kept too much in herself, her life was such she had to keep too much in herself. My wisdom came too late. She has much to her and probably nothing will come of it. She is a child of her age, of depression, of war, of fear.

Let her be. So all that is in her will not bloom — but in how many does it? There is still enough left to live by. Only help her to know — help make it so there is cause for her to know — that she is more than this dress on the ironing board, helpless before the iron.

◎ *ANNIE DILLARD*

Annie Dillard was born in 1945 in Pittsburgh and was educated at Hollins College. Dillard has taught at Western Washington University and at Wesleyan University. She has been a member of the U.S. cultural delegation to China and a board member and chairman of the Wesleyan Writers' Conference. Awards for Dillard's work include the Pulitzer Prize for Pilgrim at Tinker Creek *(1974); grants from the National Endowment for the Arts and the Guggenheim Foundation; and a History Maker Award from the Historical Society of Western Pennsylvania. Dillard's poetry appears in* Tickets for a Prayer Wheel *(1974); her fiction includes* The Living *(1992); and her nonfiction includes seven volumes, most recently* The Writing Life *(1989).*

This excerpt from The Writing Life *shows the wonderful specifics Dillard uses in her work ("pick," "gouge," "probe," "hammer") and the metaphysical and spiritual leaps she entices the reader into following. Writing becomes "an epistemological tool"—yes, and the voyage is one of discovery of the world. It requires nothing so much as courage.*

from *The Writing Life*

When you write, you lay out a line of words. The line of words is a miner's pick, a wood-carver's gouge, a surgeon's probe. You wield it, and it digs a path you follow. Soon you find yourself deep in new territory. It is a dead end, or have you located the real subject? You will know tomorrow, or this time next year.

You make the path boldly and follow it fearfully. You go where the path leads. At the end of the path, you find a box canyon. You hammer out reports, dispatch bulletins.

The writing has changed, in your hands, and in a twinkling, from an expression of your notions to an epistemological tool. The new place interests you because it is not clear. You attend. In your humility, you lay down the words carefully, watching all the angles. Now the earlier writing looks soft and careless. Process is nothing; erase your tracks. The path is not the work. I hope your tracks have grown over; I hope birds ate the crumbs; I hope you will toss it all and not look back.

The line of words is a hammer. You hammer against the walls of your house. You tap the walls, lightly, everywhere. After giving many years' attention to these things, you know what to listen for. Some of the walls are bearing walls; they have to stay, or everything will fall down. Other walls can go with impunity; you can hear the difference. Unfortunately, it is often a bearing wall that has to go. It cannot be helped. There is only one solution, which appalls you, but there it is. Knock it out. Duck.

Courage utterly opposes the bold hope that this is such fine stuff the work needs it, or the world. Courage, exhausted, stands on bare reality: this writing weakens the work. You must demolish the work and start over. You can save some of the sentences, like bricks. It will be a miracle if you can save some of the paragraphs, no matter how excellent in themselves or hard-won. You can waste a year worrying about it, or you can get it over with now. (Are you a woman, or a mouse?)

The part you must jettison is not only the best-written part; it is also, oddly, that part which was to have been the very point. It is the original key passage, the passage on which the rest was to hang, and from which you yourself drew the courage to begin. Henry James knew it well, and said it best. In his preface to *The Spoils of Poynton,* he pities the writer, in a comical pair of sentences that rises to a howl: "Which is the work in which he hasn't surrendered, under dire difficulty, the best thing he meant to have kept? In which indeed, before the dreadful *done,* doesn't he ask himself what has become of the thing all for the sweet sake of which it was to proceed to that extremity?"

So it is that a writer writes many books. In each book, he intended several urgent and vivid points, many of which he sacrificed as the book's form hardened. "The youth gets together his materials to build a bridge to the moon," Thoreau noted mournfully, "or perchance a palace or temple on the earth, and at length the middle-aged man concludes to build a wood-shed with them." The writer returns to these materials, these passionate subjects, as to unfinished business, for they are his life's work.

It is the beginning of a work that the writer throws away.

A painting covers its tracks. Painters work from the ground up. The latest version of a painting overlays earlier versions, and obliterates them. Writers on the other hand, work from left to right. The discardable chapters are on the left. The latest version of a literary work begins somewhere in the work's middle, and hardens toward the end. The earlier version remains lumpishly on the left; the work's beginning greets the reader with the wrong hand. In those early pages and chapters anyone may find bold leaps to nowhere, read the brave beginnings of dropped themes, hear a tone since abandoned, discover blind alleys, track red herrings, and laboriously learn a setting now false.

Several delusions weaken the writer's resolve to throw away work. If he has read his pages too often, those pages will have a necessary quality, the ring of the inevitable, like poetry known by heart; they will perfectly answer their own familiar rhythms. He will retain them. He may retain those pages if they possess some virtues, such as power in themselves, though they lack the cardinal virtue, which is pertinence to, and unity with, the book's thrust. Sometimes the writer leaves his early chapters in place from gratitude; he cannot contemplate them or read them without feeling again the blessed relief that exalted him when the words first appeared — relief that he was writing anything at all.

That beginning served to get him where he was going, after all; surely the reader needs it, too, as groundwork. But no.

Every year the aspiring photographer brought a stack of his best prints to an old, honored photographer, seeking his judgment. Every year the old man studied the prints and painstakingly ordered them into two piles, bad and good. Every year the old man moved a certain landscape print into the bad stack. At length he turned to the young man: "You submit this same landscape every year, and every year I put it on the bad stack. Why do you like it so much?" The young photographer said, "Because I had to climb a mountain to get it."

A cabdriver sang his songs to me, in New York. Some we sang together. He had turned the meter off; he drove around midtown, singing. One long song he sang twice; it was the only dull one. I said, You already sang that one; let's sing something else. And he said, "You don't know how long it took me to get that one together."

How many books do we read from which the writer lacked courage to tie off the umbilical cord? How many gifts do we open from which the writer neglected to remove the price tag? Is it pertinent, is it courteous, for us to learn what it cost the writer personally?

> You write it all, discovering it at the end of the line of words. The line of words is a fiber optic, flexible as wire; it illumines the path just before its fragile tip. You probe with it, delicate as a worm. . . .

When you are stuck in a book; when you are well into writing it, and know what comes next, and yet cannot go on; when every morning for a week or a month you enter its room and turn your back on it; then the trouble is either of two things. Either the structure has forked, so the narrative, or the logic, has developed a hairline fracture that will shortly split it up the middle — or you are approaching a fatal mistake. What you had planned will not do. If you pursue your present course, the book will explode or collapse, and you do not know about it yet, quite.

In Bridgeport, Connecticut, one morning in April 1987, a six-story concrete-slab building under construction collapsed, and killed twenty-eight men. Just before it collapsed, a woman across the street leaned from her window and said to a passerby, "That building is starting to shake." "Lady," he said, according to the Hartford *Courant*, "you got rocks in your head."

You notice only this: your worker — your one and only, your prized, coddled, and driven worker — is not going out on that job. Will not budge, not even for you, boss. Has been at it long enough to know when the air smells wrong; can sense a tremor through boot soles. Nonsense, you say; it is perfectly safe. But the worker will not go. Will not even look at the site. Just developed heart trouble. Would rather starve. Sorry.

What do you do? Acknowledge, first, that you cannot do nothing. Lay out the structure you already have, x-ray it for a hairline fracture, find it, and think about it for a week or a year; solve the insoluble problem. Or subject the next part, the part at which the worker balks, to harsh tests. It harbors an unexamined and wrong premise. Something completely necessary is false or fatal. Once you find it, and if you can accept the finding, of course it will mean starting again. This is why many experienced writers urge young men and women to learn a useful trade.

Every morning you climb several flights of stairs, enter your study, open the French doors, and slide your desk and chair out into the middle of the air. The desk and chair float thirty feet from the ground, between the crowns of maple trees. The furniture is in place; you go back for your thermos of coffee. Then, wincing, you step out again through the French doors and sit down on the chair and look over the desktop. You can see clear to the river from here in winter. You pour yourself a cup of coffee.

Birds fly under your chair. In spring, when the leaves open in the maples' crowns, your view stops in the treetops just beyond the desk; yellow warblers hiss and whisper on the high twigs, and catch flies. Get to work. Your work is to keep cranking the flywheel that turns the gears that spin the belt in the engine of belief that keeps you and your desk in midair. . . .

◎ *NATALIE GOLDBERG*

Natalie Goldberg is a writer, poet, and teacher who lives in Taos, New Mexico. Her books include Writing Down the Bones: Freeing the Writer Within *(1986),* Wild Mind: Living the Writer's Life *(1990), and* Long Quiet Highway: Waking up in America *(1993), a memoir of her journey of awakening from a suburban childhood to become a student of Zen Buddhism.*

"Walking Between the Raindrops," from Long Quiet Highway, *first appeared in the* New Age Journal. *Goldberg is a passionate observer of her life and growth as a writer; she inspires others, informed by her Buddhist practice, to begin the journey of writing: "Every moment is enormous, and it is all we have."*

Walking Between the Raindrops

By accident, not intended, not even wanted, I had a deep awakening experience in front of a sixth-grade class I was teaching in the Northwest Valley in Albuquerque, New Mexico. I was wearing a white button-down blouse, gray slacks. I had my hair pulled back with a barrette. I was standing near the third row, the blackboard with a map of the world pulled down was behind me, and

I was twenty-six years old. I was an ardent atheist — only "lit-er-a-chure" would save me. I had studied Descartes, Kant, Plato. I believed in reason, rationality. I had been hired in the middle of the school year; the veteran teacher of eleven years had quit because she couldn't control this particular group of Hispanic and Indian kids, and I was next in line to try my fortitude and courage. This was my first time in a contracted teacher's position. I had received my teaching certification six months before, in Ann Arbor, Michigan. I said yes immediately when Mr. Jones, the school district personnel manager, called me. He said that the other teacher was taking a leave of absence to pursue a Ph.D. It wasn't true. *She* told me she was beat, exhausted, and she also told me which kids to watch out for, when I visited the class on her last day of duty. I wasn't even supposed to teach English, the only thing I knew. I was supposed to teach social studies, a subject I knew nothing about. I was in New Mexico, naïve about the state, its culture and customs.

That morning, three men in suits had appeared at our classroom door. They knocked.

"Yes," I said, "please, class, be still." The class was never still. They did not become still then, either, but they were curious. They half sat in their seats.

"We're from Cuba," one of the men said. "We're here to study your school."

"Cuba! Come in. Come in." I ran to the blackboard and stood before the world map.

"Now, who can point out Cuba for me?"

Skinny Roberto ran down the aisle between two rows of desks. He pointed his finger to Costa Rica. I adjusted it to Cuba.

"Yes, that's it." I turned to the three men. "How did you pick our school?"

They looked bewildered. One said, "Our principal sent us," and they quickly excused themselves.

The lunch bell rang. The kids ran out the door. I went to the teacher next door.

"Mrs. Martinez, you're not going to believe this. There were three men here from Cuba! Can you imagine? They picked our school."

She looked up from her desk. She was about to pop a Chiclet into her mouth.

"Miss Goldberg, they came from Cuba, *New Mexico.* Not Havana, Cuba. Cuba's a small town north of here."

"Oh," I said, and backed out of her class. My face turned red.

I sat down at the steel desk in my classroom, opened a drawer, took out a container and scooped strawberry yogurt into my mouth. I rubbed the chest bone above my heart. It was sore. The night before I had been so busy writing a short story about my grandfather's orange bowl that I forgot two eggs I'd left on the stove to boil. Suddenly I smelled something burning and jerked up from my desk and bolted into the kitchen. As I turned the corner I ran into the refrigerator; the handle hit me hard in the chest. I fell back, staggered, and saw stars. They were the same stars I'd seen the weekend before on a wall painting at the palm reader's.

I had been driving down highway 25 just outside of Albuquerque when I passed a small adobe house with a huge white sign of a red hand with red lettering. KNOW YOUR FUTURE. I quickly swung into the driveway. I thought to myself, what are you doing? I don't believe in this.

I knocked at the door. A seventeen-year-old Chicano girl answered. I lied and said I was a student so I could get the two-dollar discount she told me about. I followed her through a dining room, past a brown velvet couch, a television set, and a black velvet painting of a tiger hanging on a yellow wall, and into a back room separated from the rest of the house by a curtain of beads.

Christ, a wooden sculpture of his head, was on the wall, and next to it that painting of gold stars on a blue-black background.

I thought, oh, Jesus, I don't believe in this.

She told me to hold out my hand.

I held it out.

"Um, you're very sure of yourself. Your whole way of seeing and understanding is going to change."

Oh, yeah, I thought. "When's this going to happen?"

"Soon."

"How soon?"

"Very, very soon."

I rolled my eyes. I argued with her. That wasn't going to happen. "Anything else?" I asked.

"You're going to go someplace you've never been before. Where you know no one. Into the deep north. You'll do this for the love of a man." She held my hand.

Oh, brother, I thought. I was a strong feminist. I wasn't going to drop everything for a man. "Yeah, when will this happen?" I asked.

"Not for a long while. In the future."

I had had enough. I pulled my hand away. I put it forward again. I started to ask about writing, I pulled it back again.

I paid her the three dollars and left and forgot about it.

When I ran into the refrigerator handle, I remembered the palm reader, the dusty road, the turquoise sky, the rock cliffs behind her house, and the star painting behind her left shoulder.

Stunned, I turned off the stove. The eggshells were burned brown and the pot was black. There was an awful smell in my apartment. I threw the eggs and pot in the garbage.

My chest was still hurting. I had fifteen minutes before the kids returned to the class. There were paper planes on the floor, at least fourteen of them. Paper clips, textbooks, pencils, empty Frito-Lay orange-and-red cellophane bags, a whistle, three sweaters, and two pairs of sneakers also were on the floor. The wooden desks with attached chairs were in jagged rows, some turned all the way around and facing each other.

After I finished my yogurt and dumped the container in the wastebasket, I just sat at my desk and waited for the bell to ring.

When it did, the kids charged into the class in jean jackets and sweatshirts. It was April. They ran to their seats.

I stood up in the middle of "Please, please, be quiet," and suddenly stopped. The place where my chest was sore — it was opening, opening red and enormous like a great peony, and it was radiating throughout my body. I felt the blood flowing in my hands and legs. I turned and looked out the window. I looked at the smoky appearance of the spring cottonwoods near the parking lot. Any day now they would break into leaf. There was a spindly Russian olive near our window. Suddenly it looked beautiful. Then I had one simple vision: I saw myself wandering in autumn fields and I felt that nothing, nothing else was important. This was a profound feeling, a big feeling. It wasn't a passing, momentary flash. I knew I had to stay true to that one vision.

Understand, I had no idea what was happening. It wasn't some glorious enlightenment that many of us imagine and wish for. I was frightened. I didn't want it. I just wanted to be a writer and to earn a living keeping this class in front of me quiet. I didn't understand what was going on, and I had no clue about those autumn fields. Just then, there was a fistfight in the corner between Henry and Anita, the toughest girl in the class, and the spectators were enthusiastic. I had signed a contract, my first. I hated my job; I wasn't qualified for it — which, in this case, meant keeping control of everyone — but that didn't matter. I was going to get through it. I had two months until the end of school and now something was inside me and I had to stop that fight.

When I got home that night I called a friend.

"Gabrielle, my heart opened in front of the class. Nothing makes sense."

"I don't know what you're talking about," she replied. She was an intellectual. She, too, had read Kant, Descartes, Henri Bergson, Aristotle.

I hung up. None of my friends wanted to hear about it. They all were like the person I'd been before this afternoon in class: atheists, intellectuals.

At two in the morning, I bolted up in bed, wide awake. I got up and walked into the living room, sat down on the couch and stared at the kitchen clock over the refrigerator in the other room. My mind was totally blank. I just stared. I didn't go back to sleep until five A.M. I had to wake up for school at seven. I was exhausted the whole next day in class.

This waking up and staring in the middle of the night continued for three weeks. It became clear that I should quit my job and go to the mountains. Simultaneous with this clear feeling was another voice in me: "What! Are you crazy? You've signed a contract. If you quit, you won't get another one. The mountains! You're a city girl. You don't know anything about the mountains!"

The kids continued to run around the classroom. I became quite fond of several of them, and I was tired from no sleep and strung out between my heart and my teacher's contract.

Finally on one Monday in school, without plan or thought, I went next door to Mrs. Martinez and asked her to watch the class. I marched down the just-waxed linoleum corridor lined with tan lockers to the principal's office. I have no idea what I said to him as I sat across from him at his large brown desk, because while my mouth, connected with my body, spoke one thing, my busy mind was screaming at me, "What are you doing? You're crazy. You're finished! You'll starve in a gutter." I must have been eloquent, though, because when I was finished, Mr. Peterson, the principal, stood up, gave me a strong handshake, and said, "I understand completely. And if you ever want a job again, just call me."

I felt such relief. I flew down the hall back to my class. I was free. This was my last week trying to get the kids in their seats. As a matter of fact, when I entered the class again, after thanking Mrs. Martinez for watching them, I thought, "What the hell. Let them do what they want. They do it anyway." I sat behind my desk the rest of the afternoon, smiling. We all seemed happier and, given freedom, they seemed less unruly.

On Tuesday, I took attendance and then lined them up at the door. I didn't have a plan but I was sure one would emerge. I marched them outside and along the weeded road. Just being outside made us all happy. We walked for a quarter of a mile and I saw the STAFF OF LIFE sign in the distance. I remembered it was a food co-op on five acres of land, with swings and paths and an herb garden. We headed toward it, and for the whole morning the kids gathered in small groups, played, and were content. The co-op people were thrilled. They were getting a chance to educate the youth. They ran out intermittently with samples of organic carrots and roasted corn. Anita even said she could definitely taste the difference between organic and nonorganic carrots and she liked the organic better, said she was going to ask her mom to buy some.

Each day of that week we did something different. I trusted something inside me, instead of what I thought I should do, and the kids responded. Because I was leaving soon, I didn't feel the restraints of the public school. It was as though that institution was no longer between me and the kids, that massive brick structure had crumbled, a new path had opened, a new way to be together. It wasn't all obvious to me at the time, but it was the beginning of something new.

On Thursday it rained. The kids were dismayed. We wouldn't be able to leave the building.

"Nonsense," I said. "It's not cold out and it's not raining hard. Let's get very still." I waited for them to become still and they did, unlike a few weeks ago.

"When we go out and enter the rain, see if you can walk between the drops." I paused. "If we do get wet, don't worry — it's New Mexico!" In one enormous rush, I felt the whole glory of the state. "We'll dry quickly."

I led them to the front door. They were excited and a little nervous. We were breaking a rule: You couldn't get wet by rain, only by swimming in pools, by sprinklers, showers, and never in school. I was happy, fearless.

I stood by the door. "I will demonstrate. All of you watch and then you can follow." They stood huddled in the entryway. I stepped out, no raincoat, no umbrella, my palms up and open in supplication to water. I stepped along the sidewalk.

I went up to a bush, picked a twig, turned to face the group and said, "Ahhh, sagebrush smells best in the rain. Come slowly and enter it."

They stepped away from the building like the patients in the movie *King of Hearts* who had been freed from the insane asylum. They stepped out into the rain gingerly, tenderly, and were delighted.

On Friday, I stood in front of the blackboard. "I have something to tell you." They were all attentive. "Today is the last day of the week and the last day I'll be here." There was an awkward, stunned silence. "Look, I know, this has been a tough year for you. Let's face it, none of you were dolls. You weren't that well behaved." Alvaro, Roberto, and Eloy smirked. "But this week was a great week." They all nodded. "I want you to remember it. It's important. All of you get in your seats" — they were leaning against bookshelves and sitting on top of desks — "and when you do, I want you to close your eyes and put out your hands." I walked around and placed a Hershey's Kiss in each kid's palm. "Now unwrap it, and all on the same count, when I say yes, put it on your tongue, close your eyes and your mouth, let it melt slowly, and remember this week. Promise to never forget it, no matter what else happens in your life." I switched off the classroom lights.

I felt sad and happy when I left that day. I had begun to redeem something from a long time ago, all that deadness I had felt as a child.

◎ *MAXINE KUMIN*

Maxine Kumin was born in Philadelphia in 1925. She received her B.A. and M.A. from Radcliffe. She lives on a farm in Warner, New Hampshire, where she breeds horses. Kumin has published several volumes of poetry as well as novels, short stories, essays, and more than twenty children's books. Kumin has won the Pulitzer Prize (for Up Country*, 1972), the Academy of American Poets Fellowship, and the Levinson Award from* Poetry *magazine. Kumin held the position of Poetry Consultant to the Library of Congress (a post now called Poet Laureate of the United States) in 1980–1981.*

"Menial Labor and the Muse," a meditative essay on the relation between physical labor and mental work, was first published in TriQuarterly *in 1989. Kumin often finds, in the repetitive labor of her days, abundant mental space for her "best ruminations."*

Menial Labor and the Muse

An all-day rain of the mizzly seductive sort, compounded by snow fog; twilight began this day and will mediate it until fully dark.

Before settling in at my desk I've distributed an extra bale of hay to the horses, making a quick trip from house to barn in my slicker and muck boots. The whole main floor of the barn is packed, this time of year, with last August's second cutting, a mix of timothy and brome grass, mostly without the seed heads. The bales are still green, so sweet it makes me salivate as I inhale their aroma which cries *summer!* on the winter air. I have never understood why some entrepreneur has yet to capture the scent and market it as a perfume. Doesn't everyone melt, smelling new hay? I must have been a horse in the last incarnation or had a profound love affair in some sixteenth-century hayloft.

A perspicacious student once pointed out to me that it rains or snows in a large percentage of my poems. She's right, of course, though I hadn't ever thought of the connection.

Stormy days are my best writing days. The weather relieves me of my Jewish-Calvinist urgency to do something useful with one or another of the young stock, to longe or drive or ride the current two-, three- or four-year old. Or, in season, to cut around the perimeters of the pastures, work that's known as *brushing out.* Or clean out and re-bed the run-in sheds and the central area under the barn my friend Robin calls the motel lobby. No need to bring the vegetable garden into this, or the sugar bush of a hundred maple trees. We probably won't be setting any taps this March. Acid rain and the depredations of the pear thrip that followed have weakened the trees to a possibly fatal point.

This year's wood is in, all split and stacked. Next year's is already on the ground, split in four-foot lengths to dry. It snowed before we could get two truckloads of manure on the garden, though. Victor says we'll have a thaw, that there is still time. He's still puttying and caulking as we button up for the hard months. *Still* is the wrong word, as there is no beginning and no apparent end. Outside water faucets are drained and closed off, heating element installed in the watering trough, and so on.

Writing and well-being. In the most direct, overt and uncomplicated way, my writing depends on the well-being that devolves from this abbreviated list of chores undertaken and completed.

One set of self-imposed deadlines nurtures the other: something harshly physical each day, the reward being a bone-tired sense of equipoise at nightfall. A daily session at the desk even when, as Rilke warned, nothing comes. I must keep holy even disappointment, even desertion. The leaven of the next day's chores will redeem the failed writing, infuse it with new energy or at the very least allow me to shred it while I await the Rilkean birth-hour of a new clarity.

The well-being of solitude is a necessary component of this equation. A "Good! No visitors today" mentality isn't limited to snowstorms or Monday mornings. On the contrary, this feeling of contentment in isolation pervades every good working day. My writing time needs to surround itself with empty stretches, or at least unpeopled ones, for the writing takes place in an area of suspension as in a hanging nest that is almost entirely encapsulated. I think of the oriole's graceful construction.

This is why poems may frequently begin for me in the suspended cocoon of the airplane, or even in the airport lounge during those dreary hours of layovers. There's the same anonymity, the same empty but enclosed space, paradoxical in view of the thousands of other travelers pulsing past. But I have no responsibility here. I am uncalled upon and can go inward.

My best ruminations take place in the barn while my hands (and back) are busy doing something else. Again, there's the haunting appeal of enclosure, the mindless suspension of doing simple, repetitive tasks — mucking out, refilling water buckets, raking sawdust — that allows those free-associative leaps out of which a poem may occasionally come. And if not, reasons the Calvinist, a clean barn is surely a sign of the attained state of grace. Thus I am saved. And if the Muse descends, my androgynous pagan Muse, I will have the best of both worlds.

◎ *ALICE CHILDRESS*

Alice Childress was born in 1920 in Charleston, South Carolina. At the age of five she moved to Harlem, where she was raised by her grandmother, Eliza Campbell, who taught her the power of storytelling and encouraged her to write. Childress trained as an actress and was a founding member of the American Negro Theatre in the early 1940s. Her writing career spanned over forty years, and included the publication of at least a dozen plays, as well as novels, children's books, screenplays, and essays. Childress was the first African American woman to see her play (Gold through the Trees, *1952) professionally produced in New York, and the first to receive an Obie Award, for* Trouble in Mind *(1956). In the early 1950s she initiated the first union off-Broadway contracts, establishing equity standards. She received the first Paul Robeson Award for Outstanding Contributions to the Performing Arts, the Coretta Scott King Award, and a Rockefeller Foundation grant. Childress died in 1994 in Queens, New York.*

Written for the American Negro Theatre in 1949, Florence *began Childress's career as a playwright. Childress directed and starred in the play, which is set in a segregated waiting room of a Southern railway station. Childress's writings consistently addressed issues of gender and class as well as of race.*

Florence

Place: A very small town in the South.

Time: The present.

Scene: A railway station waiting room. The room is divided in two sections by a low railing. Upstage center is a double door which serves as an entrance to both sides of the room. Over the doorway stage right is a sign "Colored," over the doorway stage left is another sign "White." Stage right are two doors . . . one marked "Colored men" . . . the other "Colored women." Stage left two other doorways are "White ladies" and "White gentlemen." There are two benches . . . one on each side. The room is drab and empty-looking. Through the double doors upstage center can be seen a gray lighting which gives the effect of early evening and open platform.

At rise of curtain the stage remains empty for about twenty seconds. . . . A middle aged Negro woman enters, looks offstage . . . then crosses to the "Colored" side and sits on the bench. A moment later she is followed by a young Negro woman about twenty-one years old. She is carrying a large new cardboard suitcase and a wrapped shoebox. She is wearing a shoulder strap bag and a newspaper protrudes from the flap. She crosses to the "Colored" side and rests the suitcase at her feet as she looks at her mother with mild annoyance.

MARGE: You didn't have to get here so early mama. Now you got to wait!

MAMA: If I'm goin' someplace . . . I like to get there in plenty time. You don't have to stay.

MARGE: You shouldn't wait 'round here alone.

MAMA: I ain't scared. Ain't a soul going to bother me.

MARGE: I got to get back to Ted. He don't like to be in the house by himself. [*She picks up the bag and places it on the bench by Mama.*]

MAMA: You'd best go back. [*Smiles.*] You know I think he misses Florence.

MARGE: He's just a little fellow. He needs his mother. You make her come home! She shouldn't be way up there in Harlem. She ain't got nobody there.

MAMA: You know Florence don't like the South.

MARGE: It ain't what we like in this world! You tell her that.

MAMA: If Mr. Jack ask about the rent. You tell him we gonna be a little late on account of the trip.

MARGE: I'll talk with him. Don't worry so about everything. [*Places suitcase on floor.*] What you carryin', mama . . . bricks?

MAMA: If Mr. Jack won't wait . . . write to Rudley. He oughta send a little somethin'.

MARGE: Mama . . . Rudley ain't got nothin' fo himself. I hate to ask him to give us.

MAMA: That's your brother! If push comes to shove, we got to ask.

MARGE [*places box on bench*]: Don't forget to eat your lunch . . . and try to get a seat near the window so you can lean on your elbow and get a little rest.

MAMA: Hmmmm . . . mmmph. Yes.

MARGE: Buy yourself some coffee when the man comes through. You'll need something hot and you can't go to the diner.

MAMA: I know that. You talk like I'm a northern greenhorn.

MARGE: You got handkerchiefs?

MAMA: I got everything, Marge.

MARGE [*wanders upstage to the railing division line*]: I know Florence is real bad off or she wouldn't call on us for money. Make her come home. She ain't gonna get rich up there and we can't afford to do for her.

MAMA: We talked all of that before.

MARGE [*touches rail*]: Well, you got to be strict on her. She got notions a Negro woman don't need.

MAMA: But she was in a real play. Didn't she sent us twenty-five dollars a week?

MARGE: For two weeks.

MAMA: Well the play was over.

MARGE [*crosses to Mama and sits beside her*]: It's not money, Mama. Sarah wrote us about it. You know what she said Florence was doin'! Sweepin' the stage!

MAMA: She was *in* the play!

MARGE: Sure she was in it! Sweepin'! Them folks ain't gonna let her be no actress. You tell her to wake up.

MAMA: I . . . I . . . think.

MARGE: Listen Ma. . . . She won't wanna come. We know that . . . but she gotta!

MAMA: Maybe we shoulda told her to expect me. It's kind of mean to just walk in like this.

MARGE: I bet she's livin' terrible. What's the matter with her? Don't she know we're keepin' her son?

MAMA: Florence don't feel right 'bout down here since Jim got killed.

MARGE: Who does? I should be the one goin' to get her. You tell her she ain't gonna feel right no place. Mama, honestly! She must think she's white!

MAMA: Florence is brownskin.

MARGE: I don't mean that. I'm talkin' about her attitude. Didn't she go into Strumley's down here and ask to be a sales girl? [*Rises.*] Now ain't that somethin'? They don't hire no Colored folks.

MAMA: Others besides Florence been talkin' about their rights.

MARGE: I know it . . . but there's things we can't do cause they ain't gonna let us. [*She wanders over to the "White" side of the stage.*] Don't feel a damn bit different over here than it does on our side.

[*Silence.*]

MAMA: Maybe we shoulda just sent her the money this time. This one time.

MARGE [*coming back to "Colored" side*]: Mama! Don't you let her cash that check for nothin' but to bring her back home.

MAMA: I know.

MARGE: [*restless . . . fidgets with her hair . . . patting it in place*]: I oughta go now.

MAMA: You best get back to Ted. He might play with the lamp.

MARGE: He better not let me catch him! If you got to go to the ladies' room take your grip.

MAMA: I'll be alright. Make Ted get up on time for school.

MARGE [*kisses her quickly and gives her the newspaper*]: Here's something to read. So long Mama.

MAMA: G'bye, Margie baby.

MARGE [*goes to door . . . stops and turns to her mother*]: You got your smelling salts?

MAMA: In my pocketbook.

MARGE [*wistfully*]: Tell Florence I love her and I miss her too.

PORTER [*can be heard singing in the distance.*]

MAMA: Sure.

MARGE [*reluctant to leave*]: Pin that check in your bosom, Mama. You might fall asleep and somebody'll rob you.

MAMA: I got it pinned to me. [*Feels for the check, which is in her blouse.*]

MARGE [*almost pathetic*]: Bye, Ma.

MAMA [*sits for a moment looking at her surroundings. She opens the paper and begins to read.*]

PORTER [*offstage*]: Hello, Marge. What you doin' down here?

MARGE: I came to see Mama off.

PORTER: Where's she going?

MARGE: She's in there; she'll tell you. I got to get back to Ted.

PORTER: Bye now. . . . Say, wait a minute, Marge.

MARGE: Yes?

PORTER: I told Ted he could have some of my peaches and he brought all them Brandford boys over and they picked 'em all. I wouldn't lay a hand on him but I told him I was gonna tell you.

MARGE: I'm gonna give it to him!

PORTER [*enters and crosses to the "White" side of waiting room. He carries a pail of water and a mop. He is about fifty years old. He is obviously tired but not lazy*]: Every peach off my tree!

MAMA: There wasn't but six peaches on that tree.

PORTER [*smiles . . . glances at Mama as he crosses to white side and begins to mop*]: How d'ye do, Mrs. Whitney . . . you going on a trip?

MAMA: Fine, I thank you. I'm going to New York.

PORTER: Wish it was me. You gonna stay?

MAMA: No, Mr. Brown. I'm bringing Florence . . . I'm visiting Florence.

PORTER: Tell her I said hello. She's a fine girl.

MAMA: Thank you.

PORTER: My brother Bynum's in Georgia now.

MAMA: Well now, that's nice.

PORTER: Atlanta.

MAMA: He goin' to school?

PORTER: Yes'm. He saw Florence in a Colored picture. A moving picture.

MAMA: Do tell! She didn't say a word about it.

PORTER: They got Colored moving picture theatres in Atlanta.

MAMA: Yes. Your brother going to be a doctor?

PORTER [*with pride*]: No. He writes things.

MAMA: Oh.

PORTER: My son is goin' back to Howard next year.

MAMA: Takes an awful lot of goin' to school to be anything. Lot of money leastways.

PORTER [*thoughtfully*]: Yes'm, it sure do.

MAMA: That sure was a nice church sociable the other night.

PORTER: Yes'm. We raised 87 dollars.

MAMA: That's real nice.

PORTER: I won your cake at the bazaar.

MAMA: The chocolate one?

PORTER [*as he wrings mop*]: Yes'm . . . was light as a feather. That old train is gonna be late this evenin'. It's number 42.

MAMA: I don't mind waitin'.

PORTER [*lifts pail, tucks mop handle under his arm. Looks about in order to make certain no one is around. Leans over and addresses Mama in a confidential tone*]: Did you buy your ticket from that Mr. Daly?

MAMA [*in a low tone*]: No. Marge bought it yesterday.

PORTER [*leaning against railing*]: That's good. That man is mean. Especially if he thinks you're goin' north. [*He starts to leave . . . then turns back to Mama.*] If you go to the rest room use the Colored men's . . . the other one is out of order.

MAMA: Thank you, sir.

MRS. CARTER [*a white woman . . . well dressed, wearing furs and carrying a small, expensive overnight bag. She breezes in . . . breathless . . . flustered and smiling. She addresses the porter as she almost collides with him*]: Boy! My bags are out there. The taxi driver just dropped them. Will they be safe?

PORTER: Yes, mam. I'll see after them.

MRS. CARTER: I thought I'd missed the train.

PORTER: It's late, mam.

MRS. CARTER: [*crosses to bench on the "White" side and rests her bag*]: Fine! You come back here and get me when it comes. There'll be a tip in it for you.

PORTER: Thank you, mam. I'll be here. [*As he leaves.*] Miss Whitney, I'll take care of your bag too.

MAMA: Thank you, sir.

MRS. CARTER [*wheels around . . . notices Mama*]: Oh. . . . Hello there. . . .

MAMA: Howdy, mam. [*She opens her newspaper and begins to read.*]

MRS. CARTER [*paces up and down rather nervously. She takes a cigarette from her purse, lights it. Takes a deep draw. She looks at her watch. Speaks to Mama across the railing*]: Have you any idea how late the train will be?

MAMA: No mam. [*Starts to read again.*]

MRS. CARTER: I can't leave this place fast enough. Two days of it and I'm bored to tears. Do you live here?

MAMA [*rests paper on her lap*]: Yes, mam.

MRS. CARTER: Where are you going?

MAMA: New York City, mam.

MRS. CARTER: Good for you! You can stop "maming" me. My name is Mrs. Carter. I'm not a southerner really.

MAMA: Yes'm . . . Mrs. Carter.

MRS. CARTER [*takes handkerchief from her purse and covers her nose for a moment*]: My God! Disinfectant! This is a frightful place. My brother's here writing a book. Wants atmosphere. Well he's got it. I'll never come back here ever.

MAMA: That's too bad, mam . . . Mrs. Carter.

MRS. CARTER: That's good. I'd die in this place. Really die. Jeff . . . Mr. Wiley . . . my brother. . . . He's tied in knots, a bundle of problems . . . positively knots.

MAMA [*amazed*]: That so, mam?

MRS. CARTER: You don't have to call me mam. It's so southern. Mrs. Carter! These people are still fighting the Civil War. I'm really a New Yorker now. Of course I was born here . . . in the South I mean. Memphis. Listen . . . am I annoying you? I've simply got to talk to someone.

MAMA [*places newspaper on bench*]: No, Mrs. Carter. It's perfectly alright.

MRS. CARTER: Fine! You see Jeff has ceased writing. Stopped! Just like that! [*Snaps fingers.*]

MAMA [*turns to her*]: That so?

MRS. CARTER: Yes. The reviews came out on his last book. Poor fellow.

MAMA: I'm sorry, mam . . . Mrs. Carter. They didn't like his book?

MRS. CARTER: Well enough . . . but Jeff's . . . well Mr. Wiley is a genius. He says they missed the point! Lost the whole message! Did you read . . . do you . . . have you heard of *Lost My Lonely Way?*

MAMA: No, mam. I can't say I have.

MRS. CARTER: Well it doesn't matter. It's profound. Real . . . you know. [*Stands at railing upstage.*] It's about your people.

MAMA: That's nice.

MRS. CARTER: Jeff poured his complete self into it. Really delved into the heart of the problem, pulled no punches! He hardly stopped for his meals. . . . And of course I wasn't here to see that he didn't overdo. He suffers so with his characters.

MAMA: I guess he wants to do his best.

MRS. CARTER: Zelma! . . . That's his heroine. . . . Zelma! A perfect character.

MAMA [*interested . . . coming out of her shell eagerly*]: She was colored, mam?

MRS. CARTER: Oh yes! . . . But of course you don't know what it's about do you?

MAMA: No, miss . . . Would you tell me?

MRS. CARTER [*leaning on railing*]: Well . . . she's almost white, see? Really you can't tell except in small ways. She wants to be a lawyer . . . and . . . well, there she is full of complexes and this deep shame you know.

MAMA [*excitedly but with curiosity*]: Do tell! What shame has she got?

MRS. CARTER [*takes off her fur neckpiece and places it on bench with overnight bag*]: It's obvious! This lovely creature . . . intelligent, ambitious, and well . . . she's a Negro!

MAMA [*waiting eagerly*]: Yes'm, you said that. . . .

MRS. CARTER: Surely you understand? She's constantly hating herself. Just before she dies she says it! . . . Right on the bridge. . . .

MAMA [*genuinely moved*]: How sad. Ain't it a shame she had to die?

MRS. CARTER: It was inevitable . . . couldn't be any other way!

MAMA: What did she say on the bridge?

MRS. CARTER: Well . . . just before she jumped. . . .

MAMA [*slowly straightening*]: You mean she killed *herself?*

MRS. CARTER: Of course. Close your eyes and picture it!

MAMA [*turns front and closes her eyes tightly with enthusiasm*]: Yes'm.

MRS. CARTER [*center stage on "White" side*]: Now . . . ! She's standing on the bridge in the moonlight. . . . Out of her shabby purse she takes a mirror . . . and by the light of the moon she looks at her reflection in the glass.

MAMA [*clasps her hands together gently*]: I can see her just as plain.

MRS. CARTER [*sincerely*]: Tears roll down her cheeks as she says . . . almost! almost white . . . but I'm black! I'm a Negro! and then . . . [*turns to Mama*] she jumps and drowns herself!

MAMA [*opens her eyes. Speaks quietly*]: Why?

MRS. CARTER: She can't face it! Living in a world where she almost belongs but not quite. [*Drifts upstage.*] Oh it's so . . . so . . . tragic.

MAMA [*carried away by her convictions . . . not anger . . . she feels challenged. She rises*]: That ain't so! Not one bit it ain't!

MRS. CARTER [*surprised*]: But it is!

MAMA [*during the following she works her way around the railing until she crosses about one foot over to the white side and is face to face with Mrs. Carter.*]: I know it ain't Don't my friend Essie Kitredge daughter look just like a German or somethin'? She didn't kill herself! She's teachin' the third grade in the colored school right here. Even the bus drivers ask her to sit in the front seats cause they think she's white! . . . an' . . . an' . . . she just says as clear as you please . . . "I'm sittin' where my people got to sit by law. I'm a Negro woman!"

MRS. CARTER [*uncomfortable but not knowing why*]: . . . But there you have it. The exception makes the rule. That's proof!

MAMA: No such a thing! My cousin Hemsly's as white as you! . . . an' . . . an' he never. . . .

MRS. CARTER [*flushed with anger . . . yet lost . . . because she doesn't know why*]: Are you losing your temper? [*Weakly.*] Are you angry with me?

MAMA [*stands silently trembling as she looks down and notices she is on the wrong side of the railing. She looks up at the "White Ladies Room" sign and slowly works her way back to the "Colored" side. She feels completely lost*]: No, *mam.* Excuse me please. [*With bitterness.*] I just meant Hemsly works in the colored section of the shoe store. . . . He never once wanted to kill his self! [*She sits down on the bench and fumbles for her newspaper.*]

[*Silence.*]

MRS. CARTER [*caught between anger and reason . . . she laughs nervously*]: Well! Let's not be upset by this. It's entirely my fault you know. This whole thing is a completely controversial subject. [*Silence.*] If it's too much for Jeff . . . well naturally I shouldn't discuss it with you. [*Approaching railing.*] I'm sorry. Let *me* apologize.

MAMA [*keeps her eyes on the paper*]: No need for that, mam.

[*Silence.*]

MRS. CARTER [*painfully uncomfortable*]: I've drifted away from . . . What started all of this?

MAMA [*no comedy intended or allowed on this line*]: Your brother, mam.

MRS. CARTER [*trying valiantly to brush away the tension*]: Yes. . . . Well I had to come down and sort of hold his hand over the reviews. He just thinks too much . . . and studies. He knows the Negro so well that sometimes our friends tease him and say he almost seems like . . . well you know. . . .

MAMA [*tightly*]: Yes'm.

MRS. CARTER [*slowly walks over to the "Colored" side near the top of the rail*]: You know I try but it's really difficult to understand you people. However . . . I keep trying.

MAMA [*still tight*]: Thank you, mam.

MRS. CARTER [*retreats back to the "White" side and begins to prove herself*]: Last week . . . Why do you know what I did? I sent a thousand dollars to a Negro college for scholarships.

MAMA: That was right kind of you.

MRS. CARTER [*almost pleading*]: I know what's going on in your mind . . . and what you're thinking is wrong. I've . . . I've . . . eaten with Negroes.

MAMA: Yes, mam.

MRS. CARTER [*trying to find a straw*]: . . . And there's Malcom! If it weren't for the guidance of Jeff he'd never written his poems. Malcom is a Negro.

MAMA [*freezing*]: Yes, mam.

MRS. CARTER [*gives up, crosses to her bench, opens her overnight bag and takes out a book and begins to read. She glances at Mama from time to time. Mama is deeply absorbed in her newspaper. Mrs. Carter closes her book with a bang . . . determined to penetrate the wall that Mama has built around her*]: Why are you going to New York?

MAMA [*almost accusingly*]: I got a daughter there.

MRS. CARTER: I lost my son in the war. [*Silence . . . Mama is ill at ease.*] Your daughter . . . what is she doing . . . studying?

MAMA: No'm. She's trying to get on the stage.

MRS. CARTER [*pleasantly*]: Oh . . . a singer?

MAMA: No, mam. She's . . .

MRS. CARTER [*warmly*]: Your people have such a gift. I love spirituals . . . "Steal Away," "Swing Low, Sweet Chariot."

MAMA: They are right nice. But Florence wants to act. Just say things in plays.

MRS. CARTER: A dramatic actress?

MAMA: Yes, that's what it is. She been in a Colored moving picture, and a big show for two weeks on Broadway.

MRS. CARTER: The dear, precious child! . . . But this is funny . . . no! it's pathetic. She must be bitter . . . *really* bitter. Do you know what I do?

MAMA: I can't rightly say.

MRS. CARTER: I'm an actress! A dramatic actress. . . . And I haven't really worked in six months. . . . And I'm pretty well known. . . . And everyone knows Jeff. I'd like to work. Of course, there are my committees, but you see, they don't need me. Not really . . . not even Jeff.

MAMA: Now that's a shame.

MRS. CARTER: Your daughter . . . you must make her stop before she's completely unhappy. Make her stop!

MAMA: Yes'm . . . why?

MRS. CARTER: I have the best of contacts and *I've* only done a few *broadcasts* lately. Of course, I'm not counting the things I just wouldn't do. Your daughter . . . make her stop.

MAMA: A drama teacher told her she has real talent.

MRS. CARTER: A drama teacher! My dear woman, there are loads of unscrupulous whites up there that just hand out opinions for. . . .

MAMA: This was a colored gentleman down here.

MRS. CARTER: Oh well! . . . And she went up there on the strength of that? This makes me very unhappy. [*Puts book away in case, and snaps lock.*]

[*Silence.*]

MAMA [*getting an idea*]: Do you really, truly feel that way, mam?

MRS. CARTER: I do. Please . . . I want you to believe me.

MAMA: Could I ask you something?

MRS. CARTER: Anything.

MAMA: You won't be angry mam?

MRS. CARTER [*remembering*]: I won't. I promise you.

MAMA [*gathering courage*]: Florence is proud . . . but she's having it hard.

MRS. CARTER: I'm sure she is.

MAMA: Could you help her out some, mam? Knowing all the folks you do . . . maybe. . . .

MRS. CARTER [*rubs the outside of the case*]: Well . . . it isn't that simple . . . but . . . you're very sweet. If I only could. . . .

MAMA: Anything you did, I feel grateful. I don't like to tell it, but she can't even pay her rent and things. And she's used to my cooking for her. . . . I believe my girl goes hungry sometime up there . . . and yet she'd like to stay so bad.

MRS. CARTER [*looks up, resting case on her knees*]: How can I refuse? You seem like a good woman.

MAMA: Always lived as best I knew how and raised my children up right. We got a fine family, mam.

MRS. CARTER: And I've no family at all. I've got to! It's clearly my duty. Jeff's books . . . guiding Malcom's poetry. . . . It isn't enough . . . oh I know it isn't! Have you ever heard of Melba Rugby?

MAMA: No, mam. I don't know anybody much . . . except right here.

MRS. CARTER [*brightening*]: She's in California, but she's moving East again . . . hates California.

MAMA: Yes'm.

MRS. CARTER: A most versatile woman. Writes, directs, acts . . . everything!

MAMA: That's nice, mam.

MRS. CARTER: Well, she's uprooting herself and coming back to her first home . . . New York . . . to direct "Love Flowers" . . . it's a musical.

MAMA: Yes'm.

MRS. CARTER: She's grand . . . helped so many people . . . and I'm sure she'll help your . . . what's her name.

MAMA: Florence.

MRS. CARTER [*turns back to bench, opens bag, takes out pencil and address book*]: Yes, Florence. She'll have to *make* a place for her.

MAMA: Bless you, mam.

MRS. CARTER [*holds handbag steady on rail as she uses it to write on*]: Now let's see . . . the best thing to do would be to give you the telephone number . . . since you're going there.

MAMA: Yes'm.

MRS. CARTER [*writing address on paper*]: Your daughter will love her . . . and if she's a deserving girl. . . .

MAMA [*looking down as Mrs. Carter writes*]: She's a good child. Never a bit of trouble. Except about her husband, and neither one of them could help that.

MRS. CARTER [*stops writing, raises her head questioning*]: Oh?

MAMA: He got killed at voting time. He was a good man.

MRS. CARTER [*embarrassed*]: I guess that's worse than losing him in the war.

MAMA: We all got our troubles passing through here.

MRS. CARTER [*gives her the address*]: Tell your dear girl to call this number about a week from now.

MAMA: Yes, mam.

MRS. CARTER: Her experience won't matter with Melba. I know she'll understand. I'll call her too.

MAMA: Thank you, mam.

MRS. CARTER: I'll just tell her . . . no heavy washing or ironing . . . just light cleaning and a little cooking . . . does she cook?

MAMA: Mam? [*Slowly backs away from Mrs. C. and sits down on bench.*]

MRS. CARTER: Don't worry. That won't matter with Melba. [*Silence. Moves around rail to "Colored" side, leans over Mama.*] I'd take your daughter myself, but I've got Binnie. She's been with me for years, and I can't just let her go . . . can I?

MAMA [*looks at Mrs. C. closely*]: No, mam.

MRS. CARTER: Of course she must be steady. I couldn't ask Melba to take a fly-by-night. [*Touches Mama's arm.*] But she'll have her own room and bath, and above all . . . security.

MAMA [*reaches out, clutches Mrs. C.'s wrist almost pulling her off balance*]: Child!

MRS. CARTER [*frightened*]: You're hurting my wrist.

MAMA [*looks down, realizes how tight she's clutching her, and releases her wrist*]: I mustn't hurt you, must I.

MRS. CARTER [*backs away rubbing her wrist*]: It's all right.

MAMA [*rises*]: You better get over on the other side of that rail. It's against the law for you to be here with me.

MRS. CARTER [*frightened and uncomfortable*]: If you think so.

MAMA: I don't want to break the law.

MRS. CARTER [*keeps her eye on Mama as she drifts around railing to bench on her side. Gathers overnight bag*]: I know I must look like a fright. The train should be along soon. When it comes, I won't see you until New York. These silly laws. [*Silence.*] I'm going to powder my nose. [*Exits into "White Ladies" room.*]

PORTER [*singing offstage.*]

MAMA [*sits quietly, staring in front of her . . . then looks at the address for a moment . . . tears the paper into little bits and lets them flutter to the floor. She opens the suitcase, takes out notebook, an envelope and a pencil. She writes a few words on the paper.*]

PORTER [*enters with broom and dust pan*]: Number 42 will be coming along in nine minutes. [*When Mama doesn't answer him, he looks up and watches her. She reaches in her bosom, unpins the check, smooths it out, places it in the envelope with the letter. She closes the suitcase.*] I said the train's coming. Where's the lady?

MAMA: She's in the *ladies'* room. You got a stamp?

PORTER: No. But I can get one out the machine. Three for a dime.

MAMA [*hands him the letter*]: Put one on here and mail it for me.

PORTER [*looks at it*]: Gee . . . you writing to Florence when you're going to see her?

MAMA [*picks up the shoe box and puts it back on the bench*]: You want a good lunch? It's chicken and fruit.

PORTER: Sure . . . thank you . . . but won't you . . .

MAMA [*rises, paces up and down*]: I ain't gonna see Florence for a long time. Might be never.

PORTER: How's that, Mrs. Whitney?

MAMA: She can be anything in the world she wants to be! That's her right. Marge can't make her turn back, Mrs. Carter can't make her turn back. "Lost My Lonely Way"! That's a book! People killing themselves 'cause they look white but be black. They just don't know do they, Mr. Brown?

PORTER: Whatever happened don't you fret none. Life is too short.

MAMA: Oh, I'm gonna fret plenty! You know what I wrote Florence?

PORTER: No, mam. But you don't have to tell me.

MAMA: I said "Keep trying." . . . Oh, I'm going home.

PORTER: I'll take your bag. [*Picks up bag and starts out.*] Come on, Mrs. Whitney. [*Porter exits.*]

[*Mama moves round to "White" side, stares at signs over door. Starts to knock on "White Ladies" door, changes her mind. As she turns to leave, her eye catches the railing; she approaches it gently, touches it, turns, exits. Stage is empty for about six or seven seconds. Sound of train whistle in distance. Slow curtain.*]

◎ KATE BRAID

Kate Braid is a journeywoman carpenter and poet who lives in Vancouver and who teaches construction at the British Columbia University of Technology. She is a founder of Canadian Women in Trades and Technology. Her poems appear in magazines and anthologies, including East of Main. *She has published* Building the Future: Profiles of Canadian Women In Trades *(1989). Her first book of poems,* Covering Rough Ground, *was published in 1991.*

" 'Girl' on the Crew" was first published in Room of One's Own *and has been anthologized in* If I Had a Hammer: Women's Work in Poetry, Fiction, and Photographs *(1990). The poem shows that Braids' sense of humor has stood her in good stead; her courage and skill at the construction site show up the male coworkers who had harassed her at the outset.*

"Girl" on the Crew

The boys flap heavy leather aprons at me
like housewives scaring crows
from the clean back wash.
    Some aprons.   Some wash.
They think if the leather is tough enough
if the hammer handle piercing it is long enough
I will be overcome with primordial dread
or longing.

They chant construction curses at me:
    Lay 'er down!   *Erect those studs!*
and are alarmed when I learn the words.
They build finely tuned traps, give orders I cannot fill
then puzzle when a few of their own
give me passwords.

I learn the signs of entry,
dropping my hammer into its familiar mouth
as my apron whispers *O-o-o-h Welcome!*

I point my finger and corner posts spring into place
shivering themselves into fertile earth at my command.
The surveyors have never seen such accuracy.

I bite off nails with my teeth
shorten boards with a wave of my hand
pierce them through the dark brown love knots.
They gasp.

I squat and the flood of my urine digs
whole drainage systems in an instant.
The boys park their backhoes, call their friends
to come see for themselves or they'd never believe it.

The hairs of my head turn to steel and join boards
tongue-in-groove
like lovers along dark lanes.
Drywall is rustling under cover
eager to slip over the studs at my desire.

When I tire, my breasts grow two cherry trees
that depart my chest
and offer me shade, cool juices
while the others suck bitter beans.

At the end of the day the boys are exhausted
from watching.
They fall at my feet and beg for a body like mine.
I am too busy dancing to notice.

LAURIE BLAUNER

Laurie Blauner was born in 1953 in New York City and now makes her home in Seattle, Washington. She was educated at Kenyon College, at Sarah Lawrence College, and at the University of Montana. Her poems have appeared in journals such as The American Poetry Review, The Nation, College English, *and* Poetry. *She has published three books of poetry, most recently* Children of Gravity *(1995), which won the King County Publication Award. Other recognition for her work includes a grant from the National Endowment for the Arts. Besides writing, Blauner is interested in the visual arts, especially painting, photography, and printmaking. She did the cover art for* Children of Gravity, *an original collagraph.*

"The Invention of Imagination" is from Children of Gravity. *The speaker describes her surroundings in a typical neighborhood and in a typical house, where "Every morning the songs of the phone begin." But through dream, through imaginative re-creation, the speaker reaches the poem's surprising conclusion — a foreign landscape to which the speaker has been transported.*

The Invention of Imagination

The sound of your clock is rain
troubling the window. The house of
narcissus, ivory dominoes, and spiders waiting.

And this is the blare of work: the dusk of
your favorite time, watching the widow across the street
dig up flower bulbs like gnarled moons following
one another into days. Each night you think it will
never end. Every morning the songs of the phone begin.
You daydream of a mottled horse brushing flies
from his hind legs, the color photograph of the latest
criminal's execution, the men you will meet.
It's time to push the boulder up the hill
again, think about sharing necessities,
the household of your heart. *This is*
your first day in Paris. You watch a man in a beret
selling bread and the buildings crumple
like paper at the shadows of your feet.

◎ *KATHRYN STRIPLING BYER*

Of "The Carpenter" the poet has told us: "As someone raised on a farm, I have always found the land and the habitations built upon it profoundly important. When my grandfather's house burned, I felt it was somehow my work as a poet to build it up again, but this time out of words. I began to see a poem as a structure in and of itself, a habitation that could offer its own kind of shelter and repose" (letter to M. Kallet, 1996). (For more on Byer, *see page 389.)* *This poem appears in* The Girl in the Midst of the Harvest *(1986).*

The Carpenter

From ashes I rebuild my grandfather's house.
It is slow labor. Whatever is left
I must gather. My hip pockets bulge
with coals the roof scattered like seed.
I hoist tangled wire onto my shoulders
and stumble forth, huffing and puffing,
to search the debris for a nail straight enough
to be hammered. As soon as I find it,
I pound with conviction but no skill.
I hold up my battered blue thumb to the sky
and I curse as magnificently
as my grandfather ever did, calling on

bird, beast, and cosmos to judge his incompetence.
Tears streak my dirty cheeks. Each day I quit
and each day I start over again,
using buckets of glue if I must, and
a patience I hardly knew I had inherited.

I have one window already aloft
in my grandmother's kitchen. Above the remains
of her teacups and crockery, it frames the oak
sifting light through its branches
like wheat. If the glass is cracked
I do not notice. By spring
I will see the big kettle secure
on the stove and the stove-pipe ascending.
The bread will rise endlessly. Butter will come
in the earthenware churn. Let the roof wait
for winter. My grandfather's house always
was airy with a sly breeze,
the pig stink all night long in summer.
I slept under cracks where the winking rain
entered, so why should I mind
the bad weather? I work best when I take
my time, coaxing woolly worms into a tin can
and letting them go again, dreaming
the night sky unfolds like a blueprint I learn
to read. Sometimes I dawdle with scrap iron
and bed-springs until it is dawn. Unembarrassed,
I sing the old ditties. Hey diddle-
diddle, I dance by the light of the moon
and feel lonely, already at home
here. I talk to the rubble. I swear
by the toil of my two clumsy hands I will

make of this junk-pile a dwelling place
yet. When I hammer the last nail straight
into the last sagging beam, I will
spit on the edge of my shirt and sit down
on a barrel to scrub my face clean.
I will not look my Sunday-best,
but I cannot wait forever.
The hinges will creak as I open the front door
and call out my grandfather's name.
In the silence that answers, I step
slowly over the threshold,

believing that each board supports me.
I stand in my grandfather's house again.

◎ BARBARA CROOKER

Barbara Crooker was born in 1945 in Cold Spring, New York. She received a B.A. from Douglass College and an M.S. in English from Elmira College. Crooker is the author of six books of poetry, the most recent being Obbligato *(1992). She has published her poetry in numerous magazines, including* Yankee, The Christian Science Monitor, *and* Organic Gardening. *She has received fellowships from the Pennsylvania Council on the Arts in Literature and has won the NEA and* Passages North *Emerging Writers Competition. She offers writing workshops and teaches English in addition to caring for her children.*

"The Last Woman in America to Wash Diapers" was originally published in Footwork Magazine *and has been anthologized in* If I Had a Hammer: Women's Work in Poetry, Fiction, and Photographs *(1990). Crooker's sense of humor about the drudgery of washing diapers makes this poem a triumph from its title to the hilarious last three lines.*

The Last Woman in America to Wash Diapers

The last woman in America to wash diapers
lugs the full pail down to the first floor,
heaves it in the washer, makes it spin its offal load.
How many diapers has she sloshed in the toilet,
how many neatly folded stacks has she raised skyward,
soft white squares of cotton, pieces of cloud,
how many double and triple folds has she pinned
on little bottoms? How many nights
of checking beds did she find those buns
raised in the air, loaves resting on a bakery shelf?
She knows the power of bleach, the benefits of rinsing.
On winter nights, when the snow comes pouring down
in glittery drifts, she sees Ivory Flakes,
their slippery iridescence. When it comes
to dealing with the shit in her life,
nothing else is so simple, so white, so clean.

◎ LINDA HOGAN

"What Has Happened to These Working Hands?" is a praise poem found in Linda Hogan's Savings *(1988). Like prayer, the structure of this poem is based on repetition, suggesting the power of women and the power of ritual. The earliest poems were prayers to the gods, praising their attributes which composed the universe. Here women's hands, women's work, and the culture built by women are the source of praise.* *(For more on Hogan, see page 146.)*

What Has Happened to These Working Hands?

They opened the ground and closed it around seeds.
They added a pinch of tobacco.
They cleaned tired old bodies
        and bathed infants.
They got splinters from the dried-out handles of axes.
The right one suspected what the left was doing
        and the arms began to ache.
They clawed at each other when life hurt.
They pulled at my hair when I mourned.
They tangled my hair when I dreamed poems.
As fists they hit the bed
        when war spread again throughout the world.
They went crazy and broke glasses.
They regretted going to school where they became so soft
        their relatives mistook them for strangers.
They turned lamps off and on
        and tapped out songs on tables,
        made crosses over the heart.
They kneaded bread.
They covered my face when I cried,
        my mouth when I laughed.
"You've got troubles," said the left hand to the right,
        "Here, let me hold you."
These hands untwisted buried roots.
They drummed the old burial songs.
They heard there were men cruel enough to crush them.
They drummed the old buried songs.

◎ *FRANCES McCUE*

Frances McCue, born in 1962, received a B.A. from the University of New Hampshire and an M.F.A. from the University of Washington. McCue is a poet and critic living in Snohomish, Washington. Her first book of poems, The Stenographer's Breakfast *(1992) won the Barnard New Women Poets Prize. Since then, McCue's poems have appeared in many literary magazines.*

"The Stenographer's Breakfast" is the title poem of McCue's first collection of poetry. The poem also appeared in Ms. *in 1993. McCue's poem reveals the mind of a stenographer as she goes about her work, this day assisting men who interrogate a widow about the circumstances of her husband's death. The stenographer is the distanced observer but not one without heart or heartache of her own. She comes to reveal, slowly, how she prefers the regimented life of filing, typing, and transcribing compared to "the alternative chaos" of the world.*

The Stenographer's Breakfast

I

Legs pinched together, I play the machine
sidesaddle, fingers bobbing from the keys like I'm pulling
laundry from a trough. History dictates
such wrong-headed order which I *digest,*
resuscitate as *skill, employ*— a wry design
to sit off-center and transcribe
roomfuls of men, their ties loosened,
interrogating the next of kin.

Aside: *To take dictation* means I watch each speak,
turn my face, read lips and leap — *space* —

from one to the other.
Today there are three of them.
Across the table, a widow props her body up,
answering as she can.
When they called me here
to conference table, stiff-backed chair,
I dedicated my serving them as a prayer
for this woman. I prepared

to be the voyeur, the silent ear,
the widow's distillery of truth and relay.

The government of such a room —
Never stop the proceedings. Speak when spoken to —
prevents an active defense. What this group of men
delivers is some quest for accuracy,
but I know this technique
depends on the distance between man and paper,

chair and door, woman and her role.
All this talk might well have been
over a telegraph, the way the tap-tap clicks
and bounces back. The lawyers only call the widow in
so they may watch her eyes and face
to find, by chance, if she wished her husband dead.
In a skirt, ascot-necked and jacket
tight, I blend right into them, take my place and offer

Shorthand: a lack, understaffed, decoding and
recoding, carry language to its core.

And more — the world of facts brought to bear
on whatever questions they ask of her.
Your husband, did he provide for you?
The day he died, what was it that he wore?
I'll revive it later, fill the gaps.
Umm hmm. Cough. Cough. included as the manual says.
Such faith I have in sounds not yet
formed as words, shy riddles and intrusions

into code. *Interruptions are difficult*
but essential to include in any transcript.

II

Clerk smart, each step parts my raincoat
as if I'm crossing through brambles
or over tracks. This is the walk from the office
when the keypunch and earphones
shinny down my bones, and patter skin.
Not long, and I can't distinguish between my own
footfall and the street, my eye from market
or kiosk — I can't help transcribing

everything. *The curb stiffens like a brow.*
Cars unscrew the pavement. Time releases
the tower's clock from its confines.

A back alley considers revealing some trauma,
my reason for clipping forward. And the walls,
what do they reflect, as wainscot and gargoyle
lift to frame my stroll?
Even these coordinates weaken to arcs,

tease my decoding mind —
flit of paper, twirl of can.
Today, taking dictation from the men,
word by word, I took the widow's life,
pushed its tiny pulse through the chords.
After the flush of pity, I could only be
stoic. And tomorrow, as I translate
those symbols, the marks like stray hairs

on the tickertape — they will spell out phrases:
I don't know. He just stopped breathing.
There's nothing else to say.
He turned blue.
And the pinched sobs, to chart as stage directions,
what the manual dictates as *the witness cries,*
or in some other case, *the witness gestures,*
the witness faints.

You know the joke: The Stenographer's Breakfast
is a cup of coffee and a Winston. On the bare stage

with table and placemat, the secretary
empties her life before she goes into work.
When I reach the stairs
and my rooms, even the absent-minded move,
a nod to the dog, flip of the light switch
is some calculated truth. I document the area,
and think how heaven must be some version
of a waiting room — the widow's husband

lingering on a cloud-swollen couch.
Here in my walk-up,
I can look out to a sky
blown into dome by breath
while somewhere overhead
Galileo milks the stars
one at a time.
Like my keys, his notes

test the pure relay of truth,
but the truth is quick and small

however bright. And in this time
when each place is earmarked
by hordes, purity frustrates me
as heaven does. How can I help
loving the chronological
seductions of file and box?
Imagine the alternative chaos.

◎ *ENID SHOMER*

Enid Shomer was born in 1944 in Washington, D.C. She was educated at Wellesley College (B.A.) and the University of Miami (M.A.) Shomer has published several volumes of verse, including Florida Postcards *(1990),* Stalking the Florida Panther *(1990), and* This Close to the Earth *(1992), as well as* Imaginary Men *(short stories, 1993). Among her many awards are the Eve of St. Agnes Prize, the Washington Prize in Poetry, the Celia B. Wagner Award, the Wildwood Poetry Prize, and the Randall Jarrell Poetry Prize. Shomer has also received poetry fellowships from the National Endowment for the Arts and from the state of Florida.*

Shomer notes: " 'The Tomato Packing Plant Line' grew out of my experience working at a packing and juicing plant on an Israeli kibbutz. In the weird surreality often engendered by monotonous labor, I became intensely aware of the tomatoes' shape, size, color, etc. and of the primal correspondences between them and the women who sorted them" (letter to M. Kallet, 1996).

The Tomato Packing Plant Line

Bumped and rolling jovially
down the conveyor the tomatoes
dance in   a press of faces
the shine on their skins like smiles
the stem ends chipper as cowlicks.

Young women remove the mistakes —
harelips   two-headed ones   gashed ones
with papery crosshatched scars.
Tiny ones too are removed
to be juiced with the freaks.

At the far end hemmed in by boxes
the old women sort the tomatoes

the largest and the perfect ones first.
Their hands   like their eyes
know the swell before ripeness.
It is something they flaunted
on Fridays   a gust that inflated
box-pleated skirts into bells
as they stepped into dusk
hands washed white of tomatoes
which did not survive
their ripeness.

◎ *ANITA SKEEN*

Anita Skeen was born in 1946 and grew up in Big Chimney, West Virginia. A professor of English at Michigan State University, she has also taught at Wichita State University and has given poetry readings and workshops across the country. Skeen's teaching has won her many awards, including the Regent's Award for Teaching at Wichita State University. She has worked in the Poets-in-Schools Program and has been a member of the board of directors of the University of Kansas Commission for the Humanities. Skeen has published in numerous magazines and anthologies, and she has two volumes of poetry to her credit: Each Hand a Map *(1986) and* Portraits.

"The English Teacher, in Mid-Life" was written as part of a series of dramatic monologues, Speaking in Tongues. *It is an honest portrait of the emotional roller-coaster that teaching can be, especially if one has a passionate commitment to literature and to the students. As the poet says, "I think most students never know how they, too, can teach the teacher."*

The English Teacher, in Mid-Life

Today my life scrawls out
before me in misspellings and red ink,
a paragraph with no topic sentence,
a term paper interesting
to no one at all. Surely
I who have lived so many years
with Hamlet and Ishmael,
Hester Prynne and Martha Quest
can escape this life

of other peoples' lives,
this constant ministry
of words. I stand before
my students, Moses with tablets
in a foreign tongue, the Ten Commandments
for an "A." But I am
no old-time prophet
nor precursor of the Divine,
I cannot heal their fragments,
rescue their dangling participles
from sin, resurrect their breathless
themes. I cannot give words
their autumn hues nor can I bring
the loon's cry to desert ears.
I can make no choir of the dumb.
Each day language fails me
more and more. There are no words
to explain how the Brontës wrote
what they wrote or why
Virginia Woolf waded out
to sea. How do I tell them
what made Thoreau
search out Walden Pond?
The page lies dead, the pencil
a remembrance of things
past, a dinosaur bone.
Something Grandpa stuck
behind his ear. Something
broken and blunt.
The chains of paper
weigh more than chains of iron.
They rattle in my sleep.
Then, she comes to me, holding forth
a piece she has written
like communion bread. I receive it
and read the words mixing together,
yeast and flour. She, too, has a life
of secret snows and dreams
deferred. We have more in common
than she knows. We schedule
an appointment for this same time
next week.

◎ LOIS-ANN YAMANAKA

Lois-Ann Yamanaka was born in 1961 in Ho'olehua, Molokai. Her first book of poetry was Saturday Night at the Pahala Theatre *(1993). She has published in many literary magazines and anthologies including* Bamboo Ridge: The Hawaii Writer's Quarterly; Hawaii Review; Michigan Quarterly Review; Dissident Song: A Contemporary Asian American Anthology; *and* The Female Body. *Her book's title poem, "Saturday Night at the Pahala Theatre," was selected for the Pushcart Prize.*

In "Turtles," the narrator, who speaks in dialect, is Asian American — a descendent of Japanese or Korean immigrants — working-class and poor, a young teenager from an abusive family. In the small plantation town on the Big Island, Bernie, the shopowner, is one of the few kind characters in this hard-hitting book of poems.

Turtles

On the wall in Bernard's Taxidermy Shop
is two big, green turtles. They all shiny.
Bernie, he use varnish, make um look wet.
Bernie say, before could catch turtles
for the shell or for meat, but now,
he say not suppose to catch turtles
or else the police going arrest you.
He say, when you catch a turtle,
the turtle he cry a tear
from his big, wet eye.
Bernie seen um when he went fish
down South Point side.

He ask if I ever taste turtle meat.
He say, *Ono you know.*
I tell my wife cook
the frozen turtle meat one night
and you come over try some.
Ask your mama first.
I thinking about the tear from the turtle eye.
I tell Bernie I no like.

Bernie say the turtle eggs
look like ping pong balls.
He tell me, his friend Melvin,
the lifeguard down Punalu'u beach,
seen turtle fin marks in the sand

couple weeks ago so him and Bernie
wen' put all the eggs in one hole
and wen' put one cage over so nobody vandal um.

Late one Saturday afternoon,
I was at Bernie's shop helping him sweep up
the loose feathers, this white chemicals,
and sheep wool off the floor,
the phone wen' ring and was Melvin.
Bernie stay all panic on the phone.
Okay, okay. I going close the shop.
C'mon, he tell me. *No need sweep.*
C'mon, c'mon. The turtles hatching.
We neva going to see this our whole life again.
Us get in the Jeep and drive fast down Punalu'u.
No speed, Bernie, I tell him,
bumbye Officer Gomes give you one ticket.
But Bernie, he no listen.
When us get there, close to night time.
Get Melvin and his girlfriend, Teruko.
Bernie's wife stay too —
she work the lei stand down the beach.
The little turtle babies,
they pop their head
right out the black sand.
They all black too.
And when one 'nother one about to come up,
the sand cave in little bit
around the turtle head.
Turtles, they know by instinct
where is the ocean, Bernie tell. *Watch.*
And he turn one baby turtle backwards to the mountain.
Then the turtle he turn
his own self around
and run to the water.

Get plenny. They all running to the water.
They shine when the wave hit them.
And their heads stay bob up
and down in the ocean.
Plenny little heads.
Bernie pick one up and give um to me.
Like take um home?
Take um, take um, he tell me.

I think about the turtles on Bernie wall.
They look like they crying too.
Nah, I tell him. *I no like um.*
I take the baby turtle to the water edge,
his eye all glassy, the whole body shine,
and I put um down.
No cry now, I tell um,
No cry.

◎ *MAY SARTON*

May Sarton was born in Belgium in 1912. The family moved to Cambridge, Massachusetts, when World War I began. Sarton declined a scholarship to Vassar, apprenticing instead at the Civic Repertory Theater in New York. She founded and directed her own theater for three years before turning to writing as a career. Sarton was a prolific writer with more than fifty books to her credit, including poetry, journals, novels, essays, plays, and children's books. She considered herself primarily a poet. Solitude is a key theme, and she actively pursued solitude in her own life, as her journals show. Sarton died in 1995 and was buried in Nelson, New Hampshire, the town where she had purchased her first house in 1958. Before her death, Sarton had received seventeen honorary Doctor of Letters degrees.

"The Work of Happiness" was first published in May Sarton's The Lion and the Rose *(1948). For Sarton, a creative life is "the work of happiness," involving solitude and silence and writing. Happiness is earned — and Sarton had worked for sixty years at writing poetry. On her grave in Nelson, New Hampshire, the marker simply reads:*

May Sarton
Poet
1912–1995

The Work of Happiness

I thought of happiness, how it is woven
Out of the silence in the empty house each day
And how it is not sudden and it is not given
But is creation itself like the growth of a tree.
No one has seen it happen, but inside the bark
Another circle is growing in the expanding ring.
No one has heard the root go deeper in the dark,

But the tree is lifted by this inward work
And its plumes shine, and its leaves are glittering.

So happiness is woven out of the peace of hours
And strikes its roots deep in the house alone:
The old chest in the corner, cool waxed floors,
White curtains softly and continually blown
As the free air moves quietly about the room;
A shelf of books, a table, and the whitewashed wall —
These are the dear familiar gods of home,
And here the work of faith can best be done,
The growing tree is green and musical.

For what is happiness but growth in peace,
The timeless sense of time when furniture
Has stood a life's span in a single place,
And as the air moves, so the old dreams stir
The shining leaves of present happiness?
No one has heard thought or listened to a mind,
But where people have lived in inwardness
The air is charged with blessing and does bless;
Windows look out on mountains and the walls are kind.

INTERVIEW

Finding the Muse: An Interview with May Sarton

by Marilyn Kallet

MAY SARTON

Marilyn Kallet's interview with May Sarton took place on July 21, 1991, at Sarton's home. The dialogue was brief because of Sarton's illness. Though in the interview Sarton states that she has stopped writing poetry, she actually experienced a resurgence of poetry in her last four years. The interview reveals Sarton's tenacity and self-discipline—despite vicious attacks on her work in her middle years, she persisted in her art.

MK: You wrote a beautiful poem called "Friendship & Illness" in 1990. Was that your last poem?
MS: Yes, last year. I wrote it in August.
MK: Have there been others since then?
MS: No. The one great advantage of having to write a Christmas poem is that I do it. And if I didn't have that compulsion and feel I must get it done, I probably wouldn't have written some of my best poems. "The Nativity," the one about the painter Piero della Francesca, who affected me so deeply, that was a Christmas poem [*SSE* 157].
MK: "Christmas Light," with its quiet lines, ". . . . pure light / Stayed on, stayed on"—that's another [*SN* 27]. So sometimes in order to get to your inspiration, you have to get kick-started. How long have you been doing the Christmas poems?
MS: Thirty years or so. But I stopped for a long time, when the list got to be a thousand. I felt: I'm not a factory. Just writing the addresses was exhausting. I had no secretary. And so I gave it up for twenty years. Only quite recently a fan,

William Ewert, who loves to do special editions, said, "Wouldn't you write a poem, and we'd do it for you?" He does it for nothing, and then he sells them. It's wonderful. He gets wonderful people to illustrate. It's just great!

MK: "Friendship & Illness" is very spare, resonant, and moving. It seemed to be an invitation to your friends to come and see you. Literally, that we should take you up on it.

MS: Yes, I think it really was. . . . I was afraid of sending it. It seemed too personal, not enough about Christmas. But people have loved it. Many people tell me that they've framed it. Amazing!

MK: Let's talk about "the muse," a subject that has been crucial to your work. . . . Has the muse always been a passionate, feminine source for you?

MS: Yes, the muse has always been a woman. I have had more than one male lover, but never a male muse. And the muses, the women, were, by no means, all lovers. The muse is someone who captures the imagination. . . .

MK: Yet, in your writings the donkey has been a muse. Bramble [Sarton's cat] was a muse.

MS: Animals more than people.

MK: And trees.

MS: Trees. Yes, that's true. It's very puzzling. I just don't know. I really don't. The muse is possession by the imagination. It was very often someone older than I, though not always someone obvious like Eva Le Gallienne, whom I adored, and who was very glamorous. But I think I wrote only one poem for her. One of the great muses in my life was Katharine Taylor, the head of Shady Hill School when I was ten or eleven. I wrote many poems for her. . . . I started to say that it was not until I was over forty that I could begin to think of myself as a woman and not a young man. So, in all the early poems, the romantic poems, I am "he."

MK: I went through that also. I didn't realize I was a "she" in my work until 1968, as ridiculous as that sounds.

MS: There you are! I'm so glad to hear that. . . . We didn't believe in ourselves as women.

MK: It's not necessarily that. At the time, it just wasn't part of the common currency of speech to differentiate our pronouns; we didn't think about the implications of using "he" as a generic pronoun. We naïvely thought "he" was everybody.

MS: Yes, exactly. . . . Finally, someone said to me about the last, fairly recent "Phoenix" poem — which ended with something about "sing his thrilling song" — she said: "Why don't you say 'her'?" ["The Phoenix Again," *SN* 76]. And I said to myself, "Why not?" [laughter].

MK: I think we've all come through that. Even Adrienne Rich's poems are traditional in the beginning; her models are traditional male poets. She moved on.

MS: Yes. I knew her then. She was the same kind of poet as I was — like Millay and Elinor Wylie. Rich has certainly grown!

MK: Before I move on to ask about the historical placement of your work, I want to ask you if the muse is still here for you.
MS: No.
MK: Yet, on some level it must be, because you wrote that poem, "Friendship & Illness."
MS: But then *I* was the muse. Someone said to me, "You must become your own muse." I think in a way that's true. That's what happens.
MK: I love that idea! We embrace ourselves.
MS: Yes, in a way. There is a poem about the last muse being the sea. The poem begins, "Never has the sea been maternal to me or kind" [*SN* 73]. But, in a way, perhaps the last muse has been this house, this environment where I've written a great deal. . . . Juliette Huxley has been a muse, but you see I haven't written poems for her for thirty years. She was one of the great muses. I wrote the sonnet sequences for her in Paris. "Those images remain" — that sequence, those were to her. There were many poems to her [*CP* 144–47].
MK: Is she still living?
MS: Yes, she's over ninety. There's a whole book of my letters to her that Norton will publish when she dies. She gave permission to me, but I'm sure she doesn't realize what's there. They're really lovely letters, not sexual. But I think if she saw the book, she might say, "I never said that!" It's too ticklish.
MK: We had talked before about the difficulty of placing your work in a historical context, since your writing spans sixty years. In fact, you saw this difficulty as one reason why there has been some neglect of the poetry, more so than of the other genres you have worked in. Having begun to write poetry in the 1930s, you might be dismissed by contemporary critics as being old-fashioned — without their taking a more serious look.
MS: I think that's so. Helen Vendler, poetry critic for the *New Yorker,* said of my work in a review: "derivative and not interesting" [556]. I think that was the general attitude. It looked as though I were like everyone else, but I really wasn't. I was doing things like "A Divorce of Lovers" [*CP* 201–8], saying things that hadn't been said before. And that *they* didn't get.
MK: Then Vendler did not read your work closely?
MS: That's right.
MK: Your work shows the pervasive influence of the modern poets Yeats and Valéry.
MS: Yes, Yeats and Valéry were the two major influences, absolutely. Yeats, partly because he grew so much and changed his style.
MK: And he was lyrical.
MS: Lyrical too. He was everything. His last poems are like rocks.
MK: The language has been "worked." Your poems are polished, too.
MS: That's what I feel. That's what I want.
MK: Was Valéry more of an influence than Mallarmé?
MS: Mallarmé was not an influence. No, Valéry. Louise Bogan and I translated a

lot of Valéry together. . . . *Metamorphosis* was one literary magazine that printed quite a few [seven]. I did all the work. This tickled Louise. She would go over the poems and make a few suggestions. I would have worked ten hours on a poem. She couldn't put them into form; I could. She was a good critic in some ways. She was helpful. But she got the credit for a lot she didn't do. . . . I didn't mind; I enjoyed it. . . . We both enjoyed this working relationship.

MK: Did the poetry cross-pollinate?

MS: She was a muse, certainly. She wasn't writing then. She was at a very bad time in her life when we met. This was in the 1950s and '60s. Her poetry was out of print. You know how terrible that feels.

MK: I know how it feels. It doesn't seem right. I mean, here you are still alive and yet the book is dead!

MS: Yes, yes. Then they did a selected poems, thank God, and she got back. . . . And she got very good reviews, deserved, well deserved.

MK: Did you influence one another in your work?

MS: She influenced me by her poetry enormously. She was extremely — I think now I can say it — jealous of me. So, she never gave me a good review. And this was at a time when she could have made all the difference. She chose not to. It was very painful.

MK: You mentioned in one interview that you were influenced by Walt Whitman.

MS: He was one of the poets I knew best and loved most when I was fourteen. One of my first great influences. . . . And then I went to other poets to study form. . . . I read Donne and Marvell. I got very excited about all that.

MK: Are there any contemporary poets you feel strongly about?

MS: There aren't many . . . Constance Hunting, who has just had a book of poetry brought out. I think she's an absolutely remarkable poet. She edits Puckerbrush Press, and she has many books. . . . William Heyen, I also admire him tremendously. He's a German who's been able to write about the Holocaust. That's so rare.

MK: William Stafford was kind enough to copy over a note that you had written to him, where you say that regularly you receive a letter from some reader who is just discovering your poetry. I was happy to hear that.

MS: I think I said I get such a letter at least once a week. Yes. Once a week is a lot!

MK: Does that make you feel better about this whole enterprise?

MS: Yes, it does. It does!

MK: It seems like you've always been a poet foremost — heart, soul and mind, a poet.

MS: That's right. That's why you must read the first novel. . . .

MK: Recently, I had a talk with Joy Harjo, who is Native American, and some of her poems are influenced by prayers, specifically by the form of a Navajo prayer. I asked her whether she saw a connection between poetry and prayer, and she said, "Yes, of course," as though this were perfectly obvious. I would like to ask you the same question.

MS: I feel that too. I feel it very much. Yes, I've gone so far as to say my poems are between me and God; my novels are communication with other people. I would write poems even if I were in solitary confinement, but I would not write novels, and I don't think I would write a journal.

MK: At some points of your life, you must have felt like you were in solitary confinement.

MS: Yes, I have. I went to Nelson because I felt that I had to withdraw, that the literary world would eventually come to me. At that moment I was in the wilderness, and I thought I'd better go to the real wilderness and be there. And it has worked out. But I've just been reading my letters to Bogan to help Susan Sherman make some choices for the book of letters she is editing. There were some very painful letters after the Shapiro review of the selected poems came out at Christmas. The collection was *Cloud, Stone, Sun, Vine,* six volumes of my poems selected. The review appeared in the *New York Times:* "May Sarton is a bad poet"... That was it. And he ended the review, "I'm sorry to have had to do this" [5].

MK: At least he realized he had something to apologize for.

MS: Yes. I was terribly ill, I became violently sick. I almost died of it; I really did.

MK: The review attacked you at the core — how could you not be affected?

MS: Yes, that's right. In front of 5 million people, I was called "a bad poet." He blamed me for doing sonnets, and he did a whole book of sonnets ten years later. Oh, what a rat! Well, this is the anti-woman thing.

MK: You think that's it?

MS: Oh, I'm sure it was. When you think of Ciardi.... We were all in a group together — Wilbur, Eberhart, Ciardi, and John Holmes. We met five times a year to criticize each other's poems.... It was very interesting.... Well, Ciardi wrote a book about writing poetry and in the introduction he told all about that group and never mentioned that I was in it!... I didn't exist, period.

MK: For those of us for whom poetry is such a meaningful activity, and for whom this recession amounts to a repression of the arts, it's heartening to have a model of someone who's been kicked down so many times and for such a long time and whose poetry has thrived.

MS: I kept going — well, I had to. I think it's because I finally decided to give up all ideas of ever being successful or read or criticized. That was when I went to Nelson. I sort of closed the door on ambition, I think that's what I'm saying. And so finally, recognition came. But it might not have. And that's the hell!

MK: Whether it comes or doesn't — whatever "it" is — at least having taken control of your life you can be more at peace with yourself.

MS: Yes, that's right.

WORKS CITED

Heyen, William. *Erika: Poems of the Holocaust.* St. Louis: Time Being Books, 1990.

Hunting, Constance. *Between The Worlds: Poems, 1983–1988.* Orono: Puckerbrush Press, 1990.

Sarton, May. *Collected Poems (1930–1973)*. New York: Norton, 1974.

———. *May Sarton: Among the Usual Days: Illustrated Portrait of the Poet in Unpublished Letters, Journals, and Poems*. Ed. Susan Sherman. New York: Norton, 1993.

———. *Sarton Selected: An Anthology of the Journals, Novels, and Poems of May Sarton*. Ed. Bradford Dudley Daziel. New York: Norton, 1991.

———. *The Silence Now*. New York: Norton, 1988.

———, trans. "Palm." By Paul Valéry. *Metamorphosis* 4 (1964): 7.

Shapiro, Karl. "Voices That Speak to the Critic in Very Different Rhythms." Rev. of *Cloud, Stone, Sun, Vine: Poems, Selected and New*, by May Sarton. *New York Times Book Review* 24 Dec. 1961, Sun. ed.: 4–5.

Vendler, Helen. "Recent American Poetry." *Massachusetts Review* 8 (1967): 541–60.

Friendship & Illness

Christmas, 1990

Through the silences,
The long empty days
You have sat beside me
Watching the finches feed,
The tremor in the leaves.
You have not left my mind.

Friendship supplied the root —
It was planted years ago —
To bring me flowers and seed
Through the long drought.

Far-flung as you are
You have seemed to sit beside me.
You have not left my mind.

Will you come in the new year?
To share the wind in the leaves
And the finches lacing the air
To savor the silence with me?
It's been a long time.

May Sarton

Many Loves

Many Loves

◎ ◎ ◎

THE STEREOTYPE OF WOMEN'S LIVES WOULD feature love as its primary focus. It is quite likely that the thematic sections in this anthology implicitly argue that that stereotype is a myth. Of course women's lives are also filled with work and with the issues they deal with in their cultures. Women's lives resonate with work, people, complications, politics, and money — and yet love is indeed present in women's lives, most likely in many more guises than typical pictures show.

This section of *Worlds in Our Words* explores the many different kinds of attachment women have: love for other women, love for children, love for men, and love for friends and relatives, of course. There is much more, however. The selections following will show the complexity of love in women's lives and will reveal the depth of the emotion we call love. Some selections will reveal the moral issues and entanglements women face as they deal with love. Some writers will retell myths of love and sexual attraction, updating them for our time. And some writers here announce and celebrate love in lyric joy, love in its brief and famous intensity. "Many Loves," then, is the complex nexus weaving women's hearts together.

J. California Cooper's story "The Magic Strength of Need" paints a portrait of a nineties woman who is ahead of her time. Burlee goes through a transformation and awakening similar to the ugly duckling's. She builds her life the best way she knows how. If she ignores, for a while, the male friend who could change her life around, that seems all to the good: if he is true, he will wait. Burlee almost misses out on the love this man has to offer, but she has built such a rich life without him we're sure she goes to him free of need.

Pam Houston's "How to Talk to a Hunter" has a lot to say about men and women, physical love and attraction, and why women put up with relationships that seem far from ideal. By the end of the story, the female narrator, trying to break free and using her head more and more, seems to be coming into her own.

"Cousins" by Jeanne McDonald shows the layers and fractures of familial love from the point of view of a sixteen-year-old girl. Though the protagonist longs for adulthood, she is watching from the sidelines as aunts marry and as her own mother and father go through marital difficulties. The story reaches its resolution when she goes out in a boat with her cousin and glimpses for the first time how flux will have to be accepted, perhaps even embraced.

Variety and complexity also shine through in nonfiction. Both "Love and Learn" by Lucy Ferriss and "Between Girls" by Lisa Springer cast an eye back on a past love. With hindsight, each writer sees love differently than she saw it at the time. Ferriss contemplates the boundaries of love between teacher and student. Unlike her own teachers, Ferris chooses not to act on her tender feelings for a student. What she gains by cautiousness is the possibility of a lifelong friendship.

Springer's piece is tinged with regret as she remembers past hurts she inflicted on a friend. The central question in this poignant and precisely remembered story is the difference it might have made had the author known more about lesbianism. With chronological age, then, some maturity comes, and with it comes some forgiveness, too, of our earlier lost and confused selves.

Anne Lamott's diary entry "December 3" and Nancy Willard's "The Friendship Tarot" are celebratory pieces where love shines through. A single mother raising baby Sam on her own, Lamott writes a glowing, tender description of the day of his baptism. Looking at adult women friends, Willard's piece depicts many scenes as she unfolds the story of her friendship with Ilse. Theirs is a friendship of cats, of art, of work, and of the pain of history.

Janet Neipris's play *The Agreement* is a hilarious and poignant view of divorce and its effects. The Matchetts have separated, and both are going through the awkardnesses of middle-aged dating. When they meet with lawyers to iron out a divorce agreement, they surprise themselves by remembering many good times in their past life together.

Poets are the bards of love. The poems in this section sing of the permutations of love and loss. One lover may experience many kinds of love, many shades of emotion. And one's "lovers," in a sense, may be of many types: one physical, one spiritual, one earthly, one of the heavens. Paula Gunn Allen and Maya Angelou retell the myth of Adam and Eve in their poems. Eve, a fox in Allen's version, winds up in confrontation with Adam. Olga Broumas and Tess Gallagher celebrate sensual love; sensuous waves move their poems along. Barbara L. Greenberg envisions love as a moral education, while Marilyn Hacker's "Self" is an education in the physical and the pleasures of self-love.

Love is complex and contains its reverse, perhaps — in love we are vulnerable and fragile, open to being hurt, open to the old wounds of past loves. June Jordan, Sharon Olds, and Molly Peacock write powerful versions of love's dangerous side. To Jordan physical love is ultimately as renewing as the seasons; snow blankets earth much as a lover holds the beloved. For Olds, the first night with her lover is a change in the history of her universe. As always with Olds's poems, there is an admirable physicality: the speaker likens herself to an animal, newborn, her lover's face "about to be imprinted" in her memory. Peacock finds strangeness in her self, a self she thought she knew but that now surprises her with its tenuous readiness for love.

Adrienne Rich's "XIX" describes how we persist in love, despite its difficulty, despite life's difficulties. And for lesbians, as for any two people, love will not be easy: "two women together is a work / nothing in civilization has made simple, / two people together is a work / heroic in its ordinariness. . . ." Cathy Song celebrates physical and sensual love in "The White Porch," a poem of lushness and texture. The daughter dreams all day of the night and of her lover's arrival, in contrast to the mother in her "tight blankets." Finally, in "Angels in Winter," Nancy Willard celebrates a love beyond the lover — perhaps a realm of spiritual love, and love for those who have gone before us. The speaker recognizes how "whatever I try to hold perishes."

In the interview with Nancy Willard that concludes this section, the writer speaks of a correspondence in poetry that she initiated with writer Jane Yolen. When the two writers finally met, it felt to Willard as though they'd met "in a former life." As in her essay "A Friendship Tarot," Willard shows an example of the many-faceted jewel of love.

◎ *J. CALIFORNIA COOPER*

J. California Cooper was born in Berkeley, California. She attended technical high school and various colleges. Cooper's published works include A Piece of Mine *(1984),* Homemade Love *(1986), and* Some Soul to Keep *(1987). Works in progress include a novel, a collection of short stories for children, and a collection of stories for adults.*

"The Magic Strength of Need" is from Homemade Love. *Cooper is known for her exuberant style and frequent use of exclamation points to convey a speaker's feelings. The story seems to begin on such a harsh note that the reader may fear to go on, but we learn that Burlee is a model of strength.*

The Magic Strength of Need

There's magic in every life, I do believe! You just got to find it! I don't know how to explain it, but I do know it's not the kind of magic you read about that changes everything like for Cinderella. The real magic is something you got to think on, work on! It's a job! But it's the thing that brings your life through and you have some happiness. It's a hard job cause you don't never know which way the magic is going. You got to have some kind of good sense. Common sense!

Sometime, the magic fools you! It be setting there like a big unlucky, ugly . . . unwanted something! A person will walk over it, step on it, throw it out, beat it up, hide it! Drown it in alcohol! Send it into a coma with dope! Mildew it with tears or just kick it to the side as they go out to dance! Some folks never find it!

Now, I'ma show you what I mean!

There was a girl named Burlee was born the seventh child to a big, poor family. Burlee was what is called ugly! Even very ugly! The world got a lot to pay for messing up a lotta people's minds with all that division stuff! Now, rich and poor and North and South divides things up and that's okay with things like that that can't feel nothing. But when they made ugly and pretty, they was messing with people's minds! Their lives!

I'ma tell you something! God didn't make no ugly people! Man did! Talking about what was pretty and what was ugly. If it's somebody for everybody, then everybody is pretty to somebody! And it wasn't none of them people's business who started this ugly-pretty business to get in everybody's business like they did! You ever notice that somebody the world says is ugly, you might even agree, but when you get to know that person, you don't see ugly no more?! That goes to show you! God didn't make ugly people! Man did!

Burlee's life started off wrong cause her mama meant to name her "Berylee." A nurse who just passed right on through her life and out, looked down at Burlee and decided she had just the right look for "Burlee" and put that down. Some people are like that. Run in your life and run out, leaving you something you got to deal with the rest of your life!

Anyway, Burlee . . . was ugly. I mean ugly! Even her mama knew that. Look like Burlee knew it too, cause she looked mad right from the minute they put her in her mother's arms! Her mama said, "Hm! Hmmm! Well, things will get better." But they didn't. Burlee stayed ugly.

She was a quiet baby, just lay around looking mean. She had plenty to cry about too! Wasn't much food (well, seven kids, you know) and her diapers always wet making little sores on her baby-soft behind. She grown now and still got some of the marks! Little eyes be matted sometimes with something and nose all runny cause not enough heat for the house. They paid rent but nobody ever fixed that little house up! Paint rotted away, peeling walls, mildew even grew on the walls, and it was almost too cold for rats in there. Anyway, Burlee suffered all what being one of seven kids will make you suffer when your family is poor. The mama can try all she want too, she can't be everywhere doing everything at the same time! And sometime the dear sweet man be laying in your bed waiting for you to get through doing your work so you can come to bed and he can give you the start of something big that will wear you out some more in another nine months! He may not mean to, but, see, he may think you his magic! Thats a real funny valentine, ain't it?

However which way it was . . . Burlee was the last one cause her mama said she must be the bottom of the barrel!

Naturally, she went through the whooping cough and measles, mumps, and some of them things left little marks on Burlee's face to make that matter worse.

As she grew up, she wore all the hand-me-downs that made it down to her, went barefoot and without everything else when she had to.

As she got older, she made a secret place somewhere and would go off to that place and sit all day and think. I don't know all she was thinking of but I do know she was like a lot of people who want things. Things they see other people have. She was sick and tired and shamed of being laughed at and called "U-ga-ly!" She didn't have nothin . . . but her mama, who held her lots of times cause she knew Burlee needed it! They would talk.

"Burlee, don't cry. Don't pay no tention to what them kids say."

Burlee would cry back, "Mama, I can't help it!"

Mama would say, "You can help anything, Burlee."

Burlee would sniffle, "I try, Mama."

Mama would pet and rub. "You not ugly to me. And pretty ain't everything! Pretty is as pretty do!"

Through the warmth of her mother's love, Burlee would whisper, "What does pretty do, Mama?"

Mama would hold her closer. "Pretty go to school, study harrrrd, and learn how not to need nobody but herself!"

Burlee would smile a little. "I do that Mama. That don't make me pretty!"

Mama would smile back. "Yes it do! A little more every day! You watch and see. It adds up! You learn all you can! When you gets through learning, you gon see something!" Then another child would need Mama, cause children are jealous of each other sometimes! Mama would give Burlee a quick squeeze and turn to the next one. She was a thin, wiry woman, but she had strength she got from somewhere. She said it was from God. She had told her husband the Lord said to her, "Stop makin love" (cause she was tired). He said, "Then what I'm sposed to do?" She answered, "I don't know. You got to ask the Lord that!"

Anyway, Burlee did study hard. She was smart too! Quick to learn but always stayed in the background of things. Silent. All during high school she still went to sit in her quiet secret place, thinking. She knew what she wanted now.

Mama was bending from the weight of life . . . and was tired, very tired. When Burlee hugged her now, she would tell her, "Just hold on, Mama. I'll take care of you! I may not be getting pretty, but I am getting smart! I'm gonna find me a *rich man* and he gon marry me! I will sit you down! We'll both sit down!" Being sat down is a lotta people's dream.

Mama would smile, nod, and pat Burlee as she looked at her uncomely daughter with the shoulders and bust wider than any other part of her body. She looked like an exclamation point! Wasn't any curves and her head sat down in her shoulders with hardly no neck!

"Just be a good girl, Burlee," Mama would sigh.

"I'm too smart to be bad, Mama!" Burlee would smile and hug her one more time before some other child took over. Off she would go to her secret place and sit and dream, cause she was serious about marrying up with a Rich Man. Didn't know where they were or who they were, but they were out there! Didn't care was he black or white, just rich!

Now, it's somebody for everybody, I don't care who you are nor what you look like! At least one! Burlee had one who liked her by name of Winston. Winston wasn't too good-looking either, but he was better lookin than Burlee. The girls didn't pay him no mind. He was always leaning against some wall or tree, looking at things going on round him. He liked sports but had to work to help his mama and wasn't even in school too much, just enough to get by. He would walk home with Burlee sometime, telling her he liked her. Catching up to her he would say, "I'm going your way, Burlee." She'd fling over her shoulder, "Not far!" He'd reach for her books, she'd snatch her arm away. He'd be hurt.

"How come you don't like me, Burlee? I ain't done nothin to you! I'm always tryin to help you!" He use to fight the other kids bout callin her names. He never did 'low nobody to hurt her if he could help it. He got whipped hisself sometime but that never did stop him!

She would ease up. "I like you, Winston, you alright. I just ain't got no time for you!"

Reaching for crumbs again, he would say, "I know you get lonely sometime, Burlee. I even know you goes off by yourself."

Burlee would snap, "Ain't cause I'm lonely! And I told you to stop watching me! Leave me alone!"

Winston smiled. "Can't help it cause I'm lonely. I ain't got nobody, you don't go with nobody, why can't we keep company?"

Just before she ran off Burlee would snap, "Cause you too poor! I don't want nothin to do with no poor man! You just ain't rich enough!"

Winston hollered after her, "Money, ain't everything! And where you gon find a rich man?!"

Which is the question Burlee thought about in her secret place that day. Which question made her come up with the idea that rich men go shopping in department stores and own em to! She was going to get a job in one and find her man! She got a part-time job fore she graduated.

She started to wearing all that makeup she got on discount to cover her pimply skin. She looked a mess! Thick pancake makeup, blue or green eye shadow, bright red lipstick and rouge, black pencil round her eyes and false eyelashes so thick and stiff with that stuff that goes on them. If she'd fallen down and hit her face it would have cracked cause it was that stiff! She looked worser . . . ugly plus ridiculous! Winston told her so and she took to hating him for it. Then her boss at the store told her if she kept wearing makeup like that, she could only clean up in the stockrooms instead of all over the store. She changed.

Now, she hung out, or rather I should say, the cleanest place in the store was round the offices where she could watch the men going in all dressed up in their suits. She was learning things too, cause she now knew the ones who owned the store were not dressed up or flashy like the ones who only worked there! After she cut down on the makeup, she decided to work more over by the beauty shop so she could maybe learn how to work on her face. Besides all the hair stuff, she saw people doing fingernails and toenails, facials and stuff like that!

Burlee didn't make much money, ain't hardly no need to say it, but she saved. From the money she insisted on giving her mama she saved 50¢ a week for four weeks to get one of them man-u-cures! The lady who gives em, a regular poor woman, thought Burlee was crazy, but took her money anyway and gave her a quick, lousy man-u-cure for her four weeks of saving and dreaming! Ain't it funny how most people, poor people, will cheat people just like themselves? And kiss the yes-yes-yes of somebody with money who wouldn't give them the time of day in return? Well, they do it all the time!

Anyway, them painted nails of Burlee's was scratched up and gone in two days! The first day she just looked at em and waved her hands in everybody's face! The second day her boss told her her work was suffering. Burlee got to work and the nails got wiped out, scratched up! Now, she didn't want to save four weeks for two days, so she decided to learn how to do it herself! That was the magic working, don't you see?! She asked the nail lady and the nail lady begrudged telling her, thinking Black folks always trying to take over things they didn't belong in. But she knew it was in the phone book, so she told her. Burlee signed up for the hand course. They didn't want her, but what the hell! Money is money!

Burlee really saved then! Her mama helped her cause she wanted her daughter to want something, to do something for herself! Sit in a chair and do white folks' nails, stead of in the kitchen or somewhere with a mop and broom! Burlee went! She practiced on her mama, which made them both happy! Little happinesses are awful good too!

Naturally, she was looking round her at school and learned about the hair. They didn't teach nothing bout no Black hair and Burlee wondered why and where she could go to learn it. There was nowhere, she was told. No school for Black hair! The magic again! Burlee talked to the only Black beautician she knew, who drank beer and smoked as she straightened and curled. She had been doing hair thirty years or so, and Burlee asked the woman to teach her. The woman thought of the competition mongst the already small clientele til Burlee said she would pay her. So, on to saving again! She learned, but she only wanted to do her own hair. She also learned she would like to own a Black hairdresser school. She talked to her mama again. Her mama offered to try to make a small loan if Burlee would pay it. She also talked to Winston, who still came around. He was working and saving his money so he could be rich someday, plus still helping his mother! That man really loved Burlee. She didn't want him from nothing!

Winston offered to give her his savings. Burlee said no to that, but would give him 25 percent of the business. That happened.

She found a small, tired-out office where a doctor used to be and rented it, getting the first three months free in exchange for cleaning, painting, and fixing it up. The landlord planned to put her out when all the work was done, so when she asked for the contract in writing, he and his wife refused! That sent Burlee to her secret place to sit and think!

When Burlee came out of that secret place, she went to the landlord and told them the bank (there was none) wanted the written agreement to give her the loan for a year's rent. Well, money and loans was part of their world so they gave her a written agreement, which Burlee put away.

She had already offered the hairdresser who had taught her, 25 percent to teach in the "Beauty College," as she now called it. You know, that hairdresser, who had long ago given up dreams and hopes except for some good man to come along, looked up at Burlee and saw a little light in her life! She accepted and took some of her little savings and got a teaching license. Before they knew it the ads was in the paper and the school was open! And doing alright!

Burlee, with 50 percent, took over the books. Winston, with 25 percent, kept it clean after leaving his regular job. Watching Burlee with his love in his eyes! The teacher, with 25 percent, taught! Plenty people came and brought their $5.00 cause it cost $8.00 at a regular shop and didn't always look any better! The students paid too, that was the main idea, so all in all Burlee was doing all right! She was saving steady and in a year or so, added a small supply shop that was 100 percent hers.

She hadn't got married yet but she was a good saver, so in a few years she bought a better home for her mama and daddy and told those sisters and brothers still at home to get out in the world and make their own way. Now!

Burlee was still looking for a rich man, but the magic was working through her!

Burlee, also, got out more and visited beauty shops and learned about that makeup stuff! Her nails were pretty all the time now, free, and she didn't have to do them herself! Pretty was still on her mind, along with that rich man. She asked one of the white ladies she met about teaching makeup at her college. The woman frowned, but Burlee said, "Just one day a week. I'll pay you good!" The woman smiled and soon was teaching. Burlee learned. Her makeup improved and the college did too. The customers were mixed colors now and she had some Latin students, so she got a Latin teacher. Just going on, chile!

Winston wanted to get married, still, but he always got the same old answer. He wasn't rich! But I'll tell you this! He was saving!!

Now, Burlee had done come in contact with all kinds of women and was always talking bout a rich man. One old one, who hustled the hard way for her living, told Burlee she couldn't get no rich man living in no house like the one she shared with her mama! Said Burlee didn't have nothing but a room! How a rich man gonna look at somebody living in a room in a house with they mama and think they deserve *him,* a rich man?! "And where your furs?" (the woman went on) "Your diamonds?" (she laughed) "And look at your clothes! Look at you! What a rich man gon see to want you for?"

Now, Burlee got mad! The magic always come when Burlee start thinking! She knew bout her clothes, but she was kinda tight with her money and, remember, she had responsibilities, her mama and all, you know! That's a long word, ain't it? Anyway, she had looked at clothes and the prices of what she liked was too high! Sides, she didn't have nowhere to go noway! She looked all over and found a lady who could sew to beat the band and wasn't doing nothing but sitting round the house getting fat. She ordered a couple outfits out of a book and paid well, but less!

Burlee also started looking round for another house, found one, a nice one, and paid down on it and was almost moving in when her father got sick. The magic worked again and she decided to stay with her mama and help her daddy and she rented the new house out. Got good rent for it! In a short time she took the basement, had Winston fix it up, and she opened a seamstress shop and school called "Fix-its." Winston got 25 percent of the business for his help. Burlee hated to give him money! Her bank accounts was getting on, chile!

She was still planning on that rich man tho. Burlee was doing all this for HIM!

Burlee's body started giving her problems round bout midnight on most nights, and all day and night on the rainy ones! She looked around her, carefully, cause she wanted to wait for her rich man, give him something special, you know? Most men want that something *special!*

I know a woman had five husbands and told every one of them but the first one that the last one had raped her first and she had married him because she couldn't bear to be had by a man she was not married to! *And* that *he* was the first man she had ever given herself to! They *all* had loved her!

Anyway, Burlee was having these messages from her body bout some attention! Now, Winston, being in her face a lot and she trusted him, believed he loved her and thinking she could handle him, she told him he could be her lover. That magic is somethin!

She was thinking of satisfaction and he was thinking of love, so she got more out of it than he did! But, again, because he loved her, he was one happy, satisfied man! He thought Burlee and marriage were getting closer. Everything they had was already tied up!?! So!

Burlee was amazed at this feeling she felt *with* Winston but her inexperience didn't know that kind of lovemaking came with love, so she still didn't feel she felt anything *for* Winston! But a big chunk of her heart was moving over, following that big chunk of her body, into a warm, secret place inside her. The magic working again! She didn't treat him no better outside the bed tho, and she saw him only when she wanted to!

"Are you busy tonight, Mr. Winston?" She called him that in front of other people.

"What time are you thinking of, Burlee?" He just wasn't phony at all!

"I'll let you know as soon as I can, *Mr.* Winston!"

"Alright, Burlee! I blieve I'm free!" He went home to get the house he had bought ready.

But one day she said, "Are you busy tonight, Mr. Winston?"

He being a little tired of her wanting, but not wanting, him, said, "Yes, Miz Burlee. Yes, I am!"

Burlee like to broke her neck when she turned it so fast she fell off that stool she was perched on! She left the college early that day and didn't even go by the other shops! Just went home and locked up in her secret place in her mind, worried! Thinking bout Winston, not wanting to. Hating him . . . she thought!

Burlee thought she would never ask him again! For the next two months or so, she didn't! Then winter came . . . and the rains. She made sure he asked her . . . and she went . . . for a while.

Thinking she was getting way off her plans for her life, she took a trip East to look over the rich men. She let a travel agency set up her schedule and she stayed at the best hotel, ate at the best places, saw theater. Always dressed . . . and always lonely. Happy, pleased, but lonely anyway. She didn't meet anyone who paid her special attention so she went home and opened up a Bar-B-Q place and served it with cloth napkins, tablecloths and real plated silver and champagne!

Everyone came! 25 percent was Winston's again and he helped her. They still made love sometime but she urged him to love someone else. He used to look down at her, when she got through moaning and groaning and hollering under him, while she told him he should find someone to love him. He thought she was crazy!

Winston became more thoughtful, giving the matter of someone else serious thought. He started taking someone he already knew out. A stash of his, I guess. The stash was a good-looking woman and she showed she liked Winston . . . a lot! She's the one who gave him birthday presents, valentine cards and Easter eggs. Cooked him breakfast sometimes, when he let her. Left pretty little notes under his pillow, if she was inside. Pretty little notes under his door, if she was outside. He wouldn't give her a key.

Burlee noticed he was pretty busy.

"Well!! I guess I lost my loving buddy?!" She smiled.

"No. You don't have to lose me!" came the reply.

"Yes I do!" she snapped back. "I don't want no disease! Who knows who else that sorry-looking woman is screwing!" She walked away.

It must have made Winston mad, cause a month or so later when Burlee said, "Are you busy this evening, Mr. Winston?" with that special light in her eyes, Winston answered, "Yes! I got a date with that beautiful woman who screws!" Then he walked away.

Couple weeks later, Burlee went to the West Coast to check on her rich man. She had plenty money now. She looked real good. She was dressed! That woman surely dressed! She moved in some fairly nice circles now and everyone knew she had that money, all them houses and business! She met her rich man! Extended her trip so they could get to know each other better, talk more. The talk finally moved to marriage cause Burlee was not going to sleep with him til it did! The commitments were almost made and he took her to his large, rambling house. The Mercedes and the Rolls in the garages. The swimming pool, the cabanas, the cook, the maid, the gardener, the thick carpets and plush luxurious furniture. Upstairs to his enormous seven-by-seven bed with the fur spread and the soft lights! Burlee was in seventh heaven! Picturing herself walking up and down these stairs, days and nights, surveying all that was hers! My, my!

She unpacked her beautiful nightgown, bought just for this occasion. Slipped as best she could between satin sheets and waited for him to come to her. A little frightened, but smiling.

Soon he came with glasses of champagne. He talked gently and softly, as he turned on the overhead lights and got into the bed and . . . grabbed her with fingers and arms that felt more like steel than flesh! He pinched and twisted the nipples of her soft human breast, then grabbed a handful of the same soft breast and squeezed hard, very hard! A thought arrived just before the small scream came. "Does he think this feels good?" He let go, so she didn't hit him, just threw her arm out, knocking over the glass of champagne she had placed on the bedside table when she was smiling. It spilled into the bed on the fine satin sheets! She was looking to see what she had done when his steel-trap hand trapped her in that warm, soft little space that is very special to us ladies. It was painful! He then pressed his hard, dry lips against hers and the hard, wet tongue through them, and proceeded to roll over on her in what I would personally call stupid jerky movements! Trying to tear the beautiful gown out the way! Did he think that was sexy? Burlee almost screamed again as it flashed through her mind all the days and nights of this there would be if she married the rich man! He was struggling around on top of her now and the only soft thing on his body wouldn't work! His face had a strange leer on it just before he raised from biting her breast, hard, and dove under the covers to sink his teeth into her leg! Burlee was confused a moment and overwhelmed by a totally new experience with what she called love! Only for a moment tho, because before even she knew it, she had thrown the cover back and slapped the living shit out of the man! Now, you can slap someone pretty hard, but to get the living shit slapped out of you . . . is to really be hit! He screamed and grabbed his rich head that the toupee had flown off of, at the same time Burlee got up! His teeth fell from her thigh as she hit the floor and grabbed her things, rushing her exclamation point body down them beautiful stairs onto the plush carpet, where she dressed and called a cab!

The rich man came rushing down the stairs screaming, "What's the matter with you? Are you crazy?"

Burlee answered with conviction, "Nothing now! I'm alright!"

He gasped, "*You're* alright?! Look at my face! Look at what you've done!"

As she went out the door, she said, "You look at it! I surely do not want to see it again!"

Slam! went the door!

She went straight to the airport from the hotel, waited for her plane and flew home . . . wanting *something* with all her mighty heart!

Burlee rested, had to, the first day she got home. She thought all night practically. Didn't once think of them businesses! She took herself out to dinner the next night . . . alone! She thought about the years that were passing while she fooled around with a dream that was getting raggedy!

She had plenty money! Houses! Everything but . . . *something!* She was living good, but . . . she wasn't LIVING!

Her little heart under that fine soft breast and them expensive materials, yearned and yearned.

The lobster was like cotton, tasteless. The champagne was expensive dishwater. She had ordered what she loved most but it didn't taste like nothing! She put the silver fork down and thought some more.

"What have I done with my life? What am I doing with it?" The magic was working! Her eyes filled with tears. To stop them she took a deep breath and looked around the room to see who could see she was crying. That's when she saw Winston sitting there with his good-looking girlfriend! Without knowing why, she got mad! She'd been sitting there wanting SOMETHING. Wasn't he SOMETHING?

She got up and, looking like a mad exclamation point, she pointed herself toward Winston and walked over to him and said, "I want to see you! I want to talk to you!"

Calmly Winston replied, "I'm busy now, Miz Burlee!"

Burlee looked at the woman. "No, you ain't busy! I said I want to *see* you!"

Winston stood up. "I said I was busy, so I am busy! Can't you see us sitting here?! What's wrong with you!?"

Burlee was almost crying. "You ain't busy! You ain't never been busy when I want to talk to you, Winston! I want to talk to you, now!" She grabbed his shoulders and shook him.

He firmly grabbed her hands and removed them and, looking into her eyes, said, "If you are through eating your dinner all by yourself, go home! Go somewhere! I'm not stopping my life anymore for you to get on or get off whenever it pleases you!!"

Burlee bent her head, standing all alone, sniffling. "I got to talk to you . . . about you . . . about me. About . . . about life!"

Winston waited a few seconds, looking at her and at his girlfriend, who didn't know how to look. He said, "Go home, Burlee. I'll be by there when I am finished!"

Burlee looked at the astonished woman. "Take her home first!"

Winston sighed, "Go home, Burlee." He walked her to her car. She grabbed him and pleaded. "Come now! Pleassssse come now!" (We all know how that is.)

Winston remained silent, looking at her. "What did you find out there in the West that got you so ready for me?"

Burlee screamed at him. "Do you still love me?"

Winston opened her car door. "Get in, go home. I'll be there soon."

She got in, but as he walked back to the club she screamed, "You promised you would love me forever! Don't you lie to me!"

He turned. "I didn't say I'd *wait* forever tho!"

"Forever ain't over!" she screamed!

"No, you told me to find somebody else!" he threw back.

She looked tired. "I didn't know I was lyin. Oh hell! Winston, can't you see I love you . . . now. I want you to love me . . . now."

He looked at her for a long time, turning his head to the side. She looked up at him, feeling the very air against her perspiring, hot skin, felt the very sweat in her armpits, the very real need in her soul.

He smiled. "I'll be over in a little while."

She left thinking, "He's almost rich!"

Later, he did go by. Yes, they talked a long time. Yes, he still loved her. Seems some people is just for some people! Yes, he made love to her, the kind she understood. Yes, they soon got married.

Burlee lately gave Winston a little son and named it Winston Burl. I'm glad they got that over with and out the way before they had a daughter!

I see her sometimes. She is happy. Winston takes care more of the business cause she takes care more of the house. She wants to! Says she done worked enough in her life for three people. Says all these white women tryin to get out in the workplace, don't understand that that's where her people been all the time! Say she tryin to get out of it! She still takes care the money and the books tho! She also got her pet projects. She holds free classes every week for poor young girls and boys she gets from schools, to teach them how not to feel left out of life. Burlee always looks carefully over them youngsters for the ones the world might call "Ugly." She asks them to do *her* a favor, and sends them through all her beauty stuff for a week, free. So they will know how to do something for themselves to make themself feel better! When they smile at their new selves in a mirror, Burlee laughs a deep, happy laugh and sends them on their new way.

There is magic in life, if you can find it. It's a job tho! Oh yes, you got to carpet, where she dressed and called a cab!

The rich man came rushing down the stairs screaming, "What's the matter with you? Are you crazy?"

Burlee answered with conviction, "Nothing now! I'm alright!"

He gasped, "*You're* alright?! Look at my face! Look at what you've done!"

As she went out the door, she said, "You look at it! I surely do not want to see it again!"

Slam! went the door!

She went straight to the airport from the hotel, waited for her plane and flew home . . . wanting *something* with all her mighty heart!

Burlee rested, had to, the first day she got home. She thought all night practically. Didn't once think of them businesses! She took herself out to dinner the next night . . . alone! She thought about the years that were passing while she fooled around with a dream that was getting raggedy!

She had plenty money! Houses! Everything but . . . *something!* She was living good, but . . . she wasn't LIVING!

Her little heart under that fine soft breast and them expensive materials, yearned and yearned.

The lobster was like cotton, tasteless. The champagne was expensive dishwater. She had ordered what she loved most but it didn't taste like nothing! She put the silver fork down and thought some more.

"What have I done with my life? What am I doing with it?" The magic was working! Her eyes filled with tears. To stop them she took a deep breath and looked around the room to see who could see she was crying. That's when she saw Winston sitting there with his good-looking girlfriend! Without knowing why, she got mad! She'd been sitting there wanting SOMETHING. Wasn't he SOMETHING?

She got up and, looking like a mad exclamation point, she pointed herself toward Winston and walked over to him and said, "I want to see you! I want to talk to you!"

Calmly Winston replied, "I'm busy now, Miz Burlee!"

Burlee looked at the woman. "No, you ain't busy! I said I want to *see* you!"

Winston stood up. "I said I was busy, so I am busy! Can't you see us sitting here?! What's wrong with you!?"

Burlee was almost crying. "You ain't busy! You ain't never been busy when I want to talk to you, Winston! I want to talk to you, now!" She grabbed his shoulders and shook him.

He firmly grabbed her hands and removed them and, looking into her eyes, said, "If you are through eating your dinner all by yourself, go home! Go somewhere! I'm not stopping my life anymore for you to get on or get off whenever it pleases you!!"

much warmer than yours, and he'll give you a key, and just like a woman, you'll think that means something. It will snow hard for thirteen straight days. Then it will really get cold. When it is sixty below there will be no wind and no clouds, just still air and cold sunshine. The sun on the windows will lure you out of bed, but he'll pull you back under. The next two hours he'll devote to your body. With his hands, with his tongue, he'll express what will seem to you like the most eternal of loves. Like the house key, this is just another kind of lie. Even in bed; especially in bed, you and he cannot speak the same language. The machine will answer the incoming calls. From under an ocean of passion and hide and hair you'll hear a woman's muffled voice between the beeps.

Your best female friend will say, "So what did you think? That a man who sleeps under a dead moose is capable of commitment?"

This is what you learned in college: A man desires the satisfaction of his desire; a woman desires the condition of desiring.

The hunter will talk about spring in Hawaii, summer in Alaska. The man who says he was always better at math will form the sentences so carefully it will be impossible to tell if you are included in these plans. When he asks you if you would like to open a small guest ranch way out in the country, understand that this is a rhetorical question. Label those conversations future perfect, but don't expect the present to catch up with them. Spring is an inconceivable distance from the December days that just keep getting shorter and gray.

He'll ask you if you've ever shot anything, if you'd like to, if you ever thought about teaching your dog to retrieve. Your dog will like him too much, will drop the stick at his feet every time, will roll over and let the hunter scratch his belly.

One day he'll leave you sleeping to go split wood or get the mail and his phone will ring again. You'll sit very still while a woman who calls herself something like Patty Coyote leaves a message on his machine: she's leaving work, she'll say, and the last thing she wanted to hear was the sound of his beautiful voice. Maybe she'll talk only in rhyme. Maybe the counter will change to sixteen. You'll look a question at the mule deer on the wall, and the dark spots on either side of his mouth will tell you he shares more with this hunter than you ever will. One night, drunk, the hunter told you he was sorry for taking that deer, that every now and then there's an animal that isn't meant to be taken, and he should have known that deer was one.

Your best male friend will say, "No one who needs to call herself Patty Coyote can hold a candle to you, but why not let him sleep alone a few nights, just to make sure?"

* * *

The hunter will fill your freezer with elk burger, venison sausage, organic potatoes, fresh pecans. He'll tell you to wear your seat belt, to dress warmly, to drive safely. He'll say you are always on his mind, that you're the best thing that's ever happened to him, that you make him glad that he's a man.

Tell him it don't come easy, tell him freedom's just another word for nothing left to lose.

These are the things you'll know without asking: The coyote woman wears her hair in braids. She uses words like "howdy." She's man enough to shoot a deer.

A week before Christmas you'll rent *It's a Wonderful Life* and watch it together, curled on your couch, faces touching. Then you'll bring up the word "monogamy." He'll tell you how badly he was hurt by your predecessor. He'll tell you he couldn't be happier spending every night with you. He'll say there's just a few questions he doesn't have the answers for. He'll say he's just scared and confused. Of course this isn't exactly what he means. Tell him you understand. Tell him you are scared too. Tell him to take all the time he needs. Know that you could never shoot an animal, and be glad of it.

Your best female friend will say, "You didn't tell him you loved him, did you?" Don't even tell her the truth. If you do, you'll have to tell her that he said this: "I feel exactly the same way."

Your best male friend will say, "Didn't you know what would happen when you said the word 'commitment'?"

But that isn't the word that you said.

He'll say, "Commitment, monogamy, it all means just one thing."

The coyote woman will come from Montana with the heavier snows. The hunter will call you on the day of the solstice to say he has a friend in town and can't see you. He'll leave you hanging your Christmas lights; he'll give new meaning to the phrase "longest night of the year." The man who has said he's not so good with words will manage to say eight things about his friend without using a gender-determining pronoun. Get out of the house quickly. Call the most understanding person you know that will let you sleep in his bed.

Your best female friend will say, "So what did you think? That he was capable of living outside his gender?"

When you get home in the morning there's a candy tin on your pillow. Santa, obese and grotesque, fondles two small children on the lid. The card will say something like, From your not-so-secret admirer. Open it. Examine each carefully made truffle. Feed them, one at a time, to the dog. Call the hunter's machine. Tell him you don't speak chocolate.

Your best female friend will say, "At this point, what is it about him that you could possibly find appealing?"

Your best male friend will say, "Can't you understand that this is a good sign? Can't you understand that this proves how deep he's in with you?" Hug your best male friend. Give him the truffles the dog wouldn't eat.

Of course the weather will cooperate with the coyote woman. The highways will close, she will stay another night. He'll tell her he's going to work so he can come and see you. He'll even leave her your number and write "Me at Work" on the yellow pad of paper by his phone. Although you shouldn't, you'll have to be there. It will be you and your nauseous dog and your half-trimmed tree all waiting for him like a series of questions.

This is what you learned in graduate school: in every assumption is contained the possibility of its opposite.

In your kitchen he'll hug you like you might both die there. Sniff him for coyote. Don't hug him back.

He will say whatever he needs to to win. He'll say it's just an old friend. He'll say the visit was all the friend's idea. He'll say the night away from you has given him time to think about how much you mean to him. Realize that nothing short of sleeping alone will ever make him realize how much you mean to him. He'll say that if you can just be a little patient, some good will come out of this for the two of you after all. He still won't use a gender-specific pronoun.

Put your head in your hands. Think about what it means to be patient. Think about the beautiful, smart, strong, clever woman you thought he saw when he looked at you. Pull on your hair. Rock your body back and forth. Don't cry.

He'll say that after holding you it doesn't feel right holding anyone else. For "holding," substitute "fucking." Then take it as a compliment.

He will get frustrated and rise to leave. He may or may not be bluffing. Stall for time. Ask a question he can't immediately answer. Tell him you want to make love on the floor. When he tells you your body is beautiful, say, "I feel exactly the same way." Don't, under any circumstances, stand in front of the door.

Your best female friend will say, "They lie to us, they cheat on us, and we love them more for it." She'll say, "It's our fault. We raise them to be like that."

Tell her it can't be your fault. You've never raised anything but dogs.

* * *

The hunter will say it's late and he has to go home to sleep. He'll emphasize the last word in the sentence. Give him one kiss that he'll remember while he's fucking the coyote woman. Give him one kiss that ought to make him cry if he's capable of it, but don't notice when he does. Tell him to have a good night.

Your best male friend will say, "We all do it. We can't help it. We're self-destructive. It's the old bad-boy routine. You have a male dog, don't you?"

The next day the sun will be out and the coyote woman will leave. Think about how easy it must be for the coyote woman and a man who listens to top-forty country. The coyote woman would never use a word like "monogamy"; the coyote woman will stay gentle on his mind.

If you can, let him sleep alone for at least one night. If you can't, invite him over to finish trimming your Christmas tree. When he asks how you are, tell him you think it's a good idea to keep your sense of humor during the holidays.

Plan to be breezy and aloof and full of interesting anecdotes about all the other men you've ever known. Plan to be hotter than ever before in bed, and a little cold out of it. Remember that necessity is the mother of invention. Be flexible.

First, he will find the faulty bulb that's been keeping all the others from lighting. He will explain in great detail the most elementary electrical principles. You will take turns placing the ornaments you and other men, he and other women, have spent years carefully choosing. Under the circumstances, try to let this be a comforting thought.

He will thin the clusters of tinsel you put on the tree. He'll say something ambiguous like, Next year you should string popcorn and cranberries. Finally, his arm will stretch just high enough to place the angel on the top of the tree.

Your best female friend will say, "Why can't you ever fall in love with a man who will be your friend?"

Your best male friend will say, "You ought to know this by now: Men always cheat on the best women."

This is what you learned in the pop psychology book: Love means letting go of fear.

Play Willie Nelson's "Pretty Paper." He'll ask you to dance, and before you can answer he'll be spinning you around your wood stove, he'll be humming in your ear. Before the song ends he'll be taking off your clothes, setting you lightly under the tree, hovering above you with tinsel in his hair. Through the spread of the branches the all-white lights you insisted on will shudder and blur, outlining the ornaments he brought: a pheasant, a snow goose, a deer.

The record will end. Above the crackle of the wood stove and the rasp of the hunter's breathing you'll hear one long low howl break the quiet of the frozen night: your dog, chained and lonely and cold. You'll wonder if he knows enough to stay in his dog house. You'll wonder if he knows that the nights are getting shorter now.

◎ *JEANNE McDONALD*

Born in 1935, Jeanne McDonald grew up in Virginia and graduated from the College of William and Mary. Now a managing editor at the University of Tennessee in Knoxville, she has published short stories in American Fiction, Memphis Magazine, Better Homes and Gardens, Special Report: Fiction, River City Review, *and* Phoebe, *and in anthologies including* Lovers *and* Love's Shadow. *In 1989, McDonald won the Tennessee Arts Commission/Alex Haley Literary Fellowship. A chapter of her novel-in-progress will appear in* Homeworks, *the bicentennial volume sponsored by the Tennessee Arts Commission (1966).*

According to McDonald, " 'Cousins,' first published in Special Report: Fiction *(1989), grew out of a conversation with a friend about his daughter. The relationship was strained. . . . I tried to imagine the kind of interaction he and his daughter might have, and thus Sophie, the narrator of 'Cousins,' was born in my mind. I put her into the story with her father, whom I called Frank, and let them work out the plot by virtue of their characters. In order to survive the uneven relationship intact, Sophie has to make the transition from girlhood to womanhood, but the journey is bittersweet" (letter to M. Kallet, 1996).*

Cousins

"It's always the women who suffer," Aunt Helen says. She is standing at the sink, her pregnant stomach blooming against the chipped enamel rim, sunburned arms plunged deep into the steaming dishwater. Here in the kitchen is where the women do their serious talking every night after supper while the men play cards in the living room, the acrid blue smell of their cigars floating back to us in the thick, humid air. That is all we have of them — that and their closed, muted laughter.

It seems to me, in this, my sixteenth summer, that all the important issues decided in this family have been made during vacations in the kitchen of this musty mountain cabin, with its bare swinging lightbulb and worn floorboards: Helen's decision to become pregnant at forty, Debbie's resolution to leave Grover for a younger man, and this year — my mother's determination to divorce my father.

Though none of us has seen a newspaper for days, Helen remembers all the current atrocities against women and children, the names of the victims and the towns where the incidents took place. "Did you hear," she says now, shifting her weight a little, and I notice the thick knot of blue veins at her ankle, "about that baby over in Nashville that crawled under the car and his daddy — his own *daddy* — ran over him? God, how could a man live with a thing like that?"

I wonder if Helen fears for the safety of the baby growing inside her, if she worries about the number of its fingers and toes, if she in fact foresees its early death in a swimming pool or under the wheels of the family car. I wonder if other people's horrors seem applicable to her own life, as they do to mine. Her husband, Earl, is the younger of my father's two brothers. He is quiet and slow, and when Helen passes him in a room she rubs his head as if he were a large, lovable dog. Earl pats her stomach and grins when Helen does that. He's easy.

Marty, standing by the sink, is the new wife — the *second* wife — of the middle brother, mischievous Grover, the uncle who cuts figures from old Sears catalogues and pastes them up on the oil paintings in the living room, the seascapes and pastoral scenes that are hung — too high — above the faded blue sofa. It is Grover who ties our sneakers and baits our hooks and waits for the children along the trail to the lake, helping them as they struggle with their cargos of lawn chairs and towels and lunches in plastic shopping bags. My father, Frank, the oldest of the three brothers, is the serious one. His smiles these days are given only rarely, like special gifts that have been hidden and saved for a special occasion.

Marty dries dishes with a spectacular rhythm, piling up the crazed, heavy china on the counter. Her hand flies across the ridged drainboard, grabs a dish, swipes the linen towel across it, then stacks it on the column of plates, which is beginning to lean a little, like the Tower of Pisa. She looks at me and winks. I like her, she fits in fine here. None of the women misses Debbie, Grover's first wife, who was moody and complained continually about rain and the mold and having to use the outside toilet. Marty this year has brought along her son from her first marriage — Tony, who is about my age, and the two kids from Grover's marriage to Debbie. The baby, Elizabeth, keeps waking up in the middle of the night and crying for her mother — for Debbie.

I lean my elbows on the countertop and watch my mother, Sarah, thinking how nice she looks, dusky and tan, her hair touched by sun. She's retrieving dishes from Marty's endless stack and putting them away in the open cupboards, drying the places that Marty in her haste has missed. A cigarette hangs from her lips. Smoking is a pleasure she's found only recently, just when all her friends and my father have given it up. In fact, since Daddy has stopped, he won't sleep in the double bed with her any more because he says he hates the smell of tobacco. The cigarettes, I know now, are only an excuse.

Mom leans back against the sink, dragging on her Lucky, her eyes squinting against the spiraling smoke. "You'll get wrinkles," I tell her. "You'll look old before your time."

"Fine with me, Sophie." She throws back her head and laughs. "I keep waiting for that — getting old. Maybe I'll get fat and wear a muumuu. Why not? I'll pin my hair up in a bun and throw away my mascara. I swear, it would be a relief to make up my mind once and for all that it's over — this whole business with men."

"Not yet, Sarah." Helen puts a wet hand on her stomach. I imagine I see a tiny elbow or foot lift the faded print of her smock, a smock I recognize as having been traded back and forth over the years among all the sisters-in-law, and suddenly I feel left out, too old to be ignored and too young to be initiated into all the histories and mysteries of their lives. "No," Helen says, "not until you make sure you don't need another man."

"Helen!" My mother shoots her an accusing look and glances over at me quickly. She reaches out to hug me, and her wet dish towel clings to my bare sunburned arm. I shrug her off and head for the screen door to the porch.

"Sophie, honey, I'm sorry," Helen says. She shakes her head. "Me and my big mouth."

"Come on back, Sophie," Mom calls, but I'm gone, out into the thick black night. The porch is closed in by darkness and the syrupy perfume of pine. I climb into the hammock and pull the rough cotton netting close around my arms. I'm in a cocoon. From here I can see into the kitchen, where Marty has her arm around my mother's shoulders and Helen is shaking her head, her lips moving as she scrubs at a skillet. Their voices, sifting through the rusty screen, seem far away, as if they were people in a movie. Through the other window I see the men bending over the round oak table in the living room, hear the soft slap of their cards as they sit around the table playing blackjack.

I can hear the children, too, in the back bedrooms, wrestling on the musty-smelling bunks that have been wet on and accidentally rained on for Lord knows how many years. Tony is off somewhere alone, as usual. He disappears every night after supper and later comes in out of the dark and beds down in a sleeping bag on the porch. Sometimes I see him there when I get up in the morning, his curly black hair flattened down with the mist, his lashes dark against his smooth, suntanned face. But he doesn't talk much — to me or anyone. I can see that that is hard on his mother and Grover, they want everyone to like him.

Once at supper I thought I saw him looking at me, but who could tell what he was thinking?

From this angle I can see my father's profile with its broad forehead, the straight, strong nose and thick mustache. I love his rugged handsomeness and his rare, beautiful smile. The other brothers look up to him, you can tell that. It is almost as if they flirt with him, encouraging his laugh or some kind of response to their jokes and stories. "Hey Frank," they say, "listen to this one." They all smoke and drink and play their cards and reminisce about high school and growing up and fishing and grouse hunting and the deer they expect to shoot, come winter — nothing the women can relate to. Nor are they meant to. This is the men's vacation, the men's cabin. The rest of us are here simply because we are the children and the wives.

We all know that the men would prefer to be alone, the way they are in the winter when they come up here to hunt deer. Driving home then with the buck tied to the hood of the car, they are tired and bearded and smell of cigars, wood fires, whiskey, and steely mountain air, and when my father says good-bye to the others at the door he stands for a long time watching Earl's station wagon drive away into the clear, cold night.

Last year they came up into the mountains and hunted on horseback because of the heavy snow, and just at dusk my father's horse threw him and galloped away. It took Daddy two hours to get back to the cabin on foot, pushing along on his frozen boots. Earl and Grover were already out looking for him, they had been frightened when the horse came back with the empty saddle. I would have thought he'd be angry, but he laughed when he repeated the story and his voice dropped at the end, with a kind of longing, when he told about trudging up the snowy mountainside. Every time he tells that story I can imagine the sky milky with moonlight, the rhododendrons piled high with pale drifts of snow, and the vast blue silence of the forest. I can even hear my father's thudding heartbeat as he lifts his icy feet and pulls his cap down closer over his ears.

For a long time he has not smiled at me. I used to say it. I used to say, "I love you, Daddy," and he would glance at me obliquely and say, "Thank you, Sophie."

Thank you?

Earlier this evening after supper I stood behind his chair to read his hand and I saw how the glare from the hanging lamp reflected off the faces of his cards and flew up from the shiny red and white checkered oilcloth on the table, so that sometimes he had to tilt his draw a little to see it just right. There was a moon-shaped cut from a fishhook on the flat, broad thumb of his right hand.

I leaned against his shoulder, felt the smooth muscle move under his cotton shirt. There were white criss-crossed lines in his thick, sunburned neck. But he tensed under my touch, shifted his weight in the pressed-back chair and gave me a little nudge toward the kitchen. "Go help your mom, Sophie. You're standing in my light."

I think about that again and let my heart give in to grieving for myself. I know it isn't my mother I'm angry at, or Helen, or even my father. I'm angry at life — maybe at God — for not letting things go the way I want them.

In a minute the screen door pushes open and my mother comes out. "Sophie, is that you?" she says.

"No."

She laughs. She pads over toward me in her bare feet. "May I get in with you?"

"Oh, Mom, get serious."

"No, really, baby, let me in." Before I can resist, she's tipping the edge of the netting toward her and climbing in with me. She throws me off balance, and for a minute the hammock bucks crazily and I laugh with her. In spite of everything I laugh, and then I begin to cry. She wraps her arm around me and her skin is full of heat from the kitchen and it feels good in the cool darkness to be warmed like that.

We swing silently for a while. She holds me and smooths my hair, the way she has done since I was a baby. I can tell that she is looking at Daddy. "Do you think he's handsome?" I ask.

She laughs. "Frank? I think he is *definitely* handsome."

"Then why don't you love him anymore?"

She stiffens a little, but her fingers continue to stroke my hair. "I do love him, Sophie. Maybe I just don't *like* him anymore."

She rocks the hammock with her body and holds me closer, so that my face is pressed into her neck. She smells of Ivory soap and the baby oil she rubs on her skin in the sun. Her voice is low, hypnotic. "When I married your daddy, I thought I was the luckiest girl in the world. Honestly, honey, some days I would just sit and *look* at him and feel happy. But there were other times. . . . Sophie, I never told you this — he left me to go on a hunting trip when you were due to be born and by the time he came home, you were three days old. And it went on like that — my loving Frank more than I loved myself and Frank loving Frank more than he loved me. I'm tired, Sophie. I can't do that anymore."

"You're giving up," I say. "You're giving up after all this time."

She pulls my face up and smiles at me in the faded brown darkness. I can see tears glistening in her eyes. "You'll understand some day, Sophie, when you're more of a woman yourself." She hugs me again, but I am rigid, I am unyielding.

"Look up there, Sophie," she says finally, her tone brightening deliberately. "It's the old moon. See how the crescent curves to the left? That means it's in the last quarter."

"The old moon?" I say. "I've never heard of such a thing. You don't know what you're talking about. You don't know anything." I wrench myself from her grasp, tumble out of the hammock and run off the porch, leaving my mother clinging to the sides of the netting, rocking alone in the dark. I hurry away from the cabin, anticipating the place in the trail where a huge root buckles up out of the satiny gray dirt. I try not even to *think* about bears and copperheads. There's nothing else here, I know, that can hurt me, but my heart is pounding against whatever could be lingering in the heavy undergrowth and behind the fat, peeling vines.

Finally I come to the clearing, the wide basin of water. Here the moon is directly overhead and the cold, brilliant stars are burning bright white holes in the sky. As my eyes adjust to the dark, I see the thick planks of the dock, the swimming platform in the middle of the lake, and there, sitting in the moored rowboat, is somebody whose ruby-ended cigarette is making a swift, defined arc against the black water. I call out. "Tony?"

For a minute he doesn't answer. My hand is poised on the railing of the dock, my foot on the last plank, ready to run. Already I have an image of myself tearing through the woods, something with talons and yellow eyes breathing down my neck. But finally he says, "Who wants to know?" and my heart slows down. Carefully, I make my way to the end of the dock and sit down. The sweet, grassy fragrance of his cigarette permeates the air, and against my dangling legs the hairy rope of the mooring groans a little. The lake smells rich and darkly golden from the day's heat. "Me," I said. "Sophie."

He turns his head out toward the lake, but he's talking to me. "Sophie? What kind of name is that anyway?"

He's heard my name before. I decide not to answer. This is what my father calls a rhetorical question. That's what he always says when Mom asks him things like, "Do you really expect me to believe that you were working until midnight?"

Once, after one of those arguments, my father winked at me and said, "Sophie, I get blamed for everything I do." I laughed, but later, hearing my mother cry in the bathroom, I wish I hadn't. As much as I want him to love me, I never wanted to take sides against her.

I swing my feet beneath the dock and watch Tony. It's the first time we've really talked. "Are you Italian?" I say.

"No," he says, "American."

I laugh. "Well I know that, silly. So what's your real name? Anthony?" He doesn't answer. He reminds me of James Dean, only darker. He's moody, sort of, and I sense that in the blackness he is squinting because the end of the joint he's smoking fattens up for a minute as he draws deeply. "My name isn't short for anything," I tell him. "It's just Sophie."

Tony's not impressed. He shifts his weight and the water slaps at the sides of the boat in a half-hearted way. I'm beginning to see better now, and then I realize he's standing up, making his way toward the bow. His cigarette looks like a distant comet as he throws it into the lake and there's a sound like a quick kiss as it hits the water.

He reaches out his hand. "Come on," he says, "I'll take you for a boat ride."

That's funny. This is my father's boat, and Tony is the newcomer. But he's playing the host, which is all right, really, I want someone to take care of me. He senses my hesitation, though, feels the pull of my fingers against his. "Come on, *Sophie*," he says, throwing the weight of his voice on my name, "I won't bite."

For balance I rest my hands on the sides of the boat and lower myself into the bow seat. Tony faces me in the center, fitting the oars into the rowlocks, which whine a little as he backpaddles and we drift out over the satin field of the lake.

"So where do you go every day?" I ask, watching the semicircle of trees beginning to bear down on us from the opposite shore.

He takes his time answering. "Places. Around. Too many people up at that cabin."

"I know what you mean," I say. "Nobody up there speaks my language."

He laughs. Finally he laughs. I like the way he leans forward as he rows, his shoulders a broad, shadowed curve. In the half light the line of his arms blends into the smooth sculptured handle and loom of the oar and then the blade, connecting glassily with the water, painting dark concentric circles on the face of the lake. "So why do you come here every year, then?" he asks.

"My parents make me," I say, though that is not the truth. "Only next year, I don't know — I think they're splitting up. If they do, I don't know where I'll be, who I'll live with." I stop. I've said too much. I lean over and dip my hand into the lake. "Who knows?"

That touch of the warm water makes me homesick for this place, even before I've left it. Why did I lie to Tony about it? It's wonderful, really, the sweet rich smell of the earth and trees, the moist fleshy soil, the lake in the daylight a silky green. I love the way the breeze feathers the water and the sunlight bounces off it like tiny, bright constellations.

Suddenly I remember how I could smell the sun on my father's shoulders when I leaned over him back at the cabin, the way his hands looked safe and comfortable. I can't breathe, I think I'll die if my parents separate. Why does my father have to be so hard, so unyielding?

But he still has his tender moments, my daddy. Sometimes he picks up Elizabeth, tosses her high into the air and then catches her, the way he used to catch me. I've watched her expression as she falls back into his hands, as his face looms larger beneath her. She laughs and I remember that feeling — ecstasy, release, then the comfort of the thick, solid fingers folding around my ribs, the rough kiss of welcome back.

He's taken me fishing with him, has patiently untangled my lines, has shown me the brown speckled trout floating dreamily against the ruffled leaves on the bottom of the stream. Once he took me hunting. I remember the dogs yapping around us, the grouse rising straight up from the brush in a spiral of feathers and splintering twigs and then the sudden explosion of the shotgun and the brilliant silence afterwards, falling into the woods like weightless fragments of light. I cried to see the blood on the beautiful mottled feathers of the bird, but on the way home we stopped at the country store and he bought me a slab of cheddar cheese and a Coke so icy it hurt my head. He laughed with the men on the porch, showed them his grouse and his daughter with equal pride. Then in the car he told me how he loves to listen to those men, how he loves their tall tales and their slow, blunt way of talking. I fell asleep with my head against the soft shoulder of his chamois hunting shirt, and when he carried me into the house, I didn't want to let go of the day.

Yet the next morning he closed up again, retreated into his own world, a place he won't share with me or my mother. We know by now he is never going to let us in all the way. When my father gets in one of his moods around his brothers, they just scratch their heads and walk away from it. "Frank's clammed up," they say. That's all. They accept it.

Tony pushes the oars forward. The boat rebels momentarily, bumps against the easy gliding thrust of its own rhythm. "You'll live through all this," Tony says. "I did."

"When did *your* dad leave?" I ask. I want to learn what kind of armor I need to put on. I want to anticipate my wounds.

"Three years ago. Mom went crazy. First she just laid around in her bathrobe, crying. Then she started going out every night. She met Grover in a bar."

"Grover is all right," I say. "Grover is okay."

"Yeah," says Tony. "I guess."

"He'll be good to her." There is silence, only the scrape of the oarlock. I trail my hand in the water. "Feel this," I tell Tony, "the lake is still warm from the sun."

He reaches over the side to test the temperature. "Want to go in?"

My breath snags for a minute in my chest. "Right now? What'll we wear?"

He laughs. "Our birthday suits. Come on. It's dark."

My hands grip the sides of the boat. "I hardly know you."

"Jesus," he says, "I won't look. It's dark outside, haven't you noticed? Besides, if my mom is married to your uncle, doesn't that make us cousins?"

Cousins.

He stands up in the boat, turns his back, and strips before I know it, and he's over the side with hardly a splash.

There's the silver flash of his body beneath the surface, then a long, trailing ripple. He comes up sputtering, and his laugh echoes across the wide expanse of the lake. "Hurry up. This feels great."

I peel off my shorts and underwear before I have time to lose my nerve. My pulse is beating needles in my fingertips and suddenly I do it, I'm in. The water closes around me thickly, like a cold dark curtain. Under the surface everything is navy blue and I lift my head and the air in my lungs shoots me to the surface where Tony is waiting, treading water.

"Okay?" he says, and when he sees that I am, he strikes out, away from the boat, his arms flashing white in the night. I follow, pulling hard, holding my head up, keeping parallel to the dark margin of trees to my left. In a minute Tony slows down. He's floating and I stop, too, leaning into the water now and relaxing a little, feeling good. The water lifts my breasts. I'm drifting in the silky envelope of the lake, the cool cradling darkness. "Look up there, Tony," I tell him. As I lift my hand a sparkling arc of water sprays against the surface. My arm has never looked so graceful, so beautifully made. "That's the old moon. See how the crescent curves to the left?"

He's quiet for a minute, looking up. I hear his breathing and the soft paddle of his arms against the water. "How do you know that?" he asks finally.

"I don't know. It's something I heard somewhere."

He smiles at me. I can see his teeth gleam. "What about tomorrow, Sophie?" he asks. My name when he says it sounds like a kiss.

"What about it?" I'm suddenly beginning to feel pretty — powerful, almost. For the first time in my life, I feel in control.

"Let's do something together tomorrow," he says. "Just you and me."

Suddenly I hear my mother's voice skimming toward me, like one of the smooth round pebbles my father has taught me to throw across the lake. "Sophie, is that you out there?"

I'm wishing that it had been my father who had come looking for me, I'm wishing that he had been the one to worry. But I give in to it now. I know it will always be my mother who does the searching, the worrying. "I'm with Tony," I call back, and he laughs softly. My voice echoes once, then once again, against the trees on the other side. "We'll be out in a minute."

"Be careful," she says.

These are her favorite words.

Tony reaches out his hand and I take his fingers in mine and we turn over and kick our way back to the boat, watching the pale sliver of moon and the purple sky and the black fringe of trees. At the boat, he lifts me up, fitting his hands around my waist right about where my daddy used to catch me, at the base of my rib cage.

I know I should be careful. I know I should slow down a little and think about where this is leading, but I also sense that it is the nature of women to fling themselves headlong into the arms of danger even when they recognize that it is only thinly disguised as love.

Dressed again, with the boat heading for the pale rectangle of the dock, I turn my back to Tony and face into the breeze, listening to the sip of the oars against the water and thinking about what might happen tomorrow and the day after that and the rest of the week, thinking about how maybe now I can stop worrying so much about my father and let Tony teach me a few things.

As we tie up the boat, we hear voices from the cabin. The men are a little drunk, but it's all right, they're having a good time, singing old hymns, harmonizing. What can it hurt?

Tony and I walk up the path, our fingers locked together. We see the silhouettes of the men as they lean together against the porch railing. From here I can't even tell which one is my father.

There's no sign of the women. I wonder about them, where they are now, what they're doing. I imagine them in the back rooms, putting the children to bed.

And after they have turned out the lights, they will stand by the windows and stare out into the dark woods. What they remember, what they anticipate, I can only imagine. Yet I realize now that the legacy of women is not instruction but support — Marty's comforting touch in the kitchen, my mother's voice floating across the lake. Somehow, through these gestures, the women have been teaching me the peculiar intricacies of love throughout the summers of my life.

All Tony knows of me now is the weight of my hand in his, the length of my fingers measured against his own. For a minute I loosen my grasp and let my arm swing free in the cool darkness, just to convince myself that I can do it. If I needed to, if I wanted to, I could walk alone up the path to the cabin, where my mother is waiting, worrying, and my father stands laughing with his brothers on the porch.

◎ *LISA SPRINGER*

Lisa Springer was born in Queens in 1956 and now lives in New York City. Her fiction pieces and essays have been published in Ikon, Cover, *and* California Today *and in the new anthology* Surface Tension: Love, Sex, and Politics Between Lesbian and Straight Women *(ed. Meg Daly). Springer grew up in the Middle East, where her father was a diplomat. She returned to the United States and received her B.A. from Barnard College and her M.F.A. from Warren Wilson. She teaches at New York University, and is currently working on a novel and a collection of narrative personal essays that explore the many aspects—political, social, sexual—of her life as a lesbian.*

Of "Between Girls," Lisa Springer comments: "During my own adolescence I wish that I had been able to read about girls' sexual feelings for each other. But this is a subject that is hardly ever written about. . . . Like all of my work, this essay deals with the difficulties for lesbians of understanding our private lives in a world that offers little discussion, no rituals, and minimal acceptance of same gender sexual love. I feel there is an urgent need for more and more writing about women loving women" (letter to M. Kallet, January 15, 1996).

Between Girls

In high school in Iran I was in love with my best friend Miriam. We had a passionate emotional closeness, and I remember moments with her in minute detail; the feel of the physical world around us remains clearer to me than anything surrounding me in the present. But she wasn't a lesbian, and at the time I didn't know I was. Now, with the knowledge of who I am, I can go back to those sharp memories and make sense of the emotional confusion that colored our interactions, and I can understand the detours our relationship took — like the time I had an affair with her father.

Our dynamic, a battle for domination, began the first day we met. She was twelve and I thirteen when she transferred to the French school I was attending. On a clear September day, with the particular bright blue sky of high altitude, we stood in the courtyard of the school, lined up to walk past the woman who would inspect our uniforms. Miriam stood very straight, wearing a red skirt that peeked out beneath her immaculately ironed blue smock. I asked about her life, and she answered in English with the British accent she had acquired at her last school.

I learned that her parents, an Iranian father and a French mother, wanted her to work on her French now that she had perfected her English. She lived in the northern part of the city, up a steep hill, in a house with a big yard and several dogs. In the afternoons, she was very busy with piano and Farsi lessons, but after she finished her studies, she was allowed to go horseback riding. Weekends she liked to ski and summers — of course — she spent at the seaside in France.

I felt poor and scruffy in comparison. My parents were both American, which seemed much less exotic to me. Both from immigrant families, one Irish and one German, they were proud of my father's steady ascent to the position of mid-level officer in the Foreign Service. I lived with them and my five brothers and sisters in a small house that we were told we were "fortunate" to have. That morning, my mother had dug my smock out of a box and it was wrinkled and smelled like old clothes. I was wearing plaid yellow pants that were too short and revealed my white socks. After school, if I was lucky, I would play Monopoly with my siblings. I had never had a private lesson in anything.

I found Miriam beautiful. Her straight dark brown hair had the weight of a cascade of water rushing down a mountain. It glistened in the sun and I considered touching it to see if it felt like silk. Her eyes, set close together, made her seem vulnerable, while her rigid back made her seem unapproachable, even snobbish.

Although this first interaction left me with the conviction that Miriam was perfect, the too-close eyes a new definition of beauty, I found my admiring self a little idiotic. I felt that Miriam already had too much power over me. I turned away from her, for the first time. This would happen again and again.

I walked over to my friend Yasmine and kissed her on both cheeks. "Plaid pants that are a bit short are the rage in the United States," I told her. I didn't look back to see if Miriam was watching me.

Yasmine, as always, was wearing her smock open, revealing a black mini skirt underneath. She and I were planning a little rebellion against the school rule that we had to keep our smocks closed. We would convince our classmates to cut off all the buttons on their uniform by the next morning. While I thought about Miriam's perfectly pressed clothes, Yasmine and I walked up and down the row of students telling our friends that the uniform infantilized us and we needed to take charge of our own destinies.

I ignored Miriam for a good half hour. Then I turned to her. "Welcome to the school," I said, as an afterthought, as if I didn't care. I explained that she should cut the buttons off her uniform that night.

"My mother wouldn't want me to do that," she said.

I laughed. "I wouldn't let my mother run *my* life," I said, knowing as I said it that this was an easy way to put her down.

Our rebellion failed and Yasmine and I began smoking cigarettes in the bathroom. Meanwhile, Miriam sat in the front of the class, and I watched her from the back row. The barrettes in her hair changed frequently. I memorized the stiffness of her shoulders. She invited me to her house on the hill to play on her trampoline in the afternoons, after her lessons. And one afternoon, she told me about the plum trees in the garden in her family's house on an island in France and the jam they made from them.

"We eat it with fromage blanc. You'll love it."

This is how I learned that I would go with her to France. For years, it surprised me that Miriam invited me anywhere, even though she did so regularly. I had the total self-absorption of a person in love. I thought about Miriam all the time, but I never wondered about her feelings. I thought about the way she finished a plate of fromage blanc and plum jam, bringing the plate up to her mouth and licking it. I remembered her telling me that hands symbolized a person's being better than any other part of the body. But I never wondered what it was like to be her and how she might feel about me. I never thought that she liked me and that I could hurt her, too.

One afternoon during that first summer at the house on the island in France, Miriam felt sad and wanted to stay at home reading and listening to music. She assumed I would do whatever she did. She informed me that we wouldn't be going out that day. I felt trapped inside the house and trapped being on her turf. Miriam didn't say that she needed me and I didn't say I was waiting to hear that I made a difference to her. I told her I had other plans and she attacked.

"I invited you because my parents think that vacations are more fun for me if I have a friend."

The rounded wood door, set into a stone wall at the end of the garden, stood open. I held my bicycle—Miriam's from the previous year—away from me, ready to jump on.

"I am not your paid companion," I said.

"My father is making this trip possible for you," Miriam said.

"I'm going to play with Caroline," I replied.

"She's my friend," Miriam said.

"And now she's mine."

I bicycled down the little alley that led to the center of town. Vines with delicate flowers peeped through stone walls. My wheels crunched small pebbles and my heart pounded.

"I am not Miriam's possession," I told myself. "I am not the friend of the year, like the bicycle of the year, the new model."

Caroline's house lay beyond the square at the center of town, behind a church. From a balcony off her bedroom, we could see the tiled sloping roofs of the houses in the center of town. We sang American songs. Caroline told me she was really happy that I was there for the summer. When Caroline said this, I thought about Miriam for the first time that afternoon. I decided that Caroline probably liked me better than she did Miriam.

Now, twenty years later, I wonder how Miriam felt, spending the afternoon alone. Her friend listened to her closely and then disappeared when she most needed her. Her friend admired her but surrounded herself with other people, even when she stayed at Miriam's own house. She acted as if she was at a hotel, coming and going as she pleased. I'm sure that at that moment, Miriam vowed to invite a different friend the following year.

But as the summer approached the next year, Miriam began sharing her dreams of being back in France. She talked about the plum jam and fromage blanc. This time, I too had memories that added details to the idea of summer on the island. I remembered watching Miriam's eyes as she licked her plate clean. They crossed just a little at the same time that they lost their focus. She seemed completely involved in what she was doing. I tried licking my own plate but found that it was not as satisfying as it looked when Miriam did it. She also talked about riding our bikes in the salt marshes. "We should be more athletic this summer," she said. I noticed the word "we" and didn't even wonder whether I would accept her unspoken invitation. Miriam never formally invited me and I never stated that I would come. We fell back into my being part of her vision of the summer.

Miriam found my independence a challenge. We continued to dance around each other's desires, my running away a sure-fire way of confirming that I could affect her, even if I only believed it during the moment of her anger. And so, year after year, I watched her dark body become tan, telling her as we sat on the beach that her knees were fine.

"They're too thick for my body, fat even," she said.

"They're glorious," I said.

"You're lying," she said.

"Okay," I admitted, although I had been telling the truth. Her knees separated her well-defined solid thighs from her much finer calves. This seemed perfect to me, a combination of strength and delicacy in each leg, the knees incidental in themselves but beautiful as part of the whole.

I tried to explain something of this to her. "If you look at any one part of a body closely, really closely, separate from the others, especially a joint, it's bound to be ugly."

When Miriam stood on the beach and shook her hair behind her, I was reminded of the beautiful power of a horse. She held her head high, and moved her limbs in the wind, as if getting ready to unleash the energy held inside her body. Beneath her small firm breasts, her stomach was completely flat, descending sharply, like the sheer drop of a cliff to the ocean. Her legs with their thick knees seemed like the perfect base for this sculpture. I didn't think Miriam had a complaint.

She must not have believed me, because we had the conversation again and again, the summers blending into one another, our sentences one year merely variations on those of the previous year. One year, she brushed my hair for a long long time.

"I feel so insecure," she said. "I have so many complexes."

I didn't answer and I didn't move. I believed that I had a monopoly on insecurity and so I didn't need to say anything to console Miriam. I didn't move because I wanted her to continue to touch my hair, and I feared that a motion on my part might give her the idea of stopping. By staying in the exact same position, I willed her to do the same, to brush my hair forever. I kept my head tilted forward, and looked at the couch cushion, white with a burgundy flower sewn on. My neck hurt after a while, and I wondered about how we would make the transition from touching to not touching. But although I sat rigid the whole time she had her hand on my head, inside my body my nerves were jumping around frenetically, anything but still, dancing and playing as if nothing else in the world mattered.

Interestingly, it was she who initiated our most physical and intimate moments. I thought about brushing her hair too much to actually be able to do it. And one afternoon, I thought about kissing her stomach.

We were playing at her house in Tehran when Miriam told me she wanted to take me to a secret place. We walked through the trees to the back of the garden, Miriam leading me by the hand. We came to a clearing. To my great surprise, Miriam unbuttoned her jeans and lay down on the ground, face forward. She wiggled her body like a snake, pushing herself up against the dirt and the grass.

"I love the earth," she said. "And when I put my naked body up against, I feel close."

I stood watching Miriam, wondering why it had never occurred to me to put my stomach up against the earth. I wished I was Miriam because I wanted to be spontaneous and sensual and free. I imagined myself undressing and rolling my body in the sand at the beach. I would do this — another day. On this day, desire was imprisoned inside my body. I wanted to reach out and touch Miriam but instead I reached up and moved a curl away from my forehead. I wanted to lie down in the grass next to her but my legs felt like tree trunks that had roots in this spot. I hated my immobility.

When Miriam rose, her face was flushed. "Beautiful," I thought. I looked at the pieces of grass that had molded themselves into the flesh around her belly button. That's when I thought about kissing her stomach, placing my lips up against it and pressing them into her flesh.

Instead, I kissed her boyfriend. Miriam went to the mountains for a weekend with her father. The excuse was that he had just bought a new sports car and wanted to try it out. I always felt envious of their closeness and shut out from the oddly romantic aspects of their relationship. That weekend, at a party, when Miriam's boyfriend followed me into an empty dark room and began to kiss me, I didn't push him away.

It didn't take long for Miriam to find out what had happened. On a bus going up to the ski resort two hours north of Tehran, she told me she knew I had made out with her boyfriend.

"He told me the two of you kissed for a little over an hour," Miriam said. "He removed your bra from beneath your pink sweater and played with your breasts."

I looked out the window at the treeless mountains covered with blinding snow. Miriam's bluntness shocked me. I really didn't want to hear the whole scene described. I had been there and wanted to forget about it.

"He said that he was aroused because, after all, he's a boy and you're a girl and you were lying on a bed together touching one another, but he doesn't feel that you're very passionate."

I listened, feeling that I had little choice. I was the one who had committed the sin, and I was thankful that Miriam was speaking to me at all.

She continued. "You kiss in a tentative way and your breasts are very white and soft. He took off his shirt, but you didn't touch his chest. He said you seemed afraid of it."

I looked for a break in the monotony of the landscape but saw white in all directions. I wanted to tell Miriam that she shouldn't go out with that boy. He kissed roughly and had been most pleased when I was awkward. He loved conquest and humiliating his partner. Besides, he was hairy and too strong and insensitive and boring and self-involved.

I knew I had little right to criticize him. But I thought about the hairs that peeked out of his nostrils and the leer on his face, and I convinced myself that I had to speak up.

"He's always unfaithful to you," I said softly, looking down at my lap.

"At least he's honest," Miriam said. "That's more than I can say for you."

Miriam and I skied separately that day but rode home together, exhausted, sleeping on each other's shoulders. Half asleep, the bus jolting us through darkness, I felt the sharp pain of contrition. I deeply regretted spending the two unpleasant hours with her boyfriend. I vowed to be a better, more loyal, and understanding friend.

I believe that I sincerely intended this. But the intensity of my response to Miriam twisted my feelings into a multitude of desires. I wanted to have her, to be her, to hurt her. And it was often when I hurt her that I came closest to having her.

One summer, Miriam's father planned a party at the house on the island that included his friends as well as Miriam's. Late at night, he and I danced together, close. I saw Miriam walking around the room picking up empty glasses while I felt her father's hands slide up and down my back. She sat in a chair and watched us for a few minutes before she came up to us and pushed us away from each other.

"Come out to the garden," she said.

In the garden, she did all the talking. My head was spinning from drink as I heard her say that we had gone too far and had no respect for anything, including her feelings. I felt deeply ashamed of myself but exhilarated to know that she cared.

During my first year in college, I received a telegram from Miriam's father inviting me to go with him to the Bahamas or Las Vegas, whichever I preferred. Standing in front of hundreds of grey mailboxes on the first floor of my dorm, I read the line, "The beach or gambling?" and I remembered Miriam's reproaches. I immediately sent my answer, "The Bahamas." I had a fantasy that Miriam would be on the trip with us, reprimanding us. I had seen pictures from trips that Miriam had taken with her father to exotic places. The two of them in a pink jeep, the two of them with snakes. I imagined that I could jump into the picture too, no longer just the friend that Miriam invited along, no longer a second-class citizen. I could become a real member of the family, another daughter with whom the father was in love, Miriam's sister.

Her father and I sat beneath a palm tree sipping drinks with multicolored umbrellas in them. Behind us, in a cage, a parrot repeated the five words of its vocabulary. We had just had sex and I felt confused and sad and didn't understand why.

"How do you think you would feel if Miriam were in this same position?" I asked, trying to make sense of my own feelings. "For example, if she were having an affair with my father?"

Miriam's father leaned back in his chair and laughed. It was the laugh of a man at a poker game whose adversary has told a joke, a staged laugh accompanied by a hand slap on the table and a thrown back head. And then he stopped as suddenly as he had begun.

"She wouldn't be," he said coldly.

Of course not. Miriam never took more than tiny steps away from her own family. When we lived together in Tehran, she didn't like to spend the night at my house. She needed to take care of her dogs and she didn't want to leave her mother. I invited her to the Caspian Sea with my family for a four-day weekend in a cottage at a middle-class resort, but she decided to spend the time with a new horse at the stables. She had a completely full life with school and lessons and vacations, parents and a boyfriend and me, her best friend. Miriam didn't have the constant longing that consumed me during my adolescence. I looked and looked for something I could not find.

In my mind, I tore up the picture I had created of Miriam and me with her father in a pink jeep with snakes around our necks. I decided that I didn't want to stay in the Bahamas for the full five days we had planned. We left the palm trees and the parrot and spent the rest of the day at travel agencies finding a flight back to New York.

As we were about to land at Kennedy, Miriam's father had an idea.

"We could have a quickie in the bathroom at the airport."

He looked at his watch.

"I have three hours before my flight for Paris takes off. It wouldn't even have to be so quick."

"No, thanks," I responded.

I wanted something. I could taste it in the extra saliva in my mouth. I could see it in the brightness that my desire cast on the colors around me. I didn't want to have furtive sex with Miriam's father in a public bathroom at Kennedy Airport. Still, I wanted something.

I took a taxi back to my dorm with the twenty dollars Miriam's father gave me. I watched the lights of the city moving past me and tried to find the right cool distant tone in which to inform my friends, "It was hot in the Bahamas and I couldn't focus on my reading of Marx." In truth, I was ashamed of running away from Miriam's father. I wanted to be more mature, able to have wild affairs without emotion. I thought this was the solution to my confusion and yearning.

What would have happened if I had known that I wanted to make love with Miriam? I had all the evidence I needed but was missing one vital clue: the awareness of attraction between women, between girls.

I can't really know what the gift of information would have done for my life. Perhaps I would now be writing my memories of a first sweet romance with Miriam. Perhaps not. Still, whatever the shape of my life, looking back, I wish I had known what was going on. Understanding would have opened up choices.

I didn't see Miriam for a year after the trip to the Bahamas. On the first night of my arrival at the house in France, I told her about college, about the way American universities work, and about the men I had slept with. Always more graphic than I, she brought up the question of circumcised versus uncircumcised penises. She wondered how a woman's pleasure was affected.

"I've never noticed the difference," I said.

"Even with Papa?" she asked.

I felt humiliated and tricked. We had been speaking for several hours in a friendly way, and all the while she knew that I had betrayed her. I had been boasting of my experience, portraying myself as a woman of the world. "I've had sex with five men," I had said. The words came back to me, sounding superficial, mocking me. Miriam had set the whole thing up, organizing the conversation so that it would lead to her question, "Even with Papa?"

"He's not circumcised, you know," Miriam said.

Actually, I didn't know, and this added to my humiliation. I was a liar and a fraud. Neither a good friend nor a woman of the world. Having allowed me to pretend to be both, Miriam sat tall in her chair and looked at me without pity.

"You've had sex with at least one uncircumcised man," she said. "Surely you can say something about the difference."

I felt stuck in the particular space I occupied in the air, as if my silhouette had been cut out and placed there. I couldn't move or say anything.

"Or you could say something about the experience. Just about the experience with Papa."

I looked down at the thick dark wood of the table. I thought about the many hours that Miriam and I had spent at this very table over the years, talking and talking, trying to figure out the world and ourselves.

I had missed her enormously during that year. Being in the same room with her, I remembered her smell, especially strong at the point where her neck joined her shoulders. I remembered that she loved the sand and the ocean water and rabbit with mustard sauce.

Eventually, Miriam spoke. "I've known you for many years," she said. "And never, in all that time, have you been at a loss for words."

I looked up and saw that she was smiling. I didn't dare return the smile.

"I'm glad to know I have power over you," Miriam said.

I smiled then. This was as close as Miriam would come to admitting that I mattered to her.

"You must be tired from your trip," Miriam said. "It's time to go to bed. Tomorrow we'll go sailing."

I wanted to stay up all night listening to our favorite Neil Young album from the previous year. When the sky turned light, we could go to the bakery and get a fresh loaf of hot bread, bring it back to the room at the end of the yard where I always slept, and eat it with butter and strawberry jam. Then we could go to the beach and sleep all day in the warm sun, waking up every once in a while to run into the ocean.

"You're right," I said. "It's late."

I kissed Miriam on the right cheek and then on the left cheek and went alone through the yard to my little room. The green and yellow bedspread that had kept me company for many summers greeted me.

◎ LUCY FERRISS

Lucy Ferriss was born in St. Louis in 1954 and was educated at Pomona College, San Francisco State University, and Tufts University. She is the author of three novels; the latest, Against Gravity *(1996), received the Pirate's Alley Faulkner Prize for Fiction. Her other awards include a grant from the National Endowment for the Arts, the George Bennett Memorial Fellowship, the Irene Leache Award for Fiction, and the River City Award for Fiction. She chairs the committee on multicultural literature for the Associated Writing Program, and she directs the creative writing program at Hamilton College in New York. Her personal essays have appeared in the* New York Times, Boston Magazine, *and other periodicals.*

As Ferriss writes in a letter to Marilyn Kallet, "The subject matter of 'Love and Learn' arose from a moment when, having constructed a myth of my young womanhood full of notions of romance and fate, I realized that I had been exploited and damaged rather than honored by an older man's attentions. No good could have come of raging at events seventeen years in the past; rather, I looked at my own situation—a position of relative power—and tried to consider the merits of both erotic feeling and its restraint while I put that past (not a unique one, I suspect) in perspective" (1996).

Love and Learn

I had a crush this spring. The object of my affections was a kind, intelligent, good-looking man, a talented writer, an athlete, a lover of children. I have reason to think he was attracted to me. There was just one problem: he was my student, 22 to my 37.

Sixteen years ago, I had a crush on one of my professors. Since the attraction was returned, the result seemed inevitable: a student-teacher affair. His being married, like my being married now, doesn't enter this particular equation; I believe he loved his wife, as I love my husband. He was considerably older than I, but since we weren't entering into a lifelong alliance, the difference in our ages only enforced the attraction. So did our respective roles as mentor and student: the passion of learning keeps a ready pace with that of Eros.

So why, now that time has reversed my role, has the inevitable come to seem the impossible? Some of it, certainly, has to do with gender roles. In the world as we know it, women make themselves available and men make the first move. But men make that move when they have a fair chance of success, and that pretty well precludes a student approaching a married woman in a position of power. Some of it has to do with age and standards of attraction. When I was 21, it seemed natural to be attracted to a 40-year-old man. Sure, he could have used rippling muscles and flashing blue eyes; but confidence, astuteness and, of course, interest in me counted for far more. Whereas, this spring, there seemed to be plenty of wise and authoritative women around, but the ideal was one of firm curves, smooth skin, shiny hair. Against my college peers, my professor had no contestants: for me today, the battle is lost before it begins.

Much of the difference lies in what I have to lose, versus what my long-ago professor had to lose. When I think of myself, back then, it seems I was the brave one: risking my heart for someone who (so long as his wife didn't find out) could take or leave the affair and still maintain his secure, middle-aged life. For me, now, a tempestuous romance with a 22-year-old invites disaster: even if no one "found out," my self-respect, my career, my bond with my husband and children would all be threatened. What would be gained are a few of those moments between a man and a woman that come about only when sexual tension has dissolved into intimacy. Not enough to tip the balance.

Some of it, finally, has to do with feminism. When I was an undergraduate, virtually no charges of sexual harassment were pressed, and being seduced by one's professor was viewed more as privilege than as exploitation. Now that some headway has been made on that difficult front, it seems callous, at best, to try to seduce in one's turn. What happened to me, back then, was not altogether good; I cannot assume that my student is any more sophisticated or able to "handle" such abuse of power than I was, simply because he is a man.

And yet. Putting aside (again) all questions of morality, the turnabout seems unfair. Now that I have some perspective on him, my professor seems to have had quite a saucy time of it. He had only to initiate things, and that exhilarating encounter with youth was his. I, on the other hand, sense my caricature like a second self (desperate aging lady teacher, Miss Jean Brodie run amok). So I miss out on the delightful nuances in class, the heated intellectual debates after lovemaking.

Or do I? Now, when I look back on my rather stereotypical affair, what I remember is how young and lovely I felt. I assume he enjoyed my mind, for I have a good mind — but the A's seemed a foregone conclusion, once we had begun, and my thoughts and feelings about the larger world seemed extraneous, possibly silly.

My student and I, on the other hand, forced to hammer out a platonic friendship outside the classroom, have found out about one another more slowly, more spontaneously. I know that he renamed himself, in a burst of rebellion, when he was 6; that he doesn't believe in the sorts of epiphanies that literature tries to hand us; that he'll be teaching ghetto kids next year. I guess he knows a similar array of minor facts about me. He's spent time with my family, and they have guessed at my sentimental attachment and like him anyway. If we manage to keep in touch, there are no limits to the growth of this friendship; if we lose touch, it will not be because we didn't go to bed together. So perhaps mine is the richer reward, after all.

Am I saying that the introduction of sex into the mentor relationship is destructive, pure and simple? No, for two reasons. The first is obvious: some teachers and students marry and live happily ever after. The second is that sex is already there. There's a magnetic charge in this exploring of frontiers, a uniqueness to the relationship (there will be other students, other teachers, but never *this* one, *now*). One feels, for a time, nothing but affection for this other person. And there's a great challenge to the ego, which wants to believe it's *me* that's set this relationship spinning, and not the various coincidences of time and place and mutual desire.

What I am saying is that, unlike other relationships between woman and man (man and man, woman and woman), where it often seems sexual romance is a prerequisite to the delights of the spirit, the bond between teacher and learner has already opened the gate to the magic garden. *It doesn't get any better than this*, one wants to say. Sexual relations are almost redundant, and they can destroy. This is true not just in academe, but in all places where teachers and learners dwell — the office, the volleyball court, the volunteer committee. Have male mentors always known this truth? Perhaps — or perhaps it takes the very set of circumstances I've listed, things that work against hasty sex, for the privilege and fun of platonic mentoring to manifest itself.

I taught better this spring than I ever have. Classes came alive and — especially since I was trying hard not to play favorites — the give-and-take ranged more widely than it has before. Like anyone with a crush, I tried to look terrific all the time, which meant being healthier and more animated. In a strange twist, I probably noticed and appreciated my female students — my rivals — more than I have in the past. If I could judge only by my spirits and performance, I'd pray for an attraction to resist every semester.

I took my young friend to the airport, to see him out of town. He asked for a big hug and he got it. Goodbye, thanks for everything, keep in touch. No regrets . . . except one, going way back. And it's really only a wish that things somehow could be different. That I, too, had a teacher out there — one who had had a crush on me years ago but did nothing about it — that there was a friendship like that still growing, for me.

◎ *ANNE LAMOTT*

Anne Lamott is the author of four novels: Hard Laughter *(1980)*, Rosie *(1983)*, Joe Jones *(1985), and* All New People *(1989). Her book on overcoming writer's block is called* Bird by Bird *(1994). A past recipient of a Guggenheim Fellowship, she has been the book review columnist for* Mademoiselle *and a restaurant critic for* California *magazine. Lamott lives in San Rafael, California.*

"December 3" is the complete diary entry for one day in 1989 of Lamott's journal, Operating Instructions: A Journal of My Son's First Year *(1993). A single parent, Lamott's journal is by turns brutally honest and hilariously funny.*

December 3

Sam was baptized today at Saint Andrew's. It is almost too painful to talk about, so powerful, so outrageous and lovely. Just about every person I adore was there. They were the exact people I would invite to my wedding.

Everyone cried, or at any rate, lots of people did — all those old faces of the people at my church, and all the younger people, too, and my family and best friends, everyone clapping and singing along with the choir. All these old left-wing atheist friends singing gospel music. The singing was extraordinary, the choir of these beautiful black women and one white man, singing to Sam and me. A friend of nearly twenty years, Neshama, from Bolinas, described the two of us as looking very tremulous and white and cherished. Out of this broken-down old church, out of the linoleum floors and the crummy plastic stained-glass windows, came the most wonderful sounds anyone had ever heard, because of the spirit that moved the day.

Sam was just great, although I must say I took the liberty of dosing him with perhaps the merest hint of Tylenol beforehand so he wouldn't weep or whine too much during the service. He wore the baptism gown that my cousin Samuel had worn fifty years ago, very Bonnie Prince Charlie, very lacy and high Episcopalian, with a plain little white cap.

For the huge party at Pammy's afterward, he changed into his one-piece cow outfit. It was a wonderful party. Everybody mingled like mad, except me, and everyone got to hang out in the garden because it was such a beautiful day. I kept feeling that God was really showing off. The party felt like the secular portion of the show.

I've always kept the various parts of my life compartmentalized, but today all the important people from all aspects of my life were finally brought together: my sweet nutty family, in droves; my reading group; people I have worked with at magazines over the years; old lovers; and the women I have loved most in my life. It was my tribe. It felt like Brownian motion, all of these friends who had been strangers to one another bumping off each other in the garden.

Inside Pammy's house, the sun streamed through the windows, and there were vases of flowers everywhere, dozens of vases, hundreds of flowers of every possible color and shade, some arranged as if by pros, some like crazy hairdos.

It was like a Haight-Ashbury wedding. Emmy and Bill brought a whole roast turkey, and everyone else brought the most beautiful dish he or she knew how to make. Mom and Dudu had been in charge of recruiting the food, and there were beautiful bowls and plates of food on every inch of tabletop and counter. My brilliant old friend Leroy from Petaluma, who has been a permanent member of my food review squad for years, told my mother that the food was so exquisite that after eating, one heard the "Triumphal March" from Verdi's *Aida*, had visions of elephants, camels, cannons. My mother was so proud, so high from the whole thing that she could have chased down an airplane.

The kid made a haul, fantastic toys and clothes and books for the little emir. Dudu and Rex started a savings account for him; my reading group gave us a check for a small fortune. Except for the fact that there was folk music on the stereo, it was like the wedding scene in *The Godfather.*

A bunch of other babies were there, all of them about Sam's age, and they were all so much more robust than Sam. He is a skinny little guy. When I mentioned this to Neshama, she said very kindly that the other babies looked like babies on steroids while Sam was a baby on spirit. I had to hide in a back room with him practically the whole time because I was too overwhelmed, amazed, and profoundly grateful at how loved Sam is and how loved I am. It made my stomach ache.

Now I am sitting here on the futon in the living room, Sam asleep beside me, the kitty sniffing at him with enormous interest as if I had accidentally brought a perfectly broiled Rock Cornish game hen to bed with me. I have spent so much of my life with secret Swiss-cheese insides, but I tell you — right now, Mama, my soul is full.

◎ *NANCY WILLARD*

Nancy Willard's work has received many awards, including an O. Henry Award for best short story; National Endowment for the Arts grants in poetry and in fiction; and the John Newbery Medal and the Caldecott Honor Book Award from the American Library Association for A Visit to William Blake's Inn: Poems for Innocent and Experienced Travelers *(1981). Willard's books include seven volumes of poetry, most recently* Water Walker *(1990), more than twenty children's books, most recently* The High Rise Glorious Skittle Skat Roarious Sky Pie Angel Food Cake *(1990); and seven volumes of stories, criticism, and essays, most recently* Telling Time: Angels, Ancestors, and Stories *(1993). She teaches in the English department at Vassar College.*

"The Friendship Tarot" initially appeared in Between Friends: Writing Women Celebrate Friendship, *edited by Mickey Pearlman (1994), for which Willard*

was asked to submit an essay. Willard comments on this essay in her interview with Patricia Clark (page 578).

The Friendship Tarot

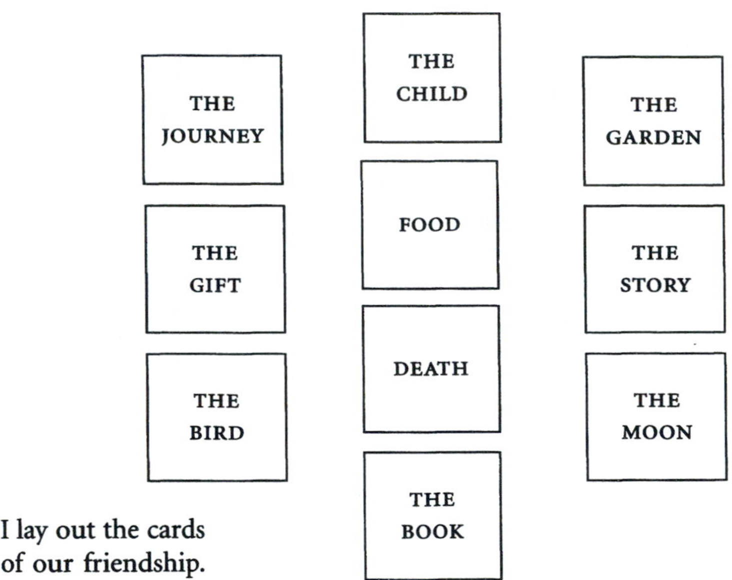

I lay out the cards
of our friendship.

THE CHILD

The card shows a child with chocolate on his face wandering through an art gallery in downtown Poughkeepsie devoted — for two weeks — to illustrations from children's books. Ilse Vogel and I have not met, but we both have work in this show. In one room stands the six-foot doll's house I made when I was writing *A Visit to William Blake's Inn.* In the next room hang Ilse's meticulous pen-and-ink drawings for her book *Dodo Every Day.*

What I saw: an elegant woman with white hair, a knitted cloche, and eyes that missed nothing.

What she saw: a woman with a seven-year-old boy whose face was smeared with chocolate.

What I thought: Who is this remarkable person?

What Ilse thought: Her child has a dirty face, but does she worry about it? No. And neither does the child.

THE GARDEN

The card shows two married couples eating dinner in a garden: Eric and me, Howard and Ilse. Four artists: one painter (Howard), one photographer (Eric), one writer (me), and Ilse, who can't be pinned down to one category since she illustrates her own stories. The dinner Ilse has prepared is exquisite. Butter blooms in a little pot; Ilse has sculpted it into the face of a sunflower. Howard helps her carry dishes from the tiny kitchen into the Francesa, a shelter shingled in nasturtiums and morning glories. The front is entirely open to view; over the edge of the second story dangle the tails of four sleeping cats. Once it was a rickety outbuilding for storing tools. Now it is paved with round river stones chosen and put into place years ago by Ilse. Shortly after she'd laid the last stone, she felt chest pains. The day she came home from the hospital, Howard filled the house with anemones.

Ilse heaps seconds on our plates without asking us and tells us they bought this small yellow house in the country because they loved the apple tree blooming outside the kitchen window. The soil is rocky but the garden is full of flowers; Ilse has put out one hundred and four pots of flowers. When a large tabby springs from behind one of them, Ilse explains that they are down to ten cats.

"Ten cats!" exclaims Eric.

"We have only two," I add apologetically.

Is this the first step into friendship? Ilse knows right away she can discuss the excellence of cats without boring me: Velvet Paws, Parsley, Comedy Cat, Mr. Goldie, Chives. Summer and winter the ten cats that live with Howard and Ilse sleep in the garage at night.

Winter and summer the two cats that live with Eric and me sleep at the foot of our bed so they can watch over us.

THE JOURNEY

The card shows three people in a car headed for New York. Ilse wears the same knitted cloche she wore at the gallery, and Howard's hat is the identical shade of oatmeal. When I remark on this, Ilse explains that she knitted them both.

We three are traveling to New York to see *The Tin Drum*. On the way, Ilse explains that she lived in Berlin all during the war, so naturally she's curious to see this film.

Of the movie I remember only a few scenes, not because the film was forgettable but because of what happened on the trip back.

THE STORY

The card shows a woman talking and a woman listening.

I am riding in the back seat of the car and I lean forward and ask, "Ilse, was it really like that in Germany?"

Ilse answers by telling me about the day the Russians marched into Berlin.

"When the Russians came so close to the house, you could hear them talking and shouting. And all the inhabitants of the house were sitting in the bunkers except me, because I hated to be down there with the Nazis. I was in my apartment with a friend of mine. And then we heard shooting and voices, and then we heard a sound as if masses and masses of water would come rushing in, and then my friend said, 'Oh, something has hit the canister of gasoline,' and within seconds I saw the flames and the gasoline floating in under the doorway of my apartment, and everything was in flames. There was just one window where we could get out. We crossed the yard to the door of the bunker and went inside and then the house did burn with tremendous speed. Smoke came and people started to pray and to sing, and others cursed and screamed. I sat with my friend and we held hands and I said, 'This is the end, there's no way out.' And my friend had a little flute with him which he always carried. I'll show it to you tomorrow—I still have it. He pulled it out and played a little Bach sonata for us, to comfort us."

She tells me how she worked in the Resistance against Hitler, hiding Jews in her apartment and printing passports to smuggle them out of Germany. Two hours later we are back in Poughkeepsie.

"Ilse," I say, "have you written this down?"

"It's not a story for children," she says. "And I can't find the right voice to tell it."

"You must tell it," I say, "so people don't forget." Ilse asks to use the bathroom. When she emerges she says with a smile, "I'm so glad your house isn't neat all the time."

THE GIFT

The card shows a restaurant strung with red and green lights.

The week before Christmas, Ilse and Howard and Eric and I meet for lunch at Dickens. Ilse calls ahead so that we can have the same table we had last year—a table intended for six. She tells the waitress we are expecting another person, a man, and during the meal she laments his bad manners—why couldn't he have phoned? She brings the snapshots we took of each other last year. In the snapshots we are always opening presents. Here I am, opening the present Ilse made for me: a muff, to keep my hands warm. It is made of brown corduroy, lined with synthetic lamb's wool, and decorated in orange and turquoise and lavender: braid, felt hearts, pyramids, and silver beads, each bead no bigger than a mustard seed. It has a corduroy strap and a pocket, into which Ilse has tucked a bright red handkerchief.

Since I ride a bicycle to class and my arms are usually full of books, I seldom have the leisure to use a muff unless I decide to take a muff-walk: a walk with no other purpose than exercise and pleasure. Which is probably why Ilse gave it to me.

This year Howard gives Eric a book of Vuillard's paintings and Ilse gives me a Waring hand-held blender which, she assures me, will make cooking much easier.

Eric gives Howard a photograph he took inside the conservatory of the New York Botanical Gardens and I give Ilse a set of flannel sheets and pillowcases printed with cats.

FOOD

The card shows dinner tables, side by side.

When we eat dinner at their house, they serve hors d'oeuvres and drinks in the living room or the garden, just for the four of us. Ilse makes the salad dressing. The courses arrive in succession at the proper time.

When they eat dinner at ours, I am famished from having skipped lunch to meet with students, and I rush everything to the table at once. The salad dressing is Paul Newman's finest, the cake is the handiwork of the Aurora Café Bakery. The last time I baked a cake, it collapsed like an old hat and I filled in the holes and cracks with frosting, which made it astonishingly heavy but quite tasty. Howard warned Ilse not to eat it.

"All that chocolate is bad for your heart," he said softly.

She smiled and took another bite.

THE MOON

The card shows four people perched on top of the world.

Ilse phones us in great excitement. Tonight, if we stand on a certain hill a mile from their house, we can watch the sun go down and the moon come up, all at the same time. She has checked the weather; the sky will be clear.

The road to the hill runs past stables and pastures broken by white fencing into parcels that give expensive horses enough room to run free by keeping them apart from each other. Howard regrets that the landscape feels so owned.

When we climb out of the car and look east and west from the crest of the windy hill, the valley sweeps broadly around us; could we see the Hudson if we knew where to find it?

As the sun slides into its nest of light behind the Catskills, the moon rises silently, secretly. She is so pale and thin that she might be the shed carapace of some large round animal. As darkness gathers, she grows solider, more golden.

"In German, the moon is masculine," says Ilse. "And the sun is feminine."

I can't think of another language in which those genders are assigned to my old friends in the sky.

Ilse says she is trying to write about those last days before the fall of Berlin, but she is not yet ready to read me what she has written.

The card shows an empty cage in a garden.

Ilse phones us — can we come over and see the dove? It seems that the postmistress in their little town of Bangall runs an animal adoption service on the side, and she has presented Ilse with a dove.

When we arrive, Ilse has put its cage on a pile of stones in the garden, like an altar to flight. The cage is made of the sticks that Ilse gathered in the yard, but it is very small, and when Eric and I approach, the dove beats her wings against the bars. All during dinner she makes endearing noises.

"You can't imagine how we enjoy hearing that wonderful sound," says Ilse. "And the cats don't seem to notice her."

We sit outside and watch the singular stars arrive, one by one, like notes in a music box winding down to silence.

The next day I telephone Joanne, a friend of mine who does excellent carpentry, and ask her to make a catproof cage for Ilse's dove. I tell her it should be made of sticks gathered in a forest and it should be huge. Ilse's birthday is two weeks away — could she possibly have it finished by then?

Two weeks later, Joanne drives up with a cage nearly as tall as herself on her truck. It is a gazebo, a minaret, a chapel, it is the mother of all birdcages. I phone Howard and tell him we want to deliver it as a surprise to Ilse, who likes surprises but does not like unexpected visitors. Howard can tell her whatever he likes; we will arrive with the cage at eleven o'clock on Thursday.

When we appear, the two of them are sitting in the garden, attended by Velvet Paws. Joanne and I carry the cage across the lawn. Ilse is speechless with astonishment. That is just the way I hoped she would be.

"You've given me exactly what I wanted!" she exclaims.

The dove takes to the cage at once. Soon it no longer feels like a cage; Ilse adds branches and leaves and nasturtiums and she removes the bottom so that the dove sits directly on the grass. How good the grass feels on her little coral feet! All night long she enjoys dewfall and moonrise and starshine. When the sun warms the dark world, Howard arrives with her breakfast.

One morning Howard goes to feed the dove and finds a dash of bloody feathers. There is a snake in Eden; nothing but a snake could insinuate itself into so stout a cage.

Ilse mourns her dove. All winter the cage is filled only with cream-colored twigs and the curious seedpods that catch her eye in the garden. One day the postmistress telephones her. A relative of the slain dove has recently laid a clutch of eggs; two of them hatched. Would Ilse like two doves? Howard snakeproofs the cage. It is spring again and the voices of Ilse's doves are heard in the land.

DEATH

The card shows a shelf on which Ilse has arranged the skulls of their cats. After their deaths, she digs them up. The skulls are light and beautiful as parchment.

"Some people think it's a strange thing to do," she says, "but see how beautiful their bones are!"

When I cook chicken, I save not only the wishbone but the breastbone. Scrubbed clean and dried, the breastbone looks like a mask or a saddle intended for an animal unaccustomed to carrying passengers. On the apple tree in our back yard hang the shells of half a dozen horseshoe crabs I found on Cape Cod. Anyone passing the tree would take it for the site of a secret ceremony devoted to saving what holds us up but is never seen under the living flesh.

THE BOOK

The card shows pages falling and gathering like snow.

Ilse is now seriously at work on her stories about life in Germany under Hitler. Howard is typing them for her. The stories arrive in the mail, one by one, in white envelopes bordered with a green stripe.

Without telling her, I am sending them to my editor at Harcourt Brace.

Velvet Paws has had her kittens behind a canvas of Howard's which he imprudently left leaning against an upstairs wall. Ilse invites us to view the kittens. Eric and I sit in the living room of the little white house and wait for the great moment. We wait and wait. And suddenly here is Ilse, presenting them to us in a basket lined with violets and strawberry leaves, as if she had just picked them in the garden.

Later, as we are leafing through a box of old photographs, I pull out a picture of two blond girls standing side by side: Ilse and her twin sister, Erika, who died of diphtheria when they were nine.

"Which one is you?" I ask.

Ilse is not sure.

"Perhaps that one, with the knees bent a little. Erika was born first and she always was the more courageous one."

Eight years ago, when I published my first novel, *Things Invisible to See*, I dedicated it to Ilse and Howard.

Today I open the book of Ilse's stories, *Bad Times, Good Friends*, and find it is dedicated to Eric and me. Over the dedication is Ilse's pen-and-ink drawing of a dove turning into a woman. She is flying over a bed of pansies, carrying three tulips in one hand and pointing to our names with the other.

"They didn't want a dove-woman on the dedication page," says Ilse. "I had to fight for it."

◎ *JANET NEIPRIS*

Janet Neipris chairs the dramatic writing program at New York University's Tisch School for the Arts. Her plays have been staged at theatres including the Arena State Theatre in Washington, D.C., the Goodman Theatre in Chicago, and, in New York City, the Harold Clurman Theatre, the Cubiculo, the Manhattan Theatre Club, and the Women's Project of the American Place Theatre. She has also written for television. Neipris attended Tufts University and received her M.A. in English from Simmons College and later an M.F.A. from Brandeis University, where she received a Sam Shubert Playwriting Fellowship. Among other honors, she has received a National Endowment for the Arts Fellowship in playwriting, a Rockefeller Foundation grant, and an A. W. Alton Jones Grant.

The Agreement *was originally commissioned by the Public Broadcasting System as a radio drama. The stage adaptation premiered at the Philadelphia Festival for New Plays in 1985, directed by Julianne Boyd. The play appeared in* Best Short Plays *in 1986.*

The Agreement

CHARACTERS

SYBIL MATCHETT
SIGMUND MATCHETT
ALICE BAILEY, *her lawyer*
LESTER OSTERMEYER, *his lawyer*
BORIS, *Sybil's date*
ALICIA, *Sigmund's date*
JUDGE ALBERT BELLOWS

[*Casting note: The same actor may play both Boris and Judge Bellows.*]

SCENE ONE

Time: Early evening.
Place: California. Sybil Matchett's apartment. Sybil is with her date, Boris. Her children are in an adjoining room.

SYBIL [*holding up a glass*]: To rainy nights in California.

BORIS [*holding up his glass*]: To rainy nights [*pause*] *and love* in California. So, do you find it exciting writing for the movies?

SYBIL: Love it, and I've certainly never met a live stunt man before. What's the hardest stunt you ever did?

BORIS [*as in "Ooh, this is hard"*]: The hardest stunt?

SYBIL: The hardest stunt . . .

BORIS: Well, I did this horror film and there's this forest fire . . .

SYBIL [*cutting him off and turning to the direction of the children*]: Stop it! Stop it! Just eat your sushi! [*Back to Boris, shrugging.*] Kids. They like to shred it to aggravate me. Excuse me.

BORIS: No big deal. [*Continuing.*] *So*, the entire world is enveloped by this forest fire. . . . [*Imitating the fire starting in spots over the world, jumping around.*] Woo . . . Woo . . . Woo! Everything's burning! Poof! [*Pause.*] Actually, just the parts that have forests.

SYBIL: Naturally.

BORIS: See, it starts out as this *love* story. What I'm talking about is . . . let me show you . . . [*Getting ready to jump.*] This is *perfectly* safe. Don't worry.

SYBIL: No. I'm *perfectly* calm. [*To the children.*] I hear you in there! If you're not going to eat it, stop throwing it! [*Back to Boris.*] This is really hard. *They're* jumping around, and *you* are . . .

BORIS: *SO*, it's this *love* story, and his girlfriend is down there in this forest burning, and he has to put her out . . . so he parachutes . . . like this [*Parachuting, landing on the couch beside her, listing towards her.*] Terrible film. . . . But what do you think of my landing?

SYBIL: I'm impressed. [*To the children, without getting up.*] Just go watch Big Bird! [*Back to Boris.*] In the winter, Sigmund — that's my ex — takes them to Florida to his mother's mobile home where they play Bingo all week at her Activity Center. This year he brought his girlfriend, Auntie Bambi. The children said she combed her hair a lot. She also got bored with playing Bingo, so they went to Disney World where Sigmund and she wore matching Mickey Mouse shirts. [*To the children.*] You are nearing the end of my rope!

BORIS: Here, let me help you. [*Getting up, yelling at the children.*] Hey kids! Listen to your mother! HEY! HEY! [*Back to Sybil.*] So when do they go to sleep?

SYBIL: When they get tired.

BORIS: When is that usually?

SYBIL: It varies.

BORIS: I think it would be good if we could relax.

SYBIL: I am certainly trying.

BORIS [*breathing in on the "Re" and out on "lax"*]: Re-lax. Re-lax. [*Sybil follows him, and they do the relaxation exercise in unison.*] Re-lax. Re-lax. Now when's your trial?

SYBIL: It's a pre-trial. Next week in New York. Thank you for asking.

BORIS: And how long have you been separated?

SYBIL: One year, eight months.

BORIS: Been dating?

SYBIL: I haven't slept with anybody yet if that's what you mean.

BORIS: How come?

SYBIL: Nobody's asked me.

BORIS: I'm asking you.

SYBIL: Boris, do you think I'll get the Russian samovar his Aunt Millie gave us, because it was *his* aunt, but she gave it to me, but I think I'm going to give him the pictures of the kids, seeing I have the real thing.

BORIS [*exasperatedly*]: RE-LAX. RE-LAX, LAX, LAX.

End of scene.
Lights fade down slowly on the above scene then up on the next scene

SCENE TWO

Time: Early evening.
Place: Sigmund Matchett's Manhattan apartment. Sigmund and his date, Alicia, are eating, almost finished with dinner.

ALICIA: Marvelous spaghetti avec pesto sauce, Sigmund.

SIGMUND: Thank you. It's my specialty. Don't bother twirling it around the fork. Just let it hang. So I have this house on the island which costs me a thousand dollars a month upkeep and it rains every damn weekend this summer.

ALICIA: What a shame. Pauvre [*pronouncing the "e" as in "eggs"*] Sigmund.

SIGMUND: A thousand dollars a month shame.

ALICIA: I thought psychiatrists were rich, the urban population à la Woody Allen being trés neurotic.

SIGMUND: Not ones paying for the past *and* the present.

ALICIA: That sounds very psychological.

SIGMUND: It isn't. More scotch?

ALICIA: Merci, but no.

SIGMUND: An after dinner drink? Crème de cacao, crème de menthe, Manischewitz?

ALICIA: One scotch was fine. Beautiful view you have of Central Park.

SIGMUND: Thank you . . . It's curious, Alice . . .

ALICIA [*interrupting*]: Alicia.

SIGMUND: Forgive me.

ALICIA: My name's Alicia.

SIGMUND: Alicia.

ALICIA: Thank you.

SIGMUND: You know, it's curious, Alicia . . . I forgot what I was going to say, I got so concerned with the name. Oh yes, I was going to ask you if you were free next weekend.

ALICIA: I don't care for the Hamptons, thank you. They don't touch me.

SIGMUND: I see. They don't touch you.

ALICIA: And I think touching's important. How long were you married, Sigmund?

SIGMUND: Ten years. Well, perhaps we can make other arrangements.

ALICIA: I've never been to the Virgin Islands.

SIGMUND: Neither have I. The Virgin Islands touch you?

ALICIA: Vastly.

SIGMUND: Vastly. . . . Could you watch your ashes, Alicia. That's French country fabric on the sofa, $18.99 a yard.

ALICIA: Have you ever been to Europe?

SIGMUND: When I was in the Army.

ALICIA: My former husband was in Korea.

SIGMUND: Good for him.

ALICIA: His name was Stanley, as in Marlon Brando in *Streetcar Named Desire.*

SIGMUND: Good for Stanley.

ALICIA: He had a dark fear of intimacy, unlike Brando. So what do you think about the Virgin Islands?

SIGMUND: I can't. I have a pre-trial coming up.

ALICIA: Oh. I thought you were already divorced.

SIGMUND: Well, for all purposes, I am.

ALICIA: Well for my purposes I wish you'd told me, because I only date *completely* free men, though I have to tell you, you make a terrific pesto sauce. [*Starting to leave.*]

SIGMUND: I grate the cheese myself. Asiago. That's my secret. Not Parmesan. Asiago — A-S-I-A-G-O.

ALICIA: Well, I certainly admire that.

SIGMUND: But make sure it's fresh. Sometimes they say it's fresh when it's not fresh at all. Deceit is a dreadful thing in our society, you know.

ALICIA: And when you're free absolutely, sans doubt, I'd consider a return. I'll just catch a cab. Goodnight, Sigmund.

[*She exits as Sigmund muses, unaware, in a way, that she's gone, more preoccupied.*]

SIGMUND: Unfortunately, *she* took the Cuisinart, because that's the way to *really* pulverize cheese, but I'm demanding it back because I know she never uses it because she never figured out which parts go where on anything. Sybil's very unmechanical. I also want the little Mexican god we bought in Guadalajara because she insisted it looked like me. It's actually a rendering of the god, Quetzalcoatal. She called him "Quetzal." It rhymes with "pretzel." Do you know she was late for our wedding ceremony? We had to pay overtime for the hall.

End of scene.

[*Lights fade down, fade up on Manhattan courtroom interior.*]

VOICE [*over loud speaker system*]: Court of the Southern District of New York, Probate Division, Judge Albert Bellows presiding. First Case, Farrow versus Farrow.

SCENE THREE

Time: Morning, one week later.
Place: Manhattan Courthouse Corridor. We see Alice Bailey.
Sybil enters, breathless, somewhat disheveled.

SYBIL: Am I late? The plane was late. There were seagulls on the runway.

ALICE: Relax. We're fifth in line. We'll just go over some things here in the corridor.

SYBIL: I'm sorry, Mrs. Bailey. I'm always late. I was late for my own wedding.

ALICE: Beautiful day for a divorce, Mrs. Matchett. We'll probably be here all day. They're booked solid.

SYBIL: It drove Sigmund crazy, my being late, because he's so compulsive. He said it was part of my complicated neurosis.

ALICE: Just take a seat on the bench until we're called. And Judge Bellows may not call you and Dr. Matchett in on a pre-trial. He dislikes being involved with the inevitable emotions of the adversaries.

SYBIL: What does that mean?

ALICE: The judge gets the information from the lawyers, and then we lawyers translate the information to you, and you say yes or no. [*Pause.*] It eliminates the middle man.

SYBIL: Us.

ALICE: Precisely. You wait outside while the lawyers talk to the judge. Now what were the taxes on your house in California last year?

SYBIL: Well, I should think it would help the judge if he could see the real people.

ALICE: The taxes . . .

SYBIL: They're somewhere here. . . . [*Dumping out the contents of her bag.*] The children gave me this candy bar [*pulling out a melted candy bar and credit cards*] as a goodbye present at the airport, which was cute, but it's melting all over my credit cards.

ALICE: This is no joking matter, Mrs. Matchett. I need the tax figures.

SYBIL: I think I'm not hearing you on purpose because I'm scared.

ALICE [*sharply*]: Well, no one would know it. You look awfully gorgeous.

SYBIL: Thank you. It's an Oscar de la Renta. He does this dot thing.

ALICE: You might have done better to dress down.

SYBIL: You mean to dress a little poor.

ALICE: Precisely. It would be in better taste.

SYBIL: What a dilemma, because I wanted to feel good too. [*Still searching.*] Here it is. . . . [*Taking out the paper.*] Two sixty-four Mullholland Drive, four thousand, six hundred dollars.

ALICE: Good.

SYBIL: Why is it good?

ALICE: It's high. Your expenses are high. That's good. We'll have a better case against the enemy.

SYBIL: The enemy . . .

ALICE: Regarding medical and dental, are your children currently undergoing orthodonture or do you plan orthodonture?

SYBIL: Are you kidding? Have you looked in their father's mouth?

ALICE: Truthfully, I'm thorough, but no.

SYBIL: Awful. The children have dreadful malocclusions, and Sigmund comes from a long line of malocclusers, so it's his side that they get the bad bite from, so I feel he ought to be responsible.

ALICE: We're not talking about right or wrong here, Mrs. Matchett.

SYBIL [*breaking in*]: But their bite . . .

ALICE: I can only promise a good fight, not justice.

SYBIL: God!

ALICE: There's no agreement made in heaven. A good agreement is only what's good for both parties.

SYBIL: That's very philosophical, Mrs. Bailey.

ALICE: Thank you. And your husband and Mr. Ostermeyer, his counsel, are late.

SYBIL: And Sigmund has awful vision. I think we ought to put something in the agreement about future opthomological care. When you think about the things that *could* happen in the future because *he* was their father.

ALICE: Just wait until you meet your husband's counselor, Lester Ostermeyer, if you think you've got trouble now. And I thought your husband was always on time.

SYBIL: He might have a queasy stomach. Sigmund's stomach turns over when he's nervous. I used to make him hot water and lemon juice.

ALICE: Dr. Matchett is also asking for his exercycle, Mrs. Matchett.

SYBIL: That's ridiculous. He hasn't used it in ten years. He hasn't used a lot of things in ten years.

ALICE: Divorce has wrought many changes.

SYBIL: Someone said he gained twenty pounds after I left.

ALICE: He looked quite trim when he came to my office.

SYBIL: Was he wearing a vest? I bet he was wearing a vest.

ALICE: He could have been. Yes.

SYBIL: Well, watch out. He hides everything under vests. Do you think he's attractive?

ALICE: Are you kidding? Those blue eyes? That head of hair?

SYBIL: Head of hair? He must have had a transplant. Was he wearing glasses?

ALICE: Not that I recall. What were the utilities last year, Mrs. Matchett?

SYBIL: I knew it. Contact lenses. He probably had plastic surgery too. I may not even recognize him. He's a very vain person, Mrs. Bailey. I think the judge ought to know this. I had to fight him for the mirror every morning. Did you notice his nervous tic?

ALICE: Quite frankly, I found his eyes distracting, so I tried not to look into them.

SYBIL: No. It's in his left knee. It goes off at three-minute intervals. It developed shortly after we married. All of a sudden the knee just pops out like a cuckoo clock.

ALICE: I wouldn't mention that.

SYBIL: Mention what?

ALICE: That it happened *after* you were married. Discretion is the name of the game here.

SYBIL: Well I'm certainly not responsible, Mrs. Bailey, for everything that happened *after* we were married.

ALICE: Potentially.

SYBIL: God!

ALICE: Dr. Matchett also mentions a sheepdog.

SYBIL: Snowflake.

ALICE: He just stated *The* Sheepdog.

SYBIL: He slept with it.

ALICE: Every night?

SYBIL: Uh-huh.

ALICE: Let me get this down. [*Writing.*] Slept with sheepdog. . . . Were you in the same bed with Dr. Matchett and his sheepdog?

SYBIL [*adamant*]: Our sex life was very [*hesitation*] hot. I tested out the range listed in *Cosmopolitan*'s quiz.

ALICE: I'm trying to make a case for you here, Mrs. Matchett. This is the name of the game. Now you understand this could qualify as sexual deprival and / or depravity. What exactly did Dr. Matchett do with this dog, Mrs. Matchett?

SYBIL: I bought Snowflake in the stuffed animal department of F.A.O. Schwartz. Sigmund kept it on top of the bed as you would a toss pillow.

ALICE: That *is* a bummer.

VOICE [*offstage*]: Next case . . . Connely versus Connely.

ALICE [*reading from her list*]: The Sam Francis painting of Point Bobo at Sunset.

SYBIL: Point *Lobo,* Mrs. Bailey, *Lo-Bo.*

ALICE [*reading*]: Also asking for the Cuisinart, the sailboat . . .

SYBIL [*surprised*]: What?

ALICE: Well, he can *ask* for anything he wants.

SYBIL: Whose side are you on, Mrs. Bailey?

ALICE: It doesn't mean he's going to get it.

[*Lester Ostermeyer and Sigmund Matchett enter, deeply involved in discussion, looking at papers.*]

ALICE: There he is! That's Mr. Ostermeyer, his counselor, the man with him. Don't worry, Mrs. Matchett. You know what they say about me. That my knife goes in so quietly you never see the blood.

SYBIL: Sigmund looks terrible. I hate the hair.

ALICE: Just be charming to him. A little honey never hurts.

SYBIL: His back is bothering him. I can tell by the way he's walking crooked. Oh, God!

ALICE: Just be calm and don't give them any information. And be advised that your husband's counselor, Lester Ostermeyer, is going through a divorce himself.

SYBIL [*whispering as the men come nearer*]: Is that good?

ALICE: Oh, no. That's bad. Very bad.

SYBIL [*repeating*]: Very bad.

ALICE: He hates all women now. His wife ran away with her secretary.

[*Lights fade out then up on corridor outside courtroom. It is fifteen minutes later.*]

ALICE: My client, Sybil Matchett, is requesting ownership of the sailboat, *The Sybil.*

SIGMUND: Sybil can't even sail.

ALICE: She could learn to sail, Dr. Matchett.

SYBIL: I could learn to sail.

LESTER: That boat gives *my* client inordinate seasonal pleasure.

ALICE: I'm sure. I understand he does a lot of "springy" entertaining on board.

LESTER: He's too busy working so he can make his payments to Mrs. Matchett.

ALICE: Not too busy working to take a vacation in Florida last year.

LESTER: To visit his aged mother.

SIGMUND: My aged mother.

SYBIL: My foot, Sigmund.

ALICE: And snuck a trip in to Disney World, four days at the folksy Dutch Inn, one hundred and forty dollars a night.

SIGMUND: I object! That was for two rooms and I had the children.

SYBIL: Auntie Bambi slept in *his* room I'll bet.

LESTER: My client has every right to participate in social contact with the opposite sex.

ALICE: Your client took some bunny on a trip.

LESTER: Bambi LeClair is a social worker.

ALICE: Oh I'll bet she is with a name like that. [*Turning back to the case.*] My client, as noted in document one hundred and fifty-nine [*reading*] is asking for the following: the property on West 83rd Street in Manhattan and the furnishings thereof, the summer property on Long Island and the furnishings *thereof*, the piece of land purchased jointly, and let me add hastily, in Spanish Lakes, located in the deserted desert of Arizona.

SIGMUND: Oh, boy, another tall tale.

LESTER: May I understand, Mrs. Bailey, the only thing *not* under contest is the children, custody awarded to *your* client.

SYBIL [*to Alice*]: Is that a win or lose?

ALICE: Please refrain from any comments, Mrs. Matchett.

LESTER: That's right, Mrs. Matchett, a little restraint here and on your MasterCharge.

SIGMUND: I'll drink to that.

ALICE: You're out of order, Mr. Ostermeyer, and your client.

LESTER: You're never going to get what you're asking for, Mrs. Bailey. You must think I'm representing Rockefeller here.

ALICE: You're going to be weeping in your scotch, Lester Ostermeyer. I'm warning you.

LESTER: Blow it out your bloomers, Alice. Where are we on the list?

ALICE: Two more cases before us, and I doubt we'll come to any agreeable agreement here today since your client is making outrageous demands.

LESTER: Just wait until we get into her artsy-crafty life in sunny California.

ALICE: Who *is* Bambi LeClair?

LESTER: We understand Sybil Matchett associates with women — *a lot!*

ALICE: Sybil Matchett is a model mother.

LESTER: But can she bake an apple pie?

SYBIL: Yes, I can.

SIGMUND: Yes, she can! She certainly can. I was married to her, so I know.

SYBIL: I wish this was over, Sigmund.

SIGMUND: It takes a lot of digging to bury the past, Sybil.

VOICE [*offstage*]: Next case, Wolf versus Wolf.

[*Lights fade, spot on Sigmund downstage.*]

SIGMUND: The day I asked her to marry me, in Truro, Massachusetts, which means "truth" and is on Cape Cod, was sunny. We were invited guests for that weekend. It was August, 1969, and the nights were already beginning to get cold. Sharon Tate and her friends had just been murdered, John Kennedy had been dead for six years and Robert Kennedy for one. That weekend in Truro, we rowed across the lake in a brown wooden boat to a beach where the sign said "Private, No Trespassing." It was hazy and the fog was beginning to roll in. I thought then that I wanted to be with you forever. "I'll love you forever," I said. The name of the boat was "Someday."

[*Lights down on Sigmund and up on Sybil downstage.*]

SYBIL: If you want to know why I married him, the beginning of everything, I would have to tell you pea soup. He was a senior at Amherst and had an apartment over Russo's Liquors. He invited me for the weekend. I was a junior at Wellesley and it cost eleven dollars round trip on the Peter Pan Bus Lines. I arrived in a well-underway snowstorm and we made soup together, he peeling the carrots, me adding the peas. We ate it, sitting at a four-legged maple table by the window, with French bread, which we dipped. Outside the snow was falling on the spruce trees in the public park. It was green and white outside and in. Afterwards we made love, of course.

[*Lights fade, then up again on courtroom corridor.*]

SYBIL: It was a B minus over C plus marriage which was hard to leave.

SIGMUND: We had our differences.

SYBIL: Which are nobody's business.

ALICE: The specifics would be helpful, Matchetts.

SIGMUND: No touching privates, please.

LESTER: I don't know how you expect us to fight this case without ammunition.

SIGMUND: God, all we want is an agreement.

ALICE: Cut the baloney, doctor. You preyed on this woman, demanding favors, refusing coffee of the instant type, laughing at her large buttocks.

SYBIL: Mrs. Bailey, please!

SIGMUND: Thank you.

SYBIL: No dirty linen.

SIGMUND: We'll wash our own.

SYBIL: And I don't have large buttocks.

SIGMUND: No, she doesn't.

SYBIL: Thanks, darling.

SIGMUND: The pleasure's mine.

LESTER [*officially*]: The marriage has irretrievably broken down.

ALICE [*officially*]: Non-aligned chemistry.

SIGMUND: We simply grew in different ways.

SYBIL: Like a cactus and a violet.

ALICE: My client is also demanding the bicycle built for two.

LESTER: My client is not shipping a tandem bike cross-country.

ALICE: Then *my* client will forget to send *your* client the slides. They'll slip her mind.

LESTER: Which you must admit is already pretty slippery. Things just fall in and out of it.

SYBIL: Wait a minute. You're talking about me. He's talking about me, Sigmund. He's insulting me.

SIGMUND: All's fair.

SYBIL: What's fair? How you came in the middle of the night and absconded with our entire set of classical records?

SIGMUND: It was three o'clock on a Sunday afternoon, I'd just flown in from New York, I was visiting my two children, and she said "Take anything, I don't care."

ALICE [*to Sybil*]: My God, is this true? You said, "Take anything"?

SYBIL: I didn't care at the moment.

ALICE: My client was crazed from temporal disappointment.

SIGMUND: Sybil was never crazed. She is a very rational woman.

SYBIL: Thank you, Sigmund.

SIGMUND: You're welcome, and she lives in California, so what would she want with classical records?

SYBIL: Right. We're too busy tossing about on the tennis courts.

LESTER: I suggest they split the collection—he'll take Bach through Liszt, and she'll get Mozart through Wagner.

ALICE: I object. Then my client loses Rachmaninoff and Tchaikovsky.

SYBIL: And I love the Russians.

SIGMUND: God, you can't have the world!

SYBIL: He has all our books, a green leather bound version of *The Rubaiyat of Omar Khayyám* which he inscribed "To my sweetheart, and the night shall be filled with music," boxed in his mother's basement.

SIGMUND: Safe in Mamaroneck.

SYBIL: Molding away. How is your mother?

SIGMUND: She had a heart attack and is in a recuperative home.

SYBIL: A home! My God! Couldn't your sister Helen take her in?

ALICE: Keep to the necessary confusions, please. We are about to be called. State your requests clearly.

LESTER: In tangible terms.

SYBIL: Twenty-five.

SIGMUND: Thousand?!

SYBIL: Until there's a change in my situation.

SIGMUND: Like what?

SYBIL: Success.

SIGMUND: I heartily wish it for you.

SYBIL: From the depths of your pocketbook, I'm sure.

ALICE: Let me remind you, visitation rights have to be settled.

SIGMUND: I want the children every summer.

SYBIL: Fine.

SIGMUND: For two weeks.

LESTER: In any state my client wishes.

ALICE [*to Sybil*]: You don't have to agree to any location lock-in.

SYBIL: Then I won't. I have no idea what state I'll be in.

ALICE: All my client wants is a sense of security. She wants Dr. Matchett to put his assets *not* in wine or women, but in his family. Trust funds.

SIGMUND: Security comes from within.

LESTER: A-men.

SYBIL: Sigmund always talks like a psychiatrist when it comes to money because he's cheap.

SIGMUND: If Sybil were to lay all the baubles I've given her in a straight line, they would stretch across the lobby of the Plaza Hotel where I took her on her honeymoon.

SYBIL: *Our* honeymoon, Sigmund, *OUR*.

[*Lights fade out. Spot up on Sigmund downstage.*]

SIGMUND: I wanted everything to be perfect. I was very much in love with her. I ordered the bridal suite. There were mirrors on the ceiling.

[*Lights down on Sigmund, up on Sybil downstage.*]

SYBIL: We brought our own candles. Hand dipped. I was nervous. The ceiling had mirrors. I couldn't look. I was very young and Sigmund was the world.

[*Lights fade, then up on courtroom corridor.*]

SIGMUND: She kept telling me she felt sick, at fifty-five dollars a night in those days.
SYBIL: I kept telling him I felt nauseous.
SIGMUND: I told her I loved her.
SYBIL: I told him I thought I was going to throw up.

[*Lights fade up on Sigmund.*]

SIGMUND: We had dreams, trips we wanted to make, children we wanted to have, how we were special . . . lucky.

[*Lights fade, up on Sybil.*]

SYBIL: Sigmund was wise about things no one else was wise about, and he knew all the verses to "My Darling Clementine," which he sang to me lying in bed at the Plaza Hotel. He sang them off key, which was the only way he knew, lying there, the city sounds outside us. . . . [*Singing a little off key.*] "You are lost and gone forever, La dee da da, da da dee."

[*Lights fade and up on Sigmund.*]

SIGMUND: We read *The Prophet* aloud to each other by candlelight in the beginning. Her hair was brown and silky, and we promised never to take anything for granted, like our luck. But it turned out that luck had nothing to do with anything.

[*Lights fade back up on courtroom corridor.*]

SIGMUND: Mrs. Matchett threw up on our wedding night.
ALICE: I don't find that evidence of anything to my client's detriment.
SYBIL: Well, I was much better in the morning.
SIGMUND: The next morning I had breakfast sent up.
SYBIL: It came on a silver tray with a red rose.
SIGMUND: Which was wilting. I ordered fresh strawberries out of season. It was December.
SYBIL: It was snowing and carriages were lined up in the park.

SIGMUND: She said she wanted to go out for a ride in the snow, so we did.

SYBIL: Three times around the park. I said, "Let's ride until the sun comes out."

SIGMUND: Only it never did.

SYBIL: So we went back to the room.

SIGMUND: Back to bed.

SYBIL: They had white satin sheets.

SIGMUND: And she threw up again.

SYBIL: Well, it turned out I had the flu.

ALICE: My client requests full medical and dental.

SIGMUND: Only I refuse to pay for another gum job. She already had one gum job, and if she doesn't floss, it's not my fault.

SYBIL: I stimulate with toothpicks every night.

LESTER: My client does, however, deed to his soon-to-be-former wife, their jointly owned cemetery plots.

ALICE: My client accepts.

SYBIL: I do not! They don't even have a view. He bought them in the most crowded part of the cemetery, way in the back, because it's cheaper.

SIGMUND: That's my Sybil! Always has to be a star!

SYBIL: I'm *not* your Sybil anymore, and I've decided to be cremated anyway. Everyone in California is cremated.

SIGMUND: That's the American way. Out of sight, out of mind.

LESTER: Let's just divide the plots evenly then.

SYBIL: I'm not being buried next to him.

ALICE: Then I'll take them. I have no need for front and center.

LESTER: Thank you, Mrs. Bailey.

ALICE: Let's get under way then.

LESTER: To proceed.

SIGMUND: I want the Cuisinart returned.

SYBIL: The Cuisinart's broken.

SIGMUND [*to Sybil*]: What did you do to it?

SYBIL: I don't think an avocado should harm a Cuisinart.

SIGMUND: No. Not unless you put it in with the pit. Where's the warranty?

SYBIL: I lost it.

SIGMUND: WHAT?

ALICE: My client says she has lost it.

SIGMUND: My lawyer can hear what your client, who is my wife, says. I'm telling you, Lester, she's highly irresponsible. I don't know, letting the children go off with her.

SYBIL [*sarcastically*]: Then take them, please, Sigmund.

SIGMUND [*to Sybil*]: I wouldn't want to hog all the assets. On the other hand, candidly, Sybil is a highly eccentric and bizarre personality. And an oral compulsive. Twinkies by the ton, undercover.

SYBIL: He is a highly rigid and obsessive person, an anal compulsive.

ALICE: Sounds like the perfect match.

SYBIL: Mrs. Bailey, whose side are you on?

LESTER: How was your wife's eccentricity manifested, Dr. Matchett?

SIGMUND: When driving she would only make *left* turns, refused to make rights.

SYBIL: I'm afraid of rights. He knows that.

SIGMUND: We would just drive around and around and . . . it also severely limited our sexual activity.

ALICE: I should also mention, then, that Dr. Matchett, a highly revered psychiatrist, wears his bunny slippers to bed because he says they make him feel more secure. I mean he already has his stuffed sheepdog.

SIGMUND: I have poor circulation.

SYBIL: The bunny slippers have little blue furry ears and button eyes.

SIGMUND: Why don't I tell them how you slept with your mouth open.

SYBIL: I have a deviated septum.

SIGMUND: Which causes a loud locomotive-like sound.

LESTER [*to Sybil*]: In other words, Mrs. Matchett snores. And I also understand you have a hot tub in your backyard. Who's been in your tub lately, Mrs. Matchett? And how hot is it? Rub a dub dub, three men in a tub.

ALICE: I consider these innuendos highly unprofessional.

LESTER: Come on, Alice, you're defending a hot chick here. Admit it.

SYBIL: I am not a hot chick.

SIGMUND: My wife is definitely not a hot chick.

SYBIL: Thank you, Sigmund.

LESTER [*to Sigmund*]: I'm your lawyer and I'm simply trying to establish here that Mrs. Matchett is a rotten mother and that you owe her nothing.

SIGMUND: But that's not true. Sybil is a very dedicated mother . . . scouts, cake sales, bedtime stories, the whole bit — four stars.

LESTER: Oh, terrific, Dr. Matchett, that's terrific! Keep it up!

ALICE: In my opinion, Mrs. Matchett is one of the most beautiful women to ever come across my desk.

LESTER [*to Alice*]: Well, no one asked for your opinion.

ALICE: My colleague here seems to think my opinion is worthless.

LESTER: You women think you're the only ones in the world who ever poached an egg, prepared a report, and looked gorgeous — all on the same day.

ALICE: I think you should be disqualified for that sexist statement.

LESTER: I'm not quitting now, just when the juices are beginning to run.

SYBIL: Well, don't count on my juice, Ostermeyer.

SIGMUND: Mrs. Matchett and I came for an agreement, not a carnage. I want this stopped, Lester.

LESTER: You want a case or not, Dr. Matchett?

SIGMUND: You're harassing my wife.

ALICE: You are, Lester. You are in contempt of the court and my client.

LESTER [*to Alice*]: You haven't got a case and you know it. Sybil Matchett's crazy, a highly eccentric personality, classified according to the American Psychiatric Association under file #509, "Bizarrity as a Classical Disorder."

ALICE: Come on, Lester, everyone knows all psychiatrists are nuts, including your client.

LESTER: My client is paying me a hundred dollars an hour to determine exactly who the crazy one is.

SIGMUND: Don't remind me.

SYBIL [*to Sigmund*]: You're shaking.

SIGMUND: It's my stomach.

SYBIL: No, I think it's your knee.

VOICE [*offstage, over loud speaker*]: Next case . . . Matchett versus Matchett.

SYBIL: That's us!

VOICE [*offstage*]: Counselors only.

SIGMUND: What does that mean?

LESTER: The judge is going to try and mediate without you and Mrs. Matchett there.

ALICE: Around the corner, there's a small cafe. You two go off and have a drink.

LESTER: Have yourselves a Bloody Mary.

ALICE: We'll deal with the judge. We know what you're fighting for. And on the boat, *The Sybil*, Sybil, how much is it worth roughly?

SYBIL: Why don't you let Sigmund have it. To tell the truth, I don't know the bow [*pronounced "ow"*] from the rudder.

LESTER: Aha! She admits it!

ALICE: She admits nothing. Come on, Lester. The judge is waiting. *This* is war!

[*Lights fade out.*]
End of scene.

SCENE FOUR

Time: One half hour later.
Place: "A Small Cafe."
Sybil and Sigmund are seated at a table. Jazz plays. They have a drink and a sandwich.

SIGMUND: I thought you don't drink.

SYBIL: I do now. I like your contacts.

SIGMUND: I got a transplant.

SYBIL: I'm working on a word processor.

SIGMUND: I've learned to cook on a wok.

SYBIL: I joined a spa.

SIGMUND: I'm taking a Great Books Course at Columbia. We read Plato last week.

SYBIL: I finally read *The Brothers Karamazov.*

SIGMUND: I miss the kids.

SYBIL: They miss you. Julie had the lead in the Thanksgiving Play. She was Pocahontas.

SIGMUND: I know. She wrote me.

SYBIL: I have the pictures. [*Taking them out.*]

SIGMUND [*peeking a look*]: She's pretty. She has your mouth. [*Then abruptly.*] Beautiful day today. Warm. Sunny.

SYBIL: Feels like home, breathing in all those good Manhattan fumes. I miss New York.

SIGMUND: More happens on any given day *in a closet in New York* than in an entire city anyplace in America.

SYBIL: We don't have good jazz in L.A. Nobody's blue, I guess. [*Offering him a cigarette.*] Cigarette?

SIGMUND: No, thanks. I gave up smoking too.

[*Sybil lights up.*]

SYBIL: Too?

SIGMUND: Too. You didn't notice I wasn't smoking in the courthouse this morning?

SYBIL: I guess you weren't.

SIGMUND: No, I wasn't.

SYBIL: Well, I'm impressed.

SIGMUND: Well, you should be.

SYBIL: Please don't tell me what I should be.

SIGMUND: It was a long process. I was hypnotized five times. I'm in a trance right now. [*Pause.*] I've decided not to ask for the other night table. I don't want to break up a matched pair.

SYBIL: Thank you.

SIGMUND: And I know you'll be sad to learn that my Uncle Al died last month. Zap. Just like that. I think he died of loneliness with Aunt Celia gone.

SYBIL: Gone?! Sigmund!

SIGMUND: I mean you go to the other side of the continent, you expect life to stop.

SYBIL: You could have called me.

SIGMUND: We *are* getting divorced!

SYBIL: Well, I still like your family. It was you I didn't like. [*Pause.*] I don't know what to do with our wedding pictures.

SIGMUND: I don't know what to do with your father's pocket watch your mother gave me. Better head back for the courthouse. Maybe they've come to a decision. [*Calling.*] Waitress!

SYBIL [*interior*]: It was the thickest pea soup this side of Austria, and we ate it sitting at a four-legged maple table by the window.

SIGMUND: Before we go back, I have something to tell you. You were a winning wife. You're funny, you're warm, I love your face and your meatless moussaka and the shape of your mouth which is bowshaped which is what the kids are, and I don't know what happened. I just got crazy. I don't know what it is I wanted . . . I still don't.

SYBIL: You wanted a divorce. You said you didn't love me anymore.

SIGMUND: I hate going to sleep by myself at night and waking up all alone on Sundays which are terrible. Where's the waitress? [*Calling.*] Miss! [*Pause, then abruptly.*] How's your social life?

SYBIL: Dating a lot. How's yours?

SIGMUND: Dating a lot. [*Pause.*] It stinks. That's correct. I date a lot. I have dated twenty-two women in the past year, and I have noted a certain pattern; they jog, they drink white wine spritzers, and make quiche on request. Oh, the quiches I've conquered, the millions of mushrooms and brocollae.

SYBIL: Well, no one can do eggs once over light the way you can.

SIGMUND: Last winter I went up to Bromley. I rode past our house. They let the maples get too high; they block the whole view of the mountains.

SYBIL: That was a good house.

SIGMUND: We made love that time in front of the fireplace after the kids went to sleep.

SYBIL: Stop. You're making me crazy. It's history.

SIGMUND: It's our history. [*Pause.*] Why did you stop coming to bed when I went up to bed? Staying downstairs . . . ?

SYBIL: I was afraid you wouldn't ask me if I wanted to.

SIGMUND: But if you didn't come, how could I ask you?

[*Lights fade.*]
End of scene.

SCENE FIVE

Time: Same time.
Place: Lights fade up on judge's chambers. Judge Bellows, Alice Bailey, and Lester Ostermeyer.

JUDGE: They all want it all, but you can't give them what there isn't nor can you divide what's indivisible.

ALICE: You can't fight over the contents of an empty pocketbook, your honor.

LESTER: And you can't argue over the water in an empty well, sir.

JUDGE: Precisely.

LESTER: What, then, is your proposal on the periodontal care, Judge Bellows?

JUDGE: Brush better. Brush three times a day. Your gums are your own responsibility.

ALICE: This agreement appears in order, judge. We'll present it to the Matchetts.

JUDGE: If they can't agree, tell them they'll have to come to court, but there's a four-year back-up, by which time no one will remember *or* care anymore about who gets the pet cat.

ALICE: Dog.

JUDGE: See, I've already forgotten. And without passion there are no victories. Good afternoon, counselors. Pleasure to see the A Team together again, stopping at nothing. Oh, and Lester, how's yours going?

LESTER: Fine thank you, sir. Very civilized. Since we can't come to any decisions yet, my wife is occupying the bottom floor of our home, and I have the top. She's got the kitchen, so I'm simply taking all my meals out . . . but I got the bathroom, which seemed more essential.

JUDGE: I'd say so. Good luck with the Hatchetts. Tell them I said compromise is the cornerstone of conciliation.

ALICE: You bet, your honor.

JUDGE: And Alice, how's the big romance going? Any chance of wedding bells?

ALICE: Nothing ringing this year, your honor. Always hoping.

JUDGE: Just keep your sunny side up—NEXT!

[*Lights fade out.*]
End of scene.

SCENE SIX

Time: Immediately following.
Place: Courthouse corridor.

ALICE: There they are! [*Calling.*] Dr. and Mrs. Matchett! Here we are! [*To Lester.*] They're a handsome couple, don't you think? Wholesome.

LESTER: We're divorcing them, Alice.

SYBIL: What did Judge Bellows say?

LESTER: You'd better agree today. If you hesitate, you'll forget why you're getting a divorce in the first place.

ALICE: We may be coming very close to an agreement here.

[*Note: Both lawyers write quickly on legal pads during next scene.*]

LESTER [*rapidly*]: To him, all statuary.

ALICE [*rapidly*]: To her, all paintings.

LESTER: To him, all loose lamps.

ALICE: To her, all fixed lighting.

LESTER: To each, all gifts from the other's family.

ALICE: As in *his* Aunt Millie's samovar to *her.*

LESTER: And *her* mother's silver service to *him* as *he* polished it.

ALICE: As the party of either side claims it was their charms which wooed the other's family, in contrast to their own.

LESTER: Wherein the adage familiarity breeds contempt.

SIGMUND [*to Sybil*]: I thought I might come out to California for Christmas.

SYBIL: Last Christmas Day the kids and I went to a movie with another divorced family. It was supposed to be a comedy, but it was very sad and we all cried.

LESTER: I think we're getting close on this agreement.

SIGMUND: I think you took my bathrobe when you left, Sybil.

ALICE: Before we tie things up here, Dr. and Mrs. Matchett, we'll have to renegotiate the life insurance.

SIGMUND: My green velour robe.

SYBIL: I wear it around.

SIGMUND: It's a *real* robe.

SYBIL: Yes, it is.

LESTER [*to Sigmund*]: If you let her keep the lithograph of Rodin's "The Screaming Woman" and the Cuisinart . . .

ALICE [*breaking in*]: Which is broken. [*To Sybil, who is staring into Sigmund's eyes.*] Mrs. Matchett, pay attention here. Your whole future's at stake.

SYBIL: Hardly over a Cuisinart.

ALICE: We are working our way *up*, if you please. Now his lawyer's carved out a three-year plan, at the end of which, he disclaims all responsibility.

SIGMUND: That's ridiculous. I don't disclaim responsibility in three years.

LESTER: Well, if you insist on continuous support, then Mrs. Matchett should give you some of the furniture as collateral. We are talking *the* major pieces.

ALICE: That's crazy.

SIGMUND: I agree. That's crazy, Lester. The kids and her have to live, sleep, work, eat, sit in a chair, do whatever it is people do every day to use up the time.

LESTER [*to Sigmund*]: This is a battle. We're fighting here to divide the spoils.

SIGMUND: We sound like vultures.

ALICE: No room for sentiment here. This is a courthouse. She gets to keep all the jewelry Dr. Matchett *gifted* her, without attachments.

LESTER [*writing it down*]: No attachments.

ALICE: All liquid assets are divided equally since he is probably hiding what he *really* has in some bank in New Jersey.

LESTER: There is nothing in New Jersey.

SIGMUND: That's right.

LESTER: Try not to hold up progress, the two of you. We're committed to getting you a rock solid agreement. [*Quickly continuing.*] He gets to keep the French Oriental.

SYBIL: Sigmund doesn't even *like* the French Oriental.

SIGMUND: I didn't even know we *had* a French Oriental.

SIGMUND: What about WAM? Do you still belong to WAM?	SYBIL: Women Against Men? Yes, they have a West Coast Branch; but Sig, it's nothing personal.
ALICE: All the real estate to her.	LESTER: Then everything in the houses to him.
SIGMUND: Oh, nothing personal.	SYBIL: It's a political issue with me. And I joined because I was angry at you for making me punch a time clock.
ALICE: Who wants an empty house?	LESTER: We are talking value here, not utility.

[*Note: Above speeches should be timed to end at the same time. Though characters speak over each other, the lawyers don't miss a word.*]

ALICE: He made you punch a time clock, Mrs. Matchett?

SIGMUND: I just wanted to equalize the load. . . . Why don't you ask her about the time she and her friends from WAM put a rabbit in the bed . . . a live one, I might add.

SYBIL: Simply to remind you of *your* responsibility in the birth control process.

LESTER: She put a rabbit in your bed?

[*Note: The next section occurs rapidly.*]

ALICE: And on the insurance, he adds the dismemberment amendment, God forbid.

LESTER: God forbid.

SIGMUND: God forbid.

ALICE [*writing*]: So on this twenty-fifth day of August, the party of the first part agrees with the party of the second part . . .

LESTER [*breaking in*]: You're really getting a fine agreement here, Dr. Matchett. Everything spelled out.

ALICE: So everyone goes away happy.

LESTER: Final check. [*Checking his list.*] Routine clauses on cohabitation and other deviations from the norm will in effect negate this contract.

ALICE: Wipe it out.

LESTER: And we would simply start from scratch.

ALICE [*breaking right in.*] Now if you'll both sign this paper, Mr. Ostermeyer and I will write it up and you could be divorced this afternoon. [*Pushing the paper at Sigmund.*]

LESTER: In the next hour.

SIGMUND: As simple as that. [*He does not sign right away but ignores the paper.*]

ALICE: This agreement will not be considered final, of course, for six months, so both of you would have to wait that period to remarry.

SYBIL: To remarry . . .

ALICE: Most difficult settlement since Ford versus Ford. I can't believe it's almost over. Just sign here, Mrs. Matchett . . . [*holding out the paper to Sybil*] and you'll be divorced, out in the world with the rest of us, out in the marketplace. You'll receive a xeroxed copy.

[*Sybil does not move to sign.*]

LESTER [*to Sigmund*]: Just sign your John Doe here and you're a free man.

SIGMUND [*interior*]: The night she left I kept thinking, if I get up the next morning and start the day with orange juice, everything will be okay.

SYBIL [*interior*]: I didn't stop crying until Indiana. And the moonlight does not shine along the Wabash. The kids were silent all the way across the country. Not one fight. Thank you, I thought, for something. By the time we got to the Black Hills, I couldn't remember why we had started out.

SIGMUND: Sybil, we're all alone in our lives and nobody knows. We could die of something and no one would know.

SYBIL: I know.

LESTER: People are waiting to lock up. [*Holding out the document to Sigmund.*] X marks the spot. [*Handing him the pen. Pause. Sigmund signs.*]

ALICE: Mrs. Matchett. . . . [*Holding out the document and pen.*] Your signature . . . [*pause*] AND IT'S . . . [*Sybil signs*] OVER!

LESTER: It's over, Dr. Matchett! It's over!

SYBIL [*quietly*]: It's over.

SIGMUND: All over.

SYBIL: Wait a minute! You forgot the children!

LESTER: The children.

ALICE: The children.

SIGMUND: How could you forget the children?

ALICE: Well, they're *your* children.

LESTER: You could have reminded us.

ALICE [*holding out her lists*]: Look at all these items we're juggling. You need the memory of an elephant. [*Looking over the list.*] She got the swings on the outdoor equipment clause.

LESTER: So he gets the children, no strings attached.

SYBIL: Wait a minute. I'm not giving up any children.

LESTER: We all have to make do with partial rewards.

SYBIL: Tell it to Santa Claus.

SIGMUND: The children are hers.

ALICE: I move we put the children on a rider.

LESTER [*writing*]: *Ride* the children.

SIGMUND: I mean they're ours, but I can't make the home Sybil does. I think we'll arrange this between us. Don't you think, Sybil.

SYBIL: We prefer to arrange matters between us privately. [*Pause.*] We'll separate and divide them ourselves.

LESTER [*packing up*]: Everything then is in order and accord.

ALICE [*packing up*]: Congratulations, Mr. Ostermeyer. [*Shaking his hand.*]

LESTER [*saluting*]: I salute you, Mrs. Bailey. A lovely agreement.

ALICE: Good afternoon, Dr. Matchett, Mrs. . . . [*correcting herself*] Sybil Matchett. [*Looking out the window.*] Blue skies, white clouds, birds singing. . . . It's a beautiful day for a divorce.

LESTER: An exquisite day for a divorce.

[*Lester and Alice exit. Pause.*]

SIGMUND: And it's over.

SYBIL: All over. [*Interior.*] It was green and white outside and in. Afterwards we made love, of course.

SIGMUND [*interior*]: I'll love you forever, I said. The name of the boat was "*Someday.*"

SYBIL: Sometimes when I'm on a date, I call the man Sigmund by mistake. I forget. Maybe I'll always forget, or never forget. . . . Oh, God, I'm embarrassed. Could you give me a lift to the airport?

SIGMUND: Maybe you never will. When I go to bed at night, I always make sure the pillows are together, even though no one's there. Come on, Sybil. [*Pause.*] To the airport.

The End

PAULA GUNN ALLEN

"Eve the Fox" is from Skins & Bones *(1988) by Paul Gunn Allen (see page 387). The poem retells the encounter of Adam and Eve in the book of* Genesis, *in colloquial language that depicts Eve as "a fox" and Adam as "the hunk / who was twiddling his toes."*

Eve the Fox

Eve the fox swung
her hips appetizingly, she
sauntered over to Adam the hunk
who was twiddling his toes and

devising an elaborate scheme
for renaming the beasts: Adam
was bored, but not Eve for she
knew the joy of swivelhips
and the taste of honey on her lips.
She was serpent wise and snake foolish,
and she knew all the tricks of the trade
that foxy lady, and she used them
to wile away the time: bite into this,
my hunky mate, she said, bending
tantalizingly low so her warm breasts
hung like peaches in the air. You
will know a thing or two when I get
through to you, she said, and gazed
deep with promise into his squinted eyes.
She admired the glisten of sweat and light
on his ropey arms, that hunky man of mine,
she sighed inside and wiggled deliciously
while he bit deep into the white fleshy
fruit she held to his lips. And wham-bam,
the change arose, it rose up in Adam
as it had in Eve and let me tell you
right then they knew all
they ever wanted to know about knowing,
and he discovered the perfect curve of her
breasts, the sweet gentle halfmoon of her belly,
the perfect valentine of her vulva,
the rose that curled within the garden
of her loins, that he would enter like bees,
and she discovered the tender power
of his sweat, the strong center of his
muscled arms, she worshipped the dark hair
that fell over his chest in waves.
And together riding the current of this
altogether new knowing they had found,
they bit and chewed, bit and chewed.

◎ *MAYA ANGELOU*

Maya Angelou was born Marguerite Johnson in 1928 in St. Louis, Missouri. I Know Why the Caged Bird Sings *(1970), a moving and often humorous account of her childhood in segregated Arkansas, was nominated for a National Book Award. Since then Angelou has published five more volumes of autobiography and five collections of poetry, among them* And Still I Rise *(1978);* Shaker, Why Don't You Sing *(1983);* Now Sheeba Sings the Song *(1987); and* I Shall Not Be Moved *(1990). Angelou's career has included singing, acting, screenwriting and songwriting. In 1977, she was nominated for an Emmy for her role in the television production of Alex Haley's* Roots. *She is one of the few women members of the Directors Guild. On January 20, 1993, Angelou read her poem "On the Pulse of the Morning" at President Bill Clinton's inauguration. Angelou holds the Reynolds Chair at Wake Forest University.*

"Known to Eve and Me" is from Maya Angelou's I Shall Not Be Moved. *The poem (compare with Allen's "Eve the Fox") retells an encounter in the Garden of Eden from the point of view of a sensuous black girl who, instead of being horrified by the "guileless" serpent, embraces him. The coiled lines of the poem and the glittering images seduce the reader's attention with their appeal to the senses. Eve's puncture wound becomes the source of her own snake-like power.*

Known to Eve and Me

His tan and golden self,
coiled in a threadbare carapace,
beckoned to my sympathy.
I hoisted him, shoulders above
the crowded plaza, lifting
his cool, slick body toward the altar of
sunlight. He was guileless, and slid into my embrace.
We shared seeded rolls and breakfast on the mountaintop.
Love's warmth and Aton's sun
disc caressed
his skin, and once-dulled scales
became sugared ginger, amber
drops of beryl on the tongue.

His lidless eye slid sideways,
and he rose into my deepest
yearning, bringing
gifts of ready rhythms, and
hourly wound around

my chest,
holding me fast in taut
security.
Then, glistening like
diamonds strewn
upon a black girl's belly,
he left me. And nothing
remains. Beneath my left
breast, two perfect identical punctures,
through which I claim
the air I breathe and
the slithering sound of my own skin
moving in the dark.

◎ *OLGA BROUMAS*

Olga Broumas was born in 1949 in Greece and was educated at the University of Pennsylvania and the University of Oregon. Broumas has worked as a writer as well as a professor of English and a poet-in-residence. She has received a Guggenheim fellowship, and she is a founder and associate faculty member of Freehand, a learning community of women writers and photographers in Provincetown, Massachusetts. Broumas won the Yale Series of Younger Poets competition for her Beginning with O *(1977). Since then she has published five additional books of poetry and translations, most recently* What I Love: Selected Translations of Odysseas Elytis *(1986).*

"Lullaby" is from Broumas's Beginning with O. *Stanley Kunitz, the judge who chose Broumas's book as the winner of the 1977 Yale Series of Younger Poets competition, called the book "as much a political statement as it is an impassioned lyric outburst."*

Lullaby

I see you, centered
along the long
axis of the house, as I come in

to your wide perspective
that endless corridor, the light
drawling forever on the lip of darkness, your long
skin radiant, its stubborn resistance
to summer tan. I see you
signaling like a white flag

in the square of your mother's crocheted
and labyrinth quilt. Brown,

black, amber, white, and that treacherous
red like a border around
the luminous hull
of your body. You leaned

into me like a ship embracing
the waters it was meant to shun, the dangerous
undertow it was meant to float on
and not claim. My love

this love has not been
forbidden. It's one risk: sailing
down through the warm laterals of the heart
to a windless bay. One of our mothers prays for this song

to survive
her own deafened ears, the other
pieces together a second quilt, one that will
cover us, not for shame, nor
decency, but

as the chill
streetlights fluoresce on our light sleep, finally
tucking us in, for warmth.

◎ *TESS GALLAGHER*

"Sea Inside the Sea" is from Moon Crossing Bridge *(1992). Tess Gallagher says, "The poem was possibly written in 1991." In this wonderfully sensual poem the lovers drink in wave after wave of their lovemaking, having gone deep into the "body-ness of the body." The poet is giving herself back to love and to life, after years of grieving for her husband. (For more on Gallagher, see page 144.)*

Sea Inside the Sea

How well he knows he must lift out
the desolate Buddha, unfurl the scroll
raked anciently with its dragon's claw
of waiting. Silk banner embossed

with the myriad invigorations of the blood
pulling the tide toward us
until our bodies don't hoard eternity
but are spun through with a darting vehemence,
until the abundant thing made of us spikes free
of even its ripening, that moan of white fingers at a depth
that strips the gears of the soul.

I lick salt of him from under his eyes,
from the side of the face. Prise open each wave
in its rising, in its mouth-to-breast-to-groin.
A velvet motionlessness where the halo
lingers as if between two endless afternoons
in which a round presence, most quiet and
most unquiet, is tended. Because love
has decided and made a place of us.
Has once again asked its boldest question
as an answer.

We are the lucidity of salt, jealous
even of its craving. It follows
its thirst with its neck outstretched
so like the shy deer
who come down from the mountain.
They run their quick tongues
over the wet ribbons of seaweed. But we are so far inside
the body-ness of the body, that the hieroglyphics of their hoofprints
inscribe the many-paired lips of the sea's cave mouth
which, even now, drinks wave onto wave.

We are overspent into awakening like the pinched scent
of aniseed that carries its sex
as a bruising. He lifts himself like an answer
in which love, as it knows not to speak
but is many-chasmed, says, "Ask me. Ask me
anything." Again, his palm passes over
the mute belly, passes and repasses.
Her gold and silver rings in a heap
on the headboard. His naked hand. Hers
more naked. The sea turned back nightlong
by the blackened tide of her hair
across no shore.

◎ *BARBARA L. GREENBERG*

Barbara L. Greenberg was born in 1932 in Boston. She has published a book of stories, Fire Drills *(1982), and her fiction has appeared in* Epoch, Moment, The Yale Review, The Iowa Review, The Ohio Review, *and* Northwest Review. *Greenberg has published two volumes of poetry,* The Spoils of August *(1974) and* The Never-Not Sonnets *(1989). Her poems have appeared in* Quickly Aging Here: Some Poets of the 1970's *(1969) and* Rising Tide: 20th Century American Women Poets *(1973). Greenberg also writes plays. She divides her time between Newton and Gloucester, Massachusetts.*

"When I Think of My Happy Ending" is the last poem in Greenberg's book-length sequence of sonnets, The Never-Not Sonnets. *She wrote all these sonnets during the summer of 1988 and refers to them as "colloquial," playing against the sonnet tradition.*

When I Think of My Happy Ending

When I think of my happy ending and who I owe
garlands and citations to, your name is not
on the list. When I conclude by saying, "They know who
they are," you still aren't who I mean. I mean *her*
and her stiletto heel, and what she did for me.
I'm also referring to *him*, the great tattooer.
I mean the way the clergy (God bless them for trying)
opposed my sense of life-on-earth as brute harassment
with their own sense of life-on-earth as godly harassment.
I have in mind the pain I fattened on when you-know-who
went mad, and certain poems, and strong music,
and the raking beauty of nature I glimpsed through a veil—
so when my first love touched me, I was ready for him;
and when you said, "Speak up!" I was ready for you also.

◎ *MARILYN HACKER*

Marilyn Hacker was born in the Bronx in 1942. She has taught creative writing at several universities. Hacker is the author of seven books of poetry, including Presentation Piece *(1974), which was a Lamont Poetry Selection and won a National Book Award. She has also received a Lamda Literary Award from the Gay and Lesbian*

Publishers and Booksellers Association for Going Back to the River *(1992). Hacker was editor of the* Kenyon Review *from 1990 to 1994.*

Hacker's poem "Self" can be found in Going Back to the River. *The volume includes many sensual, lyrical love poems. Although most of her love poems are addressed to others, "Self" focuses on the physical, sexual, and emotional pleasures of self-love, a rebellious act for women in our society.*

Self

I did it
differently:
moistened two
fingers in my mouth,
touched
with curiosity,
desire, what I'd
squeezed spasms from before
to get to sleep.
As I would touch an
other's
fullness, blood-ripe
(I was from dreaming
her pleasure
pleasuring
me), I felt
myself, touched
what she would touch me
to, what I
treasured (unexamined),
and ignored.
Velvety, floriform
animal breathes
body-wet like a parched
snail, water;
still, dry,
slicked to a bearing
rolls in place
rooted
where I learned to love
entering; am entered.

Pleasure connects
those parts, nerves whose duty is delight:
a self-contained utopian
dialogue on the beautiful: quintessentially human.

◎ SHARON OLDS

"First Night" is found in Satan Says *(1980). This poem explores the personal mythology of love, of being sexual, and specifically of being a woman writer married to a psychiatrist in New York. "First Night" expresses a fierce and tender love with a sense of humor. Olds mythologizes the impact of the first sexual experience with the beloved. Personal events are made large— historical, geographical, anthropological — as the poet's metaphors express the importance of her new "blood bond" with her partner.* *(For more on Olds, see page 148.)*

First Night

I lay asleep under you,
still and dark as uninhabited
countryside, my blood slowly
drying between us, the break in my flesh
beginning to heal, open, a border
permanently dissolved.
The inhabitants of my body began to
get up in the dark, pack, and move.

All night, hordes of people
in heavy clothes moved south in me
carrying houses on their backs, sacks of
seed, children by the hand, under
a sky like smoke. Grazing grounds
shifted by hundreds of miles. Certain animals,
suddenly, were nearly extinct,
one or two odd knobby
shapes in opposite parts of the land.
Other forms multiplied,
masses of deep red wings
pouring out of nowhere. Rivers changed course,

the language turned
neatly about
and started to go the other way.
By dawn the migrations were completed. The last
edge of the blood bond dried,
and like a newborn animal about to be imprinted
I opened my eyes and saw your face.

MOLLY PEACOCK

Molly Peacock was born in 1947 in Buffalo, New York. She was educated at the State University of New York at Binghamton and at Johns Hopkins University. Her work has been honored with a Creative Artists Public Service award and an award from the Ingram Merrill Foundation. Recently she has served as president of the Poetry Society of America. Peacock has published three volumes of poetry, most recently Take Heart *(1989).*

"How I Come to You" is from Take Heart. *Peacock is interested in the formal qualities of poetry and has written that "rhyme has become a kind of organizer of my poetic world. Just as recognition of the patterns of my experience helps me to understand my life, so recognition of the patterns of sound helps me to structure my experiences into art."*

How I Come to You

Even a rock
has insides.
Smash one and see
how the shock

reveals the rough
dismantled gut
of a thing once dense.
Making the cut

into yourself,
maybe you hoped
for rock solid through.
That hope I hoped,

too. Dashed
on my rocks was my wish

of what I was. Angry,
dense and mulish,

I smashed myself
and found my heart
a cave, ready to be
lived in. A start,

veined, unmined.
This is how I come to you:
broken,
not what I knew.

◎ *ADRIENNE RICH*

"XIX" is one of a series of twenty-one love poems found in the center of The Dream of a Common Language *(1978). These poems trace the course of a relationship in which the poet has chosen "something new" — to love her partner "with all of her intelligence" (from "Splittings"). Nevertheless, two women loving each other in a world that offers violence instead of support — a world unprepared for them — makes loving on day-to-day basis "heroic." Because she has* chosen *this love, the narrator does not place blame for the failures of the relationship, marked by the end of this series.* *(For more on Rich, see page 217.)*

from *Twenty-One Love Poems*

XIX

Can it be growing colder when I begin
to touch myself again, adhesions pull away?
When slowly the naked face turns from staring backward
and looks into the present,
the eye of winter, city, anger, poverty, and death
and the lips part and say: *I mean to go on living?*
Am I speaking coldly when I tell you in a dream
or in this poem, *There are no miracles?*
(I told you from the first I wanted daily life,
this island of Manhattan was island enough for me.)
If I could let you know —
two women together is a work
nothing in civilization has made simple,

two people together is a work
heroic in its ordinariness,
the slow-picked, halting traverse of a pitch
where the fiercest attention becomes routine
— look at the faces of those who have chosen it.

JUNE JORDAN

June Jordan was born in New York City in 1936 and attended Barnard College. She is a poet, playwright, essayist, and activist with twenty-three books to date, including June Jordan's Blueprint for Poetry for the People *(1995);* Haruko/Love Poems *(1995);* Living Room *(poetry, 1985);* Passion *(poetry, 1980);* On Call *(essays, 1988); and* Technical Difficulties *(essays, 1992). She has received a Rockefeller Grant, the Prix de Rome in Environmental Design, a fellowship from the National Endowment for the Arts, a National Association of Black Journalists Achievement Award, and most recently a Lila Wallace–*Reader's Digest *Writer's Award. Jordan is professor of African American Studies at the University of California at Berkeley.*

"Poem Toward the Bottom Line" is from Jordan's Passion. *As the poet said in a recent interview with Renee Olander: "I'm very much dedicated to intelligent love, and trying to develop connections . . . so that we can move to a good place, here and throughout the world." Jordan's writing class at Berkeley is helping to develop this intelligence: ". . . every person needs to know how to write poetry because that means every person will know what it is to be accurate about what she or he feels or thinks or needs, so that she or he takes command of this common currency, our language" (*AWP Chronicle, *Feb. 1995).*

Poem Toward the Bottom Line

Then this is the truth: That we began here
where no road existed even
as a dream: where staggered scream and grief inside
the howling air where hunched against
the feeling and the sounds of beast we moved
the left and then the right leg: stilted terminals
against infinity against amorphous omnivores
against the frozen vertigo of all
position: there we moved against
the hungering for heat for ease we moved

as now we move against each
other unpredictable around the corner
of this sweet occasion. Or as now the earth
assumes the skeletal that just the snow that just
the body of your trusting me can capture

tenderly enough.

CATHY SONG

"The White Porch" opens the second section of Cathy Song's Picture Bride *(1982). This section, titled "Sunflower," evokes the bold colors of both the flower and of Georgia O'Keeffe's painting. In this sensual love poem, Song quietly and slowly allows the scene to unfold as the narrator waits for her lover. "There is this slow arousal," the narrator confides. As the poem proceeds with its tempting imagery of food and bright colors, it seems that waiting is almost as wonderful as her lover's arrival. (For more on Song, see page 153.)*

The White Porch

I wrap the blue towel
after washing,
around the damp
weight of hair, bulky
as a sleeping cat,
and sit out on the porch.
Still dripping water,
it'll be dry by supper,
by the time the dust
settles off your shoes,
though it's only five
past noon. Think
of the luxury: how to use
the afternoon like the stretch
of lawn spread before me.
There's the laundry,
sun-warm clothes at twilight,
and the mountain of beans

in my lap. Each one,
I'll break and snap
thoughtfully in half.

But there is this slow arousal.
The small buttons
of my cotton blouse
are pulling away from my body.
I feel the strain of threads,
the swollen magnolias
heavy as a flock of birds
in the tree. Already,
the orange sponge cake
is rising in the oven.
I know you'll say it makes
your mouth dry
and I'll watch you
drench your slice of it
in canned peaches
and lick the plate clean.

So much hair, my mother
used to say, grabbing
the thick braided rope
in her hands while we washed
the breakfast dishes, discussing
dresses and pastries.
My mind often elsewhere
as we did the morning chores together.
Sometimes, a few strands
would catch in her gold ring.
I worked hard then,
anticipating the hour
when I would let the rope down
at night, strips of sheets,
knotted and tied,
while she slept in tight blankets.
My hair, freshly washed
like a measure of wealth,
like a bridal veil.
Crouching in the grass,
you would wait for the signal,
for the movement of curtains
before releasing yourself

from the shadow of moths.
Cloth, hair and hands,
smuggling you in.

NANCY WILLARD

"Angels in Winter" is from Willard's book Among Angels *(1995), for which she collaborated with writer Jane Yolen. Beginning with the experience of making snow angels with her son, Willard's speaker then ruminates on snow and angels. She laments, in some sense, the human tendency of trying to hold onto things that vanish, though she remains sympathetic to our plight, how "tame and defenseless" we are as a race.* *(For more on Willard, see page 535.)*

Angels in Winter

Mercy is whiter than laundry,
great baskets of it, piled like snowmen.
In the cellar I fold and sort and watch
through a squint in the dirty window
the plain bright snow.

Unlike the earth, snow is neuter.
Unlike the moon, it stays.
It falls, not from grace, but a silence
which nourishes crystals.
My son catches them on his tongue.

Whatever I try to hold perishes.
My son and I lie down in white pastures
of snow and flap like the last survivors
of a species that couldn't adapt to the air.
Jumping free, we look back at

angels, blurred fossils of majesty and justice
from the time when a ladder of angels
joined the house of the snow
to the houses of those whom it covered
with a dangerous blanket or a healing sleep.

As I lift my body from the angel's,
I remember the mad preacher of Indiana

who chose for the site of his kingdom
the footprint of an angel and named the place
New Harmony. Nothing of it survives.

The angels do not look back
to see how their passing changes the earth,
the way I do, watching the snow,
and the waffles our boots print on its unleavened face,
and the nervous alphabet of the pheasant's feet,

and the five-petaled footprint of the cat,
and the shape of snowshoes, white and expensive as tennis,
and the deep ribbons tied and untied by sleds.
I remember the millions who left the earth;
it holds no trace of them

as it holds of us, tracking through snow,
so tame and defenseless
even the air could kill us.

INTERVIEW

Finding and Gathering and Dreaming: An Interview with Nancy Willard

by Patricia Clark

NANCY WILLARD

The interview with Nancy Willard was conducted by telephone in January 1996. Willard was at home in Poughkeepsie, New York where a recent blizzard had left "drifts up to my shoulders." After a discussion of the weather, she moved on to talk of angels, of collaboration and friendship during book projects, and of her proudest accomplishment — "always the next book."

PC: As a writer who works in many different genres, I'm wondering, what do you call yourself? I mean, besides Nancy? [*laughter*]

NW: I call myself just a writer. I can't really explain why I work in different genres.

PC: And you've done enough writing by now, do you then trust that impulse when it comes? Something occurs to you, and it's poetry?

NW: Oh yes. The work chooses its own form. The model I love is Blake, who didn't separate his painting from his poetry on the page. I like working on projects that bring the arts together.

PC: And do you think we too falsely keep things apart?

NW: I don't know if *falsely* is the right word. There are many different ways of doing things.

PC: Has it created any problems for you, with publishing, for example?

NW: It's hard to say. The audiences for children's books and adult books are so separate. And I was writing for adults long before I wrote and illustrated books for children.

PC: Which was the first genre you started in?

NW: Oh, I started with poetry. And that remains the genre I most enjoy working in.

PC: Are you currently working on things?

NW: [*laughter*] Yes, I'm always working on things.

PC: Even with teaching, and . . . ?

NW: Oh yes.

PC: Are you able to do both?

NW: Yes. You learn to carry the work around in your head and use all the odd scraps of time you can find.

PC: Let me ask you about your essay "The Friendship Tarot," and how you came up with that structure for your essay.

NW: I should say that I'm not a very informed reader of the Tarot deck, but I certainly know some of the images. What interested me about the Tarot was the method of using images to convey a nexus of ideas. When I was asked to write a piece on friendship for that particular book, I thought, Well, instead of writing about the friendship, what if I simply presented the friendship the way a single Tarot image presents its subject, making it as concrete as possible. And if I presented it, I would do it in scenes. That would make it as concrete as possible.

When you write about friendship in this way, you don't necessarily pick the most obvious events. You record some fragment of conversation or some flick of the eye that carries more meaning than a generalized chronicle of the friendship.

It's not such an odd idea, really, because dreams follow that structure. A dream unwinds in a series of scenes with no editorial overvoice telling you what it means. Even if you can't explain your dream, you can usually narrate it. You can tell what happened.

PC: And the other thing is, too, that with the structure of the images, or the Tarot cards, the reader can, in a sense the cards can, create different kinds of synapses for different people, then, I suppose?
NW: Sure. The narrative changes when you change the order of the images. You're free from the chronology of events. But there's still a structure.
PC: So more psychologically true, in a way?
NW: I suppose, since it has to try to be psychologically true when you use that method.
PC: Do you feel that friendship has been important to your work?
NW: I don't know. You know, there are so many different kinds of friendship. I mean, you meet people in so many different ways. Ilse, I've known her for a very long time.

The book that I wrote with Jane Yolen, *Among Angels*, started out as a correspondence in poetry. I wanted to try an exchange of poems with another writer on a given topic. I picked angels because angels have always interested me. Then I thought, with whom can I have this exchange? Knowing Jane's work — she's a wonderful folklorist and fiction writer — and having met her several times, I suggested we try it. And we got to know each other through our work. When we finally came together last fall to do some readings from the book, we felt we'd met in a former life. We were already old friends. When you meet someone through her work, you skip the small talk. You meet at a much deeper level.
PC: So you would recommend that as a way of knowing someone?
NW: Well, it's an odd way to meet someone. But it was a very interesting thing to try.
PC: And then you and Jane did some readings together?
NW: Yes, we tried to read them the way we wrote them, back and forth, as if we were talking to each other. We took a completely open approach to our subject.
PC: But you were trying to address a particular subject?
NW: Yes. I would address whatever her poem suggested, and then I'd send her my poem. She'd find something in mine — an image, maybe, or an idea — to start her off on a poem, which she'd send to me. Back and forth. We asked nothing about each other's religious backgrounds. I didn't know she was Jewish, and I don't know if she realized I was Christian. When I wrote about the Christian mystic Jacob Boehme, she wrote about the Old Testament Jacob. Though we found ourselves playing off the two points of view, we never planned it. We just let things happen. I think we both knew when the book was finished.
PC: Now where did this idea come from?
NW: I got it from reading a wonderful book by Marvin Bell and William Stafford, *Segues*. It's a far-ranging correspondence in poems which they started exchanging after they returned from the Midnight Sun Writers' Conference in Fairbanks. I thought it would be so interesting to focus on one subject, like a meditation, and I've sometimes suggested to students who are struggling with

their own writing to keep a focused journal. For example, I kept a journal for one year in which I recorded how I spent my time as a writer. The first entries deal with how I worked on particular writing projects, conversations about writing, meetings with editors and such. But very soon I found myself including other things, because everything that happened to me seemed to be part of the writing — the act of sitting down at the blank page is only part of the process. The rest is the finding and gathering and dreaming over material before you ever write a word.

I've asked students to keep a journal which focuses on their own childhoods. And the first entry in many of them reads, "I can't remember anything about my childhood." But when you know you're going to be writing in it several times a week, those memories do come back to you. And the memories that come back are not the ones recorded in snapshots. The look of light on the kitchen floor, the smell outside when the last snow melts — those memories stay close to the senses. I remember the arrangement of the canned goods in the kitchen cupboard. I learned to read by studying those labels with pictures of carrots and peas and the name of each thing clearly written above it. I've noticed that when students keep these kinds of journals, their own writing becomes more concrete. The journal opens doors to parts of themselves they'd forgotten.

PC: Sure, and do you think it helps students not simply to record day-to-day events in their lives?

NW: Yes. It reminds them that we don't just live in the present. In a way, that was part of what I wanted to do when I wrote the angel poems with Jane. The topic freed us.

PC: And did you ever get stuck?

NW: We never did. Because the approach was so open and because we were two very different people working from two different locations, her poems and where she took me in them were always a nice surprise. And I think the same thing happened to her.

PC: And you were on for the ride.

NW: Yes, it was wonderful!

PC: Were you trying anything particular in terms of prosody or form?

NW: No. I guess we used the forms each of us felt comfortable with. We only included a couple in meter and rhyme, and those were mine. One of them was a Christmas carol, since all the carols I know are in meter and rhyme. Jane wrote hers in free verse. And then we went on to other things.

PC: I was re-reading your poetry last night in your children's books — *Pish-Posh, The Sorcercer's Apprentice*, and *William Blake's Inn* — and I loved what you do there with meter and rhyme.

NW: Well, meter and rhyme is easier for children to remember than free verse. And children love to hear and say poems out loud. If the poems of Mother Goose had been composed in free verse, I fear they would never have survived.

PC: Wasn't it Theodore Roethke who talked a lot about learning rhythm and rhyme from nursery rhymes?

NW: Oh, yes, he has a wonderful essay called "Some Remarks on Rhythm" in which he analyzes the rhythm in several Mother Goose rhymes and goes on to how Auden uses those same rhythms in his own poetry. It was Auden who said that some books are only for adults because they presuppose adult experience, but there is no good children's book that is only for children. He was speaking of Lewis Carroll. When you write a book for children, you are writing for the child in everybody.

PC: What books do you feel were especially important to your development as a writer?

NW: Two kinds of literature have stayed with me: the fairy tales I read as a child and the poems I memorized when I was in high school — Shakespeare's songs and lots of Emily Dickinson. And of course, *Songs of Innocence* and *Songs of Experience.*

PC: What advice would you have for young writers or for those interested in going into writing as a profession?

NW: What will help a young writer to succeed is the capacity to deal with failure. If you look into the dark corners of the workrooms of many writers, you will find a great many manuscripts either rejected by editors or by the writer herself. I don't throw my failures away, because I find myself going back to those manuscripts to steal an image or a bit of dialogue to use in a story or poem that is not a failure.

PC: Which of your books are you proudest of?

NW: The answer is always the same: my next one.

PC: What are your upcoming projects?

NW: Well, three books are supposed to come this fall: a new book of poems, a picture book called the *Good Night Blessing Book* I wrote and illustrated for children, and a nonfiction book, *Cracked Corn and Snow Ice Cream,* which uses a lot of oral history I collected from my own family.

Spirit and Song

Spirit and Song

◎ ◎ ◎

THOUGH *SPIRIT* IS DIFFICULT TO DEFINE, expressions of spirit pervade writings by women. For some writers, such as May Sarton and Mary Oliver, spirit is an activity of being, a going out of one's self in which one experiences connectedness with nature and with the divine. Access to this heightened state of awareness, this wider sense of life, is for these writers a practice of daily conversation with mystery and possibility. Writing is the meditation that helps them to focus their attention both within and on the gleaming particulars of this world. For others, such as Joyce Carol Thomas and Adrienne Marcus, the sacred is found in sanctified places, such as the church or synagogue. The power of language, of song, of voice, especially of prayer, comes through in these writings by women.

According to some writers, *spirit* can best be experienced in solitude. In solitude the writer can listen for the murmurings or for the thunder of spirit. Whether in solitude or in community, the writers represented here bring to their work a quality of attention that is the opposite of the busyness that one finds in the office or at the mall.

Music and song, the human voice as an instrument of spirit, also pervade writings by women that express our spirituality. Our metaphors for the ineffable are limited — we speak of *going deep within* ourselves, or of being *uplifted* — but music defies boundaries, carrying us beyond ourselves and words. The writings in this section weave together themes of spirit and song, suggesting that music *is* the language of spirit.

"Melodies lifted them up to a higher place and never let them down," Joyce Carol Thomas says of her characters in "Young Reverend Zelma Lee Moses." In Thomas's story the church provides the center for the action. Thomas combines humor and seriousness, narrative and poetry, to convey song's power to make connections with community, with the beloved, and with the sacred. Zelma Lee Moses's youthfulness enables her to grow through her mistakes, and the readers can enjoy learning with her. Adrianne Marcus's "The Paincaller" takes place during the Days of Awe, the ten days in the Jewish calendar that fall between the High Holy Days of Rosh Hashonah and Yom Kippur. Hannah and Rivkah help us to see that spirit at times originates in pain.

In "Singing" by George Ella Lyon, *spirit* means the courage to persist in what is right. Jeanie, the young heroine, defies racial prejudice in her efforts to join an all-white choir, the "Belle Notes." In Sylvia Watanabe's "Talking to the Dead," the main character, Yuri, requires years to grow into the courage of her calling — she is a singer / healer in the oral tradition, restoring the world through the power of her songs. Set in Hawaii, this story takes us back to older, tribal magic, to nature with its powerful spirits.

The nonfiction selections in this chapter reflect both personal and larger-than-personal concerns. Yet the tone of each, mingling quietness and sound, seriousness and awe, unites these writings. Each has the hallmarks of religious as well as aesthetic experience.

May Sarton's excerpt from *Plant Dreaming Deep* meditates on solitude. In this memoir Sarton recorded the personal drama of living alone in her first house, in Nelson, New Hampshire. Sarton readers will recognize the town in which her *Journal of a Solitude* (1973) was also composed, as she continues the habit of meditating upon and composing a woman writer's life each day, alone. Sarton compares this discipline to music.

Paula Gunn Allen's "A New Wrinkle" does not consist of primarily personal meditations, but rather Allen's retelling of Native American myths about Spider Grandmother, the goddess whose dreaming and singing brought forth the four quadrants of the earth. In the oral tradition from which Allen's work originates, language has the power to create worlds.

In Gioia Timpanelli's meditation on the soul, poetry and prose draw close in an incantation summoning a release from stasis. Creativity and spirituality cannot be forced, though writing, like prayer, reminds us that we yearn for "the fertile rain," for birth and growth. The sound of doors being opened and slammed shut is the soul's cue that the sensual music of the natural world is returning.

Ntozake Shange's "boogie woogie landscapes" is a performance piece, a long poem in dramatic form. Many voices sing to Layla, the dreamer at the center of the story. The presence of these spirits — some welcome, some nightmarish — can come through in dreams, defying walls, teaching the dreamer about herself. Spirit is complex, "more than heart" — it is "the consequence of being real."

Poets are guardians of spirit in their rhythms and sounds, which help language to resonate. In "Lullaby," Louise Glück finds holiness in the ordinary, in "summer's deep sweetness filling the open window." Glück's poem is an inner conversation, quiet as breathing, with a difficult God whom she has been wooing through her poetic voice.

The music turns louder, becomes hotter in Joy Harjo's "Healing Animal," where the influence of jazz can be heard and seen in the dynamic lines. An urban poet of Muskogee origin, Harjo still holds to the healing power of word and song. Linda Hogan, who is of Chickasaw origin, sings the power of the drum to help us dream back to "the deepest world," to the time before our birth. Marilyn Kallet's "Passover" begins in narration, with a memory of several generations observing the ritual Passover seder. Music rises at the end of the poem to carry the story over a wider geography than the family table. Marge Piercy's "Wellfleet Sabbath" evokes the newness that the Jewish Sabbath can bring, the sense of renewal waiting in the ordinary, evoked by ritual. In Colette Inez's "Mary at the Cave" the poet receives and participates in her own revisioning of biblical lore — a "touch-vision," where the dancing muse is generous.

In Ellen Bryant Voigt's "Song and Story" a mother sings to her unconscious daughter in a hospital room. Her song has mythic dimensions, going back to Orpheus and ancient rituals of harvest and resurrection. In her singing, the mother longs to strengthen the daughter's heartbeat, to bring her back from the coma. In "The Motion of Songs Rising" by Navajo poet Luci Tapahonso, prayers combined with traditional songs and dances offer another view of spirit in which the singers and the earth are restored to balance.

Elaine Zimmerman's "To Essie Parrish," dedicated to the memory of the Pomo shaman, reflects in the tight, spiraling motion of the poem the ways in which the shaman takes illness into herself and then through ritual dance and song restores balance to both the sick person and to the world.

The interview with Joy Harjo provides insight into the connectedness of all the arts for Harjo. Writing, music, and art are of special importance to her. Harjo talks about her beginning as a writer and also about her band and her hours of practice on the saxophone. In Harjo's work, spirit is the work of integrating a life, drawing together traditional and contemporary arts, poetry, politics, courage, and religious experience.

◎ *JOYCE CAROL THOMAS*

"Young Reverend Zelma Lee Moses" was written expressly for a volume of short stories, A Gathering of Flowers: Stories About Being Young in America *(1990). Joyce Carol Thomas is the editor of that volume as well as a contributor. Other contributors include Maxine Hong Kingston, Al Young, and Ana Castillo. These multicultural stories about growing up in America appeal to young adults and to adults as well.* *(For more on Thomas, see page 285.)*

Young Reverend Zelma Lee Moses

A hoot owl feasted round eyes on the clapboard building dipped in April shadow at the edge of a line of magnolia and redbud trees.

The owl peered through the budding branches until he focused on the kitchen, in which a mother, brown and fluffy as buttermilk biscuits, stood by the muslin-draped window, opening glass jars of yams, okra, tomatoes, spinach, and cabbage and stirred the muted colors in a big, black cast-iron pot. Then she raised the fire until she set the harvest green and red colors of the vegetables bubbling before fitting the heavy lid in place and lowering the flame.

She watched the blaze, listening to the slow fire make the food sing in low lullaby.

When it was time, she ladled the stew onto warmed platters, sliced warm-smelling red-pepper corn bread into generous wedges, and poured golden tea into three fat clay mugs.

"Dinner!" her voice sang.

"Coming, Mama," said tall Zelma, who was leaning over stoking the fire in the wood fireplace. Her shadow echoed an angular face, backlit by the light from the flames.

When she turned around, her striking features showed misty black eyes in a face which by itself was a chiseled beauty mark. Indeed, she gave the phrase "colored woman" its original meaning. She was colored, with skin the sugar brown of maple syrup.

At the kitchen table she sat between her aging parents. Her father, his earthen face an older, darker, lined version of Zelma's, his hair thick as white cotton and just as soft and yielding to Zelma's touch, started the blessing.

"We thank thee for this bountiful meal. . . ."

"May it strengthen us in our comings and goings," Zelma continued.

"Lord, do look down and watch over us for the work that lies ahead," chanted the father and daughter together.

"And bless the hands of the cook who prepared this meal."

"Amen," said the mother.

They ate as the quiet light outside their window began to fall in whispers. Zelma told time by how long the fire in the fireplace at their backs danced. She counted the dusky minutes in how long it took to clear the table, to clean and place the dishes in their appointed places in the cabinet, to scrub the black cast-iron pot until it gleamed black as night.

Then it was the hushing hour, the clock of the trees and the sky and the flying crickets said, "Come, let us go into the house of the Lord." And they started out, hands holding hands, down the red clay dusty road together.

Before long they were joined by Mother Augusta, a pillar of the community and cornerstone of the church.

The eighty-year-old Mother Augusta, who like a seer was frequently visited by psychic dreams, enjoyed a reputation as the wrinkleless wonder because her face was so plump no lines could live there, causing folks to say, "She either a witch or she been touched by God." Today Mother Augusta kept up a goodly pace with her wooden cane. Augusta and her late husband had broken the record for the longest continuous years of service as board members to the church. She was a live oak living on down through the years and keeping up the tradition now that her husband was gone on.

Today as the family walked along, Mother Augusta smiled at Zelma, thinking it was just about wedding time for the young woman. The older Mother Augusta's head flooded with memories of Zelma and how she had always been special, but one memory stood out from the rest. One April memory many years back.

The Bible Band of preschoolers had come marching into the church that Easter looking so pretty, and all the children serious, strict-postured, the girls with black braids laced with ribbons like rainbows. A few with hot-iron curls.

Each of the ten children had stepped forward and given a biblical recitation, a spring poem, and short song. The church house nodded, a collection of heads in a show of approval as one child with pink ribbons sat down.

Another reciter in a little Easter-egg-yellow child's hat stood up and delivered an age-old poem. Finishing, she gave a sigh of relief, curtsied, and took her seat.

Then Zelma, pressed and curled, stepped forward, her maple hands twisting shyly at the sleeves of her lavender-blue and dotty-green organdy dress. In white cotton stockings and ebony patent leather shoes so shiny and carefully walked in no mud scuffed the mirror bright surface, her feet just wouldn't stay still. Zelma couldn't get settled; she nervously listed from one foot to the other.

She started her speech in an expressionless, singsong tone. No color anywhere near it. It was a typical Bible Band young people's performance that the whole church endured, as yet another duty, as yet another means of showering encouragement upon the young.

Zelma recited:

"It's raining, it's raining;
The flowers are delighted;
The thirsty garden greens will grow,
The bubbling brooks will quickly flow;
It's raining, it's raining, a lovely rainy day."

Now instead of curtsying and sitting herself down, Zelma stared suddenly at the crucifix above the sanctuary door.

She stared so hard until every head followed her gaze that had settled on the melancholy light beaming on the crucifix.

Then in a different voice she started to speak.

"And Jesus got up on the cross and He couldn't get down."

Mother Augusta had moved forward in her seat as if to say, "Hear tell!"

And Zelma went on like that, giving her own interpretation of the crucifixion, passion making her voice vibrate.

An usher moved forward to stop her, but Mother Augusta waved the usher back.

"Well?" said Mother Augusta.

"If He could have got down, He would've," Zelma supposed.

Zelma talked about stubbing her toe, about how much it hurt, and she reported the accident she had of once stepping on a rusty nail.

"If one nail could hurt so bad, how painful the Christ nails piercing Him in His side must have been," Zelma decided.

"And so I think He didn't get down, because you see," she added in a whisper, "something was holding Him there.

"It was something special."

"Yes?" called Mother Augusta just as a deacon moved to herd the child to her pew. Bishop Moses waved the deacon back.

"I know He wanted to get down. Why else would He have said, 'My Lord, my Lord, why hast Thou forsaken me?' "

"Amen," said the first usher.

"But you see," said Zelma, "something was holding my Lord there, something was nailing Him to that old rugged cross, and it wasn't just metal nails."

Now the entire church had gotten into the spirit with young Zelma.

"Wasn't just metal nails," sang the church in response.

"It was nails of compassion."

"Nails of compassion," repeated the church.

"He was nailed with nails of sorrow," Zelma preached.

"Nails of sorrow," the church rang out.

"Nailed for our iniquity," Zelma called.

"Nailed," the church responded.

"He was nailed, he was bruised for our transgression."

Then Zelma let go. "The nail, the nail that wouldn't let Him down, the nail that would give Him no peace, the nail that held Him there was the nail of love."

"Love," shouted the church.

"Jesus," Zelma said, in a lower muted voice, "Jesus got up on the cross and He couldn't get down, and because He couldn't get down, and because He couldn't get down, He saved a world in the name of a nail called Love!"

It was all told in rhythms.

As the church went ecstatic with delight, somebody handed Zelma her guitar.

Another child hit the tambourine.

And the music started talking to itself.

"She been called to preach," announced Mother Augusta.

Bishop Moses, scratching his getting-on-in-years head, was as thunderstruck as the other members of the congregation. He flitted from one to the other as they stood outside in the church yard to gossip and to appraise the service.

One of the elder deacons opened his mouth to object, starting to say something backward, something about the Bible saying fellowship meant fellows not women, but the eldest sister on the usher board proclaimed, "God stopped by here this morning!"

Who could argue with that?

This evening as Augusta walked long with Zelma's family skirting the honeysuckle-wrapped trees of the Sweet Earth woods, they eagerly approached that same church, now many years later. Two mockingbirds singing and chasing each other in the tulip trees just by the tamed path leading into the church house reminded Mother Augusta that it was almost Easter again.

Spring was lifting her voice through the throats of the brown thrashers and the wood thrushes and the wild calls coming from the woods.

And in the light colors of bird feathers, beauty spread her charm all over the land.

Inside the church a wine-red rug stitched with Cherokee roses led the way down the center aisle around a pot-bellied stove and continued up three steps. Behind the lectern sat three elevated chairs for Bishop Benjamin Moses, Zelma Lee Moses, and any dignitary who might come to visit. Then behind the three chairs perched seats for the choir members who filled them when the singers performed formally and on Sundays.

The church had been there so long that the original white paint on the pew armrests had been worn and polished by generations of the members' hands until in spots the pure unadulturated rosewood peeked through.

The Bishop opened the weeknight service by saying a prayer. All over the building the members stood, knelt, sat, waiting for the rapture.

Soon Testimony Service was over and the congregational singing had been going on for some time before they felt that special wonder when the meeting caught fire. First they felt nothing and then they all felt the spirit at one time.

The soul-thrilling meters, the changing rhythms, the syncopated tambourine beats trembled inside every heart until they were all of one accord.

Stripes of music gathered and fell across the people's minds like lights.

Melodies lifted them up to a higher place and never let them down.

The notes rang out from the same source: the female, powerhouse voice of Zelma Lee Moses. She bounced high on the balls of her feet as she picked the guitar's steely strings, moving them like silk ribbons. The congregation felt the notes tickling from midway in their spines and on down to the last nerve in their toes.

Zelma gave a sweet holler, then lowered her voice to sing so persuasively that the people's shoulders couldn't stay still, just had to move into the electrifying rhythm and get happy.

Zelma gospel-skipped so quick in her deep-blue robe whirling with every step she took, somebody had to unwrap the guitar from around her neck. She was a jubilee all by herself.

And the people sang out her name, her first two names, so musically that they couldn't call one without calling the other: *Zelma Lee.*

Perfect Peace Baptist Church of Sweet Earth, Oklahoma, sat smack-dab in the middle of a meadow near the piney woods. This zigzag board wooden building with the pot-bellied stove in its center served as Zelma Lee Moses's second home.

Here she sang so compellingly that shiny-feathered crows from high in the treetops winged lower, above the red clay earth, roosted on black tupelo tree branches, peeked in the church window and bobbed their heads, flapped their glossy feathers, cawing in time to the quickened-to-perfection, steady beat.

Reverent Zelma Lee Moses closed her eyes and reached for the impossible note made possible by practice and a gift from God. Row after row of worshippers commenced to moaning watching her soul, limited only by her earthly body, full and brimming over, hop off the pulpit. She sang, "Lord, just a little mercy's all I need."

And she didn't need a microphone.

"Look a yonder, just a skipping with the gift and the rhythm of God." Mother Augusta over in the Amen Corner clapped her hands in syncopated time. At home, Sister Moses, Zelma's blood mother, was the woman of the house, but in the sanctuary Mother Augusta, the mother of the church, was in charge.

Zelma began and ended every sermon with the number "Lord, Just a Little Mercy's All I Need."

The sound tambourined and the Sweet Earth sisters swooned and swooned, the ushers waved their prettiest embroidered handkerchiefs under the noses of the overcome, but they couldn't revive the fainting women as long as young Reverend Zelma Lee Moses dipped into her soul and crooned.

> "*Lord, just a little mercy's all I need.*
> *If I have sinned in any way,*
> *Down on my knees I'll stay and pray,*
> *Lord, just a little mercy's all I need.*"

How her silver voice swooped over the words, coloring them a mystery color that did not exist except in the mind which received it, forgot it, then gave it back.

Daniel, a newcomer who'd only been in town for one year, wanted Zelma to pay him some attention; how she had stayed unattached puzzled him. He knew the statuesque Reverend Zelma Lee Moses easily attracted men. On this third visit to church Daniel saw how men flocked like butterflies to Zelma's color-rich flower garden, to the sunbows in her throat every time she opened her mouth to preach or sing. Out flew the apricot hues of hollyhock. The gold of the goldenrod, the blue pearl of Jacob's ladder. Daniel got a little jealous watching Zelma study the fellows, her camera eyes pausing on one young man's skin that rivaled the brown feather colors of a red-tailed hawk. Her admiring gaze directed briefly at the young man made Daniel itch around the collar. He turned neon red inside watching her watching him.

But it was on Daniel that Zelma's camera stopped scanning and focused. She saw his skin flirting with light, his inky hair accepting the brilliance like a thirsty canvas accepts a crown of black beads dabbed by a painter's shimmering brush.

His eyes shone with such a joy-lit intensity of sparkling double black flecked with the silver crescents of the moon that looking into them made her want to die or live forever.

Now Zelma, already so touched with talent that limousined producers from New York came down and waved rock and roll contracts in front of her, wanted to ask Daniel his opinion of the intricate offers.

"What do you think about this here music contract," she asked him one night after service.

"Rock and roll? I don't know. Seems to me you ought to keep singing gospel. But take your time," he advised after studying the papers.

"Time," she said thoughtfully, and when she looked in Daniel's eyes, she knew he was just thinking about what was best for her.

"Think I'll write gospel right next to rock and roll," she said.

"Makes sense to me," said Daniel.

"What you studying to be?" she asked.

"How do you know I'm studying anything?" he teased.

"You're getting lots of books in the mail."

"Oh that! I'm studying to be an electrician or a bishop like your daddy," he said, handing the music recording agreement back to her.

"So that's why you're always carting the Bible and those big mail-order books around?"

"That's the truth," he acknowledged with a grin.

"An electrical bishop."

"An electrician-bishop," said Daniel.

"Uh-hm," said Zelma Lee in her most musical speaking voice.

When she took her time about signing the contracts, the producers resorted to recording her mellifluous gospel voice to see if they could find someone else to match it who wouldn't study too long over the words in their contracts. But they never could.

Nobody else had that red clay memory in her throat, fat gold floating in the colored notes.

So they returned to try again and again until the young singer, after understanding as best she could all the small print and inserting the part about gospel, took pen in hand and signed the document.

That night her voice rivered out melodies so clear that when the music company visitors from the outside world heard the rhythms rinsed in some heavenly rain, they either thought of art or something dangerous they could not name.

Since the producers were coming with music on their minds, they only thought of songs and never perceived the threat.

The producers seemed so out of place in that place that welcomed everybody, common and uncommon, that they sometimes giggled suddenly without warning and thought that instead of stained glass they saw singing crows dressed in polka dot hats looking in the windows.

When they packed up their recording gear and stood on the outside of the church by the side of the road where the wild irises opened their blue mouths, Mother Augusta, leaning on her cane, bent an ear to the limousine and commented, "Say, good sirs, that motor's running so soft on this long machine you can hear the flowers whisper. Umph, umph, umph!"

"What?"

The music merchants leaned back in their accordion cars and waved the chauffeur forward. They eased on down the road shaking their heads, couldn't figure out what she was talking about.

One said to the other, "Whispering flowers? Another one of those old Oklahoma fogeyisms."

"No doubt," agreed his partner, hugging the hard-earned contract to his breast.

Reverend Zelma Lee Moses only sang so the people could rejoice.

"A whole lot of people will rejoice when you sign this contract," the producer had said.

"Will?" said Zelma.

"Of course I'll be one of them." The record company man smiled as he extended the pen.

And more people did rejoice about a year after she'd signed the contract.

The echo of colors flew across the airwaves. The song "A Little More Mercy" made women listening to the radio as they pressed clothes still their irons in the middle of rough, dried collars, watching the steam weave through the melody.

Daniel, in his pine-thick backyard chopping wood, his head awash in the sound, wondered at the miracle of vinyl, catching a voice like that and giving it back so faithfully, reached inside the open kitchen window and turned up the homemade radio he had assembled with his own hands. The sound flowed out to him even more distinctly. He raised the ax, chopping more rhythmically, clef signs scoring the wood.

More and more people rejoiced.

Both Zelma's mothers, Augusta and her natural mother, ended up with limousines, if they wanted them, turning the dials to their favorite gospel stations, which always played their favorite artist to the additional accompaniment of limousine tires dancing down the road.

Zelma only sang so the people could rejoice.

And therein lay the danger. Preachers who had that kind of gift had to be around folks who loved them, for the devil stayed busy trying to stick the old pitchfork in. Zelma kept herself too wrapped up with her gift to notice the devil's works; those around her had to be aware, wary, and protective.

She preached one Sunday 'til her voice rang hoarse with power and her guitar hit a note so high it rang heaven's doorbell. And all up and down the rows, women stood up, their tambourines trembling like rhinestones.

Palm Sunday, the Sunday when visiting congregations from as far away as New Orleans, Louisiana, arrived with their clothes speckled with the Texas dust they passed through to get to Sweet Earth, Oklahoma, and the new gospel recording star; the visiting Louisiana choir, hot from their journey, crowded the choir stands to overflowing and mopped sweat from their curious brows.

Palm Sunday in Sweet Earth at Perfect Peace Baptist Church, the deacons with trembling hands, babies sucking blisters on their thumbs, folks so lame they had to wheel themselves in wheelchairs, eyeglassed teachers, and farmers with weed cuts persisting around their scrubbed nails, all stepped out, in shined shoes, pressed suits, spring dresses, and assorted hats, coming to hear the female preacher perform on Palm Sunday, and she didn't disappoint them; she preached until her robe stuck to her sculptured body, wringing wet. She preached until dear Daniel, in an evergreen shirt of cotton and linen, Daniel so handsome she could squeeze the proud muscles straining against his shirt sleeves, until Daniel who had been tarrying for a year on the altar, dropped his tambourine and fell out in the sanctuary overcome by the holy spirit.

A cloud of "Hallelujah's" flew up like joy birds from the congregation when Daniel got religion. Still the Sweet Earth saints in front of Zelma with their mouths stretched open on the last syllable of Hallelujah, had not *shouted*, had not danced in the spirit.

Only one mover shook loose in the whole flock of them. And that was dimpled Daniel, an earth angel dressed in light and leaf green and smelling of musky sweet spring herbs, stepping all up and down and inside the gospel beat, a human drum.

It was just about time for Zelma to wind up the sermon and finish with the song "Lord, Just a Little Mercy's All I Need."

And she felt as if she hadn't done her job at all if she couldn't get ten sisters and several deacons moved from their sanctified seats.

The visiting choir voices behind her had sunk and their volume diminished. She was used to more call and response and certainly much more shouting.

"Why's this church so cold?" she asked.

Stopped in the middle of her sermon and asked it.

What she could not see behind her were the visiting choir members being carried off the stage one by one. The entire soprano section of the New Orleans New Baptist Church Youth Choir had danced until they fainted, until only one or two straggly alto voices were left.

The Sweet Earth congregation gazed so amazed at the rapture and the different shouting styles of the Louisiana choir that they settled back and, instead of joining in the commotion, sat transfixed on their chairs like they were in a downtown theater watching a big city show on tour.

Nobody told Zelma she had preached so hard that she had set a record for the number of folks falling out in one sermon.

She wasn't aware of the record she'd just broken because she couldn't see the Louisiana choir behind her, she only saw dear Daniel in a golden trance, speaking in tongues, Daniel who made her feel like an angel every time she beheld his face.

When she pronounced Daniel "saved" and accepted him into the church, she made a silent promise, looking into Daniel's deep dark gaze, finding her passion in the curve of his molasses-colored lips.

Before the week-long revival was over Daniel would be proud of her.

And then it came to her, not from God but from the soft place in the center of her soul-filled passion.

She would do what nobody else had done.

Come Sunday, the crowning day of the revival, young Reverend Zelma Lee Moses would fly.

"On Easter Sunday," she announced, talking to the Church but looking Daniel in the eyes, "on the last day of the revival, on the day Christ came forth from the tomb, Church, it's been given me to fly."

Their opened mouths opened even wider.

The New Orleans New Baptist Youth Choir, scheduled to be in concert in Louisiana on Easter Sunday, took a vote and sent back word that their Oklahoma stay would be extended and that the Sunday School Choir would have to sing two extra numbers instead to make up for their absence.

Since the Reverend Zelma Lee Moses's voice had moved over them like a mighty wind, knocking them from their perches in the choir stand and rendering them senseless from the mighty impact of her spirit, they could not leave, even if they wanted to.

"Young Reverend Zelma Lee Moses's gonna fly come Sunday evening," the ecstatic choir director chanted over the Oklahoma-to-Louisiana telephone wires.

That very night, beneath her flower garden patched quilt, Mother Augusta dreamed. First she saw Zelma Lee inside the church, making the announcement about flying, then she saw a red-dressed she-devil down in her hell home listening to Zelma's promise to fly on Sunday. Slack-jawed, the devil looked up at the church and the people being moved like feathers and got jealous.

"Flying on Sunday? Zelma Lee's gonna fly!" The next day these two phrases lit up the telephone wires in Sweet Earth.

The funny thing about all of this, of course, was that passion was playing hide-and-seek.

Daniel wanted Zelma as much as Zelma wanted him, but she did not know this.

"I want this Zelma," Daniel whispered to himself in the still hours of the night when the lightning bugs flew like earth stars outside his window. It was then he spoke, forgetting his Sweet Earth enunciation, in the lyrical thick accent of the swamp place from which he came.

As experienced with women as Daniel was he had never seen anybody like Zelma, and so he studied her carefully; he slowly wondered how to approach her. He didn't want to make even one false move.

Just seeing her was sometimes enough to take his breath away. Zelma had already stolen his heart when he saw her sitting in the pulpit between the visiting evangelist and Bishop Moses that first Sunday he visited Perfect Peace.

Because the visiting evangelist preached, Zelma was not required to speak or sing. It was her presence alone that had attracted him. He didn't even know she could talk, let alone sing. Even quiet she was a sight.

Hearing her sing on his second Sunday visit brought him to his knees. Folks thought he had fallen down to pray.

Eventually he did kneel to pray all the subsequent Sundays, but his belly still quivered like Jell-O even now remembering what the woman did to his mind.

And Zelma had never had so much as one boyfriend before. Since she was a preacher's daughter, she was expected, when it came to passion, to wait 'til her appointed time. Music had been her passion; music had been enough.

Then came Daniel. When she looked at Daniel, her heart opened on a door to a God she had not known was even there.

Daniel she wanted to impress even though he was already smitten.

Anything she did beyond being who she already was was needless, was superfluous, but young Zelma didn't know this.

As Mother Augusta might have said, "Humph. The devil found work."

The first thing Zelma did wrong was she built a short platform out of the wrong wood and didn't ask the deacons of the church to help her out.

"Didn't ask nobody nothing," complained Deacon Jones, he was so mad his trembling bottom lip hung down almost to his knees. "Got to drive a nail in at the right angle or it won't hold!"

Second thing Zelma did wrong was she went downtown to some unsanctified, whiskey-drinking folks and had them sew some wings onto her robe;

looking like vultures roosting, they sewed crooked, leaving tobacco smoke lingering in the cloth.

"You don't tell sinning people nothing sacred," Mother Augusta clucked in a chastising voice to whoever's ears were free to listen.

"Sinning people! They nature is such that they misunderstand the mysteries.

"If they see trumpets on your head, they refer to them as horns.

"Now and then you run across an exception, but half the time they don't know *what* they looking at," said Mother Augusta.

And too, the seasoned women in the church primped their mouths and got offended, because for as long as they could remember they had personally sewn the sacred robe with the smoke blue thread that had been blessed and sanctified in a secret ritual that nobody discussed, lest a raven run away with their tongue.

"Who knows what them drunk people put in them wings?"

Mother Augusta, the human *Jet* and *Ebony* combined, kept a running oral column going among the older people all the revival days approaching Easter Sunday.

In the meantime Mother Augusta wanted to have words with the young preacher, but the members of the New Orleans New Baptist Youth Choir kept Zelma so occupied the female preacher didn't even have time for her own Sweet Earth congregation.

Even her own father, the retired Bishop Benjamin Moses, couldn't get a word in edgewise. Between counseling the New Orleans young folk, Zelma studied the Bible in the day and slept in the church house at night after falling out exhausted from continuous prayer. In the wee hours of the morning she slipped home, where her mother had prepared steaming hot bathwater and laid out fresh clothes. She refused her mother's platters of peppergrass greens, stewed turkey wings and Sunday rice, including her favorite dewberry biscuits. She was fasting and only took water.

But the community fed the Louisiana visitors. The gray-haired, white-capped mothers of the church, mothers of the copper kettles and porcelain pans, kept their kitchens bustling with younger Sweet Earth women. They instructed these sisters of the skillet in the fine art of baking savory chicken-and-dressing and flaky-crusted peach cobblers.

"Put a little more sage in that corn bread.

"Make that dumpling plumper than that," Mother Augusta ordered, throwing out to the birds a pan of dough that didn't pass her inspection.

She personally turned over each peach, seeing with her farsighted eyes what stronger, younger eyes often missed.

The young Louisiana people stood around, underfoot, mesmerized by Zelma, but Mother Augusta saw what they couldn't see and what Zelma's mother's eyes wouldn't see.

She prayed, Mother Augusta did.

Zelma prayed, but her love for Daniel had her all puffed up and half-drunk with passion.

Come Easter Sunday she would fly, then after church she would offer Daniel her hand, and if he held it much longer than friendly, they would be companions.

Every night she preached and promised to fly on Sunday.

Every night the crowd got thicker.

By Sunday night the standing-room-only audience pushed and elbowed each other in competition with the cawing crows for a low, window-level place on the tupelo branches above the clay by the window.

Oh, the crowd and the crows!

The church house sagged, packed to the rafters. And Mother Augusta ordered the carpenter to check the floor planks because they might not be able to take the whipping she knew Zelma was going to give them once she got started stomping the floor and making the Bible holler.

"Tighten that board over yonder," she ordered.

Another sound that added to the clamor was the hum of more buses arriving from New Orleans. Some members back home in the Louisiana church were so intrigued by the choir's decision to remain in Sweet Earth that they boarded yet another bus and struck out for northeast Oklahoma to see what the excitement was all about, driving on through the sleepless night so they could reach Perfect Peace in time for Sunday service and the promised night of miracles.

The New Orleans contingency was so glad to have made it in time, they entered the church swaying down the aisle, fingers circling circles in the air, uncrossed feet whipping up the holy dance.

As the evening lengthened, something softened in the air. Maybe it was the effect of the full moon.

The Reverend Zelma Lee Moses preached about wings that Sunday night.

The soft shadows cast by the full moon looked like veils hanging over the sanctuary.

She took her text from Psalms.

"Read, Brother Daniel!"

Daniel opened his Bible and quoted, "Keep me as the apple of thy eye, hide me under the shadow of thy wings.

"And He shall cover thee with his feathers, and under his wings shalt thou trust: his truth shall be thy shield and buckler."

"Read!"

Daniel found the next Psalm and continued, "Be merciful unto me, O God, be merciful unto me: for my soul trusteth in thee: yea, in the shadow of thy wings will I make my refuge. . . ."

"Read!"

". . . Who layeth the beams of his chambers in the waters; who maketh the clouds his chariot: who walketh upon the wings of the wind."

Now the great flying moment the Sweet Earth people had been anticipating for a whole week arrived. The spectacle that the New Orleans visitors awaited was here at last.

As she approached the platform, the young Zelma Lee Moses began to sing the closing number, "Lord, just a little mercy's all I need."

One sister let out a long, low holler. Transfigured, a ghost took over her throat, and it was like a special spirit had flown in through the open church window; like the miracle of the cross, Christ ascending into heaven would be repeated in another way.

It was too crowded for the people to cut loose. They swayed backward, swooned; and the crush of their numbers held each member up.

Now Zelma Lee Moses approached the foot of the launching platform, the platform built without consulting the deacons.

She mounted it and spread the arms of her robe, revealing the drunk-people-made wings.

And the congregation hushed.

Neither crowd nor crows flapped.

Young Zelma Lee Moses leaped!

But instead of being taken by a mighty wind into the rafters above the gaping crowd, she plopped, sprawled, spread out on the oak floor at the feet of the frowning deacons, under the scrutinizing gaze of Mother Augusta, dragging her wings in the sawdust.

"The hem's crooked. And the thread's red wrong." Mother Augusta pointed, almost choking.

"Caw!" sang a crow.

Zelma scrambled back up, sure that the Lord had not forsaken her.

Maybe all she needed was a little speed to prime her wings: Recalling the way kites had to be hoisted, remembering her long adolescent legs running down the weed fields fast and far enough before the kite yielded to the wind and took off, she opened her hands and spread her wings.

And with her long arms out as far as she could fling them, she ran, up and down the aisles, her arms moving up and down, her hands making circles. Up and down the aisles.

Up. Down.

Fast, faster.

Up. Down.

Fast. Faster.

She ran past her future sweetheart-to-be and Daniel saw that she could not fly.

And she could not fly.

Finally her mother said, "Daughter?"

And the people got mad.

"Limp-winged!" somebody said in an un-Christian voice.

They chased her on out of the church house. Out across the weed field like a carnival of people chasing a getting-away kite. They ran her under the full moon, under the crows shadowing and cawing above them and on into the woods. She disappeared right through a grove of white oak and yellow pines. The last thing Daniel saw was Zelma's left foot, looking like a wing, as she slipped farther into the piney woods.

The people stopped right at the lush wildness, which was a curtain of green forest pulled like a secret against the place where unknown lakes and streams flowed and where wild foxes and all sorts of untamed creatures roamed.

Daniel was the only one who could have followed her there into the wildness, for he knew wild places like the back of his hand. But the look Zelma had shot him had said No.

And then he remembered that the piney woods was a natural bird refuge. There also doves flew in the thicket, marsh hens strutted proud, and quail called across the muddy and winding Sweet Earth River. He saw Zelma trembling there among the white and golden lilies and the singing crows. And Daniel knew this red earth of willow trees, dogwoods, and redbuds could hypnotize a person like Zelma who had wings in her feet, until it would be difficult for her to leave its allure.

As the church people ended their chase, he also stopped. It seemed as if she had been gone for weeks already. But instead of following her, he did the best thing: He turned back with the others.

Mother Augusta now raised her trembling hand and directed the choir to sing Zelma's favorite number, "Lord, Just a Little Mercy's All I Need," which they began singing softly, and she conducted the song so that it slowed down to a soothing pace. Finally the Louisiana choir dispersed, gathered their belongings, got on board and continued their sweet, wafting music on the midnight bus as they started out for home and Louisiana.

"She'll be back," Mother Augusta promised Daniel, who was sitting by the altar, head sadly bowed, looking long-faced, sifting the sawdust through his fingers, sawdust Zelma Lee Moses made rise by pounding the oak into powder while doing one of her gospel-skipping holy dances.

"She'll be back," Mother Augusta repeated in a knowing voice, then added as she took apart the launching platform, "This church is full of God's grace and mercy. Zelma's seen to that." She was remembering Zelma's invisible flight of the soul every time she looked at Daniel.

"When?" asked Daniel in that deep baritone voice.

"In three days," Mother Augusta answered, mumbling something about God making humans just a little bit lower than the angels.

"Being a little spryer than a timeworn woman, she didn't know she couldn't fly," sighed Mother Augusta. "Yet we hear her flying every Sunday morning on the radio."

"Well then why did the people come if they knew she couldn't fly?" asked Daniel, forgetting the miracle of the sawdust in his hand and the clef notes in the wood he chopped that radio afternoon when Zelma's first record came over the airwaves.

"Listen," said Mother Augusta.

"I'm listening."

"They came for the same reason they got mad," answered Mother Augusta. "They didn't want to miss it just in case she could." The elderly woman paused, then added, "When she realizes she already can fly, she'll be back. Take a lesson from the crow. Why should a bird brag about flying — that jet bird just spreads two easy wings. When Zelma knows that lesson, and she will know it, she'll return, she'll sure enough return."

The next day the women gathered in the morning pews and Mother Augusta offered up a prayer of early thanks.

The deacons joined in, serving the women broomwheat tea, gathering the cloth to help the sisters in the sanctuary sew a new gown fit for a child of God.

Somebody started lining a hymn.

It started out as a low moan.

Then it grew until it was full to bursting.

It exploded and the right word dropped from a mouth, scooted along the floor, lifted its head, flapped in place, flew up and became a note hanging from the light bulb in the rafters of the church.

A moan. A lyric.

And it went on like that, from moan to lyric.

Until the song was fully realized.

Three long days passed with the people sitting, waiting, sewing, singing.

Mother Augusta was lining a hymn and she was lining a hem.

And on the third day, and on the third day they heard the crows gathering around the church.

But they did not open their beaks.

The hymn stopped, circled the light bulb above their heads.

The sound of silence.

The sound of waiting.

The the next sound they heard was the door of the church opening softly.

"Who is it?" Daniel asked.

"Sh!" Mother Augusta whispered.

Nobody turned around except the waiting silence.

The silence stood up and opened its welcome arms.

Zelma.

Zelma Lee.

Zelma Lee Moses.

On the third day Zelma Lee Moses, looking a little down at the heel, stepped through Perfect Peace, paused and put on her long sanctified robe of invisible wings, picked up her guitar, mounted the steps to the pulpit, opened her mouth, and began to sing a crescendo passage in a higher voice with light wings glittering in the fire-singed notes, "Lord, just a little mercy's all I need."

And she looked at Daniel with a look that some folks claimed she got from talking to the devil for three days. But this was not true.

The look was all mixed up with angels, mockingbird flights, burnished butterflies, and tree-skimming kites.

After the service Daniel took her hand and held it longer than friendly.

When Zelma glanced up at the crucifix it seemed to her that Jesus, through a divine transformation, was winking through His pain. Or maybe it was just the effect of the morning sun kindling His expression, beaming only on those muscles of the mouth that brightened the corners of His lips.

As they left the church they walked under the crucifix over the doorway.

As if he too saw the same expression on the Christ, Daniel squeezed Zelma Lee's hand tighter. And she could feel electricity pulse back and forth from his fingers to hers.

And they flew away to a place where wings grew from their ribs.

And they were standing still flying.

◎ SYLVIA WATANABE

Sylvia Watanabe's "Talking to the Dead" was first published in Bamboo Ridge: The Hawaii Writers' Quarterly *in 1989. The story was subsequently chosen by William Abrahams for inclusion in* Prize Stories 1991: The O. Henry Awards. *It is also the title story in Watanabe's first book, about which she has said: "I first began writing because I wanted to record a way of life which I loved and which seemed in danger of dying away." (For more information on Watanabe, see page 363.)*

Talking to the Dead

We spoke of her in whispers as Aunty Talking to the Dead, the half-Hawaiian kahuna lady. But whenever there was a death in the village, she was the first to be sent for — the priest came second. For it was she who understood the wholeness of things — the significance of directions and colors. Prayers to appease the hungry ghosts. Elixirs for grief. Most times, she'd be out on her front porch, already waiting — her boy, Clinton, standing behind with her basket of spells — when the messenger arrived. People said she could smell a death from clear on the other side of the island, even as the dying person breathed his last. And if she fixed her eyes on you and named a day, you were already as good as six feet under.

I went to work as her apprentice when I was eighteen. That was in '48 — the year Clinton graduated from mortician school on the G.I. Bill. It was the talk for weeks — how he returned to open the Paradise Mortuary in the very heart of the village and brought the scientific spirit of free enterprise to the doorstep of the hereafter. I remember the advertisements for the Grand Opening — promising to modernize the funeral trade with Lifelike Artistic Techniques and Stringent Standards of Sanitation. The old woman, who had waited out the war for her son's return, stoically took his defection in stride and began looking for someone else to help out with her business.

At the time, I didn't have many prospects — more schooling didn't interest me, and my mother's attempts at marrying me off inevitably failed when I stood to shake hands with a prospective bridegroom and ended up towering a foot above him. "It's bad enough she has the face of a horse," I heard one of them complain.

My mother dressed me in navy blue, on the theory that dark colors make everything look smaller: "Yuri, sit down," she'd hiss, tugging at my skirt as the decisive moment approached. I'd nod, sip my tea, smile through the introductions and small talk, till the time came for sealing the bargain with handshakes all around. Then, nothing on earth could keep me from getting to my feet. The go-between finally suggested that I consider taking up a trade. "After all, marriage isn't for everyone," she said. My mother said that that was a fact which remained to be proven, but meanwhile, it wouldn't hurt if I took in sewing or learned to cut hair. I made up my mind to apprentice myself to Aunty Talking to the Dead.

The old woman's house was on the hill behind the village, just off the road to Chicken Fight Camp. She lived in an old plantation worker's bungalow with peeling green and white paint and a large, well-tended garden out front — mostly of flowering bushes and strong-smelling herbs.

"Aren't you a big one," a voice behind me said.

I started, then turned. It was the first time I had ever seen the old woman up close.

"Hello, uh, Mrs., Mrs., Dead," I stammered.

She was little — way under five feet — and wrinkled, and everything about her seemed the same color — her skin, her lips, her dress — everything just a slightly different shade of the same brown-grey, except her hair, which was absolutely white, and her tiny eyes, which glinted like metal. For a minute, those eyes looked me up and down.

"Here," she said finally, thrusting an empty rice sack into my hands. "For collecting salt." And she started down the road to the beach.

In the next few months, we walked every inch of the hills and beaches around the village.

"This is *a 'ali'i* to bring sleep — it must be dried in the shade on a hot day." Aunty was always three steps ahead, chanting, while I struggled behind, laden with strips of bark and leafy twigs, my head buzzing with names.

"This is *awa* for every kind of grief, and *uhaloa* with the deep roots — if you are like that, death cannot easily take you." Her voice came from the stones, the trees, and the earth.

"This is where you gather salt to preserve a corpse," I hear her still. "This is where you cut to insert the salt," her words have marked the places on my body, one by one.

That whole first year, not a single day passed when I didn't think of quitting. I tried to figure out a way of moving back home without making it seem like I was admitting anything.

"You know what people are saying, don't you?" my mother said, lifting the lid of the bamboo steamer and setting a tray of freshly-steamed meat buns on the already-crowded table before me. It was one of my few visits home since my apprenticeship — though I'd never been more than a couple of miles away — and she had stayed up the whole night before, cooking. She'd prepared a canned ham with yellow sweet potatoes, wing beans with pork, sweet and sour mustard cabbage, fresh raw yellow-fin, pickled egg plant, and rice with red beans. I had not seen so much food since the night she'd tried to persuade her younger brother, my Uncle Mongoose, not to volunteer for the army. He'd gone anyway, and on the last day of training, just before he was shipped to Italy, he shot himself in the head when he was cleaning his gun. "I always knew that boy would come to no good," was all Mama said when she heard the news.

"What do you mean, you can't eat another bite," she fussed now. "Look at you, nothing but a bag of bones."

I allowed myself to be persuaded to another helping, though I'd lost my appetite.

The truth was, there didn't seem to be much of a future in my apprenticeship. In eleven and a half months, I had memorized most of the minor rituals of mourning and learned to identify a couple of dozen herbs and all their medicinal uses, but I had not seen — much less gotten to practice on — a single honest-to-goodness corpse.

"People live longer these days," Aunty claimed.

But I knew it was because everyone — even from villages across the bay —

had begun taking their business to the Paradise Mortuary. The single event which had established Clinton's monopoly once and for all had been the untimely death of old Mrs. Pomadour, the plantation owner's mother-in-law, who'd choked on a fishbone during a fundraising luncheon of the Famine Relief Society. Clinton had been chosen to be in charge of the funeral. He'd taken to wearing three-piece suits — even during the humid Kona season — as a symbol of his new respectability, and had recently been nominated as a Republican candidate to run for the village council.

"So, what are people saying, Mama," I asked, finally pushing my plate away.

This was the cue she had been waiting for. "They're saying that That Woman has gotten herself a new donkey," she paused dramatically.

I began remembering things about being in my mother's house. The navy blue dresses. The humiliating weekly tea ceremony lessons at the Buddhist Temple.

"Give up this foolishness," she wheedled. "Mrs. Koyama tells me the Barber Shop Lady is looking for help."

"I think I'll stay right where I am," I said.

My mother drew herself up. "Here, have another meat bun," she said, jabbing one through the center with her serving fork and lifting it onto my plate.

A few weeks later, Aunty and I were called just outside the village to perform a laying-out. It was early afternoon when Sheriff Kanoi came by to tell us that the body of Mustard Hayashi, the eldest of the Hayashi boys, had just been pulled from an irrigation ditch by a team of field workers. He had apparently fallen in the night before, stone drunk, on his way home from Hula Rose's Dance Emporium.

I began hurrying around, assembling Aunty's tools and bottles of potions, and checking that everything was in working order, but the old woman didn't turn a hair; she just sat calmly rocking back and forth and puffing on her skinny, long-stemmed pipe.

"Yuri, you stop that rattling around back there!" she snapped, then turned to the Sheriff. "My son Clinton could probably handle this. Why don't you ask him?"

Sheriff Kanoi hesitated. "This looks like a tough case that's going to need some real expertise."

"Mmmm." The old woman stopped rocking. "It's true, it was a bad death," she mused.

"Very bad," the Sheriff agreed.

"The spirit is going to require some talking to."

"Besides, the family asked special for you," he said.

No doubt because they didn't have any other choice, I thought. That morning, I'd run into Chinky Malloy, the assistant mortician at the Paradise, so I happened to know that Clinton was at a morticians' conference in the city and wouldn't be back for several days. But I didn't say a word.

Mustard's remains had been laid out on a green Formica table in the kitchen. It was the only room in the house with a door that faced north. Aunty claimed that you should always choose a north-facing room for a laying-out so the spirit could find its way home to the land of the dead without getting lost.

Mustard's mother was leaning over his corpse, wailing, and her husband stood behind her, looking white-faced, and absently patting her on the back. The tiny kitchen was jammed with sobbing, nose-blowing relatives and neighbors. The air was thick with the smells of grief — perspiration, ladies' cologne, last night's cooking, and the faintest whiff of putrefying flesh. Aunty gripped me by the wrist and pushed her way to the front. The air pressed close — like someone's hot, wet breath on my face. My head reeled, and the room broke apart into dots of color. From far away I head somebody say, "It's Aunty Talking to the Dead."

"Make room, make room," another voice called.

I looked down at Mustard, lying on the table in front of me — his eyes half-open in that swollen, purple face. The smell was much stronger close up, and there were flies everywhere.

"We're going to have to get rid of some of this bloat," Aunty said, thrusting a metal object into my hand.

People were leaving the room.

She went around to the other side of the table. "I'll start here," she said. "You work over there. Do just like I told you."

I nodded. This was the long-awaited moment. My moment. But it was already the beginning of the end. My knees buckled and everything went dark.

Aunty performed the laying-out alone and never mentioned the episode again. But it was the talk of the village for weeks — how Yuri Shimabukuro, assistant to Aunty Talking to the Dead, passed out under the Hayashis' kitchen table and had to be tended by the grief-stricken mother of the dead boy.

My mother took to catching the bus to the plantation store three villages away whenever she needed to stock up on necessaries. "You're my daughter — how could I *not* be on your side?" was the way she put it, but the air buzzed with her unspoken recriminations. And whenever I went into the village, I was aware of the sly laughter behind my back, and Chinky Malloy smirking at me from behind the shutters of the Paradise Mortuary.

"She's giving the business a bad name," Clinton said, carefully removing his jacket and draping it across the back of the rickety wooden chair. He dusted the seat, looked at his hand with distaste before wiping it off on his handkerchief, then drew up the legs of his trousers, and sat.

Aunty picked up her pipe from the smoking tray next to her rocker and filled the tiny brass bowl from a pouch of Bull Durham. "I'm glad you found time to drop by," she said. "You still going out with that skinny white girl?"

"You mean Marsha?" Clinton sounded defensive. "Sure, I see her sometimes. But I didn't come here to talk about that." He glanced over at where I was sitting on the sofa. "You think we could have some privacy?"

Aunty lit her pipe and puffed. "There's nobody here but us. . . . Yuri's my right hand. Couldn't do without her."

"The Hayashis probably have their own opinion about that."

Aunty waved her hand in dismissal. "There's no pleasing some people. Yuri's just young; she'll learn." She reached over and patted me on the knee, then looked him straight in the face. "Like we all did."

Clinton turned red. "Damn it, Mama! You're making yourself a laughingstock!" His voice became soft, persuasive. "Look, you've worked hard all your life, but now, I've got my business — it'll be a while before I'm really on my feet — but you don't have to do this," he gestured around the room. "I'll help you out. You'll see. I'm only thinking of you."

"About the election to village council, you mean!" I burst out.

Aunty was unperturbed. "You considering going into politics, son?"

"Mama, wake up!" Clinton hollered, like he'd wanted to all along. "The old spirits have had it. We're part of progress now, and the world is going to roll right over us and keep on rolling, unless we get out there and grab our share."

His words rained down like stones, shattering the air around us.

For a long time after he left, Aunty sat in her rocking chair next to the window, rocking and smoking, without saying a word, just rocking and smoking, as the afternoon shadows flickered beneath the trees and turned to night.

Then, she began to sing — quietly, at first, but very sure. She sang the naming chants and the healing chants. She sang the stones, and trees, and stars back into their rightful places. Louder and louder she sang — making whole what had been broken.

Everything changed for me after Clinton's visit. I stopped going into the village and began spending all my time with Aunty Talking to the Dead. I followed her everywhere, carried her loads without complaint, memorized remedies and mixed potions. I wanted to know what *she* knew; I wanted to make what had happened at the Hayashis' go away. Not just in other people's minds. Not just because I'd become a laughingstock, like Clinton said. But because I knew that I *had* to redeem myself for that one thing, or my moment — the single instant of glory for which I had lived my entire life — would be snatched beyond my reach forever.

Meanwhile, there were other layings-out. The kitemaker who hung himself. The crippled boy from Chicken Fight Camp. The Vagrant. The Blindman. The Blindman's dog.

"Do like I told you," Aunty would say before each one. Then, "Give it time," when it was done.

But it was like living the same nightmare over and over — just one look at a body and I was done for. For twenty-five years, people in the village joked about my "indisposition." Last year, when my mother died, her funeral was held at the Paradise Mortuary. I stood outside on the cement walk for a long time, but never made it through the door. Little by little, I had given up hope that my moment would ever arrive.

Then, one week ago, Aunty caught a chill after spending all morning out in the rain, gathering *awa* from the garden. The chill developed into a fever, and for the first time since I'd known her, she took to her bed. I nursed her with the remedies she'd taught me — sweat baths; eucalyptus steam; tea made from *ko'oko'olau* — but the fever worsened. Her breathing became labored, and she grew weaker. My few hours of sleep were filled with bad dreams. In desperation, aware of my betrayal, I finally walked to a house up the road and telephoned for an ambulance.

"I'm sorry, Aunty," I kept saying, as the flashing red light swept across the porch. The attendants had her on a stretcher and were carrying her out the front door.

She reached up and grasped my arm, her grip still strong. "You'll do okay, Yuri," the old woman whispered hoarsely, and squeezed. "Clinton used to get so scared, he messed his pants." She chuckled, then began to cough. One of the attendants put an oxygen mask over her face. "Hush," he said. "There'll be plenty of time for talking later."

The day of Aunty's wake, workmen were repaving the front walk and had blocked off the main entrance to the Paradise Mortuary. They had dug up the old concrete tiles and carted them away. They'd left a mound of gravel on the grass, stacked some bags of concrete next to it, and covered them with black tarps. There was an empty wheelbarrow parked on the other side of the gravel mound. The entire front lawn was roped off and a sign put up which said, "Please use the back entrance. We are making improvements in Paradise. The Management."

My stomach was beginning to play tricks, and I was feeling a little dizzy. The old panic was mingled with an uneasiness which had not left me ever since I had decided to call the ambulance. I kept thinking maybe I shouldn't have called it since she had gone and died anyway. Or maybe I should have called it sooner. I almost turned back, but I thought of what Aunty had told me about Clinton and pressed ahead. Numbly, I followed the two women in front of me through the garden along the side of the building, around to the back.

"So, old Aunty Talking to the Dead has finally passed on," one of them, whom I recognized as the Dancing School Teacher, said. She was with Pearlie Mukai, an old classmate of mine from high school. Pearlie had gone years ago to live in the city, but still returned to the village to visit her mother.

I was having difficulty seeing — it was getting dark, and my head was spinning so.

"How old do you suppose she was?" Pearlie asked.

"Gosh, even when we were kids it seemed like she was at least a hundred."

" 'The Undead,' my brother used to call her."

Pearlie laughed. "When we misbehaved," the dancing teacher said, "my mother used to threaten to send us to Aunty Talking to the Dead. She'd be giving us the licking of our lives and hollering, 'This is gonna seem like nothing, then!' "

Aunty had been laid out in one of the rooms along the side of the house. The heavy, wine-colored drapes had been drawn across the windows, and all the wall lamps turned very low, so it was darker in the room than it had been outside.

Pearlie and the Dancing School Teacher moved off into the front row. I headed for the back.

There were about thirty of us at the wake, mostly from the old days — those who had grown up on stories about Aunty, or who remembered her from before the Paradise Mortuary.

People were getting up and filing past the casket. For a moment, I felt faint again, but I remembered about Clinton (how self-assured and prosperous he looked standing at the door, accepting condolences!), and I got into line. The Dancing School Teacher and Pearlie slipped in front of me.

I drew nearer and nearer to the casket. I hugged my sweater close. The room was air conditioned and smelled of floor disinfectant and roses. Soft music came from speakers mounted on the walls.

Now there were just four people ahead. Now three. I looked down on the floor, and I thought I would faint.

Then Pearlie Mukai shrieked, "Her eyes!"

People behind me began to murmur.

"What, whose eyes?" The Dancing School Teacher demanded.

Pearlie pointed to the body in the casket.

The Dancing School Teacher peered down and cried, "My God, they're open!"

My heart turned to ice.

"What?" voices behind me were asking. "What about her eyes?"

"She said they're open," someone said.

"Aunty Talking to the Dead's eyes are open," someone else said.

Now Clinton was hurrying over.

"That's because she's not dead," still another voice put in.

Clinton looked into the coffin, and his face turned white. He turned quickly around again, and waved to his assistants across the room.

"I've heard about cases like this, someone was saying. "It's because she's looking for someone."

"I've heard that too! The old woman is trying to tell us something."

I was the only one there who knew. Aunty was talking to *me*. I clasped my hands together, hard, but they wouldn't stop shaking.

People began leaving the line. Others pressed in, trying to get a better look at the body, but a couple of Clinton's assistants had stationed themselves in front of the coffin, preventing anyone from getting too close. They had shut the lid, and Chinky Malloy was directing people out of the room.

"I'd like to take this opportunity to thank you all for coming here this evening," Clinton was saying. "I hope you will join us at the reception down the hall."

While everyone was eating, I stole back into the parlor and quietly — ever so quietly — went up to the casket, lifted the lid, and looked in.

At first, I thought they had switched bodies on me and exchanged Aunty for some powdered and painted old grandmother, all pink and white, in a pink dress, and clutching a white rose to her chest. But the pennies had fallen from her eyes — and there they were. Open. Aunty's eyes staring up at me.

Then I knew. In that instant, I stopped trembling. This was *it:* My moment had arrived. Aunty Talking to the Dead had come awake to bear me witness.

I walked through the deserted front rooms of the mortuary and out the front door. It was night. I got the wheelbarrow, loaded it with one of the tarps covering the bags of cement, and wheeled it back to the room where Aunty was. It squeaked terribly, and I stopped often to make sure no one had heard me. From the back of the building came the clink of glassware and the buzz of voices. I had to work quickly — people would be leaving soon.

But this was the hardest part. Small as she was, it was very hard to lift her out of the coffin. She was horribly heavy, and unyielding as a bag of cement. It seemed like hours, but I finally got her out and wrapped her in the tarp. I loaded her in the tray of the wheelbarrow — most of her, anyway; there was nothing I could do about her feet sticking out the front end. Then, I wheeled her through the silent rooms of the mortuary, down the front lawn, across the village square, and up the road, home.

Now, in the dark, the old woman is singing.

I have washed her with my own hands and worked the salt into the hollows of her body. I have dressed her in white and laid her in flowers.

Aunty, here are the beads you like to wear. Your favorite cakes. A quilt to keep away the chill. Here is *noni* for the heart and *awa* for every kind of grief.

Down the road a dog howls, and the sound of hammering echoes through the still air. "Looks like a burying tomorrow," the sleepers murmur, turning in their warm beds.

I bind the sandals to her feet and put the torch to the pyre.

The sky turns to light. The smoke climbs. Her ashes scatter, filling the wind.

And she sings, she sings, she sings.

◎ *ADRIANNE MARCUS*

Adrianne Marcus was born in 1935 in Everett, Massachusetts. She grew up in Fayetteville, North Carolina but spent her summers in New England with her grandparents. Marcus was educated at San Francisco State University. She has published four books of poetry and a chapbook, and her short stories have appeared in several magazines. Her fiction includes Carrion House: World of Gifts *(1980), a humor book cowritten with William Dickey and Wayne Johnson, and* Photojournalism: Mark and Leibovitz *(1974). Marcus has won two Borestone Mountain Poetry Awards, a National Endowment for the Arts fellowship, and fellowships from Yaddo and Ossabaw Island. She has worked as a food and travel writer, and she taught at the College of Marin for eleven years.*

Marcus goes to the Virginia Center for the Creative Arts to finish stories and novels. "That's where 'The Paincaller' happened. I had no intention of writing this story, and the only basis in reality was the fact that my back had gone out a year before and that a Russian healer worked on it and got me up and running again. But all the rest is sheer invention. Thank God for invention. The story literally 'did itself' in two days. I made very few changes" (letter to M. Kallet, 1996).

The Paincaller

"It's like having filaments of pain pulled out," Hannah is explaining to her friend Michael, while trying to move the pillow around to the small of her back in one more futile attempt to find a less excruciating phone position. "Like taking threads out of a needle."

"How strange," Michael replies. "Does it hurt when she does it?"

"Not hurt," she says, "more like tingling." Hannah tries to straighten, leans back against the pillow like some foreign potentate. "Hold on, Michael, I have to put the phone down and rearrange my body," she is reassembling herself into a Lego block mechanism. A curve by number, a long lumpy arc along the border of the bed. If only her leg didn't itch.

She remembers, years ago, a doctor telling her that itching was really subliminal pain. Now she understands. She is irritated. Trips canceled. Jobs lost. How can one be a travel consultant if one can't leave the bed?

"Well, if it doesn't get better soon, we can get you a good chiropractor or acupuncturist," Michael is advising. Michael is very Marin County; he likes alternative medicine, or the thought of alternative medicine better than he likes the idea of Kaiser or Blue Cross. The only things Michael consumes are strange amino acid combinations, Smart cocktails, as Michael calls them, along with his pills: Cal-Mag, DHEA, Fundamental Sulfur. Nothing as simple as Vitamin C. Unless it is distilled from pesticide-free rose hips.

Hannah doesn't reply. After all, she has chosen a healer herself. Certainly that qualifies as alternative medicine. The worst part is, her doctor at Kaiser not only understood but announced that as long as Hannah didn't drive to see the healer, it couldn't do any harm. The doctor added that she had known a woman who once worked in their own physical therapy department whose hands, she was sure, could heal. Instead of being validated, Hannah felt as if she were being condescended to. Like a child needing reassurance.

"I'll see what the MRI shows on Tuesday, then go from there," Hannah concludes. She wants to get off the phone, not to hear Michael extol other ways of spending money. Particularly since Hannah hasn't earned any lately.

The conversation completed, Hannah goes back to her book. She reads the same paragraph over and over again before putting the book face down, defying her own rule about bending the spine. Something about discs and spines. She finds it grimly humorous that the hard disk on her computer at the office has just crashed barely two weeks after her back has seemingly done the same thing. Trivial, she thinks. Trivia. Trivet. That's what her leg feels like. A trivet that holds her body up. Only this trivet is operating with one leg lame. She picks up the phone and calls her contact in Tunisia. The trip has to be put off. Endless explanations. He is not kind and understanding. If this tour is delayed, it backs up others. Where will he get another guide? She suggests names. Apologizes again. After all, she tells herself, he has over a month's notice to replace her.

"Do you feel this?"

Hannah lies face down on her stomach and the question that Rivka asks takes a moment to reach her. "It feels warm," Hannah replies.

"Yah," Rivka continues to slap her hands together, "that's where pain is." Hannah cannot see what it is Rivka does, but knows, somehow, that it involves running hands above her back and pulling the pain from her. Hannah feels a current of heat, followed by a cooling. She imagines warmth radiating down her leg, then the cool air descends behind it. Riding the thermals. Soaring.

Rivka is saying something. "I'm sorry, what did you ask me?" Hannah keeps her questions simple, since Rivka speaks little English, having been in this country only 11 months.

"Not good here. Very hot."

"Is heat how you know where the problem is?"

"I feel heat. When better, cool."

Rivka's phrases are hesitant, spoken in a halting cadence as if each word had to be separately weighed, evaluated, but her hands continue moving over Hannah, pulling the pain out. Hannah begins to relax, inhaling the strange odor that comes from the blanket on which she is lying — an odor that smells like a combination of tearoses and musk. Foreign. But soothing.

The hour is up. Rivka helps Hannah rise, then stands in front of her, an attractive woman in her forties, her dark hair haloed out about her thin, white face. Hannah knows Rivka works at a large department store during the day, in the auditing department, and treats her clients, who have managed to find her by word of mouth, in the evening or on her days off. During their four healing sessions, she has gleaned this much.

Hannah is trying to dress as quickly as she can. Her movements are stiff, uncoordinated. Rivka offers her a hand and Hannah supports herself while trying to get her right leg into her slacks. "I'll be glad when I can walk again," trying not to wince as she finally puts her shoe on. "I have only been to Russia once. But with an Intourist guide. They would not let us go anywhere else, but Yalta, Odessa, Sochi, and Leningrad. And one day in Moscow."

"Hurts still?" Rivka seems more concerned with the leg than whether or not Hannah has visited her homeland.

"Not as much. Tell me, how did you know you had this gift?"

"Always. Is from God." Rivka's face is calm, open.

"Did you, I mean, were you able to do this in Russia?" Hannah is trying to imagine more than she has seen of Russia, and all she can think of is vast scenes of snow as in *Doctor Zhivago,* or the onion towers of Moscow. Yalta with its verdant hills. The tea gardens. Somehow Russia is so large it defeats her efforts to place it in neat categories, as she can a smaller country such as Switzerland, canton by canton, or France, province by province, according to food.

"Yah. But I . . . careful. How you say? Secret."

"Secretive." Hannah knows that geography quite well. She has learned to be secretive.

"Only friends. Family." Rivka lets out a small sigh.

"Do you still have family in Russia?" Hannah is curious, trying to imagine how one could just pull roots and leave. Go to a country where even the language is unknown. Make a new life. Heal people who are not friends or family.

"Yah." Rivka cautioned, "Now. You walk slow. Not much on leg." The conversation is terminated. Hannah is led out, helped down the stairs to the car, like a precious dowager.

This is a typical exchange with Rivka since the sessions started two weeks ago. Hannah tries to relax; and suddenly she can feel the pain beginning to subside, as if it is a tide beginning to turn, to recede. Giddily, she thinks, I could get up and walk. Or dance, even. The thought amuses her, but she keeps silent.

Gingerly, she straightens herself in the car, trying to favor her leg, and drives home. Strangely enough, the leg does not hurt as much this evening.

When Hannah gets the results of her MRI, she is relieved. No evident damage to the disk; it showed a clear channel. "No. The problem is with the muscles in the back. You've caused them to spasm, and that's triggered off the sciatic nerve. You've simply got to rest and give it a chance to unspasm; all your moving around doesn't help, and before you ask me . . ." the doctor says in her unsympathetic voice, as if this were something Hannah has done on purpose just to annoy her, "no. You can't fly. You can't go to Brazil or New York or even Fresno. Airplane seats weren't designed for the human body in the first place. They cripple people who don't have back problems, never mind those who have sciatic nerve problems." Having made her speech, the doctor looks at Hannah again and decides to add one final grace note: "And if you lose weight, that will help. Put less strain on that back," she concludes, closing the chart. "I'm going to prescribe another muscle relaxant," she reaches for her pad.

"No thanks. The last one rendered me nearly comatose," Hannah puts her hand up, as if to ward off demons.

"It does keep you off that leg."

"And in a state resembling vegetative indolence. I'll simply stick with what doesn't hurt."

She limps back out to the car, thinking of her back as the ultimate traitor. She hadn't really meant to do wrong, it was just she was in a hurry to get up the stairs, tripped and fell forward, catching herself on her hands and knees. It hadn't even hurt at first. The next day she felt a twinge in her leg; hour by hour the pain grew, got progressively worse. Now she feels like Igor, the limping assistant in an ongoing horror movie, only the movie is hers.

At home, she picks up the phone and dials Rivka. "Can you see me this evening? I seem to need another couple of sessions."

A long pause. Hannah imagines Rivka riffling through her daily diary of pain, and finding out where she can fit an errant leg and back.

"8:30 is o.k.?"

"Fine. I'll be there."

Arriving early, Hannah is able to park the car almost in front of the stucco apartment building; she sees that two of the fake stones that border the entire building have fallen off; underneath the stucco is the color of watery cement. Then she notices the skid marks on the ground. Obviously, someone has backed a car into the wall.

As Rivka opens the door, Hannah catches the scent of tomatoes and cabbage cooking. For an instant she is back in her childhood, in her Grandmother's house, the smell of borscht and the taste of potatoes and sour cream almost palpable. The smell unlocks the house on Blue Hill Avenue in Roxbury and she remembers her bedroom that looked out over the streetcar tracks, over the Shawmut Theater, and how she had thought, as a child, that her radio, brought so carefully 800 miles from home, would still get the same stations as it had in North Carolina. Her Grandfather, in his broken English, patiently explaining how here it will get new stations in Boston.

Rivka is smiling at her. "You are better? Look happy."

"I was just remembering something from long ago. My Grandmother's house."

"She live here in San Francisco?"

"Oh, no. She lived in Boston. Or near Boston. They had a bakery. But your apartment smells like hers used to."

"We just have supper. My husband home late tonight."

Hannah took off her slacks and lay face down on the familiar single bed. "What does he do?"

"Work in petrol station."

"What did he do in Russia?"

"Taught in the conservatory."

"Music?"

"Yah. Concert pianist and teacher."

"Why doesn't he teach here?"

"His English is no good enough yet. And there are no jobs. We play concerts both until we apply to leave. Then, no jobs in Russia either."

"You said you have relatives still there?"

"Yah. Mother. Father. Brother. All physicians."

"Will they come over?"

"No. Now you be quiet and I work."

This time the warmth is further down the leg, and radiates out from the calf to the ankle. As Hannah turns, the pain shoots up her leg. "Oh," she gasps, involuntarily.

"Hurt here?" Rivka touches her lightly.

"Up a bit."

The warmth grows stronger, and is followed by a perceptible chill. The pain begins, once again, to recede by waves.

"Where does the pain go?" Hannah asks, as she begins to dress.

"Back to air. Where it belong."

Were there clusters of pain out there, groups, like clouds, waiting to descend on people? Did pain travel in straight lines until it finds a willing victim?

Over the following week Hannah gathers bits and pieces of Rivka: the new Russian version of the old pogroms was to not allow Jews to hold important jobs. If they showed any political leanings, there would be a sudden departure — like Rivka's brother, who was called for one evening at dinnertime and had been taken away; six years would pass before he would be "repatriated" and allowed to return home, but by then he was a broken man who shuffled to a menial job, no longer even considered a physician.

When Rivka married David, they were considered good enough party members and talented enough to rate a two-room apartment in Moscow, but as the children came, the tides went back and forth, so they did not apply for more room; all lived in the same two-room apartment. Publicly, Rivka and David were praised as top Russian artists. Privately, because they were Jews, they had few friends. It was dangerous to have Jews as friends.

"We come here, we can be real Jews. And this year, we have Good New Year. Go to Shul."

Hannah is almost embarrassed; she has forgotten that next week begins the High Holy Days. So much she takes for granted. Going to the synagogue. Praying when and if she wants to. Even not going if she doesn't want to, or forgetting because she is on the road, working. Like last year.

It is Rosh Hashonah eve. Hannah dresses to go to the synagogue, which is really not the usual synagogue, but has been moved to the Masonic temple out on 19th Avenue to accommodate the twice a year Jews who appear, as she does, during the High Holy Days. This is the conservative temple her friends belong to. The reason she has joined is that she likes the choir, which consists of a great range of old and young members of the congregation, some of whom can sing and others who are patently off-key, but equally sincere. Somehow this makes it human and makes God almost believable to Hannah.

She goes, as she always does, with her friend, Michael, who likes the ceremony and particularly likes the female cantor. "She would have been great in a New Wave band," he whispers to Hannah, as they take their seats, halfway back in the auditorium, behind the expensive seats.

"Shah," she retorts, jabbing him lightly in the ribs.

Hannah remembers services she went to growing up in North Carolina. At first, it was Orthodox, and men sat downstairs, women and children upstairs in the stifling heat of September. Later, it became more conservative, but her own disenchantment grew. In Hebrew school, she learned that she would never be allowed on the Bimah, the altar, because she was female. Not to hold the sacred scrolls, the Torah, not to participate in the prayers. When she asked her father why, he said it was the way it was. That was the way it had always been. Women should stay home and take care of the house. Men prayed. God rewarded both.

Hannah thought it stupid then, and stupid now. But here, at B'nai Emmanuel, the women take an active part. They lead prayers. They open the doors of the ark. They stand on the Bimah. And Hannah responds, as the old melodies swell in her throat, as she remembers what she thinks she has forgotten.

The Rabbi gives a sermon that begins with his trip to Israel, his feeling of wonder and awe. And how he feels at coming home: the same feeling of wonder and awe. That we are free here to worship, to praise God in so many ways. Hannah has no choice except to listen and let her mind drift over the walls of the Masonic Auditorium where the various wise men are rendered. No women, she notices, grace the temple.

As she and Michael are leaving, she sees Rivka. She calls her. Rivka turns and smiles. Rivka has her head covered, in deference to God, the way women in Hannah's childhood wore hats in the synagogue.

They hug. Wish each other a Happy New Year in Hebrew. Introduce one to another. "I didn't know you went here," Hannah starts.

"Most Russian here. Yah. Leg good?"

"Oh, much better. A happy and healthy New Year."

Rivka looks at her, says, "You no travel; leg want to stay home."

"What?" Hannah is puzzled by the remark.

"Body tell you. Stay. What you look for, here. Not there."

A slight twinge answers. The leg is trying to speak.

Rivka stands apart from the crowd that is getting ready to leave, having shaken the Rabbi's hand, having wished one and all a happy and healthy New Year.

These are the Days of Awe, the ten days between Rosh Hashonah and Yom Kippur, when one seeks reconciliation, forgiveness for anyone offended in the previous year. What is it Rivka must atone for? Hannah wonders. She thinks of a family left behind, of always being afraid to say the few words Rivka has just said to her. Incredible courage even to speak. And of herself, running from place to place, trying to assimilate all that is foreign.

Rivka trying to assimilate all that is unforeign.

"I will see you Yom Kippur?" Hannah smiles.

"Yah. I pray. We pray," Rivka includes everyone in her joy.

Yom Kippur.The highest Holy Day. The Day of Atonement, when the names will be written into the Book of Life, who will live the following year and who will die. Hannah knows, logically, that part of her dismisses this as poetic myth, but a deeper part remembers. Something in her comes back, like pain or prayers, sent skyward, dissipating.

Cole Porter, she recalls, used to write music in the "Jewish scale" for Broadway. In a minor key. "My Heart Belongs to Daddy." He knew his audience was Jewish and they would respond to music that just stopped this side of pain. Perhaps it is like childbirth gone through, the pain forgotten, but still there as a residual memory. Just under the surface, ready to be born, other kinds wait.

Out of the fading memories of childhood, growing up in a Southern town, she sees herself making up stories to other children for why she wasn't in school during the High Holy Days. Inventing reasons. Wanting to belong and not belonging. Of her parents, inside the synagogue, praying for an entire day, not leaving, the weather hot and clinging, her father swaying in front of the altar, wearing a white kittle, white for forgiveness, chanting and pleading to God, who may or may not be listening, to God as both ritual and belief.

Does God hear pain easier than joy? Hannah wonders. Is that why the music is so sad? She does and does not believe. If there is a book of life, her name is in small letters. She walks slowly, with Michael, back to her car, back to a world that is racing past her. She smells the past: mothballs and furs that have come out of storage for this night, men in their suits and ties, everyone should look fine in the presence of a God whom no one can see, but to whom they sing.

And it is a song of pain, of repentance, of asking. It is a song she knows as it wells up inside her, unbidden, to flow up into the long, anchored night.

◎ *GEORGE ELLA LYON*

George Ella Lyon was born in 1949 in Harlan, Kentucky. Raised in the southern Appalachians, near all four of her grandparents, she grew up on stories. Educated at Centre College, the University of Arkansas, and Indiana University, she works as a freelance writer and teacher in Lexington, Kentucky. Her books include Catalpa *(poems, 1993);* Come a Tide *(picture book, 1990), and* Borrowed Children *(novel for young readers, 1988). She is the editor of* Common Ground: Contemporary Appalachian Poetry *(1985). Married to musician Steve Lyon, she has two sons.*

Lyon writes, " 'Singing' is from a collection called Choices: Stories for Adult New Readers, *which I wrote while working with literacy students and tutors in Harlan. As a high school freshman in 1963, I was in a group like the Belle Notes when a singer like Jeanie tried out. I finished the story in January, 1989, on the day of George Bush's inauguration" (letter to M. Kallet, 1996).*

Singing (Jeanie)

I'll be 40 in the spring. It's one of those can't-be-true things that's really going to happen. All I have to do is breathe through three more months. Most of the time I don't care. Shoot, I say, time is just a hallway to Heaven. Who cares about the numbers on the doors?

But there are other times when I look at my kids. Clyde is 14, Jessie is 11. I looked at them Sunday getting ready for the Martin Luther King march. I'm 40 years old, I thought. My momma scrubbed floors so I could get an education. I saw Watts burn, I saw King killed. And Malcolm X and Medgar Evers. I saw the Selma march and watched the 1968 convention on TV. I marched to get my hair cut, to eat in a restaurant, to try on clothes in the store. Do Clyde and Jessie have to do it all over again?

Marching is not the hardest part. Going to jail isn't even the hardest, not if you go together. Sometimes the hardest parts are the everyday things, the ones you do alone. They don't get on TV. Let me tell you about one of those.

I was 14, Clyde's age, when they closed the black school in Cardin and sent us all to the white school on the hill. Why didn't they come to our school? "Not big enough," the papers said. "Not a suitable location." Not good enough for white kids, they meant. White kids don't do well with rats in the gym.

Anyway, we had to try to fit where we weren't wanted, where we didn't belong to anything. The ball teams took the boys in right away. They wanted to win. But what were girls supposed to do? I could survive without the pep club, the paper staff. The thing I really missed was the chorus. Cardin High didn't have one. It had a choir for boys and a singing club for girls, the Belle Notes. I told all this to Momma.

"Try out," she said.

"Oh, Momma, I can't do that. They meet in each other's houses."

"So? Ain't their houses good enough for you?"

"Momma —"

"I know what you're thinking." She looked up from the ironing board. "You're thinking they don't want you, and you're probably right. But they ain't heard you sing. Ain't nobody in Cardin, nobody I expect in this whole end of Kentucky, that can open just one mouth and sound like you."

It's no credit to me, but she was telling the truth. My voice was a thing I just came with, like some fancy feature on a car. If I had brushed my hair and dollar bills had fallen out, I couldn't have been more surprised.

"Besides," Momma went on, "somebody's got to do it."

"Do what?"

"Be the first. Like your great-granddaddy."

"I know."

"Don't tell me what you know. You don't know anything about slavery time. None of us does. Nothing but what the old folks told us, and we got to keep that alive. Stories is where we come from. You pay attention. And you try out for that choir. You owe it to your people."

"I just wish . . ."

"What, Jeanie?"

"I don't know."

"You wish it wasn't so hard?"

"Yes."

"You and the rest of Creation." She was wiping sweat from her forehead with a handkerchief. It was one of those years when September was hotter than

August. "But in your voice you got something, Jeanie. God give you something you can *use*."

I signed up.

The tryouts were held in the music director's living room. There was a grand piano, a brand-new couch, 25 white Belle Notes, 12 white hopefuls, and me. Mr. Henley said they would choose 8 new members. We drew numbers to get the order in which we would sing. I was fifth.

The first two girls had voices that sounded like mice. The third was better, but she didn't have the nerve to breathe. The fourth girl, whose braces made spit catch around her mouth, sang "God Bless America" with plenty of feeling and no tune at all. Then it was my turn.

I started out quiet. I didn't shake the vases on the mantel till I got to "From the mountains / to the prairies." I never did really let loose. They had all they needed and more than they deserved. When I finished, the girls just sat there. The one with braces started to clap, but her friends stared her down.

"Very good, Jean," Mr. Henley said. "I believe Brenda Wilcox is next."

Brenda Wilcox sang the song in neat jerks, as if she were a music box. The next girl was good, though. Not a great voice but solid. And on it went. In the end there were two useful voices, two good voices, and me. That left them three choices for favorites, relatives, etc.

When it was done, everybody who tried out had to go to the family room while the Belle Notes voted. It took a long time. I kept looking at the red-plaid rug that was better than any coat my family owned. Then we were called back. We'd have refreshments, Mr. Henley said, while he counted the votes.

His wife brought out Cokes, cookies, and chip-and-dip. I took a few chips but could not swallow a bite. Strangest thing. I had to take what was in my mouth and hide it in a napkin, then put that on the paper plate and hope nobody saw. To keep from thinking about it, I tried to account for the smells in that house. No soap, no sweat, no cooking. What did these people do?

Then Mr. Henley came in with the results. Everybody listened.

The four girls I picked were chosen. Besides them, the Belle Notes took one of the mice, the music box, a girl who had no rhythm whatsoever, and the director's daughter. They did not take me.

"Sorry," everyone said. "Try again next year."

Well, from what I've said about my momma, you know I kept trying. The last year two other black girls tried, too. None of us made it. It was ten years before that choir had a single Black Note. You ever hear piano played only on the white notes? Not much music.

I used to think my activist days didn't start till I got to college. The end of the sixties and all that. But now when anybody asks what I did in the Movement, the first thing I tell them is, "I sang."

◎ *MAY SARTON*

"Silence was the food I was after . . ." is an excerpt from "With Solitude for My Domain," which is taken from Sarton's memoir, Plant Dreaming Deep *(1968). Here Sarton reflects on the "flowing, changing light" as it "plays a constant silent fugue." Terms from painting, music, and writing echo one another in this expression of spirit (this poetical technique of describing one sense in terms of another is called* synaesthesia*). A pioneer in women's literature, Sarton demonstrated in lines such as these that a woman writer living alone is not to be pitied or considered incomplete. On the contrary, the poet finds fulfillment and even ecstacy in her relationship with light and shadow. Only in sustained solitude could the author experience such revelations.* *(For more on Sarton, see page 484.)*

"Silence was the food I was after . . ."

Silence was the food I was after, silence and the country itself — trees, meadows, hills, the open sky. I had wanted air, light, and space, and now I saw that they were exactly what the house had to give. The light here is magic. Even after all these years, it still takes me by surprise, for it changes with every hour of the day and with every season. In those first days it was a perpetual revelation, as sunlight touched a bunch of flowers or a piece of furniture and then moved on. Early in the morning I watched it bring alive the bronzed-gray of the bird's-eye maple of mother's desk in my study and make the flowers in the wreaths suddenly glow. In the afternoon, when I lay down for an hour in the cosy room, I saw it dapple the white mantelpiece and flow in waves across the wall there. And when I went into the kitchen to make tea, there it was again, lying in long dazzling rectangles on the yellow floor. This flowing, changing light plays a constant silent fugue, but in those first days I had still to learn how different the music is as the seasons come and go. In January and February the light as brilliant as snow is reflected on the white walls. In summer the light turns green; the shadows become diffuse. This, my first experience of it, was in October of course, and in October one's eye is pulled outward, to look out and up into fiery bowers of maple leaves or, early in the morning, across frost-silvered meadows.

Inside and out I found myself in a world that kept me in a state of perpetual Mozartian joy. I can still remember the first time I witnessed the windows of the barn shining bright red in the afterglow, and the first time that same afterglow took the low hills all around the village so that, although we were already in darkness, we lay in a luminous purple bowl, and the first time I saw the church steeple spot-lit, dazzling white against dark wind clouds.

All those first days the light said, "Go outdoors!" But it also said, "Stay inside!" And ever since, I have been torn by all the lives I live here and the difficulty of choosing any one at any given moment. Those first days I often chose "inside"; the house had to be rebuilt first as a physical being — that job was now nearly accomplished — but just as important was the intangible structure, the way things chose to happen day by day, or the way I chose to make them happen, as I began, quite consciously, to build the metaphysical frame.

> "What I possessed was all my own,
> Yet not to be possessed at all;
> And not a house or even hearthstone,
> And never any sheltering wall.
>
> There solitude became my task,
> No shelter but a grave demand,
> And I must answer, never ask,
> Taking this bridegroom by the hand."

I knew, from having watched my father hack down the incredible amount of work he accomplished day by day and year by year, how supportive a routine is, how the spirit moves around freely in it as it does in a plain New England church. Routine is not a prison, but the way into freedom from time. The apparently measured time has immeasureable space within it, and in this it resembles music.

◎ *PAULA GUNN ALLEN*

According to Allen's preface to Grandmothers of the Light, *these oral tradition stories span our continent. As in Leslie Marmon Silko's writings, stories are the author's connection to sacred power. In her telling of the story of Spider Grandmother, or Thinking Woman, Allen uses evocative and rhythmical language to create a prose poem appropriate for this Great Goddess, who was motivated to sing awake all creation by her desire to share the beauty and power of her songdream.* *(For more on Allen, see page 387.)*

A New Wrinkle

In *Schat-Chen,* his small book about the Keres (Queres) of Laguna and Acoma, John Gunn writes:

> "Their theory [concerning Thinking Woman] is that reason (personified) is the supreme power, a master mind that has always existed,

which they call Stich-tche-na-ko. This is the feminine form for thought or reason. She had one sister, Shro-tu-na-ko, memory or instinct [nako means woman]. Their belief is that Stich-tche-na-ko is the creator of all, and to her they offer their most devout prayers." Hamilton A. Tyler remarks, in reference to Gunn's comment, "However lofty a conception this goddess may be, it seems that when she has a form it is that of a spider, and in the popular mind she is often equated with Spider Grandmother."

Spider Grandmother, the major deity of the Keres, is weaver and thinker: she thinks, therefore we are. Though she is "supreme" — the thought sounds wrong put in those terms and read from a Western perspective where "supreme" means king or pope or dictator — she is not alone. There isn't an "only," just as there isn't a beginning as such. Surely, the Western mind inquires, something comes before her, something made her. Surely the universe has a beginning, and an end. But like their stories, which go on and on, Indians seem to believe that life itself does not have endings. And, if that is so, then what use is there of beginnings.

I have depicted Spider Grandmother as a Great Goddess whose medicine power is so vast (or whose own being is so complete and focused) that she brings thoughts or ideas into being. In my sense of her, she is akin to Wind. Indeed it is said she is Wind's Grandmother. That is because she makes movement, and from movement all else derives.

She is, like her Maya counterpart Xmucané, a weaver of life. She is also humble and small, a trait highly valued by the modest and unaffected people of Laguna and Acoma, among whom Gunn gathered his stories and sharpened his understanding. I think his stories about her approach the Keres conception because he married my grandmother, Mita Atseye Gunn, who I am sure told him about Old Spider Woman from her woman's perspective. Perhaps what he rendered as "memory or instinct" might better be termed "collective unconscious" despite the perils involved in using that term, because the wisdom contained in the being of her sister Shro-to-nako is the wisdom embedded in the bones and cells of her people. But her intelligence goes beyond human beings; it permeates the land — the mountains and clouds, the rains and lightning, the corn and deer. The reference to Spider Woman's sister Shro-tu-nako reminds us that the Goddess is multiple, that sisterhood extends to the farthest reaches of the universe, and that soroates were viable social systems that thrived for centuries — not merely as a wish or theory, but as factually as the Keres themselves.

Thinking Woman (S'ts'tsi'naku, Tse-che-nako, Sussistinako, Stich-tche-nako, Ts'its'nako) and her cohorts Nau'ts'ity (Nautset, Naotsete, Nautsete) and Ic'sts'ity (Ic'ts'ity, Icsity, Utset, Iyatiku) create and recreate the cosmos giving shape, form, and meaning to all that is. As she thinks, so we are. Spider lives everywhere and presides in Shipap, the underground source of life of the people, where she sits on Iyatiku's shoulder and advises her.

Ooma-oo, long ago. The Spider was in the place where only she was. There was no light or dark, there was no warm wind, no rain or thunder. There was no cold, no ice or snow. There was only the Spider. She was a great wise woman, whose powers are beyond imagining. No medicine person, no conjurer or shaman, no witch or sorcerer, no scientist or inventor can imagine how great her power is. Her power is complete and total. It is pure, and cleaner than the void. It is the power of thought, we say, but not the kind of thought people do all the time. It's like the power of dream, but more pure. Like the spirit of vision, but more clear. It has no shape or movement, because it just is. It is the power that creates all that is, and it is the power of all that is.

In that place where she was alone and complete with her power, she thought about her power, how it sang to her, how she dreamed from it, how she wished to have someone to share the songdream with her. Not because she was lonely, but because the power's song was so complete, she wished for there to be others who could also know it. She knew this was the power's wish just as it was hers. For she and her power were together and of one mind. They were two, but they were the same thing.

So she thought to the power once and knew a rippling, a wrinkling within. Then she knew she was old, and wrinkled, and that the power's first song was a song of great age. The wrinkling became tighter, more spidery, stronger. It became in one place. She named that place Northwest. She knew the wrinkling had folded up on itself, enfolded on itself. She knew much of the universe, the great power, was contained within. Later the earth would be ripples and wrinkles, spidery lines of power folded and enfolded into a tight moving shape, and it would also hold the great power within, like a mother holds new life. Others would also imitate this time: walnuts and acorns, apples and pineapples, cactuses and mountains, even the oceans would be like that. And humans, five-fingered beings, would grow wrinkled in their skin and brains, in honor of this time when she and the power made a song to form new life, new beings.

She was so happy with what she knew, so full of awe at the beauty of the song, that she thought again. And again she knew the rippling, the wrinkling, the running of spidery lines along the edges of the forming pouch of the power's song, the folding and enfolding into a shape that held some of the power of all that is within. She knew that the place of that pouch, that bundle of her thought, her song, was in the Northeast. So humming and singing, she shaped them. Humming and singing, she placed them where they belonged. That was how the directions came into being. How the seasons came to be.

She thought in her power to each of the bundles and continued singing. She sang and sang. She sang the power that was her heart, the movement that is the multiverse and its dancing. The power that is everywhere and that has no name or body, but that is just the power, the mystery. She sang, and the bundles began to move. They began to sing, to echo her song, to join it. They sang their heart's song, that was the same as Spider's heart song, that was the heart song of great mystery, the power that moves. The song seemed to deepen as she heard other hearts singing. The song seemed more free, it seemed stronger. The two who rose up from the bundles with their singing each had a bundle of her own. And in each bundle the life of the universe rested, waiting until it was sung into life.

Spider named each of the beings, one she named Ic'sts'ity and the other she named Nau'ts'ity. They were not human beings, but supernatural beings. They did not have physical bodies because they were much vaster than even a planet, even a star. A star couldn't contain all they were and knew, all they thought.

Spider told each of them that they were to make more beings, so that the song could go on and on, so that she and the power could share the beauty with more and more beings. She told them that they would take from their pouches a part of the song and would sing it into fullness, into ripeness. They would need to sing the mystery in the way of thought to bring the lives in their bundles into being. They understood her directions because they were the song and the mystery. All of it and only a small piece of it. It was much vaster than they, and yet they could sing it into different shapes of being, different ways of singing, different parts of the great being song.

Ic'sts'ity began to sing a new chant: way-a-hiyo, way-a-hiyo, way-a-hiyo, way-a way-ay-o. She sang and sang, thinking to her bundle, and around them as she sang swirling, whirling globes of light began to form. They began pushing outward in a great whirling spiral, a great wheeling multitude of stars, all singing as they circled and wheeled like great geese upon the void. As they spiraled outward, they grew larger and brighter. Around and around the still, invisible center where Spider, Ic'sts'ity and Nau'ts'ity sang. They whirled, the outer ones flinging themselves farther and farther from the center, great arms forming in the spiral dance, following the lines of the song, the lines of the power, reaching out farther and farther into the mystery, carrying the song in their light, in their fingers, making both the darkness and the light as they danced, finding the power coming to them from the darkness, flinging it out from them in the light. The power danced in the void, in the light, in the midnight reaches of the gleaming dark. It sang.

Then Nau'ts'ity began to sing her thought to her bundle. Aam-i-humm, humm, humm, aam-i-humm, humm, humm, aam-i-o, o, o, o, aam-i-o, o, o, o, aam-i-o. The song changed again as Spider and Ic'sts'ity joined her song, and from the brilliant globes of light new shapes spun out, dancing around and around the lights, giving shape and solidity to the darkness, carrying the spin of the song into new places, more solid, more full. The planets sang, new beings awakening, joining their minds and hearts to the huge chorus, singing their parts of the heart song. The power shaped and dipped, wheeled and danced, and over vast reaches it took on forms it hadn't known.

Satisfied with their work, Spider turned to her granddaughters and smiled as she chanted. In their begetting they would make many worlds, and upon some of them human beings would sing in the same way as she and her granddaughter-sisters sang. On those same worlds, feathered beings would swoop and wheel as the great fires around her did. And on them, life would press its way from the place of the Spider singing into the place of individual songs. And that would be far away from the place where the three stood. It would be right among them as they stood and sang in the void, surrounded by the wheeling lights and the great swooping dark.

WORKS CITED

Gunn, John M. *Schat-Chen: History, Traditions, and Narratives of the Queres Indians of Laguna and Acoma.* Albuquerque: Albright and Anderson, 1977; New York: AMS, 1977 (reprint).

Tyler, Hamilton A. *Pueblo Gods and Myths.* Norman: University of Oklahoma Press, 1964.

GIOIA TIMPANELLI

Gioia Timpanelli was born in New York in 1936. She is one of the earliest and most central figures in the worldwide revival of storytelling, having told stories for over thirty years. For twelve years she wrote and produced literature programs for public television, and she received two Emmy awards for the series Stories from My House. *She won the Women's National Book Association Award for bringing the oral tradition to the American public (1987). Her publications include* Tales for the Roof of the World *(1984) and* Stones for the Hours of the Night *(1975). Most recently her stories have been published in* Sacred Stories, *(1993), and* Walking Swiftly *(1992).*

"There Are Times" is a meditation on spiritual stasis and renewal. Its lyrical cadences create a bridge between poetry and prose. The essay itself is a bridge, a prelude to a story about sudden and profound changes in a woman's life. Of the meditation's link to music, Timpanelli says, "The soul attunes its ear to the sound of the world." (Conversation with M. Kallet, May 20, 1996.)

There Are Times

There are times when the soul is tested. The body feels sore, the mouth dumb, the big red hands hang useless on their arms. Time passes. Surely, the soul will have its way. It lolls. Time passes. And the soul waits. Nothing happens. Come on, MAKE something happen. Make lists! There are always urgent things to do, things to do. Things for this morning, for today, for next week, for an entire month. But then a laziness takes hold. Nothing on the list proves as urgent as this lethargy, so the lists are left out in the sun in a shopping bag, become bleached, illegible, are rained on and finally forgotten under the beach chair. No, not lists, certainly not lists. Poor, dear, little, papers. It's too heavy a burden for them. Minutes pass, hours, maybe a year, possibly a decade. At last, the soul is refreshed in the sweet company it has made for itself.

Then one day it gets up and stretches. Today is not like yesterday. The soul notes the difference. To the neighbors, opening and slamming shut their doors, nothing seems to have happened. Nothing at all. Finally, now, the soul lifts its arms and with its graceful hands brings down the fertile rain.

◎ NTOZAKE SHANGE

Ntozake Shange was born in Brooklyn, New York. She received a B.A. from Barnard and an M.A. from the University of California. Her African name means "she who comes with her own things" and "she who walks like a lion." An accomplished novelist and poet, she is perhaps best known for for colored girls who have considered suicide / when the rainbow is enuf, *a choreopoem which won an Obie Award in 1977. Recently she has published a poem for all ages:* I live in music *(1994). Her awards include Woman of the Year from* Mademoiselle, *and the Audelco Award for Best Playwright from the Black Theatre Alliance. Shange has taught creative writing, literature, and women's studies at several universities, including Sonoma College, Mills College, and the University of California at Berkeley.*

Shange's boogie woogie landscapes *is from* three pieces *(1981). It is a "choreopoem": poetry, music, dance and drama are blended. The "visions, dreams & memories" in this play are those of Layla, the main character. The other characters are "night-life companions" or "dream-memories." This piece was first presented at the New York Shakespeare Festival's Poetry at the Public series in 1979.*

boogie woogie landscapes

CAST

layla an afro-american woman, 20–30. the visions, dreams & memories in this play are hers. she must be able to dance.
night-life companions (n.l.c. — dream-memories):
n.l.c. #1 young woman, should move well.
n.l.c. #2 a woman.

n.l.c. #3 older woman, should be able to sing.
n.l.c. #4 a man, layla's lover.
n.l.c. #5 young man, should sing & move well.
n.l.c. #6 a man, must be a dancer.

this is a geography of whimsy, fantasy, memory & the night: a bedroom. the bedroom of layla ("born at night": arabic), an all-american colored girl. there is what furniture a bedroom might accommodate, though not too much of it. the most important thing is that a bedroom is suggested: the windows that overlook somewhere; an object that might be a bed; another that might be a night table. the mirrors that we see ourselves in / comin in or goin out / in our full regalia or in layers of our own sweat.

the walls of the bedroom are designed to permit at least one or two of the night-life companions (dream-memories) to enter or exit at will. they cd just as easily come from beneath the bed or behind curtains, from under a chair, etc., but that wd not be appropriate to the night-life of an adult, and layla is an adult when we begin.

aside from the night-life companions, layla also entertains a trio of musicians. the musicians sometimes reflect her consciousness, but more often than not, they side with the night-life interlopers, attempting to refine layla's perceptions of herself and her past.

[*layla enters her bedroom, to music we will recognize as her theme song. she is obviously returning from a night at the disco. this is revealed by her clothing, the movements she makes (as if she were dancing alternately with 3 or 4 different partners), & by musical quotations laced thru her theme. the band enters virtually thru the walls, giving us the first instance of the presence of spirits & an attitude toward life that makes fantasies tangible. layla dances to recreate her evening & to explore her present feelings which include a sense of dislocation & confusion, for the disco is over & she is in her bedroom with 3 made-up musicians. layla takes notice of the audience. begins*]

layla
dontcha wanna be music/ dontcha wanna be music/ dontcha wanna
be daybreak & ease into fog/ a cosmic event like sound/ & rain
yah/ like rain
like when a woman can walk down gold street
feeling like she's moved to atlantis
when the mine's been closed a hundred years
& the only gold is music seepin thru fog
it's what we call a marine intrusion

interlopin visions & lost deities findin the way home
cuz we dont recognize what's sacred anymore

oh dontcha wanna be music n ease on into the fog/ like
rain & sun/ like daybreak/ dontcha wanna be . . .

[*the six night-life companions (n.l.c.) enter thru the walls, chanting in unison at first.*]

n.l.c.'s [*in unison*]
she is trapped in black & white/ she is trapped in black & white

layla [*to n.l.c.'s; she is startled & defensive*]
dontcha wanna be music & ease into the fog?
dontcha wanna be like rain/ like a cosmic event . . .

n.l.c. #2
she never thought people places or ideas were anything
but black & white

[*layla is overwhelmed by the visitors/ who take charge & begin to act out their stories.*]

n.l.c. #1
a macadam road & black bark trees
singed grass in soot dirt & a house
more like a cave/ she's black too
not tar like but a shade lighter than
the sky that envelops her legs while
she walks/ headlights frighten her
where she is from the sun is ochre
& daylight no different from sleep/
her most serious problem is how
to stop walking on this road the
color of pitch/ this path slippin off
exploration with long sticks leads nowhere/
she is trapped in black & white/ without shadows
she cannot lean against anything/
the earth has no depth because she cannot hold it
she cannot go away/ the horizon implies three dimensions

n.l.c. #3
if she were to try to bump into a tree/ she
wd go thru it unmarked/ no things
have taste/ or weight/ she is as facile
as air at 14 years old/ she wonders if

anyone has penetrated the chiaroscuro of her life
she is a deeper gray than the shutters of her house.

n.l.c. #2
her hair tangles the wind like billie holiday's voice/
her tears fall behind her blacker than her songs/
she follows these back to her house
where she howls/ for anything red.

layla
inside the cave i imagine i can
cook something to eat/ but my hands dont work
the skillet burns up/ my mother's smoke
scars my arms/ my mouth blurts some phrase
i wd have a fierce yellow
but i don't know what that is.

n.l.c. #4
she tries to stumble on something to stop
this charcoal life/ she goes from room to room
like a tractor in the grapes of wrath/ but
everything she touches gets blacker & more nondescript/
"that's it"/ she says

layla
smudges/ I'm soft graphite
i'm clumsy & reckless/ i'm a hazard to definitions

n.l.c. #5
she threw herself on her bed & her sobs
roused her so/ she began to beat the walls
her fists matted the surface with grime/
she turned to the doors/ rubbin her face
across the thresholds/ she created ebony blurs
that she cdnt even reach less she leave a furrow
of slate fingerprints/ she made things black

n.l.c. #6
indistinguishable. only someone else accustomed to
overwhelming darkness/ cd see her under the bed
tryin not to wipe her tears
she didnt want anything as black as the palms of her hands
to touch her

n.l.c. #1
she was black enuf awready/ dawns held no surprises.

layla
I feel like an oven

n.l.c. #1
all black & crusty/ with a huge space to fill up
with something/ she ate newspapers/ the black & white pages/
thinking news of the outside world wd soothe her hunger.
but she started to eat her books/ even the gothic novels/
the frank yerby slaves/ made her ill/ but she chewed
foxes of harrow & swallowed *mandingo*/ like her joy
she had hidden these pages in a great box under her bed/
no one understood where the newspapers disappeared to/
but she knew it didnt matter/ cuz the outside world waz
black & white & thin like where she lived. she cd
read in the dark/ & eventually only ate *the new york times*/
the newsprint of the *times* waznt cheap like local papers
or gritty like the *philadelphia inquirer*
but as she tore the pages/ HELP WANTED first/ then
REAL ESTATE/ stuffing them in her mouth/ she never thought
people places or ideas were anything but black & white/
no one printed books in colors/ plus she waznt sure
what colors were/ till she discovered jesus/ on the radio/
the voice/ with cadence like her grandma's
but deep/ & husky.

n.l.c. #4
hello jesus/ jesus is with us tonite
& there is a great light shining in yr soul.

layla
amen/ amen.

n.l.c. #2
as jesus came closer to her heart the way
the deep voice waz sayin/ she knew the sun waz yellow
& warm/ cuz the sun got in her throat & pushed a brilliant
glow of shout from her/ not only heaven/ but the world
waz bathed in the gold of his love. she ran in the
sunlight of herself thru the house praisin god/
lettin her laughter wash thru the darkness of night.

n.l.c. #6
& she stood in a arc of yellow so bright
her mother came runnin to see what waz the matter/
even tho the child had laid a daffodil glaze

to the whole house/ the mother cd not see
jesus had released her to the warmth of herself.
the mother waz cold/ & thought the rush of color
from her daughter's mouth/ too blazing & niggardly
for her household. no more deep voices on the radio.

n.l.c. #3
no/ jesus does not like noise/ & his light shines
in the church & the blessing & the lord's prayer
using trespasses/ not debts. we owe no debts.

n.l.c. #2
& the daffodils crawled back into the child's mouth
but she never forgot again that even if jesus
didnt hear her sayin hello/ something made her wanna
say hello/ cuz she had a glowin inside her that changed the world.
now she cd touch her face with the palms of her hands
she usedta sit on/ those black hands
now caressed her with forsythia delicacy
her soul waz filled with daffodils/ tulips spread in her cheeks.

layla
I waz growin beyond this singed & reluctant plane/
I discovered dimensions/ & hope.

n.l.c. #4
there are horizons. there are different dawns.

n.l.c. #3
not here/ but out there somewhere/ or maybe
in my hands/ these black hands.

n.l.c. #5
the corn waz yellow/ under the heavy sheaths of husk
the corn waz yellow/ as she was bright under the crust
of herself. the sunrise was piqued with gold
like her voice winding thru the limbs of trees
on the thin road she no longer walked/ she sailed
the gravel & the sticks she held as a mast for herself.
at the door/ she drew in all this color.
the spinach was ashen still & the grim boilin water
for black teas/ greeted her with cackles, shrieks &
ignorance of her tastes/ once under the bed & starving
she let out a gust of light/ & lay it about her like
other girls she didnt know might have lined up their dolls/

she studied the legs & arms of herself/ the hair & lips
of herself/ before the burst of spirit let her hold herself.

n.l.c. #3
she had withdrawn from the hugs of her mother her father
her grandmother & those other lil blk things who lived with her/
the sisters & brothers who had found no colors/
who still left huge slurs of gray all around/
she held herself in her light/ feeling sorry for the rest.
if she let them near her/ they might smudge this precious secret/
this soft fire she waz/ she wd never do that/ she waz selfish
she wd never even tell them there waz something more
than black & white skinny lives & black & white shutters/
& black cries & white yelps/ she wd never tell them
but/ as she thought these black & white thoughts/
she heard the lil blk things/ brothers & sisters/
making sounds like horses surrounded by coyotes/
sounds like Rodan & someone falling from a 16th floor
thru the glass/ to sidewalks/ sounds like a crowd/
peering at smashed bodies.

n.l.c. #1
she ran/ she ran leaving blurts of yellow & smudges of gray
thru the halls. everything she touched as she stumbled
toward the noise was golden & black/ she had forgotten to
put her spirit back / she ran into a wave of heat
she had never felt/ a rush of scarlet came cross her body/
threw her over the porch to reach the ankle of one of
the little black things. red/ she saw red/ & the lil
black things' tears were orange as she grabbed their faces
& her brightness wiped the fire from their brows/
they were charred now/
as thin scrawny cheap white men made down the road
laughin out the windows of their thin scrawny truck.

n.l.c.'s [*in unison*]
niggahs/ niggahs/ go home/ go home/ niggahs!

n.l.c. #6
the lil black things/ pulled to her & whimpered lil black whys/
"Why did those white men make red of our house/ why did those
white men want to blacken even the white doors of our house/
why make fire of our trees/ & our legs/ why make fire/
why laugh at us/ say go home/ arent we home/ arent we home?"

n.l.c. #2
she saw red. she saw senseless blazes in her arms.
carrying the lil black things into the house/ the black
& white house/ the smudges of children were a cacophony
of colors. now they all knew/ if you can see black
you can see/ yellow/ that softness/ that glow that wipes tears
& holds close/ but holding soft & close/ means danger/
makes you see red/ to orange/ to make fury
to champion the tendermost.

layla
i drew the lil black things with me under my bed
& wiped the scarlet stains from their mouths
with the light of myself.

n.l.c. #4
even these smudges of children/ these lil black things/
cdnt dim the brightness of her. she cd tell them/
but even she didnt know why
the thin scrawny white men in a truck laughin
had made a fire/ to char these black limbs
til they fell abt the fields/ like dry old leaves.

n.l.c. #2
she got too big to hide under her bed/
she didnt really want to hide any more.
the warmth of her waz sought & cherished by the smudges
of children/ even they shared the lil color they had dug
from themselves/ the glow & the ravage of red/
the orange leaps that spattered cross the sky.
there waz the thin black road & the frail charcoal of dusk here/
but morning breeze curved their lips & left the treasured
aszure hue of dreams on their cheeks. she grew to expect colors/
& the memories of acres of indistinguishable black mosses/
walls of shadow creepin between/ long thin steps/
her own dark paths/ & the hungers she knew that opaque night
the thin white men in a truck/ spread sick crimson round her mouth/
the blue of dream in her arms/ these violet memories
rounded her body so/ gave depth to her gaze.
she waz too full of black & white & skinny life
besides/ her eyes were chestnut brown.

[*throughout the telling of the story of the black & white two-dimensional planes, the night-life companions have been as mobile as imaginable, coming & going freely thru the walls. they have also been assisted in the telling of their tale by the trio of musicians layla thought wd entertain her. layla's responses, in addition to the verbal ones, have been to dance what she knew of what they said/ or to reject it by repeating, "dontcha wanna be music & ease into fog." if the truths of the n.l.c.'s came too close.*]

n.l.c.'s [*in unison*]
she waz too full for a black & white & skinny life
she waz too full for a black & white & skinny life

layla [*underneath them*]
when a woman can walk down gold street
feelin like she's moved to atlantis
when the mine's been closed a hundred years
& the only gold is music seepin thru fog
it's what we call a marine intrusion.
interlopin visions & lost deities/ findin the way home/
like thieves/ cuz we dont recognize what's sacred anymore

n.l.c.'s [*in unison, under layla, as they exit*]
remember what's sacred/ what's sacred anymore/ remember
what's sacred/ anymore?

layla [*cont'd*]
women in big hats wit lilies behind their ears
women in blk & white scarves dance on stairways with
bougainvillea & clouds/ men in jeans & honest faces.
music offers solace/ offers some kinda way to reach out/
to ring bells on gold street/ not tin pan alley
but montezuma's preciousness/ a marine intrusion
natural as tides/ learnin to pray. to give more of yrself
than ya think ya have/ diggin below the bottom of what's possible/
& so clean/ like a expensive gangster/ a tibetan shaman's
prophesy/ marine intrusion/ like wind
like winds make fires/ make dust swirl
make us catch ourselves/ fly against our will
til we like it/ til we know we waz meant to soar/
to be free/ in truth/ in silence.
more ourselves & music/ like a voice we cannot speak in/
a voice to move thru/ more than heart
marine intrusion's a meteorological phenomenon/ like rain
like rain & sun/ like c'mon   c'mon
the consequence of bein real/ unpredictable as the weather
sure as the sun risin/ the sweet comeuppance of risk . . .
if ya wear a lotus in yr hair/ it'll fly wit the horn

to another space. marine intrusion movin soft movin strong/
you cant hurt ya.
dontcha wanna be music/ dontcha wanna be/ dontcha wanna/
dontcha wanna be daybreak & ease into fog/ a cosmic event/
sound/ & rain. yeah/ like rain.

[*layla is relieved that the excitement has ceased. she is alone again, having convinced us that we can join in her reveries. she becomes languid, and prepares for bed, i.e., sleep. enter n.l.c. #4, the man who loves her.*]

n.l.c. #4
you drink continually from a scarlet wine glass
& let yr brazziere straps slip/ round/ yr shoulders
yr hair is acorns/ yr hair is like a bundle of dreads
round up on themselves/ you sit on glass & look at us
with eyes as unfamiliar as your simplicity.
you rest your hands on light/ make yrself/ over & over
you are your own mirror/ yr own déjà-vu/ i, yr accomplice.
yr beauty is irreducible/ yr hair acorns.

layla [*nonchalantly*]
as a child I threw these brown concentric miracles
to the bears in the park where colored children cd play/
as a child I knew acorns as toys/ as the ends of trees
I cd not climb.

n.l.c. #4
yr hair is acorns/ you rest on glass/ quick
as a sailboat heeling/ yr wine glass barely braizes yr lips/
vermelho tambem/ yr nails unpainted/ ridiculously inviting
you sit here in carved glass/ in mirrors/ on light/
in sepia caves/ only i imagine/ i sleep near you
you are not afraid of the dark/ the wine simply eases
the flowers from yr cheeks to my dreams/ the red goblet
signals my white stallions to trot
now/ we are ready for the vision/ we are the silk blossoms
of the fica/ needin sun/ lil water/ daily care.

layla
my feet get dirty sometimes/ i like to walk in soil.

n.l.c. #4
you sit on embroidered glass in a beige brazziere/
you can do without seashells.

layla
i am sometimes naked/ but mostly i wear my past/
the pinafores & white socks that shamed me.

n.l.c. #4
this woman with acorn hair/ can be caressed
can stimulate even men with leica eyes
you drink "du vin blanc bon" on glass so old
even white men approach with reverence.
my lover/ the acorn hair woman.

layla
how i've known myself among you.

n.l.c. #4
the one whose head cd not be touched/ the woman too tough
to tossle & fling to the sky/ who rests on glass
& mirrors/ light/ memory/ the woman with no red lights.

layla
only a red glass/ full of love.

n.l.c. #4
a red glass so close to yr lips/ not unlike a kiss
not at all like my lips/ but constant & always possible.
you put yr hope where you can have it
you sleep with me on laced glass/ in caves swollen with beauty/
i put my dreams in yr goblet.

layla
i sleep more easily now/ my love in that scarlet cup.

[*n.l.c. #4 exits*]
i can almost taste you/ my brazziere/ fallin from my shoulder.
i almost believe/ you gave me this.

[*layla looks hoping to see the man who loves her, but instead there are two women, very agitated & aggressive, coming toward her. layla tries to gather her clothes, crouches near what might be her bed.*]

n.l.c. #1
what are they gonna do/ take the windows & doors from
our houses/ leave us lil boxes no man can enter for fear of
electrocution/ bar us from the streets/ at threat of
life imprisonment: alternative number 1: all the men
are locked in boxes with no windows & no doors/ we can come
& go as we please/ at any hour/ any day.

n.l.c. #3
alternative number 2: all the men are sent to new jersey
& the women's army air corps guards all tunnels & bridges/
airport, bus & train stations to make sure that no men invade
the state during rape prevention month. since there are
actually 50 states in the union/ i imagine we cd pair off
& alternate during the year/ so at any time maybe some 25
states wd be free of rape for a month.

n.l.c #1
all the yng men who go to cuba & come back with stories about
how the yng women in cuba walk abt with no fear in their streets/
these yng men are sent out in the streets of new york
with bull horns. they are given prime time 60-second spots
to tell eyewitness news the story of how there is no rape
in cuba. the city of new york supplies transportation for
the thousands of women in the boxes/ or for the thousands
of women waiting for the men to go to new jersey/ to go to
cuba where rape is treason.

n.l.c. #3
women shd go everywhere in 2's after dark. women who dont
have friends or want to take a walk alone/ have to stay in
or getta police dog. also women walking alone/ or rather
in 2's after dark/ must counter rumors that the only thing
2 women wd want to do without a man is to fuck each other/
in this case/ they are still preventing rape.

n.l.c. #1
self-defense classes are offered free by the state during
working hours to all women. self-defense classes are given
in the streets to all unemployed women. self-defense classes
are mandatory for our children/ from age 3/ to prevent rape.

n.l.c. #3
every convicted rapist must be in a parade thru times square
during rape prevention month. all the porno houses will be
closed down during this parade/ no one shall be able to see
any sexual violence/ there will be the annual rapists' parade
instead.

n.l.c. #1
give us guns.

n.l.c. #3
unless the streets are made safe for us/ we shall call a

general strike/ in factories/ at home/ at school.
we shall say we cannot come to work/ it is not safe.

n.l.c. #1
rape victims are given prime time 60-second spots to say
what happened to them. the governor/ the mayor/ & the entire
city council will personally see the rape victim/ apologize
for the municipal negligence/ the failure of the state
to provide secure living space/ & the state pays for all debts
incurred by the crime they survived. in addition/ all women
who died or who demonstrated remarkable courage & integrity
during rape attacks are given congressional medals of honor.

n.l.c. #3
or the purple heart.

n.l.c. #1 & #3 [*in unison*]
we shall have streets/ schools & monuments named after all
these women & children/ they died for their country.

[*n.l.c. #5 shouts as if he were a newsboy in the thirties.*]

n.l.c. #5
EXTRA EXTRA/ READ ALL ABOUT IT!
EXTRA EXTRA/ READ ALL ABOUT IT!

[*cont'd, confidentially to the audience.*]

the *ny times* has never asked me what i think abt a goddamn thing.
the *ny times* has never excused himself to take a leak
no/ the *times* has never helped in times of need
or offered his seat to a pregnant woman on the irt
as a matter of fact
at breakfast the *times* is quite rude
interruptin conversations in any language
unless i insist on sittin under the table
so i cd talk to people's knees
i've never been able to communicate with someone
whose nose is in the *times*/ also i'd like
to mention i've never seen the *times* dance
can the *ny times* dance
can the *times* get down
i mean/ in habana/ everybody knows fidel can mambo
a revolutionary rhumba/ if fidel can do it/ it
cant be so hard to love yr people n keep in step/
at the same time/ everybody in the ford assembly line
cd do it/ the folks in soweto cd do it/ i mean think

n dance at the same time/ but i've never heard tell
of the *ny times* takin notice of that moment when
"CASTRO LEADS HABANA IN NATIONAL RHUMBA" just
like they make no mention of the fact that jimmy carter
cant dance to any rhythm known to man.
(perhaps/ he cd do it on the moon/ that's aristocratic/
dont ya think/ not many people cd get there/ the secret
service wdnt have much to do/ on the moon/ all white
n barren n free of anybody who looks like me/ on the
moon jimmy carter cd do a foxtrot or some peckerwood
derivation thereof/ the ayatollah is very formal/ but
brezhnev n carter cd have the first disco contest on
the moon/ with afghanistan as the prize)
still i wd like to get the *ny times* out of my social life
the next time someone asks me if i have seen the paper/
i'll say/ i've seen more news than is fit to print
& yes we have deliveries everyday/ discounts to
households that understand the rhythm of our lives
n speak colloquial universal language/ we go
person to person/ block to block/ any way ya wanna get it
any way ya wanna get it/ we got it
EXTRA EXTRA READ ALL ABOUT IT:
ZIMBABWE CELEBRATES FIFTY YEARS OF INDEPENDENCE
EXTRA EXTRA READ ALL ABOUT IT:
THOUSANDS OF WRITERS FLOCK TO INTERNATIONAL CONFERENCE
ON FREE SPEECH IN ARGENTINA
EXTRA EXTRA READ ALL ABOUT IT:
WHITE SOUTH AFRICANS DENIED ENTRY TO THE UNITED STATES
AS WAR CRIMINALS.
EXTRA EXTRA READ ALL ABOUT IT:
NOT ONE AFRO-AMERICAN CHILD WHO CANT READ & WRITE/
CELEBRATION OF CAMPAIGN AGAINST NATIONAL ILLITERACY
EPIDEMIC HELD IN BED-STUDY
that's how i see it, today. now that's the news that's
fit to print.
EXTRA EXTRA READ ALL ABOUT IT/
EXTRA EXTRA READ ALL ABOUT IT

[*then fanfare hits like at the apollo for the james brown review. n.l.c. #5, who is an r&b star, enters—or rather, leaps in.*]

n.l.c. #6
can i have a word   the word wid you   like the spinners

waz talkin about a MIGHTY LOVE
MIGHTY MIGHTY MIGHTY MIGHTY LOVE

layla
that grabs me/ i'm thinkin black & realizin colored.
cant stand no man to be calling me BABEE to my face

n.l.c. #1
but if i bear some stylistics du-wah.
BETCHA BY GOLLY WOW to me/ dontcha know i wanna give it away!
baby: YOU MAKE ME FEEL SO BRAND NEW . . . so brand new.

n.l.c. #3
& there's another strut i cant do widout:
satiné suits & lamé cuffs/ volcano blue crepe shirts
& heavy chests/ like muhammed all gone & learned
to charm a lady/ sweep a child to womanhood/ from the stage
make mama scream/ & she dont know that man's name.

n.l.c.'s & layla [*in unison, singing from* WHY DO FOOLS FALL IN LOVE]
UE WAH UE WAH EU WAH OW HAAAAaaa

n.l.c. #1
the audacity of the blues! rock me daddy/ roll me daddy
rock n roll me at the bijou/ de uptown/ in soldan's gym
saw jackie tear his shirt/ throw it to us/
smokey leanin over da lights/ sighin for us

n.l.c. #5
oo oo ooooooo baby babeeeee. . . . .

n.l.c.'s & layla [*in unison, singing*]
LET ME BUILD YOU A CASTLE . . .

layla
bring all the hornplayers i know/ gonna sing & shout
like the babysitter's tryin to entertain us/

n.l.c. #3
do the chicken. do the slop. chantels gonna chiffon
& pearl appliqué theyselves all over dis room

n.l.c. #1 [*singing*]
& MAYBE   IF I PRAY EVERY DAY   YOU'LL COME BACK TO ME

n.l.c.'s & layla [*in unison*]
& i'ma rock   & i'ma roll

n.l.c. #3
in all of them free music blues.

n.l.c. #5
joseph bowie knows what i'm talkin bout/
the art ensemble jumped the r&b train headin for saturn
on saturday nite is colored/ i ant lyin

n.l.c. #1
& them flyin capes/ exaggerated broken hearts/ teasin me
when the drifters go down them railroad tracks
there she goes

n.l.c.'s & layla [*in unison, singing*]
THERE GOES MY BABY   MOVIN ON DOWN THE LINE

n.l.c. #5
archie & frank lowe/ whatchu blowin bout?
there she goes   there she goes.

n.l.c. #3 [*singing*]
IT S A BLK & BLUE HOLIDAY

n.l.c. #5
in atlantic city/ club harlem/ bein colored on the 4th of july!

n.l.c.'s & layla [*in unison, singing*]
& I'MA LOOKIN   I'M LOOKIN   I'M LOOKIN
OH LOOKIN FOR A LOVE   TO CALL MY OWN

n.l.c. #3
& i aint particular/ what kinda guitar you got
long as/ you can play me/ that song

layla
rock me   daddy   roll me   daddy
bring me them rhythms & blues
i'ma neo-afrikan lady BUT:

n.l.c.'s & layla [*à la O. Redding* SATISFACTION]
I GOTTA GOTTA GOTTAGOTTA

n.l.c. #5
get me some rock & rollssss!
c'mon albert/ where are you at

n.l.c. #3
yeah, albert/ where are you at/ i'ma ride yr ribald squeal
like chuck berry roosters in st. louis

n.l.c. #5
sun-ra & horace/ bring all them heliotropical folks
to this heah ROCK N ROLL PREVIEW

layla
bring me some ol roots/ irresistible!

n.l.c.'s & layla [COME GO WITH ME]
BA DA DADA DADA DA DAD A DUMM

n.l.c. #5
listen, cecil mcbee

n.l.c. #1
listen heah/ ike turner got me all gainst the wall
& i waznt goin nowhere

layla
i waznt goin nowhere/ nowhere but home

n.l.c.'s
i waznt goin nowhere . . . nowhere but home . . . i waznt
goin nowhere . . .

layla
YOU BETTAH TELL SOMEBODY TO MEET ME!

n.l.c. #3
TELL SOMEBODY TO MEET ME & tell me somethin good . . .
tell me that you love me YEAH
bring a lil delfonics in yr smile

n.l.c. #1
march clifford thornton all round in thru heah!

n.l.c. #3
rock me daddy

layla
roll me daddy

n.l.c. #5
deliver yrself!

n.l.c.'s & layla [*in unison, singing*]
SO FIIIINE YEEAH MY BABY'S SO DOGGONE FINE

n.l.c. #3
& free/ & sing it to me/ SING it to me

layla
i'ma neo-afrikan lady/ but

n.l.c.'s & layla [*singing*]
I GOTTA GOTTA GOTTA GOT GOT GOTTA

layla
i gotta have me some of that rock n roll for de new land.

[*the company freezes. enter n.l.c. #2.*]

n.l.c. #2
we waz a house fulla chirren who waz fulla the dickens cordin to grandma. there waz me & my 2 sisters & my brother & my 2 cousins/ too smart for our own good & nothin but trouble for the ladies who looked after us while mama waz at work & papa went to the hospital.

[*n.l.c.'s begin to mime actions as described.*]

we cd watch little rock & eisenhower or american bandstand/ then wait til waz the day for colored at the Y/ or play beat-em-up in the yard. or wrestle wid the white boys from texas down the street. i usedta like to dig holes in damp ground & line the worms up on the sidewalk/ my brother liked to set things on fire/ & my sister liked to beat me up til i told on her/ then pull my top braid that wasnt pressed cuz it waz summer & a waste of money/ til some of my hair wd actually come out in her hand. my littlest sister liked to write "pussy" in nail polish behind the refrigerator/ & my cousins rode bikes

[*n.l.c.'s freeze.*]

up on the private catholic girls' school til the police came/ they waz only twelve/ but the officer saw my mama waznt no regular colored woman/ so he just warned her bout the attitude folks in st. louis had toward nigras/ & since she waz from the north & her chirren waznt "customed to tradition"/ he'd let it go on by. this time.

[*n.l.c.'s begin miming action.*]

well. we ran bernice off cuz she cdnt cook nothin but hard stiff grits & didnt 'low none of us to run up & down the stairs or rub the goldfish together. & she always tol mama when one of them fresh boys wd come by to talk to me on the front porch. but she never cd figure out which one of us waz stealin her change & buyin snickers & new jack sets

n.l.c. #3
now/ which one of you is stealin my change/ & buyin snickers & new jack sets?

n.l.c. #2
MAMA! BERNICE IS IMAGININ THINGS! so mama fired her.

[*n.l.c.'s improv gleeful goodbyes to n.l.c. #3; she exits. n.l.c.'s move stage left & sit back to back, as if under a tree.*]

n.l.c. #2
there waz a tree in fronta the house

[*she joins the group & sits.*]

alla us usedta sit by it & think of things to do. watch the earth roll under the clouds/ waz the only time we knew peace/ cuz in the house waz grandma

[*n.l.c. #1 gets up, moves center. she is grandma.*]

raisin cain her own self/ cuz somebody rode down the street on the bike/ free-handed/ or somebody trampled mr. noble's carnations & it waz one of us/ so there wasnt no calm in the house/ til regina came.

[*layla gets up, begins dance. she is regina.*]

doin the slop. listenin to tina turner. eavesdroppin on roscoe & regina when they slipped to the side porch & waz feelin on each other. regina waz a high-school drop-out/ but she waz pretty/ wid spit curls & big bangs over her eyes. & she wore tight skirts & bernard's ring on a chain round her neck. she took us to sumner high

[*n.l.c.'s rise, begin dancing.*]

where the baddest basketball team for colored waz/ to see smokey robinson & the miracles sing "shop around"/ & she let us dance on the stage. when regina waz wid us/ even grandma let us alone. she waz so busy seein to it that roscoe didnt stay long & regina didnt forget she waz a lady/ grandma forgot all about us.

[*n.l.c.'s mime learning to french kiss.*]

then/ in the middle of little willie john & regina's friends showin us how to "french kiss"/ grandma came lookin for her fan. & mama fired regina for bein a bad influence.

[*n.l.c.'s improv sad goodbyes to layla; she exits. the mime of actions continues.*]

the house got crazy. mama tryin to feed nine people & make lunches for five/ put each one of us at a different bus stop. cuz a integration/ none of us went to the neighborhood school/ my own school was 15 miles away/ so grandma tried to help/ & she got real nervous tryin to please mama/ & be in her room cryin cuz none of us wd mind. waz all the time sassin her. forcin her to cut switches off the hedges to whip our legs/ when we waz the only granchirren she had. i had had just about enuf & ran off a couple of times. & mr. robinson at the pharmacy by the trolley stop always called mama to tell her what line i got on/ & then the trolley driver wd stop & let a police on/ who took me back/ & i came home from mrs. maureen's fulla beauty parlor gossip a child had no right to hear/ & when i tried to listen to blues on the radio/ somebody wd turn it off

[*n.l.c. #5 mimes turning radio off; he is daddy.*]

& 'cuse me of tryin my best to be a niggah. so mama went away

[*n.l.c. #3 exits.*]

for a while & daddy brushed our braids to a point like a dunce's cap & then patted them down. he gave us way too much money for lunch & tol grandma she waz overworkin her heart so he wd have to get someone to come in til mama figured out whether she waz comin back.

[*n.l.c.'s exit, except for #2.*]

it was sposed to be a secret bout mama not bein sure whether she wanted to live wid us/ but i knew. & cuz i didnt want the others to worry & cuz they were becomin bothersome/ i didnt say nothin bout it. & when carrie came i figured everythin wd always be awright. now carrie was a big woman/ bigger than any woman on my mama's side or daddy's/ even aunt marie who waz sposed to have talked in tongues & run a farm all by herself cdnt have been as big as carrie. & carrie straightened her hair so funny/ it made her look even bigger/ cuz she didnt curl it/ just ran a hot comb thru it/ so it pointed out in all directions/ like a white man's crew cut. & she had pierced ears/ like aunt mamie's who waz 90/ & the ears liked ta touch her shoulders/ they waz so long & narrow/ but more n alla that/ carrie wore two house dresses at the same time. one up til lunch & the other up til she went to her rooms on the top floor/ where the white folks who lived there before us/ left all this junk/ scrapbooks & crinolines & things. carrie tied her dresses wid a rope/ a real thick rope. not like one for hanging clothes/ but like one for makin a swing on a tree/ & she always wore it/ even when she changed house dresses. & carrie wdnt use none of the bathrooms/ even tho there oughtta have been enuf for her/ cuz there waz one on each floor/ but carrie usedta say/ she liked the latrine in the cellar cuz that's what her mama had in arkansas/ & that's where she went. of course, my mama didnt know that.

[*n.l.c. #3 enters.*]

mama came home. we had a party. carrie started bein more proper/ not cursin or drinkin so much/ & never mentionin men anymore/ it just waznt the same/ but the house sure did run good. me & my sisters stopped fightin in the bed/ & i didnt run off/ the boys stopped stealin things/ & my brother started makin up songs like chuck berry steada burnin up every thing. we usedta play like we waz the shirelles & mama wd sing christian gospel songs.

[*n.l.c. #3 begins singing* HIS EYE IS ON THE SPARROW.]

like paul robeson/ not like the man at the church carrie took us to sometimes/ where we cd play tambourines & get a spirit. just bout the time vanita/ my very best friend/ got to wear stockings insteada anklets/ mama took us aside for a talk bout things women shd know/ & i checked everything she told me wid carrie. & carrie said mama waz almost right/ but it waznt necessary to keep yr dress down/ yr knees locked/ & yr head high/ all the time. just when some no good niggah came round did ya need to do alla that pre-cautionin. on fridays/ carrie stayed gone til monday mornin/ she came back just in time to help me get everybody's lunch together & make daddy's breakfast/ cuz mama

[*n.l.c. #3 exits.*]

skipped that meal for her figure. & i waz gettin to be real important/ cuz carrie had shown me how to fix just about every thing we ate/ how to starch clothes/ & wax the crevises on the stairway/ how to clean crystal & silver/ what to say when some one called. I always usedta shout "mama, it's somebody colored," or, "daddy it's a white man"/ but carrie showed me how to be right/ & to sweep all under the bed & turn the blinds at midday so the sun wdnt bleach the furniture.

[*n.l.c.'s enter. begin miming the action.*]

so when carrie didnt come this one monday morning, i figured i wd cover for her. i cda done a good job, too/ cept mama & grandma kept askin where waz carrie/ & wdnt let me do none of the stuff i knew how to do/ widout tellin me their way/ which waznt the way carrie showed me. so i got in a fight wid em/ & they cused me of bein a impudence & not havin respect. & as i waz movin the glasses outta the dishwasher/ to pour juice for us/ my dumb brother dropped his shoe he cdnt tie in between my legs/ & all the glasses shattered cross the floor

n.l.c. #1 [*holds her heart*]
lord lord. please be careful.

n.l.c. #3 [*angry, ad lib cursing*]
goddamn! watch what yr doin . . . look what you've done . . .

n.l.c. #2
& mama waz cursin/ & the phone rang.

[*all n.l.c.'s except #2 & #3 freeze.*]

n.l.c. #3
carrie/ where are you?

n.l.c. #2
i waz sweepin up the glass/ & carrie musta been goin round the bush/ cuz finally mama looked sick & said

n.l.c. #3
JAIL! well/ why?

n.l.c. #2
i know for sure carrie said "cuz i hadta cut a friend of mine" . . .

n.l.c. #3
cut a friend of yrs? cut a friend of yrs! carrie. come pick up yr things & yr last check/ cuz there's no way in the world you cd expect me to let a criminal look after my chirren!

[*n.l.c.'s exit except #3, who stands frozen.*]

carrie musta come while we were at school/ when i came home alla her things were gone/ but i found some of the rope she usedta tie round her waist by the latrine downstairs in the cellar. my sisters & my brother & my cousins/ didnt even realize what happened/ our losin carrie & all . . .
& i never mentioned my feelins to mama/ cuz then she wd just remind me/ that i always pick the most niggerish people in the world to make my friends. & then she wd list mavis & freddie & charlenetta & linda susan (who waz really po white trash) so i didnt say nothin. i just took carrie's place in the house/ & did everythin like she wda/ cept i did use the regular bathrooms/ & prayed for her like she prayed for the one of her chirren waz most dead. cdnt see how anybody didnt know carrie wdnt cut nobody/ less they hurt her a whole lot. not less she hurt a whole lot. carrie wdnt cut nobody/ not less they hurt her a whole lot . . . i cdnt see . . .

[*n.l.c. #2 exits, repeating last lines a little.*]
[*n.l.c. #3 turns to exit; turns back, crosses downstage.*]

n.l.c. #3
it's not so good to be born a girl/ sometimes.

[*she turns to exit again, & turns back.*]

that's why societies usedta throw us away/ or sell us/ or play with our vaginas/ cuz that's all girls were good for. at least women cd carry things & cook/ but to be born a girl is not good sometimes/ some places/ such abominable things cd happen to us. i wish it waz gd to be born a girl everywhere/ then i wd know for sure that no one wd be infibulated/ that's a word no one wants us to know. infibulation is sewing our vaginas up with cat-gut or weeds or nylon thread to insure our virginity. virginity insurance equals infibulation. that can also make it impossible for us to live thru labor/ make it impossible for the baby to live thru labor. infibulation lets us get infections that we cant mention/ cuz disease in the ovaries is a sign that we're dirty anyway/ so wash yrself/ cuz once infibulated we have to be cut open to have/ you know what/ the joy of the phallus/ that we may know nothin about/ ever/ especially if something else not good that happens to little girls happens: if we've been excised. had our labia removed with glass or scissors. if we've lost our clitoris because our pleasure is profane & the presence of our naturally evolved clitoris wd disrupt the very unnatural dynamic of polygamy. so with no clitoris/ no labia & infibulation/ we're sewn-up/ cut-up/ pared down & sore if not dead/ & oozing pus/ if not terrified that so much of our body waz wrong & did not belong on earth. such thoughts lead to a silence/ that hangs behind veils & straightjackets/ it really is not so good to be born a girl when we have to be infibulated, excised, clitorectomized & STILL be afraid to walk the streets or stay home at night. i'm so saddened that being born a girl makes it dangerous to attend midnight mass unescorted. some places if we're born girls & someone else who's very sick & weak & cruel/ attacks us & breaks our hymen/ we have to be killed/ sent away from our families/ forbidden to touch our children. these strange people who wound little girls are known as attackers/ molesters & rapists. they are known all over the world & are proliferating at a rapid rate. to be born a girl who will always have to worry not only abt the molesters/ the attackers & the rapists/ but also abt their peculiarities: does he stab too/ or shoot? does he carry an axe? does he spit on you? does he know if he doesnt drop sperm we cant prove we've been violated? these subtleties make being a girl too complex/ for some of us & we go crazy/ or never go anyplace. some of us have never had an open window or a walk alone, but sometimes our homes are not safe for us either. rapists & attackers & molesters are not strangers to everyone/ they are related to somebody/ & some of them like raping & molesting their family members better than a girl-child they don't know yet. this is called incest, & girl children are discouraged from revealing attacks from uncle or daddy/ cuz what wd mommy do? after all/ daddy may have seen to it that abortions were outlawed in his state/ so that mommy might have too many children to care abt some "fun" daddy might be having with the 2-yr-old/ she's a girl after all/ we have to get used to it. but infibulation, excision, clitorectomies, rape & incest are irrevocable life-deniers/ life stranglers & disrespectful of natural elements. i wish these things wdnt happen anywhere anymore/ then i cd say it waz gd to be born a girl everywhere.

even though gender is not destiny/ right now being born a girl is to be born threatened; i want being born a girl to be a cause for celebration/ cause for protection & nourishment of our birthright/ to live freely with passion/ knowing no fear that our species waz somehow incorrect. & we are now plagued with rapists & clitorectomies. we pay for being born girls/ but we owe no one anything/ not our labia, not our clitoris, not our lives. we are born girls to live to be women who live our own lives/ to live our lives. to have/ our lives/ to live. we are born girls/ to live to be women . . .

[*n.l.c. #3 exits thru the walls/ n.l.c. #4 enters, searching for her.*]

n.l.c. #4

she waited on me on the 7th floor corner flat/ our children
wanderin from room to room   ghosts   ghost children
effie   althea   rosalie/ diphtheria deserted blonde
colored girls/ bright-migrant children never runnin
carolinian hills/ never utterin gullah accents/ slurrin words
like bajans/ mountain folk/ they wandered

rosalie   althea   effie/ in white lace dresses
starched for the wake/ celebrated births on 52nd street
swallowed/ like placenta/ when there is/ nothin else
when you rear yr young in dark closets/ like a stray cat
she waited on me by the door/ opened to auntie's room
from my side of the family/ uncles from charleston/
a loyal bartender/ &/ children in bodies
only hintin of ochre soil/ she lingered by the corrupted window
by the fire escape/ soot-sprinkled plants laughed at her
meticulous ventures/ washin sills/ diapers/ my carpeter's
trousers. her hair/ languid in the nape of her neck
a thick wad of soft nap/ above the mole/ she wanted a bob
a fashionable diversion/ to save pushin thick braids off
her chest while she leaned/ over steamin laundry/ the baby
the father/ & the graves. she waited on me at the kitchen
table/ heaped with buttered rice n okra/ heaped with linen napkins
from the allendale wedding/ the children in bodies gorged
themselves on halves of biscuits/ they prided themselves
for lovin me/ the father/ & they waited. & she drew sketches
of her mother/ who had died/ her sisters/ who had died
her father who had died in jacksonville & left her to speak
too proper for a workman/ too poor/ for somethin better
& i waz solid/ waz handsome/ waz kind & delivered her north
delivered her too many to suckle/ & still sass me.

she waited/ her hair so heavy/ her head hung down to fondle
the baby/ warm the baby/ move the baby from colored manhattan
take the baby north to freedom/ to the bronx/ she waited for
deliverance/ for me to return/ from tendin the fire/
from passin for irish/ from the bar where faster women rolled/
from the garveyites sneerin at pale niggahs all livin together
in special wings of tenements/ she waited & she mumbled . . .

[*n.l.c. #5 enters. he is the surviving son of the man speaking.*]

n.l.c. #5
she poured grease over turnip greens/ asked the haitian roomer
to move/ for workin voodoo on the baby/ dyin/ from scarlet fever
warm the baby/ pray/ save the child. he loved his own.
he loved his own. she sweat & brought breath to his blood.
& he lied to the world/ looked over his shoulder/ every step/
to see the burnin cross/ feathers/ ruins of farms/ his father's
tools. she waited by the bed/ fingerin his tuskegee photo/
the carpenter's shop/ the colored pioneers.
the baby waz purple/ foamin at the mouth/ she waited for christ
to reveal himself/ she sang/ compulsively/ to soothe the baby/
ease his entry/ the door never opened

n.l.c. #4
i lay in the cellar/ fractured/ crumbled/ over uneven casing
i crawled without my body/ thru sicilian ashes/
jewish cadavers moanin in the beams/ i crawled to my children
rosalie   althea   effie in white lace dresses starched
for the wake/ roamin from room to room/ swallowed like placenta
my woman waitin/ receivin the spirits/ carolina screams
branded up country slaves/ i made the journey/ to deliver her
to freedom/ the carpenter/ tendin to his own/ movin north
to the bronx.

[*n.l.c. #4 exits.*]
[*n.l.c. #1 and #6 enter with a burst of energy; n.l.c. #5 exits slowly. n.l.c. #1 addresses n.l.c. #6.*]

n.l.c. #1
shall we go to jonestown or the disco
i cd ware red sequins or a burlap bag
maybe it doesnt matter
paradise is fulla surprises

n.l.c. #6
& the floor of the disco changes colors/
like special species of vipers

n.l.c. #1
no real musicians appear after 2:00 there is no dining out

n.l.c. #6
shout hallelujah/ praise the lord!

n.l.c. #1
but shall i go to jonestown or the disco?
if jesus wont fix it/ the deejay will.
my step is off or on
my arms are sweatin in the spotlights twirlin or the sun

n.l.c. #6
pick those tomatoes/ & join us in prayer!

n.l.c. #1
a tango might excite the crowd
a bolero give us salvation

n.l.c. #1 & #6 [*in unison*]
freak freak freak

n.l.c. #1
maybe i shd really consider the blue silk
every one at the office is looking for me on tv
tonite/ if i win i might die/ jesus help me
the kingdom comes

n.l.c. #6
god moves in mysterious ways & koolaid is all we cd handle

n.l.c. #1
even my aunt promised not to miss us
our children will be so proud/ gd dancers are gd lovers/
but shall i go to jonestown or the disco?
good lovers get married/ god shares the covenant
of marriage/ & marriage is the dance of life/ oh
we get so happy/ we so happy it's sin & we might die

n.l.c. #1 & #6 [*in unison*]
thank-you jesus

n.l.c. #1
god loves bringing wealth from the wilderness

n.l.c. #6
yes lord

n.l.c. #1
at the disco we shout the praises of the almighty
i wrap my arms around you til the end

n.l.c. #6
are you ready/ are you ready to/ freak

n.l.c. #1
we came here to feel good

n.l.c. #6
thank-you jesus

n.l.c. #1
to give joy & form to the world

n.l.c. #6
thank-you jesus

n.l.c. #1
we came here/ yes lord
in our desire/ in hairshirts & satin
yes/ oh to praise the power & the glory
amylnitrate makes you wanna die/ or dance yrself to death
amylnitrate makes you wanna die/ or dance yrself to death
why go to jonestown/ amen/ i say why go to jonestown

n.l.c. #6
yes lord/ i'ma go to the disco/ where i cd dance myself to death

n.l.c. #1 & #6 [*own rhythms*]
shout hallelujah/ praise the lord
shout hallelujah/ praise the lord
shout hallelujah/ praise the lord
shout hallelujah/ praise the lord.

[*n.l.c. #1 dances off.*]

n.l.c. #6
elegance in the extreme/ gives style to the hours
of coaxing warmth/ outta no where.
elegant hoodlums/ elegant intellectuals/ elegant ornithologists
elegant botanists/ but elegance in the extreme helps most
the stranger who hesitates to give what there is
for fear of unleashing madness

(which is sometimes uninvolved in contemporary mores/
archetypal realities or graciousness). elegant cab drivers.
elegant derelicts/ elegant surgeons/ elegant trash.
elegant priests/ elegant dieticians/ elegant nymphomaniacs/
elegant discos/ elegant shoes/ elegant elevator operators/
elegant salesmen/ elegant negroes . . . elegant/ elegant/ elegant!
in the absence of extreme elegance/ madness can set right in
like a burnin gauloise on japanese silk. though highly cultured/
even the silk must ask how to burn up discreetly.
elegance. elegance. elegance.

[*n.l.c.'s enter & freeze, as layla begins offstage.*]

layla [*o.s.*]
i want to say these things to you/ mostly cuz yr not here.
if you were here we wd kiss/ rub all denim thru . . .
i speak to you a lot/ when i'm alone. i want to tell you
i cannot stop smoking kools/ forget the militia in panama
all brown & bald in gestapo boots . . .

[*music begins as layla enters, surrounded by her night-life companions.*]

paradise has her own ugliness: the man on the boat
from dusseldorf/ chasing me to dance with a "colored"/
the first in his life/ this my april in the north atlantic.
at dusk the sea is sultry/ we are not her lovers & she treats
us so.
did you know i have so many secrets i believe are yrs/
what of me? i need you to have & still cant imagine
you ever thot i wanted you to see the posters in rio/
guerilleros' faces taped to steel/ remind me of our struggle.
we merge in our eccentricity/ this penchant for the right to live.
peter tosh awready said: "everybody's talkin abt peace, i
talkin abt justice"/ our kiss is desperate/ long awaited/
known immediately/ unequivocal & not enuf.
tupac amaruo knew what to do. i imagine you in guadalajara
on the back of a donkey/ the 3-yr-old pickpocket will seduce you.
this is not the first time i've swallowed bad white wine/
i've been betrayed by escalators before/ no one knows
you've planted here/ no one knows you find wine tricklin
from my body/ our champagne still squirts from my braids/
even now i am not empty . . . such things i wd say/ tho cecil taylor
long ago passed quevy station/ in the cemetery there
i smelled myself in soil/ bitter & french/ dark & falling apart
in my hand . . . i wd say to you/ a marimba might civilize me/

a fashion fair in bangkok suffocate my sense of style.
jessica swears the yng men in manila dance well/ but
have no minds. i want to hold you in this/ so you might know
what i bring you/ my mouth is full & broad/ my tongue
cluttered with syllables & desire/ even this has not come out
straight/ so many days uprooted/ each time i fly i know again
memory & desire are relentless/ when yr not here to talk to
i speak my most precious/ lay out the mystery/ the devastation/
my honor/ i cant even catch yr eye/ so i trace the skies
with/ these hidden things/ ces choses perdues/
that you might find me/ in the night/ when i am flying.
i want to tell you i cannot stop smoking kools/ forget
the militia in panama/ all brown & bald in gestapo boots/
dontcha wanna be music/ & ease into the fog
dontcha wanna be like rain/ a cosmic event/ like sound . . .

[*layla's night-life companions come alive & join her in the chant/ then slowly disappear thru the walls as layla goes back to sleep/ but the chant is heard as the lights fade.*]

◎ *LOUISE GLÜCK*

"Lullaby" is from Louise Glück's most recent book of poems, The Wild Iris *(1992). The voices in the poems constitute an "impassioned polyphonic exchange" between a god and the natural world. A lullaby is an evening song, a dusk and sleep song.* *(For more on Glück, see page 391.)*

Lullaby

Time to rest now; you have had
enough excitement for the time being.

Twilight, then early evening. Fireflies
in the room, flickering here and there, here and there,
and summer's deep sweetness filling the open window.

Don't think of these things anymore.
Listen to my breathing, your own breathing

like the fireflies, each small breath
a flare in which the world appears.

I've sung to you long enough in the summer night.
I'll win you over in the end; the world can't give you
this sustained vision.

You must be taught to love me. Human beings must be
    taught to love
silence and darkness.

◎ JOY HARJO

"Healing Animal" is from In Mad Love and War. *Harjo states, "in tribal traditions, poetry and music aren't separate (the ancient Greeks recognized this holistic reality) and [I'm] incorporating my saxophone playing and the work of other musicians into both the writing and performance" (personal statement, 1995). Words and music both have the power to heal, Harjo reminds us, in this poem that in its "fluid shape" resembles a jazz improvisation. John Coltrane's "A Love Supreme" has been a continual source of inspiration to Harjo.* *(For more on Harjo, see page 65.)*

Healing Animal

(For L. N. and Michael Harper)

On this day when you have needed to sleep forever,
to forgive the pained animal kneading
                                        your throat,
Sleep, your back curled against my belly.
I will make you something to drink,
                                        from a cup of frothy stars
from the *somewhere there is the perfect sound*
called up from the best-told stories
                                        of benevolent gods,
who have nothing better to do.
                                        And I ask you
what bitter words are ruining your soft-skinned village,
because I want to make a poem that will cup
                                        the inside of your throat

like the fire in the palm of a healing animal. Like
the way Coltrane knew love in the fluid shape
of a saxophone
that could change into the wings of a blue angel.
He tasted the bittersweet roots of this crazy world,
and spit them out into the center of our musical
jazzed globe.
Josiah's uncle brought his music
to the Papago center of the world
and music climbed out of his trombone
into the collected heartbeat of his tribe.
They had never heard anything like it,
but it was the way they had remembered, the way
"Chief" Joe Moore must have known when he sang
for the very first time
through the brass-boned monster.
All through the last few nights I have watched you fight for yourself
with the eyes I was warned against opening.
You think you are asleep
when you turn off the lights, and we blend into the same
hot-skinned sky.
The land called miracle is the daughter you never died for and she
stands at the edge of the bed with her slim hand
against your cheek.
Your music is a crystal wall with a thousand mouths, kin to trains and
sounds that haven't yet been invented,
and you walk back and forth
through it to know it won't betray you.
And in the last seconds before the breaking light,
when you are nearly broken with the secret antelope
of compassion,
when the last guardian angel has flown west to the Pacific
to see someone else through their nightly death,
a homefire is slowly kindled in the village of your body.
And the smoke of dawn turns all your worded enemies
into ashes that will never rise.
Mythic cattle graze in your throat, washing it with milk.
And you will sing forever.

◎ *LINDA HOGAN*

"Drum" is from Linda Hogan's The Book of Medicines *(1993). Here the poem is a means of journeying back to humankind's beginnings in water, to the "oldest place" that the poet can reach within. The beat of the poem becomes the more subtle equivalent of the traditional drum, which can alter consciousness with its rhythmical insistence. (For more on Hogan, see page 146.)*

Drum

Inside the dark human waters
of our mothers,
inside the blue drum of skin
that beat the slow song of our tribes
we knew the drifts of continents
and moving tides.

We are the people who left water
to enter a dry world.
We have survived soldiers and drought,
survived hunger
and living
inside the unmapped terrain
of loneliness.
That is why we have thirst.
It is why
when we love
we remember our lives in water,
that other lives fall through us
like fish swimming in an endless sea,
that we are walking another way
than time
to new life, backwards
to deliver ourselves to rain and river,
this water
that will become other water
this blood that will become other blood
and is the oldest place
the deepest world
the skin of water
that knows the drum before a hand meets it.

◎ *MARILYN KALLET*

Marilyn Kallet was born in Montgomery, Alabama, in 1946. A poet, translator, editor, and essayist, she attended Jackson College, Tufts University, and Rutgers. Kallet is the author of six books, including a translation of Paul Eluard's Last Love Poems, *and most recently she edited* A House of Gathering: Poets on May Sarton's Poetry *(1993). With Judith Ortiz Cofer she is currently assembling a book of personal essays entitled* Sleeping with One Eye Open: A Survival Guide for Creative Women. *Kallet won the Tennessee Arts Commission Literary Fellowship in poetry in 1988. She is professor of English at the University of Tennessee at Knoxville, where she has directed the creative writing program since 1986.*

Kallet says, " 'Passover' was written in the spring of 1988 while I was on leave from teaching and while I was recovering from a serious illness. I took long walks in the fields across from my house, and poems seem to come into me whole out of the air." Passover is the Jewish holiday commemorating the release of Jews from slavery in Egypt, and it is also a time of commemorating those who died in the Holocaust and remembering those who still are not free. "At the ritual meal we drink four cups of wine, eat haroset *— apples and nuts soaked in wine to remind us of the bricks the Jews used for Pharaoh's buildings — and we eat matzoh ball soup — the trick is to keep the matzoh balls light, so they float."*

" 'How to Get Heat Without Fire' was written in 1980, and underscored my commitment to poetry. The end of the poem summons an intense state of listening, such as jazz musicians practice when they play improvisations." The poem was first published in Carolina Quarterly *in 1983.*

Passover

My father heads our table,
his cheeks flushed from the first cup of wine.
At sunset he left his wallet upstairs
with bags of quarters from the vending machines.
He's making jokes and laughing with his mouth shut,
giving us his bright side — boy, clown, inventor.
Tonight by candlelight even the sullen teenagers
are cheerful, my sister Elaine and I,
glowing from apples and walnuts soaked in wine.
Aunt Marilyn is alive, sitting across from me.
Her breasts are hers again, untouched by cancer.
The New York Grandma is beside her
in a cotton housedress, two lines of berry lipstick
pressed on her faded mouth.

She's laughing, "Oy, stop it, Harry!" as my father
teases her. Letting go of want and pogroms.
My mother is no longer a martyr.
Pharaoh has set her free so she can recline,
testing her frothy matzoh-balls,
delighting in all she has created.
This is Passover, an invitation
to our freer selves to join us,
an invitation to the poor to come and dine.

My father loved kids, especially poor ones,
seeing himself starving back in Brooklyn.
He liked to buy ice cream for any hungry child
he found hanging around the stand.
The prayer book tells us, "The dead shall live on earth
in the good deeds they performed here,
and in the memory of those who live after them."
That's it, no big party, though this evening
circulating like sad music in the fragrant air
all the Jews who ever lived are still alive.

How to Get Heat Without Fire

Beneath the dark floor
there has always been love,
but the trick is,
how to get down to it?
Shall I tear my way down
like a tiger clawing
the floorboards, when this
tearing down is what scarred you?
Whose mother is there
in the dark trying hard
to hide you from the memory
of the floorboards in flame?
How to get heat without fire?
To coax light open?
To ease you new into
the world if I am not
a mother, or a beloved?
Pull back? Peel back dead

bark, pull back the boards
we trample, throw each other
down on and through some days?
Turn the floor into a pool
we can dive deep into,
cradle the mothers,
let the animals swim their ways?
Has music ever saved anyone?
Then I will reenter my life
as sound,
as notes strung like pearls
that you have yearned
to enter.
I will be sound,
I will be sound,
and silence,
listening.

◎ *MARGE PIERCY*

Marge Piercy was born in Detroit, Michigan, in 1936. She was educated at the University of Michigan and Northwestern University. She has written eleven novels consisting of realistic and utopian fiction, and twelve books of poetry, among them Breaking Camp *(1968),* To Be of Use *(1973),* The Moon Is Always Female *(1980),* Circles on the Water: Selected Poems *(1982),* Stone, Paper, Knife *(1983),* My Mother's Body *(1985),* Available Light *(1988), and* Mars and Her Children *(1992). The University of Michigan Press published her* Parti-Colored Blocks for a Quilt: Poets on Poetry *(essays, reviews, and interviews, 1982). Piercy edited* Early Ripening: American Women's Poetry Now *(1987). She currently lives in a communal household in Wellfleet, Massachusetts.*

"Wellfleet Sabbath" appears in Available Light. *Its quatrains display Piercy's openness to the natural spirituality of her environment, here Wellfleet. The poem celebrates the Jewish Sabbath, which begins on Friday night and lasts through Saturday and which is a sacred time of joy, rest, and reflection. Traditionally women light and bless the candles — "sweet beeswax"; there is also a blessing over the wine — shining "its red lantern of joy." The "Shekinah," the mystical Bride of God, enters the home at the Sabbath—here she comes in on a simple "seaside sparrow."*

Wellfleet Sabbath

The hawk eye of the sun slowly shuts.
The breast of the bay is softly feathered
dove grey. The sky is barred like the sand
when the tide trickles out.

The great doors of the sabbath are swinging
open over the ocean, loosing the moon
floating up slow   distorted   vast, a copper
balloon just sailing free.

The wind slides over the waves, patting
them with its giant hand, and the sea
stretches its muscles in the deep,
purrs and rolls over.

The sweet beeswax candles flicker
and sigh, standing between the phlox
and the roast chicken. The wine shines
its red lantern of joy.

Here on this piney sandspit, the Shekinah
comes on the short strong wings of the seaside
sparrow raising her song and bringing
down the fresh clean night.

◎ *ELLEN BRYANT VOIGT*

Voigt's "Song and Story" combines the narrative-lyric with myth to sing a contemporary and personal version of the archetypal journey through hell. The rhythms of a heart monitor suggest to the narrator the sounds of the sea, of oars, and of scythes. The poem includes stanzas resembling folk songs, invoking an old peasant woman; Orpheus, proto-poet; Eurydice, his stolen love; and Procne, whose tongue was cut out when she told the truth about having been raped—the gods took pity on her, and turned her into a swallow. Like a loom the poem shuttles between the present and ancient journeys, between song and story, ending with the consolations of song. *(For more on Voigt, see page 155.)*

Song and Story

for Allen Grossman

The girl strapped in the bare mechanical crib
does not open her eyes, does not cry out.
The glottal tube is taped into her face;
bereft of sound, she seems so far away.
But a box on the stucco wall, wired to her chest,
televises the flutter of her heart —
news from the pit — her pulse rapid and shallow,
a rising line, except when her mother sings,
outside the bars: whenever her mother sings
the line steadies into a row of waves,
song of the sea, song of the scythe

old woman by the well, picking up stones
old woman by the well, picking up stones

When Orpheus, beating rhythm with a spear
against the deck of the armed ship, sang
to steady the oars, he borrowed an old measure:
broadax striking oak, oak singing back,
the churn, the pump, the shuttle sweeping the warp
like the waves against the shore they were pulling toward.
The men at the oars saw only the next man's back.
They were living a story — the story of desire,
the rising line of ships at war or trade.
If the sky's dark fabric was pierced by stars,
they didn't see them; if dolphins leapt from the water,
they didn't see them. Sweat beaded their backs
like heavy dew. But whether they came to triumph
or defeat, music ferried them out
and brought them back, taking the dead and wounded
back to the wave-licked, smooth initial shore,
song of the locust, song of the broom

old woman in the field, binding wheat
old woman by the fire, grinding corn

When Orpheus, braiding rushes by the stream,
devised a song for the overlords of hell
to break the hearts they didn't know they had,
he drew one from the olive grove —
the raven's hinged wings from tree to tree,

whole flocks of geese crossing the ruffled sky,
the sun's repeated arc, moon in its wake:
this wasn't the music of pain. Pain has no music,
pain is a story: it starts,
Eurydice was taken from the fields.
She did not sing — you cannot sing in hell —
but in that viscous dark she heard the song
flung like a rope into the crater of hell,
song of the sickle, song of the hive

old woman by the cradle, stringing beads
old woman by the cradle, stringing beads

The one who can sing sings to the one who can't,
who waits in the pit, like Procne among the slaves,
as the gods decide how all such stories end,
the story woven into the marriage gown,
or scratched with a stick in the dust around the well,
or written in blood in the box on the stucco wall —
look at the wall:
the song, rising and falling, sings in the heartbeat,
sings in the seasons, sings in the daily round —
even at night, deep in the murmuring wood —
listen — one bird, full-throated, calls to another,
little sister, frantic little sparrow under the eaves.

◎ *COLETTE INEZ*

Colette Inez was born in 1931 in Brussels, Belgium to a French mother (a medievalist scholar) and an American father (a priest), who placed her in a Catholic orphanage. She joined foster parents in New York in 1939 and later earned a degree from Hunter College. She has since published many books of poetry, including The Woman Who Loved Worms *(1972),* Alive and Taking Names *(1977),* Family Life *(1988), and* Getting Under Way: New and Selected Poems *(1993). Among many other honors, Inez has been the recipient of a Guggenheim Foundation fellowship, two National Endowment for the Arts Fellowships, a Pushcart Prize, and a New York Foundation for the Arts fellowship, and the Kreymborg Award from the Poetry Society of America. Inez has taught poetry in the writing program at Columbia University since 1983.*

"Mary at the Cave" was composed in Knoxville, Tennessee, in April 1996, when Colette Inez was writer-in-residence. A classroom writing exercise about imagining an ancestor and receiving a gift from her sparked the poem. The images become more

sensual and the rhythm intensifies as the poem proceeds. The ancient connection between poetry and dance can be felt here; body and spirit are one.

Mary at the Cave

Mary-mother comes to me from the mouth
of the cave, places her hand
on my shoulder, says:
"I know the desert's secret of water,

the shudder of lilies where bees feed."
She lowers her veil and instructs:
"My arm will circle
your waist and yours around mine.

Twirl your hips, your dark rough curls.
We will infuriate the earth with our pounding
bare feet until the sky breaks,
flinging bones of rain inside our song."

She tells me: "I am Mary of Nazareth,
a sister in the ritual of raising the dead
with a woman's hand,
of subduing the serpent."

She taps her drum. She counts that cadence
in our blood. Mary-mother, Mary-sister,
her many bracelets catch the light.
We drink the water of consoling words,

snap our fingers in a dance,
pouring our rhythms to the wind,
oiled bodies, scented hair, tribal women
with secrets to share in the desert.

◎ *LUCI TAPAHONSO*

"The Motion of Songs Rising" is from Tapahonso's collection Sáanii Dahataał / The Women Are Singing *(1993; see also page 229). Tapahonso blends Navajo and English, verse, chant, and prose to re-create the holy Navajo Night Chant, which restores balance to the universe and to those who participate in the ceremony.*

The Motion of Songs Rising

The October night is warm and clear.
We are standing on a small hill and in all directions,
around us, the flat land listens to the songs rising.
The holy ones are here dancing.
The Yeis are here.

In the west, Shiprock looms above the desert.
Tsé bit'a'í, old bird-shaped rock. She watches us.
Tsé bit'a'í, our mother who brought the people here on her back.
Our refuge from the floods long ago. It was worlds and centuries ago,
yet she remains here. Nihimá, our mother.

This is the center of the night
and right in front of us, the holy ones dance.
They dance, surrounded by hundreds of Navajos.
                    Diné t'óó àhayóí.
                    Diné t'óó àhayóí.
We listen and watch the holy ones dance.
                    Yeibicheii.
                    Yeibicheii.
                    Grandfather of the holy ones.

They dance, moving back and forth.
Their bodies are covered with white clay
and they wave evergreen branches.
They wear hides of varying colors,
their coyote tails swinging as they sway back and forth.
All of them dancing ancient steps.
They dance precise steps, our own emergence onto this land.

They dance again, the formation of this world.
They dance for us now — one precise swaying motion.
They dance back and forth, back and forth.
As they are singing, we watch ourselves recreated.

Éí áłts'íísígíí shił nizhóní. The little clown must be about six years old. He skips lightly about waving his branches around. He teases people in the audience, tickling their faces if they look too serious or too sleepy. At the beginning of each dance, when the woman walks by to bless the Yeis, he runs from her. Finally, after the third time, she sprinkles him with corn pollen and he skips off happily. 'éí shił nizhóní.

The Yeis are dancing again, each step, our own strong bodies.
They are dancing the same dance, thousands of years old. They are here
for us now, grateful for another harvest and our own good health.
                    The roasted corn I had this morning was fresh,
                    cooked all night and taken out of the ground this
                    morning. It was steamed and browned just right.

They are dancing and in the motion of songs rising,
our breathing becomes the morning moonlit air.
The fires are burning below as always.
                                        We are restored.
                                        We are restored.

◎ *ELAINE ZIMMERMAN*

Elaine Zimmerman was born in 1950 in New York. She is a poet and psychotherapist who turned her love of language and change to politics. Zimmerman has worked for the California and Connecticut legislatures as well as for national organizations seeking to make policy innovations for women, children, and families. She is known for community organizing, crafting national policy agendas, and public speaking to inspire action among constituencies. She has published poetry, as well as numerous articles on the politics of change.

Zimmerman writes, "I wrote this poem for Essie Parrish after hearing her speak and watching her cure her husband of cancer through a healing ceremony. Essie Parrish was the Shaman of the Pomo tribe in northern California. I heard Essie Parrish at the University of California, Berkeley, and then viewed a film of her chanting and dancing to heal her husband. After the viewing, I was taken over by the sounds, the power, the shift of worlds. The first line of the poem stayed with me for days, repetitively and in a chant. It was only when the poem came out, and it did just that, that I was able to get back to my life and its routines. I believe it was her strength, her sounds, and her willingness to be transformed that took hold of me" (letter to M. Kallet, 1996).

To Essie Parrish

shaman of Pomo
breaks   the center
pole
in the roundhouse   turning

as the spirit
gives her
tongue,   her call
shatters stone.
birds take flight
        against the weight
of falling mountains,
        fly to clouds
above the roundhouse
cawing   to her   calling:
o lady bending
        to the sucking
of your marrow
by three separate   worlds,
o lady trembling
as the skin   disappears
and the blood   turns
        to song,
what sounds
are they
howling
in the tips
of your fingers?
what steps
are they
dancing in the
vessels of your
eyes?
your body magnet
pulls toward the
sick one
limbs quivering
at the touch
of the spirit,   evil
in the man,   shrilling
your calls   sucking
the whole
of his madness   spitting out
        his venom
breathing in
        your song.
shaman of Pomo
return

the center
pole
in the roundhouse.
    birds sing
    upon the mountains.

INTERVIEW

In Love and War and Music: An Interview with Joy Harjo

by Marilyn Kallet

JOY HARJO

Marilyn Kallet's interview with Joy Harjo took place on April 19, 1991, and was completed by telephone on September 16, 1992. They met and talked in the sitting room of Harjo's hotel in Knoxville. Particularly impressive was Harjo's openness — her assumption that honest communication would take place — and her patience. In Knoxville as part of an NEA Audience Development Grant, Harjo also taught high school classes at Oak Ridge High School, and gave a reading and held an informal discussion at the University of Tennessee. This interview was published in The Kenyon Review *in 1993. (For more on Harjo, see page 65.)*

MK: What were your beginnings as a writer?

JH: I could look at this in a couple of ways. One is to look at the myths and stories of the people who formed me in the place where I entered the world. . . . Another way is to look at when I first consciously called myself a writer. I started writing poetry when I was pretty old, actually — I was about twenty-two. I committed to poetry the day I went in to my painting teacher who mentored me and expected a fine career in painting for me, and told him I was switching my major to poetry. I made the decision to learn what poetry could teach me. It was a painful choice. I come from a family of Muskogee painters. My grandmother and my great-aunt both got their B.F.A.s in art in the early 1900s. And from the time I was very small you could always find me drawing, whether it was in the dirt or on paper. That was one thing that made me happy. . . . I always said that when I grow up I am going to be a painter, I am going to be an artist. Then I made the decision to work with words and the power of words, to work with language, yet I approach the art as a visual artist. From childhood my perceptions were through the eye of a painter. I feel any writer serves many aspects of culture, including language, but you also serve history, you serve the mythic structure that you're part of, the people, the earth, and so on — and none of these are separate.

MK: It seems like almost any question we ask about your writing, about your cultural background, is going to lead us in the same paths of discussion about your family life, your tribal life, and your life as a writer.

JH: Well, they are not separate, really. Though the way I've come to things is very different from, say, Beth Cuthand, who is a Cree writer from Saskatchewan, or Leslie Silko from Laguna. There's a tendency in this country to find one writer of a particular ethnicity and expect her to speak for everyone and expect her experience to be representative of all Native women and all Native people. My experience is very different from Silko's and Cuthand's, although it's similar in the sense of a generational thing, of certain influences on us and influences we have on each other. But my experience has been predominantly urban. I did not grow up on a reservation — we don't even have a reservation. There are more rural areas where the people are. I'm not a full-blood, and yet I am a full member of my (Muskogee) tribe, and I have been a full member of my tribe since my birth into the tribe. I find some people have preconceived ideas — I was talking to this guy on the plane and he says, "Well, you don't fit my idea of an Indian." What does that mean? I think for most people in this country, it means to be a Hollywood version of a Plains tribe, as falsely imagined 100 or 150 years ago. Most people in this country have learned all they know about Indian people from movies and television. . . .

MK: Certain books have helped to popularize Plains culture. *Black Elk Speaks* is taught most often at the university. . . .

JH: And even then it's a perversion of what it means to be an Indian in this country — how do you translate context? Within my tribe you have people who are very grounded in the traditions and are very close to the land. Then you have people who are heavily involved in church; some are involved in both; some live in Tulsa, which is where I grew up; others live all over but are still close to that place which is home. It is more than land — but of the land — a tradition of mythologies, of ongoing history . . . it forms us.

MK: What is there specifically in the Muskogee culture that lends itself to poetry?

JH: That's like asking what is it in life that lends itself to poetry . . . it's the collective myth balanced with history.

MK: When you talk about particulars of individuals and tribes, you are continually breaking down conventions and stereotypes. Does that become tiresome for you?

JH: Yes, it does. I find that wherever I speak I always get asked more questions having to do with culture than with writing.

MK: You must feel like a cultural missionary sometimes. . . .

JH: Right. I feel like I'm having to explain something that's not really easily explainable.

MK: Among your friends, and among the other writers you mentioned, surely you don't have to keep explaining.

JH: No. There's no need. Culture just is. Certainly I'm always asking myself questions about how we came to be, and how we're becoming, and who we are in this world. . . .

MK: In terms of your own background, were there people in your family who loved words? Where does your love of language come from?

JH: Probably from both sides. I have a grandfather, my father's grandfather, who is a full-blooded Creek Baptist minister. I often feel him and I know much of what I am comes from him (including my stubbornness!). I know that he had a love for words and he spoke both Muskogee and English. My mother used to compose songs on an old typewriter. I think she loved the music more than the words, she wasn't particularly a wordsmith, but could translate heartache. From her I learned Patsy Cline and other "heartbreak country."

MK: Do you remember what made you write that first poetry in your twenties?

JH: Yes, very distinctly. The urge was the same urge I had to make music. Around that time was the first time I heard music in poetry, heard Native writers like Leslie Silko and Simon Ortiz read their work. I also heard Galway Kinnell for the first time, his was one of the first poetry readings I ever attended. I became friends with Leo Romero whose dedication to poetry impressed me. He was always writing and reading his work to me. I witnessed process and began writing my own pieces. Of course, the first attempts were rather weak. Like newborn colts trying to stand just after birth. . . .

MK: You attended the M.F.A. Program in Creative Writing at the University of Iowa. Was that helpful to you?

JH: Well, I have to take into consideration my age when I went — I was in my mid-twenties. I was a single mother. I arrived at this strange country with two small children — my daughter was three years old. I knew no one, did not know the place or the people. About the university setting — I felt like I had walked into a strange land in which I had to learn another language. This comes from being of Native background, from the West, but it also comes from being a woman in that institution. I heard the director say once to a group of possible funders — I was one of the people they chose to perform for them in the workshop — he told them that the place was actually geared for teaching male writers, which is honest; it was true, but I was shocked. I remember Jayne Ann Phillips and I looking at each other, like "Can you believe this? Then why are we sitting here?" Certainly I think I learned a lot about technique. I also learned that what was most important in a poem had nothing to do in some ways with what I thought was most important. I felt like the art of poetry had broken down into sterile exercises. And yet, I admire some of the work of those people who taught me. But the system had separated itself from the community, from myth, from humanhood.

MK: But you saw it through?

JH: I did see it through. I wanted to walk away. One way I made it through was through the help of people like Sandra Cisneros — through close ties to the Indian and Chicano communities, to the African American community, to women's groups.

MK: Have you been able to bring back some of the technical skill you learned to what you consider fundamental?

JH: Yes. You can have the commitment to writing, the fire, but you can write crummy poems. Certainly you need technique. I guess what I'm saying is that I felt values were out of balance.

MK: What was missing?

JH: Heart. And yet some of the poets who taught me there had heart in their poems. But sometimes I felt like what was more important was the facade of being a poet. It became more of an academic pursuit than a pursuit of what it means to live. Granted, I was young and I had a lot of misconceptions to work through.

MK: Could you say more about your true teachers of poetry, those who have influenced your work?

JH: I feel like Galway Kinnell has been a teacher, even though I have never met him. I love his work. I think that what he has is a beautiful balance between technique and music. He is such a poet. He's a poet's poet with the music . . . and that's important to me. Of course James Wright. Richard Hugo. Adrienne Rich. I admire her sheer audacity. In the face of everything she learned from the fathers, given the time when she grew up and her own father's admonitions, still she became herself.

MK: I see that in your work, too. I don't know if you are aware of how daring your work is, and how dangerous!

JH: I'd better be! I love the work of Audre Lorde; she has also been one of my teachers.

MK: In the dedication to *In Mad Love and War* you affirm that "the erotic belongs in the poetry, as in the self." Can you elaborate?

JH: It has taken me years to divest myself of Christian guilt, the Puritan cloud that provides the base for culture in this country . . . or at least to recognize the twists and turns of that illogic in my own sensibility. In that framework the body is seen as an evil thing and is separate from spirit. The body and spirit are not separate. Nor is that construct any different in the place from which I write poetry. There is no separation. See Audre Lorde's "Uses of the Erotic: The Erotic as Power" for a viable definition of the erotic. Again, there is no separation.

MK: Feminist writings and lesbian feminist writings have been very important to you, your work?

JH: Yes, they have.

MK: Are there other writers who have been important to you that we should know about?

JH: Yes. I can think of a lot of writers who are important to me—Leslie Silko, for instance, whom I met shortly after I started writing. I actually took a fiction class from her at UNM as an undergraduate. . . . I especially liked our wine breaks in our office, the stories as we listened to Fleetwood Mac, watched for rain. . . . There are a lot of people . . . Beth Brant, Louis Oliver, June Jordan. . . .

MK: You dedicated the poem "Hieroglyphics" (from *In Mad Love and War*) to June Jordan. Why did she get that one?

JH: Well, it's a long story.

MK: It's a wonderful poem. It moves time and space, defying boundaries. Maybe June Jordan has a mythic imagination that can comprehend those leaps?

JH: Yeah. I mean she is somebody you can talk to like that and you can't talk to everyone that way. Sometimes in a poem you assume you can.

MK: Maybe you assume that because you need to make the poems accessible. You want people to feel like you are talking to them. *In Mad Love and War* is a breakthrough in terms of form and content. How do you feel about being formally inventive?

JH: I don't know. I don't really know what I'm doing.

MK: You lean into the unknown in those lines and see what happens?

JH: Yes, I do. I don't analyze. I mean certainly analysis is also part of the process of writing, but it's not primary. It comes later in the process.

MK: In part it's probably discipline that lets you explore. Discipline from the habit of years of writing. Do you write daily?

JH: I don't. I try to! [*laughter*] Well, do you?

MK: No, of course not! We were talking before about having families and having lives, and here you are in Knoxville. I mean, how are you supposed to write every day? Though William Stafford writes every day, even when he's traveling.

JH: Writing is a craft and there's something to doing it or you lose it. I used to paint and draw, and was quite a good artist, but I can't do it at the same level anymore. It's not that I've lost it but I'd have to get my chops together, so to speak, practice.

MK: Do you regret the decision to give up painting?

JH: I don't know that I regret it, but I certainly miss painting. That particular language was more familiar to me than the literary world. . . .

MK: What can you do in poetry that painting could not achieve?
JH: Speak directly in a language that was meant to destroy us.
MK: You have focused on your writing and on your music.
JH: Yes. If I'm not writing I'm thinking about it, or looking at things — I feel this infuses my vision. I'm listening for stories and listening to how words are put together and so on.
MK: Living a "writer's life"?
JH: Yes.
MK: The theme of music gets into your poetry when you dedicate poems to Billie Holiday or make reference to Coltrane. But I also sense the influence of jazz on your forms.
JH: Well, that wasn't conscious. I think it's coming out of playing the saxophone. I realized recently that I took it up exactly when I entered academe. I don't feel like I've become an academic but if you're going to be in that place, certainly it's going to rub off on you. [*laughter*]
MK: So you needed some way back to the body?
JH: Yes. Anyway, it was a time when I started teaching at the University of Colorado, Boulder. I had run from teaching in universities. I remember applying once years ago for the University of Texas, El Paso, and then I couldn't make it to MLA because I had no money. I preferred to keep my own hours, worked freelance, doing screenplay writing and readings and workshops — somehow the money always came in — but it's a tough existence, you have to have a lot of faith. I got a position as assistant professor at the University of Colorado, Boulder. I wrote "We Must Call a Meeting" right after I started teaching there because I was afraid that in that atmosphere, in that place, I was going to lose my poetry. That was around the time I started playing tenor sax. I play tenor and soprano now, but I realize that in a way it was a way to keep that poetry and keep that place.
MK: Keep your sanity, keep your juice!
JH: Yeah. I mean you pick up the saxophone again, I suppose it's like writing poetry, you are picking up the history of that. Playing saxophone is like honoring a succession of myths. . . . I never thought of this before but: the myth of saxophone and here comes Billy Holiday and there's Coltrane. I love his work dearly, especially "A Love Supreme." That song has fed me. And all of that becomes. When you play you're a part of that, you have to recognize those people.
MK: There's a very strong sense of community in your work, community of musicians you address; community of other writers, community of women. . . . I want to ask you about your great-aunt, to whom you dedicated *She Had Some Horses*.
JH: She's the relative I was closest to, and my life in some ways has uncannily paralleled hers. I miss her dearly. I always felt like I dropped into an alien family almost — maybe most people do — but when she and I got together, then I felt akin. She was very interested in art — she was a painter and was very sup-

portive of the Creek Nation Museum in Okmulgee, and donated most of her paintings to them. She traveled. We followed the same routes. Like her, I left Oklahoma for New Mexico — I was sent to an Indian boarding school in Santa Fe. It was a school for the arts, very innovative in its time, sort of like an Indian *Fame* school. When I left Oklahoma to go to high school there, in a way it saved my life. . . . In my travels I often met relatives of people that she knew. I have a necklace that Maria Martinez gave her — Maria, the potter from San Ildefonso. [My great-aunt] was someone who was married for six months and didn't like it and got a divorce, and spent a lot of time driving — she liked traveling Indian country — and also opened a jewelry shop.

MK: So there's movement, dynamism, in your family, and that restlessness. . . .

JH: Yes. Through her and her life I understand myself more clearly, and I love her dearly and miss her.

MK: Did she live long enough to see the book dedicated to her?

JH: No. She died before my father . . . in '82.

MK: But she knew you were a poet?

JH: Oh yes. She was real proud of that.

MK: What's new in your work that you feel comfortable talking about?

JH: The music, what I've been actively involved in to the tune of two or three hours a night (that's a lot of time!) is working with my band *Poetic Justice*. We're working on a show, putting together performances of my poems.

MK: Earlier you mentioned that you were frustrated about your music — why?

JH: I want to be farther along than I am. The music is still not as far along as the poetry. I fooled around with the sax for about seven years; I've played really seriously for only two years. . . . I want to play more and spend more time with it.

MK: What has the audience response been like?

JH: Our first gig we played in Santa Rosa, California, as part of a show of Indian performers called Indian Airobics, and most recently in Minneapolis. There we were brought in by The Loft. The audiences loved us. We're still rather raw in actual practice, we've very recently come together, but there's something we make as a band with the music and poetry that is rather exciting.

MK: I recently read a selection of autobiographical prose that you did, called "Family Album" (*The Progressive*, March 1992). Are you still working on the autobiographical writing?

JH: I'm working on a manuscript of autobiographical writings. I call it: "A Love Supreme; Stories, Poems, and Parables." There's much interest in it.

MK: So it's a mixture of several genres. The "Family Album" piece has passages of poetry in it.

JH: Yes, I think it's all one. I work within that assumption.

MK: You mentioned once before that you were putting together a book called "Reinventing the Enemy's Language." Are you still working on that?

JH: Yes. It's an anthology of Native women's writings. The original concept was to include writings from North and South America. We have one piece from a Native woman from El Salvador. We also received some prose from Rigoberta Menchu as well as from Wilma Mankiller, Cherokee Chief. We have work in it from Canada — it's quite wide-ranging, and includes many genres.

MK: What else is going on with your work? How far did you get with your essay on poetry and jazz?

JH: Oh, it's getting there. I have rewriting, rethinking to do. Some of the pieces are meant particularly for music. We're rearranging and performing two tunes of Jim Pepper's. Jim was a friend of mine, a fine jazz saxophone player who integrated jazz and tribal forms with music. He's the same tribe, Muskogee (or Creek) as well as Kaw Indian from Oklahoma. He died recently and I wanted to play a tribute for him. So we decided on "Witchi Tia To," for which he is most famous, and "Lakota Song" — which isn't an original tune but his arrangement is unique of this Lakota woman's love song. I "sing" the women's part on tenor sax. For "Witchi Tia To" I read a poem as a tribute to him, "The Place the Musician Became a Bear on the Streets of a City Meant to Kill Him."

MK: It's an intimate cosmic dance! You're doing so many things — we haven't touched on all of them — you're active in tribal life, you've been traveling to various tribal ceremonies, you teach, give workshops and readings. How do you find time to do it all? How do you make time for your writing?

JH: I was blessed with energy. I also try to integrate each aspect of my life. The poetry I mix with the music. And so on . . . though sometimes I just lose it. Then get back up again. I get excited about the possibilities and permutations of sound, about the color blue, for instance.

MK: I want to ask you whether there is a connection between poetry and politics, and poetry and prayer. Are these intermingled?

JH: Of course.

MK: In the back of *In Mad Love and War,* there's a poem based on a Native traditional form. . . .

JH: Which comes out of the Beauty Way Chant. I used to speak Navajo fairly well. I know that it's influenced my writing.

MK: I've been told that it's a very difficult language.

JH: It's a beautiful language. I love the way that you can say things in that language. So that's been a powerful influence.

MK: How did you learn Navajo?

JH: When I was a student at UNM I took Navajo Language for a year and a half. I had a wonderful teacher the first year, Roseanne Willink, a Navajo from western New Mexico. We had a great time in there. I remember making up jokes and then starting dreaming in Navajo. I don't know my own language, and wish to learn.

MK: Was your family bilingual?

JH: No, my father's mother had died when he was young. His father married a white woman. He had a lot of difficulties as a child. He was beaten a lot by his dad, and sent to a military school in Ponca City, Oklahoma. I think being Creek — which he was proud of — became a very painful thing for him.

MK: No wonder he had such a hard time coping. You spoke earlier about his alcoholism. He had so much to contend with as such a young person.

JH: Yes, he did. But anyway, back to your earlier question — for me there's always a definite link between poetry and prayer. I think that you can say that a poem is always a prayer for whomever you're speaking of. "Eagle Poem" at the end [of *In Mad Love and War*] is most obviously a prayer. You could look at all poems as being a prayer for our continuance. I mean even the act of writing, to be creative, has everything to do with our continuance as peoples.

The Place the Musician Became a Bear

for Jim Pepper

I think of the lush stillness of the end of a world, sung into place by
singers and the rattle of turtles in the dark morning.

When embers from the sacred middle are climbing out the other side of
stars.

When the moon has stompdanced with us from one horizon to the
next, such a soft awakening.

Our souls imitate lights in the Milky Way. We've always known where
to go to become ourselves again in the human comedy.

It's the how that baffles. A saxophone can complicate things.

You knew this, as do all musicians when the walk becomes a necessary
dance to fuel the fool heart.

Or the single complicated human becomes a wave of humanness and
forgets to be ashamed of making the wrong step.

I'm talking about an early morning in Brooklyn, the streets the color of
ashes, do you see the connection?

It's not as if the stars forsake us. We forget about them. Or remake the
pattern in a field of white crystal or of some other tricky fate.

We never mistook ourselves for anything but human.

The wings of the Milky Way lead back to the singers. And there's the
saxophone again.

It's about rearranging the song to include the subway hiss under your
feet in Brooklyn.

And the laugh of a Bear who thought he was a human.

As he plays that tune again, the one about the wobble of the earth spinning so damned hard it hurts.

Happiness

Happiness

◎ ◎ ◎

OFTEN HAPPINESS COMES NOT AS SOMEthing reached for or sought after, but as the by-product of work, or daily living, or any ordinary activity. Happiness can catch us unaware. And there are as many varieties of happiness as there are kinds of love or kinds of work. Happiness seems like a fitting close to *Worlds in Our Words* since it is underrecognized as a part of women's lives. Part of living is celebration and recognizing the joyful times that gleam throughout our lives, veins of gold that we must treasure as much as we honor struggle.

The fiction selections in "Happiness" show three different situations where female characters reach a happy peace with themselves and others after a difficult struggle. In Laurie Colwin's "Another Marvelous Thing," Billy Delielle has given birth at last to her first baby. However, the child is too small to leave the hospital, and Billy and her husband must cope with the feelings this engenders. As often happens, happiness occurs in moments that might seem ordinary to an onlooker. For Billy, simply being able to walk down the street with her family "just like everyone else" fills her heart with joy.

"Don't Explain" by Jewelle Gomez shows happiness in a more subdued moment. Though the story is set in Boston in 1959, it is permeated with the smoke and sultriness of Billie Holliday and the 1930s. The story moves subtly to show Letty her inner self and the pain and isolation she has endured for being a lesbian. Wonderful and surprising, then, is the reaching out to Letty by her young coworker Delia. Though she is untrusting, though she is sure that her life is meant for pain alone, Letty comes to find a place of unexpected happiness in her companionship with other women by the end of Gomez's tender story.

By contrast, Pam Houston's "A Blizzard Under Blue Sky" takes place outdoors, where the main character interacts with nature and with her two dogs. The unnamed female narrator is struggling with depression and she feels sure that winter camping will be the tonic she needs. Though the night turns out to be an especially cold one, though she can hardly sleep for fear of freezing to death, she rises with a sense of renewal.

Another instance of happiness found in self-realization comes in Judith Cofer's personal essay "More Room," where Cofer describes the transformation of her grandmother. A woman with eight children, she had her husband build an addition onto the house with each new child. The latest addition, we learn, is not for a new baby but for her husband, exiled to give Mama freedom from childbearing. Cofer emphasizes that "even now . . . she still emanates the kind of joy that can only be achieved by living according to the dictates of one's own heart."

Exercise of one's freedom is one way to happiness; another way is through the imagination. In "Just Reading" by Jamaica Kincaid, the narrator describes her delightful winter pastime of reading gardening supply catalogues. The author particularly enjoys catalogues for potatoes, ordinarily the humblest of foods. In Kincaid's prose, potatoes might be orchids, they are so lovingly described.

Luci Tapahonso's memoir also celebrates the ordinary, in this case trips into town with the family. The periodic trips to Farmington for supplies and for laundry facilities is sketched vividly and compellingly. At day's end, driving back, the father would sing and the mother would join him. Peace, security, and happiness blended, and the children would sleep until they reached home. The song of the parents twined around their childhood dreams.

Generosity is another movement-of-spirit that may result in happiness, as we see in *Am I Blue* by Beth Henley, in which two awkward and inexperienced teenagers are drawn together. By the play's end John Polk and Ashbe make an important connection with one another. When the play opens, it seems unlikely that the two will connect at all. Ashbe has shoplifted and attempts to hide under John Polk's raincoat at a table in a bar. They begin to talk, and before long Ashbe has invited John to her apartment. There, after mutual admissions of self-doubt, Ashbe and John reach out to each other.

The poetry selections for "Happiness" also show imaginative moments, moments of self-realization and of making connections with others. Alice Friman's "The Good News" takes the humorous, imaginative leap to the viewpoint of mosquitoes: how do they look at a juicy human walking into their territory?

Talking with one's women friends, eating and laughing, creating rituals — all these occur in Tess Gallagher's "Crêpes Flambeau" and in Davi Walders's "Reflections in Green Glass." Gallagher paints a wonderful scene of communion with friends in a restaurant: "The brandy / is aflare in a low blue hush and golden / now and red where he [the waiter] spills / the brown sugar saved / to make our faces wear the sudden burst." And in Davi Walders's poem two women at fifty laugh and drink together — the world is theirs in their closeness and shared experience.

A brilliant and sharply realized moment of selfhood is the treasure of

"The Moment" by Patricia Hampl. Here is an ordinary, prosaic moment in a parking garage transformed by sharp details and a sudden unexplained rush of good feeling. Healing can occur anywhere, any time, the poem tells us. "The moment" is a paradigm for an illumination in our time — rather than searching for immortality we find bliss in the moment that takes us out of ordinary time.

Exuberance and delight are expressed in Colette Inez's poem "Good News! Nilda Is Back." The speaker notices a sign at a beauty shop announcing Nilda's return, and she dances an associative train of thought imagining Nilda's life. The sound of the name triggers the verbal dance in the poet's lines. Wherever she has been, Nilda now "cha chas up the aisles," enlivening the city. In "So Much Happiness" Naomi Shihab Nye paints an exuberant picture of domestic happiness. Part of the pleasure she experiences is in the sense of the fleeting quality of happiness; it cannot stay, so surely we must "take no credit" for it. Linda Pastan's "The Happiest Day" is similar to Nye's poem in its celebration of daily living. We look back and suddenly we realize, "Ah, there we were happy!"

Denise Levertov's "O Taste and See" is a skillful celebration of sensual life, and it pairs nicely with "August" by Mary Oliver. In spare, condensed language Levertov spins her poem from the sight of a subway poster that Levertov sees as an invitation to experience "all that lives / to the imagination's tongue. . . ." The berry picker in Oliver's "August" similarly delights in the world, eating berries, conscious of "this happy tongue."

Another sensual poem composed in tercets is Alicia Ostriker's "Mother in Airport Parking Lot." All of the life cycle is packed into this song of temporary release from motherly cares. Ostriker's wit helps her to savor the moment.

Joyce Carol Thomas's "Sisters" finds happiness and magic in the ordinary, as two sisters run past prejudice into the field of "golden weeds," the world of their own vitality and gifts for observing. Seemingly effortless, this hard-won poem resembles Langston Hughes's poetry for all ages.

The interview with Joyce Carol Thomas contains joyful reflections on work, children, food, and spirit. Thomas's recipe for sweet potato pie is included so that the reader may share the palpable delights of this conversation. Thomas is eager to credit those who have given her strength, especially her mother. Despite a childhood without financial riches, Thomas celebrates abundance in her work. The connection between poetry and prayer is a real one for her: "I say 'Thank you God' when I write a poem that works."

Whether it is accidental wonder or a wrought, crafted experience, happiness is abundantly evident in the concluding writings of *Worlds in Our Words.* The voices of these writers may linger after the final page is turned and the book put aside. Laughter and richness may stay with the reader along with the her delightful winter pastime of reading gardening supply catalogues. The author particularly enjoys catalogues for potatoes, ordinarily the humblest of foods. In Kincaid's prose, potatoes might be orchids, they are so lovingly described.

Luci Tapahonso's memoir also celebrates the ordinary, in this case trips into town with the family. The periodic trips to Farmington for supplies and for laundry facilities is sketched vividly and compellingly. At day's end, driving back, the father would sing and the mother would join him. Peace, security, and happiness blended, and the children would sleep until they reached home. The song of the parents twined around their childhood dreams.

Generosity is another movement-of-spirit that may result in happiness, as we see in *Am I Blue* by Beth Henley, in which two awkward and inexperienced teenagers are drawn together. By the play's end John Polk and Ashbe make an important connection with one another. When the play opens, it seems unlikely that the two will connect at all. Ashbe has shoplifted and attempts to hide under John Polk's raincoat at a table in a bar. They begin to talk, and before long Ashbe has invited John to her apartment. There, after mutual admissions of self-doubt, Ashbe and John reach out to each other.

The poetry selections for "Happiness" also show imaginative moments, moments of self-realization and of making connections with others. Alice Friman's "The Good News" takes the humorous, imaginative leap to the viewpoint of mosquitoes: how do they look at a juicy human walking into their territory?

Talking with one's women friends, eating and laughing, creating rituals — all these occur in Tess Gallagher's "Crêpes Flambeau" and in Davi Walders's "Reflections in Green Glass." Gallagher paints a wonderful scene of communion with friends in a restaurant: "The brandy / is aflare in a low blue hush and golden / now and red where he [the waiter] spills / the brown sugar saved / to make our faces wear the sudden burst." And in Davi Walders's poem two women at fifty laugh and drink together — the world is theirs in their closeness and shared experience.

A brilliant and sharply realized moment of selfhood is the treasure of

she got out of bed at dawn and saw that the meadow was full of sea gulls who congregated each morning before the sun came up.

The nursery was an enormous room painted soft yellow. When Billy went to take the one short walk a day allowed her, she found herself averting her eyes from the neat rows of babies in their little plastic bins, but once in a while she found herself hungry for the sight of them. Taped to each crib was a blue (I'M A BOY) or pink (I'M A GIRL) card telling mother's name, the time of birth, and birth weight.

At six in the morning the babies were taken to their mothers to be fed. Billy was impressed by the surprising range of noises they made: mewing, squawking, bleating, piping, and squealing. The fact that she was about to have one of these creatures herself filled her with a combination of bafflement, disbelief, and longing.

For the past two months her chief entertainment had been to lie in bed and observe her unborn child moving under her skin. It had knocked a paperback book off her stomach and caused the saucer of her coffee cup to jiggle and dance.

Billy's husband, Grey, was by temperament and inclination a naturalist. Having a baby was right up his street. Books on neonatology and infant development replaced the astronomy and bird books on his night table. He gave up reading mysteries for texts on childbirth. One of these books had informed him that babies can hear in the womb, so each night he sang "Roll Along Kentucky Moon" directly into Billy's stomach. Another suggested that the educational process could begin before birth. Grey thought he might try to teach the unborn to count.

"Why stop there?" Billy said. "Teach it fractions."

Billy had a horror of the sentimental. In secret, for she would rather have died than showed it, the thought of her own baby brought her to tears. Her dreams were full of infants. Babies appeared everywhere. The buses abounded with pregnant women. The whole process seemed to her one half miraculous and the other half preposterous. She looked around her on a crowded street and said to herself: "Every one of these people was *born*."

Her oldest friend, Penny Stern, said to her: "We all hope that this pregnancy will force you to wear maternity clothes, because they will be so much nicer than what you usually wear." Billy went shopping for maternity clothes but came home empty-handed.

She said, "I don't wear puffed sleeves and frilly bibs and ribbons around my neck when I'm not pregnant, so I don't see why I should have to just because I am pregnant." In the end, she wore Grey's sweaters, and she bought two shapeless skirts with elastic waistbands. Penny forced her to buy one nice black dress, which she wore to teach her weekly class in economic history at the business school.

Grey set about renovating a small spare room that had been used for storage. He scraped and polished the floor, built shelves, and painted the walls pale apple green with the ceiling and moldings glossy white. They had once called this room the lumber room. Now they referred to it as the nursery. On the top of one of the shelves Grey put his collection of glass-encased bird's nests. He already had in mind a child who would go on nature hikes with him.

As for Billy, she grimly and without expression submitted herself to the number of advances science had come up with in the field of obstetrics.

It was possible to have amniotic fluid withdrawn and analyzed to find out the genetic health of the unborn and, if you wanted to know, its sex. It was possible to lie on a table and with the aid of an ultrasonic scanner see your unborn child in the womb. It was also possible to have a photograph of this view. As for Grey, he wished Billy could have a sonogram every week, and he watched avidly while Billy's doctor, a handsome, rather melancholy South African named Jordan Bell, identified a series of blobs and clouds as head, shoulders, and back.

Every month in Jordan Bell's office Billy heard the sound of her own child's heart through ultrasound and what she heard sounded like galloping horses in the distance.

Billy went about her business outwardly unflapped. She continued to teach and she worked on her dissertation. In between, when she was not napping, she made lists of baby things: crib sheets, a stroller, baby T-shirts, diapers, blankets. Two months before the baby was due, she and Penny went out and bought what was needed. She was glad she had not saved this until the last minute, because in her ninth month, after an uneventful pregnancy, she was put in the hospital, where she was allowed to walk down the hall once a day. The sense of isolation she had cherished — just herself, Grey, and their unborn child — was gone. She was in the hands of nurses she had never seen before, and she found herself desperate for their companionship because she was exhausted, uncertain, and lonely in her hospital room.

Billy was admitted wearing the nice black dress Penny had made her buy and taken to a private room that overlooked the park. At the bottom of her bed were two towels and a hospital gown that tied up the back. Getting undressed to go to bed in the afternoon made her feel like a child forced to take a nap. She did not put on the hospital gown. Instead, she put on the plaid flannel nightshirt of Grey's that she had packed in her bag weeks ago in case she went into labor in the middle of the night.

"I hate it here already," Billy said.

"It's an awfully nice view," Grey said. "If it were a little further along in the season I could bring my field glasses and see what's nesting."

"I'll never get out of here," Billy said.

"Not only will you get out of here," said Grey, "you will be released a totally transformed woman. You heard Jordan — all babies get born one way or another."

If Grey was frightened, he never showed it. Billy knew that his way of dealing with anxiety was to fix his concentration, and it was now fixed on her and on being cheerful. He had never seen Billy so upset before. He held her hand.

"Don't worry," he said. "Jordan said this isn't serious. It's just a complication. The baby will be fine and you'll be fine. Besides, it won't know how to be a baby and we won't know how to be parents."

Grey had taken off his jacket and he felt a wet place where Billy had laid her cheek. He did not know how to comfort her.

"A mutual learning experience," Billy said to his arm. "I thought nature was supposed to take over and do all this for us."

"It will," Grey said.

Seven o'clock began visiting hours. Even with the door closed Billy could hear shrieks and coos and laughter. With her door open she could hear champagne corks being popped.

Grey closed the door. "You didn't eat much dinner," he said. "Why don't I go downstairs to the delicatessen and get you something?"

"I'm not hungry," Billy said. She did not know what was in front of her, or how long she would be in this room, or how and when the baby would be born.

"I'll call Penny and have her bring something," Grey said.

"I already talked to her," Billy said. "She and David are taking you out to dinner." David was Penny's husband, David Hooks.

"You're trying to get rid of me," Grey said.

"I'm not," Billy said. "You've been here all day, practically. I just want the comfort of knowing that you're being fed and looked after. I think you should go soon."

"It's too early," said Grey. "Fathers don't have to leave when visiting hours are over."

"You're not a father yet," Billy said. "Go."

After he left she waited by the window to watch him cross the street and wait for the bus. It was dark and cold and it had begun to sleet. When she saw him she felt pierced with desolation. He was wearing his old camel's hair coat and the wind blew through his wavy hair. He stood back on his heels as he had as a boy. He turned around and scanned the building for her window. When he saw her, he waved and smiled. Billy waved back. A taxi, thinking it was being hailed, stopped. Grey got in and was driven off.

Every three hours a nurse appeared to take her temperature, blood pressure, and pulse. After Grey had gone, the night nurse appeared. She was a tall, middle-aged black woman named Mrs. Perch. In her hand she carried what looked like a suitcase full of dials and wires.

"Don't be alarmed," Mrs. Perch said. She had a soft West Indian accent. "It is only a portable fetal heart monitor. You get to say good morning and good evening to your baby."

She squirted a blob of cold blue jelly on Billy's stomach and pushed a transducer around in it, listening for the beat. At once Billy heard the sound of galloping hooves. Mrs. Perch timed the beats against her watch.

"Nice and healthy," Mrs. Perch said.

"Which part of this baby is where?" Billy said.

"Well, his head is back here, and his back is there and here is the rump and his feet are near your ribs. Or hers, of course."

"I wondered if that was a foot kicking," Billy said.

"My second boy got his foot under my rib and kicked with all his might," Mrs. Perch said.

Billy sat up in bed. She grabbed Mrs. Perch's hand. "Is this baby going to be all right?" she said.

"Oh my, yes," Mrs. Perch said. "You're not a very interesting case. Many others much more complicated than you have done very well and you will, too."

At four in the morning, another nurse appeared, a florid Englishwoman. Billy had spent a restless night, her heart pounding, her throat dry.

"Your pressure's up, dear," said the nurse, whose tag read "M. Whitely." "Dr. Bell has written orders that if your pressure goes up you're to have a shot of hydralazine. It doesn't hurt baby — did he explain that to you?"

"Yes," said Billy groggily.

"It may give you a little headache."

"What else?"

"That's all," Miss Whitely said.

Billy fell asleep and woke with a pounding headache. When she rang the bell, the nurse who had admitted her appeared. Her name was Bonnie Near and she was Billy's day nurse. She gave Billy a pill and then taped a tongue depressor wrapped in gauze over her bed.

"What's that for?" Billy said.

"Don't ask," said Bonnie Near.

"I want to know."

Bonnie Near sat down at the end of the bed. She was a few years older than Billy, trim and wiry with short hair and tiny diamond earrings.

"It's hospital policy," she said. "The hydralazine gives you a headache, right? You ring to get something to make it go away and because you have high blood pressure everyone assumes that the blood pressure caused it, not the drug. So this thing gets taped above your bed in the one chance in about fifty-five million that you have a convulsion."

Billy turned her face away and stared out the window.

"Hey, hey," said Bonnie Near. "None of this. I noticed yesterday that you're quite a worrier. Are you like this when you're not in the hospital? Listen. I'm a straight shooter and I would tell you if I was worried about you. I'm not. You're just the common garden variety."

Every morning Grey appeared with two cups of coffee and the morning paper. He sat in a chair and he and Billy read the paper together as they did at home.

"Is the house still standing?" Billy asked after several days. "Are the banks open? Did you bring the mail? I feel I've been here ten months instead of a week."

"The mail was very boring," Grey said. "Except for this booklet from the

Wisconsin Loon Society. You'll be happy to know that you can order a record called 'Loon Music.' Would you like a copy?"

"If I moved over," Billy said, "would you take off your jacket and lie down next to me?"

Grey took off his jacket and shoes, and curled up next to Billy. He pressed his nose into her face and looked as if he could drift off to sleep in a second.

"Childworld called about the crib," he said into her neck. "They want to know if we want white paint or natural pine. I said natural."

"That's what I think I ordered," Billy said. "They let the husbands stay over in this place. They call them 'dads.' "

"I'm not a dad yet, as you pointed out," Grey said. "Maybe they'll just let me take naps here."

There was a knock on the door. Grey sprang to his feet and Jordan Bell appeared.

"Don't look so nervous, Billy," he said. "I have good news. I think we want to get this baby born if your pressure isn't going to go down. I think we ought to induce you."

Billy and Grey were silent.

"The way it works is that we put you on a drip of pitocin, which is a synthetic of the chemical your brain produces when you go into labor."

"We know," Billy said. "Katherine went over it in childbirth class." Katherine Walden was Jordan Bell's nurse. "When do you want to do this?"

"Tomorrow," Jordan Bell said. "Katherine will come over and give you your last Lamaze class right here."

"And if it doesn't work?"

"It usually does," said Jordan Bell. "And if it doesn't, we do a second-day induction."

"And if that doesn't work?"

"It generally does. If it doesn't, we do a cesarean, but you'll be awake and Grey can hold your hand."

"Oh what fun," said Billy.

When Jordan Bell left, Billy burst into tears.

"Why isn't anything normal?" she said. "Why do I have to lie here day after day listening to other people's babies crying? Why is my body betraying me like this?"

Grey kissed her and then took her hands. "There is no such thing as normal," he said. "Everyone we've talked to has some story or other — huge babies that won't budge, thirty-hour labors. A cesarean is a perfectly respectable way of being born."

"What about me? What about me getting all stuck up with tubes and cut up into little pieces?" Billy said, and she was instantly ashamed. "I hate being like this. I feel I've lost myself and some whimpering, whining person has taken me over."

"Think about how in two months we'll have a two-month-old baby to take to the park."

"Do you really think everything is going to be all right?" Billy said.

"Yes," said Grey. "I do. In six months we'll be in Maine."

Billy lay in bed with her door closed reading her brochure from the Loon Society. She thought about the cottage she and Grey rented every August in Jewell Neck, Maine, on a lagoon. There at night with blackness all around them and not a light to be seen, they heard hoot owls and loons calling their night cries to one another. Loon mothers carried their chicks on their back, Billy knew. The last time she had heard those cries she had been just three months pregnant. The next time she heard them she would have a child.

She thought about the baby shower Penny had given her — a lunch party for ten women. At the end of it, Billy and Grey's unborn child had received cotton and wool blankets, little sweaters, tiny garments with feet, and two splendid Teddy bears. The Teddy bears had sat on the coffee table. Billy remembered the strange, light feeling in her chest as she looked at them. She had picked them both up and laughed with astonishment.

At a red light on the way home in a taxi, surrounded by boxes and bags of baby presents, she saw something that made her heart stop: Francis Clemens, who for two years had been Billy's illicit lover.

With the exception of her family, Billy was close only to Grey and Penny Stern. She had never been the subject of anyone's romantic passion. She and Grey, after all, had been fated to marry. She had loved him all her life.

Francis had pursued her: no one had ever pursued her before. The usual signs of romance were as unknown to Billy as the workings of a cyclotron. Crushes, she had felt, were for children. She did not really believe that adults had them.

Without her knowing it, she was incubating a number of curious romantic diseases. One day when Francis came to visit wearing his tweed coat and the ridiculously long paisley scarf he affected, she realized that she had fallen in love.

The fact of Francis was the most exotic thing that had ever happened in Billy's fairly stolid, uneventful life. He was as brilliant as a painted bunting. He was also, in marked contrast to Billy, beautifully dressed. He did not know one tree from another. He felt all birds were either robins or crows. He was avowedly urban and his pleasures were urban. He loved opera, cocktail parties, and lunches. They did not agree about economic theory, either.

Nevertheless, they spent what now seemed to Billy an enormous amount of time together. She had not sought anything like this. If her own case had been presented to her she would have dismissed it as messy, unnecessary, and somewhat sordid, but when she fell in love she fell as if backward into a swimming pool. For a while she felt dazed. Then Francis became a fact in her life. But in the end she felt her life was being ruined.

She had not seen Francis for a long time. In that brief glance at the red light she saw his paisley scarf, its long fringes flapping in the breeze. It was amazing that someone who had been so close to her did not know that she was having a baby. As the cab pulled away, she did not look back at him. She stared rigidly frontward, flanked on either side by presents for her unborn child.

The baby kicked. Mothers-to-be should not be lying in hospital beds thinking about illicit love affairs, Billy thought. Of course, if you were like the other mothers on the maternity floor and probably had never had an illicit love affair, you would not be punished by lying in the hospital in the first place. You would go into labor like everyone else, and come rushing into Maternity Admitting with your husband and your suitcase. By this time tomorrow she would have her baby in her arms, just like everyone else, but she drifted off to sleep thinking of Francis nonetheless.

At six in the morning, Bonnie Near woke her.

"You can brush your teeth," she said. "But don't drink any water. And your therapist is here to see you, but don't be long."

The door opened and Penny walked in.

"And how are we today?" she said. "Any strange dreams or odd thoughts?"

"How did you get in here?" Billy said.

"I said I was your psychiatrist and that you were being induced today and so forth," Penny said. "I just came to say good luck. Here's all the change we had in the house. Tell Grey to call constantly. I'll see you all tonight."

Billy was taken to the labor floor and hooked up to a fetal heart monitor whose transducers were kept on her stomach by a large elastic cummerbund. A stylish-looking nurse wearing hospital greens, a string of pearls, and perfectly applied pink lipstick poked her head through the door.

"Hi!" she said in a bright voice. "I'm Joanne Kelly. You're my patient today." She had the kind of voice and smile Billy could not imagine anyone's using in private. "Now, how are we? Fine? All right. Here's what we're going to do. First of all, we're going to put this IV into your arm. It will only hurt a little and then we're going to hook you up to something called pitocin. Has Dr. Bell explained any of this to you?" Joanne Kelly said.

"All," said Billy.

"Neat," Joanne Kelly said. "We *like* an informed patient. Put your arm out, please."

Billy stuck out her arm. Joanne Kelly wrapped a rubber thong under her elbow.

"Nice veins," she said. "You would have made a lovely junkie.

"Now we're going to start the pitocin," Joanne Kelly said. "We start off slow to see how you do. Then we escalate." She looked Billy up and down. "Okay," she said. "We're off and running. Now, I've got a lady huffing and puffing in the next room so I have to go and coach her. I'll be back real soon."

Billy lay looking at the clock, or watching the pitocin and glucose drip into her arm. She could not get a comfortable position and the noise of the fetal heart monitor was loud and harsh. The machine itself spat out a continual line of data.

Jordan Bell appeared at the foot of her bed.

"An exciting day — yes, Billy?" he said. "What time is Grey coming?"

"I told him to sleep late," Billy said. "All the nurses told me that this can take a long time. How am I supposed to feel when it starts working?"

"If all goes well, you'll start to have contractions and then they'll get stronger and then you'll have your baby."

"Just like that?" said Billy.

"Pretty much just like that."

But by five o'clock in the afternoon nothing much had happened.

Grey sat in a chair next to the bed. From time to time he checked the data. He had been checking it all day.

"That contraction went right off the paper," he said. "What did it feel like?"

"Intense," Billy said. "It just doesn't hurt."

"You're still in the early stages," said Jordan Bell when he came to check her. "I'm wiling to stay on if you want to continue, but the baby might not be born till tomorrow."

"I'm beat," said Billy.

"Here's what we can do," Jordan said. "We can keep going or we start again tomorrow."

"Tomorrow," said Billy.

She woke up exhausted with her head pounding. The sky was cloudy and the glare hurt her eyes. She was taken to a different labor room.

In the night her blood pressure had gone up. She had begged not to have a shot — she did not see how she could go into labor feeling so terrible, but the shot was given. It had been a long sleepless night.

She lay alone with a towel covering one eye, trying to sleep, when a nurse appeared by her side. This one looked very young, had curly hair, and thick, slightly rose-tinted glasses. Her tag read "Eva Gottlieb." Underneath she wore a button inscribed EVA: WE DELIVER.

"Hi," said Eva Gottlieb. "I'm sorry I woke you, but I'm your nurse for the day and I have to get you started."

"I'm here for a lobotomy," Billy said. "What are you going to do to me?"

"I'm going to run a line in you," Eva Gottlieb said. "And then I don't know what. Because your blood pressure is high, I'm supposed to wait until Jordan gets here." She looked at Billy carefully. "I know it's scary," she said. "But the worst that can happen is that you have to be sectioned and that's not bad."

Billy's head throbbed.

"That's easy for you to say," she said. "I'm the section."

Eva Gottlieb smiled. "I'm a terrific nurse," she said. "I'll stay with you."

Tears sprang in Billy's eyes. "Why will you?"

"Well, first of all, it's my job," said Eva. "And second of all, you look like a reasonable person."

Billy looked at Eva carefully. She felt instant, total trust. Perhaps that was part of being in hospitals and having babies. Everyone you came in contact with came very close, very fast.

Billy's eyes hurt. Eva was hooking her up to the fetal heart monitor. Her touch was strong and sure, and she seemed to know Billy did not want to be talked to. She flicked the machine on, and Billy heard the familiar sound of galloping hooves.

"Is there any way to turn it down?" Billy said.

"Sure," said Eva. "But some people find it consoling."

As the morning wore on, Billy's blood pressure continued to rise. Eva was with her constantly.

"What are they going to do to me?" Billy asked.

"I think they're probably going to give you magnesium sulfate to get your blood pressure down and then they're going to section you. Jordan does a gorgeous job, believe me. I won't let them do anything to you without explaining it first, and if you get out of bed first thing tomorrow and start moving around you'll be fine."

Twenty minutes later, a doctor Billy had never seen before administered a dose of magnesium sulfate.

"Can't you do this?" Billy asked Eva.

"It's heavy-duty stuff," Eva said. "It has to be done by a doctor."

"Can they wait until my husband gets here?"

"It's too dangerous," said Eva. "It has to be done. I'll stay with you."

The drug made her hot and flushed, and brought her blood pressure straight down. For the next hour, Billy tried to sleep. She had never been so tired. Eva brought her cracked ice to suck on and a cloth for her head. The baby wiggled and writhed, and the fetal heart monitor gauged its every move. Finally, Grey and Jordan Bell were standing at the foot of her bed.

"Okay, Billy," said Jordan. "Today's the day. We must get the baby out. I explained to Grey about the mag sulfate. We both agree that you must have a cesarean."

"When?" Billy said.

"In the next hour," said Jordan. "I have to check two patients and then we're off to the races."

"What do you think," Billy asked Grey.

"It's right," Grey said.

"And what about you?" Billy said to Eva.

"It has to be done," Eva said.

Jordan Bell was smiling a genuine smile and he looked dashing and happy.

"Why is he so uplifted?" Billy asked Eva after he had dashed down the hall.

"He loves the OR," she said. "He loves deliveries. Think of it this way: you're going to get your baby at last."

Billy lay on a gurney, waiting to be rolled down the hall. Grey, wearing hospital scrubs, stood beside her holding her hand. She had been prepped and given an epidural anesthetic, and she could no longer feel her legs.

"Look at me," she said to Grey. "I'm a mass of tubes. I'm a miracle of modern science." She put her hand over her eyes.

Grey squatted down to put his head near hers. He looked expectant, exhausted, and worried, but when he saw her scanning his face he smiled.

"It's going to be swell," Grey said. "We'll find out if it's little William or little Ella."

Billy's heart was pounding but she thought she ought to say something to keep her side up. She said, "I knew we never should have had sexual intercourse." Grey gripped her hand tight and smiled. Eva laughed. "Don't you guys leave me," Billy said.

Billy was wheeled down the hall by an orderly. Grey held one hand, Eva held the other. Then they left her to scrub.

She was taken to a large, pale green room. Paint was peeling on the ceiling in the corner. An enormous lamp hung over her head. The anesthetist appeared and tapped her feet.

"Can you feel this?" he said.

"It doesn't feel like feeling," Billy said. She was trying to keep her breathing steady.

"Excellent," he said.

Then Jordan appeared at her feet, and Grey stood by her head.

Eva bent down. "I know you'll hate this, but I have to tape your hands down, and I have to put this oxygen mask over your face. It comes off as soon as the baby's born, and it's good for you and the baby."

Billy took a deep breath. The room was very hot. A screen was placed over her chest.

"It's so you can't see," said Eva. "Here's the mask. I know it'll freak you out, but just breathe nice and easy. Believe me, this is going to be fast."

Billy's arms were taped, her legs were numb, and a clear plastic mask was placed over her nose and mouth. She was so frightened she wanted to cry out, but it was impossible. Instead she breathed as Katherine Walden had taught her to. Every time a wave of panic rose, she breathed it down. Grey held her hand. His face was blank and his glasses were fogged. His hair was covered by a green cap and his brow was wet. There was nothing she could do for him, except squeeze his hand.

"Now, Billy," said Jordan Bell, "you'll feel something cold on your stomach. I'm painting you with Betadine. All right, here we go."

Billy felt something like dull tugging. She heard the sound of foamy water. Then she felt the baby being slipped from her. She turned to Grey. His glasses had unfogged and his eyes were round as quarters. She heard a high, angry scream.

"Here's your baby," said Jordan Bell. "It's a beautiful, healthy boy."

Eva lifted the mask off Billy's face.

"He's perfectly healthy," Eva said. "Listen to those lungs." She took the baby to be weighed and tested. Then she came back to Billy. "He's perfect but he's little — just under five pounds. We have to take him upstairs to the preemie nursery. It's policy when they're not five pounds."

"Give him to me," Billy said. She tried to free her hands but they were securely taped.

"I'll bring him to you," Eva said. "But he can't stay down here. He's too small. It's for the baby's safety, I promise you. Look, here he is."

The baby was held against her forehead. The moment he came near her he stopped shrieking. He was mottled and wet.

"Please let me have him," Billy said.

"He'll be fine," Eva said. They then took him away.

The next morning Billy rang for the nurse and demanded that her IV be disconnected. Twenty minutes later she was out of bed slowly walking.

"I feel as if someone had crushed my pelvic bones," Billy said.

"Someone did," said the nurse.

Two hours later she was put into a wheelchair and pushed by a nurse into the elevator and taken to the Infant Intensive Care Unit. At the door the nurse said, "I'll wheel you in."

"I can walk," Billy said. "But thank you very much."

Inside, she was instructed to scrub with surgical soap and to put on a sterile gown. Then she walked very slowly and very stiffly down the hall. A Chinese nurse stopped her.

"I'm William Delielle's mother," she said. "Where is he?"

The nurse consulted a clipboard and pointed Billy down a hallway. Another nurse in a side room pointed to an isolette — a large plastic case with porthole windows. There on a white cloth lay her child.

He was fast asleep, his little arm stretched in front of him, an exact replica of Grey's sleeping posture. On his back were two discs the size of nickels hooked up to wires that measured his temperature and his heart and respiration rates on a console above his isolette. He was long and skinny and beautiful.

"He looks like a little chicken," said Billy. "May I hold him?"

"Oh, no," said the nurse. "Not for a while. He mustn't be stressed." She gave Billy a long look and said, "But you can open the windows and touch him."

Billy opened the porthole window and touched his leg. He shivered slightly. She wanted to disconnect his probes, scoop him up, and hold him next to her. She stood quietly, her hand resting lightly on his calf.

The room was bright, hot, and busy. Nurses came and went, washing their hands, checking charts, making notes, diapering, changing bottles of glucose solution. There were three other children in the room. One was very tiny and had a miniature IV attached to a vein in her head. A pink card was taped on her isolette. Billy looked on the side of William's isolette. There was a blue card and in Grey's tiny printing was written "William Delielle."

Later in the morning, when Grey appeared in her room he found Billy sitting next to a glass-encased pump.

"This is the well-known electric breast pump. Made in Switzerland," Billy said.

"It's like the medieval clock at Salisbury Cathedral," Grey said, peering into the glass case. "I just came from seeing William. He's much *longer* than I thought. I called all the grandparents. In fact, I was on the telephone all night after I left you." He gave her a list of messages. "They're feeding him in half an hour."

Billy looked at her watch. She had been instructed to use the pump for three minutes on each breast to begin with. Her milk, however, would not be given to William, who, the doctors said, was too little to nurse. He would be given carefully measured formula, and Billy would eventually have to wean him from the bottle and onto herself. The prospect of this seemed very remote.

As the days went by, Billy's room filled with flowers, but she spent most of her time in the Infant ICU. She could touch William but not hold him. The morning before she was to be discharged, Billy went to William's eight o'clock feeding. She thought how lovely it would be to feed him at home, how they might sit in the rocking chair and watch the birds in the garden below. In William's present home, there was no morning and no night. He had never been in a dark room, or heard bird sounds or traffic noise, or felt a cool draft.

William was asleep on his side wearing a diaper and a little T-shirt. The sight of him seized Billy with emotion.

"You can hold him today," the nurse said.

"Yes?"

"Yes, and you can feed him today, too."

Billy bowed her head. She took a steadying breath. "How can I hold him with all this hardware on him?" she said.

"I'll show you," said the nurse. She disconnected the console, reached into the isolette, and gently untaped William's probes. Then she showed Billy how to change him, put on his T-shirt, and swaddle him in a cotton blanket. In an instant he was in Billy's arms.

He was still asleep, but he made little screeching noises and wrinkled his nose. He moved against her and nudged his head into her arm. The nurse led her to a rocking chair and for the first time she sat down with her baby.

All around her, lights blazed. The radio was on and a sweet male voice sang, "I want you to be mine, I want you to be mine, I want to take you home, I want you to be mine."

William opened his eyes and blinked. Then he yawned and began to cry.

"He's hungry," the nurse said, putting a small bottle into Billy's hand.

She fed him and burped him, and then she held him in her arms and rocked him to sleep. In the process she fell asleep, too, and was woken by the nurse and Grey, who had come from work.

"You must put him back now," said the nurse. "He's been out a long time and we don't want to stress him."

"It's awful to think that being with his mother creates stress," Billy said.

"Oh, no!" the nurse said. "That's not what I mean. I mean, in his isolette it's temperature controlled."

Once Billy was discharged from the hospital she had to commute to see William. She went to the two morning feedings, came home for a nap, and met Grey for the five o'clock. They raced out for dinner and came back for the eight. Grey would not let Billy stay for the eleven.

Each morning she saw Dr. Edmunds, the head of neonatology. He was a tall, slow-talking, sandy-haired man with horn-rimmed glasses.

"I know you will never want to hear this under any other circumstances," he said to Billy, "but your baby is very boring."

"How boring?"

"Very boring. He's doing just what he ought to do." William had gone to the bottom of his growth curve and was beginning to gain. "As soon as he's a little fatter he's all yours."

Billy stood in front of his isolette watching William sleep.

"This is like having an affair with a married man," Billy said to the nurse who was folding diapers next to her.

The nurse looked at her uncomprehendingly.

"I mean you love the person but can only see him at certain times," said Billy.

The nurse was young and plump. "I guess I see what you mean," she said.

At home William's room was waiting. The crib had been delivered and put together by Grey. While Billy was in the hospital, Grey had finished William's room. The Teddy bears sat on the shelves. A mobile of ducks and geese hung over the crib. Grey had bought a secondhand rocking chair and had painted it red. Billy had thought she would be unable to face William's empty room. Instead she found she could scarcely stay out of it. She folded and refolded his clothes, reorganized his drawers, arranged his crib blankets. She decided what should be his homecoming clothes and set them out on the changing table along with a cotton receiving blanket and a wool shawl.

But even though he did not look at all fragile and he was beginning to gain weight, it often felt to Billy that she would never have him. She and Grey had been told ten days to two weeks from day of birth. One day when she felt she could not stand much more Billy was told that she might try nursing him.

Touch him on his cheek. He will turn to you. Guide him toward the breast and the magical connection will be made.

Billy remembered this description from her childbirth books. She had imagined a softly lit room, a sense of peacefulness, some soft, sweet music in the background.

She was put behind a screen in William's room, near an isolette containing an enormous baby who was having breathing difficulties.

She was told to keep on her sterile gown, and was given sterile water to wash her breasts with. At the sight of his mother's naked bosom, William began to howl. The sterile gown dropped onto his face. Billy began to sweat. All around her, the nurses chatted, clattered, and dropped diapers into metal bins and slammed the tops down.

"Come on, William," Billy said. "The books say that this is the blissful union of mother and child."

But William began to scream. The nurse appeared with the formula bottle and William instantly stopped screaming and began to drink happily.

"Don't worry," the nurse said. "He'll catch on."

At night at home she sat by the window. She could not sleep. She had never felt so separated from anything in her life. Grey, to distract himself, was stenciling the wall under the molding in William's room. He had found an early American design of wheat and cornflowers. He stood on a ladder in his blue jeans carefully applying the stencil in pale blue paint.

One night Billy went to the door of the baby's room to watch him, but Grey was not on the ladder. He was sitting in the rocking chair with his head in his hands. His shoulders were shaking slightly. He had the radio on, and he did not hear her.

He had been so brave and cheerful. He had held her hand while William was born. He had told her it was like watching a magician sawing his wife in half. He had taken photos of William in his isolette and sent them to their parents and all their friends. He had read up on growth curves and had bought Billy a book on breast-feeding. He had also purloined his hospital greens to wear each year on William's birthday. Now *he* had broken down.

She made a noise coming into the room and then bent down and stroked his hair. He smelled of soap and paint thinner. She put her arms around him, and she did not let go for a long time.

Three times a day, Billy tried to nurse William behind a screen and each time she ended up giving him his formula.

Finally she asked a nurse, "Is there some room I could sit in alone with this child?"

"We're not set up for it," the nurse said. "But I could put you in the utility closet."

There amidst used isolettes and cardboard boxes of sterile water, on the second try William nursed for the first time. She touched his cheek. He turned to her, just as it said in the book. Then her eyes crossed.

"Oh, my God!" she said.

A nurse walked in.

"Hurts, right?" she said. "Good for him. That means he's got it. It won't hurt for long."

At his evening feeding he howled again.

"The course of true love never did run smooth," said Grey. He and Billy walked slowly past the park on their way home. It was a cold, wet night.

"I am a childless mother," Billy said.

Two days later William was taken out of his isolette and put into a plastic bin. He had no temperature or heart probes, and Billy could pick him up without having to disconnect anything. At his evening feeding when the unit was quiet, she took him out in the hallway and walked up and down with him.

The next day she was greed by Dr. Edmunds.

"I've just had a chat with your pediatrician," he said. "How would you like to take your boring baby home with you?"

"When?" said Billy.

"Right now, if you have his clothes," Dr. Edmunds said. "Dr. Jacobson will be up in a few minutes and can officially release him."

She ran down the hall and called Grey.

"Go home and get William's things," she said. "They're springing him. Come and get us."

"You mean we can just walk out of there with him?" Grey said. "I mean, just take him under our arm? He barely knows us."

"Just get here. And don't forget the blankets."

A nurse helped Billy dress William. He was wrapped in a green and white receiving blanket and covered in a white wool shawl. On his head was a blue and green knitted cap. It slipped slightly sideways, giving him a raffish look.

They were accompanied in the elevator by a nurse. It was hospital policy that a nurse hold the baby, and hand it over at the door.

It made Billy feel light-headed to be standing out of doors with her child. She felt she had just robbed a bank and got away with it.

In the taxi, Grey gave the driver their address.

"Not door to door," Billy said. "Can we get out at the avenue and walk down the street just like everyone else?"

When the taxi stopped, they got out carefully. The sky was full of silver clouds and the air was blustery and cold. William squinted at the light and wrinkled his nose.

Then, with William tight in Billy's arms, the three of them walked down the street just like everyone else.

JEWELLE GOMEZ

Jewell Gomez was born in 1948 in Boston. She received degrees from Northeastern University and the Columbia School of Journalism. Her publications include two volumes of poetry, The Lipstick Papers *(1980) and* Flamingoes and Bears *(1987), and the novel* The Gilda Stories *(1991). A prolific book reviewer and public speaker—primarily on lesbian and gay issues—she has worked for PBS and taught women's studies, literature, and writing courses. Currently she lives in New York and is director of the literature program at the New York State Council of the Arts. Her writing is inspired by having participated in the antiwar movement of the 1960s and 70s, by her understanding of race and class issues, and by her lesbianism.*

"Don't Explain" was first published in 1987 in Love, Struggle and Change *and has been included in the* Penguin Book of Lesbian Short Stories. *The story reveals Gomez's sense of the dignity of working-class women of color as well as the importance for her of fighting isolation by belonging to a lesbian community.*

Don't Explain

BOSTON 1959

Letty deposited the hot platters on the table, effortlessly. She slid one deep-fried chicken, a club-steak with boiled potatoes and a fried porgie platter down her thick arm as if removing beaded bracelets. Each plate landed with a solid clink on the shiny Formica, in its appropriate place. The last barely settled before Letty turned back to the kitchen to get Bo John his lemonade and extra biscuits and then to put her feet up. Out of the corner of her eye she saw Tip come in the lounge. His huge shoulders, draped in sharkskin, barely cleared the narrow door frame.

"Damn! He's early tonight!" she thought but kept going. Tip was known for his generosity, that's how he'd gotten his nickname. He always sat at Letty's station because they were both from Virginia, although neither had been back in years. Letty had come up to Boston in 1946 and been waiting tables in the 411 Lounge since '52. She liked the people: the pimps were limited but flashy; the musicians who hung around were unpredictable in their pursuit of a good time and the "business" girls were generous and always willing to embroider a wild story. After Letty's mother died there'd been no reason to go back to Burkeville.

Letty took her newspaper from the locker behind the kitchen and filled a large glass with the tart grape juice punch for which the cook, Mabel, was famous.

"I'm going on break, Mabel. Delia's takin' my station."

She sat in the back booth nearest the kitchen beneath the large blackboard which displayed the menu. When Delia came out of the bathroom Letty hissed to get her attention. The reddish-brown skin of Delia's face was shiny with a country freshness that always made Letty feel a little warm.

"What's up, Miss Letty?" Her voice was soft and saucy.

"Take my tables for twenty minutes. Tip just came in."

The girl's already bright smile widened, as she started to thank Letty.

"Go 'head, go 'head. He don't like to wait. You can thank me if he don't run you back and forth fifty times."

Delia hurried away as Letty sank into the coolness of the overstuffed booth and removed her shoes. After a few sips of her punch she rested her head on the back of the seat with her eyes closed. The sounds around her were as familiar as her own breathing: squeaking Red Cross shoes as Delia and Vinnie passed, the click of high heels around the bar, the clatter of dishes in the kitchen and ice clinking in glasses. The din of conversation rose, levelled and rose again over the juke box. Letty had not played her record in days but the words spun around in her head as if they were on the turntable:

> . . . right or wrong don't matter
> when you're with me sweet
> Hush now, don't explain
> You're my joy and pain.

Letty sipped her cool drink; sweat ran down her spine soaking into the nylon uniform. July weather promised to give no breaks and the fans were working overtime like everybody else.

She saw Delia cross to Tip's table again. In spite of the dyed red hair, no matter how you looked at her, Delia was still a country girl: long and self-conscious, shy and bold because she didn't know any better. She'd moved up from Anniston with her cousin a year before and landed the job at the 411 immediately. She worked hard and sometimes Letty and she shared a cab going uptown after work, when Delia's cousin didn't pick them up in her green Pontiac.

Letty caught Tip eyeing Delia as she strode on long, tight-muscled legs back to the kitchen. "That lounge lizard!" Letty thought to herself. Letty had trained Delia: how to balance plates, how to make tips and how to keep the customer's hands on the table. She was certain Delia would have no problem putting Tip in his place. In the year she'd been working Delia hadn't gone out with any of the bar flies, though plenty had asked. Letty figured that Delia and her cousin must run with a different crowd. They talked to each other sporadically in the kitchen or during their break but Letty never felt that wire across her chest like Delia was going to ask her something she couldn't answer.

She closed her eyes again for the few remaining minutes. The song was back in her head and Letty had to squeeze her lips together to keep from humming aloud. She pushed her thoughts on to something else. But when she did she always stumbled upon Maxine. Letty opened her eyes. When she'd quit working at Salmagundi's and come to the 411 she'd promised herself never to think about any woman like that again. She didn't know why missing Billie so much brought it all back to her. She'd not thought of that time or those feelings for a while.

She heard Abe shout a greeting at Duke behind the bar as he surveyed his domain. That was Letty's signal. No matter whether it was her break or not she knew white people didn't like to see their employees sitting down, especially with their shoes off. By the time Abe was settled on his stool near the door, Letty was up, her glass in hand and on her way through the kitchen's squeaky swinging door.

"You finished your break already?" Delia asked.

"Abe just come in."

"Uh oh, let me git this steak out there to that man. Boy he sure is nosey!"

"Who, Tip?"

"Yeah, he ask me where I live, who I live with, where I come from like he supposed to know me!"

"Well just don't take nothing he say to heart and you'll be fine. And don't take no rides from him!"

"Yeah, he asked if he could take me home after I get off. I told him me and you had something to do."

Letty was silent as she sliced the fresh bread and stacked it on plates for the next orders.

"My cousin's coming by, so it ain't a lie, really. She can ride us."

"Yeah," Letty said as Delia giggled and turned away with her platter.

Vinnie burst through the door like she always did, looking breathless and bossy. "Abe up there, girl! You better get back on station. You got a customer."

Letty drained her glass with deliberation, wiped her hands on her thickly starched white apron and walked casually past Vinnie as if she'd never spoken. She heard Mabel's soft chuckle float behind her. She went over to Tip, who was digging into the steak like his life depended on devouring it before the plate got dirty.

"Everything alright tonight?" Letty asked, her ample brown body towering over the table.

"Yeah, baby, everything alright. You ain't workin' this side no more?"

"I was on break. My feet can't wait for your stomach, you know."

Tip laughed. "Break! What you need a break for, big and healthy as you is!"

"We all gets old, Tip. But the feet get old first, let me tell you that!"

"Not in my business, baby. Why don't you come on and work for me and you ain't got to worry 'bout your feet."

Letty sucked her teeth loudly, the exaggeration a part of the game they played over the years. "Man, I'm too old for that mess!"

"You ain't too old for me."

"Ain't nobody too old for you! Or too young neither, looks like."

"Where you and that gal goin' tonight?"

"To a funeral," Letty responded dryly.

"Aw woman get on away from my food!" The gold cap on his front tooth gleamed from behind his greasy lips when he laughed. Letty was pleased. Besides giving away money Tip liked to hurt people. It was better when he laughed.

The kitchen closed at 11:00 P.M. Delia and Letty slipped out of their uniforms in the tiny bathroom and were on their way out the door by 11:15. Delia looked even younger in her knife-pleated skirt and white cotton blouse. Letty did feel old tonight in her slacks and long-sleeved shirt. The movement of car headlights played across her face, which was set in exhaustion. The dark green car pulled up and they slipped in quietly, both anticipating tomorrow, Sunday, the last night of their work week.

Delia's cousin was a stocky woman who looked forty, Letty's age. She never spoke much. Not that she wasn't friendly. She always greeted Letty with a smile and laughed at Delia's stories about the customers. "Just close to the chest like me, that's all," Letty often thought. As they pulled up to the corner of Columbus Avenue and Cunard Street, Letty opened the rear door. Delia turned to her and said, "I'm sorry you don't play your record on your break no more, Miss Letty. I know you don't want to, but I'm sorry just the same."

Delia's cousin looked back at them with a puzzled expression but said nothing. Letty slammed the car door shut and turned to climb the short flight of stairs to her apartment. Cunard Street was quiet outside her window and the guy upstairs wasn't blasting his record player for once. Still, Letty lay awake and restless in her single bed. The fan was pointed at the ceiling, bouncing warm air over her, rustling her sheer nightgown.

Inevitably the strains of Billy Holiday's songs brushed against her, much like the breeze that fanned around her. She felt silly when she thought about it, but the melodies gripped her like a solid presence. It was more than the music. Billie had been her hero. Letty saw Billie as big, like herself, with big hungers, and some secret that she couldn't tell anyone. Two weeks ago, when Letty heard that the Lady had died, sorrow enveloped her. A refuge had been closed that she could not consciously identify to herself or to anyone. It embarrassed her to think about. Like it did when she remembered Maxine.

When Letty first started working at the 411 she met Billie when she'd come into the club with several musicians on her way back from the Jazz Festival. There the audience, curious to see what a real, live junkie looked like, had sat back waiting for Billie to fall on her face. Instead she'd killed them dead with her liquid voice and rough urgency. Still, the young, thin horn player kept having to reassure her: "Billie you were the show, the whole show!"

Once convinced, Billie became the show again, loud and commanding. She demanded her food be served at the bar and sent Mabel, who insisted on waiting on her personally, back to the kitchen fifteen times. Billie laughed at jokes that Letty could barely hear as she hustled back and forth between the abandoned kitchen and her own tables. The sound of that laugh from the bar penetrated her bones. She'd watched and listened, certain she saw something no one else did. When Billie had finished eating and gathered her entourage to get back on the road she left a tip, not just for Mabel but for each of the waitresses and the bartender. "Generous just like the 'business' girls," Letty was happy to note. She still had the two one dollar bills in an envelope at the back of her lingerie drawer.

After that, Letty felt even closer to Billie. She played one of the few Lady Day records on the juke box every night during her break. Everyone at the 411 had learned not to bother her when her song came on. Letty realized, as she lay waiting for sleep, that she'd always felt that if she had been able to say or do something that night to make friends with Billie, it might all have been different. In half sleep the faces of Billie, Maxine and Delia blended in her mind. Letty slid her hand along the soft nylon of her gown to rest it between her full thighs. She pressed firmly, as if holding desire inside herself. Letty could have loved her enough to make it better. That was Letty's final thought as she dropped off to sleep.

Sunday nights at the 411 were generally mellow. Even the pimps and prostitutes used it as a day of rest. Letty came in early and had a drink at the bar and talked with the bartender before going to the back to change into her uniform. She saw Delia through the window as she stepped out of the green Pontiac, looking as if she'd just come from Concord Baptist Church. "Satin Doll" was on the juke box, wrapping the bar in cool nostalgia.

Abe let Mabel close the kitchen early on Sunday and Letty looked forward to getting done by 10:00 or 10:30, and maybe enjoying some of the evening. When her break time came Letty started for the juke box automatically. She hadn't played anything by Billie in two weeks; now, looking down at the inviting glare, she knew she still couldn't do it. She punched the buttons that would bring up Jackie Wilson's "Lonely Teardrops" and went to the back booth.

She'd almost dropped off to sleep when she heard Delia whisper her name. She opened her eyes and looked up into the girl's smiling face. Her head was haloed in tight, shiny curls.

"Miss Letty, won't you come home with me tonight?"

"What?"

"I'm sorry to bother you, but your break time almost up. I wanted to ask if you'd come over to the house tonight . . . after work. My cousin'll bring you back home after."

Letty didn't speak. Her puzzled look prompted Delia to start again.

"Sometime on Sunday my cousin's friends from work come over to play cards, listen to music, you know. Nothin' special, just some of the girls from the office building down on Winter Street where she work, cleaning. She, I mean we, thought you might want to come over tonight. Have a drink, play some cards . . ."

"I don't play cards much."

"Well not everybody play cards . . . just talk . . . sitting around talking. My cousin said you might like to for a change."

Letty wasn't sure she liked the last part: "for a change," as if they had to entertain an old aunt.

"I really want you to come, Letty. They always her friends but none of them is my own friends. They alright, I don't mean nothin' against them, but it would be fun to have my own personal friend there, you know?"

Delia was a good girl. Those were the perfect words to describe her, Letty thought smiling. "Sure honey, I'd just as soon spend my time with you as lose my money with some fools."

They got off at 10:15 and Delia apologized that they had to take a cab uptown. Her cousin and her friends didn't work on Sunday so they were already at home. Afraid that the snag would give Letty an opportunity to back out, Delia hadn't mentioned it until they were out of their uniforms and on the sidewalk. Letty almost declined, tempted to go home to the safe silence of her room. But she didn't. She stepped into the street and waved down a Red and White cab. All the way uptown Delia apologized that the evening wasn't a big deal and cautioned Letty not to expect much. "Just a few friends, hanging around, drinking and talking." She was jumpy and Letty tried to put her at ease. She had not expected her first visit would make Delia so anxious.

The apartment was located halfway up Blue Hill Avenue in an area where a few blacks had recently been permitted to rent. They entered a long, carpeted hallway and heard the sounds of laughter and music ringing from the rooms at the far end.

Once inside, with the door closed, Delia's personality took on another dimension. This was clearly her home and Letty could not believe she ever really needed an ally to back her up. Delia stepped out of her shoes at the door and walked to the back with her same, long-legged gait. They passed a closed door, which Letty assumed to be one of the bedrooms, then came to a kitchen ablaze with light. Food and bottles were strewn across the pink and gray Formica top table. A counter opened from the kitchen into the dining-room, which was the center of activity. Around a large mahogany table sat five women in smoke-filled concentration, playing poker.

Delia's cousin looked up from her cards with the same slight smile as usual. Here it seemed welcoming, not guarded as it did in those brief moments in her car. She wore brown slacks and a matching sweater. The pink, starched points of her shirt collar peeked out at the neck.

Delia crossed to her and kissed her cheek lightly. Letty looked around the table to see if she recognized anyone. The women all seemed familiar in the way that city neighbors can, but Letty was sure she hadn't met any of them before. Delia introduced her to each one: Karen, a short, round woman with West Indian bangles up to her pudgy elbow; Betty, who stared intently at her cards through thick eyeglasses encased in blue cat-eye frames; Irene, a big, dark woman with long black hair and a gold tooth in front. Beside her sat Myrtle, who was wearing army fatigues and a gold Masonic ring on her pinky finger. She said hello in the softest voice Letty had ever heard. Hovering over her was Clara, a large red woman whose hair was bound tightly in a bun at the nape of her neck. She spoke with a delectable southern accent that drawled her "How're you doin" into a full paragraph that was draped around an inquisitive smile.

Delia became ill-at-ease again as she pulled Letty by the arm toward the French doors behind the players. There was a small den with a desk, some books and a television set. Through the next set of glass doors was a livingroom. At the record player was an extremely tall, brown-skinned woman. She bent over the wooden cabinet searching for the next selection, oblivious to the rest of the gathering. Two women sat on the divan in deep conversation, which they punctuated with constrained giggles.

"Maryalice, Sheila, Dolores . . . this is Letty."

They looked up at her quickly, smiled, then went back to their preoccupations: two to their gossip, the other returning to the record collection. Delia directed Letty back toward the foyer and the kitchen.

"Come on, let me get you a drink. You know, I don't even know what you drink!"

"Delia?" Her cousin's voice reached them over the counter, just as they stepped into the kitchen. "Bring a couple of beers back when you come, OK?"

"Sure, babe." Delia went to the refrigerator and pulled out two bottles. "Let me just take these in. I'll be right back."

"Go 'head, I can take care of myself in this department, girl." Letty surveyed the array of bottles on the table. Delia went to the dining-room and Letty mixed a Scotch and soda. She poured slowly as the reality settled on her. These women were friends, perhaps lovers, like she and Maxine had been. The name she'd heard for women like these burst inside her head: bulldagger. Letty flinched, angry she had let it in, angry that it frightened her. "Ptuh!" Letty blew air through her teeth as if spitting the word back at the air.

She did know these women, Letty thought, as she stood at the counter smiling out at the poker game. They were oblivious to her, except for Terry. Letty remembered that was Delia's cousin's name. As Letty took her first sip, Terry called over to her. "We gonna be finished with this game in a minute Letty, then we can talk."

"Take your time," Letty said, then went out through the foyer door and around to the living-room. She walked slowly on the carpet and adjusted her eyes to the light, which was a bit softer. The tall woman, Maryalice, had just put a record on the turntable and sat down on a love seat across from the other two women. Letty stood in the doorway a moment before the tune began:

> Hush now, don't explain
> Just say you'll remain
> I'm glad you're back
> Don't explain . . .

Letty was stunned, but the song sounded different here, among these women. Billie sang just to them, here. The isolation and sadness seemed less inevitable with these women listening. Letty watched Maryalice sitting with her long legs stretched out tensely in front of her. She was wrapped in her own thoughts, her eyes closed. She appeared curiously disconnected, after what had clearly been a long search for this record. Letty watched her face as she swallowed several times. Then Letty moved to sit on the seat beside her. They listened to the music while the other two women spoke in low voices.

When the song was over Maryalice didn't move. Letty rose from the sofa and went to the record player. Delia stood tentatively in the doorway of the living-room. Letty picked up the arm of the phonograph and replaced it at the beginning of the record. When she sat again beside Maryalice she noticed the drops of moisture on the other woman's lashes. Maryalice relaxed as Letty settled on to the seat beside her. They both listened to Billie together, for the first time.

◎ *PAM HOUSTON*

"A Blizzard Under Blue Sky" first appeared in Walking with the Twilight: Women Writers of the Southwest *(1994). Pam Houston is a contributing editor at* Elle *and* Ski *magazines. The idea of a "retreat" into nature to soothe the spirit is an idea Houston shares with Ernest Hemingway in his "Big Two-Hearted River" or in fishing scenes in* The Sun Also Rises. *(For more on Houston see page 508.)*

A Blizzard Under Blue Sky

The doctor said I was clinically depressed. It was February, the month in which depression runs rampant in the inversion-cloaked Salt Lake Valley and the city dwellers escape to Park City, where the snow is fresh and the sun is shining and everybody is happy, except me. In truth, my life was on the verge of more spectacular and satisfying discoveries than I had ever imagined, but of course I couldn't see that far ahead. What I saw was work that wasn't getting done, bills that weren't getting paid, and a man I'd given my heart to weekending in the desert with his ex.

The doctor said, "I can give you drugs."

I said, "No way."

She said, "The machine that drives you is broken. You need something to help you get it fixed."

I said, "Winter camping."

She said, "Whatever floats your boat."

One of the things I love the most about the natural world is the way it gives you what's good for you even if you don't know it at the time. I had never been winter camping before, at least not in the high country, and the weekend I chose to try and fix my machine was the same weekend the air mass they called the Alaska Clipper showed up. It was thirty-two degrees below zero in town on the night I spent in my snow cave. I don't know how cold it was out on Beaver Creek. I had listened to the weather forecast, and to the advice of my housemate, Alex, who was an experienced winter camper.

"I don't know what you think you're going to prove by freezing to death," Alex said, "but if you've got to go, take my bivvy sack, it's warmer than anything you have."

"Thanks," I said.

"If you mix Kool-aid with your water it won't freeze up," he said, "and don't forget lighting paste for your stove."

"Okay," I said.

"I hope it turns out to be worth it," he said, "because you are going to freeze your butt."

When everything in your life is uncertain, there's nothing quite like the clarity and precision of fresh snow and blue sky. That was the first thought I had on Saturday morning as I stepped away from the warmth of my truck and let my skis slap the snow in front of me. There was no wind and no clouds that morning, just still air and cold sunshine. The hair in my nostrils froze almost immediately. When I took a deep breath, my lungs only filled up halfway.

I opened the tailgate to excited whiners and whimpers. I never go skiing without Jackson and Hailey: my two best friends, my yin and yang of dogs. Some of you might know Jackson. He's the oversized sheepdog-and-something-else with the great big nose and the bark that will shatter glass. He gets out and about more than I do. People I've never seen before come by my house daily and call him by name. He's all grace, and he's tireless, he won't go skiing with me unless I let him lead. Hailey is not so graceful, and her body seems in constant indecision when she runs. When we ski she stays behind me, and on the downhills she tries to sneak rides on my skis.

The dogs ran circles in the chest-high snow while I inventoried my backpack one more time to make sure I had everything I needed. My sleeping bag, my Thermarest, my stove, Alex's bivvy sack, matches, lighting paste, flashlight, knife. I brought three pairs of long underwear — tops and bottoms — so I could change once before I went to bed, and once again in the morning, so I wouldn't get chilled by my own sweat. I brought paper and pen, and Kool-Aid to mix with my water. I brought Mountain House chicken stew and some freeze-dried green peas, some peanut butter and honey, lots of dried apricots, coffee and Carnation instant breakfast for morning.

Jackson stood very still while I adjusted his backpack. He carries the dog food and enough water for all of us. He takes himself very seriously when he's got his pack on. He won't step off the trail for any reason, not even to chase rabbits, and he gets nervous and angry if I do. That morning he was impatient with me. "Miles to go, Mom," he said over his shoulder. I snapped my boots into my skis and we were off.

There are not too many good things you can say about temperatures that dip past twenty below zero, except this: They turn the landscape into a crystal palace and they turn your vision into Superman's. In the cold thin morning air the trees and mountains, even the twigs and shadows, seemed to leap out of the background like a 3-D movie, only it was better than 3-D because I could feel the sharpness of the air.

I have a friend in Moab who swears that Utah is the center of the fourth dimension, and although I know he has in mind something much different and more complicated than subzero weather, it was there, on that ice-edged morning, that I felt on the verge of seeing something more than depth perception in the brutal clarity of the morning sun.

As I kicked along the first couple of miles, I noticed the sun crawling higher in the sky and yet the day wasn't really warming, and I wondered if I should have brought another vest, another layer to put between me and the cold night ahead.

It was utterly quiet out there, and what minimal noise we made intruded on the morning like a brass band: the squeaking of my bindings, the slosh of the water in Jackson's pack, the whoosh of nylon, the jangle of dog tags. It was the bass line and percussion to some primal song, and I kept wanting to sing to it, but I didn't know the words.

Jackson and I crested the top of a hill and stopped to wait for Hailey. The trail stretched out as far as we could see into the meadow below us and beyond, a double track and pole plants carving through softer trails of rabbit and deer.

"Nice place," I said to Jackson, and his tail thumped the snow underneath him without sound.

We stopped for lunch near something that looked like it could be a lake in its other life, or maybe just a womb-shaped meadow. I made peanut butter and honey sandwiches for all of us, and we opened the apricots.

"It's fabulous here," I told the dogs. "But so far it's not working."

There had never been anything wrong with my life that a few good days in the wilderness wouldn't cure, but there I sat in the middle of all those crystal-coated trees, all that diamond-studded sunshine, and I didn't feel any better. Apparently clinical depression was not like having a bad day, it wasn't even like having a lot of bad days, it was more like a house of mirrors, it was like being in a room full of one-way glass.

"Come on, Mom," Jackson said. "Ski harder, go faster, climb higher."

Hailey turned her belly to the sun and groaned.

"He's right," I told her. "It's all we can do."

After lunch the sun had moved behind our backs, throwing a whole different light on the path ahead of us. The snow we moved through stopped being simply white and became translucent, hinting at other colors, reflections of blues and purples and grays. I thought of Moby Dick, you know, the whiteness of the whale, where white is really the absence of all color, and whiteness equals truth, and Ahab's search is finally futile, as he finds nothing but his own reflection.

"Put your mind where your skis are," Jackson said, and we made considerably better time after that.

The sun was getting quite low in the sky when I asked Jackson if he thought we should stop to build the snow cave, and he said he'd look for the next good bank. About one hundred yards down the trail we found it, a gentle slope with eastern exposure that didn't look like it would cave in under any circumstances. Jackson started to dig first.

Let me make one thing clear. I knew only slightly more about building snow caves than Jackson, having never built one, and all my knowledge coming from disaster tales of winter camping fatalities. I knew several things not to do when building a snow cave, but I was having a hard time knowing what exactly to do. But Jackson helped, and Hailey supervised, and before too long we had a little cave built, just big enough for three. We ate dinner quite pleased with our accomplishments and set the bivvy sack up inside the cave just as the sun slipped away and dusk came over Beaver Creek.

The temperature, which hadn't exactly soared during the day, dropped twenty degrees in as many minutes, and suddenly it didn't seem like such a great idea to change my long underwear. The original plan was to sleep with the dogs inside the bivvy sack but outside the sleeping bag, which was okay with Jackson the super-metabolizer, but not so with Hailey, the couch potato. She whined and wriggled and managed to stuff her entire fat body down inside my mummy bag, and Jackson stretched out full-length on top.

One of the unfortunate things about winter camping is that it has to happen when the days are so short. Fourteen hours is a long time to lie in a snow cave under the most perfect of circumstances. And when it's thirty-two below, or forty, fourteen hours seems like weeks.

I wish I could tell you I dropped right off to sleep. In truth, fear crept into my spine with the cold and I never closed my eyes. Cuddled there, amid my dogs and water bottles, I spent half of the night chastising myself for thinking

I was Wonder Woman, not only risking my own life but the lives of my dogs, and the other half trying to keep the numbness in my feet from crawling up to my knees. When I did doze off, which was actually more like blacking out than dozing off, I'd come back to my senses wondering if I had frozen to death, but the alternating pain and numbness that started in my extremities and worked its way into my bones convinced me I must still be alive.

It was a clear night, and every now and again I would poke my head out of its nest of down and nylon to watch the progress of the moon across the sky. There is no doubt that it was the longest and most uncomfortable night of my life.

But then the sky began to get gray, and then it began to get pink, and before too long the sun was on my bivvy sack, not warm, exactly, but holding the promise of warmth later in the day. And I ate apricots and drank Kool-Aid flavored coffee and celebrated the rebirth of my fingers and toes, and the survival of many more important parts of my body. I sang "Rocky Mountain High" and "If I Had a Hammer," and yodeled and whistled, and even danced the two-step with Jackson and let him lick my face. And when Hailey finally emerged from the sleeping bag a full hour after I did, we shared a peanut butter and honey sandwich and she said nothing ever tasted so good.

We broke camp and packed up and kicked in the snow cave with something resembling glee.

I was five miles down the trail before I realized what had happened. Not once in that fourteen-hour night did I think about deadlines, or bills, or the man in the desert. For the first time in many months I was happy to see a day beginning. The morning sunshine was like a present from the gods. What really happened, of course, is that I remembered about joy.

I know that one night out at thirty-two below doesn't sound like much to those of you who have climbed Everest or run the Iditarod or kayaked to Antarctica, and I won't try to convince you that my life was like the movies where depression goes away in one weekend, and all of life's problems vanish with a moment's clear sight. The simple truth of the matter is this: On Sunday I had a glimpse outside of the house of mirrors, on Saturday I couldn't have seen my way out of a paper bag. And while I was skiing back toward the truck that morning, a wind came up behind us and swirled the snow around our bodies like a blizzard under blue sky. And I was struck by the simple perfection of the snowflakes, and startled by the hopefulness of sun on frozen trees.

◎ *JAMAICA KINCAID*

"Just Reading" appeared in 1993 in the New Yorker, *the periodical for which Jamaica Kincaid is a staff writer (see page 419). Kincaid admits to a love of gardening catalogues that keep her "warm" in the winter; one that she particularly admires "is the most beautiful catalogue I receive each year; it is simple, like a hymn."*

Just Reading

On the day, a few weeks ago, that the temperature was ten below zero, the Ronniger's Seed Potatoes catalogue arrived, and that was the cheeriest thing, for I spent the afternoon sitting in a bathtub of hot water, trying to satisfy a craving for overchilled ginger ale and oranges, and reading this little treasure. It is the most beautiful catalogue I receive each year; it is simple, like a hymn. (I was brought up a Methodist, and I am thinking of the first one that was in my children's hymnal, "All Things Bright and Beautiful.") It is plain, humble, and comforting — the opposite of the White Flower Farm catalogue, which is sumptuous, showy, and expensive-looking. Ronniger's is printed on newsprint, and it has photographs that might have been taken with a not very good camera, or by someone who was not a particularly good photographer, or a combination of the two. But the photographs are adorable. They are of people doing one thing or another with potatoes, or of machinery used in the cultivation of potatoes, or of potatoes just by themselves, in a bowl or some other household container. It is a catalogue only of potatoes and a few things that might enhance the flavor of a potato (onions, garlic, salt) or might make a potato grow better (a cover crop of alfalfa or clover). There is a particularly appealing picture of a young boy gathering potatoes; he has a look of blissful concentration on his face, as if the world outside the cultivation of the potato were completely closed to him. But this is only conjecture on my part; it could very well be that this boy is deeply familiar not only with the cultivation of the potato but with its history, with the crucial part it played in his ancestors' diet and, therefore, development as a people.

The process of receiving and reading catalogues may not be as important to my garden as my weeding is, but that is the way I begin the gardening year. The very big, showy ones, like the White Flower Farm and Wayside Gardens catalogues, are psychological lifts: I never read them; I only look again and again at the pictures. The best catalogues for reading are not unlike wonderful books; they plunge me deep into the world of the garden, the growing of the things advertised (because what are these descriptions of seeds and plants but advertisements?), and that feeling of being unable to tear myself away comes over me, and I look out the window at the garden, which is blankets upon blankets of white, and see it filled with the things described in the catalogue I am reading.

It is in such a state that I read the Ronniger's Seed Potatoes catalogue. Here is a description of an early-maturing potato called the Dazoc: "Talk about a delicious red potato . . . we found this one in our neighborhood on the Moyie River Road, grown since 1953 by Bud Behrman, who claims it came from North Dakota and has long since disappeared from commercial markets. Yet, he and his brother have zealously kept it going over the years. Round red deep eyes, excellent flavor, delicious baked and great hash browns, stores well. Bud and family eat them 'til the next crop produces new potatoes." This seemingly straightforward description of a kind of potato provided many hours of deliberation and fantasy on my part: How many kinds of early-maturing potatoes can I grow this year? Should Dazoc be among them? Surely a potato grown by someone named Bud Behrman and eaten regularly by him and his family must be a good potato. And the Behrmans — who are the Behrmans? I imagined the Behrman family as the nicest people ever. When I was young and living far away from my family, my life was almost completely empty of domestic routine, and so I made a fetish of the way ordinary people in families lived inside their homes. I read women's magazines obsessively and would often cook entire meals (involving meats in tins, and frozen vegetables) from the recipes I found in them. One year, I made an entire Thanksgiving dinner that was the same Thanksgiving dinner a family somewhere in the Midwest ate every year. This meal was featured in one of the magazines I read all the time, and the portrayal of these people and their food was so compelling to me that not only did I make the entire meal but, after a friend and I ate it, I called up the Midwestern family and told them what I had done; they were perplexed and flattered. I believe that that meal brought to an end that particular expression of alienation in my life. It was the memory of this that made me not order the Dazoc potato but remain content with simply imagining the Behrmans and their potato dinners.

Then I moved on to the plantsman Shepherd Ogden and the catalogue he puts out with his wife, The Cook's Garden. It is from him that I always get my lettuce and other salad greens, and a beet called Formanova, which he describes this way (the descriptions are written by him; he is a writer). "An old favorite of ours and for good reason. Very tender and sweet, with a unique carrot shape that makes it easy to peel and slice. Can be planted closer than other main crops for high yields." But this beet isn't shaped like a carrot at all. It is shaped like a penis, and I always refer to it that way, I call it the penis-shaped beet. This used to be my favorite catalogue to read before I discovered Ronniger's, and it remains high on the list of the catalogues I read over and over just for the descriptions. I know Shepherd Ogden well; he had been the previous tenant of the first house I lived in here in Vermont, and each year when I read his catalogue it is quite like talking to him. When I first met Shep, he mystified me; he is a very tall man who moves much too swiftly for his height, and he speaks as swiftly as he moves. I finally understood him when, one day, he told me that until he was eighteen years old he was five feet tall, and then suddenly he grew twelve inches in twelve months, but throughout his teenage years he thought of himself as a short person, and he never got over that. Knowing him in that way, I read his catalogue and feel that he is speaking directly to me.

I am having a minor infatuation with the Shepherd's Garden Seeds catalogue (no relation to Shep Ogden's catalog), so I ended up ordering more than I meant to from them. But the description of the Kidma cucumbers was hard to resist: "Developed for eating out of hand, they are perfect when picked at 5 to 8 inches long. These cucumbers are not marketed commercially because they are too delicate to stand shipping." This is the luxury of the kitchen garden — growing things that you cannot buy at the store. And from Shepherd's Garden Seeds I also got Chioggia Striped beets (described as an Italian variety), which I tried late last summer at a friend's house; they revealed pink-in-white circles when sliced, and they were delicious plain, without a vinaigrette or butter. And I ordered Blue Lake string beans, which I have never grown; they are the most common string beans to grow, and, perversely, for just that reason I wanted to have them this year. But it was in the seeds for flowers that I lost myself: three packets each of Old Spice and Early Mammoth sweet peas. Where I will put them all, I don't know yet, but they'll all have to go in; there's no such thing as too many sweet peas. I also ordered packets of rose campion, cottage pinks, foxglove, stock, and double Canterbury bells.

I plan to plant all these flowers, along with some love-in-a-mist (from Smith & Hawken), daylilies, platycodon, malva, and many other flowers I find beautiful in themselves, completely disregarding the great Gertrude Jekyll's admonitions about color schemes, complementary or contrasting. Lately I have been immersed in her writing, and it was this extraordinary pleasure that the arrival of the spring catalogues interrupted. In her book "Colour Schemes for the Flower Garden" (which is hard to find in this country, and which I just happened to come across in Borders Bookshop, in Ann Arbor, Michigan) she says, "I am strongly of opinion that the possession of a quantity of plants, however good the plants may be themselves and however ample their number, does not make a garden; it only makes a *collection.*" And, again, "Given the same space of ground and the same material, they may either be fashioned into a dream of beauty, a place of perfect rest and refreshment of mind and body — a series of soul-satisfying pictures — a treasure of well-set jewels; or they may be so misused that everything is jarring and displeasing. To learn how to perceive the difference and how to do right is to apprehend gardening as a fine art." All that and much more of what she says about beauty and art in the garden is perfectly true — but what if all the flowers I love and want very much to grow are, when seen together, all wrong, all jarring and displeasing? When I lived in my old house and had just started gardening and knew even less than I do now, I decided one day to place a large square bed in the middle of my small lawn. It seemed an odd thing to everybody — everybody told me so — but I just went ahead and put things I liked in this square: white peonies, pink peonies, some yellow lupines, some Johnny-jump-ups, and some portulaca, and then, on one edge, lavender and oregano. I found this quadrangle beautiful and used to sit for long stretches in a chair and gaze at it; at the time I was much in love with lupines.

Devotion to what I love, or might love, has caused me to order six rugosa Alba, a Reine des Violettes, and a Madame Isaac Pereire — all roses — from Wayside Gardens. I wanted four Paul's Himalayan Musk from them, too — this is a great rambler, pink, which I had planned to run up some old apple trees (an idea not unique to me; I got it from Gertrude Jekyll) — but they were sold out. The rugosa Alba I shall put in an opening near the road; I don't know how they will look, but they will be full of thorns, so the deer won't eat them. They might keep the deer out, that is. I could make a barrier against the deer from many things that grow naturally around here — honeysuckle is something many people use in this way, also spirea and hydrangea — and the idea of staying in harmony with your surroundings is another one of Gertrude Jekyll's laws, but I very much want a hedge of coarse white roses, with red hips later on. The Reine des Violettes, too, might be strange — I believe I am opposed to blue roses — but once I saw a picture of it I began to imagine it in the corner, at the far end of my new stone wall, alone with some Canterbury bells, blue and pink platycodon (White Flower Farm), and blue and white campanula. In a large order to White Flower Farm that I made — this went against my promise to myself not to order too much from them, because they are expensive and they seem so conceited in their advertisements, but their daylilies are the best I have ever grown — were six Canada lilies. They look best surrounded by masses of green grass and brown tree trunks; that is how I saw them when I first fell in love with them, in a field across from my first house in Vermont, the house that Shep Ogden used to occupy. They are tall, with stems two fingers thick and modest-sized, cadmium-color, cup-shaped flowers, their heads bent down as if in a demonstration of humility. And where to put these? There is a part of my garden that I could call the woodland garden, but I won't (I don't like giving nicknames to places in my garden); that is where the Canada lilies will go, along with some ferns that I am just beginning to love and some perennial foxgloves. I don't know how this will look. I may not only violate established rules of gardening but also not please me in the end at all.

In the Park Seed catalogue I saw some beautiful portulaca. When I think of this little spready plant with short, spiny yet succulent leaves and roselike flowers, I think of it by itself, isolated, disregarding how it might fit into the garden as a whole. My love for this plant is no longer a mystery to me. Last summer, as I knelt over it, fretting about its health (fretting is the most common of all the moods that a gardener can have; a gardener frets even when things are going well), the origins of my feeling for it became clear to me. When I was little and lived in Antigua, my mother used to leave me in the care of a woman who, once we were alone, would take me to visit a friend of hers, a man, whose name I cannot remember. They would talk for a while and then disappear inside — to have sex, I realized some time later — leaving me all by myself outside. He lived in a small yellow house, and the shutters, which they would close up when they were inside, were painted a vivid blue. In the front of the house was a little walkway, and on either side of the walk were two banks carpeted with this flower, portulaca, which we called bachelor's buttons, and which behaves like a perennial there. These portulaca were crimson and deep purple, and I used to dance up and down around them, pretending that I was a little girl from somewhere else. From that garden I could see the sea, and sometimes a locomotive, pulling cars loaded with sugarcane, would pass by, for the house was near the railroad tracks. The woman and I would return to her home, and she always had a bag full of brown sugar, the raw kind, only a stage away from being molasses; she would sometimes give me a lump of it to eat. She and my mother had an enormous fight when my mother found out about our trips to the man's house, but they would have had an enormous fight anyway; people there always do.

Gertrude Jekyll's nurse told her that dandelions were "Nasty Things," and wouldn't allow her to pick them and carry them home. I learned this in a biography of Miss Jekyll written by a woman named Sally Festing, which I read intermittently—in between the spring catalogues and Gertrude Jekyll's own writing. I identify strongly with the pain writers experience when they are criticized, so I don't want to say too loudly how unsatisfying I found this book. It's possible that the nurse's disapproval of dandelions was an event that led to the person Gertrude Jekyll became and her choice of vocation, but the author doesn't say; this kind of speculation doesn't seem to interest her. This book is very decent and discreet—just the qualities I want in a friend, but not in a book I am reading. Was Gertrude Jekyll ever in love with anyone? Did she ever have sex? That's just the kind of thing I like to know about other people. Gertrude Jekyll had many close friendships with women; the book does say that. And it says that she knew John Ruskin; she was much influenced by his ideas about art. But I wanted to know what Gertrude thought of the fact that an English court had annulled Ruskin's marriage, which had never been consummated. Apparently he had been horrified to discover, on his wedding night, that his wife had pubic hair, she was not smooth and hairless like the nude statues he so admired. (All this I read somewhere else, though.) This biography skips happily along, and then surprises you with a new piece of information. I carried around in my head the fact that the architect Edwin Lutyens and his wife, Emily, were very much in love, and then all of a sudden I read that Emily had become involved in some way not at all clear to me with Krishnamurti, and that Edwin turned up to visit Gertrude in the company of Lady Victoria Sackville and her daughter Vita. I guessed that Edwin and Lady Victoria Sackville were having an affair. Sometimes he called Gertrude Bumps, and sometimes Woozle. She was an ugly woman, and very conscious of it. What better way to divert attention from herself than to make pronouncements about correctness and beauty in the garden? What a perfect example of making a virtue of your own neuroses!

As I finish writing this, the thermometer outside my door reads eighteen below zero. I now *know* that spring will never come. I shall spend the rest of my life reading seed and plant catalogues, and books about gardens and the people connected to them.

◎ LUCI TAPAHONSO

"It Was a Special Treat" is a reminiscence from Tapahonso's collection Sáanii Dahataał/ The Women Are Singing *(see page 229). The narrator reflects on family trips and the feeling of security induced by hearing her father sing Navajo songs.*

It Was a Special Treat

Trips to Farmington were a special treat when we were children. Sometimes when we didn't get to go along, we cried so hard that we finally had to draw straws to decide fairly who would get to go. My oldest brother always went because he drove, my other brother went because he helped carry laundry, my father went because he was the father, and my mother went because she had the money and knew where to go and what to buy. And only one or two kids were allowed to go because we got in the way and begged for things all the time.

We got up early on the Saturdays that we were going to town — we would get ready, sort laundry, and gather up pop bottles that we turned in for money. My father always checked the oil and tires on the pickup, and then he and my brothers would load the big laundry tubs, securing the canvas covers with heavy wooden blocks. We would drive out of the front yard, and the unfortunate ones who had to stay home waved good-bye sullenly. The dogs chased the truck down the road a ways before turning home.

In Farmington, we would go to the laundry first. It was always dark and clammy inside. We liked pulling the clothes out of the wringer even though my mother was nervous about letting us help. After that, we drove downtown and parked in the free lot north of Main Street. Sometimes my father got off at the library, and we picked him up after we finished shopping. Someone always had to "watch" the pickup, and usually the one who was naughty at the laundry had to sit in the pickup for two or three hours while everyone else got to "see things" around town. If my father didn't go to the library, the kids were off the hook, naughty or not, because he waited in the pickup and read "The Readers Digest."

When we stopped at Safeway, our last stop, it was early evening. My mother would buy some bologna or cooked chicken in plastic wrapped trays and a loaf of bread. We would eat this on our way home. After the groceries were packed in securely under the canvas and wooden blocks, we talked about who we saw, what we should have bought instead of what we did buy (maybe we could exchange it next time), then the talking would slow down and by the time we reached the Blue Window gas station, everyone but my father was sleepy.

He would start singing in Navajo in a clear, strong voice and once in a while, my mother would ask him about a certain song she heard once. "Do you know it? It was something like this . . ." and she would sing a bit, he would catch it and finish the song. We listened half asleep. I would whisper to my sister, "He sounds like those men on Navajo Hour." "I know. It's so good," she'd answer, and we'd sleep until we reached home.

◎ JUDITH ORTIZ COFER

"More Room" is from Judith Ortiz Cofer's memoir, Silent Dancing: A Partial Remembrance of a Puerto Rican Childhood *(1990; see page 31). This essay centers on Mamá, Judith's maternal grandmother, who is the source of many lessons about surviving as a woman in this world, as well as a source of courage and pride to her granddaughter. This particular essay is on Mama's choice to "own her nights" — to sleep separately from her husband in order to have freedom from pregnancy.*

More Room

My grandmother's house is like a chambered nautilus; it has many rooms, yet it is not a mansion. Its proportions are small and its design simple. It is a house that has grown organically, according to the needs of its inhabitants. To all of us in the family it is known as *la casa de Mamá.* It is the place of our origin; the stage for our memories and dreams of Island life.

I remember how in my childhood it sat on stilts; this was before it had a downstairs. It rested on its perch like a great blue bird, not a flying sort of bird, more like a nesting hen, but with spread wings. Grandfather had built it soon after their marriage. He was a painter and housebuilder by trade, a poet and meditative man by nature. As each of their eight children were born, new rooms were added. After a few years, the paint did not exactly match, nor the materials, so that there was a chronology to it, like the rings of a tree, and Mamá could tell you the history of each room in her *casa*, and thus the genealogy of the family along with it.

Her room is the heart of the house. Though I have seen it recently, and both woman and room have diminished in size, changed by the new perspective of my eyes, now capable of looking over countertops and tall beds, it is not this picture I carry in my memory of Mamá's *casa*. Instead, I see her room as a queen's chamber where a small woman loomed large, a throne-room with a massive four-poster bed in its center which stood taller than a child's head. It was on this bed where her own children had been born that the smallest grandchildren were allowed to take naps in the afternoons; here too was where Mamá secluded herself to dispense private advice to her daughters, sitting on the edge of the bed, looking down at whoever sat on the rocker where generations of babies had been sung to sleep. To me she looked like a wise empress right out of the fairy tales I was addicted to reading.

Though the room was dominated by the mahogany four-poster, it also contained all of Mamá's symbols of power. On her dresser instead of cosmetics there were jars filled with herbs: *yerba buena, yerba mala*, the making of purgatives and teas to which we were all subjected during childhood crises. She had a steaming cup for anyone who could not, or would not, get up to face life on any given day. If the acrid aftertaste of her cures for malingering did not get you out of bed, then it was time to call *el doctor*.

And there was the monstrous chifforobe she kept locked with a little golden key she did not hide. This was a test of her dominion over us; though my cousins and I wanted a look inside that massive wardrobe more than anything, we never reached for that little key lying on top of her Bible on the dresser. This was also where she placed her earrings and rosary at night. God's word was her security system. This chifforobe was the place where I imagined she kept jewels, satin slippers, and elegant sequined, silk gowns of heartbreaking fineness. I lusted after those imaginary costumes. I had heard that Mamá had been a great beauty in her youth, and the belle of many balls. My cousins had other ideas as to what she kept in that wooden vault; its secret could be money (Mamá did not hand cash to strangers, banks were out of the question, so there were stories that her mattress was stuffed with dollar bills, and that she buried coins in jars in her garden under rosebushes, or kept them in her inviolate chifforobe); there might be that legendary gun salvaged from the Spanish-American conflict over the Island. We went wild over suspected treasures that we made up simply because children have to fill locked trunks with something wonderful.

On the wall above the bed hung a heavy silver crucifix. Christ's agonized head hung directly over Mamá's pillow. I avoided looking at this weapon suspended over where her head would lay; and on the rare occasions when I was allowed to sleep on that bed, I scooted down to the safe middle of the mattress, where her body's impression took me in like a mother's lap. Having taken care of the obligatory religious decoration with a crucifix, Mamá covered the other walls with objects sent to her over the years by her children in the States. *Los Nueva Yores* were represented by, among other things, a postcard of Niagara Falls from her son Hernán, postmarked, Buffalo, N.Y. In a conspicuous gold frame hung a large color photograph of her daughter Nena, her husband and their five children at the entrance to Disneyland in California. From us she had gotten a black lace fan. Father had brought it to her from a tour of duty with the Navy in Europe (on Sundays she would remove it from its hook on the wall to fan herself at Sunday mass). Each year more items were added as the family grew and dispersed, and every object in the room had a story attached to it, a *cuento* which Mamá would bestow on anyone who received the privilege of a day alone with her. It was almost worth pretending to be sick, though the bitter herb purgatives of the body were a big price to pay for the spirit revivals of her story-telling.

Mamá slept alone on her large bed, except for the times when a sick grandchild warranted the privilege, or when a heartbroken daughter came home in need of more than herbal teas. In the family there is a story about how this came to be.

When one of the daughters, my mother or one of her sisters, tells the *cuento* of how Mamá came to own her nights, it is usually preceded by the qualifications that Papá's exile from his wife's room was not a result of animosity between the couple, but that the act had been Mamá's famous bloodless coup for her personal freedom. Papá was the benevolent dictator of her body and her life who had had to be banished from her bed so that Mamá could better serve her family. Before the telling, we had to agree that the old man was not to blame. We all recognized that in the family Papá was as an *alma de Dios*, a saintly, soft-spoken presence whose main pleasures in life, such as writing poetry and reading the Spanish large-type editions of *Reader's Digest*, always took place outside the vortex of Mamá's crowded realm. It was not his fault, after all, that every year or so he planted a baby-seed in Mamá's fertile body, keeping her from leading the active life she needed and desired. He loved her and the babies. Papá composed odes and lyrics to celebrate births and anniversaries and hired musicians to accompany him in singing them to his family and friends at extravagant pig-roasts he threw yearly. Mamá and the oldest girls worked for days preparing the food. Papá sat for hours in his painter's shed, also his study and library, composing the songs. At these celebrations he was also known to give long speeches in praise of God, his fecund wife, and his beloved island. As a middle child, my mother remembers these occasions as a time when the women sat in the kitchen and lamented their burdens, while the men feasted out in the patio, their rum-thickened voice rising in song and praise for each other, *compañeros* all.

It was after the birth of her eighth child, after she had lost three at birth or in infancy, that Mamá made her decision. They say that Mamá had had a special way of letting her husband know that they were expecting, one that had begun when, at the beginning of their marriage, he had built her a house too confining for her taste. So, when she discovered her first pregnancy, she supposedly drew plans for another room, which he dutifully executed. Every time a child was due, she would demand, *more space, more space.* Papá acceded to her wishes, child after child, since he had learned early that Mamá's renowned temper was a thing that grew like a monster along with a new belly. In this way Mamá got the house that she wanted, but with each child she lost in heart and energy. She had knowledge of her body and perceived that if she had any more children, her dreams and her plans would have to be permanently forgotten, because she would be a chronically ill woman, like Flora with her twelve children: asthma, no teeth, in bed more than on her feet.

And so, after my youngest uncle was born, she asked Papá to build a large room at the back of the house. He did so in joyful anticipation. Mamá had asked him special things this time: shelves on the walls, a private entrance. He thought that she meant this room to be a nursery where several children could sleep. He thought it was a wonderful idea. He painted it his favorite color, sky blue, and made large windows looking out over a green hill and the church spires beyond. But nothing happened. Mamá's belly did not grow, yet she seemed in a frenzy of activity over the house. Finally, an anxious Papá approached his wife to tell her that the new room was finished and ready to be occupied. And Mamá, they say, replied: "Good, it's for *you.*"

And so it was that Mamá discovered the only means of birth control available to a Catholic woman of her time: sacrifice. She gave up the comfort of Papá's sexual love for something she deemed greater: the right to own and control her body, so that she might live to meet her grandchildren — me among them — so that she could give more of herself to the ones already there, so that she could be more than a channel for other lives, so that even now that time has robbed her of the elasticity of her body and of her amazing reservoir of energy, she still emanates the kind of joy that can only be achieved by living according to the dictates of one's own heart.

◎ *BETH HENLEY*

Beth Henley was born in Jackson, Mississippi, in 1952. After she had attended Southern Methodist University and the University of Illinois, she became an actress and playwright. In 1981, she was awarded a Pulitzer Prize for her play Crimes of the Heart, *which has also been made into a film. This award marked the first time the prize has been awarded prior to a play's Broadway opening. Henley has also received the New York Drama Critics Circle award and the Oppenheimer award. She lives in Los Angeles.*

Henley's play Am I Blue *(1972) was written as part of a drama class assignment while Henley was an undergraduate at Southern Methodist University. Daniel Halpern selected the play for his collection* Antaeus, *which celebrates "the play as an act of 'recorded' literature . . . to be read at leisure."*

Am I Blue

CHARACTERS

JOHN POLK *Seventeen*

ASHBE *Sixteen*

HILDA *Thirty-five, a waitress*

STREET CHARACTERS BARKER, WHORE, BUM, CLAREECE

Settings: A bar, the street, the living room of a run-down apartment
Time: Fall 1968

The scene opens on a street in the New Orleans French Quarter on a rainy blue bourbon night. Various people: a whore, bum, street barker, Clareece appear and disappear along the street. The scene then focuses on a bar where a piano is heard from the back room playing softly and indistinctly "Am I Blue?" The lights go up on John Polk, who sits alone at a table. He is seventeen, a bit overweight and awkward. He wears nice clothes, perhaps a navy sweater with large white monograms. His navy raincoat is slung over an empty chair. While drinking, John Polk concentrates on the red-and-black card that he holds in his hand. As soon as the scene is established, Ashbe enters from the street. She is sixteen, wears a flowered plastic rain cap, red galoshes, a butterfly barrette, and jeweled cat eyeglasses. She is carrying a bag full of stolen goods. Her hair is very curly. Ashbe makes her way cautiously to John Polk's table. As he sees her coming, he puts the card into his pocket. She sits in the empty chair and pulls his raincoat over her head.

ASHBE: Excuse me . . . do you mind if I sit here, please?

JOHN POLK [*looks up at her — then down into his glass.*]: What are you doing hiding under my raincoat? You're getting it all wet.

ASHBE: Well, I'm very sorry, but after all, it is a raincoat. [*He tries to pull off coat.*] It was rude of me, I know, but look, I just don't want them to recognize me.

JOHN POLK [*looking about*]: Who to recognize you?

ASHBE: Well, I stole these two ashtrays from the Screw Inn, ya know, right down the street. [*She pulls out two glass commercial ashtrays from her white plastic bag.*] Anyway, I'm scared the manager saw me. They'll be after me, I'm afraid.

JOHN POLK: Well, they should be. Look, do you mind giving me back my raincoat? I don't want to be found protecting any thief.

ASHBE [*coming out from under coat.*]: Thief — would you call Robin Hood a thief?

JOHN POLK: Christ.

ASHBE [*back under coat*]: No, you wouldn't. He was valiant — all the time stealing from the rich and giving to the poor.

JOHN POLK: But your case isn't exactly the same, is it? You're stealing from some crummy little bar and keeping the ashtrays for yourself. Now give me back my coat.

ASHBE [*throws coat at him*]: Sure, take your old coat. I suppose I should have explained — about Miss Marcey. [*Silence.*] Miss Marcey, this cute old lady with a little hump in her back. I always see her in her sun hat and blue print dress. Miss Marcey lives in the apartment building next to ours. I leave all the stolen goods as gifts on her front steps.

JOHN POLK: Are you one of those kleptomaniacs? [*He starts checking his wallet.*]

ASHBE: You mean when people all the time steal and they can't help it?

JOHN POLK: Yeah.

ASHBE: Oh, no. I'm not a bit careless. Take my job tonight, my very first night job, if you want to know. Anyway, I've been planning it for two months, trying to decipher which bar most deserved to be stolen from. I finally decided on the Screw Inn. Mainly because of the way they're so mean to Mr. Groves. He works at the magazine rack at Diver's Drugstore and is really very sweet, but he has a drinking problem. I don't think that's fair to be mean to people simply because they have a drinking problem — and, well, anyway, you see I'm not just stealing for personal gain. I mean, I don't even smoke.

JOHN POLK: Yeah, well, most infants don't, but then again, most infants don't hang around bars.

ASHBE: I don't see why not, Toulouse Lautrec did.

JOHN POLK: They'd throw me out.

ASHBE: Oh, they throw me out, too, but I don't accept defeat. [*Slowly moves into him.*] Why it's the very same with my pick-pocketing.

[*John Polk sneers, turns away.*]

It's a very hard art to master. Why, every time I've done it I've been caught.

JOHN POLK: That's all I need is to have some slum kid tell me how good it is to steal. Everyone knows it's not.

ASHBE [*about his drink*]: That looks good. What is it?

JOHN POLK: Hey, would you mind leaving me alone — I just wanted to be alone.

ASHBE: Okay. I'm sorry. How about if I'm quiet?

[*John Polk shrugs. He sips drink, looks around, catches her eye; she smiles and sighs.*]

I was just looking at your pin. What fraternity are you in?

JOHN POLK: SAE.

ASHBE: Is it a good fraternity?

JOHN POLK: Sure, it's the greatest.

ASHBE: I bet you have lots of friends.

JOHN POLK: Tons.

ASHBE: Are you being serious?

JOHN POLK: Yes.

ASHBE: Hmm. Do they have parties and all that?

JOHN POLK: Yeah, lots of parties, booze, honking horns; it's exactly what you would expect.

ASHBE: I wouldn't expect anything. Why did you join?

JOHN POLK: I don't know. Well, my brother — I guess it was my brother — he told me how great it was, how the fraternity was supposed to get you dates, make you study, solve all your problems.

ASHBE: Gee, does it?

JOHN POLK: Doesn't help you study.

ASHBE: How about dates? Do they get you a lot of dates?

JOHN POLK: Some.

ASHBE: What were the girls like?

JOHN POLK: I don't know — they were like girls.

ASHBE: Did you have a good time?

JOHN POLK: I had a pretty good time.

ASHBE: Did you make love to any of them?

JOHN POLK [*to self*]: Oh, Christ —

ASHBE: I'm sorry — I just figured that's why you had the appointment with the whore — 'cause you didn't have anyone else — to make love to.

JOHN POLK: How did you know I had the, ah, the appointment?

ASHBE: I saw you put the red card in your pocket when I came up. Those red cards are pretty familiar around here. The house is only about a block or so away. It's one of the best, though, really very plush. Only two murders and a knifing in its whole history. Do you go there often?

JOHN POLK: Yeah, I like to give myself a treat.

ASHBE: Who do you have?

JOHN POLK: What do you mean?

ASHBE: I mean which girl.

[*John Polk gazes into his drink.*]

Look, I just thought I might know her is all.

JOHN POLK: Know her, ah, how would you know her?

ASHBE: Well, some of the girls from my high school go there to work when they get out.

JOHN POLK: G.G., her name is G.G.

ASHBE: G.G. — Hmm, well, how does she look?

JOHN POLK: I don't know.

ASHBE: Oh, you've never been with her before?

JOHN POLK: No.

ASHBE [*confidentially*]: Are you one of those kinds that likes a lot of variety?

JOHN POLK: Variety? Sure, I guess I like variety.

ASHBE: Oh, yes, now I remember.

JOHN POLK: What?

ASHBE: G.G., that's just her working name. Her real name is Myrtle Reims; she's Kay Reims's older sister. Kay is in my grade at school.

JOHN POLK: Myrtle? Her name is Myrtle?

ASHBE: I never liked the name, either.

JOHN POLK: Myrtle, oh, Christ. Is she pretty?

ASHBE [*matter-of-fact*]: Pretty, no she's not real pretty.

JOHN POLK: What does she look like?

ASHBE: Let's see . . . she's, ah, well, Myrtle had acne, and there are a few scars left. It's not bad. I think they sort of give her character. Her hair's red, only I don't think it's really red. It sort of fizzles out all over her head. She's got a pretty good figure — big top — but the rest of her is kind of skinny.

JOHN POLK: I wonder if she has a good personality.

ASHBE: Well, she was a senior when I was a freshman; so I never really knew her. I remember she used to paint her fingernails lots of different colors — pink, orange, purple. I don't know, but she kind of scares me. About the only time I ever saw her true personality was around a year ago. I was over at Kay's making a health poster for school. Anyway, Myrtle comes busting in screaming about how she can't find her spangled bra anywhere. Kay and I just sat on the floor cutting pictures of food out of magazines while she was storming about slamming drawers and swearing. Finally, she found it. It was pretty garish — red with black and gold-sequined G's on each cup. That's how I remember the name — G.G.

[*As Ashbe illustrates the placement of the G's she spots Hilda, the waitress, approaching. Ashbe pulls the raincoat over her head and hides on the floor. Hilda enters through the beaded curtains spilling her tray. Hilda is a woman of few words.*]

HILDA: Shit, damn curtain. 'Nuther drink?

JOHN POLK: Ma'am?

HILDA [*points to drink*]: Vodka Coke?

JOHN POLK: No, thank you. I'm not quite finished yet.

HILDA: Napkins clean.

[*Ashbe pulls her bag off the table. Hilda looks at Ashbe, then to John Polk. She walks around the table, as Ashbe is crawling along the floor to escape. Ashbe runs into Hilda's toes.*]

ASHBE: Are those real gold?

HILDA: You again. Out.

ASHBE: She wants me to leave. Why should a paying customer leave? [*Back to Hilda.*] Now I'll have a mint julep and easy on the mint.

HILDA: This preteen with you?

JOHN POLK: Well — I — No — I —

HILDA: IDs.
ASHBE: Certainly, I always try to cooperate with the management.
HILDA [*looking at John Polk's ID*]: ID, 11-12-50. Date 11-11-68.
JOHN POLK: Yes, but — well, 11-12 is less than two hours away.
HILDA: Back in two hours.
ASHBE: I seem to have left my identification in my gold lamé bag.
HILDA: Well, boo hoo. [*Motions for Ashbe to leave with a minimum of effort. She goes back to table.*] No tip.
ASHBE: You didn't tip her?
JOHN POLK: I figured the drinks were so expensive — I just didn't —
HILDA: No tip!
JOHN POLK: Look, miss, I'm sorry. [*Going through his pockets.*] Here, would you like a — a nickel — wait, wait here's a quarter.
HILDA: Just move ass, sonny. You, too, Barbie.
ASHBE: Ugh, I hate public rudeness. I'm sure I'll refrain from ever coming here again.
HILDA: Think I'll go in the back room and cry. [*Ashbe and John Polk exit. Hilda picks up tray and exits through the curtain, tripping again.*] Shit. Damn curtain.

[*Ashbe and John Polk are now standing outside under the awning of the bar.*]

ASHBE: Gee, I didn't know it was your birthday tomorrow. Happy birthday! Don't be mad. I thought you were at least twenty or twenty-one, really.
JOHN POLK: It's okay. Forget it.
ASHBE [*as they begin walking, various blues are heard coming from the nearby bars*]: It's raining.
JOHN POLK: I know.
ASHBE: Are you going over to the house now?
JOHN POLK: No, not till twelve.
ASHBE: Yeah, the pink-and-black cards — they mean all night. Midnight till morning. [*At this point a street barker beckons the couple into his establishment. Perhaps he is accompanied by a whore.*]
BARKER: Hey, mister, bring your baby on in, buy her a few drinks, maybe tonight ya get lucky.
ASHBE: Keep walking.
JOHN POLK: What's wrong with the place?
ASHBE: The drinks are watery rotgut, and the show girls are boys.
BARKER: Up yours, punk!
JOHN POLK [*who has now sat down on a street bench*]: Look, just tell me where a cheap bar is. I've got to stay drunk, but I don't have much money left.
ASHBE: Yikes, there aren't too many cheap bars around here, and a lot of them check IDs.
JOHN POLK: Well, do you know of any that don't?

ASHBE: No, not for sure.

JOHN POLK: Oh, God, I need to get drunk.

ASHBE: Aren't you?

JOHN POLK: Some, but I'm losing ground fast. [*By this time a bum who has been traveling drunkenly down the street falls near the couple and begins throwing up.*]

ASHBE: Oh, I know! You can come to my apartment. It's just down the block. We keep one bottle of rum around. I'll serve you a grand drink, three or four if you like.

JOHN POLK [*fretfully*]: No, thanks.

ASHBE: But look, we're getting all wet.

JOHN POLK: Sober, too, wet and sober.

ASHBE: Oh, come on! Rain's blurring my glasses.

JOHN POLK: Well, how about your parents? What would they say?

ASHBE: Daddy's out of town and Mama lives in Atlanta; so I'm sure they won't mind. I think we have some cute little marshmallows. [*Pulling on him.*] Won't you really come?

JOHN POLK: You've probably got some gang of muggers waiting to kill me. Oh, all right — what the hell, let's go.

ASHBE: Hurrah! Come on. It's this way. [*She starts across the stage, stops, and picks up an old hat.*] Hey look at this hat. Isn't it something! Here, wear it to keep off the rain.

JOHN POLK [*throwing hat back onto street*]: No, thanks, you don't know who's worn it before.

ASHBE [*picking hat back up*]: That makes it all the more exciting. Maybe it was a butcher's who slaughtered his wife or a silver pirate with a black bird on his throat. Who do you guess?

JOHN POLK: I don't know. Anyway, what's the good of guessing? I mean, you'll never really know.

ASHBE [*trying the hat on*]: Yeah, probably not. [*At this point, Ashbe, and John Polk reach the front door.*] Here we are. [*Ashbe begins fumbling for her key. Clareece, a teeny-bopper, walks up to John Polk.*]

CLAREECE: Hey, man, got any spare change?

JOHN POLK [*looking through his pockets*]: Let me see — I —

ASHBE [*coming up between them, giving Clareece a shove*]: Beat it, Clareece. He's my company.

CLAREECE [*walks away and sneers*]: Oh, shove it, Frizzels.

ASHBE: A lot of jerks live around here. Come on in. [*She opens the door. Lights go up on the living room of a run-down apartment in a run-down apartment house. Besides being merely run-down, the room is a malicious pigsty with colors, paper hats, paper dolls, masks, torn-up stuffed animals, dead flowers and leaves, dress-up clothes, etc., thrown all about.*] My bones are cold. Do you want a towel to dry off?

JOHN POLK: Yes, thank you.

ASHBE [*she picks a towel up off of the floor and tosses it to him*]: Here. [*He begins drying off as she takes off her rain things; then she begins raking things off the sofa.*] Please do sit down. [*He sits.*] I'm sorry the place is disheveled, but my father's been out of town. I always try to pick up and all before he gets in. Of course he's pretty used to messes. My mother never was too good at keeping things clean.

JOHN POLK: When's he coming back?

ASHBE: Sunday, I believe. Oh, I've been meaning to say —

JOHN POLK: What?

ASHBE: My name's Ashbe Williams.

JOHN POLK: Ashbe?

ASHBE: Yeah, Ashbe.

JOHN POLK: My name's John Polk Richards.

ASHBE: John Polk? They call you John Polk?

JOHN POLK: It's family.

ASHBE [*putting on socks*]: These are my favorite socks, the red furry ones. Well, here's some books and magazines to look at while I fix you something to drink. What do you want in your rum?

JOHN POLK: Coke's fine.

ASHBE: I'll see do we have any. I think I'll take some hot Kool-Aid myself. [*She exits to the kitchen.*]

JOHN POLK: Hot Kool-Aid?

ASHBE: It's just Kool-Aid that's been heated, like hot chocolate or hot tea.

JOHN POLK: Sounds great.

ASHBE: Well, I'm used to it. You get so much for your dime it makes it worth your while. I don't buy presweetened, of course, it's better to sugar your own.

JOHN POLK: I remember once I threw up a lot of grape Kool-Aid when I was a kid. I've hated it ever since. Hey, would you check on the time?

ASHBE [*she enters carrying a tray with several bottles of food coloring, a bottle of rum, and a huge glass*]: I'm sorry we don't have Cokes. I wonder if rum and Kool-Aid is good? Oh, we don't have a clock, either. [*She pours a large amount of rum into the large glass.*]

JOHN POLK: I'll just have it with water, then.

ASHBE [*she finds an almost empty glass of water somewhere in the room and dumps it in with the rum*]: Would you like food coloring in the water? It makes a drink all the more aesthetic. Of course, some people don't care for aesthetics.

JOHN POLK: No, thank you, just plain water.

ASHBE: Are you sure? The taste is entirely the same. I put it in all my water.

JOHN POLK: Well —

ASHBE: What color do you want?

JOHN POLK: I don't know.

ASHBE: What's your favorite color?

JOHN POLK: Blue, I guess. [*She puts a few blue drops into the glass — as she has nothing to stir with, she blows into the glass, turning the water blue.*] Thanks.

ASHBE [*exits. She screams from kitchen*]: Come on, say come on, cat, eat your fresh good milk.

JOHN POLK: You have a cat?

ASHBE [*off*]: No.

JOHN POLK: Oh.

ASHBE [*she enters carrying a tray with a cup of hot Kool-Aid and Cheerios and colored marshmallows*]: Here are some Cheerios and some cute little colored marshmallows to eat with your drink.

JOHN POLK: Thanks.

ASHBE: I one time smashed all the big white marshmallows in the plastic bag at the grocery store.

JOHN POLK: Why did you do that?

ASHBE: I was angry. Do you like ceramics?

JOHN POLK: Yes.

ASHBE: My mother makes them. It's sort of her hobby. She is very talented.

JOHN POLK: My mother never does anything. Well, I guess she can shuffle the bridge deck okay.

ASHBE: Actually, my mother is a dancer. She teaches at a school in Atlanta. She's really very talented.

JOHN POLK [*indicates ceramics*]: She must be to do all these.

ASHBE: Well, Madeline, my older sister, did the blue one. Madeline gets to live with Mama.

JOHN POLK: And you live with your father.

ASHBE: Yeah, but I get to go visit them sometimes.

JOHN POLK: You do ceramics, too?

ASHBE: No, I never learned . . . but I have this great pot holder set. [*Gets up to show him.*] See I make lots of multicolored pot holders and send them to Mama and Madeline. I also make paper hats. [*Gets material to show him.*] I guess they're more creative, but making pot holders is more relaxing. Here, would you like to make a hat?

JOHN POLK: I don't know, I'm a little drunk.

ASHBE: It's not hard a bit. [*Hands him material.*] Just draw a real pretty design on the paper. It really doesn't have to be pretty, just whatever you want.

JOHN POLK: It's kind of you to give my creative drives such freedom.

ASHBE: Ha, ha, ha, I'll work on my pot holder set a bit.

JOHN POLK: What time is it? I've really got to check on the time.

ASHBE: I know. I'll call the time operator. [*She goes to the phone.*]

JOHN POLK: How do you get along without a clock?

ASHBE: Well, I've been late for school a lot. Daddy has a watch. It's 11:03.

JOHN POLK: I've got a while yet.

ASHBE [*Twirls back to her chair, drops, and sighs.*]

JOHN POLK: Are you a dancer, too?

ASHBE [*delighted*]: I can't dance a bit, really. I practice a lot is all, at home in the afternoon. I imagine you go to a lot of dances.

JOHN POLK: Not really, I'm a terrible dancer. I usually get bored or drunk.

ASHBE: You probably drink too much.

JOHN POLK: No, it's just since I've come to college. All you do there is drink more beer and write more papers.

ASHBE: What are you studying for to be?

JOHN POLK: I don't know.

ASHBE: Why don't you become a rancher?

JOHN POLK: Dad wants me to help run his soybean farm.

ASHBE: Soybean farm. Yikes, that's really something. Where is it?

JOHN POLK: Well, I live in the Delta, Hollybluff, Mississippi. Anyway, Dad feels I should go to business school first; you know, so I'll become, well, management minded. Pass the blue.

ASHBE: Is that what you really want to do?

JOHN POLK: I don't know. It would probably be as good as anything else I could do. Dad makes good money. He can take vacations whenever he wants. Sure it'll be a ball.

ASHBE: I'd hate to have to be management minded. [*John Polk shrugs.*] I don't mean to hurt your feelings, but I would really hate to be a management mind. [*She starts walking on her knees, twisting her fists in front of her eyes, and making clicking sounds as a management mind would make.*]

JOHN POLK: Cut it out. Just forget it. The farm could burn down and I wouldn't even have to think about it.

ASHBE [*after a pause*]: Well, what do you want to talk about?

JOHN POLK: I don't know.

ASHBE: When was the last dance you went to?

JOHN POLK: Dances. That's a great subject. Let's see, oh, I don't really remember. It was probably some blind date. God, I hate dates.

ASHBE: Why?

JOHN POLK: Well, they always say that they don't want popcorn and they wind up eating all of yours.

ASHBE: You mean, you hate dates just because they eat your popcorn? Don't you think that's kind of stingy?

JOHN POLK: It's the principle of the thing. Why can't they just say, yes, I'd like some popcorn when you ask them. But, no, they're always so damn coy.

ASHBE: I'd tell my date if I wanted popcorn. I'm not that immature.

JOHN POLK: Anyway, it's not only the popcorn. It's a lot of little things. I've finished coloring. What do I do now?

ASHBE: Now you have to fold it. Here . . . like this. [*She explains the process with relish.*] Say, that's really something.

JOHN POLK: It's kind of funny looking. [*Putting the hat on.*] Yeah, I like it, but you could never wear it anywhere.

ASHBE: Well, like what, anyway?

JOHN POLK: Huh?

ASHBE: The things dates do to you that you don't like, the little things.

JOHN POLK: Oh, well just the way they wear those false eyelashes and put their hand on your knee when you're trying to parallel park and keep on giggling and going off to the bathroom with their girlfriends. It's obvious they don't want to go out with me. They just want to go out so that they can wear their new clothes and won't have to sit on their ass in the dormitory. They never want to go out with me. I can never even talk to them.

ASHBE: Well, you can talk to me and I'm a girl.

JOHN POLK: Well, I'm really kind of drunk and you're a stranger . . . Well, I probably wouldn't be able to talk to you tomorrow. That makes a difference.

ASHBE: Maybe it does. [*A bit of a pause, and then, extremely pleased by the idea, she says*] You know we're alike because I don't like dances, either.

JOHN POLK: I thought you said you practiced . . . in the afternoons.

ASHBE: Well, I like dancing. I just don't like dances. At least not like — well, not like the one our school was having tonight. . . . They're so corny.

JOHN POLK: Yeah, most dances are.

ASHBE: All they serve is potato chips and fruit punch, and then this stupid baby band plays and everybody dances around thinking they're so hot. I frankly wouldn't dance there. I would prefer to wait till I am invited to an exclusive ball. It doesn't really matter which ball, just one where they have huge golden chandeliers and silver fountains and serve delicacies of all sorts and bubble blue champagne. I'll arrive in a pink silk cape. [*Laughing.*] I want to dance in pink!

JOHN POLK: You're mixed up. You're probably one of those people that live in a fantasy world.

ASHBE: I do not. I accept reality as well as anyone. Anyway, you can talk to me, remember. I know what you mean by the kind of girls it's hard to talk to. There are girls a lot that way in the small clique at my school. Really tacky and mean. They expect everyone to be as stylish as they are, and they won't even speak to you in the hall. I don't mind if they don't speak to me, but I really love the orphans, and it hurts my feelings when they are so mean to them.

JOHN POLK: What do you mean — they're mean to the orpheens? [*Notices pun and giggles to self.*]

ASHBE: Oh, well, they sometimes snicker at the orphans' dresses. The orphans usually have hand-me-down, drab, ugly dresses. Once Shelly Maxwell wouldn't let Glinda borrow her pencil, even though she had two. It hurt her feelings.

JOHN POLK: Are you best friends with these orphans?

ASHBE: I hardly know them at all. They're really shy. I just like them a lot. They're the reason I put spells on the girls in the clique.

JOHN POLK: Spells, what do you mean, witch spells?

ASHBE: Witch spells? Not really, mostly just voodoo.

JOHN POLK: Are you kidding? Do you really do voodoo?

ASHBE: Sure, here I'll show you my doll. [*Goes to get doll, comes back with straw voodoo doll. Her air as she returns is one of frightening mystery.*] I know a lot about the subject. Cora she used to wash dishes in the Moonlight Café, told me all about voodoo. She's a real expert on the subject, went to all the meetings and everything. Once she caused a man's throat to rot away and turn almost totally black. She's moved to Chicago now.

JOHN POLK: It doesn't really work. Does it?

ASHBE: Well, not always. The thing about voodoo is that both parties have to believe in it for it to work.

JOHN POLK: Do the girls in school believe in it?

ASHBE: Not really; I don't think. That's where my main problem comes in. I have to make the clique believe in it, yet I have to be very subtle. Mainly, I give reports in English class or Speech.

JOHN POLK: Reports?

ASHBE: On voodoo.

JOHN POLK: That's really kind of sick, you know.

ASHBE: Not really. I don't cast spells that'll do any real harm. Mainly, just the kind of thing to make them think — to keep them on their toes. [*Blue drink intoxication begins to take over and John Polk begins laughing.*] What's so funny?

JOHN POLK: Nothing. I was just thinking what a mean little person you are.

ASHBE: Mean! I'm not mean a bit.

JOHN POLK: Yes, you are mean — [*picking up color*] and green, too.

ASHBE: Green?

JOHN POLK: Yes, green with envy of those other girls; so you play all those mean little tricks.

ASHBE: Envious of those other girls, that stupid, close-minded little clique!

JOHN POLK: Green as this marshmallow. [*Eats marshmallow.*]

ASHBE: You think I want to be in some group . . . a sheep like you? A little sheep like you that does everything when he's supposed to do it!

JOHN POLK: Me a sheep — I do what I want!

ASHBE: Ha! I've known you for an hour and already I see you for the sheep you are!

JOHN POLK: Don't take your green meanness out on me.

ASHBE: Not only are you a sheep, you are a *normal* sheep. Give me back my colors! [*Begins snatching colors away.*]

JOHN POLK [*pushing colors at her*]: Green and mean! Green and mean! Green and mean! et cetera.

ASHBE [*throwing marshmallows at him*]: That's the reason you're in a fraternity and the reason you're going to manage your mind, and dates — you go out on dates merely because it's expected of you even though you have a terrible time. That's the reason you go to the whorehouse to prove you're a normal man. Well, you're much too normal for me.

JOHN POLK: Infant bitch. You think you're really cute.

ASHBE: That really wasn't food coloring in your drink, it was poison! [*She laughs, he picks up his coat to go, and she stops throwing marshmallows at him.*] Are you going? I was only kidding. For Christ sake, it wasn't really poison. Come on, don't go. Can't you take a little friendly criticism?

JOHN POLK: Look, did you have to bother me tonight? I had enough problems without — [*Phone rings. Both look at phone; it rings for the third time. He stands undecided.*]

ASHBE: Look, wait, we'll make it up. [*She goes to answer phone.*] Hello — Daddy. How are you? . . . I'm fine . . . Dad, you sound funny . . . what? . . . Come on, Daddy, you know she's not here. [*Pause.*] Look, I told you I wouldn't call anymore. You've got her number in Atlanta. [*Pause, as she sinks to the floor.*] Why have you started again? . . . Don't say that. I can tell it. I can. Hey, I have to go to bed now, I don't want to talk anymore, okay? [*Hangs up phone, softly to self.*] Goddamnit.

JOHN POLK [*he has heard the conversation and is taking off his coat*]: Hey, Ashbe — [*She looks at him blankly, her mind far away.*] You want to talk?

ASHBE: No. [*Slight pause.*] Why don't you look at my shell collection? I have this special shell collection. [*She shows him collection.*]

JOHN POLK: They're beautiful, I've never seen colors like this. [*Ashbe is silent, he continues to himself.*] I used to go to Biloxi a lot when I was a kid . . . one time my brother and I, we camped out on the beach. The sky was purple. I remember it was really purple. We ate pork and beans out of a can. I'd always kinda wanted to do that. Every night for about a week after I got home, I dreamt about these waves foaming over my head and face. It was funny. Did you find these shells or buy them?

ASHBE: Some I found, some I bought. I've been trying to decipher their meaning. Here, listen, do you hear that?

JOHN POLK: Yes.

ASHBE: That's the soul of the sea. [*She listens.*] I'm pretty sure it's the soul of the sea. Just imagine when I decipher the language. I'll know all the secrets of the world.

JOHN POLK: Yeah, probably you will. [*Looking into the shell.*] You know, you were right.

ASHBE: What do you mean?

JOHN POLK: About me, you were right. I am a sheep, a normal one. I've been trying to get out of it, but now I'm as big a sheep as ever.

ASHBE: Oh, it doesn't matter. You're company. It was rude of me to say.

JOHN POLK: No, because it was true. I really didn't want to go into a fraternity. I didn't even want to go to college, and I sure as hell don't want to go back to Hollybluff and work the soybean farm till I'm eighty.

ASHBE: I still say you could work on a ranch.

JOHN POLK: I don't know. I wanted to be a minister or something good, but I don't even know if I believe in God.

ASHBE: Yeah.

JOHN POLK: I never used to worry about being a failure. Now I think about it all the time. It's just I need to do something that's — fulfilling.

ASHBE: Fulfilling, yes, I see what you mean. Well, how about college? Isn't it fulfilling? I mean, you take all those wonderful classes, and you have all your very good friends.

JOHN POLK: Friends, yeah, I have some friends.

ASHBE: What do you mean?

JOHN POLK: Nothing — well, I do mean something. What the hell, let me try to explain. You see it was my "friends," the fraternity guys that set me up with G.G., excuse me, Myrtle, as a gift for my eighteenth birthday.

ASHBE: You mean, you didn't want the appointment?

JOHN POLK: No, I didn't want it. Hey, ah, where did my blue drink go?

ASHBE [*as she hands him the drink*]: They probably thought you really wanted to go.

JOHN POLK: Yeah, I'm sure they gave a damn what I wanted. They never even asked me. Hell, I would have told them a handkerchief, a pair of argyle socks, but, no, they have to get me a whore just because it's a cool-ass thing to do. They make me sick. I couldn't even stay at the party they gave. All the sweaty T-shirts and moron sex stories — I just couldn't take it.

ASHBE: Is that why you were at the Blue Angel so early?

JOHN POLK: Yeah, I needed to get drunk, but not with them. They're such creeps.

ASHBE: Gosh, so you really don't want to go to Myrtle's?

JOHN POLK: No, I guess not.

ASHBE: Then are you going?

JOHN POLK [*pause*]: Yes.

ASHBE: That's wrong. You shouldn't go just to please them.

JOHN POLK: Oh, that's not the point anymore; maybe at first it was, but it's not anymore. Now I have to go for myself — to prove to myself that I'm not afraid.

ASHBE: Afraid? [*Slowly, as she begins to grasp his meaning.*] You mean, you've never slept with a girl before?

JOHN POLK: Well, I've never been in love.

ASHBE [*in amazement*]: You're a virgin?

JOHN POLK: Oh, God.

ASHBE: No, don't feel bad, I am, too.

JOHN POLK: I thought I should be in love —

ASHBE: Well, you're certainly not in love with Myrtle. I mean, you haven't even met her.

JOHN POLK: I know, but, God, I thought maybe I'd never fall in love. What then? You should experience everything — shouldn't you? Oh, what's it matter, everything's so screwed.

ASHBE: Screwed? Yeah, I guess it is. I mean, I always thought it would be fun to have a lot of friends who gave parties and go to dances all dressed up. Like the dance tonight — it might have been fun.

JOHN POLK: Well, why didn't you go?

ASHBE: I don't know. I'm not sure it would have been fun. Anyway, you can't go — alone.

JOHN POLK: Oh, you need a date?

ASHBE: Yeah, or something.

JOHN POLK: Say, Ashbe, ya wanna dance here?

ASHBE: No, I think we'd better discuss your dilemma.

JOHN POLK: What dilemma?

ASHBE: Myrtle. It doesn't seem right you should —

JOHN POLK: Let's forget Myrtle for now. I've got a while yet. Here, have some more of this blue-moon drink.

ASHBE: You're only trying to escape through artificial means.

JOHN POLK: Yeah, you got it. Now, come on. Would you like to dance? Hey, you said you liked to dance.

ASHBE: You're being ridiculous.

JOHN POLK [*winking at her*]: Dance?

ASHBE: John Polk, I just thought —

JOHN POLK: Hmm?

ASHBE: How to solve your problem —

JOHN POLK: Well —

ASHBE: Make love to me!

JOHN POLK: What?

ASHBE: It all seems logical to me. It would prove you weren't scared, and you wouldn't be doing it just to impress others.

JOHN POLK: Look, I — I mean I hardly know you —

ASHBE: But we've talked. It's better this way, really. I won't be so apt to point out your mistakes.

JOHN POLK: I'd feel great stripping a twelve-year-old of her virginity.

ASHBE: I'm sixteen! Anyway, I'd be stripping you of yours just as well. I'll go put on some Tiger Claw perfume. [*She runs out.*]

JOHN POLK: Hey, come back! Tiger Claw perfume, Christ.

ASHBE [*entering*]: I think one should have different scents for different moods.

JOHN POLK: Hey, stop spraying that! You know I'm not going to — well, you'd get neurotic or pregnant or some damn thing. Stop spraying, will you!

ASHBE: Pregnant? You really think I could get pregnant?

JOHN POLK: Sure, it'd be a delightful possibility.

ASHBE: It really wouldn't be bad. Maybe I would get to go to Tokyo for an abortion. I've never been to the Orient.

JOHN POLK: Sure, getting cut on is always a real treat.

ASHBE: Anyway, I might just want to have my dear baby. I could move to Atlanta with Mama and Madeline. It'd be wonderful fun. Why, I could take him to the supermarket, put him in one of those little baby seats to stroll him about. I'd buy peach baby food and feed it to him with a tiny golden spoon. Why, I could take colored pictures of him and send them to you through the mail. Come on — [*Starts putting pillows onto the couch.*] Well, I guess you should kiss me for a start. It's only etiquette; everyone begins with it.

JOHN POLK: I don't think I could even kiss you with a clear conscience. I mean, you're so small, with those little cat-eye glasses and curly hair — I couldn't even kiss you.

ASHBE: You couldn't even kiss me? I can't help it if I have to wear glasses. I got the prettiest ones I could find.

JOHN POLK: Your glasses are fine. Let's forget it, okay?

ASHBE: I know, my lips are too purple, but if I eat carrots, the dye'll come off and they'll be orange.

JOHN POLK: I didn't say anything about your lips being too purple.

ASHBE: Well, what is it? You're just plain chicken, I suppose —

JOHN POLK: Sure, right, I'm chicken, totally chicken. Let's forget it. I don't know how, but somehow this is probably all my fault.

ASHBE: You're darn right it's all your fault! I want to have my dear baby or at least get to Japan. I'm so sick of school I could smash every marshmallow in sight! [*She starts smashing.*] Go on to your skinny pimple whore. I hope the skinny whore laughs in your face, which she probably will because you have an easy face to laugh in.

JOHN POLK: You're absolutely right; she'll probably hoot and howl her damn fizzle red head off. Maybe you can wait outside the door and hear her, give you lots of pleasure, you sadistic little thief.

ASHBE: Thief — was Robin Hood — Oh, what's wrong with this world? I just wasn't made for it is all. I've probably been put in the wrong world, I can see that now.

JOHN POLK: You're fine in this world.

ASHBE: Sure, everyone just views me as an undesirable lump.

JOHN POLK: Who?

ASHBE: You for one.

JOHN POLK [*pause*]: You mean because I wouldn't make love to you?

ASHBE: It seems clear to me.

JOHN POLK: But you're wrong, you know.

ASHBE [*to self, softly*]: Don't pity me.

JOHN POLK: The reason I wouldn't wasn't that — it's just that — well, I like you too much to.

ASHBE: You like me?

JOHN POLK: Undesirable lump, Jesus. Your cheeks, they're — they're —

ASHBE: My cheeks? They're what?

JOHN POLK: They're rosy.

ASHBE: My cheeks are rosy?

JOHN POLK: Yeah, your cheeks, they're really rosy.

ASHBE: Well, they're natural, you know. Say, would you like to dance?

JOHN POLK: Yes.

ASHBE: I'll turn on the radio. [*She turns on radio. Ethel Waters is heard singing "Honey in the Honeycomb." Ashbe begins snapping her fingers.*] Yikes, let's jazz it out. [*They dance.*]

JOHN POLK: Hey, I'm not good or anything —

ASHBE: John Polk.

JOHN POLK: Yeah?

ASHBE: Baby, I think you dance fine! [*They dance on, laughing, saying what they want till end of song. Then a radio announcer comes on and says the 12:00 news will be in five minutes. Billy Holiday or Terry Pierce begins singing, "Am I Blue?"*]

JOHN POLK: Dance?

ASHBE: News in five minutes.

JOHN POLK: Yeah.

ASHBE: That means five minutes till midnight.

JOHN POLK: Yeah, I know.

ASHBE: Then you're not —

JOHN POLK: Ashbe, I've never danced all night. Wouldn't it be something to — to dance all night and watch the rats come out of the gutter?

ASHBE: Rats?

JOHN POLK: Don't they come out at night? I hear New Orleans has lots of rats.

ASHBE: Yeah, yeah, it's got lots of rats.

JOHN POLK: Then let's dance all night and wait for them to come out.

ASHBE: All right — but how about our feet?

JOHN POLK: Feet?

ASHBE: They'll hurt.

JOHN POLK: Yeah.

ASHBE [*smiling*]: Okay, then let's dance. [*He takes her hand, and they dance as lights black out and the music soars and continues to play.*]

◎ *ALICE FRIMAN*

Alice Friman was born in 1933. She lives in Indianapolis. Friman is the author of five collections of poetry, the most recent being Driving for Jimmy Wonderland *(1992). Her poems have appeared in* Poetry, Shenandoah, Manoa, Georgia Review, Prairie Schooner, London Review of Books, *and* Poetry Review *(U.K.), among others. She has won three prizes from the Poetry Society of America, First Prize in the* Abiko Quarterly *International Poetry Contest (Japan), and the Award of Excellence from* Hopewell Review.

Friman wrote "The Good News" in Minnesota in July 1992. In a letter to Marilyn Kallet, she writes: "I had rented a dorm room at St. John's University — making my own writers' colony — and found myself surrounded by a flood of Catholic imagery and the most voracious mosquitoes north of the equator. This is usually how I write, weaving inner and outer worlds, but in this case, I ended up with an upbeat poem, you might even say optimistic, unusual for me" (1996).

The Good News

for the mosquitoes of Minnesota

I managed to make them
very happy.
Whenever I went out
lilies opened on their pads
like satellite dishes
and butterflies
spread their flags
to flutter the good news. I was
the Red Cross rolling in
in a white truck —
donuts and blankets
sacks of rice & powdered
milk for the babies. I was
payday for the troops
R & R and a geisha
for Saturday nights, Lucky Strikes
and a kiss before dying.
I was the Berlin airlift
and the Marshall Plan —
chicken soup in vats
and a hunk of bread, ripped off

with the back teeth. I was
hope for the young
and succor for the old
and after me, surely
faith in a second coming
for it is I who answered
their wing & their prayer
who gathered to me
the whining dispirited
and unified the multitudes.
It is for me the cathedrals
for me the bells
for I am the miracle
the sacrificial lamb.
I am the staff of life
the bread basket of this world
the loaves and fishes
the body and the blood.

TESS GALLAGHER

"Crêpes Flambeau" is from Tess Gallagher's Amplitude: New and Selected Poems *(1987). The poem was written in 1979, while the poet was first living in El Paso, Texas, with Raymond Carver.* *(For more on Gallagher, see page 144.)*

Crêpes Flambeau

We are three women eating out
in a place that could be California
or New Jersey but is Texas and our waiter
says his name is Jerry. He is pink
and young, dressed in soft denim
with an embroidered vest and, my friend says,
a nice butt. It's hard not to be intimate
in America where your waiter wants
you to call him Jerry. So why
do you feel sorry for him
standing over the flames
of this dessert?

The little fans of the crêpes are
folding into the juice. The brandy
is aflare in a low blue hush and golden
now and red where he spills
the brown sugar saved
to make our faces wear the sudden burst. We
are all good-looking and older and he
has to please us or try
to. What could go wrong? Too much
brandy? Too little sugar? Fire
falling into our laps, fire
like laughter behind his back, even
when he has done it just right, "Jerry,"
we say, "that was wonderful," for now
he is blushing at us
like a russet young girl. Our lips

are red with fire and juice.
He knows we could go on
eating long into the night until the flames
run down our throats. "Thank you,"
he says, handing us our check, knowing
among the ferns and napkins that he has
pleased us, briefly, like all
good things, dying away
at the only moment, before
we are too happy, too
glad in the pioneer decor: rough boards,
spotted horses in the frame.

◎ *PATRICIA HAMPL*

Patricia Hampl was born in 1946 in St. Paul, Minnesota. She has received degrees from the University of Minnesota and the University of Iowa. Awards for her work include a grant from the National Endowment for the Arts, a grant from the Bush Foundation, a Houghton Mifflin literary fellowship, and an Ingram Merrill fellowship. She has published two volumes of poetry, a prose poem edition called Spillville *(1987), and two volumes of memoirs:* A Romantic Education *(1981) and* Virgin Time *(1992). Hampl lives in St. Paul and is a professor of English at the University of Minnesota.*

"The Moment" first appeared in the New Yorker. *One poetry critic has noted Hampl's use of "rapturous" descriptions, and that use is evident in the transformative and transcendent occurrence in the poem's otherwise mundane, even gritty, setting.*

The Moment

Standing by the parking-ramp elevator
a week ago, sunk, stupid with sadness.
Black slush puddled on the cement floor,
the place painted a killer-pastel
as in an asylum.
A numeral 1, big as a person,
was stencilled on the cinder block:
Remember your level.
The toneless bell sounded.
Doors opened, nobody inside.
Then, who knows why, a rod of light
at the base of my skull flashed
to every outpost of my far-flung body —
I've got my life back.
It was nothing, just the present moment
occurring for the first time in months.
My head translated light,
my eyes spiked with tears.
The awful green walls, I could have stroked them.
The dirt, the moving cube I stepped into —
it was all beautiful,
everything that took me up.

◎ COLETTE INEZ

"Good News! Nilda Is Back" appeared in Inez's first book, The Woman Who Loved Worms *(1972) and is reprinted in* Getting Under Way: New and Selected Poems *(1993). While much of her work focuses on her family history, Inez has always displayed a keen eye and ear for the whimsical sights and the rhythms of the city. Here the waves of rain and hair are syncopated with the "huzzahs" and "cha chas" of Nilda.* *(For more information on Inez, see page 665.)*

Good News! Nilda Is Back

Good news! Nilda is back,
the sign huzzahs
in the Beauty Shoppe

as the rain combs
the sky over and over
like a grandmother combing
the hair of a child.

Impermanent waves
of rain on the street;
the trees are straight
but the city bends.

Nilda is back
from Guayaquil,
Quito, Ponce,
San José

to tease the gringo smiles
of blue-eyed wives
in the raining city.

And now she cha chas up the aisles
to supervise the upswept lines
of an aging lady

who does not know why Nilda comes
or why she goes
or where her hair uncurls at night
damp at the edge from waves of love.

◎ DENISE LEVERTOV

"O Taste and See" is the title poem of Denise Levertov's 1962 volume and is now available in Poems 1960–1967 *(1983; see also page 396). Many of the poems in* O Taste and See *were written during the year she was a Guggenheim fellow. Levertov's poem is a response to the Wordsworth sonnet that begins: "The world is too much with us. . . ." No, the urban poet answers, "The world is / not with us enough." Responding to a subway poster that says "O taste and see," the poet expresses her delight in the world. Here poetry takes the place of religion, and the exuberant poet is hungry for the things of this world.*

O Taste and See

The world is
not with us enough.
O taste and see

the subway Bible poster said,
meaning **The Lord,** meaning
if anything all that lives
to the imagination's tongue,

grief, mercy, language,
tangerine, weather, to
breathe them, bite,
savor, chew, swallow, transform

into our flesh our
deaths, crossing the street, plum, quince,
living in the orchard and being

hungry, and plucking
the fruit.

◎ *NAOMI SHIHAB NYE*

"So Much Happiness" is from Hugging the Jukebox, *Naomi Shihab Nye's second book of poetry, which was a National Poetry Series Winner in 1982 and which also won the 1982 Voertman Award from the Texas Institute of Letters. (For more on Nye,* *see page 70.)*

So Much Happiness

for Michael

It is difficult to know what to do with so much happiness.
With sadness there is something to rub against,
a wound to tend with lotion and cloth.
When the world falls in around you, you have pieces to pick up,
something to hold in your hands, like ticket stubs or change.

But happiness floats.
It doesn't need you to hold it down.

It doesn't need anything.
Happiness lands on the roof of the next house, singing,
and disappears when it wants to.
You are happy either way.
Even the fact that you once lived in a peaceful tree house
and now live over a quarry of noise and dust
cannot make you unhappy.
Everything has a life of its own,
it too could wake up filled with possibilities
of coffee cake and ripe peaches,
and love even the floor which needs to be swept,
the soiled linens and scratched records . . .

Since there is no place large enough
to contain so much happiness,
you shrug, you raise your hands, and it flows out of you
into everything you touch. You are not responsible.
You take no credit, as the night sky takes no credit
for the moon, but continues to hold it, and share it,
and in that way, be known.

◎ *MARY OLIVER*

Mary Oliver was born in 1935 in Cleveland, Ohio. She has published nine volumes of poetry and received numerous awards, including the Pulitzer Prize for American Primitive *(1983) and the National Book Award for* New and Selected Poems *(1992). Her* Poetry Handbook *was published in 1994, as was a new volume of poems,* White Pine. Blue Pastures *(prose) appeared in 1995. Oliver has been a fellow of the Guggenheim Foundation and the National Endowment for the Arts.*

"August," which first appeared in Country Journal, *opens Mary Oliver's* American Primitive *(1983). Its tercets, crammed with alliteration, joyfully set the tone for the volume. The poet spends the whole day "among the high / branches" picking and eating blackberries. The poet's delight is hard-earned: her arms are "ripped" from the work of picking berries. Yet the poet closes her lyric with the image of "this happy tongue."*

August

When the blackberries hang
swollen in the woods, in the brambles
nobody owns, I spend

all day among the high
branches, reaching
my ripped arms, thinking

of nothing, cramming
the black honey of summer
into my mouth; all day my body

accepts what it is. In the dark
creeks that run by there is
this thick paw of life darting among

the black bells, the leaves; there is
this happy tongue.

◎ *ALICIA OSTRIKER*

Alicia Ostriker was born in 1937 in Brooklyn, New York. She attended Brandeis University and received her M.A. and Ph.D. from the University of Wisconsin. A feminist poet and scholar, she is the author of seven books of poetry, including The Imaginary Lover *(1986) and* Green Age *(1989). A new volume of poetry,* The Crack in Everything, *is forthcoming. Her works of scholarship include* Stealing the Language: The Emergence of Women's Poetry in America *(1986),* Feminist Revision and the Bible *(1993), and* The Nakedness of the Fathers: Biblical Visions and Revisions *(1994). A professor of English at Rutgers University, Ostriker lives in Princeton, New Jersey.*

"Mother in Airport Parking Lot" is from Ostriker's The Imaginary Lover. *Elsewhere Ostriker has commented that her mind is most free when she is alone in her car. In this poem, having said goodbye to a grown child, the narrator-mother is in ecstasy. Freed of domestic responsibilities, the world seems sexual, orgasmic. The source of this rapture? "I am by myself, climbing into my car."*

Mother in Airport Parking Lot

This motherhood business fades, is almost over.
I begin to reckon its half-life.
I count its tears, its expended tissues,

And I remember everything, I remember
I swallowed the egg whole, the oval
Smooth and delicately trembling, a firm virgin

Sucked into my oral chamber
Surrendered to my mouth, my mouth to it.
I recall how the interior gold burst forth

Under pressure, secret, secret,
A pleasure softer, crazier than orgasm.
Liquid yolk spurted on my chin,

Keats's grape, and I too a trophy,
I too a being in a trance,
The possession of a goddess.

Multiply the egg by a thousand, a billion.
Make the egg a continuous egg through time,
The specific time between the wailing birth cry

And the child's hand wave
Accompanied by thrown kiss at the airport
Outside those brackets, outside my eggshell, and running

Through the parking lot in these very balmy
October breezes—what? And who am I?
The world is flat and happy,

I am in love with asphalt
So hot you could fry an egg on it,
I am in love with acres of automobiles,

None of them having any messy feelings.
Here comes a big bird low overhead,
A tremendous steel belly hurtles over me,

Is gone, pure sex, and I love it.
I am one small woman in a great space,
Temporarily free and clear.

I am by myself, climbing into my car.

◎ *LINDA PASTAN*

"The Happiest Day" is found in Pastan's Heroes in Disguise *(1991), a volume that displays a quiet insistence on the pleasures of the everyday without denying that darkness, winter, and death wait at the edges. Her descriptions of the limits of happiness give these moments a sense of grandeur.* *(For more on Pastan, see page 281.)*

The Happiest Day

It was early May, I think
a moment of lilac or dogwood
when so many promises are made
it hardly matters if a few are broken.
My mother and father still hovered
in the background, part of the scenery
like the houses I had grown up in,
and if they would be torn down later
that was something I knew
but didn't believe. Our children were asleep
or playing, the youngest as new
as the new smell of the lilacs,
and how could I have guessed
their roots were shallow
and would be easily transplanted.
I didn't even guess that I was happy.
The small irritations that are like salt
on melon were what I dwelt on,
though in truth they simply
made the fruit taste sweeter.
So we sat on the porch
in the cool morning, sipping
hot coffee. Behind the news of the day —
strikes and small wars, a fire somewhere —
I could see the top of your dark head
and thought not of public conflagrations
but of how it would feel on my bare shoulder.
If someone could stop the camera then . . .
if someone could only stop the camera
and ask me: are you happy?
perhaps I would have noticed
how the morning shone in the reflected
color of lilac. Yes, I might have said
and offered a steaming cup of coffee.

◎ *JOYCE CAROL THOMAS*

"Sisters" is included in Joyce Carol Thomas's Brown Honey and Broomwheat Tea *(1993). This is a distilled autobiography in verse for all ages, a portrait of a childhood filled with love. Though the sisters were called "gold dust twins" because of their skin color, to them the word was lovely, the color of flowers and romping in the "golden weeds." Thomas has explained that her books are "often dedicated to her children and grandchildren, and thereby in extension to all children."* *(For more on Thomas, see page 285.)*

Sisters

The gold dust twins
They call us
Because we are so dark
And all the time I'm thinking
It's the dust from the yellow flowers
sequining the Moroline, Vaseline
on our shiny legs
as we run red, ashless
through the golden weeds

◎ *DAVI WALDERS*

Davi Walders was born in 1941 in an oil camp near Big Spring, Texas. Her poems have appeared in many national journals and anthologies. She has been a Fulbright fellow and has received a National Endowment for the Humanities grant. Walders lives in Chevy Chase, Maryland, where she is an educational consultant.

"Reflections in Green Glass," a salute to women's lasting friendships, first appeared in the Frederick County Poetry Contest Winners' Anthology *(1992), in* Ms. *(1993), and in the anthology* Grow Old Along with Me, The Best Is Yet to Be *(1996). The two female characters in the poem seem conscious of being "[t]oo early to be fashionable" where they are eating supper in a bar. By the use of a repeated phrase ("out of sync"), Walders's tune finally becomes triumphant in the final stanza as the women lift their glasses together in a toast.*

Reflections in Green Glass

for C., J., and all brave women who love

Too early to be fashionable, two women perch
on stools eating *ensalada,* our faces reflected
in the glass above the bar, our backs a partition
between Catalan, coffee, and laughter. It is dusk
in Barcelona. Waiters balancing *tapas* high
in smoky air tell us what we already know.

We are out of sync, but we have taken a stand
to sit at the bar because of our feet,
our stomachs, and our desires. We will not eat
again at midnight to lie bedded in our bloat,
staring into darkness, deprived of dreams
by dinner and aging bodies that will not adjust.

We lean, tired, looking into milky green glass.
Longer than Liceu's curtain, it shimmers like rain
on old copper, encircling Piccadillos on the Passeig.
Beveled shelves, triangles of herb brandy, Chartreuse
and necks of Rioja bottles frame our silhouettes.
We are women beyond the blur of crowded tables.

Two women, dining too early, happy to be out
of the rain, damp feet warming on zinc, we talk
of friends at fifty who buy answering machines,
wait for calls, keep money hidden in drawers, open
separate accounts, begin and end careers, take lovers,
let them go, reweave, unravel, gather and lose,
tighten and loosen their hold on children, thighs,
lies and fears. Reflections dancing on green glass,
out of sync, out of touch, out of the rain,
out of laughter, out of love for women walking
in the world, we raise our *vino blanco,* saluting,
drinking in the Spanish dusk, laughing at fifty.

INTERVIEW
In a Long Line of Strong Women: An Interview with Joyce Carol Thomas

by Marilyn Kallet

JOYCE CAROL THOMAS

This interview took place at Thomas's house overlooking Norris Lake in Careyville, Tennessee, on May 26, 1994. The house is full of windows and light, a necessity for the poet. Thomas served lunch during the interview, and for dessert she had made a sweet potato pie. Her recipe is included at the end of the interview. Enjoy!

MK: How did your family happen to settle in Ponca City, Oklahoma?
JCT: I'm not sure. My father's side of the family came from Mississippi. I didn't know until very recently that my mother's mother came from Tennessee. I was in California last March helping my Aunt Corine with insurance questions. The insurance agent asked her "Where was your mother born?" She said "Tennessee." I almost fell off my chair! I had never heard this before because my mother's mother died when my mother was twelve. My mother was the oldest girl. There were five daughters and she raised the rest of them, including my Aunt Corine, the youngest. They had heard that their own mother was born in Tennessee. After I got back to Tennessee I called Aunt Lavinia, who lives in Oklahoma. She's ninety-some years old. Speaking of women who still have a lot of energy and power! At ninety, this woman herds cattle on the farm. She's very sharp mentally. She keeps the books too.

Aunt Lavinia remembered going back to Tennessee. "Which town! Which town!" I asked. I had to know. She thought it was Memphis. There's a bush growing in Aunt Lavinia's yard in Oklahoma that she brought back from Tennessee. That was a revelation.
MK: Who were the storytellers in your family?
JCT: My mother used to tell ghost stories. She was quite good. Since she was

the oldest, she was always the lead teller. She was an amazing woman who did many things well. I'm still in awe of her.

I remember one episode concerning my mother and the power of words. At the time my cousin Doris and her two daughters lived next door to us. One of the daughters, Marva, was close in age to me and my sister. The daughters were afraid of their mother's boyfriend. My mother was doing my hair. She asked Marva, "Why are you afraid of him?" "Cause he has fits," Marva said. "He just falls on the floor and he has fits and it scares all of us when he can't get his way." My mother said, "Well, the next time he has a fit, would you come and get me?" Marva said she would.

I never heard my mother raise her voice, ever. It just so happened that the next time she was doing my hair — Cleeve, that was his name — Cleeve had a fit. And my cousins came running next door. "Cousin Leona! Cousin Leona! Cleeve's having a fit!" My mother was pressing my hair, and she put the pressing comb down. Of course I was right behind her! I wanted to see what was going on. We walked over and Cleeve was on the floor and indeed he was having a fit. And Doris, their mother, was trembling afraid. My mother said, "Cleeve, get up from there. Get up from there right now." And she said it with such force — it wasn't loud — but the power of her words had this undiluted strength. He stopped and he got up. I thought, "Good Lord, who *is* my mother!" There was something in her voice that I had never heard her use before. There was something in her that she kept.

MK: Is it fair to say that your mother is the strongest influence on your life and on your creative life?

JCT: I'd say so, yes.

MK: I am trying to imagine what your mother's life was like. She had thirteen children, nine survived. Did the others die in childbirth?

JCT: Yes. I've seen pictures of my mother when she was very young. Very frail-looking. I remember her saying that after she had her first child she became "stout."

MK: Didn't we all!

JCT: Yes. She got some meat on her bones. She gained strength from having her first child.

MK: Here's a woman who was herself a creative force. What was her life like? Did you all help her?

JCT: Oh, absolutely.

MK: Did she have other aspirations besides being a mother?

JCT: If she did, I didn't know them. When would she have had time for other things? Being a mother must have been more than enough. It was a "calling" for her.

MK: Your family was not rich. There were many children, yet in your work there is never a sense of deprivation. I feel a sense throughout of plenitude and joyfulness, a sense of abundance on every level.

JCT: I'm glad.

MK: Where did the sense of fullness come from?

JCT: In my new book of poems, *Gingerbread Days,* the last words are "People are more important than things." Hearing that bird sing is more important to me than my gold watch. Where value is placed might have a lot to do with a sense of beauty and plenty. A bush gives you one flower and that's a lot.

MK: Where I came from if you didn't have matching socks and sweaters you were an outcast! [*laughter*]

I know that you admire Lewis Hyde's book *The Gift* and use it for your classes. Do you experience your own work as a gift?

JCT: I don't consciously think about it, but when you ask me, the answer is *yes.*

MK: To what extent is the work "given"? We both know how much hard work is involved, and yet. . . .

JCT: Part of it is given. For me, the demonstration of this is when I'm so deeply into it that I forget something's cooking! [*laughter*] When I'm taken away from the present and taken somewhere else by the work — that's one way of showing that this is not something that I am consciously doing. The "gift" part is that something is coming through me.

MK: You're a medium. You've told me wonderful stories about characters who've spoken to you, who tell themselves to you. I was thinking specifically about one of the characters whose name you changed. . . .

JCT: Trembling Sally! Trembling Sally used to be Trembling Slim. There was a man in my childhood named Trembling Slim. Old folks would say, "If you don't act right we're going to give you to Trembling Slim!" He probably had some condition like Parkinson's Disease, but we didn't know it.

At one point in my story I wanted to create a character who was scary and I thought of Trembling Slim, and so I was busy writing about him. And this character said, "My name is not Trembling Slim. I'm Trembling Sally." And I thought, "Whoa, yes! Yes, whatever you say!" When those kinds of things happen it is really wonderful! You feel as if you have been given a gift when a presence comes into your story and says *this is who I am.*

MK: Since you work in several different genres, I'm wondering if these presences come in different ways.

JCT: I think that kind of presence — character-presence — comes mainly in fiction, in the novels. I'm not sure about the poems. For me poetry is like breathing. It's always with me no matter what I'm working on. A poem comes and I stop and I write it down. So if poetry is a character it is a constant character. It doesn't come and go the way a Trembling Sally would. It's always there.

MK: Light is a constant in your writing. Also we often find images of poetry, music, and food. [*laughter*] Food is not as prevalent as light and music but it's often there.

JCT: Wherever the light is in the house, there I am. It was the same way in Berkeley — wherever the light was that's where you could find me. I would be right by the light, writing. Not to see better necessarily, but to find a combination of feelings — well-being, warmth. It's as though a part of me thinks that I can write better if I'm sitting near the light. Like cats. Cats follow the light too.

MK: The impulse toward light is instinctual, but also connected with inner seeing.

JCT: Yes.

MK: What about food images? Are you hungry all the time? [*laughter*]

JCT: Food was one way of showing love. We didn't have a lot of things. But my mother used to do some amazing things with food. You know how some people think their mother's food was really good, but it really wasn't? Well, my mother's was really good! After we were grown we went back and she'd cook, and it would be excellent and by then we'd have something to compare it to. . . . The food was just wonderful. One time when my mother didn't have any fruit she made a pie out of fruit juice left over from her canned peaches. With that juice left in the Mason jar she made this wonderful pie. She used butter and nutmeg. She made the crust — it was so delicious! My sister and I talk about it — she made this pie out of nothing! It was *good*! We didn't have a lot of gifts that were clothes or toys, possessions. Food is one way of showing love, cooking well with love.

MK: What role did your father play? What was he like?

JCT: He was very much a male figure. My mother would say, "That's how men are." After having so many sons, she wanted a girl baby so badly. My father took her dolls and threw them away and said, "You don't need girl dolls. If you want a girl, I'll be the one to give you a girl." She loved him. I see in a lot of men the need to control, a sense of wanting to run their lives and your life. Certainly as a unit you have to agree on certain things. But it's almost as though they are afraid of the power of women, afraid to trust it too much. He had a beautiful singing voice, he was a natty dresser, he was handsome. The whole family was handsome.

MK: In addition to speaking of individual influences on your life and work you have spoken about how the church was an early influence, inspiring your love of language. Can you say more about that? How often did you go to church as a child?

JCT: Church services were beautiful. The sounds of the biblical names — Shadrach, Meshach, and Abednego — they seemed to me to be poetic and musical. You can get a poetic sound just from a name. If there happened to be a revival going we would be there every night. I'd be so tired some nights! As far back as I can remember I heard the music and the rhythms. I was what they called a "bench baby" — a baby brought to church, put on the front pew. When she cries, everyone picks her up.

MK: That feeling of being *in* the music and rhythm comes through in the story "The Young Reverend Zelma Lee Moses." That story was told in rhythms. Church was a place where music poured into you when you were a baby on that bench, being picked up by loving hands. Was there a real person behind the character of Queen Mother Rhythm in *Where the Nightingale Sings*? [a play by Thomas and also a novel by that name].

JCT: The name, Queen Mother Rhythm, came to me, and I fell in love with it. She seems to be a composite. Mother Augusta and Young Reverend Zelma Lee Moses remind me of women I grew up around, and of some of the greatest gospel singers whose music I love. I pay tribute to those strong women with her character.

MK: Strong women are at the heart of those stories. I asked Joy Harjo whether there was a connection between poetry and prayer and she said, "Of course."

JCT: Absolutely, for me. I do feel that sense of presence and spirit and prayer and God. I say "Thank you God" when I write a poem that works.

MK: Would you like to name some of the authors to whom you wish to show gratitude?

JCT: Certainly Maya Angelou has been a wonderful supporter. I met her in 1976 when she was chosen to direct a play I wrote, *Look What a Wonder*, starring Odetta. She has been an influence. Her writing in *I Know Why the Caged Bird Sings* brings tears to my eyes. Maya used to have me over for soup.

MK: She provided you with artistic direction and soup!

JCT: That's right. She's another wonderful cook! She fixed soup and we talked. She provided the blurb on *Marked by Fire*. She gave a wonderful interview and provided this beautiful picture of herself when I edited the magazine *Ambrosia*.

MK: How long did you edit that?

JCT: Not very long. My own writing took off.

MK: Were you able to write while you were raising your four children?

JCT: Yes. Women do need to know that they can have children and still write.

MK: You must have had some strategy.

JCT: It wasn't conscious. I remember one time this little person came to my study door — one of my little neighbors. She started talking, and I talked with her. Afterward I realized that my kids didn't do that. I must have gone inside myself. They must have said, "Uh-oh, she's got that look! Let's not bother her right now. Let's go in the next room and play marbles." So it's being present and absent at the same time.

MK: I don't think everyone can do that. You somehow trained yourself to do that because you needed to write. Your children understood that they were not to interrupt you. They probably did so anyway. But they did have some sense that you were in yourself.

JCT: Yes.

MK: Did you have help?

JCT: Sometimes.

MK: It's hard, any way you slice it.

JCT: It is hard, but it's doable. If it's in you, if it's strong enough, you find a way to do it. A lot of men get up at four and write until it's time to go to work.

Think about time as being a slice of pie. You sometimes have more than at other times. Now I have more than when I was raising four children and writing. Now I teach and write. In some ways I have more. It's hard to measure that kind of time. It's not always about quantity. Sometimes it's about sitting at the right window at the right time.

MK: So, don't let anyone talk you out of that desire to write, or that sense of purpose.

JCT: A gift is to be given again. You write a book of poems, hopefully someone picks it up and they feel that they have been given to. That's important too. Not to diminish the place of children. They are central to many women. But to say that you have to do one or the other is cruel to someone who wants to write and has children.

MK: We were talking earlier about influences. You mentioned Maya Angelou. I know that you have a strong friendship with Alice Walker. Do you consider her an influence?

JCT: No. We're contemporaries. Maya is older. I think of influences as being older people. Perhaps that's cultural.

MK: Anyone else?

JCT: Ralph Ellison, who just passed. I love his work. Margaret Walker. *Jubilee* is one of the masterpieces. It has such integrity. Toni Morrison. I love her *Song of Solomon* and *Sula*. I like the way she questions our sense of what a "good woman" is. Sula too is a good woman.

MK: You mentioned a new book of poems . . .

JCT: *Gingerbread Days*. Food again! It's a tribute to the love of my father. I thought I would write a book as a tribute to all fathers, to the warmness of fathers. I go deeply into that.

MK: When will that come out?

JCT: This year, 1995.

MK: Are there other things you are working on now that you would feel comfortable talking about?

JCT: The book after *Gingerbread Days* is *I Have Heard of a Land*, which is also poetry.

MK: For young adults?

JCT: Yes, and for "all ages." *I Have Heard of a Land* remembers my own family's westward journey and focuses on the pioneer women who helped settle Oklahoma.

MK: I know that some writers have a hard time writing again after they have received major awards. Having received the National Book Award and the American Book Award, among other honors, have you had this kind of experience?

JCT: For me, there is no negative part of receiving an award. I'm always surprised by it. The writing itself is gift enough, reward enough, award enough. Then here comes this other acclamation. I view those awards as meaning the work is connecting with people, with the readers. That's what they mean to me.

MK: *Marked by Fire* was your first major award. That must have been the biggest surprise.
JCT: Let me tell you what happened. When my agent called to tell me that the book had been nominated I was so excited. I had guests for dinner, and this other writer was there. When I told them the book had been nominated, the other writer, said, "Oh well, *nominated*." My feathers fell. Then I didn't talk about it any more.

Months later, I was in my study working when my agent called. "Joyce, are you sitting down? *Marked by Fire* won the National Book Award." I said, "You're kidding!" I reflected back on my conversation with that other writer. When I asked myself how I felt, I felt humble and proud. I knew then it was an honor to be nominated. It was an honor to win.
MK: Still, it must have felt good to win with respect to that individual.
JCT: Yes, but I did not call him and rub it in! I don't write for that. The delight I feel in awards is genuine because it does mean people are in touch with what you're doing. For me, that's affirming. You're thankful and glad. I do know that for some writers the fame stops them. Whatever happens I continue to write. If someone should say, "Your work stinks," it would not stop me. The award is the result of the work, not the other way around. Once you get that straight in your mind, you are never mislead.

Joyce Carol Thomas's Sweet Potato Pie

FILLING

1 and 3/4 cups of sweet potatoes
2/3 cup of milk
1 stick of butter
1 cup of sugar
1 egg
1 teaspoon lemon flavor
1/4 teaspoon allspice

Boil the sweet potatoes until they're done, then mash them in a large bowl; add the milk, butter, sugar, egg, lemon flavor, and allspice. Stir all ingredients until they're well mixed. Pour into a 9-inch pie crust and bake at 350° for about one hour or until done.

CRUST

2 cups flour
2/3 cup margarine
Cold water

With your fingers work the margarine and the flour together until the combination is very mealy. Add about 1/5 cup of cold water, a few drips at a time, until the dough is at the desired consistency. Note: The important thing about making pie crust that is flaky is that you only want to roll out the dough once. And when you use the rolling pin, do so very gently.

ACKNOWLEDGMENTS

Paula Gunn Allen. "Weed" and "Eve the Fox" from *Skins & Bones*, © 1988. Reprinted by permission of West End Press. *"A New Wrinkle"* from *Grandmothers of the Light*, © 1991 by Paula Gunn Allen. Reprinted by permission of Beacon Press, Boston.

Maya Angelou. "Known to Eve and Me" from *I Shall Not Be Moved* © 1990 by Maya Angelou. Reprinted by permission of Random House, Inc.

Laurie Blauner. "The Invention of Imagination" from *Children of Gravity*, Owl Creek Press, © 1995 by Laurie Blauner. Reprinted with permission.

Kate Braid. "'Girl' on the Crew" from *Covering Rough Ground*, published by Polestar Book Publishers, Vancouver, B.C. Reprinted by permission of Kate Braid and Polestar.

Olga Broumas. "Lullaby" from *Beginning with O* © 1977 by Olga Broumas. Reprinted by permission of Yale University Press.

Kathryn Stripling Byer. "Dusk" and "The Carpenter" from *The Girl in the Midst of the Harvest*, © 1986 by Kathryn Stripling Byer. Reprinted with permission from Texas Tech University Press.

Lorna Dee Cervantes. "Refugee Ship" by Lorna Dee Cervantes is reprinted with permission from the publisher of *Revista Chicano-Requena, Vol. 10:1–2, A Decade of Hispanic Literature* (Houston: Arte Publico Press-University of Houston, 1982).

Alice Childress. "Florence" © 1950. Renewed 1978 by Alice Childress. Reprinted by permission of Flora Roberts, Inc.

Marilyn Chin. "First Lessons," from *Dwarf Bamboo*, Greenfield Review Press © 1987 by Marilyn Chin. Reprinted with permission of Greenfield Review Press.

Patricia Clark. "Betrayal" © Patricia Clark; first appeared in *Poetry* magazine June 1992. "Bill of Sale" © Patricia Clark. Reprinted by permission of the author.

Lucille Clifton. "Daughters," "them and us" from *The Book of Light* © 1993 by Lucille Clifton. Reprinted by permission of Copper Canyon Press.

Judith Ortiz Cofer. "More Room" and "Tales Told Under the Mango Tree" by Judith Ortiz Cofer are reprinted with permission from the publisher of *Silent Dancing: A Partial Remembrance of a Puerto Rican Childhood* (Houston: Arte Publico Press-University of Houston, 1985). "The Latin Deli" by Judith Ortiz Cofer is reprinted with permission from the publisher of *The Americas Review* Vol. 19-1, (Houston: Arte Publico Press-University of Houston, 1991). "The Art of Not Forgetting: An Interview with Judith Ortiz Cofer" is reprinted from *Prairie Schooner*, volume 68 number 4, © 1994 University of Nebraska Press.

Laurie Colwin. "Another Marvelous Thing" from *Another Marvelous Thing* by Laurie Colwin, © 1986 by Laurie Colwin. Reprinted by permission of Alfred A. Knopf, Inc.

Barbara Crooker. "The Last Woman in America to Wash Diapers" from *If I Had a Hammer: Women's Work in Fiction, Poetry, and Photographs*, edited by Sandra Haldeman Martz (Papier-Maché Press, 1990). Reprinted with permission of the author.

Elizabeth Cook-Lynn. "A Visit from Reverend Tileston" from *The Power of Horses & Other Stories* (New York: Arcade Publishers, 1990). © 1990 by Elizabeth Cook-Lynn. Permission requested.

J. California Cooper. "The Magic Strength of Need" from *Homemade Love* by J. California Cooper, © 1986 by J. California Cooper. Reprinted by permission of St. Martin's Press.

Toi Derricotte. "Touching/Not Touching: My Mother," "A Note on My Son's Face" from *Captivity* by Toi Derricotte, © 1989. Reprinted by permission of the University of Pittsburgh Press.

Annie Dillard. Excerpt from *The Writing Life* by Annie Dillard, © 1989 by Annie Dillard. Reprinted by permission of HarperCollins Publishers, Inc.

Barbara Noreen Dinnerstein. "*Bubbie*, Mommy, Weight Watchers and Me," published in *Bubbe Meisehs by Shayneh Maidelehs: An Anthology of Poetry by Jewish Granddaughters about Our Grandmothers*, ed. Lesléa Newman. 1989, Herbooks. Permission requested.

Rita Dove. "Crab-Boil" from *Grace Notes* by Rita Dove, © 1989 by Rita Dove. Reprinted with permission of the author and W. W. Norton and Company, Inc.

Rosalyn Drexler. "Room 17C" copyright © 1984 by Rosalyn Drexler. Reprinted by permission of the author.

Janice Eidus. "Robin's Nest" from *Vito Loves Geraldine*, © 1989 by Janice Eidus. Reprinted by permission of the author.

Lucy Ferriss. "Love and Learn" © 1991 Lucy Ferriss, appeared originally in *New York Times Sunday Magazine*, September 1991. Reprinted by permission of the author.

Alice Friman. "The Good News," first published in *The Cream City Review*, © by the author. Reprinted by permission of the author.

Tess Gallagher. "Each Bird Walking," "Crêpes Flambeau" © 1987 by Tess Gallagher. Reprinted from *Amplitude* with the permission of Graywolf Press, Saint Paul, Minnesota. First printed in *Willingly*, © 1984 by Tess Gallagher, publisher Graywolf Press. "Red Poppy," "Sea Inside the Sea" © 1992 by Tess Gallagher. Reprinted from *Moon Crossing Bridge* with the permission of Graywolf Press, Saint Paul, Minnesota.

Louise Glück. "The Undertaking" from *The House on the Marshland* by Louise Glück, © 1971, 1972, 1973, 1974, 1975 by Louise Glück. First published by The Ecco Press in 1975. Reprinted by permission. "Lullaby" from *Wild Iris* by Louise Glück. Copyright © 1992 by Louise Glück. First published by The Ecco Press in 1992. Reprinted by permission.

Tereze Glück. "Yellow Light" copyright © 1995 by the University of Iowa Press. Reprinted by permission of the author.

Natalie Goldberg. "Walking Between the Raindrops" from *Long Quiet Highway* by Natalie Goldberg, © 1993 by Natalie Goldberg. Used by permission of Bantam Books, a division of Bantam, Doubleday Dell Publishing Group, Inc.

Jewelle Gomez. "Don't Explain" © 1987 by Jewelle Gomez. Reprinted by permission of the author.

Barbara L. Greenberg. "When I Think of My Happy Ending" from *The Never-Not Sonnets* (University of Central Florida Press). © 1989 by Barbara L. Greenberg. Reprinted by permission of the author.

Marilyn Hacker. "Self" from *Going Back to the River* by Marilyn Hacker. Copyright © 1990 by Marilyn Hacker. Reprinted by permission of Random House, Inc.

Patricia Hampl. "The Moment." First appeared in the *New Yorker* 16 December 1985. Permission requested.

Joy Harjo. "For Alva Benson, and for Those Who Have Learned to Speak" from *She Had Some Horses* by Joy Harjo, © 1983 by Thunder's Mouth Press. Used by permission of the publisher, Thunder's Mouth Press. "For Anna Mae Pictou Aquash Whose Spirit Is Present Here and in the Dappled Stars," "Healing Animal" from *In Mad Love and War* by Joy Harjo, © 1990 by Joy Harjo. Reprinted by permission of Wesleyan University Press. "Family Album" (memoir) printed in *Partial Recall*, ed. Lucy Lippard (The New Press, 1992). "In Love and War and Music: An Interview with Joy Harjo," first published in *The Kenyon Review* New Series, Summer 1993, Vol. XV, No. 3. © Marilyn Kallet. Reprinted by permission of Joy Harjo. "The Place the Musician Became a Bear" from *The Woman Who Fell from the Sky* by Joy Harjo. Copyright © 1994 by Joy Harjo. Reprinted by permission of W. W. Norton & Company, Inc.

Beth Henley. "Am I Blue" © 1992 by Beth Henley. Reprinted by permission of the William Morris Agency, Inc. on behalf of the author.

Linda Hogan. "Geodes," "Germinal," "Elk Song," "What Has Happened to These Working Hands?" from *Savings* © 1988 by Linda Hogan. "Drum" from *The Book of Medicines* © 1993 by Linda Hogan. Coffee House Press, publisher. Reprinted by permission of the author. "Imagining a Wider Community: Talking with Linda Hogan" reprinted with permission of Linda Hogan.

Mary Hood. "How Far She Went" from *How Far She Went* (University of Georgia Press, 1984). Reprinted by permission.

Pam Houston. "How to Talk to a Hunter" reprinted from *Cowboys Are My Weakness* by Pam Houston, with the permission of W. W. Norton and Company, Inc. © 1992 by Pam Houston. Originally published in *Quarterly West.* "A Blizzard Under Blue Sky" reprinted from *Cowboys Are My Weakness* by Pam Houston, with the permission of W. W. Norton and Company, Inc. © 1992 by Pam Houston. Originally published in *Lodestar.*

Momoko Iko. "Gold Watch" copyright © Momoko Iko 1970, all rights reserved. "Gold Watch" premiered at Inner City Cultural Center, Los Angeles, March–April 1972, directed by C. Bernard Jackson.

Colette Inez. "Mary at the Cave" © Colette Inez, 1996. "Good News! Nilda Is Back" © Colette Inez. Both poems reprinted by permission of Colette Inez.

June Jordan. "Poem Toward the Bottom Line" © 1980 by June Jordan. Reprinted with the permission of the author.

Eileen Joy. "Emma" © 1992 Eileen A. Joy. Originally published in *Short Fiction By Women #3.* Reprinted by permission of the author.

Marilyn Kallet. "How to Get Heat Without Fire" © Marilyn Kallet, first printed in *Carolina Quarterly,* 1983. "Passover" © Marilyn Kallet, first printed in *Voices from the Valley,* 1995; reprinted in *International Quarterly,* 1995. Reprinted by permission.

LuAnn Keener. "The Hummingbirds" © 1995 LuAnn Keener. Reprinted by permission of the author.

Jamaica Kincaid. "Poor Visitor" from *Lucy* by Jamaica Kincaid. Copyright © by Jamaica Kincaid. Reprinted by permission of Farrar, Straus & Giroux, Inc. "Just Reading" © 1993 by Jamaica Kincaid. Originally published in the *New Yorker.* Reprinted by permission of Wylie Aitken & Stone, Inc.

Maxine Hong Kingston. "No Name Woman" from *Woman Warrior* by Maxine Hong Kingston. Copyright © 1975, 1976 by Maxine Hong Kingston. Reprinted by permission of Alfred A. Knopf, Inc.

Irena Klepfisz. "Warsaw, 1983: *Umschlagplatz*" and "1. Poland: My mother is walking down a road" (from the poem "*Bashert*") from *A Few Words in the Mother Tongue: Poems Selected and New 1971–1990* by Irena Klepfisz (Portland, OR: The Eighth Mountain Press, 1990); © by Irena Klepfisz; reprinted by permission of the author and publisher.

Maxine Kumin. "Menial Labor and the Muse," first published in *Tri Quarterly,* Vol. 75, Spring/Summer 1989. © 1989 by Maxine Kumin. Reprinted by permission of the author and Curtis Brown Ltd.

Anne LaMott. Excerpt from *Operating Instructions* by Anne LaMott. © 1993 by Anne LaMott. Reprinted by permission of Pantheon Books, a division of Random House, Inc.

Denise Levertov. "A Tree Telling of Orpheus": *Denise Levertov: Poems 1968–1972.* Copyright © 1970 by Denise Levertov. Reprinted by permission of New Directions Publishing Corp. "O Taste and See": *Denise Levertov: Poems 1960–1967.* Copyright © 1964 by Denise Levertov. Reprinted by permission of New Directions Publishing Corp.

Amy Ling. "Whose America Is It?" © 1995 by Amy Ling; first appeared in *Weber Studies* 12.1 (Winter 1995). Reprinted by permission.

Audre Lorde. "A Litany for Survival" reprinted from *The Black Unicorn* by Audre Lorde, with the permission of W. W. Norton and Company, Inc. Copyright © 1978 by Audre Lorde. "Poetry is Not a Luxury" from *Sister Outsider,* © 1984 by Audre Lorde, The Crossing Press, Freedom, CA.

George Ella Lyon. "Singing" from *Choices,* © 1989 by George Ella Lyon. Reprinted by permission of the author.

Lisa Suhair Majaj. "Recognized Futures" by Lisa Suhair Majaj, from *Unsettling America* by Maria Mazziotti Gillan and Jennifer Gillan. Copyright © 1994 by Maria Mazziotti Gillan and Jennifer Gillan. Used by permission of Viking Penguin, a division of Penguin Books USA Inc.

Adrianne Marcus. "The Paincaller" Copyright © 1996 by Adrianne Marcus. Reprinted by permission of the author.

Paule Marshall. "To Da-duh, In Memoriam," and "The Making of the Writer: From the Poets in the Kitchen," *Reena and Other Stories* (New York: The Feminist Press at the City University of New York, 1983), pp. 3–12, 95–106. © 1983 by Paule Marshall. Reprinted by permission, from Paule Marshall.

Frances McCue. "The Stenographer's Breakfast" from *The Stenographer's Breakfast.* Copyright © 1992 by Frances McCue. Reprinted by permission of Beacon Press, Boston.

Jeanne McDonald. "Cousins" originally appeared in *Special Report: Fiction,* Whittle Communications L.P., Knoxville, Tennessee, November 1989. © Jeanne McDonald. Reprinted by permission.

Colleen J. McElroy. "For My Children" reprinted by permission of Colleen J. McElroy. Copyright © 1976 by Colleen J. McElroy. "Against a Bondage of Color: An Interview with Colleen J. McElroy." Reprinted by permission.

Cassandra Medley. "Waking Women" © Cassandra Medley. Reprinted by permission of the author.

Janice Mirikitani. Excerpt from *Shedding Silence* © 1987 by Janice Mirikitani. Reprinted by permission of Celestial Arts, P.O. Box 7123, Berkeley, CA 94707.

Pat Mora. "A Walk with My Father" from *House of Houses* by Pat Mora, © 1997 by Pat Mora. Reprinted by permission of Beacon Press, Boston.

Toni Morrison. "The Birth of Denver," excerpted from *Beloved* (New York: Alfred A. Knopf, Inc., 1987). pp. 76–85. Copyright 1987 by Toni Morrison. Reprinted by permission of Toni Morrison and International Creative Management.

Thylias Moss. "Tornados" from *Rainbow Remnants in Rockbottom Ghetto Sky* by Thylias Moss, © 1991 by Thylias Moss. Reprinted by permission of Persea Books, Inc.

Gloria Naylor. Excerpt from *Mama Day.* Copyright © 1988 by Gloria Naylor. Reprinted by permission of Ticknor & Fields/Houghton Mifflin Company. All rights reserved.

Janet Neipris. "The Agreement" © 1985 by Janet Neipris. Reprinted by permission.

Sharon Niederman. "A Gift for Languages" © 1989 by Sharon Niederman. Reprinted by permission.

Kathleen Norris. "A Starfish in Mott" from *Dakota,* © 1993 by Kathleen Norris. Reprinted by permission of Ticknor & Fields/Houghton Mifflin Company. All rights reserved.

Naomi Shihab Nye. "Adios" from *Words Under the Words* © 1995 by Naomi Shihab Nye. "So Much Happiness" from *Hugging the Jukebox* © 1982 by Naomi Shihab Nye. Both poems reprinted by permission of the author.

Sharon Olds. "Bathing the New Born" from *The Wellspring* by Sharon Olds. Copyright © 1996 by Sharon Olds. Reprinted by permission of Alfred A. Knopf, Inc. "The Race" from *The Father* by Sharon Olds. Copyright © 1992 by Sharon Olds. Reprinted by permission of Alfred A. Knopf, Inc. "First Night" from *Satan Says* by Sharon Olds, © 1980. Reprinted by permission of the University of Pittsburgh Press.

Mary Oliver. "August" from *American Primitive* by Mary Oliver. Copyright © 1982 by Mary Oliver. First appeared in *Country Journal.* Reprinted by permission of Little, Brown and Company.

Tillie Olsen. "I Stand Here Ironing," copyright © 1956, 1957, 1960, 1961 by Tillie Olsen; "O Yes," copyright © 1956, 1957, 1960, 1961 by Tillie Olsen; from *Tell Me A Riddle* by Tillie Olsen. Introduction by John Leonard. Used by permission of Delacorte Press/ Seymour Lawrence, a division of Bantam, Doubleday Dell Publishing Group, Inc.

Alicia Ostriker. "Mother in Airport Parking Lot" from *The Imaginary Lover* by Alicia Ostriker, © 1986. Reprinted by permission of the University of Pittsburgh Press.

Cynthia Ozick. "The Shawl" from *The Shawl* by Cynthia Ozick. Copyright © 1980, 1983 by Cynthia Ozick. Reprinted by permission of Alfred A. Knopf, Inc.

Grace Paley. "A Conversation with My Father" from *Enormous Changes at the Last Minute* by Grace Paley. Copyright © 1971, 1974 by Grace Paley. Reprinted by permission of Farrar, Straus & Giroux, Inc.

Linda Pastan. "Family Tree" reprinted from *Imperfect Paradise* by Linda Pastan, with the permission of W. W. Norton and Company, Inc. Copyright © 1988 by Linda Pastan. "The Happiest Day" reprinted from *Heroes in Disguise* by Linda Pastan, with the permission of W. W. Norton and Company, Inc. Copyright © 1991 by Linda Pastan.

Molly Peacock. "How I Come to You" from *Take Heart* by Molly Peacock. Copyright © 1989 by Molly Peacock. Reprinted by permission of Random House, Inc.

Marge Piercy. "Wellfleet Sabbath" from *Available Light* by Marge Piercy. Copyright © 1988 by Middlemarsh, Inc., reprinted by permission of Alfred A. Knopf, Inc.

Minnie Bruce Pratt. "Down the Little Cahaba" from *Crime Against Nature* by Minnie Bruce Pratt. Copyright © 1990 by Minnie Bruce Pratt. Reprinted with permission from Firebrand Books, Ithaca, New York.

Melissa Range. "Lot's Wife" © 1996 by Melissa Range. Reprinted by permission.

Rochelle Ratner. "Bentshen Licht" from *Someday Songs*, Bkmk/University of Missouri Press, © 1992 by Rochelle Ratner. Reprinted with permission of the author.

Hilda Raz. "Junk" appeared originally in *The Confidence Woman*, ed. Eve Shelnutt, published by Longstreet Press. © 1991 by Hilda Raz. Reprinted with permission of the author.

Adrienne Rich. "XIX" of "Twenty-One Love Poems" from *The Fact of a Doorframe: Poems Selected and New, 1950–1984* by Adrienne Rich. Copyright © 1984 by Adrienne Rich. Copyright © 1975, 1978 by W. W. Norton and Company, Inc. Copyright © 1981 by Adrienne Rich. Reprinted by permission of the author and W. W. Norton and Company, Inc. "History stops for no one" from *What Is Found There: Notebooks on Poetry and Politics* by Adrienne Rich. Copyright © 1993 by Adrienne Rich. Reprinted by permission of the author and W. W. Norton and Company, Inc.

Wendy Rose. "I Expected My Skin and My Blood to Ripen" from *Bone Dance* (University of Arizona Press, 1994) © 1980 Malki Museum Press.

Sonia Sanchez. "Dear Mama" © 1989 by Sonia Sanchez. Reprinted by permission of the author.

May Sarton. "Friendship & Illness," from *Coming into Eighty* by May Sarton. Copyright © 1994 by May Sarton. Reprinted by permission of W. W. Norton and Company, Inc. "Finding the Muse: An Interview with May Sarton" first appeared in *A House of Gathering: Poets on May Sarton's Poetry* (© 1993, University of Tennessee Press), ed. Marilyn Kallet. Reprinted by permission of the University of Tennessee Press. "The Work of Happiness" from *Collected Poems 1930–1993* by May Sarton. © 1993, 1988, 1984, 1980, 1974 by May Sarton. Reprinted by permission of W. W. Norton and Company, Inc. "Silence Was the Food I Was After" excerpted from "With Solitude for My Domain" from *Plant Dreaming Deep* by May Sarton. Copyright © 1968 by May Sarton. Reprinted by permission of W. W. Norton and Company, Inc.

Nzotake Shange. "boogie woogie landscapes" from *Three Pieces* by Nzotake Shange. Copyright © 1981 by Nzotake Shange, St. Martin's Press, Inc., New York, NY.

Enid Shomer. "The Tomato Packing Plant Line" © 1992 by Enid Shomer. Appeared in *Stalking the Florida Panther* (The Word Works, 1987). Reprinted with permission of the author.

Leslie Marmon Silko. "Lullaby." Copyright © 1994 by Leslie Marmon Silko, reprinted with permission of Wylie, Aitken & Stone, Inc. "untitled, prologue to *Ceremony*," from *Ceremony* by Leslie Marmon Silko. Copyright © 1977 by Leslie Silko. Used by permission of Viking Penguin, a division of Penguin Books USA Inc.

Anita Skeen. "The English Teacher, in Mid-Life" © 1996 by Anita Skeen. Used by permission of the author.

Cathy Song. "Picture Bride," "The White Porch" from *Picture Bride* by Cathy Song (Yale University Press 1983). © Cathy Song. Reprinted by permission of Yale University Press.

Lisa Springer. "Between Girls" is reprinted with the permission of Simon & Schuster from *Surface Tension* edited by Meg Daly. Copyright © 1966 by Meg Daly.

Mariflo Stephens. "Waltzing into Heaven" © 1991 by Mariflo Stephens. Reprinted by permission of the author.

Luci Tapahonso. "Shą́ą́ Áko Dhjiníłeh/Remember the Things They Told Us," "The Kaw River Rushes Westward," "It Was a Special Treat," "The Motion of Songs Rising," from *Sáanii Dahataal/The Women Are Singing: Poems and Stories* by Luci Tapahonso. © 1993 University of Arizona Press.

Joyce Carol Thomas. "Brown Honey in Broomwheat Tea" and "Sisters" from *Brown Honey in Broomwheat Tea* by Joyce Carol Thomas, © 1993 by Joyce Carol Thomas. Reprinted with permission of HarperCollins Publishers. "Young Reverend Zelma Lee Moses" from *A Gathering of Flowers* © 1990 by Joyce Carol Thomas. Reprinted with permission of HarperCollins Publishers. "In a Long Line of Strong Women" © Joyce Carol Thomas. Reprinted by permission of Joyce Carol Thomas.

Gioia Timpanelli. "There Are Times" © 1996 by Gioia Timpanelli. Reprinted by permission. Reprinted by permission of the author.

Ellen Bryant Voigt. "Visiting the Graves" from *The Lotus Flowers* by Ellen Bryant Voigt. Copyright © 1987 by Ellen Bryant Voigt. Reprinted by permission of W. W. Norton and Company, Inc. "Song and Story" reprinted from *Two Trees* by Ellen Bryant Voigt, with the permission of the author and W. W. Norton and Company, Inc. Originally published in the *Atlantic.* Copyright © 1992 by Ellen Bryant Voigt.

Davi Walders. "Reflections in a Green Glass." Copyright © 1992 by Davi Walders. Has appeared in *Ms.*, March/April 1993; *Frederick County Poetry Contest Winners Anthology*, 1992; and *Grow Old Along with Me, the Best Is Yet to Be*, Papier-Maché Press, 1996.

Alice Walker. "Everyday Use" from *In Love & Trouble: Stories of Black Women*, copyright © 1973 by Alice Walker, reprinted by permission of Harcourt Brace & Company.

Margaret Walker. "I Want to Write" from *October Journey*. Copyright © 1973 by Margaret Walker. Reprinted by permission of Broadside Press.

Pamela Walker. "Good Shabbos" reprinted by permission of Pamela Walker.

Wendy Wasserstein. "Tender Offer" © Wendy Wasserstein 1991. First published in *Antaeus, #66, Plays in One Act.* No part of this material may be reproduced in whole or part, without the express written permission of the author or her agent.

Sylvia Watanabe. "Where People Know Me" from *Between Friends*, ed. by Mickey Pearlman (Houghton Mifflin, 1994), by Sylvia Watanabe. Copyright © 1994 Sylvia Watanabe. Used by permission of the author. "Talking to the Dead" from *Talking to the Dead* by Sylvia Watanabe. Copyright © 1992 by Sylvia Watanabe. Used by permission of Doubleday, a division of Bantam Doubleday Dell Publishing Group, Inc. "Living Among Strangers: An Interview with Sylvia Watanabe" reprinted by permission of the author.

Nancy Willard. "The Friendship Tarot" from *Between Friends*, ed. by Mickey Pearlman (Houghton Mifflin, 1994), by Nancy Willard. Copyright © 1994 by Nancy Willard. Permission requested. "Angels in Winter" from *Household Tales of Moon and Water.* Copyright © 1982 by Nancy Willard. Reprinted by permission of Harcourt Brace & Co. "Finding and Gathering and Dreaming: An Interview with Nancy Willard" printed by permission of the author.

Joyce Madelon Winslow. "Born Again" © 1993 by Joyce Madelon Winslow. Reprinted by permission of the author.

Naomi Wolf. "Hunger" from *The Beauty Myth* by Naomi Wolf. © 1991 by Naomi Wolf. Reprinted by permission of William Morrow & Company, Inc.

Lois-Ann Yamanaka. "Turtles" © 1993 by Lois-Ann Yamanaka. From *Saturday Night at the Pahala Theatre.* Copyright © 1993 by Lois-Ann Yamanaka. Published by Bamboo Ridge Press. First published in *Bamboo Ridge: The Hawai'i Writer's Quarterly.*

Elaine Zimmerman. "To Essie Parrish" originally published in *Dreamworks: An Interdisciplinary Quarterly.* © Elaine Zimmerman. Reprinted by permission of Elaine Zimmerman.

Photo Credits. Page 72: used with permission of Judith Ortiz Cofer. Pages 114 and 115: from "Family Album," printed in *Partial Recall* (The New Press, 1992). Page 157: photo by Gary Isaacs; used with permission of Linda Hogan. Page 288: courtesy of Levant & Wales, for Colleen J. McElroy. Page 403: used with permission of Sylvia Watanabe. Page 486: photo by Susan Sherman. Page 578: used with permission of Nancy Willard. Page 670: photo by Paul Abdoo, Denver, CO; used with permission of Joy Harjo. Page 752: photo by Steve Anderson; used with permission of Joyce Carol Thomas.

Index of Authors and Titles